AMERICA AND ISLAND CHINA

AMERICA AND ISLAND CHINA
A Documentary History

Edited by

Stephen P. Gibert
William M. Carpenter

UNIVERSITY
PRESS OF
AMERICA

Lanham • New York • London

Copyright © 1989 by
Stephen P. Gibert & William M. Carpenter

University Press of America,® Inc.

4720 Boston Way
Lanham, MD 20706

3 Henrietta Street
London WC2E 8LU England

Printed in the United States of America

British Cataloging in Publication Information Available

Library of Congress Cataloging-in-Publication Data

America and Island China: a documentary history/edited by Stephen
P. Gibert, William M. Carpenter.
Includes bibliographies and index.
1. United States—Foreign relations—Taiwan. 2. Taiwan—Foreign
relations—United States. 3. United States—Foreign
relations—1945- 4. Taiwan—Foreign relations—1945- I. Gibert,
Stephen P. II. Carpenter, William M.
E183.8.T3A44 1988
327.73051'249—dc19   88-13882 CIP

ISBN 0-8191-7256-1 (alk. paper)

All University Press of America books are produced on acid-free paper.
The paper used in this publication meets the minimum requirements of American
National Standard for Information Sciences—Permanence of Paper for Printed Library
Materials, ANSI Z39.48–1984.   ∞

CONTENTS

Preface...vii

1. Introduction..1

Part I

America and Island China

2. The Chinese Revolution 1911-1949, *Harold C. Hinton*...5

3. The Republic of China on Taiwan Since 1949, *Harold C. Hinton*.. 9

4. Military Milestones, *Martin L. Lasater*...27

5. Economic Relations, *Jan S. Prybyla*... 51

Part II

Documents: 1949-1978

6. Political and Diplomatic.. 71

7. Military...117

8. Economic and Technological..165

Part III

Documents: 1979-1988

9. The Taiwan Relations Act and Its Future..195

About the Authors...401

Index...403

PREFACE

The status of the Republic of China is unique. There are no close historical parallels from which to draw inferences about its future. Of the nations which the Second World War and its aftermath left split into opposing political regimes -- Korea, Vietnam, and Germany -- the Republic of China (ROC) is exceptional in being separated from its rival political entity by a formidable barrier, the 100 miles of water of the Taiwan Strait. Were it not for this geopolitical circumstance, without doubt the confrontation between the ROC and the Peoples Republic of China (PRC), which has persisted over the last three decades, would long since have been resolved by military means, in favor of the PRC. Even given the ocean barrier, Taiwan might have been subjugated were it not for the deterrent of the 1954 ROC-U.S. Mutual Security Treaty. This treaty is now officially terminated, but the United States, because of the provisions of the April 1979 Taiwan Relations Act, remains committed to assisting Taiwan in maintaining its defense against possible threats from mainland China. In creating this legislation, the Congress recognized that Taiwan was emerging as one of the most dynamic and successful of the newly industrializing countries.

The Taiwan Relations Act (TRA) -- which dictates close United States relations with a non-recognized nation -- is a unique experiment in American diplomatic history. This unprecedented innovation, as well as the growing importance of the Pacific Basin to U.S. security and economic well-being, prompted this documentary history. Many members of the U.S. Congress have taken office since the enactment of the landmark TRA legislation. Accordingly, the editors believe it is most useful to have a collection of all the important documents concerning American relations with Taiwan, together with illustrative selections of less important documents, since the establishment in 1949 of the Republic of China on the island of Taiwan.

In order to place the documents into context, brief chapters have been written on the background of the Chinese revolution, the diplomatic history of the island republic's relations with the United States since 1949, an assessment of the security connection between the United States and Taiwan with emphasis on the post-TRA period, and the American economic relationship with Taiwan.

The editors wish to thank contributing authors Harold Hinton, Martin Lasater, and Jan Prybyla. We also want to acknowledge the assistance of Georgetown University graduate student Marc Geneste, who helped us in the document compilation. We are grateful to Mary Ruth Ford, Zari Malsawma, other staff of Georgetown University's National Security Studies Program, and Marie Brewer of SRI International who undertook editing, word processing and other tasks necessary to prepare the book for publication.

William M. Carpenter   Stephen P. Gibert

CHAPTER ONE

INTRODUCTION

The communist victory in the protracted Chinese civil war in 1949 which resulted in mainland China's becoming the People's Republic of China (PRC) and the establishment of the rival Republic of China (ROC) on Taiwan ushered in the "China problem" in American foreign policy. Until Communist China intervened in the Korean war in the fall of 1950, it was likely that the United States would have recognized the newly-established People's Republic on the mainland and cut its ties with the Republic of China on Taiwan. But the PRC-American military clash in Korea resulted in a decades-long hostile relationship between the two countries which endured until National Security Adviser Henry Kissinger's trip to China in 1971. This paved the way for President Nixon's official invitation to China. While in China, PRC and U.S. officials came to a limited agreement: the Shanghai Communique of February 1972.

In the Shanghai Communique the United States acknowledged that both the PRC and Taiwan state that there is only one China and that Taiwan is a part of China. President Nixon refused, however, to terminate U.S. ties with the Republic of China on Taiwan. In December, 1978, President Carter met the three conditions which the PRC insisted upon as prerequisites to establishing formal diplomatic relations between China and the United States. These were: terminating American recognition of the Republic of China and transferring it to the PRC; abrogating the ROC-U.S. Mutual Security Treaty of 1954; and removing U.S. military forces and installations from Taiwan. President Carter did not agree to ending U.S. arms sales to Taiwan but subsequently he suspended arms sales for the one-year period required in the treaty for notification by either party of intent to terminate it.

Congress reacted quite negatively to President Carter's decision to transfer American recognition from Taiwan to the mainland. The fundamental criticism was that insufficient measures had been taken to insure Taiwan's security against a possible PRC attempt to capture the island by force. Accordingly, the Congress, under the leadership of the Senate Foreign Relations Committee, began consideration of legislation to guarantee that Washington would continue to assist Taipei to maintain its security and to provide a firm legal albeit "informal," relationship between the United States and Taiwan. This effort resulted in the Taiwan Relations Act (TRA), passed by the Congress and signed into law by President Carter in April 1979.

Since the passage of the TRA, U.S. relations with the PRC have followed an uneven course. While agreeing to disagree over American support for Taiwan, neither Beijing nor Washington has permitted the continuation of close ties between the United States and Taiwan to jeopardize the growing set of relations between China and America. Beijing has recognized that a strong U.S. presence in East Asia provides a useful counterweight to the Soviet Union. Additionally, the PRC desires to increase its trade with the United States and is especially anxious to acquire American technological assistance.

At the same time, although "tilting" toward the United States, the PRC has no interest in an alliance directed against the Soviet Union. Rather, China appears to want friendly but not close relations with both superpowers, not being drawn into the orbit of either. Accordingly, whenever China has perceived that it was becoming too closely identified with Soviet positions in world affairs, it has publicly proclaimed that three "obstacles" stand in the way of close ties between Beijing and Moscow. These are the Soviet occupation of Afghanistan, the stationing of a large number of Soviet forces on the Chinese border, and Soviet support for Vietnam's intervention in Cambodia. Even were one or more of these obstacles to be removed, it is likely that the PRC would find other issues that could be raised to keep Chinese-Soviet relations under firm control in Beijing.

Conversely, whenever Chinese officials believe relations between the PRC and the United States are becoming too close, they complain about American support for Taiwan. The Republic of China on Taiwan thus plays, albeit unwillingly, an important role in the PRC-U.S.-Soviet "Iron Triangle."

The United States shares the basic policy preferences of the PRC with regard to the triangular relationship between the two countries and the Soviet Union. Clearly the resumption of diplomatic ties between China and the United States furthers the American aim of denying the Soviet Union undue political influence in Northeast Asia. At the same time Washington recognizes that fundamental differences in ideology, philosophies of government, regard for human rights, and other factors rule out a Sino-American alliance. In any event, such an alliance would destroy any hope of improved relations with the Soviet Union and probably would result in an intensified arms race.

The Taiwan Relations Act provides the legal basis for on-going American relations with the island republic. Of course the growth of trade between the two Chinas, the easing of travel restrictions, and other interactions will affect the specifics of U.S. policy. Further, in an era of change there is always the possibility that a future Congress, unfamiliar with the history of the long and close association between Taiwan and the United States, might take actions which are inconsistent with either the letter or the broad purpose of the TRA, thus opening up entirely new and unforeseen political and security problems in the Pacific region. Many of the present members of the House of Representatives and a number of Senators were not in the Congress in 1979 when Congress enacted the Taiwan Relations Act. And, except for those members who have special foreign affairs and defense responsibilities, or who have otherwise acquired expert familiarity with U.S. East Asian policy, it cannot be expected that the majority in Congress will be fully informed on the China issue. This book, which includes all of the important documents on ROC-American relations since 1979, along with illustrative less important documents, should be of use to the Congress when considering future policy toward the PRC and Taiwan.

The documents covering the period 1949-1978 are organized into three categories: Political and Diplomatic; Military; and Economic and Technological. The fourth collection, entitled the Taiwan Relations Act and Its Future, begins with the December 15, 1978 speech by President Carter, in which he announced the switch in U.S. diplomatic relations from Taiwan to the PRC. Because of the importance of the more recent materials the fourth collection is very extensive, including 70 separate documents, some of which, such as the TRA, are reproduced in their entirety. Less critical, but nonetheless important documents, usually concerned with political and military relations, have been reduced in length by omitting less vital sections. A few less important documents, usually economic in character, have been included in the section on the Taiwan Relations Act and Its Future in order to illustrate the range of relationships between the United States and the Republic of China.

It is the firm belief of the authors that all important documents concerning United States-Taiwan relations since 1949 are included in this book and it is their hope that it will prove useful to both policymakers and scholars in the years to come.

Part I

America and Island China

THE CHINESE REVOLUTION, 1911-1949

Harold C. Hinton

The decline of the Manchu Dynasty, which had ruled China since 1644, was a long and involved process greatly complicated by pressures and influences from abroad. The dynasty's fall began with a military revolt on October 10, 1911, a date that is known to Chinese as the Double Ten and is conventionally considered to mark the beginning of the Chinese Revolution. The "last emperor," a small boy, abdicated in February 1912, and the Chinese Republic came into existence.

The Role of Sun Yat-sen

Prominent among the revolutionary leaders who had worked to overthrow the Manchus was Dr. Sun Yat-sen, a patriotic Cantonese who was outside the country at the time of the Double Ten and in fact had spent most of the preceding years abroad, both in order to escape execution at the hands of the Manchus and to collect funds and support for his activities from among overseas Chinese communities. He hurried back to China to find himself the newly elected provisional president of the revolutionary government. He also found himself without real power, and he soon resigned in favor of Yuan Shih-kai, a former high official under the Manchus who controlled a sizable army.

Sun spent the next few years in opposition to Yuan and in the formation of a new political party, the Kuomintang (the National People's Party, sometimes called the Nationalist Party or simply the Nationalists, and referred to hereafter as the KMT). Like many other patriotic Chinese, he was distressed to see Yuan Shih-kai transform himself into a dictator and then begin to have himself proclaimed emperor of a new dynasty.

After Yuan's death, which occurred in 1916 as he was trying to suppress revolts touched off by his own actions, China dissolved into virtual chaos. The republican government in Peking (Beijing) was ineffectual, and the country was dominated by a collection of provincial and regional military governors, usually referred to as warlords. With few exceptions, they misgoverned their territories, and some of them were under strong foreign influence.

For the time being, Sun Yat-sen was at a loss how to implement his political program, which he had been developing since the late nineteenth century. It is usually called the Three People's Principles (San Min Chu I), although a better translation would be the Three Principles of the People. The principles are Nationalism, Democracy, and People's Livelihood.

Nationalism refers to the political unity of the Chinese people, as well as the ethnic minorities, the overthrow of warlordism, and the expulsion of excessive foreign influence by armed force.

Democracy means the implementation of popular sovereignty through a constitutional government composed of five Yuan (branches): the Executive, Legislative, Judicial,

Examination (for candidates for elective or appointive public office), and Control (for auditing government accounts and impeaching malfeasant officials). (The Government of the Republic of China, or GRC, on Taiwan is organized today along these lines.) The state of constitutional government was to be reached through a period of "political tutelage," during which the KMT, having first unified the country by force, would exercise a monoply of political power but with the mission of educating the people in the arts of self-government.

People's Livelihood is equivalent to what today would be called the welfare state, not necessarily fullblown socialism.

The San Min Chu I might have remained on paper if Dr. Sun had not eventually found a way to acquire some real power. He did this by "tilting," beginning in 1922, toward the young Bolshevik regime in Russia, which, unlike the Western powers, was interested in helping Sun -- for its own anti-Western reasons, of course. In 1923, Lenin's Third International (the Communist International, or Comintern), which was controlled by the Bolsheviks, began to send advisers, most but not all of them Russians, as well as arms and funds to the KMT. It ordered the infant Chinese Communist Party, not only to support Dr. Sun, but to join the KMT and submit to its discipline. Comintern advisers reorganized the KMT into a reasonable facsimile of a "democratic centralist" one -- highly organized and tightly controlled from the top -- modeled on the Bolsheviks. Another important transplant from Russia was the theory and practice of an effective party-led army, whose political morale and loyalty would be ensured by a network of political officers ("commissars").

Civil War and Japanese Invasion

With these powerful new assets, the KMT rapidly became the most dynamic political force in China. Beginning in 1925, the year of Dr. Sun's death, the party's army and political organizers swept northward (in the so-called Northern Expedition) and seized control first of the lower Yangtze Valley and then (in 1928) of much of North China, including Peking (Beijing). A new KMT-controlled, government was proclaimed at Nanking (Nanjing) later in 1928, and Dr. Sun's period of Political Tutelage began. This brilliant success was complicated, however, by a serious split within the KMT.

After Dr. Sun's death in 1925, leadership of the KMT had passed to General Chiang Kai-shek, its top military commander. Far more suspicious of the Soviet Union than Dr. Sun had been, he perceived correctly that Moscow intended to use its alliance with the KMT not only to expel Western and Japanese influence from China but also to have the Chinese Communists take control eventually over the KMT by infiltrating its leading bodies and by pressuring it from below through Communist-led peasant and labor unions. Accordingly, Chiang moved forcefully in the spring of 1926 to deal with the first of these threats, and a year later to cope with the second. The Communists, severely weakened but not destroyed, retreated into the countryside.

China had been unified more in name than in fact. The effective control of the Republic of China (ROC) was limited more or less to the lower Yangtze Valley and portions of the coastal areas to the north and south of the Yangtze. Elsewhere, provincial strongmen, some of them among the warlords of the previous period, exercised real power, while in most cases acknowledging nominally the authority of the ROC. In south central China, below the Yangtze, the Communists soon began to build power bases ("soviets") in remote rural areas and to develop a Red Army that grew increasingly skilled at guerrilla warfare. The most important Communist base area turned out to be one in the province of Kiangsi (Jiangxi) led by Mao Tse-tung (Mao Zedong), a fiery young peasant organizer and a self-taught and capable guerrilla strategist. Farther north, the Japanese army seized Manchuria in 1931-32 and then began to put pressure on North China.

In spite of these and many other problems, the new government in Nanking managed during its decade there (1928-1939) to give some reality to the concept of Political Tutelage. It was recognized by most of the foreign powers, including the United States, as the legitimate government of China. It made some progress in improving China's infrastructure (railways, etc.), in enlarging its industrial base, and in dealing with agrarian problems such as tenancy.

This record, although spotty, was destroyed from the outside, not by the Communists but by the Japanese. There can be no serious doubt that the main reason why the ROC ultimately lost control of the mainland of China to the Communists was the devasting Japanese invasion of eastern China that began in 1937. Other factors, notably various errors of the KMT and the relatively effective performance of the Communists, were also significant, but less so. The KMT's errors included a growing political conservatism, increasing corruption as the war went on, strategic mistakes (such as the obvious failure to annihilate the Communists while they were in retreat during their famous Long March from South to Northwest China in 1934-1935), and an inability to control inflation during and after the war with Japan. Soviet support for the Communists and shortcomings in American support for the ROC existed but were not sufficiently important to have a decisive effect on the outcome of the Chinese civil war.

From 1937 to 1945, however, the main problem for the ROC was not the civil war with the Communists, which was in a state of partial suspense owing to the Japanese invasion, but the war against Japan. In 1937-38, Japanese forces occupied exactly the areas where the main bases of the KMT and the ROC lay -- the lower Yangtze Valley and other important coastal regions such as the one around Canton (Guangzhou). This disaster not only weakened the KMT severely but inflicted enormous human and economic damage on the occupied areas. The Communists, whose main bases by 1937 were in Northwest China, outside the area seized by the Japanese, were much less affected than was the KMT. For the Communists, the war was not so much a disaster as an opportunity; the Japanese army was the only force in China that could weaken the KMT and its armies sufficiently so that the Communists could seize power later. The success of this scenario of course required that the Japanese be defeated by someone more powerful than they, and so they were, of course, by the United States in the Pacific after 1941.

Beginning about the time of Pearl Harbor, the United States launched a program of military support for the ROC, which was regarded as a major ally in the war against Japan. General Claire L. Chennault's Flying Tigers, volunteer American pilots who were already fighting for the ROC, became the Fourteenth Air Force and by the end of the war had inflicted enormous damage on Japanese forces operating in China as well as on Japanese shipping in the China Sea. General Joseph W. Stilwell became commander of American forces in China and Burma. He worked to modernize the Chinese army but tended to be more interested in retaking Burma, from which he had been driven by the Japanese in the spring of 1942, than in the more important show in China itself. Furthermore, an escalating personal feud with President Chiang seriously impaired his usefulness and led to his relief by President Roosevelt in 1944. American support for Chiang and his government, which had previously been enthusiastic on the whole -- as shown by the invitation to Chiang to confer with Roosevelt and Churchill at Cairo in late 1943 -- cooled somewhat as a result of the Stilwell affair. But the United States still ensured that the ROC became a founding member of the United Nations and a permanent member of the Security Council in 1945. In addition, the United States provided the ROC with credits, arms, and advisers on a substantial scale.

Driven from the lower Yangtze Valley, the GRC made its wartime headquarters much farther upriver, at Chungking (Chongqing). There, in a remote rural region, it lost much of its effectiveness, in spite of American support, and increasingly developed the problems and shortcomings already mentioned.

In other remote areas farther north, the Communists, who had the great advantage of not having to operate a major government under wartime conditions, managed to escape the corruption and inflation that plagued Chungking. From their headquarters at Yenan (Yan'an), Mao Tse-tung and his colleagues generally managed to avoid disastrous battles with the Japanese, built up the Red Army, whittled away at the Japanese -- and sometimes also at the Nationalist forces -- in guerrilla actions, and conserved most of their strength for the coming postwar struggle with the KMT. In the last months, as Japanese forces withdrew from many outlying areas near the coast that they had previously occupied, Communist forces, which had become skilled at operating behind Japanese lines, rapidly filled the vacuum and expanded the territory and population under Communist control severalfold.

Defeat on the Mainland

The surrender of Japan led to the transfer by the GRC of its capital back to Nanking as the recognized government of a major victorious Allied power. In reality, however, the GRC had been greatly weakened by the war, and it proceeded promptly to overextend itself by trying to occupy territory abandoned by the Japanese, sometimes in competition with the Communists. The United States supported this effort logistically and continued to give economic and military aid to the GRC, but it was gravely concerned over the possibility that China might be devastated by a renewal of civil war and that the United States and the Soviet Union might be dragged into it on opposite sides. The United States therefore tried to work out a compromise between the two Chinese parties that would have involved a coalition government and a unified national army. The effort failed, on account of the hositility and suspicion between the two sides, and civil war broke out in earnest in 1946.

The Communists had the significant advantage of the stronger position in Manchuria, to which the Soviet occupation forces had quietly admitted them in 1945-1946, and where they had acquired stocks of surrendered Japanese weapons. They had certain other assets as well in the form of effective leadership, high morale, and experience in guerilla warfare, that began to tell as the war went on.

On the Nationalist side, inflation grew to astronomical levels after 1945. The home front was further weakened by active political opposition to the government and by increasing official crackdowns on dissent. In the field, the best American-trained units were wasted in a hopeless effort to hold Manchuria, and generalship in other theaters was usually not of the best.

In 1948 the Communists began to win a series of major victories. They completed their conquest of Manchuria in October of that year. Early in 1949, they took Peking and Tientsin (Tianjin). In the spring, it was the turn of the Yangtze Valley, and by the end of the year everything of importance except Tibet and the two islands of Hainan and Taiwan had been "liberated."

Meanwhile, the Nationalists had transferred their headquarters from Nanking and eventually out of the mainland as a whole. During 1949, some two million officials, troops, dependents, refugees, etc., moved to Taiwan, which was better situated than Hainan to serve as an offshore base from which, it was officially claimed, the mainland would some day be recovered.

CHAPTER THREE

THE REPUBLIC OF CHINA ON TAIWAN SINCE 1949

Harold C. Hinton

Defeat by the Communists on the mainland compelled the Kuomintang and the Government of the Republic of China (GRC) to move their base of operations to Taiwan in 1949. From then on, Taiwan plus some small islands off the China coast (usually known as "the offshore islands") constituted the only significant territory actually controlled by the GRC.

Consolidating the Base

Taiwan, a beautiful, subtropical island with about twice the area of Hawaii and lying one hundred miles off the China coast, was experiencing some degree of political unrest at that time. The Taiwanese population, which is Chinese and speaks a dialect of the language spoken in the province of Fukien (Fujian) on the China coast, but which was used to stable government and reasonable prosperity as a result of the period of Japanese colonial rule (1895-1945), resented a spell of misrule by officials sent from the mainland that had followed the Japanese surrender. This resentment had led to a clash between government troops and Taiwanese on February 28, 1947, in which a number of Taiwanese were killed. Subsequently the GRC introduced reforms designed to correct the worst of the existing abuses. Then there was more confusion as the result of the arrival of a few million refugees from the mainland -- troops, officials, and so on, plus their dependents -- in 1949.

At that point, however, the GRC launched an effective reform program, with some valuable technical assistance from the United States. Agricultural land that had been owned by absentee landlords, Japanese or Taiwanese, was made available on favorable terms to Taiwanese farmers, who soon became one of the most prosperous rural populations in Asia and were also allowed a considerable degree of local self-government. Similarly, formerly Japanese-owned light industrial enterprises were sold off to Taiwanese entrepreneurs. By and large, the Taiwanese majority enjoyed the greater share of the island's growing prosperity.

Political power, however, rested overwhelmingly with the minority of mainlanders. The Kuomintang and the GRC brought with them from the mainland the full governmental structure with its five Yuan (branches) that it had derived from Sun Yat-sen's teachings. They also introduced martial law, which was rationalized on the basis of the continuing Communist threat but which facilitated the suppression of political opposition and dissent. This political system was officially defended on the ground that the island was only a temporary base and that the government and armed forces would soon "return to the mainland" and retake it from the Communists. This myth grew increasingly implausible with the passage of time, but it retained some vitality at the upper levels of the system until roughly the death of President Chiang Kai-shek in 1975.[1]

The Threat from the Mainland and the American Umbrella

Even though the Chinese Communist armed forces have never had much of a capability for amphibious operations, the idea of a military and political threat from the mainland has always loomed large in the minds of the GRC and much of the population of Taiwan. To a large extent, this nervousness is the result of the enormous disparity in size between the two contestants, and specifically between the areas that they respectively control.

In this seemingly unequal contest, the United States came to serve as the "equalizer." In spite of considerable disenchantment with the GRC because of its performance on the mainland, the United States continued to recognize it as the government of the whole of China and to maintain diplomatic relations with it after 1949. To a large extent, this was because the new Chinese Communist regime on the mainland chose to treat the United States as an adversary, for reasons only one of which was the American decision to maintain official relations with the GRC.

On the other hand, at first the Truman administration was in no mood to defend Taiwan against a possible Communist attack; the policy was rather to "let the dust settle," or in other words to wait and see. Secretary of State Dean Acheson, in a celebrated speech on January 12, 1950, pointedly excluded Taiwan, as well as South Korea and Indochina, from the American defense perimeter in the Western Pacific.

This policy was strongly unacceptable to the GRC itself and to its various American friends, who included General MacArthur in Tokyo and some powerful members of Congress. Accordingly, the decision not to defend Taiwan was reversed on June 27, 1950, simultaneously with the decision to defend South Korea against the North Korean invasion that had just begun. In part, the Truman administration acted on the basis of a belief that the outbreak of war in Korea foreshadowed a general offensive in the region by the newly formed Sino-Soviet alliance (between Mao and Stalin). In addition, by extending protection to Taiwan, the Truman administration hoped to gain political support from conservative politicians for the operation in Korea, which had been launched without Congressional sanction. To be more exact, President Truman announced on June 27, 1950, that United States forces -- the Seventh Fleet, in particular -- would neutralize the Taiwan Strait, or in other words, prevent either side in the continuing Chinese civil war from attacking the other; in practice, in view of the imbalance between the two sides, it meant protecting Taiwan from the mainland much more than the other way around.[2]

When President Eisenhower came into office in January 1953, the Korean War had become a stalemate, and he and Secretary of State John Foster Dulles were determined to end it by one means or another. Accordingly, Eisenhower announced early in February 1953 that the United States, while continuing to protect the Republic of China (ROC) on Taiwan, would no longer prevent the ROC from attacking the mainland; in the political propaganda of that period, this initiative was referred to as "unleashing Chiang Kai-shek." It made no impression on the Peoples Republic of China (PRC), which had to be brought to sign a Korean armistice on terms acceptable to the United States by means of a threat to use nuclear weapons. As for the ROC, it was told privately by Secretary of State Dulles that it should not try to attack the mainland, and that if it did so it could not count on American support. This was jocularly known as the "lend leash" policy.[3]

The most important of the offshore islands held by the GRC is Quemoy (Kinmen), which lies just off the mainland port city of Amoy (Xiamen). By 1954, the Communists apparently had come to suspect that the GRC was planning offensive operations against the mainland from Quemoy, where strong ROC forces have been stationed continuously since 1949. In any event, the PRC launched an air and naval operation against Quemoy and some of the other offshore islands from September 1954 to March 1955. It was militarily unsuccessful on the whole, and its main effect was to drive the ROC and the United States together even closer than before. At the end of 1954, they concluded a mutual defense treaty covering Taiwan and certain islands immediately adjacent to it. The offshore islands were covered by the so-called Formosa Resolution, which was passed by an overwhelming vote of both houses of Congress in January 1955; it was repealed in 1974. The Formosa Resolution provided that the President could commit American forces to the defense of the offshore islands if in his judgment such a step was necessary for the defense of Taiwan itself.[4]

In August 1958, Chinese Communist forces launched an operation that, although directed immediately against Quemoy, was admittedly aimed at the "liberation" of Taiwan. Without actually engaging in combat, United States naval vessels took part in the resupply of Quemoy, and weapons capable of firing tactical nuclear warheads were deployed temporarily to the island. These actions by the United States undoubtedly contributed to the failure of the operation, which was abandoned in October. At that time, Secretary Dulles persuaded President Chiang Kai-shek to issue a statement to the effect that the recovery of the mainland would be primarily a political, not a military process.

In the spring of 1962, nevertheless, Beijing began to suspect that Taipei was contemplating offensive operations against the mainland to take advantage of the difficult conditions created by the collapse of the Great Leap Forward. The PRC responded to this perceived threat with a rapid troop buildup opposite Taiwan and a series of propaganda statements designed to determine whether the United States would support an operation by Taiwan against the mainland if one occurred. The answer to this question was no, as President Kennedy made clear at a press conference on June 27, 1962.[5]

Since then, there have been no further serious military crises in the Taiwan Strait. On the other hand, Beijing has always refused to give a "renunciation of force" pledge with respect to Taiwan, as the United States demanded that it do in a series of Sino-American talks at the ambassadorial level that began at Geneva in 1955 and moved to Warsaw in 1958.[6]

An "Island of Growth"

American military protection of Taiwan was supplemented by a large economic and military aid program that began in the early 1960s and lasted for about ten years. The main purpose of this aid was to strengthen the island's overall ability to withstand pressures from the mainland. The total amount of economic and military aid combined for the period 1950-57 was approximately U.S. $2 billion.[7]

The effectiveness of this aid was considerable and was due to at least four factors. One was the industriousness of the Taiwanese population. A second was the impressive economic and social infrastructure left behind by the Japanese. A third was in increased efficiency on the part of the GRC now that it could concentrate on administering Taiwan without having to try to control the entire mainland as well. A fourth was the fact that after the crisis of 1958, the GRC began to devote less attention to the recovery of the mainland and more to the development of Taiwan. The island was now seen, not as a temporary haven, but as a base for the indefinite future.

Already under Japanese rule, Taiwan had been basically self-sufficient in the agricultural sector, and, in fact, had been an exporter of various foodstuffs and raw materials. The GRC's land reform and rural development programs built effectively on this foundation, so that earnings from agricultural exports were able to make an indispensable contribution to the development of industry. This occurred at first in the energy and light industrial sectors, but in time also in heavy industry. In spite of some continuing problems, the combination of private initiative and governmental support has led -- by the 1980s-- to a level of prosperity that is very unusual in Asia, a status as a major trading power (especially with the United States), and the world's largest per capita accumulation of gold and foreign exchange (about U.S. $75 billion for a population of 20 million).

By the early 1960s, this progress seemed so impressive to the United States Government that Taiwan was considered an outstanding example of "self-sustaining economic growth" that no longer needed aid. Accordingly, both economic and military aid were reduced and then eliminated. Instead, the United States contributed to Taiwan's prosperity by remaining its largest single foreign market, and to its security by continuing arms sales, as well as by the Mutual Defense Treaty of 1954, which remained in effect.

"Normalization"

Nevertheless, Taiwan posed a serious policy problem for the United States. Neither the ROC nor the PRC would allow -- or will allow today -- any foreign country, including the United States, to have diplomatic relations with both simultaneously.[8] During the 1970s, for a variety of reasons -- diplomatic, strategic, commercial, etc. -- an increasing number of governments transferred recognition and diplomatic relations from Taipei to Beijing. The major holdout was the United States, primarily because of its historic ties with, and its sense of moral obligation to, the ROC. By about 1970, however, the former hostility between Washington and Beijing had diminished substantially, and each felt a pressing need for an improved relationship with the other for a number of reasons, the most urgent of which was the strategic threat to both from the Soviet Union.

Accordingly, shortly after coming into office in 1969, President Nixon and his National Security Adviser (later Secretary of State) Henry Kissinger set out to create an improved relationship with Beijing that it was hoped would culminate in "normal," or diplomatic, relations. It was realized, of course, that such a policy would involve an erosion of the American commitment to Taiwan and would be greeted with outrage in Taipei. "No government," Kissinger later wrote, "less deserved what was about to happen to it than that of Taiwan. It had been a loyal ally; its conduct toward us had been exemplary."[9]

The celebrated Shanghai Communique, signed by President Nixon and Premier Chou En-lai (Zhou Enlai) in February 1972, contained some limited American concessions to Beijing at Taiwan's expense, in terms of what was and was not included in the document. One concession was negative; the U.S. side consciously passed up the opportunity to reaffirm the American commitment to Taiwan. Also, the American team promised to reduce its military personnel and installations on Taiwan (present there largely in connection with the Vietnam war, which was "winding down") "as the tension in the area diminishes," and to remove all of them eventually. On the other hand, the United States declined to involve itself in a solution of the Taiwan question, which it insisted must be settled peacefully between the two Chinese parties themselves. In that regard, the U.S. said it would not support an independent Taiwan; this was not desired by either the PRC or the ROC authorities. "Normalization" was clearly stated as the desired ultimate state of the relationship between Washington and Beijing.[10]

Early in 1973, Washington and Beijing exchanged "liaison offices." These were official, but technically non-diplomatic; in reality, they were embassies in everything but name.[11]

Beijing continued to apply pressure in various ways for a rupture of diplomatic relations between Washington and Taipei, and for the abrogation of the Mutual Defense Treaty of 1954. From the American point of view, the main problem was that Beijing still rejected the idea of a "renunciation of force" with respect to Taiwan, and in the absence of one, the American side was reluctant to terminate the treaty. Washington's main initiative during the early Carter period was a proposal that the liaison offices be raised to the rank of embassies and that the American Embassy in Taipei be reduced to a liaison office; Teng Hsiao-ping (Deng Xiaoping) firmly rejected this idea, stating that the American relationship with Taiwan must be unofficial as well as non-diplomatic if it was to be acceptable to Beijing.

In 1978 a number of developments, especially the worsening crises in Afghanistan and Cambodia, made Washington and Beijing somewhat more flexible on the terms under which "normal" relations would be established. President Carter agreed to transfer diplomatic recognition without trying to retain any official relationship with Taiwan and Washington dropped its demand for a "renunciation of force" by Beijing. On the other hand, the U.S. insisted on abrogating the Mutual Security Treaty by giving the required one year's notice rather than simply canceling it. The U.S. did not agree to terminating arms sales to Taiwan after the expiration of the treaty, but did suspend arms transfers during the one-year period the Mutual Security Treaty remained in force. For its part, Beijing protested the idea of continued American arms sales to Taiwan but did not allow its objections to obstruct "normalization." Formal diplomatic relations were broken between Washington and Taipei and established between Washington and Beijing effective January 1, 1979.[12]

The United States and Taiwan Since "Normalization"

The termination of diplomatic relations and the mutual defense treaty did not mean a complete abandonment of Taiwan by the United States. This was not contemplated by the Carter administration, eager though it was to "normalize" relations with Beijing.

On January 26, 1979, President Carter transmitted to Congress a bill designed to regulate the new unofficial (non-diplomatic) relationship between the United States and Taiwan.[13] In the eyes of Taiwan's supporters in Congress and elsewhere in American public life, it was a highly anemic measure; in particular, it made no reference to the problem of Taiwan's future security or to the continuation of American arms sales to "the people on Taiwan," a term used officially beginning at that time to refer to the derecognized ROC, as well as everyone else on the island. Accordingly, under the leadership of the Senate Foreign Relations Committee, and various Congressional supporters of Taiwan, Congress began work on another, much stronger, piece of legislation known as the Taiwan Relations Act (TRA). It was passed by both Houses, with large majorities, in April 1979 and was then reluctantly signed by President Carter.[14]

The TRA begins by making it clear, at least indirectly, that future relations between the United States and Taiwan are to be unofficial, or non-diplomatic ("commercial, cultural, and other relations between the people of the United States and the people on Taiwan"). The first substantive section of the Act (Sec. 2) deals in strong terms with the issues of Taiwan's security and the future of American arms sales to "the people on Taiwan."

It is the policy of the United States-

(1) to preserve and promote extensive, close, and friendly commercial, cultural, and other relations between the people of the United States and the people on Taiwan, as well as the people on the China mainland and all other peoples of the Western Pacific area;

(2) to declare that peace and stability in the area are in the political, security, and economic interests of the United States, and are matters of international concern;

(3) to make clear that the United States decision to establish diplomatic relations with the People's Republic of China rests upon the expectation that the future of Taiwan will be determined by peaceful means;

(4) to consider any effort to determine the future of Taiwan by other than peaceful means, including by boycotts or embargoes, a threat to the peace and security of the Western Pacific area and of grave concern to the United States;

(5) to provide Taiwan with arms of a defensive character; and

(6) to maintain the capacity of the United States to resist any resort to force or other forms of coercion that would jeopardize the security, or the social or economic system, of the people on Taiwan.

Although the opinion has been expressed that the language of the TRA regarding the critical issue of American arms sales is permissive, it appears on a commonsense reading to be mandatory; the thrust of the House and Senate Committee Reports, the Conference Report, and statements on the floor of both houses of Congress relating to this question confirm that Congress intended to require continued arms sales of a defensive character to Taiwan.[15] Section 3 of the Act deals further with the matter of arms sales, in the following language:

(a)...the United States will make available to Taiwan such quantity as may be necessary to enable Taiwan to maintain a sufficient self-defense capability.

(b) The President and the Congress shall determine the nature and quality of such defense articles and services based solely upon their judgment of the needs of Taiwan, in accordance with procedures established by law. Such determination of Taiwan's defense needs shall include review by United States military authorities in connection with recommendations by the President and the Congress.

The TRA directs the President to inform the Congress promptly of any PRC threat to Taiwan's security. No specific American response to such a threat is prescribed or predicted in the Act, but statements by influential members of both Houses at the time of the passage of the TRA suggest that the breaking of diplomatic relations with Beijing would be a likely step and that military action, in accordance with the provisions of the War Powers Act, of course, would not be excluded.[16]

Many of the provisions of the TRA naturally are legal or technical in nature. Provisions of more substantive significance include an assertion that the United States maintains an active interest in "the human rights of all the people on Taiwan..." (Sec. 2c). Section 4 of the Act defines Taiwan in effect as a de facto state and treats its "governing authorities" as successors to all rights of the GRC -- apart from diplomatic relations, of course -- in and with respect to the United States. A technically unofficial body, the American Institute in Taiwan (AIT), is to be set up to handle the relations between the United States and Taiwan provided for by the TRA (Secs. 6-12).

After the passage of the TRA, the AIT was established, with its main office in Taipei and a branch office in the Washington area. On its side, Taipei established an analogous organization, also technically unofficial and known as the Coordination Council for North American Affairs (CCNAA), to handle its new relationship with the United States. The CCNAA maintains its head office in Washington and has ten branch offices. Formerly, the ROC operated fourteen consulates and the TRA contemplated permitting the CCNAA to have that number of branches in the United States. However, the State Department has permitted the CCNAA only ten American offices. These branch offices are in Atlanta, Chicago, Honolulu, Houston, Los Angeles, New York City, San Francisco, Seattle, Boston, and Kansas City. In terms of substantive duties, there is an important difference between that of the U.S.-sponsored AIT and the ROC-sponsored CCNAA: the AIT does not perform any functions that would normally be considered official or diplomatic, while the CCNAA does (such as the issuing of visas). This is because Taipei objects to the rupture of diplomatic relations by the United States, would like them to be restored, and in the meantime seeks to replicate formal relations as closely as possible.

Of course, Beijing resents the TRA as an act of interference in China's internal affairs and demands its repeal. Beijing was outraged when Ronald Reagan, during his 1980 presidential campaign, announced repeatedly that he intended if elected to upgrade the relationship with Taiwan to the official level by establishing a liaison office in Taipei in lieu of the AIT. A visit to the PRC by vice-presidential candidate George Bush, a former director of the United States Liaison Office in China in August 1980, did not resolve this issue to Beijing's satisfaction and evoked a series of Chinese propaganda blasts.[17] Beijing was still more infuriated when Reagan, at a news conference held on August 25, following Bush's return from China, reaffirmed his support for "normalization, " but also declared that, if elected, "I would not pretend, as Carter does, that the relationship we now have with Taiwan enacted by our Congress [in other words, the TRA] is not official."[18] This statement must have been based on insufficient information, since the TRA clearly visualizes an unofficial relationship with Taiwan.

Despite his obvious sympathy for Taiwan, after taking office President Reagan's China policy appeared to be aimed much more at cultivating the difficult but potentially important relationship with China than in reassuring Taiwan. This shift of emphasis was probably due at least in part to the influence of Secretary of State Alexander Haig, who as a former NATO commander was greatly concerned with the Soviet threat, viewed China as a useful counterweight to it, and accordingly had little interest in Taiwan.

Naturally, this was a great disappointment to Taipei, which on the basis of Reagan's campaign statements had been hoping for the fulfillment of its demands for an upgrading of the relationship at least to the level visualized in the TRA, although not necessarily to an "official" level. Specifically, Taipei wants, among other things, an increase in the number of the CCNAA's offices in the United States to fourteen, access for CCNAA personnel to United States officials in the latter's offices (rather than exclusively on private premises such as restaurants), and permission from the Department of State for personnel of the AIT headquarters in Taipei to visit the Foreign Ministry and other government departments.[19]

The reason for the official American unwillingness to make these, or any similar, concessions to Taipei was a desire not to arouse criticism and possible retaliation from Beijing, which is extremely sensitive to such matters. Beijing claims to believe, and may in fact believe, that the main single factor inhibiting Taipei from reuniting with the mainland on the basis of Beijing's repeated pledges of "autonomy" is American "interference," or in other words what remains of the United States-Taiwan relationship. In Beijing's view, the more the United States cuts back its ties with Taiwan, arms sales in particular, the more likely Taipei is to negotiate a settlement on the basis of "autonomy." This is a misperception on Beijing's part. No one on Taiwan appears to have any interest in unification with the mainland on Beijing's terms. The GRC is determined to maintain its de facto existence separate from the mainland and regards the American connection as a valuable but not necessarily indispensable means of doing this.

The biggest single irritant in Sino-American relations during the Reagan administration has been arms sales to Taiwan. It began to reach serious proportions early in the administration, when Taipei indicated that it wanted to buy the F-16, a high performance fighter aircraft that the U.S. sells to some of its allies (which Taiwan no longer is, in the formal sense).[20] This idea was turned down on policy grounds -- in other words, certain and strong objections from Beijing -- and instead American officialdom began to explore and debate the possibility of having a less capable fighter, known as the FX, developed for sale to Taiwan and perhaps other foreign clients as well.

Meanwhile, Beijing tended to be even more difficult than usual in its dealings with the United States. It reacted unfavorably to a visit by Secretary Haig in June 1981, even though he offered in principle to sell it arms, on a case-by-case basis -- the first time such an offer had been made authoritatively by an American official. Apparently Beijing feared that Haig was trying to bribe it, by means of an offer-in-principle that might never materialize, into accepting continued or even increased American arms sales to Taiwan, possibly including the FX. Beijing's concern over this question was so great that Premier Zhao Ziyang appeared unlikely to visit the United States, as he had agreed to do in response to an invitation from President Reagan in August 1981, until the Taiwan arms sale issue was settled to Chinese satisfaction.[21] Since the American side was eager for such a visit to take place, it felt that it was under considerable pressure to seek a viable compromise with Beijing. Secretary Haig was especially anxious to accommodate the PRC on this issue, which of course went beyond the FX and included the entire program of American arms and spare parts sales to Taiwan.[22]

On January 11, 1982, the State Department announced that the National Security Council had recently decided not to permit the sale of the FX to Taiwan, on the ground that "no military need for such aircraft exists," but instead to allow Taiwan to continue coproduction of the less capable F-5E, which it already had in its inventory.[23] Assistant Secretary of State for East Asian and Pacific Affairs John Holdridge was promptly sent to Beijing to explain the decision to the Chinese, presumably in the hope that they would be pleased. They were not; their objectives covered the entire range of American arms sales to Taiwan, including the F-5E, not merely the FX.[24]

The FX decision was a severe disappointment to Taipei and its American friends, especially in Congress. The administration was so concerned over the future of PRC-American relations, however, that it was willing to negotiate with Beijing on the entire issue on arms sales to Taiwan. The Chinese side made this a little easier with a statement on January 31, 1982, to the effect that it was willing to negotiate a time limit on such sales, rather than continuing to insist on their immediate termination.[25] Beijing continued, however, to threaten an unspecified downgrading of its relations with the United States if no agreement on the Taiwan arms sale issue acceptable to itself was reached.[26]

Negotiations on this sensitive matter had begun in November 1981 in Beijing and proved to be protracted and difficult. The Chinese side rejected American efforts to link a reduction (not a termination) of arms sales to Taiwan with a continuation of peaceful behavior toward Taiwan on Beijing's part. On the other hand, Beijing refrained from downgrading relations in retaliation for a sale of $60 million worth of military equipment to Taiwan announced in Washington in April 1982,[27] or for an American decision in mid-1982 to implement the previous commitment to allow coproduction of the F-5E on Taiwan to continue. Secretary Haig had apparently opposed and prevented the latter decision until his resignation in June 1981.[28]

Sino-American negotiations moved ahead rapidly in July 1982. In order to reassure Taipei and its American supporters, the Reagan administration made six unpublished commitments to Taipei on July 14, to the effect that it had not agreed to a termination date for arms sales, had not agreed to consult with Beijing prior to approving such sales, would not mediate in any way between Taipei and Beijing, had not agreed to amend the TRA, had not altered its position on sovereignty over Taiwan (which is simply that the island is part of "China"), and would not pressure Taipei to negotiate with Beijing.[29]

On August 17, 1982, the United States and China issued a joint communique announcing an agreement of sorts aimed at mutual satisfaction on the Taiwan arms sales issue.

The result was a document (which became known as Shanghai Two) that was both highly political and rather vague. The Chinese side referred to two earlier statements by Beijing to the effect that its "fundamental policy" was to "strive for a peaceful solution to the Taiwan question." It did not specifically say, although it obviously wanted to be taken as meaning, that this policy was still in effect; still less did it promise never to use force against Taiwan under any circumstances. The American side referred approvingly to the two earlier Chinese statements and strongly implied, without quite saying, that the agreement just reached on arms sales to Taiwan was conditional on continued avoidance of force in Beijing's behavior toward the island.

The American side then affirmed that, "Having in mind the foregoing statements of both sides, the United States Government states that it does not seek to carry out a long-term policy of arms sales to Taiwan, that its arms sales to Taiwan will not exceed, either in qualitative or in quantitative terms, the level of those supplied in recent years..., and that it intends to reduce gradually its sales of arms to Taiwan, leading over a period of time to a final resolution."[30]

In spite of the six pledges given the previous month, Taiwan and its American supporters were considerably distressed by the August 17 communique. The administration tried to reassure them by insisting that American fulfillment of it would be conditional on peaceful behavior toward Taiwan on Beijing's part, and by authorizing a new sale of sixty F-5E fighters, with a total price tag of $632 million, to Taiwan over the following two and one half years.[31] On its side, Beijing promptly began to attack the idea that the reduction of arms sales envisaged in the August 17 joint communique could or should be conditioned on its pursuit of a peaceful approach to Taiwan.[32]

The administration had to remain on the defensive against supporters of Taiwan and critics of the August 17 communique, who insisted among other things that it was inconsistent with the TRA. They held that to the extent there was a conflict, the TRA should prevail; Beijing maintained exactly the opposite. In March 1983, President Reagan clarified his understanding of the term "final resolution" in the August 17 joint communique: arms sales to Taiwan would be terminated when and if Taiwan reached a mutually acceptable solution of its dispute with the mainland.[33] At the same time, the administration indicated that arms sales to Taiwan would be "indexed for inflation." In other words, because of the rising cost of weapons, the total dollar amounts of the annual sales would decline only slowly (by about $20 million per year from a high of $783 million in 1983, as it turned out).[34] Since about 1983, the arms sale issue has become somewhat less acute in Washington's relations with both Taipei and Beijing, each of whom apparently realizes that it has gotten everything it is likely to get on this score, at least from the Reagan administration. Chinese Premier Zhao Ziyang said in advance that he would not make American arms sales to Taiwan a major issue during his visit to the United States in January 1984.[35]

For a time after George Shultz became Secretary of State in mid-1982, there was some hope in Taipei that his past business connections with Taiwan might produce a friendlier American policy toward the ROC.[36] This turned out not to be noticeably the case, however. If anything, Shultz's tenure saw an intensified American effort to cultivate Beijing, for example, by authorizing the export to China of a wide range of "dual use" technology (military as well as civilian), beginning in 1983. Speaking in Shanghai on February 28, 1987, Shultz made what was interpreted on both sides of the Taiwan Strait as a potentially significant departure from the previous American policy of not intervening in or even commenting on the delicate relationship between Taipei and Beijing. His words were: "We have welcomed developments, including indirect trade and increasing human interchange, which have contributed to a relaxation of tensions in the Taiwan Strait. Our steadfast policy seeks to foster an environment within which such developments can continue to take place." This appeared to represent a concession to Beijing, which has long urged the United States to put pressure on Taiwan to deal, and ultimately unify, with the mainland, and Shultz's words were indeed interpreted in that sense in Taipei.[37] This interpretation is probably correct, and the explanation appears to be twofold: in the first place, the requirements of "briefcase diplomacy," which more or less mandate some new concession during each major visit to the demanding Chinese, and quiet American concern over the recent improvement in Sino-Soviet relations and a desire to counter it to the extent possible by intensified conciliation of Beijing. In fact, however, Shultz's innovation, if that is what it was, has not been followed by any significant American involvement in the Taipei-Beijing relationship.

Although the TRA was undoubtedly the high point since "normalization" of Congressional concern for Taiwan's interests, there have been other examples of such concern. Some Congressional leaders tried without success to have the abrogation of the Mutual Defense Treaty with Taiwan nullified by the U.S. courts. And, years after the fact, there are still complaints on Capitol Hill that "normalization" had been agreed on without advance consultation with Congress, to which the Carter administration had previously committed itself. This was essentially true, and it can hardly have been a coincidence that "normalization" was announced in mid-December 1978, when Congress was in recess. More recently, Congressional activity on the subject of Taiwan has tended to take a different tack, one sometimes offensive to Taipei as well as to Beijing -- support for self-determination on the part of the native Taiwanese majority. In April 1987, a concurrent resolution was introduced -- by Senators Kennedy, Pell, Levin, and by Representatives Solarz and Leach -- demanding the implementation of "full democracy" on Taiwan, including the lifting of martial law.[38] The ROC did terminate martial law in July 1987.

The status of human rights on Taiwan has been a significant issue in the eyes of a number of Americans, both in Congress and outside it. This issue has been defused to a considerable extent by the remarkable recent gains for political and human rights on Taiwan. Before that, however, a major uproar was created for a time by the assassination in California on October 15, 1984, of an American citizen of Taiwanese ancestry, Henry Liu, by agents of Taiwan's military intelligence. Liu, a journalist, was evidently considered guilty of writing propaganda favorable to Beijing and hostile to Taipei.[39]

Despite this incident, and other ROC-American tensions since "normalization," unofficial, including cultural, contacts between the United States and Taiwan have continued to proliferate. There are about 20,000 students from Taiwan in the United States at present, for example. This multiplicity of ties clearly reflected a conscious policy on Taipei's part to cultivate public opinion in the United States for several obvious and legitimate purposes: to prevent the amendment or repeal of the TRA; to forestall possible protectionist trade measures directed against Taiwan; and to insure continued access to U.S. arms. Taiwan's efforts have met with considerable success, sufficient to arouse concern in Beijing.[40]

Taiwan's phenomenal economic performance as one of the "Four Tigers" of the Western Pacific -- the others being the Republic of Korea, Hong Kong, and Singapore -- has made it the United States' fourth largest trading partner, and the United States by far Taiwan's largest, with a current annual trade balance in favor of Taiwan of about $15 billion. From the American point of view, some aspects of this relationship have been unsatisfactory. In particular, tariffs and informal barriers have made the Taiwan market less open to American exports than the American market has been to exports from Taiwan. In addition, there have been grievances relating to intellectual property rights, including Taiwan's failure to observe U.S. copyright laws. In recent years, Taiwan has made some concessions on these issues, but not enough to satisfy the American side. This was the case, for example, at a round of talks held at the end of April 1988; the main issue was reduction of tariffs on agricultural products from the United States. The Taiwan side resisted concessions on this point, largely on account of pressure from its own farmers.[41] Like other Asian trading partners of the United States, Taiwan is deeply concerned about a possible upsurge of American protectionism.

Taiwan Since "Normalization"

"Normalization" came as a great shock to most people on Taiwan and was greeted by anti-American demonstrations. It had an unsettling effect on the politics of the island. The authorities understandably felt more nervous than ever, for a time, about perceived threats to stability and security, both domestic and external. The political opposition, largely but not entirely Taiwanese, became more active than before. Moderate elements urged progressive political reform, and restrictions on the press were in fact considerably relaxed. This step made it easier for radical activists advocating more drastic change, in some cases "independence" for Taiwan under a non-KMT government, to organize and press their views. The result was a violent confrontation in December 1979 in Kaohsiung, an important industrial port city near the southern tip of the island, between pro-government forces (including police) and dissidents. In the spring of 1980, after an open trial, stiff prison sentences were imposed on eight defendants who had been found guilty of having been ringleaders in the riot.

In the eyes of public opinion on Taiwan, this episode tended to weaken the cases of both the official conservatives and the radicals and to strengthen the position of the moderate reformers, inside and outside the government alike. Accordingly, a more liberal election law, which however still did not provide for opposition (non-KMT) political parties, was promulgated in May 1980; an unprecedentedly large number of seats were to be filled through open election on Taiwan (ignoring the mainland) in the National Assembly (76 seats), the Legislative Yuan (97 seats), and the Control Yuan (32 seats). This innovation was made significantly easier, and also more necessary, by the fact that many existing members of these bodies were elderly.

Although modest, this reform led in December 1980 to the most meaningful, or at least most free, election in the history of the Republic of China. Non-KMT candidates, known as *dang wai* (literally, outside the party), although still not allowed to organize political parties, conducted very vigorous campaigns. Although some of them ran very well and won their contests, about 80 percent of the seats at stake went to the KMT, which did well in the cities as well as in the countryside. One of the explanations for the electoral strength shown by the ruling party is undoubtedly the fact that in recent years about 70 percent of the KMT's total membership has consisted of Taiwanese choosing to work "within the system."[42]

Approximately a year after "normalization," an American observer with long experience, official and unofficial, in East Asia summarized the main threats facing Taiwan as follows: an economic recession in the world as a whole or merely in the United States, which could seriously harm Taiwan's export-driven economy; possible political polarization on Taiwan between those persons regarded as mainlanders versus those regarded as Taiwanese; serious pressures from Beijing; a succession crisis resulting from the passing of the current political leadership; and a major war somewhere in the region.[43] Fortunately, none of these threats has assumed critical proportions so far, but the possibility that one or more of them might materialize still cannot be ruled out. But Taiwan's progress toward a more democratic polity, its social stability, and economic growth are making it possible to be optimistic about its future despite its anomalous status in the international community.

In response to public opinion, the election law was revised in July 1983, and on December 3, 71 candidates were elected to the Legislative Yuan. The campaign was open and spirited. The KMT won 73 percent of the popular vote and 62 seats; all but five of the successful candidates were Taiwanese (KMT or *dang wai*). Eight women, five of them KMT members and three *dang wai*, were elected.[44]

Over the next year or two, political morale on Taiwan declined significantly. The causes of this trend included the Henry Liu affair, a serious financial scandal involving a large business conglomerate known as the Cathay Group, dissatisfaction with the types and amounts of arms being made available by the United States, and uncertainty over the best response to the proposals for unification coming from Beijing.

Beginning in late 1985, however, the KMT and the government, under vigorous leadership and prodding by President Chiang Ching-kuo, began to move in the direction of political reform and liberalization. In the spring of 1986 four new reform-minded members were elected to the KMT's Central Standing Committee. President Chiang, whose health was a matter of general concern, dealt with the obvious question of succession by stating that the next president would be a member neither of his own family nor of the military leadership. This was clearly intended to mean that the succession would be a constitutional one and that the logical successor was Vice President Lee Teng-hui, a Taiwanese.

In October 1986, in preparation for a national election, President Chiang announced that martial law and the ban on the formation of opposition parties would be lifted in the near future. The opposition chose not to wait for the fulfillment, or even the unveiling, of these pledges before taking advantage of them, because it did not wish to accept the legitimacy of the existing situation. On September 28, accordingly, 135 opposition politicians proclaimed the formation of the Democratic Progressive Party (DPP) and nominated 20 candidates for the Legislative Yuan and 22 for the National Assembly in the forthcoming election. Their program included self-determination for Taiwan, a concept that they have never officially defined, evidently because it is a matter of disagreement among them, and because it arouses instinctive distrust on the part of the KMT and the government.

The 1986 campaign was lively and sometimes violent. In the election, which was held on December 6, the DPP improved on the performance of the *dang wai* in the previous election by winning 12 seats in the Legislative Yuan and 11 in the National Assembly. Although the KMT won large majorities both of the popular vote and the seats at stake, no one denied that the DPP had done remarkably well; this was probably due to the fact that its most effective campaigners were well known and respected persons.[45]

Since the 1986 election, additional opposition parties, less impressive than the DPP, have emerged; it now appears that Taiwan may be headed for a political system of the Japanese type: a relatively open system with one dominant party and several minority opposition parties. Within the KMT, there is a disagreement between the mostly older "conservatives" and the mostly younger "reformers" about the party's proper future. The conservatives generally want it to remain as it is, a "revolutionary democratic" party striving to realize the vision bequeathed by Sun Yat-sen and unwilling to share power with other political parties. At least some of the reformers believe that the KMT should be simply a democratic party, responsive to public opinion at any given time and therefore willing in principle to share or surrender power.

President Chiang's last months were marked by two significant political developments. In July 1987, martial law was terminated. This was not done until after a new National Security Law, whose provisions are rather moderate, had been passed. One of the main effects of this two-fold process has been to legalize opposition parties -- which were still technically illegal at the time of the December 1986 election -- subject to three restrictions: they must not promote communism; must not advocate secession (i.e. a separation of Taiwan from the mainland); and they must abide by the ROC's 1947 constitution.

In September 1987, the ban on travel by residents of Taiwan to the mainland was lifted for unofficial persons with relatives in China. A considerable number were already going by way of Hong Kong, which has also served as the intermediary for a growing unofficial trade between Taiwan and the mainland, but legalization greatly increased the flow. In the government's eyes, such travel tends to counteract separatist feeling in Taiwan; in the eyes of the public, travel is one aspect of a growing interest in the mainland and in contact with it, although, of course, not necessarily in unification.[46]

On December 25, 1987, a celebration of the fortieth anniversary of the constitution was marked by noisy demonstrations and by the shouting of anti-government slogans on the part of DPP members and others in the presence of President Chiang, who had evidently never witnessed anything of this kind at least on Taiwan.[47] He was evidently shocked, and the effects may have hastened his death, which occurred on January 13, 1988.

Madame Chiang Kai-shek, who had come to Taiwan from the United States in late 1986 in connection with the centennial of her late husband's birth and was still in Taiwan, allegedly tried to influence the succession to her late stepson in favor of a mainlander.[48] This effort was brushed aside, and Vice President Lee Teng-hui succeeded constitutionally to the office with the support of the other principal leaders, Premier Yu Kuo-hua, KMT Secretary General Lee Huan, and Armed Forces Chief of Staff Hau Pei-tsun.[49] President Lee, a Taiwanese and a Presbyterian, earned a doctorate in agricultural economics in the United States before entering government service in Taiwan and becoming Mayor of Taipei, Governor of Taiwan, and Vice President.[50]

Under President Lee, the liberalizing trends that appeared in President Chiang's last years have continued. At the thirteenth KMT Congress in July 1988, Lee was elected Party Chairman by an overwhelming vote, although some reformers were disappointed that the voting was by acclamation, as in the past, rather than by secret ballot.[51] A number of reputed conservatives, including Premier Yu, were elected to the KMT Central Committee, but the highest numbers of votes went to reformers. The Congress adopted decisions permitting indirect investment by Taiwan residents in the economy of the mainland. The Congress also agreed to permit PRC residents who met certain criteria to visit Taiwan.[52]

Next to political reform, relative social stability has been a key to Taiwan's progress in recent years. To some extent at least, the basis for this is an abiding popular respect for Confucian principles, one of the most important of which is social harmony. As in Singapore, the authorities in Taiwan have supported and fostered this cultural propensity as an important asset, all the more valuable because it is essentially non-political and therefore durable. There may be an additional aspect to the official cultivation of Confucianism in Taiwan, but if so, it is more implicit than explicit; it may be thought of as a potential bridge to the people, and perhaps eventually even to the rulers, of the mainland.

The third key is of course economic growth and prosperity. Taiwan's economy continues to grow at a respectable rate and to enjoy sizable export surpluses (except with Japan), but serious problems will have to be solved in the near future if this happy situation is to persist. Taiwan's traditional labor-intensive export industries are becoming less competitive, partly due to rising wage scales and increasing labor unrest. Efforts to establish high technology industries for export purposes, notably electronics, are well under way, but significant results have not yet been achieved. The industrial sector consists largely of small, private, not very efficient firms. The service sector (banking, insurance, accounting, etc.) is poorly organized and is not making the contribution it should. Partly because of the small size of the domestic market, the economy as a whole is overly dependent on exports, and particularly on exports to the United States, which absorbs about half of them. Foreign investment in Taiwan has grown at a fairly impressive rate but is still hampered by a variety of restrictions. The economy as a whole is vulnerable to possible adverse shifts in the international economy, such as rises in the prices of fossil fuels and industrial minerals and protectionist measures, especially in the United States. The GRC is well aware of these problems and is actively looking for effective ways to cope with them. [53] One of its recent measures has been to buy substantial amounts of gold out of its ample supply of United States dollars, as a hedge against a further decline in the value of the dollar.[54]

Issues for the Future

A number of important and obvious issues are likely to dominate the evolution of Taiwan in the near future.

Will Lee Teng-hui be able to hold on to his position as the head of the state and the KMT, or will he prove to be merely a transitional successor to Chiang Ching-kuo as former Vice President C.K. Yen proved to be to Chiang Kai-shek? At present, Lee's position appears reasonably solid.

How far will liberalization and democratization of the political system go, and will there be significant instability? The process will certainly not be easy nor free of turmoil, but, as in the Philippines and the Republic of Korea, there are grounds at least for cautious optimism.

How far will Taiwan's opening to the mainland go, and in particular will Taipei actually allow visits by PRC residents? The most that can be said is that the authorities are studying and considering a wide range of possibilities, probably short of direct negotiations with Beijing.

What is the likely future of the important relationship with the United States? Trade disputes may get worse but are not likely to become unmanageable. There will probably be no significant change in the "bottom line" of American policy toward Taiwan's security, which is that Beijing must not use force against the island. On the other hand, the frequent proposals from Taipei of United States-Taiwan strategic cooperation -- American bases on the island in the event those in the Philippines should be lost, for example -- will almost certainly not be taken up, because of the importance and sensitivity of United States - PRC relations. In any case, there is a major difference of regional threat perception; to the United States, the threat is the Soviet Union, whereas to Taiwan, the threat is mainland China.

In summary, there are clearly uncertainties ahead for the Republic of China and for Taiwan-American relations. Obviously at some time in the future -- perhaps in another generation -- the present political situation may be resolved in some way or another. But present trends lead one to be optimistic about the maintenance of peace in East Asia, the future of Taiwan, and the continuation of satisfactory relations between Taiwan and the United States.

NOTES

1. Ralph N. Clough, *Island China* (Harvard University Press, 1978), pp. 33-37.

2. Edwin W. Martin, *Divided Counsel: The Anglo-American Response to Communist Victory in China* (University Press of Kentucky, 1986), especially Ch. 25.

3. David Rees, *Korea, the Limited War* (St. Martin's Press, 1964), p. 405.

4. The text (excerpted) of the treaty can be found in U.S. Senate, Committee on Foreign Relations, *Background Information Relating to Peace and Security in Southeast Asia and Other Areas* (GPO, 1970), pp. 70-72; text of the Formosa Resolution in ibid., pp. 36-37.

5. Clough, pp. 16-21.

6. Kenneth T. Young, *Negotiating with the Chinese Communists: The United States Experience, 1953-1967* (McGraw-Hill, 1968).

7. Clough, p. 16.

8. In spite of this, at least two eminent China specialists advocated some form of a "two Chinas" policy for the United States. See Robert A. Scalapino, *United States Foreign Policy: Asia* (GPO, 1959), pp. 153-155; and A. Doak Barnett, *Communist China and Asia: Challenge to American Policy* (Harper, 1960), especially pp. 472-474.

9. Henry Kissinger, *White House Years* (Little, Brown, 1979), p. 733.

10. Text in *Department of State Bulletin* (March 20, 1972), pp. 435-438.

11. Text of the joint communique establishing the liaison offices in *The New York Times* (February 23, 1973).

12. Zbigniew Brzezinski, *Power and Principle: Memoirs of the National Security Adviser, 1977-1981* (Farra, Straus, Giroux, 1983); Jaw-ling Joanne Chang, *United States China Normalization: An Evaluation of Foreign Policy Decision Making* (University of Maryland Law School, Occasional Paper/Reprints Series in *Contemporary Asian Studies*, no. 4, 1986).

13. Text in "Taiwan: Proposed Legislation," *Current Policy* (Department of State, no. 54, January 1979).

14. Text in Lester L. Wolff and David L. Simon eds., *Legislative History of the Taiwan Relations Act: An Analytic Compilation with Documents on Subsequent Developments* (St. John's University Press, 1982), pp. 288-295.

15. Ibid., pp. 92-103.

16. Ibid., pp. 67-91, 104-110.

17. *Washington Post* (August 24, 1980).

18.   Text in *New York Times* (August 26, 1980).

19.   Ibid., (January 27, 1981).

20.   *Washington Post* (March 9, 1981).

21.   Ibid., (October 31, 1981).

22.   *New York Times* (November 15, 1981).

23.   Ibid., (January 12, 1982).

24.   *Washington Post* (January 12, 1982).

25.   *New York Times* (February 1, 1982).

26.   Ibid., (March 27, 1982).

27.   *Wall Street Journal* (April 7, 1982).

28.   *Washington Post* (July 2, 1982).

29.   Wolff and Simon, pp. 323-324.

30.   Text in ibid., pp. 312-313. For press comment see *Washington Post* (August 17, 18, 1982); *New York Times* (August 18, 1982); *Wall Street Journal* (August 18, 1982).

31.   *Washington Post* (August 19, 20, 1982).

32.   *New York Times* (August 22, 1982).

33.   *Washington Post* (August 10, 1982).

34.   Cf. Robert Manning, "Still Up in Arms," *Far Eastern Economic Review* (April 14, 1983).

35.   *New York Times* (January 4, 1984).

36.   *Washington Post* (August 10, 1982).

37.   Martin L. Lasater, "Reading Tea Leaves on America's Taiwan Policy," *Wall Street Journal* (April 27, 1987).

38.   *Taiwan Update* (May, 1987).

39.   *New York Times* (March 18, 1982); *Wall Street Journal* (May 11, 1984).

40.   Ibid., (March 18, 1982); Ibid., (May 11, 1984).

41.   "Give or Take? ROC-US Trade Talk," *Hotel Magazine* (Taipei, No. 97, June 1988), pp. 10-12.

42.   John F. Copper, with George P. Chen, *Taiwan's Elections: Political Development and Democratization in the Republic of China* (University of Maryland Law School, Occasional Papers/Reprints Series in *Contemporary Asian Studies*, no. 5, 1984), pp. 60-76.

43.   James Lilley, in *Taiwan: One Year After United States-China Normalization* (GPO, 1980), pp. 140-144.

44.   Copper and Chen, pp. 93-111.

45.   John F. Copper, "Politics in Taiwan, 1985-1986: Political Development and Elections," in Hungdah Chiu (ed.), *Survey of Recent Developments in China (Mainland and Taiwan), 1985-1986* (University of Maryland Law School, Occasional Papers/Reprints Series in *Contemporary Asian Studies*, No. 2, 1987), pp. 27-47.

46.   *New York Times* (May 22, 1988).

47.   *Washington Post* (December 26, 1987).

48.   *Wall Street Journal* (February 3, 1988).

49.   Ibid., (January 14, 1988).

50.   *New York Times* (January 15, 1988).

51.   Ibid., (July 9, 1988).

52.   Ibid., (July 13, 1988).

53.   Joseph Kyle in Martin Lasater (ed.), *The Two Chinas: A Contemporary View* (Heritage Foundation, 1986), pp. 40-53.

54.   *Wall Street Journal* (June 2, 1987).

CHAPTER FOUR

MILITARY MILESTONES

Martin L. Lasater

From the Second World War to 1979

Military relations between the United States and the Republic of China (ROC) became significant during World War II, when the two countries were allies against Japan.[1] It was through American efforts that the ROC was recognized as a major power in the war and was accorded a permanent seat on the United Nations Security Council. The United States also helped the ROC secure the return of Taiwan, seized by Japan during the Sino-Japanese War of 1894-1895.

Following the Second World War, the U.S. attempted to mediate differences between the ruling Kuomintang (KMT) and the Communist Party of China (CPC). The KMT and CPC had been engaged in a prolonged civil war for control of China since 1927. Washington failed in its mediation efforts, and despite more than $2.5 billion in American aid, the KMT was defeated and forced to retreat to Taiwan in 1949.

At the time of the collapse of the ROC government on the mainland, the U.S. determined that Taiwan would soon fall to the Communists. Despite considerable domestic American pressure to help the ROC, President Harry S. Truman decided not to intervene in the expected PRC invasion of Taiwan.

The June 1950 invasion of South Korea by North Korea dramatically changed U.S. perceptions of the importance of Taiwan and resulted in a complete turnabout of U.S. policy toward the Government of the Republic of China (GRC) on Taiwan. On June 27 President Truman announced that he was interposing the Seventh Fleet between Taiwan and the mainland to prevent the two sides from attacking each other. Truman's decision was based upon U.S. concerns that the Peoples Republic of China (PRC) might use Taiwan to interfere with American military deployments in Northeast Asia during the Korean War.

When the PRC entered the conflict in October 1950, American hostility toward the mainland became firm policy. Although Washington did not follow General Douglas MacArthur's advice to allow the ROC to attack Communist China, the U.S. resumed a program of massive military and economic assistance to the ROC in 1951. The total amount of American aid extended from 1949 to 1979 was $5.98 billion, of which $4.22 billion was military assistance and $1.76 billion was economic assistance.[2] The U.S. grant military assistance program was terminated in the mid-1970s, although arms continued to be furnished Taiwan on a sales basis. Economic assistance was ended in 1965. During these years, the United States completely outfitted the ROC with U.S. weapons.

In 1954 the ROC formally became part of the American global collective security system, when the United States-Republic of China Mutual Defense Treaty was signed in response to a PRC attack against offshore islands occupied by GRC forces. American military support was given to the ROC during the Quemoy crises of 1954, 1958, and 1962.

During the Vietnam War, Taiwan was a valuable strategic asset, serving as an important logistics base for American military operations in Southeast Asia and as a "listening post" for intelligence gathering from China. Initially, Washington claimed that it was in Vietnam to stop the spread of Chinese Communist influence in Southeast Asia. A major purpose of the American war was to isolate and contain China, a U.S. policy since the Korean War. For its part, the PRC viewed the United States as an enemy with which it expected eventually to go to war.

By 1969, however, both Washington and Beijing had determined to improve bilateral relations. The key factor was American and Chinese perceptions of the Soviet Union as their primary enemy, not each other. Since China's strategic value derived from its size and proximity to the Soviet Union, Taiwan's military importance to U.S. strategy diminished as Sino-American relations improved. This development was reinforced by President Richard Nixon's announcement in Guam in July 1969 that the U.S. would reduce its military presence on the Asian mainland, including, of course, in Taiwan.

From 1970 until 1979 the U.S. and the PRC gradually moved to normalize diplomatic relations. As noted by Richard Nixon, Henry Kissinger, and Jimmy Carter, U.S.-PRC relations during this decade were driven by strategic concerns.[3] Taipei found itself increasingly isolated in the international community, having lost its membership in the United Nations, including its seat on the U.N. Security Council to the PRC in October 1971.

Although the United States was reducing its military presence on Taiwan and had downgraded its perceptions of Taiwan's military value, the Nixon, Ford, and Carter administrations continued to provide military equipment to Taiwan, as noted in Table 4-1.

Table 4-1

U.S. Military Sales to ROC, 1975-1979

Unit: U.S. $ thousand

FY Year	Foreign Military Sales	Commercial Export Licensed	Total
1975	136,094	44,982	181,076
1976	344,662	42,531	387,193
1977	148,407	46,140	194,547
1978	353,154	73,637	426,791
1979	542,627	44,547	587,174

Source: Martin L. Lasater, "Honoring the Taiwan Relations Act Strengthens East Asian Stability," Heritage Foundation Asian Studies Center *Backgrounder*, No. 47 (May 27, 1986), p. 12.

In the February 28, 1972 Shanghai Communique signed during Nixon's historic trip to China, the U.S. and the PRC set forth their respective positions on the Taiwan issue. For its part, Beijing claimed Taiwan as part of China and insisted upon the withdrawal of all U.S. forces and military installations from the island. Washington declared:

The United States acknowledges that all Chinese on either side of the Taiwan Strait maintain there is but one China and that Taiwan is part of China. The

United States Government does not challenge that position. It reaffirms its interests in a peaceful settlement of the Taiwan question by the Chinese themselves. With this prospect in mind, it affirms the ultimate objective of the withdrawal of all U.S. forces and military installations from Taiwan. In the meantime, it will progressively reduce its forces and military installations on Taiwan as the tension in the area diminishes.[4]

The Shanghai Communique remains one of the important foundations for U.S. military relations with Taiwan. The Communique linked American-Republic of China military relations to a peaceful settlement of the Taiwan issue. In other words, until mainland China and Taiwan can agree to a peaceful resolution of their differences, the United States retains the right to maintain a defense relationship with Taiwan. This policy remains in effect today.

Normalization of Sino-American Relations

In the negotiations between the United States and China leading up to the exchange of diplomatic relations on January 1, 1979, the Carter administration informed Beijing of its intention to continue supplying defensive weapons to Taiwan.[5] In the Joint Communique on the Establishment of Diplomatic Relations between the U.S. and the PRC, the U.S. accepted the PRC's demands that it terminate diplomatic relations with the ROC, withdraw all remaining American military personnel from Taiwan, and abrogate the 1954 United States-Republic of China Mutual Defense Treaty. But the joint communique also reiterated the U.S. interest in a peaceful resolution of the Taiwan issue.

These interests were spelled out in considerable detail in the 1979 Taiwan Relations Act (TRA), the most important document now governing the military relationship between the United States and Taiwan. During the congressional hearings leading up to the passage of the TRA, leaders of both political parties criticized the Carter administration for not paying enough attention to the PRC threat to Taiwan's security.[6] The security provisions of the TRA define the close military relationship between the Washington and Taipei.

Section 2 of the TRA links the future of Taiwan with U.S. security interests in the Far East. It defines American security policy in the region as:

- to declare that peace and stability in the area are in the political, security, and economic interests of the United States, and are matters of international concern;

- to make clear that the United States decision to establish diplomatic relations with the People's Republic of China rests upon the expectation that the future of Taiwan will be determined by peaceful means;

- to consider any effort to determine the future of Taiwan by other than peaceful means, including by boycotts or embargoes, a threat to the peace and security of the Western Pacific area and of grave concern to the United States;

- to provide Taiwan with arms of a defensive character;

- and to maintain the capacity of the United States to resist any resort to force or other forms of coercion that would jeopardize the security, or the social or economic system, of the people of Taiwan.

Section 3 of the Taiwan Relations Act gives specific instructions on the implementation of the above security policy. Especially important are the provisions for arms sales to Taiwan.

- In furtherance of the policy set forth in section 2 of this Article, the United States will make available to Taiwan such defense articles and defense services in such quantity as may be necessary to enable Taiwan to maintain a sufficient self-defense capability.

- The President and the Congress shall determine the nature and quantity of such defense articles and services based solely upon their judgment of the needs of Taiwan, in accordance with procedures established by law. Such determination of Taiwan's defense needs shall include review by United States military authorities in connection with recommendations to the President and the Congress.

- The President is directed to inform the Congress promptly of any threat to the security or the social or economic system of the people on Taiwan and any danger to the interests of the United States arising therefrom. The President and the Congress shall determine, in accordance with constitutional processes, appropriate action by the United States in response to any such danger.

The security provisions of the TRA were soon put to the test in the major controversy over arms sales to Taiwan during the 1980-1982 period. The issue centered on whether the U.S. should sell the ROC an advanced fighter plane to replace its ageing inventory of F-104s and F-5Es. Before turning to that issue, however, the PRC threat to Taiwan needs to be examined in order to fully appreciate the dilemma Washington faces as it provides defensive weapons to Taiwan yet tries not to undermine its strategically important relationship with Beijing.

The PRC Military Threat to Taiwan

American assessments of the PRC threat to Taiwan have been consistently low since the normalization of Sino-American relations. In part this reflects the apparent commitment by Beijing since late 1978 to pursue a policy of peaceful reunification instead of military "liberation" with respect to Taiwan. In part it also reflects hesitancy in Washington to focus public attention on the PRC threat to Taiwan. Such attention would cause supporters of Taiwan to challenge the improvement of U.S. relations with the PRC and also generate demands that more advanced weapons be sold to the Republic of China.

These low threat assessments were especially important during the sensitive 1978-1979 period of normalization of Sino-American relations, when the Carter administration had to convince Congress that the shifting of diplomatic relations from Taipei to Beijing did not harm Taiwan's security.

Secretary of Defense Harold Brown assured members of the Senate Foreign Relations Committee during the TRA hearings that "for a variety of reasons PRC military action against Taiwan is extremely unlikely for the foreseeable future."[7] Chairman of the Joint Chiefs of Staff, General David Jones, told the Committee: "Our estimates are that Taiwan does have the capability to deter any attack by the People's Republic of China now and for a considerable time into the future."[8]

But the following independent assessment of the PRC threat to Taiwan shows that while the probability of Beijing attacking Taipei is low in the near-term, the probability may increase in the future if China gains a decisive advantage in critical areas such as blockade capabilities or air superiority.

In terms of total military capabilities, the PRC clearly enjoys superiority over the ROC in most crucial categories. Only in destroyers does Taiwan have an advantage over the mainland (26 vs 15).[9] Fairly close numbers are found between Taiwan and the PRC for frigates (9 vs 31), minesweepers (8 vs 33), amphibious ships (451 vs 613), and fighter aircraft that can operate in a ground attack mode (377 vs 500). But in all other areas Taiwan is vastly outnumbered, frequently by a ratio of 10 to 1 (for example, total armed forces, total troops, infantry divisions, total naval personnel, submarines, fast attack craft, air force personnel, total combat aircraft, and fighter/interceptor aircraft). In several categories, Beijing enjoys a monopoly on weapons systems. This includes all strategic nuclear forces, naval bombers and fighter aircraft, and air force bombers. It seems clear that in a major military confrontation between the two armed forces, Taiwan would face almost certain defeat barring outside intervention on its behalf or the collapse of political will to pursue the struggle on the part of the PRC.

But since mainland China must be concerned not only with Taiwan but also with the threats from the Soviet Union, and cannot ignore disputes with India, and Vietnam, a more realistic assessment of the threat to Taiwan must focus on rival forces deployed in the Taiwan Strait region. The first threat to be considered is a PRC amphibious invasion of Taiwan. The PRC naval and air threats also will be discussed.

In terms of army personnel, some 24 regular army divisions (535,000 troops) are deployed in the Nanjing Military Region, facing Taiwan's 22 divisions (340,000 troops). The PRC also has some 90,000 Marines deployed throughout its three fleets. Taiwan's Marines total about 20,000.

Estimates of the number of divisions required to invade Taiwan successfully range upward of 40 or more. In its hearings prior to the enactment of the Taiwan Relations Act, the Senate Foreign Relations Committee found that the United States during World War II estimated that it would take 300,000 American troops to defeat 32,000 Japanese ground forces then occupying Taiwan.[10] Given the fact that the PRC and ROC ground forces in the Strait region are in rough parity, and that the People's Liberation Army (PLA) is known to suffer major weaknesses (including lack of mobility and mechanization, poor logistics, limited power projection capability, obsolescent weapons, and weak command and control capabilities), it would seem that currently the PLA army does not have the power to threaten the security of Taiwan. The PLA might be able, however, to seize the islands of Kinmen (Quemoy) and Matsu just off the coast of Fujian province, because of their close proximity to the mainland.

Other than threatening the offshore islands, the PLA would have to engage in a massive mobilization and buildup in the region before attempting an invasion of Taiwan. This could be seen by American and Taiwan intelligence sources far in advance of any immediate threat, giving both Washington and Taipei adequate time to formulate an appropriate response.

A contributing factor to the low probability of a PRC invasion of Taiwan is the lack of Chinese amphibious capabilities. It was estimated in 1979 that PRC naval vessels, including motorized junks, would be able to transport only 100,000-150,000 troops to Taiwan.[11] Troubling to Taipei, however, is the PRC's new emphasis on marine-type forces and the construction of at least thirty new landing vehicles since 1979. But American analysts believe these to be intended for use in the South China Sea, where Beijing has several territorial disputes in the Paracel and Spratly islands with Vietnam and other countries, rather than against Taiwan.

Although the threat of an amphibious invasion of Taiwan is low, a more complex and less assuring picture emerges when considering PLA naval and air deployments in the Taiwan region. The PRC East Sea Fleet has some 750 vessels, 350 of which are over 100 tons, including 5 destroyers, 16 frigates, and 40 submarines. At least 90 missile-equipped fast patrol craft are also assigned to the East Sea Fleet.

The ROC's navy includes two submarines built by the Netherlands and recently delivered to Taiwan. But the major fleet units are outdated, the earliest being commissioned in 1946. These include 13 Gearing DD-710 destroyers, updated with Hsiung Feng and Sea Chapparal missiles. Similarly updated are the Allen M. Sumner DD-692 and Fletcher DD-992 class destroyers. Taiwan has 13 outdated coastal minesweepers. In addition Taiwan has recently built 5 32-meter guided missile patrol boats with a total of 24 being planned, and 50 small missile patrol boats. Also Taiwan possesses 32 S-2 Tracker ASW aircraft, all of which are scheduled to be rebuilt by Boeing.[12]

ROC naval officers are concerned about the PRC surface fleet, particularly the many small missile attack craft that pose a formidable challenge to the larger, slower destroyers carrying the ROC's flag. Neither side possesses advanced electronic countermeasures. A missile exchange between the Russian-style Styx surface-to-surface missile (SSM) carried by PRC vessels and the Israeli-designed Gabriel-type SSM carried by Taiwan's ships would likely be determined by the number of ships and missiles brought into play. Existing ratios point to a clear PRC advantage, despite construction in recent years of missile-equipped fast attack craft by Taipei. Both sides are upgrading their anti-ship missiles. The submarines purchased by Taiwan from the Netherlands, for example, are equipped with tubes enabling them to launch subsurface-to-surface missiles such as the Hsiung Feng II.

PRC submarines pose an even greater threat to Taiwan. Only ten of the "Gearing"-type destroyers in the ROC navy have been equipped with anti-submarine rockets. The remainder are armed with anti-submarine torpedoes of approximately the same range as the torpedoes carried by PRC submarines. Although Taiwan's anti-submarine warfare (ASW) capabilities are being upgraded with American assistance, the ability of Taiwan's fleet to survive submarine attack remains questionable.

The greatest naval threat to Taiwan is a blockade. As noted by Admiral Edwin K. Snyder in his testimony before the Senate Foreign Relations Committee during its 1979 hearings on the TRA:

> The most dangerous action that the PRC could participate in right now is the declaration of an embargo on all commerce into Taiwan. She could state that Taiwan is a province of China, and that henceforth all deliveries to her "province" must clear customs through one of her seaports. She can back this declaration up by stating that a blockade exists, and any ship entering her sovereign waters -- including those surrounding Taiwan -- are subject to boarding and inspection....I don't foresee any threat of invasion of Taiwan. Invasion is unnecessary if you can destroy your enemy by starving him economically.[13]

Assessments vary as to whether a PRC blockade of Taiwan would be successful in forcing Taipei to the negotiating table.[14] Without question, such a blockade would severely damage Taiwan's economy, given its heavy dependence on trade. On the other hand, the island is self-sufficient in food production, and critical resources such as petroleum are held in three or more months' reserves. In all likelihood, a blockade's success or failure would hinge on the political will of Beijing and Taipei respectively.

Although a blockade would be relatively easy for Beijing to declare in effect, and the deployment of submarines to demonstrate a determination to enforce the blockade would unquestionably be within the capabilities of the PRC, a successful sustained blockade might be very difficult to execute without enormous expenditure of resources. For one thing, Taiwan plans to respond to a high intensity blockade -- the only type likely to be effective -- with an immediate escalation of the conflict. This would include the use of the ROC air force against mainland shipping and port targets, as well as the mining of PRC ports such as Shanghai.

Yet another factor escalating the cost of a PRC blockade of Taiwan would be the adverse reaction of the United States, Japan, Western Europe, and perhaps even the Soviet Union if their trade and ships were interfered with in a blockade of the Taiwan Strait and Bashi Channel. These are international waterways of great importance in ship-borne traffic between Northeast and Southeast Asia, as well as between the Indian and Pacific Oceans. Moreover, given the close interdependence of world trading partners -- which increasingly includes the PRC -- a blockade of Taiwan would hurt the interests of far more countries than the ROC. The PRC in effect would also be blockading itself.

Moreover, it would not be easy to stop ships calling on Taiwan. In 1984, for instance, more than 34,000 ships carrying cargoes from more than 100 nations went in and out of Taiwan's ports. The total tonnage of these ships was nearly 350 million tons. The difficulty in strangling Taiwan economically becomes obvious when one considers that in all of World War II, the U.S. sank only 8 million tons of Japanese ships.[15]

In summary, the naval blockade threat to Taiwan from the PRC is higher than the amphibious threat, although it is still relatively low given the high risks to PRC surface ships and submarines should Beijing attempt to destroy the ROC navy or blockade the island and the international political liabilities of such an action.

In terms of the air threat to Taiwan, it must be recognized that the most important single key to Taiwan's deterrence is the maintenance of qualitative air superiority over the Taiwan Strait. Air superiority would enable the ROC to exact prohibitively high costs on PRC aircraft, ships, and amphibious forces in case of an assault on the island. Under optimum conditions, air superiority might enable Taiwan to defeat attacking mainland forces.

ROC strategists believe that Taiwan's security depends on a capability to thwart a limited PRC air-sea-land attack on the island. This can be achieved through both offensive and defensive tactical air operations, until the loss of essential materiel and bases halt the PRC offensive. This strategy is based on three key assumptions. First, competing pressures on Beijing would prevent the PRC from concentrating all of its offensive power against Taiwan. Second, as the time and costs of the operation escalated, PRC planners would find the military option less and less attractive. Third, the United States and other powers would aid Taiwan diplomatically and perhaps even militarily; at least the PRC cannot be certain that third countries would remain neutral.

The air balance in the Taiwan Strait is difficult to precisely calculate. In general terms, however, Taiwan has approximately 560 combat aircraft, of which 225 are F-5Es. Other combat aircraft include 30 F-5Fs, 42 F-100A/Ds, 15 F-104As, and 80 F-104Gs. All of these aircraft would be involved in the defense of Taiwan. The PRC, on the other hand, has some 6,100 naval and air force combat aircraft, including 170 medium H-6 bombers, 630 light H-5 bombers,

500 ground attack fighter aircraft (MiG-15 and Q-5), and 4,600 other fighter aircraft. Of the latter, the J-6/B/D/E are the most important interceptors, totalling some 3,000 aircraft.

According to ROC sources, within 750 nautical miles of Taiwan the PRC stations 358 bombers, 2,855 fighter aircraft, 410 transport planes, 209 helicopters, and 134 other planes. Within 600 nautical miles there are 215 bombers, 100 ground-attack fighter aircraft, 1,100 interceptors, and 60 reconnaissance aircraft. At least seven major air bases are within 250 nautical miles of Taiwan, placing aircraft stationed there within five to seven minutes of their targets on the island.[16]

Taiwan possesses a fairly effective air-defense system. It includes two surface-to-air (SAM) systems, the Sky Bow I, which appeared to be a combination of U.S. Patriot and Improved Hawk, and Sky Bow II, a high altitude system with a 100 kilometer range. Taiwan also recently acquired from the U.S. 766 Improved Chaparral (MIM-72C/F) and 284 Sea Chaparral. On order were 370 Improved-Hawk SAMs and 170 Standard shipborne SAMs.[17]

Most American analysts assume that the PRC would lose at least 500 aircraft in a battle for air superiority over the Taiwan Strait. Some estimates range much higher. As to the outcome of such an air battle, some U.S. sources predict that within two or three weeks the ROC air force would be "neutralized."[18] ROC planners believe that the PRC would have to commit around 4,000 aircraft to overwhelm Taiwan's air defenses, and that each aircraft would last for only about four missions.[19]

Weighing these factors, one has to conclude that the air threat to Taiwan is higher than either the land or sea threat. One critical factor as to whether the air threat will increase to dangerous levels is the outcome of the race between the two Chinese governments to modernize their fighter aircraft. If Taiwan can maintain its qualitative edge, then the costs involved in attempting to resolve the Taiwan issue by force will likely remain prohibitively high.

Overall, a comparison of the military capabilities of China and Taiwan reveals a clear, but not decisive advantage for the PRC. A conclusion reached by both American and Chinese analysts is that Beijing could defeat Taipei if it is willing to pay high enough military and political costs, provided, of course, the United States or other states did not come to Taiwan's aid. The military balance remains somewhat fluid, however, because the two Chinese sides are rapidly modernizing their respective armed forces. A technological race is underway in the Taiwan Strait, the outcome of which carries major implications for the future of Taiwan.

The above threat assessment also carries implications for U.S. arms sales policy to Taiwan. If, indeed, the naval and air threats to Taiwan are significant and may be growing as the PRC modernizes its own armed forces, then the U.S. is legally committed under the Taiwan Relations Act to help Taipei field an adequate deterrence in these areas. Since Taiwan cannot hope to match the PRC in terms of quantity, the only way Taipei can maintain its defense capabilities is to modernize its forces qualitatively. This will require continued American assistance. Although such assistance carries a certain political risk in U.S. relations with the PRC, a far greater risk to U.S. national security interests in preserving peace in the Taiwan Strait would accrue if Beijing acquired a decisive military advantage over Taiwan.

As important as military capabilities are in assessing the PRC threat to Taiwan, of greater importance still is the question of Beijing's intentions to use force against Taipei. PRC leaders have stated repeatedly that they do not rule out the use of force to resolve the Taiwan issue.

One of the most explicit Chinese explanations of their intent to use force against Taiwan was General Secretary Hu Yaobang's comments to *Pai Hsing* editor Lu Keng on May 10, 1985. China cannot renounce the use of force, Hu said, "because if we make such a promise, [KMT authorities] will be all the more free from anxiety."[20] The General Secretary admitted that China was too weak presently to use force against Taiwan, but that over a period of ten years the PRC economy would develop to the point where the PLA would be strong enough to take action against Taiwan. Hu stated: "If we are economically powerful in seven, eight, or ten years, we shall be in a position to modernize our national defense. If the broad masses of the Taiwan people wish to return and a small number of people do not wish to return, it will be necessary to use some force."

In the interview Lu Keng noted that Deng Xiaoping had mentioned the possibility of imposing a blockade around Taiwan. Hu Yaobang responded: "That depends. If we have the strength to enforce a blockade and if Taiwan vehemently opposes reunification, we shall have to consider enforcing a blockade." A summary of the circumstances under which the PRC said it would use force against Taiwan appeared in the summer 1985 issue of *Foreign Affairs*. Chinese scholar Huan Guo-cang listed five conditions under which Deng Xiaoping had said China would attack Taiwan: "If Taibei leaned toward Moscow instead of Washington; if Taibei decided to develop nuclear weapons; if Taiwan claimed to be an independent state; if Taibei lost internal control as a result of the succession process; or if Taibei continued to reject reunification talks for 'a long period of time'."[21]

An historical analysis of the use of force by Beijing indicates that the military, as in other countries, is regarded by the leaders of the PRC as a useful instrument to achieve political goals.[22] But Beijing has shown itself reluctant to use the military to achieve foreign policy objectives. For example, tensions along the Sino-Soviet border caused by the 1969 Ussuri River incident were quickly cooled and the PLA prevented radical Red Guards from moving into Hong Kong. While the PRC attack on Vietnam in 1979 provides a counter example, in general, one can conclude that Beijing probably will not attempt to use force to achieve reunification with Taiwan unless it is virtually sure of success and sees no other less costly option.

Hu Yaobang's May 1985 interview with Lu Keng supports this thesis. Hu said: "The first of Chairman Mao's 16 military principles is do not fight a battle without preparation, and do not fight one in which the outcome is uncertain. If you fight, you must be sure of victory. Therefore, we have not underestimated Taiwan." Hu specifically cited the following factors as contributing to Taiwan's strength:

-China's military strength was weak because its economy was weak;

-the majority of the people of Taiwan do not as yet want to reunite with the mainland;

-the possibility exists of foreign intervention on Taiwan's behalf;

-Taiwan's armed forces, military installations, economy, and political system remain strong;

-and the United States continues to strongly support Taiwan.

Of these factors, Hu said, U.S. support for Taiwan was "the most important point."[23] It is for this reason that demonstrations of continued American support for the ROC plays a crucial role in whether the resolution of the Taiwan issue will be peaceful or violent. The most demonstrable expressions of U.S. support is the sale of modern weapons to Taipei. As long as Beijing sees adequate levels of arms sold to Taiwan to ensure that a minimal ROC deterrence is maintained in the Taiwan Strait, the probability of the use of force by the PRC will remain small -- even if China's political intentions change in favor of using force.

This logic clearly undergirded the security provisions of the 1979 Taiwan Relations Act. However, as events during 1980-1982 demonstrated, the sale of advanced modern weapons to Taiwan exact a cost in terms of Washington's political relations with Beijing. Because of the delicate nature of this calculation, the U.S. decisions in 1982 to deny Taiwan a replacement fighter aircraft and to sign the August 17 Communique limiting future arms sales to Taiwan were major milestones in the U.S.-ROC military relationship. The decisions presented serious problems for Taiwan's security. But because of the manner in which the Reagan administration interpreted the Communique, it remained possible for the United States to continue a fairly high level of arms transfers to Taiwan, particularly through commercial sales and defense technology.

The FX Issue

Despite President Carter's statement that the U.S. would continue selling defensive arms to Taiwan, Beijing was not seriously offended, since Carter unilaterally imposed a one-year moratorium on arms sales to Taiwan immediately after recognizing the PRC as the sole legal government of China. However, in June 1980, the State Department decided to permit Northrop and General Dynamics to go to Taiwan to discuss the sale of their versions of a new fighter aircraft, the so-called "FX."[24]

The FX was designed by both companies with Taiwan specifically in mind. Taipei wanted to modernize its air force with purchases from the U.S., but nothing in the U.S. inventory was thought to be suitable because of its offensive capability. The U.S. did not want to sell Taiwan weapons posing a threat to the PRC for fear of jeopardizing Sino-American relations. The Department of Defense and State Department approached Northrop and asked that company to design a new fighter plane with limited range and ground attack capability for export to Taiwan and similar countries.

Northrop designed the F-5G (or F-20, as it later became known) as a follow-on model to the F-5E/F fighter aircraft it coproduced on Taiwan. The F-5G sale was approved in principle by both the Department of Defense and State Department, but the sale was delayed because Congress wanted to give General Dynamics an opportunity to compete for the potentially lucrative contract. General Dynamics' version of the FX, the F-16-J79, was a lower performance version of the U.S. Air Force's front line fighter plane, the F-16.

The PRC interpreted U.S. efforts to sell an advanced fighter aircraft to Taiwan as a serious threat to Beijing's efforts to achieve reunification.[25] Taipei had rejected the PRC's calls for negotiations and Beijing feared that if Taiwan acquired the advanced interceptor, the island's enhanced defense capabilities would encourage the ROC's leaders to delay reunification indefinitely.

In a move which Chinese describe as "killing the chicken to scare the monkey," the PRC used the occasion of the Netherlands' November 1980 decision to sell Taiwan two submarines as an opportunity to frighten the U.S. out of selling the FX to Taiwan. Throughout December 1980 and January 1981 the PRC warned that if the submarine sale were allowed to go forward, relations between Beijing and The Hague would suffer seriously. When the

Netherlands decided to proceed with the sale, the Chinese Foreign Ministry notified the Dutch government that their relations would be downgraded to the level of charge d'affaires.

PRC statements at the time indicated that Beijing's actions were directed as much toward Washington as toward The Hague. The PRC reacted strongly to the submarine sale because of great concern in Beijing that, once in office, the Reagan administration would approve the FX sale to Taiwan. Air superiority had long been identified as the key to Taiwan's security, and the sale of the FX would give Taipei that superiority for the foreseeable future.

Recognizing this fact, Taiwan's American supporters pointed to the sale of the FX as the single most important step that President Reagan could take to protect Taiwan. Many believed that Carter had deliberately withheld the sale of advanced weapons to Taiwan to smooth Sino-American relations and did not want Reagan to follow the same course. A Senate Foreign Relations Committee report had concluded, in 1980, for example, that "the failure to approve or even address Taiwan's top priorities -- an advanced fighter (the FX), the Harpoon (naval) missile and the Standard (air defense) missile -- raised questions about the willingness of the United States to improve and modernize Taiwan's defensive military capabilities."[26]

When Reagan assumed office in 1981, the arms sales issue became an important domestic political controversy. The administration came under intense pressure, both from supporters of Taiwan who saw the FX as necessary to Taipei's defense and from those who feared that the FX sale would undermine Sino-American relations.[27] The House Subcommittee on Asian and Pacific Affairs sent a letter to President Reagan on June 18, 1981, urging him not to approve the FX on the grounds that there was no PRC military threat to Taiwan; Beijing was pursuing a policy of peaceful reunification; and the sale of an advanced fighter plane would jeopardize the delicate and mutually beneficial relations between the U.S. and China.

Other members of the House Foreign Affairs Committee sent a letter to the President on November 17 asking him to approve the sale since Beijing had refused to renounce the use of force against Taiwan and Taiwan's fighter aircraft were obsolescent. Those favoring the sale tended to believe that Beijing's threats to downgrade Sino-American relations were empty rhetoric. This group also believed that honoring the U.S. moral commitment to help Taiwan defend itself against Communist China was more important than pursuing a potential strategic alliance with the PRC. A poll conducted in the Senate in June 1981 revealed that only six senators disapproved the sale of the FX to Taiwan, while 59 senators approved. The rest were undecided or did not respond.[28]

Debate continued in Washington throughout 1981, with the administration uncertain as to what course should be followed. In December 1981 the PRC issued a number of extremely strong warnings. Perhaps to test Chinese reactions, the U.S. announced on December 29 that it was going to sell Taiwan $97 million in military spare parts. Although such transactions were common practice, the Chinese responded immediately by threatening to downgrade strategic cooperation with the U.S. should arms sales continue.[29]

The intensity of the Chinese protest against the spare parts sale to Taiwan caught the administration by surprise. Apparently, the PRC reaction tipped the scales in the decision-making process in favor of denying the FX to Taiwan. There was concern that, if the Chinese reacted so strongly to a spare parts transaction, then their response would be much stronger if the FX were sold to Taiwan. Accordingly, on January 11, 1982, the Reagan administration announced that it was not selling Taiwan the FX. The Department of State explained:

> Concerned agencies of the U.S. Government, including the Departments of State and Defense and other national security elements, have

been addressing the question of Taiwan's defense needs over a period of many months and have taken into consideration the many factors which bear on the judgments which must be made in implementing this policy....

A judgment has...been reached by the concerned agencies on the question of replacement aircraft for Taiwan. The conclusion is that no sale of advanced fighter aircraft to Taiwan is required because no military need for such aircraft exists. Taiwan's defense needs can be met as they arise, and for the foreseeable future, by replacing aging aircraft now in the Taiwan inventory with comparable aircraft and by extension of the F-5E coproduction line in Taiwan.[30]

The decision not to sell Taiwan an advanced fighter was a considerable concession to the PRC on the part of the Reagan administration. The administration believed that China's leaders would be satisfied with the FX decision and be willing to set aside the arms sales issue in order to proceed with strategic cooperation with the United States.

The administration dispatched Assistant Secretary of State John Holdridge to the PRC to explain the FX decision and to inform Beijing that Washington had also decided not to sell Taipei the Harpoon antiship missile. Contrary to American expectations, Holdridge received harsh criticism from the Chinese. Instead of praising the FX decision, the PRC lodged "a strong protest" against the extension of the F-5E coproduction line. An article in *Xinhua* stated, "The Chinese Government will never accept any unilateral decision made by the U.S. Government" on arms sales to Taiwan.[31] Beijing was signalling Washington that the arms sales issue was not resolved. China was raising its demands yet another step, insisting that the PRC be notified in advance of future sales to Taiwan. Yet another negotiating point surfaced in a January 31, 1982, *Xinhua* commentary, demanding that a certain date be set for the termination of arms sales to Taiwan. The article said that while the PRC considered U.S. arms sales an "infringement" of China's sovereignty, Beijing was willing "to negotiate with the United States for an end to the sales within a time limit." The article implied that the PRC was being reasonable on this issue in the larger strategic interests of the two sides.[32]

It was during this period that negotiations between Washington and Beijing began in earnest over what eventually became the August 17, 1982, U.S.-PRC Joint Communique. Throughout these difficult negotiations, both sides exerted intense efforts to achieve their minimal objectives. For the United States these included the right to continue to sell arms to Taiwan under conditions stipulated by the Taiwan Relations Act. Beijing's objectives included limiting future American arms sales to Taiwan under an agreement recognizing PRC sovereignty over Taiwan. Both sides wished to preserve friendly relations, although Washington was more concerned than Beijing over strategic cooperation at this point. In hindsight this differing perception of the importance of a Sino-American strategic relationship provided the PRC with insurmountable leverage over the United States.

The August 17 Communique

Throughout the period of negotiations leading up to the final communique, the PRC threatened to downgrade Sino-American relations if the arms sales issue was not resolved satisfactorily. Under the influence of Secretary of State Alexander Haig, who strongly believed in the importance of strategic cooperation with the PRC against the Soviet Union, the Reagan administration attempted to mollify Beijing. Accordingly, President Reagan sent personal letters to Deng Xiaoping, Zhao Ziyang, and Hu Yaobang.[33] Vice President George Bush was dispatched to China, and several key State Department officials made speeches. In his letter to Deng, Reagan wrote: "We will not permit the unofficial relations between the American people and the people of Taiwan to weaken our commitment to [the principle of 'one China']." And in his letter to Zhao, the President said: "We expect that in the context of progress toward a peaceful solution [to the Taiwan issue] there would naturally be a decrease in the need for arms by Taiwan."

In early July 1982 the *Washington Times* reported that the State Department had prepared a secret communique limiting future arms sales to Taiwan.[34] Senator Barry Goldwater, a leading supporter of Taiwan in the Congress, asked the State Department about this. He was told no such drafts had been prepared. The White House also queried the State Department and received a similar response.

But, as evidence unfolded, it became apparent that the State Department had indeed secretly prepared a draft communique. As Goldwater commented when this became public: "It was clear to me and to the White House that President Reagan, Vice President Bush, and National Security Adviser William Clark had been lied to by the State Department about what they were planning."[35]

According to sources within the Congress, the withholding of information about the draft communique influenced the timing of Alexander Haig's resignation as Secretary of State. When key Republican congressmen were told on June 23 of the State Department's attempt to keep the document from Congress and the White House, they reportedly became quite angry and demanded that something be done. The next day President Reagan informed Haig that he would accept the Secretary's resignation.[36]

Congressional supporters of the ROC were outraged at what they considered to be the State Department's manipulation of U.S. China policy to the detriment of Taiwan. They heavily pressured the President to make good on his promises to fully implement the arms sales provisions of the Taiwan Relations Act. During the June 23 meeting to discuss this issue, National Security Adviser William Clark told the Congressmen there would be "no backing away" from Taiwan and "no time limit on the sale of arms" to Taipei.[37] On July 9 representatives from 28 conservative groups met in Washington and warned the President that he would receive an "extremely" acrimonious" backlash from his supporters if he agreed to any cutoff of arms to Taiwan.[38]

Perhaps fearing the repercussions of undermining the conservative political support of his administration, Reagan decided that no further compromise to the PRC would be made on the arms sales issue. On July 14 the administration gave several assurances to Taiwan. As described in the official ROC statement on the August 17 Communique, Washington told Taipei that the United States:

1. Has not agreed to set a date for ending arms sales to the Republic of China;

2. Has not agreed to hold prior consultations with the Chinese communists on arms sales to the Republic of China;

3. Will not play any mediation role between Taipei and Peiping;

4. Has not agreed to revise the Taiwan Relations Act;

5. Has not altered its position regarding sovereignty over Taiwan;

6. Will not exert pressure on the Republic of China to enter into negotiations with the Chinese communists.

The administration announced in mid-July its intention to sell Taiwan the additional F-5Es promised in place of the FX. At the same time, however, the Reagan government proposed to China an agreement containing assurances that in the future it would not sell Taiwan weapons of higher quantity or quality than those sold in the past. On July 30 the President and his advisers told key Congressional supporters that this was the final offer to the PRC and that the F-5E sale would go forward in two weeks. Presidential aides explained that the assurances given Beijing were deliberately vague in order to give Washington the freedom to determine whether the flow of arms at current levels would be sufficient in the future. Implicit in the administration's explanation was Washington's right to adjust its mix of arms to Taiwan to allow for inflation, technological advances, and increased threats from the mainland.[39]

Beijing twice rejected the new proposal, but when it became apparent that the United States would proceed with the F-5E sale regardless of whether an agreement had been signed, China accepted. Those close to the negotiations reported that, until the last moment, the PRC took an extremely tough position, warning of dire consequences should the F-5E sale go forward.

The U.S.-PRC Joint Communique of August 17, 1982, established the parameters within which the U.S. can sell defensive weapons to Taiwan. The August 17 Communique, along with the 1979 Taiwan Relations Act, are the key statements of American arms sales policy to Taipei. In paragraph five of the Communique the U.S. said that it "understands and appreciates" China's fundamental policy of "striving for a peaceful resolution of the Taiwan question." Because of China's peaceful reunification policy, Washington noted that a "new situation...has emerged with regard to the Taiwan question" which created an environment in which the arms sales issue might be resolved.

Paragraph six contained substantive and controversial commitments by the United States. It stated:

Having in mind the foregoing statements of both sides, the United States Government states that it does not seek to carry out a long-term policy of arms sales to Taiwan, that its arms sales to Taiwan will not exceed, either in qualitative or in quantitative terms, the level of those supplied in recent years since the establishment of diplomatic relations between the United States and China, and that it intends to reduce gradually its sales of arms to Taiwan, leading over a period of time to a final resolution.

Disagreement arose immediately over the Communique's interpretation. The Chinese rejected any linkage between the level of arms sold to Taipei and Beijing's policy of a peaceful resolution of the Taiwan issue. The PRC considered the Taiwan issue to be strictly an internal Chinese matter. The administration, however, deliberately linked its commitment to reduce arms sales to Taiwan to a continuation of Beijing's policy of seeking only peaceful reunification with Taiwan.

On August 18, 1982, Assistant Secretary of State John Holdridge explained to the House Committee on Foreign Affairs that the U.S. was willing to sign the agreement limiting future arms sales to Taiwan because China had promised to pursue a peaceful resolution of the Taiwan issue. Holdridge said that if Beijing changed its policy, the U.S. reserved the right to increase arms sales to Taiwan. Holdridge explained:

China has announced a fundamental policy of pursuing peaceful means to resolve the longstanding dispute between Taiwan and the mainland. Having in mind this policy and the consequent reduction in the military threat to Taiwan, we have stated our intention to reduce arms sales to Taiwan gradually....While we have no reason to believe that China's policy will change, an inescapable corollary to these mutually interdependent policies is that should China change its policy, we will reassess our policy. Our guiding principle is now and will continue to be that embodied in the Taiwan Relations Act: the maintenance of a self-defense capability sufficient to meet the military needs of Taiwan, but with the understanding that China's maintenance of a peaceful approach to the Taiwan question will permit gradual reductions in arms sales.[40]

Regarding the question as to whether the TRA or the August 17 Communique takes legal precedence in American policy, the State Department explained that the Communique does not invalidate the Taiwan Relations Act. State Department Legal Advisor Davis Robinson told the Senate Judiciary Committee on September 27:

[The August 17 Communique] is not an international agreement and thus imposes no obligations on either party under international law. Its status under domestic law is that of a statement by the President of a policy which he intends to pursue....The Taiwan Relations Act is and will remain the law of the land unless amended by Congress. Nothing in the joint communique obligates the President to act in a manner contrary to the Act or, conversely, disables him from fulfilling his responsibilities under it.[41]

Another important interpretation of the Communique was given privately to Republican congressmen by the White House on August 17, 1982. During the meeting, Reagan government officials said the TRA would remain the guide for U.S. policy toward Taiwan. The Communique was described as a victory for the administration because it permitted the sale of the additional F-5Es to Taipei without resulting in the downgrading of relations with the PRC. The congressmen were assured that if one day the PRC initiated hostilities toward Taiwan, the U.S. would increase arms sales to counter the threat. An important interpretation of the qualitative and quantitative limitations referred to in paragraph six of the communique was also given. These limitations were not intended to fix the level of arms sold to Taiwan, the congressmen were told, but rather to tie weapons transfers to the level of threat existing in the Taiwan Strait.[42]

Arms Sales in the Post-Communique Period

The Reagan administration attempted to minimize the damage done to Taiwan's security by the August 17 Communique by interpreting the agreement as lacking precedence over the TRA and by linking promises of future arms sales reductions to the continuation of China's policy of peaceful reunification. More practically, the administration sold Taiwan adequate military equipment to limit the immediate adverse effects of the Communique. Two days after the Communique's release, the Reagan government announced its intention to permit Taiwan to coproduce with the Northrop Corporation an additional 30 F-5Es and 30 F-5Fs over the succeeding thirty months, a package worth $622 million.[43] Two additional sales were announced shortly thereafter for 500 Maverick air-to-ground missiles and $97 million worth of various armored vehicles. In February 1983 the U.S. sold Taiwan 66 F-104G fighters, previously owned by West Germany, for $31 million. And in July Washington sold Taipei $530 million in military equipment, including land- and sea-based Chaparral missiles for air defense, SM-1

Standard missiles for shipborne air defense, AIM-7F Sparrow radar-homing air-to-air missiles, conversion kits for M-4 tanks, tank-recovery vehicles, and aircraft spare parts. The Standard and Sparrow missiles had been sought by Taiwan for several years, and the sophisticated nature of these missiles indicated that the U.S. had begun to apply at least a minimal qualitative indexing to its arms sales as well. Significantly, the PRC reported these sales but did not protest too strongly.

A key decision was announced in March 1983, when the State Department released figures setting ceilings for arms sales to Taiwan at $800 million for fiscal year 1983 and $760 million for fiscal year 1984. These figures were highly important because they were the first indication that the U.S. had applied a quantitative index to the level of its arms sales to Taiwan in the post-Communique period. The figures for authorized sales in 1979, 1980, and 1981--- the base years referred to in the communique---were $598 million, $601 million, and $295 million, respectively. To reconcile the 1983 and 1984 figures with these base years, the State Department explained that an "inflationary index" had been applied. Thus, the $598 million of 1979 would be equivalent to $830 million in current, inflated dollars.[44]

In early July 1985 the U.S. sold Taiwan 262 Chaparral ground-to-air missiles for $94 million to replace obsolete M42 anti-aircraft guns. This sale, plus the previous year's sale of 12 C-130 transport aircraft to replace obsolete Taiwan planes, raised the critical issue of whether the August 17 Communique permitted the United States to sell Taiwan new types of equipment to replace outmoded models. Because of the difficulty in finding operational equipment of old vintage, the U.S. concluded that limited upgraded sales could be made within the framework of the Communique. The PRC protested these sales, but little attention was paid in Washington since finding identical models for replacement was impossible.

In early 1986 the U.S. sold Taiwan 200 MGM-71 TOW anti-tank missiles worth $15.6 million. And in August the administration announced another arms sale to Taiwan, a $260 million avionics package to modernize thirty S-2 maritime-surveillance and ASW aircraft. More important than individual sales, however, was the developing trend since 1986 for the U.S. to sell Taiwan advanced technology to upgrade ROC armed forces. The best examples of this type of transfers are the help American companies are giving Taiwan to develop an indigenous fighter plane, the so-called IDF, and a new class of ASW frigates.

Technology Transfers in the Post-Communique Period

What quickly becomes apparent in any assessment of the PRC air threat to Taiwan is the importance of technology. In the past the ROC has maintained a high degree of technological advantage over the PRC air force. However, with the modernization of the PLA and the restrictions on U.S. arms sales to Taiwan by the August 17 Communique, Taipei's qualitative advantage is at risk.

This issue was highlighted by the controversy surrounding the 1986 U.S. sale to the PRC of $550 million of advanced avionics for the supersonic J-8-II interceptor. American officials insisted that the sale would not adversely affect the qualitative balance of air power in the Taiwan Strait, whereas Taiwan military officials noted that the avionics package would give the PRC all-weather, day-night fighting capabilities not possessed by Taipei.

Since the mainstay of Taiwan's air deterrent is the 1950s-1960s technology found in the F-5E and F-104, Taipei has placed high priority on the acquisition of a replacement fighter plane. Until the FX decision and the August 17 Communique, Taiwan had assumed that such an aircraft could eventually be purchased from the United States. But to avoid jeopardizing relations with the PRC, Washington decided not to sell Taiwan an advanced fighter aircraft.

Unable to purchase an advanced fighter plane from the United States and finding access to other international markets closed because of PRC pressure, Taipei decided in 1982 to build its own indigenous fighter, the IDF. In 1986 this plane was described as being a single-seat fighter aircraft, with moderately swept wings.[45] Developed by Taiwan's Aero Industry Development Center (AIDC), it was undergoing tests in both Taiwan and the United States. The IDF will be powered by twin turbofan engines producing 8,350 pounds of thrust each. With an afterburner, the plane's speed should exceed Mach 1.2. The range and payload of the IDF is reported to be around that of the F-5E. The plane will be equipped with head-up display, modern electronic display and flight controls. A two-seat version will eventually be built for training purposes. Avionics are being supplied off-the-shelf, as is the new radar system. The IDF is scheduled to replace Taiwan's F-104s. AIDC contracted a number of U.S. aerospace firms for consultation and aerodynamics, static structural testing, and for wind tunnel use. The IDF is scheduled to fly as a prototype in 1989. The Reagan administration has stressed that there is no U.S. government involvement in the program.

When information about the U.S. commercial role in the IDF became known, Hu Yaobang warned that the U.S. could be violating the terms of the August 17 Communique by supplying Taiwan with advanced technology it did not already possess. Hu argued that the "transfer of technology sounds better, but it is the same thing as arms sales." Hu warned: "If it is a fact that the U.S. is using technology transfers to circumvent the limits on quantitative and qualitative increases, it would constitute bad faith. China would take a stern position and would give serious consideration to the proper measures of response."[46]

As a result of this and other technology transfers, China in 1986 attempted to persuade the U.S. to redefine the August 17 Communique to include limitations on the sale of advanced technology to Taiwan. To sound the Americans out on this possibility and to emphasize the importance China attached to the matter, Vice Foreign Minister Zhu Qizhen --who had been directly involved in negotiations over the August 17 Communique--came to Washington to protest the technology sale as a violation of the Communique. Zhu was told that U.S. government-licensed transfers of technology to the ROC were permitted under the August 17 agreement, since the Communique did not explicitly limit technology transfers but only arms sales.[47]

Many within the Reagan government were irritated at the intensity of the Chinese protests, especially since the U.S. government had just gone through a bruising bureaucratic battle to offer the PRC $550 million of advanced avionics to upgrade its F-8 interceptor. Implying that Washington was tired of Chinese protests and that sentiment existed in the administration to sell Taiwan even more sophisticated weapons if the Communique's restrictions were not in place, one administration official said privately: "If Zhu wants to declare the 17 August Communique dead, Reagan would like nothing better."[48]

Perhaps to clarify its policy on arms sales to Taiwan once and for all, Washington sent a note to Beijing in mid-August stating that the August 17 Communique stood on its own and there was no need to reinterpret or renegotiate it. As one Reagan administration source said: "We don't want to reopen negotiations with the Chinese on this score. The text is very clear. It talks of arms sales and not technology."[49]

Another significant transfer of technology took place in mid-1987, when a private U.S. shipbuilding company quietly sold Taiwan blueprints and data packages necessary to build FFG-7 Oliver Hazard Perry-class frigates, similar to the USS Stark attacked in the Persian Gulf in May. The warships, to be built in Taiwan, are intended to replace the World War II destroyers and frigates comprising the backbone of Taipei's antisubmarine warfare fleet. Six of the frigates are to be built initially, with a possible option of six more. Administration sources justified the reported $40 million sale on the grounds that it was for defensive purposes only and that the technology transfer involved did not violate the August 17 Communique.[50]

Trends Toward Commercial Sales

Since 1986 the U.S.-ROC military relationship has been characterized by greater sophistication but less publicity. There has been a marked increase in technology transfers to Taiwan. An increasingly large percentage of military sales are licensed commercial sales instead of government-to-government Foreign Military Sales (FMS).[51]   These trends are reflected in the following Table 4-2, detailing U.S. arms sales to Taiwan from FY 1980-FY 1988.

The combination of commercial sales and technology transfers are enabling Taiwan to modernize its fighter aircraft, guided missile frigates, tanks, and a wide range of missiles without creating a major diplomatic crisis in Sino-American relations. For example, Taiwan's Skysword air-to-air missile resembles the U.S. AIM-9 Sidewinder. And the Hsiung Feng II (Male Bee) anti-ship missile resembles the U.S. RGM-84 Harpoon. The Hsiung Feng II has a range of about 80 kilometers and appears to be capable of being fired from shore, air, and surface and subsurface ship launchers. In May 1988 former Secretary of Defense Caspar Weinberger and former National Security Advisor William Clark visited Taiwan. ROC Premier Yu Kuo-hwa noted that during Weinberger's term in office, the ROC had been able "to acquire sophisticated U.S. military technology for the Taiwan manufacture of tanks, a new generation of jet fighters, and warships."[52]

U.S. Interests in a Peaceful Resolution of Taiwan Issue

The military relationship between the United States and Taiwan is important to maintain because Taiwan plays a crucial role in furthering American security interests in East Asia. Taiwan's strategic value to the United States stems primarily from its ideal location astride the Taiwan Strait and Bashi Channel, two key sea lines of communications linking Northeast Asia with Southeast Asia and the Middle East. Taipei also has offered the use of its military facilities to the U.S. should it lose its bases in the Philippines. Japan, too, views Taiwan as essential to the security of its southern flank. Taiwan's strategic value may actually be increasing since Sino-Soviet relations have improved steadily since 1982. This is particularly the case during the last two years when the Soviet Union has made significant steps to remove the so-called "three obstacles" Beijing has said stand in the way of normalized Sino-Soviet relations.

Second, the United States needs to help deter a PRC attack against the ROC on Taiwan because a war in the Taiwan Strait might disrupt the flow of commerce in East Asia. Sea lanes around Taiwan would be imperiled, major ports on both Taiwan and China would be closed, petroleum imports into Japan and Korea would have to be rerouted, transits of the Seventh Fleet and Soviet Pacific Fleet might be affected, and neutral ships might be damaged.

Third, the United States and the Republic of China are "old friends" and, despite diplomatic derecognition, the U.S. cannot stand idly by and watch Taiwan taken over by the Chinese Communists. Taiwan remains firmly in the democratic camp in world politics and has offered to assist the United States in several important ways in recent years. Taiwan has offered to use part of its massive $75 billion in foreign exchange in developmental assistance

Table 4-2

TAIWAN ARMS PURCHASES FROM THE UNITED STATES, 1980-1987

Unit: U.S. $ million

Fiscal Year	FMS*	Commercial**	Total
1980	462	58	520
1981	289	67	356
1982	523	75	598
1983	699	85	784
1984	689	70	759
1985	700	55	755
1986	511	228	739
1987	510	210	720
1988 (Estimate)	600	100	700

Source: *Foreign Military Sales, Foreign Military Construction Sales and Military Assistance Facts* (Washington, DC: Defense Security Assistance Agency, Department of Defense, 1987), pp. 2-3; 12-13; 36-37. All figures are rounded to the nearest million.

*These figures represent FMS agreements, the total value of defense articles and defense services purchased by Taiwan. The actual FMS deliveries for a given fiscal year are usually considerably less.

**These figures are the total dollar value of deliveries made against purchases of munitions-controlled items by Taiwan from U.S. manufacturers.

---

programs to help strategically important countries such as the Philippines and South Pacific island-states. Taiwan has also taken major steps to reduce its $19 billion trade surplus with the United States, including the removal of most tariff and non-tariff barriers to U.S. goods and services and allowing the appreciation of the New Taiwan Dollar by nearly 50% over the last two years.

Fourth, U.S. credibility is at stake in the Taiwan issue. The strength of the U.S. commitment to Taiwan convinces other American allies and friendly states in the region that Washington intends to remain in East Asia and that its commitments can be counted on. U.S. credibility is especially important at this time because of increased Soviet military and political presence in the region.

Finally, American interests are served by U.S.-Taiwan military relations because other Asian nations do not want to see China reunited at this time. From an historical perspective, a united China is more apt to be a hegemonic China. Moreover, the PRC might not always pursue the moderate domestic and international policies of Deng Xiaoping. No one knows the future of China after Deng passes from the scene. The noncommunist nations of Asia would prefer to see a democratic Taiwan remain as an alternate model for China's development in the future.

Conclusion

Although conducted on an unofficial level, the military relationship between Washington and Taipei has remained close since the shift in U.S. diplomatic recognition to the PRC in January 1979. The U.S.-Taiwan military relationship was mandated by the Congress in the Taiwan Relations Act (TRA), signed by President Jimmy Carter on April 10, 1979.

Washington's right to maintain a military relationship with Taipei was reaffirmed in the August 17, 1982, U.S.-PRC Joint Communique. In the Communique, the United States promised to reduce future arms sales to Taiwan in exchange for Beijing's continued policy of peaceful reunification. Statements by Reagan administration officials since 1982 reaffirm American determination to continue providing Taiwan with defensive weapons until a peaceful resolution of the division of China is achieved.

There is a conflict between the TRA and the August 17 Communique which will become more apparent over the next five years. The TRA places no restrictions on defensive weapons to be sold to Taiwan. Rather, the TRA conditions such sales on Washington's interpretation of what Taiwan needs to maintain an adequate self-defense. As the PRC modernizes its armed forces, Taiwan's own armed forces need to be modernized as well. Since Taiwan does not yet possess a sufficient defense industry and is unable to purchase advanced weapons from third countries, the role of the United States remains essential in modernizing the Republic of China's military forces.

But by promising Beijing to reduce arms sales to Taiwan and by placing quantitative and qualitative limits on what it will sell to Taipei, Washington has created policy dilemma. The TRA requires the U.S. to upgrade Taiwan's armed forces, but the August 17 Communique makes such upgrading a sensitive issue in Sino-American relations. How to handle this issue is a problem all future administrations will face.

To ensure that Taiwan's security was not unduly damaged by the August 17 Communique, the Reagan administration applied certain inflationary and qualitative indexing to both commercial and FMS sales to Taiwan. Moreover, private U.S. companies were permitted to assist Taiwan through the transfer of technology to develop specific weapons systems such as fighters and frigates. If future administrations are to adhere to the TRA, then similar creative interpretations of the August 17 Communique will have to be forthcoming.

Thus far, despite self-imposed constraints, the United States maintains a substantive military relationship with Taiwan. This relationship is designed to help Taiwan deter a military attack from the PRC. It serves U.S. security interests by helping to convince Beijing to pursue only peaceful means to resolve differences with Taipei.

To date, American policy has been highly successful. From the point of view of U.S. national security interests, the military relationship between the United States and Taiwan should be continued by the next administration. Nonetheless, the conflict between the TRA and the August 17 Communique ensures that the handling of this sensitive matter will remain a major challenge to American policymakers and the United States Congress.

NOTES

1. For useful background on U.S. relations with the Republic of China, see Frederick H. Chaffee and others, *Area Handbook for the Republic of China* (GPO, 1969); *China: U.S. Policy Since 1945* (Congressional Quarterly, Inc., 1980); Frederica M. Bunge and Rinn-Sup Shinn, *China: A Country Study* (GPO, 1981); and Ralph N. Clough, *Island China* (Harvard University Press, 1978).

2. U.S. Agency for International Development, *U.S. Overseas Loans and Grants and Assistance from International Organizations* (GPO, 1984), p. 83.

3. The memoirs of these three statesmen contain extensive discussion of U.S. China relations. See Richard M. Nixon, *RN: The Memoirs of Richard Nixon* (Grosset and Dunlap, 1978); Henry A. Kissinger, *White House Years* (Little, Brown and Co., 1979); and Jimmy Carter, *Keeping Faith: Memoirs of a President* (Bantam Books, 1982).

4. The text of the Shanghai Communique and other important documents relating to the Taiwan issue can be found in Martin L. Lasater, *The Taiwan Issue in Sino-American Strategic Relations* (Westview Press, 1984).

5. Carter, p. 197.

6. One of the most useful collections of information about Taiwan's defense needs and the appropriate U.S. response can be found in the Senate hearings on the Taiwan Relations Act. See U.S. Senate, Committee on Foreign Relations, *Taiwan* (GPO, 1979). For an excellent account of congressional concerns over the security aspects of the TRA, see Lester L. Wolff and David L. Simon, *Legislative History of the Taiwan Relations Act: An Analytic Compilation with Documents on Subsequent Developments* (St. John's University Press, 1982).

7. U.S. Senate, Committee on Foreign Relations, *Taiwan*, p. 36.

8. Ibid., p. 740.

9. The comparison between PRC and Taiwan military forces is taken from International Institute for Strategic Studies *The Military Balance: 1986-1987* (London: 1986), pp. 142-45; 169-70.

10. "Legislative History, P.L. 96-8 (Taiwan Relations Act)," *U.S. Code Congressional & Administrative News* (June 1979), p. 661.

11. Ibid.

12. P.D. Jones and J.V.P. Goldrick, "Far Eastern Navies," *Proceedings* (March 1987), pp. 66-67.

13. U.S. Senate, Committee on Foreign Relations, *Taiwan*, pp. 653-654.

14. See Martin L. Lasater, ed., *Beijing's Blockade Threat to Taiwan* (Heritage Foundation, 1986).

15.   Ibid., p. 13.

16.   See Martin L. Lasater, *Taiwan: Facing Mounting Threats* (Heritage Foundation, 1987), pp. 83-24.

17.   "Taiwan," *Journal of Defense and Diplomacy* (1987), pp. 36-37.

18.   Admiral Edwin K. Snyder in U.S. Senate, Committee on Foreign Relations, *Taiwan*, p. 586.

19.   Admiral Ko Tun-hwa in Lasater, *Beijing's Blockade Threat to Taiwan*, pp. 8-9.

20.   For the text of the remarkable interview, see *Pai Hsing* (June 1, 1985) in *FBIS-China* (June 3, 1985), pp. W1-W35.

21.   Guo-cang Huan, "Taiwan: A View from Beijing," *Foreign Affairs* (Summer 1985), p. 1068.

22.   See Allen S. Whiting, *The Chinese Calculus of Deterrence: India and Indochina* (University of Michigan Press, 1975); and Ellis Joffe, *The Chinese Army After Mao* (Harvard University Press, 1987).

23.   Summarized from Hu Yaobang's interview in *Pai Hsing* (June 1, 1985) in *FBIS-China* (June 3, 1985), pp. W7-W11.

24.   For background on the fighter sale issue, see Robert G. Sutter and William de B. Mills, "Fighter Aircraft Sales to Taiwan: U.S. Policy" (Congressional Research Service, IB81157, October 28, 1981).

25.   For a discussion of U.S.-Beijing-Taipei relations concerning China's reunification, see Martin L. Lasater, *Policy in Evolution: The U.S. Role in China's Reunification* (Westview Press, 1988).

26.   U.S. Senate, Committee on Foreign Relations, *Implementation of the Taiwan Relations Act, the First Year: A Staff Report* (GPO, June 1980), p. 10.

27.   Arguments against the FX sale can be found in A. Doak Barnett, *The FX Decision: "Another Crucial Moment" in U.S.-China-Taiwan Relations* (Brookings Institution, 1981). Arguments in favor of advanced fighter sales to Taiwan can be found in Martin L. Lasater, *The Security of Taiwan: Unraveling the Dilemma* (Georgetown University, 1982).

28.   American Council for Free Asia, Press Release (Washington, D.C., June 21, 1981).

29.   See, for example, *Renmin Ribao* (December 31, 1981) in *FBIS-China* (December 31, 1981), p. B1.

30.   "No Sale of Advanced Aircraft to Taiwan, Department Statement, January 11, 1982," *Department of State Bulletin* (February 1982), p. 39.

31.   *Xinhua* (January 12, 1982) in *FBIS-China* (January 12, 1982), p. B1.

32.   Quoted in *New York Times* (February 1, 1982), p. A3.

33.   Texts of these letters can be found in Robert L. Downen, *To Bridge the Taiwan Strait* (Council for Social and Economic Studies, 1984), pp. 126-128.

34.   *Washington Times* (July 2, 1982), p. 1. See also *Washington Post* (July 2, 1982), p. A26.

35.   Ibid.

36.   Interviews by the author in Washington, D.C., June-July 1982.

37.   *Washington Post* (July 3, 1982), p. A13.

38.   Ibid. (July 9, 1982), p. A5.

39.   *New York Times* (July 31, 1982), p. A2.

40.   U.S. House, Committee on Foreign Affairs, *China-Taiwan: United States Policy* (GPO, 1982), p. 5.

41.   Prepared statement of Davis R. Robinson, Legal Advisor, Department of State, given before U.S. Senate, Committee on the Judiciary, Subcommittee on Separation of Powers (September 27, 1982), pp. 1-2.

42.   Author's interviews in Washington, D.C., August 1982.

43.   *Washington Post* (August 20, 1982), p. A16.

44.   Ibid. (March 22, 1983), p. A12.

45.   *Aviation Week and Space Technology* (April 21, 1986), p. 77.

46.   *Far Eastern Economic Review* (July 24, 1986), p. 27. See also Zhang Jingxu, "A Preliminary Analysis of the 'Taiwan Straits Military Power Balance' Theory," *Liaowang* (July 28, 1986) in *FBIS-China* (August 1, 1986), pp. B2-B4.

47.   *Washington Post* (April 25, 1986), p. A32.

48.   *Far Eastern Economic Review* (July 3, 1986), p. 11.

49.   Ibid. (August 28, 1986), pp. 26-27.

50.   *Navy News & Undersea Technology* (June 19, 1987), p. 1.

51.   See Robert Karniol, "Notable Shift in Taiwan's Arms Trade with USA," *Jane's Defence Weekly* (July 11, 1987), p. 13; and Robert Karniol, "U.S. Arms Sales to Taiwan Continue at a High Level," Ibid. (November 28, 1987), p. 1243.

52.   *Free China Journal* (May 30, 1988), p. 1.

CHAPTER FIVE

ECONOMIC RELATIONS

Jan S. Prybyla

The economic record of the Republic of China (ROC) on Taiwan over the last three decades is a textbook example of the success of the market-free enterprise principle combined with governmental intervention in support of the market,[1] in doing what an economic system is supposed to do: (a) provide people with increasing quantities and qualities of goods and services that the people want at prices they are prepared to pay; (b) to do so efficiently, that is, with the least feasible resource waste; (c) to achieve it primarily by improvements in factor productivity brought about by technological innovation; and (d) to maximize the use of voluntary agreement in organizing social activity. Under all four headings -- which together constitute economic modernization -- the ROC performance has been the opposite of that of the People's Republic of China (PRC), which the PRC has only recently begun to modify. Additionally, the process of economic modernization in the ROC has been outward-oriented. Early in its development, economic thought on Taiwan rejected the neo-Marxist dependency theory (the fear of being exploited via the economy by rapacious imperialist powers) and embraced the pragmatic doctrine of comparative advantage.

In line with that doctrine, and to its great benefit, the ROC hitched its wagon to the American star using the U.S. as an extension of its own limited market, as a source of advanced technology and investment, and as a powerful engine of growth. It is not to underrate the perspicacity of ROC domestic economic policies and the ingenuity and work ethic of the people on Taiwan, to say that the ROC's American connection and the accommodating stance taken by the United States toward Taiwan's entry into the U.S. domestic market, have been among the more important -- perhaps the key -- elements in Taiwan's economic "miracle." In the midst of charges of protectionism, it is helpful to note that in large measure the exemplary performance of ROC economy can be attributed to the ready access Taiwan has had in the past and still has to the vast goods-hungry American market (which enabled Taiwan to take advantage of economies of scale and so compete successfully in the world market for manufactures). This ready access has been due in equally large measure to American policy which, for all its zigzags, has been more consistently liberal than that of other industrialized countries (Japan and members of the European Economic Community). although bothersome details remain to be worked out -- and their potential for mischief should not be underestimated -- the United States and the ROC share a philosophical foundation in their adherence to an open market system and private property rights, a multilateral world trading system, and the principle of reciprocity and mutual benefit in commercial dealings. Because the U.S. - R.O.C. relationship goes beyond and deeper than this year's balance of trade, it is worth preserving and enlarging. Together with U.S. economic relations with Japan and South Korea (where frictions are also present), the U.S. - R.O.C. economic connection in the fields of trade and finance, besides commercially benefiting both partners, exerts an overall stabilizing influence on East Asia's Pacific rim.

In the following pages this connection will be examined in its several aspects. The emphasis will be on the period following the U.S. diplomatic "derecognition" of the ROC in January 1979. Although the main manifestations of Taiwan's economic success are well known, a brief summary of them may not be amiss.

ROC Economic Record

In the 34 years from 1952 to 1986 Taiwan's gross national product (GNP) in real terms increased at an average annual rate of 8.7 percent. In 1987 it rose a further 11 percent. Real GNP per capita rose between 1952 and 1986 at an average annual rate of 6.1 percent. Per capita real national income (at 1981 prices) increased from NT$ 16,873 in 1952 to NT$ 124,181 in 1986. At current prices and the prevailing exchange rate, per capita national income on Taiwan at the end of 1987 was US$4,989 and was expected to reach US$ 5,936 by the end of 1988.[2] These are phenomenal figures, witnessing to a growth performance rare in the world annals of economic development. By now Taiwan is no longer a developing economy or even a newly industrialized country (NIC). It is on the threshold of being an industrialized market economy, more so than Spain or Ireland, slightly less than Italy. Taiwan, as the London *Economist* put it, "has done the American thing by turning itself from a loser into a winner."

Taiwan's "American thing," however, is not always cause for joyful celebrations in Washington. Between 1952 and 1986 Taiwan's external trade rose 211 times (at current prices), with imports rising 129 times and exports 3343 times. Of the 1952 exports, 3.5 percent went to the U.S. Of 1986 exports, almost 50 percent went to the U.S. In 1952 Taiwan exports to the United States amounted to US$ 4 million. In 1986 they came to just under US$ 19 billion. By comparison, Taiwan's imports from the U.S. which were US$ 86 million in 1952, came to only US$5.4 billion in 1986. The "American thing," in other words, meant that Taiwan's exports to America (1952-1986) rose at a much faster rate than Taiwan's imports from America. The result was that in 1986 the U.S. deficit on trade with Taiwan was US$ 14.6 billion and $16 billion a year later -- more if U.S. figures are to be believed. This $16 billion Taiwan surplus on trade with the U.S. represented in 1987 84 percent of Taiwan's total $19 billion trade surplus with all countries. Together with Japan and Western Europe, the ROC has become one of the major contributors to the U.S. trade deficit, which in 1987 stood at $170 billion.

The ROC economic record is remarkable not only in quantitative terms. In the course of the three and a half decades since 1952 a revolutionary qualitative transformation of the economy has taken place. Most of it has been positive and modernizing, but there have been some accompanying costs. In 1952 consumption expenditure came to NT$ 12.7 billion. It was NT$ 1.3 trillion in 1986, a 102.4-fold increase. ("Consumption," says Adam Smith in his *Wealth of Nations*, "is the sole end and purpose of all production"). Whereas in 1964 food absorbed nearly 60 percent of total household expenditures, in 1985 the proportion of household income spent on food had fallen to 38 percent. In 1985 life expectancy at birth was 70.8 years for males and 75.8 years for females (rates comparable to the most advanced industrial countries). Today 92 percent of the population is literate; 100 percent of school-aged children are enrolled in primary schools, 100 percent of primary school graduates go to junior high schools, more than 77 percent of junior high graduates go on to senior high schools, and 85.5 percent of senior high school graduates enroll in institutions of higher education. In 1986 there were for every 100 households: 85 telephones, 35 stereo sets, 80 washing machines, 26 air conditioners, 97 refrigerators, and 94 color television sets.

The growth has been "intensive", that is, achieved primarily by improvement in the performance (productivity) of factors of production. Taking 1981 = 100, the index of labor productivity in manufacturing was 138.5 in 1986 (54.7 in 1974). The technological level of the economy has been raised -- and the really big push is only just now developing. Total spending on research and development in the ROC has increased more than 1 1/2 times since 1978 (to constitute a little over 1 percent of GNP at the present time) but lags well behind the relative expenditures for this purpose of the industrialized market economies (e.g., U.S. 2.7 percent, France 2.3 percent, Japan 2 percent). Growth has restructured the composition of domestic product and employment, away from agriculture, toward industry, commerce, financial and other services (i.e., in a modernizing direction). Whereas in 1952 agriculture contributed 36 percent of net domestic product (NDP), industry 18 percent, and commerce and other services 42 percent, in 1986 the proportions were: agriculture 6.6 percent, industry 47 percent, commerce and other services 41 percent. In 1952 agriculture employed 56 percent of the labor force, industry 17 percent, and the tertiary sector 27 percent. In 1986 these proportions were: agriculture 17 percent, industry 42 percent, tertiary sector 41 percent.

Growth had been accompanied over most of the period by nearly full employment. Over the 34 year period (1952-86) the rate of unemployment never exceeded 3 percent, and since 1965 has not exceeded 2 percent. The benefits of growth have been equitably shared, increasingly so as the product expanded. The ratio of the highest income - earning fifth's of households to the lowest fifth which was 5.3 in 1964 fell to 4.3 in 1979.[3] However, there has been some deterioration since 1980.

Table 5-1

INCOME DISTRIBUTION BY HOUSEHOLDS

Item	1953	1961	1964	1970	1975	1980	1986
Gini coefficient*	0.558	0.461	0.360	0.321	0.312	0.303	0.322
Ratio of income share of the richest 20% to that of the poorest 20%	20.5	11.6	5.3	4.6	4.3	4.2	4.6

Source: Tzong-shian Yu, "Taiwan's Economic Development: Some Implications for Developing Countries," *Economic Review*, (Taipei), No. 243, May-June 1988, p. 8.

* The lower the coefficient, the lower the inequality of income distribution.

The principal costs of the ROC's rapid modernizing growth have been the degradation of the environment, particularly air and water pollution and overcrowding of the major urban areas (Taipei, Kaoshiung) by people and cars. Some concern is also being expressed by the sharp rise in the 1980s of the crime and offender rates. The crime rate which was 28.7 cases per 10,000 persons in 1978 increased 1.6 times by 1987. In the same period the offender rate almost doubled (from 23 offenders per 10,000 persons to 44 offenders). Much of the crime is committed by juveniles, reflecting the unsettling of traditional values and life patterns in a rapidly changing society. However, by the standards of other industrialized countries (particularly the U.S.) the ROC crime and offender rates remain modest.

Table 5-2 shows the major growth indicators of the ROC economy.

Table 5-2

MAJOR GROWTH INDICATORS OF THE ROC ECONOMY
(Average annual growth rate, percent)

	1952-60	1961-70	1971-80	1981-86
Gross National Product (GNP)	8.07	9.63	9.75	7.16
GNP per Capita	4.51	6.75	7.66	5.47
Exports (goods and services)	9.37	22.43	17.20	12.0

Source: Directorate-General of Budget, Accounting and Statistics (DGBAS), *National Income of the Republic of China on Taiwan*, 1986.

Sources of ROC Economic Performance: The U.S. Connection 1952-1978

There is a fair amount of agreement regarding the sources of the ROC's exemplary economic performance. These include: an assiduous, capable, educated, motivated, and (thus far) disciplined labor force; a technocratic, pragmatic, "economics-in-command" government that initiates policies designed to help the market economy overcome market failures and help it seize competitive opportunities as these emerge in the context of world trade and finance, policies that for the most part have been remarkably successful in the past in achieving the ends they sought; a successful land reform; political and social stability; and the U.S. connection.[4]

The main components of the U.S. connection since the withdrawal of the national government to Taiwan in December 1949 have been: gains reaped by Taiwan from its supply-base position during the Korean War (1950-53); the military security the country obtained under the mutual defense treaty with the United States (effective March 1955; terminated January 1980); U.S. economic, technical,[5] and military aid from 1951 through 1968 amounting to US$ 1.6 billion; and access by Taiwan to the American market, first for urgently needed supplies and investment funds, later for Taiwan exports.

It is the last component of the U.S.-R.O.C. connection that forms the subject of our investigation. The reason is simple: The importance of external trade to Taiwan's economic and political survival is pivotal. The per capita value of Taiwan's exports has risen from US$ 14.5 in 1952 to US$ 2,056 in 1986 and the per capita value of imports from US$ 23.4 to US$1,248. In 1986 exports accounted for more than of 50 percent of GNP. As noted before, almost half of those exports (47.7 percent) went to the United States. The United States that year (and ever since 1972) was the ROC's largest trading partner with a share of 38.4 percent of total ROC trade. The ROC was the fourth largest source of U.S. imports and the eighth largest market for American export goods.[6]

The development of ROC external trade from 1952 until the year before U.S. derecognition is shown in Table 5-3. Notice the appearance in 1970 of an ROC surplus on its trade with the U.S. The surplus first emerged in 1968 (US$ 38.7 million) and has never disappeared since. Notice also the large jump in total and export trade between 1960 and 1970 (overall exports rising 9 times, exports to the U.S. nearly 30 times) and the further leap between 1970 and 1978 (overall exports rising 8.6 times, exports to the U.S. 8.9 times).

Table 5-3

ROC EXTERNAL TRADE, 1952-1978

Unit: U.S. $ thousand

| Year | Total Trade | | | Trade with U.S. | | |
	Imports	Exports	Balance	Imports	Exports	Balance
1952	187,215	116,474	-70,741	85,566	4,065	-81,501
1955	201,022	123,275	-77,747	95,543	5,400	-90,143
1960	296,780	163,982	-132,798	113,108	18,853	-94,255
1965	556,011	449,682	-103,329	176,372	95,680	-80,692
1970	1,523,951	1,481,436	-42,515	363,839	564,174	200,335
1975	5,951,650	5,308,771	-642,879	1,652,129	1,822,737	170,608
1978	11,026,931	12,687,140	1,660,209	2,376,063	5,010,378	2,634,315

Source: Taiwan Statistical Data Book (*TSDB*) 1987, p. 215.

The development of ROC external trade in the 1950s through the 1970s with overall exports growing substantially faster than imports is a reflection of two policies. The first, encouraged at the time (1950s) by the United States, was one of import substitution consisting of high tariffs, quantitative import restrictions, and overvalued exchange rates. The idea was to reduce Taiwan's hard currency expenditures by substituting as many as possible domestically produced goods for those imported from hard currency areas -- principally the United States. The second policy was one of export promotion, the main component of which was a substantial reduction in the overvalued new Taiwan dollar (NT$) exchange rate. This gathered momentum in the 1960s and continued through the 1970s. However, the export promotion policy was not pursued as a substitute for remnant policy of import substitution. The two were combined in various proportions until quite recent years. It was the combination of liberalism with regard to exports and residual (but effective) protectionism with respect to imports that some blame for Taiwan's trade surplus with most partners (except the oil exporters and protectionist Japan), particularly for the massive surplus with the United States. While combining export promotion with lingering import restriction since the 1960s, Taiwan -- some argue -- has benefited from trade enhancement measures granted it by the U.S., including the generalized system of preferences and the most favored nation clause.[7] There were, it is countered, other causes of the imbalance of U.S.-R.O.C. trade, perhaps equally important, among others, changing comparative advantage and restructuring of national economies in the context of an increasingly liberalized world movement of goods and capital, and loss of American competitiveness in world trade relative to Japan and others.

During the period 1952-78 approved private foreign investment and U.S. private investment in Taiwan developed as shown in Table 5-4. The share of U.S. private investment in total approved foreign private investment in Taiwan declined from 100 percent in the early 1950s to about 50 percent in 1978 (the other half being taken up mostly by Japan and Western Europe). For the whole period 1952-1978 total approved U.S. private investment in Taiwan came to about half a billion U.S. dollars. Together with official U.S. aid (civilian and military) total U.S. investment in the ROC before 1979 came to roughly $2 billion.

Table 5-4

PRIVATE FOREIGN INVESTMENT IN THE ROC, 1952-1978
(ROC APPROVED PROJECTS)

Unit: U.S. $ thousand

| | Investment | | U.S. Investment | Total |
Year	Cases	Amount	Cases	Amount
1952	--	--	--	--
1955	2	4,423	2	4,423
1960	8	14,338	5	14,029
1965	36	35,140	17	31,104
1970	71	109,165	16	67,816
1975	41	70,940	12	41,165
1978	66	136,719	18	69,765

Source: *TSDB* 1987, p. 270.

U.S. - R.O.C. Economic Relationship Since 1979

At the time of the U.S. diplomatic derecognition of the ROC in January 1979 fears were expressed in both the United States and Taiwan that the political break could lead to a decline in the vigorous and until then rapidly growing U.S. - R.O.C. economic connection. The fears proved to have been groundless.

Two-way trade which was US$ 7.4 billion in 1978 reached more than US$ 31 billion in 1987. Taiwan exports to the United States rose from US$ 5 billion to US$ 23.6 billion and Taiwan imports from the U.S. from US$ 2.4 billion to US$ 7.6 billion. The U.S. trade deficit with Taiwan climbed from $2.6 billion in 1978 to $16 billion in 1987. U.S. private investment (approved projects) in Taiwan, which came to a total of $500 million in the 27-years 1952-1978, registered US$ 1.3 billion in the eight years 1979-1986, or about 40 percent of total approved foreign investment.

Table 5-5

ROC EXTERNAL TRADE, 1979-1987

Unit: U.S. $ thousand

Year	Total Trade			Trade with U.S.		
	Imports	Exports	Balance	Imports	Exports	Balance
1979	14,773,700	16,103,426	1,329,726	3,380,797	5,652,243	2,271,446
1980	19,733,135	19,810,618	77,483	4,673,486	6,760,300	2,086,814
1981	21,199,551	22,611,197	1,411,646	4,765,671	8,158,392	3,392,721
1982	18,888,375	22,204,270	3,315,895	4,563,255	8,757,795	4,914,540
1983	20,287,078	25,122,747	4,835,669	4,646,443	11,333,712	6,687,269
1984	21,959,086	30,456,390	8,497,304	5,041,643	14,867,709	9,826,066
1985	20,102,049	30,722,789	10,620,740	4,746,274	14,772,990	10,026,716
1986	24,164,595	39,789,198	15,624,603	5,415,788	18,994,694	13,578,906
1987	34,506,497	53,538,217	19,031,720	7,628,346	23,637,083	16,008,737

Source: *TSDB* 1987, p. 215; *National Conditions of the Republic of China* (*NC*), Winter 1987, p. 11.

Table 5-6

PRIVATE FOREIGN INVESTMENT IN THE ROC, 1979-1986
(ROC approved projects)

Unit: U.S. $ thousand

Year	Total Investment Cases	Total Investment Amount	U.S. Investment Cases	U.S. Investment Amount
1979	73	181,483	19	80,375
1980	71	243,380	15	110,093
1981	73	356,294	25	203,213
1982	82	320,286	33	79,606
1983	100	375,382	35	93,294
1984	100	518,971	41	231,175
1985	107	660,703	42	332,760
1986	206	705,574	56	138,428

Source: *TSDB* 1987, p. 271.

The U.S. - R.O.C. trade and investment relationship during the years following U.S. derecognition of the ROC and the enactment of the Taiwan Relations Act had not only a beneficial overall effect on the economies of the two countries, but has contributed importantly to the promotion of world trade and the international division of labor. The phenomenal expansion and progressive liberalization of the world market have, in turn, contributed to the preservation, indeed sharpening, of competition in the domestic economies of the world's advanced capitalist countries and the rational restructuring of those economies in a modernizing, comparative advantage direction. The superior dynamic efficiency of the world market system compared with the quasi-barter system of central planning is thus due in large measure to the growth of increasingly uninhibited international trade and finance in which the U.S. - R.O.C. connection has played an important part.

During the same period the domestic economy of Taiwan prospered. The average annual increase in real GNP (1978-86) was 7.3 percent; 5.6 percent per capita. Employment was maintained at high levels and beginning in 1982, inflationary pressures were contained.

Table 5-7

UNEMPLOYMENT AND PRICES IN THE ROC, 1979-1986

Year	Unemployment (Percent of labor force, annual average)	Price Index (Last year = 100) Wholesale	Retail
1979	0.7	113.83	109.76
1980	0.7	121.54	119.01
1981	0.8	107.62	116.33
1982	1.2	99.82	102.96
1983	1.6	98.82	101.36
1984	1.4	100.48	99.97
1985	1.7	97.41	99.84
1986	1.6	96.65	100.70

Source: *TSDB* 1987, pp. 13, 181.

Problems of U.S. - R.O.C. Economic Connection Since 1979

Although the long-term economic relationship between the United States and the Republic of China rests on the solid foundations of a shared philosophy regarding the principles of economic organization and free trade, and although both countries are examples of the validity and success of these principles, the U.S.-R.O.C. economic connection is not without problems. These must be attended to lest they erode the relationship and cause grievous losses to both parties. Fortunately the problems are soluble, but their solution calls for a great effort of patience, mutual understanding, and compromise on both sides.

At the center of the problem lies the trade imbalance. The gap between Taiwan exports to and imports from the United States has to be reduced if only because it has become so highly politicized in the United States as to threaten Taiwan's U.S. trade with restrictive legislation by the United States Congress. In the eyes of many Americans, Taiwan has become a second Japan ready to sell but reluctant to buy. With its foreign exchange reserves of US$ 75 billion (1987), the world's largest after Japan, Taiwan is seen by some as being driven by a bullionist obsession. Taiwan, it is said, is ready to attract foreign investment but is reluctant to permit its own investment funds to flow freely abroad. Finally, Taiwan's reputation in respecting foreign intellectual property rights has been somewhat tarnished in the past and is not altogether shining bright today despite widely publicized efforts by the ROC government to stamp out this particular type of piracy. There are also those who find fault with the quality of some Taiwan-made manufacture which, they find, are not always a good bargain. Right or wrong, such charges have to be taken into consideration and the conditions which gave rise to them should be analyzed.

Taiwan Exports to the U.S. From 1980 through 1985 Taiwan exports to the United States increased at an average annual rate of 17.9 percent. In 1986 they rose 28.6 percent, and in 1987 another 24.4 percent.

The first, and correct conclusion to be drawn from this rapid progression is that American consumers like Taiwanese goods: clothing, shoes, plastic products, toys, bicycles, pleasure boats, and consumer electronics. Assuming that these consumers exercise rational choice, things are just as theory says they should be : everyone is better off. Although precise quantification is difficult, between 7 and 15 percent of the goods imported into the U.S. from Taiwan from 1980 through 1987 were sell-back items from Taiwanese-based firms that had American equity. Most bicycles sold in the United States under the Schwinn label are made in Taiwan to Schwinn specifications. General Electric is Taiwan's largest exporter. Other familiar names operating in Taiwan either directly or through some kind of subcontracting arrangement are: Texas Instruments (integrated circuits), Digital Equipment (terminals, printers, personal computers), Wang Laboratories (computer products), AOC International (color televisions), Capetronic (home audio-video systems), Mattel (toys), TRW (electronic components), IBM (computer products), Wilson Sporting Goods (sporting goods and equipment), K Mart and Sears Roebuck (miscellaneous consumer products, including home electronics, clothing, and footwear). So at least some of the competition from Taiwan "is us." This, too, is as it should be: capital migrates in search of high returns and plants are located where the comparative advantage is greatest. American firms, of course, are not the only ones doing it. With the rapid appreciation of the yen against the U.S. dollar since 1985, Japanese firms have moved quickly to establish firms in places where labor costs are lower and the local currency appreciation against the U.S. dollar has been less than that of the yen. Such locations include Taiwan, and the main purpose of the move is to export Taiwan-made Japanese goods to the United States.

Apart from the 7-15 percent of sell-back items and the Japanese goods originating in Taiwan, there are Taiwan-made goods pure and simple that American consumers appear to relish, and see no reason why their entry should be restricted by special interests. These goods originate in a large number of small firms, unlike the situation in Japan and South Korea where a few large conglomerates dominate the export trade. South Korea has 7,000 trading companies of which just nine do half of the Korean export business. The ROC has 60,000 registered trading companies, 40,000 of which account for three-quarters of Taiwan's exports. In 1985 the largest Taiwan-based export company shipped US$ 264 million's worth of goods out of total Taiwan exports that year amounting to US$ 30.7 billion. The relatively small size of Taiwan export firms is both an advantage and a drawback. The advantage lies in Taiwan's ability to point to its economy as a textbook example of rugged entrepreneurship and individual free enterprise whenever voices are raised on Capitol Hill against foreign trusts, conglomerates and oligopolists allegedly conspiring to invade the U.S. domestic market and put American firms -- saddled with antitrust laws -- out of business. It is difficult for even the most ardent protectionist in the U.S. to name the Taiwan firms that fall into this threat category. There is safety in large numbers. Taiwan sells to the U.S. few big ticket items, and the Taiwanese sellers are many when they are not American. (There are exceptions in areas such as steel, petrochemicals, cement, and shipping). Another advantage of large numbers is that Taiwan firms are fast on their feet, quick to respond to rapidly changing international market conditions. Despite their relatively small size and the constant complaints voiced by their owners about the vulnerability and need for government protection, most Taiwan firms appear to be financially more sturdy than their balance sheets and profit-loss accounts would lead one to believe. Accounting, especially tax accounting, is a creative art in Taiwan. There is a lot of unreported income and the security margins for most firms are wider than advertised. Indeed, it is estimated that were all the unreported revenues properly counted, the ROC per capita income would have to be raised by perhaps as much as 40 percent. There are, however, some disadvantages to this proliferation of small export firms. One is the difficulty these firms experience in competition with large Japanese and Korean exporters, increasingly also with mainland Chinese government corporations. The ROC government has encouraged mergers among domestic exporters but without spectacular success so far. Another possible drawback is the lack of high tech skills and scientific management, low spending on research and development, underinvestment in modern plant and equipment, and recurring cash shortages. There is also the difficulty experienced by the ROC government in policing the often buccaneer actions of the many small firms where foreign patents, copyrights, and other forms of intellectual property are concerned. The ROC has an impressive body of legislation designed to combat these unsavory practices, and it is certainly ahead of Hong Kong and Korea in this regard, but actual enforcement leaves something to be desired, partly because of the number of firms that have to be supervised.

Taiwan's exports to the United States, the nation's lifeline, are constantly threatened, as such things tend to be, from a variety of sources two of which are particularly important. The first is competition from the newly industrialized countries (NICs), especially Hong Kong, Singapore, and Korea, but others as well (Thailand, Philippines) and from developing countries, especially mainland China. In contrast to the hue and cry recurrently raised in the U.S. about Taiwan exports, the rapid increase in U.S. trade with the People's Republic of China (PRC) since 1979 and the influx of mainland goods into the U.S. are usually met with mutual congratulations and celebrity pats on the back.[8] The second threat to Taiwan's U.S. sales is connected precisely with this difference in attitude and takes the form of recurrent bouts of protectionist sentiment on the Hill accompanied by a good deal of Taiwan-bashing. In order to forestall both the competition and the bashing Taiwan's exporters with the support of the ROC government have taken a number of steps that include the following. Some operations, especially in the footwear and textile products lines have moved offshore to Thailand, the Philippines, and even to mainland China (without official approval) to take advantage of lower labor costs and escape the appreciation of the New Taiwan dollar against the U.S. currency (up about 40 percent since September 1985). It has been reported that in 1986 and 1987 at least 150 textile and footwear manufacturers have ceased operations on the island, some going bankrupt, others migrating offshore.[9] Another precautionary move is to go up-market and up-scale to high fashion apparel and leather instead of plastic footwear. Some medium-sized Taiwan clothing firms have established subcontracting arrangements with American designer label companies which seek cheaper production offshore (offshore in this instance being Taiwan). Going up-scale in shoes is proving more difficult because of the retarded state of Taiwan's tanning. Market diversification has also been sought, the potential markets being Western Europe (apparel and footwear) and mainland China. The private sector of Taiwan is now permitted to trade directly with East European countries but not with the USSR. Trade with the East European countries which had been indirect since 1980 came to US$ 121 million in 1986 and US$ 245 million in 1987. Taiwan exports included textiles, plastic goods, and electronic products. Attempts at export diversification have met, however, with protectionist restraint in all three areas but particularly in Western Europe and, more recently, on the mainland. The ROC government now allows indirect trade with the mainland (mainly through Hong Kong). For 1987 this trade has been estimated at about $2 billion (up from $1 billion a year earlier) -- the bulk of it Taiwan exports consisting mainly of consumer durables (especially electronics).

Going up-market and up-scale means restructuring the economy toward higher value-added output and higher technology goods as well as services. Shoes and apparel, the ROC government has hinted, may have to go overboard. To achieve a technological upgrading of the economy is a difficult but certainly feasible task for the ROC. The educational infrastructure, the talent and ability are there for transition to knowledge-intensive production. Expenditures on research and development are being increased, and an effort is made to attract back to Taiwan U.S.-educated scientists and engineers presently residing in the United States. The effort is apparently meeting with success. The economic and political environments on the island are increasingly appealing to many educated expatriates in possession of their green cards. In the Hsinchu Science-Based Industrial Park near Taipei living conditions are attractive even though average salaries of engineers are about half of what they are in California's Silicon Valley. To supplement their income those who return are allowed to start their own spinoff companies within two years. The Park has attracted (as of mid-1988) 82 high-tech foreign companies, 37 of them since 1985, but the Japanese are holding back. Investors receive tax exemptions on imports and exports, and access to prebuilt plants. The drive to diversify trade by enlarging the hitherto small share of socialist countries in this trade is not likely to contribute much if anything to the ROC's parallel effort to restructure its output and exports in a knowledge-intensive direction. Taiwan's new socialist partners have delicate problems, as is well known, with generating and applying state-of-the-arts technology (even moderately sophisticated technology) and with converting their domestic currencies into civilian goods, and hence into hard foreign monies. They are not models of modernization and their contribution to Taiwan's *perestroika* will be at best extremely marginal.

The prospect of mainland trade has found eager response in the Taiwan business community.[10] The businessmen argue that the ban on direct trade hampers them in their competition with the South Koreans and others, and in securing at favorable rates such mainland materials as coal, cotton, tin, leather, steel plates, rubber, granite, lumber, aluminum ingots, and electrolytic copper. Some of these are being smuggled into Taiwan from the mainland through Japanese middlemen. In their search for ways to maintain the competitiveness of their products on the world market, labor-intensive Taiwan factories have been employing (in contravention of the law) cheap foreign (mainly southeast Asian) labor under the pretext of on-the-job training in anticipation of relocation of the factories offshore.

Anticipating renewed U.S. Congressional pressure on its exports, Taiwan has stepped up its efforts to secure for itself a niche in the Japanese, West European, and Pacific markets. Exports to Europe are expected to account for about 20 percent of Taiwan's exports within five years (15 percent in 1987). Exports to Japan were expected to reach US$ 9 billion in 1988 compared to $7 billion in 1987. To penetrate these markets and enlarge its share of them (as well as those of South Korea, Thailand, Malaysia, Indonesia, Singapore, Hong Kong, Pakistan, and the Philippines), the ROC has its work cut out for itself. There is a long way to go: in 1987 the US$ 7 billion sales to Japan, US$ 4 billion to Hong Kong, US$ 1 billion to West Germany, US$ 1 billion to Singapore -- a grand total of US$ 13 billion -- compared with relatively effortless sales of US$ 23.6 billion on the American market. The concentration of Taiwan's foreign trade can be seen from Table 5-8. Note the increasing concentration of exports on the United States.

Table 5-8

CONCENTRATION OF EXTERNAL TRADE
(Percentage shares)

| Year | Exports from | | | | Imports to | | | |
	USA	Japan	FRG	Hong Kong	USA	Japan	FRG	Hong Kong
1952-60	5.9	44.7	1.5	8.3	41.3	34.5	2.9	3.0
1961-70	26.2	23.4	4.9	8.9	31.6	37.7	3.8	1.3
1971-80	37.6	13.4	4.9	7.1	23.6	34.1	4.6	1.8
1981-86	44.2	10.8	3.3	7.4	23.1	28.6	3.8	1.0

Source: See Table 5-1.

In the meanwhile the United States has served notice on Taiwan that the generalized system of preferences (GSP) under which Taiwan was treated preferentially compared with the industrialized countries, will not longer apply since Taiwan no longer fits the definition of a developing country.[11] Alarmed by the protectionist mood of Congress and the mammoth trade bill inching its way forward, Taiwan has in recent years taken bilateral steps to blunt what could prove to be a serious blow to its booming economy. In 1988 the ROC agreed in principle to sign a copyright agreement with the United States and to grant patents on foreign micro-organisms and semiconductors. Among others the U.S. wants Taiwan's 30-year copyright protection of American publications to apply to works published after 1955 and to have Taiwan put an end to the screening in Taiwan's video centers of pirated American films. The U.S. contends that such piracy entails losses amounting to US$ 100 million for American film-makers. A bilateral textile agreement provides for a lower growth rate of Taiwan textile exports to the U.S. than contemplated in pending U.S. legislation. A self-restraint system with respect to Taiwan steel exports has been reached, limiting such exports to 20,000 short tons a month. Agreement has also been reached on voluntary restriction by Taiwan of machine tool exports to the U.S., which Taiwan now wants to rescind. Finally, the export performance requirement for an automobile manufacturing joint venture with Toyota has been removed. Export performance requirements for foreign-invested firms used to be common in Taiwan. The U.S. opposition to the requirements in the Toyota stemmed from the perception that Japan's trade surplus with the U.S. was being simply redistributed (and camouflaged) among offshore places such as Taiwan and Singapore. The principal reason, it was argued by the U.S. for locating the plant in Taiwan was to export Toyotas to the U.S. (not to sell them in Taiwan) by evading the consequences of the yen's sharp appreciation against the dollar.

It should be noted that the so-called "voluntary" export restraint agreements are not an unmixed blessing. They are a form of protectionism, and thus work against consumer interests in the importing country. They provide windfall profits for exporters and encourage export cartels.

ROC Imports from the United States. If buoyant Taiwan exports to the U.S. are blamed in some quarters for causing harm to various American industries and contributing to unemployment in the affected sectors, the contentiousness is sharper on the question of U.S. exports to the ROC. Since 1979 these have shown a tendency to stagnate at between US$ 4-5 billion, with an occasional surge (as in 1987) whenever patience on the U.S. side wears dangerously thin. American and ROC analyses of the problem come up with different causes, although there is some overlapping agreement.

The American View. The U.S. contends that over the years the ROC has hampered U.S. access to the Taiwan market through restrictive import and financial policies. While other causes are at work as well, Taiwan's reluctance to allow American exports to enter the Taiwan market as easily as Taiwan exports enter the U.S. market is seen as an important and remediable reason for the trade imbalance between the two countries. What the United States asks for is not the immediate or total elimination of all Taiwan trade barriers, but evidence of genuine progress toward leveling the playing field, commensurate with what Americans perceive to be generous opportunities offered Taiwan business interests in the United States. Specifically the U.S. requests the following:

1. Further reduction of obstacles to U.S. entry into the Taiwan services market and the lifting of restrictions on U.S. firms already operating in that market. The services market includes banking, financial services, insurance and trust, motion picture production and distribution, retail marketing, advertising, and transportation (especially shipping). Among the detailed requests are those for (a) reduction of the minimum capital requirement for the opening of securities services in the ROC; (b) permission for U.S. banks to engage in securities services in the ROC; (c) permission for U.S. companies to own a majority share in Taiwan securities firms; (d) permission to open extra branches of U.S. banks in or outside Taipei. (At present foreign banks can open one branch in Taipei and one outside Taipei).[12]

2. Further removal of nontariff barriers to the entry of U.S. goods. While the proportion of so-called "permissable imports" is about 97 percent of all imports (the remainder being "controlled"), there exist many cumbersome regulations covering the importation of permissible imports and roughly two-thirds of the permissable imports still require the obtaining of import licenses which is not always automatic or expeditious.

3. Further reduction of import tariffs on 172 items, including about 60 farm products, chemical raw materials, household appliances, and other consumer goods. There is concern that the old Taiwan practice of inflating the value of imports prior to assessing import duties has not been completely discarded.

4. Removal of the ban on importation of peanuts, chicken, and animal offal. (Taiwan farmers pelted the building housing the American Institute in Taiwan with cabbages during April 1988 trade talks between the U.S. and the R.O.C.)

5. Effective enforcement of ROC laws against rampant infringement of foreign intellectual property rights. The ROC has agreed in principle to sign a copyright agreement with the U.S. and to grant patents on foreign microorganisms and semiconductors. The U.S. has requested that Taiwan's 30-year copyright protection of American publications be applicable to works published after 1955. The U.S. has also lodged protests against the screening in Taiwan's video centers of pirated American movies. The U.S. contends that this practice has caused the U.S. movie industry losses amounting to more than US$ 100 million.

6.   The U.S. is interested in seeing the depreciation of the U.S. dollar in terms of the currencies of America's major trading partners reflected more faithfully in the US$-NT$ exchange rate. To that end, the U.S. contends, the NT$ should be permitted to float freely in response to market forces.

7.   The United States is disturbed by Taiwan's apparent nonchalance (given its multibillion trade surplus with the U.S.) about "buying American" in areas where it really counts: big ticket items connected with Taiwan's current NT$ 111 billion 14 large infrastructure projects (electric power, telecommunications, harbors, highways, railroads). U.S. firms, it is claimed, were given "preferential treatment" only after planning and consulting had been completed and most procurement contracts had been assigned. Assistant U.S. Trade Representative Peter Allgeier expressed the U.S. delegation's dismay with Taiwan's (a) awarding of a mass rapid transit construction project to a French firm (US$350 million); (b)   contracting with Sweden to build a mobile radiotelephone project; (c) contracting with West Germany for an electrostatic precipitator for a Taichung power plant; and (d) with Britain for a power plant chimney project. "In each of these cases," according to Allgeier, "U.S. bidders submitted strong competitive proposals."[13]   The U.S. is also watching closely the purchasing policy of the government-owned China Airlines and the possibility of its flirtation with the European Airbus.

The ROC View. The ROC position on these issues is as follows:

1.   Much progress has been made in the last several years in liberalizing foreign access to the growing Taiwan services market. The ROC has lifted a 15-year old ban on new securities firms in May 1988. New securities agents (including foreign firms) are required to have a minimum paid-up capital of US$ 13 million and at least 10 employees, and the minimum requirement for new brokerage houses is US$ 7 million and at least 20 employees. Foreign shares in local securities firms cannot exceed 40 percent. Foreign securities firms will not be allowed to operate in Taiwan if their own countries ban Taiwan securities companies. (In 1987 the daily trading volume on the Taiwan Stock Exchange was NT$ 9.3 billion -- four times the 1986 average). Branches of American banks can now issue NT$ credit cards to tap a market where the savings rate is 40 percent of GNP. Until now only NT$ debit cards (automatic withdrawal of funds from the holder's checking account) were available to Taiwan consumers. The condition is that the foreign banks incorporate their credit card operations into Taiwan's existing debit card system. U.S. banks in Taiwan will be permitted to set up automatic deposit and withdrawal facilities using their own on-line systems. The Taiwan insurance market will be opened to U.S. insurance firms within the next three years. However, questions of capital management of these companies remain to be worked out.

2.   The ROC argues that one way to promote further reductions in nontariff restrictions on imports is for the U.S. to support the ROC's bid to join (or rejoin) international organizations devoted to trade and financial liberalization, such as the World Bank, the International Monetary Fund, and the General Agreement on Tariffs and Trade (GATT). However, ROC spokesmen warn, membership in GATT would mean, among other things, that the ROC "would no longer be able to restrict bidding on public construction projects to the U.S. and Europe."[14]   The ramifications of Taiwan's rejoining GATT are currently the subject of study of a number of groups set up by the ROC government.

3-4.   ROC tariffs have been substantially reduced over the years.   It is expected that by 1989 the average import tariff burden (total tariff revenue/total imports) will have fallen to less than 5 percent, that is, to a level comparable to that of the countries forming the Organization for Economic Cooperation and Development (OECD).   For countries (like the U.S.) which have a Most Favored Nation agreement with Taiwan, the rate would be even more favorable.   Taiwan, however, is reluctant to lower tariffs on more that 60 agricultural products or to open the Taiwan market to American chicken, animal offal, and peanuts.   "We will not consider reducing tariffs on agricultural products because we do not protect our farmers more than your country protects yours," said ROC Vice Economics Minister Wang Chien-shien at the closing ceremony of the April 1988 bilateral U.S.-R.O.C. trade talks.   The removal of barriers on the sale in Taiwan of U.S. wine, beer, and cigarettes has been interpreted in many Taiwan quarters as a dishonorable surrender to outside pressure and a "betrayal" of the Chinese people by the government.   While the undercurrent of protectionism remains strong in Taiwan, it is also admitted that "our tariff and nontariff barriers are far greater in number than those in the U.S."[15]   The issue is sensitive and politically explosive, more so now that Taiwan has moved boldly toward political democratization. ROC spokesmen point out that Taiwan has in many instances gone against the dictates of economic rationality to purchase goods in America, a procedure which involves favoring the U.S. over other import sources.   For example, the ROC government requires that 38 products be imported from the United States.   Taiwan now buys in the U.S. 100 percent of its imported soybeans, 99 percent of its imported corn, 83 percent of its tobacco leaf imports, and 64 percent of its apple imports.   It is the third largest buyer of American corn, barley, and soybeans, this despite tempting offers from America's emerging raw grain exporting competitors, among them Canada, Argentina, Brazil, France, India, and (were it not for politics) mainland China.   The problem, say ROC representatives, is that Americans just do not make the effort to sell to Taiwan: the Americans come to Taiwan as buyers; the Japanese as sellers.   Moreover, not just in raw grain; but in other goods as well, Americans often lose out on the strict grounds of competitiveness -- quality, price, and after-sale service.[16]   "Leveling the playing ground," as Americans wish, could rebound to the disadvantage of American sales, and to the Japanese taking over even more of the Taiwan market.   To counterbalance these problems, the ROC has dispatched to the U.S. over the years several "Buy American" missions which generated Taiwan purchases of around US$ 11 billion since 1978.   (The U.S. argument is that most of these purchases would have been made anyway, missions or not).   In future years, according to the ROC Board of Foreign Trade, the U.S. will find Taiwan a receptive market for pollution control devices, as well as automobiles, refrigerators, microwave ovens, and washing machines - provided they can compete on a level field.

5.   Taiwan agrees that infringement (piracy) of intellectual property rights is widespread. It points to the various legislative acts passed in recent years to curb this practice which, perhaps more than anything else, causes harm to Taiwan's reputation in the United States.   ROC authorities plead difficulties of enforcement, in part because of the very large number of firms involved in this activity.   With regard to the showing of pirated American films in Taiwan's rapidly growing number of MTV parlors, the argument is that the problem will be effectively dealt with by the recently enacted Radio and Television Broadcasting Law.

6.   The appreciation of the NT$ against the U.S. currency has gone as far as it can without serious harm being done to Taiwan's exporting interests.

7.   On the question of Taiwan's European purchases for its infrastructural projects, the ROC position is that the decision to award contracts to German, Swedish, British, and French bidders was made on economic grounds. In this matter "Taiwan upheld the principle of free trade and had given all project bid participants fair treatment." Vice Minister Wang offered to brief U.S. concerns, if they so wished, on why they failed to win the contracts against European competition. Additionally, ROC sources point out, on several occasions the ROC government instructed Taiwan firms to purchase goods from American firms, only to discover that the firms had been sold to foreign interests. This has been the case with telephone equipment. Taiwan firms were told by their government to buy the equipment only from AT&T, GTE, and ITT. In the meantime GTE was sold to Siemens of West Germany. Similar cases occurred with orders placed with American firms, which, by the time the orders were executed, had become Japanese-owned firms. These and other examples illustrate the trend toward the multinationalization of firms and trade, a situation of rapid turnover of ownership and one where firms increasingly trade with their own subsidiaries or affiliates flying foreign flags of convenience.

Additionally, the ROC claims that it has found the U.S. side unreceptive to its request to terminate the 1986 agreement which allows local magazines to advertise American cigarettes (the argument is made on the incompatible grounds that cigarette advertising encourages a health-hazard habit and that it causes hardship for local tobacco growers). Nor has the U.S. been sympathetic to the ROC suggestion that its quota on sugar exports to the United States be increased. Taiwan is also seeking a reconsideration of its voluntary restraint agreement concerning exports of machine tools to the U.S. The ROC argues that its action had not helped American machine tools manufacturers because other countries, not practicing voluntary restraint, jumped into the empty space left by Taiwan. Taiwan wishes to terminate the current five-year rice export agreement limiting Taiwan's rice exports to the U.S. when it expires in 1988. The United States wants to extend the agreement.

Savings, Investment, and Capital Flows

Some Chinese economists conclude that the large trade surplus experienced by Taiwan since the mid-1970s, which has ballooned out of control since the early 1980s, is due to a leveling-off of Taiwan's imports. From 1982 through 1986 the average annual growth rate of the trade surplus was almost 62 percent; the growth rate of exports was 12 percent a year, and that of imports under 3 percent a year. The stagnation of imports was due to a combination of causes including the already mentioned mix of export promotion and residual import substitution policies, but above all -- these economists maintain -- it was due to a huge gap between the rate of domestic savings and domestic investment. The domestic gross savings rate which was less than 10 percent of GNP in the early 1950s, rose to more than 30 percent in the 1970s, and to 38 percent in 1986, one of the highest savings ratios in the world. The domestic investment rate which was below 30 percent of GNP in the 1970s, fell to 16 percent in 1986. The gap between the savings and investment rate is thus 22 percent.[17] What is needed is to reduce that gap by lowering the saving-income ratio through a restructuring of Taiwan's socioeconomic institutions. One way contemplated by the ROC government is to abolish the tax exemption on small individual savings and encourage private domestic consumption through, among others, improvement of consumer services and advertising. The introduction of credit-debit cards, for example, has spurred a spending spree among younger consumers in the 20 to 35-age group. Another way is to push on the investment front. To make any noticeable dent in the trade gap, domestic investment would have to be increased very significantly (140 percent assuming an unchanged savings rate). Even with the government's large-scale 14 infrastructural projects, investment performance has remained relatively feeble. The short term solution is to facilitate private investment abroad through a liberalization of foreign exchange controls and development and modernization of the country's financial markets. This has been initiated recently.

On July 15, 1987 the 38-year old restrictions on foreign investment by ROC nationals were considerably relaxed. As of that date prior approval by the central bank was no longer required for any investment not exceeding US$ 5 million per year per individual. Liberalization of outward capital movements has been recommended by economists not just as an excessive reserves-reducing measure, but as a long-term financial strategy that would benefit the restructuring of Taiwan's domestic economy (including the acquisition of foreign technology and inflation control) and from the short-term standpoint of easing the tensions created by the inflated foreign exchange reserves and trade surplus. It is, however, only a beginning that will have to be reinforced by action on the import liberalization front.

Conclusions

The economy of the ROC on Taiwan is a great credit to the market idea and the vitality of free enterprise institutions working in tandem with a government that has sought to encourage, support, and invigorate the market and private property rights. In the absence of worldwide calamities, the future of Taiwan as a modern economic power is as good as assured. Taiwan represents the triumph of the middle classes. It can serve as a model for other developing societies, an attractive alternative to the meandering dead-end path followed until quite recent years by mainland China and other socialist countries.

To make doubly sure, however, Taiwan in the decades to come must work to preserve the social peace that had served it so well in the past and to do this in the context of an evolving democratic polity. This involves preserving the heritage of educational and employment opportunities, upward social mobility, and of an equitable distribution of income, and the avoidance of inflation. It necessitates constant adaptation to changes in the world market and full participation in that market through continuing liberalization of its foreign trade and investment. The recurrent protectionist threat from abroad, particularly from the United States, can be met by patient give-and-take negotiation of the issues in contention, better than through dramatic (but politically impracticable) gestures such as the formation of a U.S.-R.O.C. free trade area. Also needed in an effort, presently being undertaken, to diversify export markets. This includes attempts by Taiwan to sell a greater share of its exports to Japan and the European Economic Community and to generate -- very cautiously -- more trade with the mainland.

However, the burden rests not only with Taiwan. The longer-term liberalization of the Taiwan economy to which the ROC government appears to be committed, has to find its counterpart in U.S. efforts to deal with its own serious problems: the huge fiscal deficit, monetary policies governing growth, maintenance of a low level of inflation, appropriate exchange rate policy, and perhaps lagging competitiveness. Lastly, the ROC has to keep up its military defenses, expand its participation as a world economic power in world economic organizations, and use its proven good sense and experience in evaluating the overtures (political, social, and economic) made to it by the mainland.

NOTES

1. One measure of the private enterprise nature and privatization process of the Taiwan economy is the distribution of industrial production by ownership. (Agricultural production is almost entirely private). "Public enterprises have played an important part in offering adequate utility services and supplies of raw materials...[they] have also provided the private sector with many managers and engineers who have made a great contribution to the development of private enterprises." Tzong-shian Yu, "Taiwan's Economic Development: Some Implications for Developing Countries," *Economic Review* (the International Commercial Bank of China, Taipei, No. 243, May-June 1988), p. 13; Tzong-shian Yu, "The Relationship Between the Government and the Private Sector in the Process of Economic Development in Taiwan, ROC," *Industry of Free China* (October 1985), pp. 1-16.

2. Unless otherwise noted, the statistical data are from: Council for Economic Planning and Development, ROC, *Taiwan Statistical Data Book 1987* (*TSDB* 1987) and Bureau of Statistics, DGBAS, Executive Yuan, ROC, *National Conditions of the Republic of China* (NC, Winter 1987).

3. See Yuan-li Wu, *Income Distribution in the Process of Economic Growth of the Republic of China* (University of Maryland School of Law, Occasional Papers/Reprints Series in *Contemporary Asian Studies*, No. 2, 1977); S.C. Tsiang, "Reasons for the Successful Economic Takeoff of Taiwan," *Economic Review* (The International Commercial Bank of China, Taipei, No. 232, July-August 1986), p. 18; Tzong-shian Yu, "Taiwan's Economic Development: A Case of Growth and Equity," presented at the "International symposium on Economic Development in Chinese Society: Models and Experiences," Hong Kong (December 18-20, 1986).

4. Joseph A. Yager, *The Economic Transformation of Taiwan* (Taipei: ROC-USA Economic Council, 1986); Jon Woronoff, *Asia's "Miracle" Economies* (M.E. Sharpe, 1986).

5. Technical assistance included advice on land reform, one of the pillars of Taiwan's successful economic takeoff and social stability.

6. Chung-lih Wu: "Some Measures to Promote a More Balanced Bilateral Trade Relationship Between the ROC and the USA -- Economic and Political Implications," *Economic Review* (January-February 1988), p. 7.

7. On this combination see S.C. Tsiang, Wen Lang Chen, Alvin Hsieh, "Progress in Trade Liberalization Taiwan, Republic of China," *Economic Review* (March-April 1986), pp. 1-13.

8. On the occasion of the Sino-U.S. Symposium on Industry, Trade, and Economic Development held in Beijing in June 1988, U.S. Ambassador Winston Lord celebrated the fact that in 1987 "American imports from China shot up 32 percent to US$ 6.9 billion," and that "after Japan, the United States is the leading foreign market for Chinese products, taking more than 16 percent of the PRC's exports." He noted that in the same year PRC imports from the U.S. rose 13 percent (that is roughly one-third the PRC's exports to the U.S.) to US$ 3.5 billion, or 8.7 percent of China's imports. *Beijing Review* (June 20-26, 1988), p. 20.

9.   *The Wall Street Journal* (June 2, 1988), p. 1.

10.   A poll taken on Taiwan in 1988 revealed that more than 43 percent of the respondents thought the government should allow local businessmen to do business with the mainland, 17 percent were against, and 12 percent adopted a wait-and-see attitude. *The Free China Journal* (February 29, 1988), p. 1.

11.   On the generalized systems of preferences, see J. David Richardson, *Understanding International Economics: Theory and Practice* (Little, Brown and Company, 1980), pp. 476-481. Taiwan (as well as South Korea, Hong Kong, and Singapore) are to be dropped from the GSP in 1989. It is estimated that Taiwan benefited from the GSP to the tune of US$ 4.1 billion. *The Free China Journal* (May 2, 1988), p. 4.

12.   Foreign brokerage firms intending to set up affiliates in Taiwan must have at least 10 years operating experience in their own countries and must not have violated any securities regulations in the past three year. *The Free China Journal* (May 9, 1988), p. 1.

13.   Ibid. (May 9, 1988), p. 2.

14.   Ibid., p. 1.

15.   *Commercial Times* (Taipei) cited in Ibid. (May 2, 1988), p. 2.

16.   The argument about the alleged loss of American competitiveness is valuable for polemical purposes. The question itself, however, is more complex. For one thing, "trade figures are not the best measure of competitiveness." See "A Portrait of America's New Competitiveness," *The Economist* (June 4, 1988), pp. 57-58.

17.   Craig C. Wu, "Past Performance and Recent Development of the Taiwan Economy," *Economic Review* (May-June 1988), p.5.

Part II

Documents: 1949-1978

CHAPTER SIX

POLITICAL AND DIPLOMATIC

A list of the important political and diplomatic documents for the period 1949-1978.

1. September 21, 1949. Mao's Address to the First Plenary Session of the Chinese People's Political Consultative Conference. "The Chinese People Have Stood Up!" *Selected Works of Mao Tsetung*, Volume 5. Foreign Languages Press, Peking, 1977.

2. Proclamation of the People's Republic of China. *New York Times*, October 2, 1949, p.1 (Excerpt).

3. Shift of Capital from Nanking to Taipei. *ROC Archives*, compilation of Presidential Decrees.

4. U.S. Government criteria concerning the recognition of governments - Jessup Hearings on the nomination of Philip Jessup before a subcommittee of the Senate Foreign Relations Committee. October, 1951. pp. 615-616.

5. U.S. Secretary of State Acheson's Statement rejecting recognition of People's Republic of China - Hearings on the Military situation in the Far East before the Senate Armed Services and Foreign Relations Committees, June 1951. pp. 1671-1672.

6. December 30, 1949 National Security Council Document (NSC 48-2) Discussion regarding potential split between PRC and USSR. *Foreign Relations of the United States, 1949*, Volume VII, Part 11. U.S. Government Printing Office, Washington, DC, 1976. pp. 1215-1220.

7. Representation of Member States in the United Nations, January 1950, *Yearbook of the United Nations, 1950*, Columbia University Press in cooperation with the United Nations, New York, 1951. pp. 421-429.

8. U.S. Secretary of State Acheson's Statement on U.S. Military Involvement in Formosa. *U.S. Department of State Bulletin*, Volume 22, January 16, 1950. p. 80.

9. 1950 - United States Proposals for strengthening the United Nations system in order to meet possible future aggression; The "United for Peace" Resolution. *American Foreign Relations, 1950*, Volume II, U.S. Government Printing Office, Washington, DC. pp. 303-311.

10. U.S. Secretary of State Acheson's Statement on U.S. defense perimeter in Pacific Area, January 1950. *U.S. Department of State Bulletin*, Volume 22, January 23, 1950. pp. 115-116.

11. U.N. Resolution concerning the intervention of the People's Republic of China in Korea, *Documents on American Foreign Relations*, Volume XIII, 1951. U.S. Government Printing Office, Washington, DC. pp. 451-453.

12. U.N. Resolution concerning additional measures to meet the aggression in Korea, *Documents on American Foreign Relations*, Volume XIII, 1951. U.S. Government Printing Office, Washington, DC, pp. 452-453.

13. 1953 Congressional Resolution rejecting admission of PRC to the U.N. Public Law
     195, August 5, 1953, *U.S. Statutes at Large*, 83rd Congress, 1st Session, 1953, Volume
     67. U.S. Government Printing Office, Washington, DC. p. 372.

14. 1956 Congressional Resolution rejecting admission of PRC to the U.N. Public Law
     853, July 31, 1956, *U.S. Statutes at Large*, 84th Congress, 2nd Session, 1956, Volume
     70. U.S. Government Printing Office, Washington, DC. p. 735.

15. Statement by Secretary of State Dulles, September 4, 1956. *Department of State
     Bulletin*, September 22, 1958. pp. 445-446.

16. October 24, 1958 Joint ROC-U.S. Communique in Which Chiang Kai-Shek Renounces
     use of Force to Recover the Mainland. News Item, Chinese News Agency, Taipei,
     October 24, 1958.

17. 1960 Congressional Resolution rejecting admission of PRC to the U.N. Public Law
     86-704, September 2, 1960, *U.S. Statutes at Large*, 86th Congress, 2nd Session, 1960,
     Volume 74. U.S. Government Printing Office, Washington, DC. p. 779.

18. 1965 Congressional Resolution rejecting admission of PRC to the U.N. Public 89-273,
     October 20, 1965, *U.S. Statutes at Large*, 89th Congress, 1st Session 1965, Volume 79.
     U.S. Government Printing Office, Washington, DC. p. 1003.

19. 1970 Congressional Resolution rejecting admission of PRC to the U.N. Public Law
     91-472, October 21, 1970, *U.S. Statutes at Large*, 91st Congress, 2nd Session, Volume
     84, Part I. U.S. Government Printing Office, Washington, DC. p. 1044.

20. President Nixon's Annual Report to the Congress, February 25, 1971. *U.S. Foreign
     Policy for the 1970s: A Report to the Congress by Richard Nixon*, February 25, 1971.
     pp. 91, 107-108.

21. July 15, 1971 Statement by President Nixon announcing his acceptance of invitation
     to visit People's Republic of China. *U.S. Department of State Bulletin*, volume 65, July-
     September 1971, p. 121.

22. August 2, 1971 Secretary of State Rogers regarding US position on expulsion of ROC
     from United Nations, Department of State Press Release 166, August 2, 1971,
     Department of State Bulletin, Aug. 1971.

23. September 25, 1971 "Albanian" Resolution regarding the representation of the PRC
     on the Security Council of the United Nations. U.N. document A/L.630 and Add. 1
     and 2; in General Assembly, *Official Records: 26th Session Annexes*, Agenda item 93,
     pp. 3-4.

24. September 27, 1971 "Important Question Resolution" ROC representation in the
     United Nations. UN document A/L.632 and Add. 1 and 2 in General Assembly
     Official Records: 26th Session Annexes, Agenda item 93, pp. 3-4.

25. September 27, 1971 The "Dual Representation" Resolution. UN document A/L.633
     and Add. 1 and 2; text in General Assembly *Official Records: 26th Session Annexes*,
     Agenda item 93, pp. 3-4.

26.   October 4, 1971 Address by Secretary of State Rogers to the General Assembly regarding Representation of PRC in the UN. Department of State Press Release 227. *Department of State Bulletin*, October 25, 1971, pp. 439-441.

27.   October 25, 1971 Restoration of the PRC in the United Nations. General Assembly Resolution. General Assembly *Official Records: 26th Session*, Supplement No. 29 (A/8429).

28.   October 26, 1971 Secretary of State Rogers statement concerning admission of PRC to the United Nations: Implications of the Assembly's Action. Department of State Press Release 246, text from *Department of State Bulletin*, November 15, 1971, p. 541.

29.   November 15, 1971 Statement by Ambassador George Bush to the General Assembly regarding admission of PRC to the UN. USUN Press Release 187; text from *Department of State Bulletin*, December 20, 1971, pp. 715-716.

30.   Joint Communique issued at Shanghai 1972. *Public Papers of the Presidents of the United States: Richard Nixon*, 1972, U.S. Government Printing Office, Washington, DC, 1974. pp. 376-379.

31.   1974 "Repeal of the Formosa Resolution". In Public Law 93-475, October 26, 1974, *U.S. Statutes at Large*, 93rd Congress, 1974, Volume 88. U.S. Government Printing Office, Washington, DC. p. 1955.

P&D1   THE CHINESE PEOPLE HAVE STOOD UP

September 21, 1949

Fellow Delegates,

The Political Consultative Conference so eagerly awaited by the whole nation is herewith inaugurated.

Our conference is composed of more than six hundred delegates, representing all the democratic parties and people's organizations of China, the People's Liberation Army, the various regions and nationalities of the country and the overseas Chinese. This shows that ours is a conference embodying the great unity of the people of the whole country.

It is because we have defeated the reactionary Kuomintang government backed by U.S. imperialism that this great unity of the whole people has been achieved. In alittle more than three years the heroic Chinese Pople's Liberation Army, an army such as the world has seldom seen, crushed all the offensives launched by the several million troops of the U.S.-supported reactionary Kuomintang government and turned to the counter-offensive and the offensive. At present the field armies of the People's Liberation Army, several million strong, have pushed the war to areas near Taiwan, Kwangtung, Kwangsi, Kweichow, Szechuan and Sinkiang, and the great majority of the Chinese people have won liberation. In a little more than three years the people of the whole country have closed their ranks, rallied to support the People's Liberation Army, fought the enemy and won basic victory. And it is on this foundation that the present People's Political Consultative Conference is convened.

Our conference is called the Political Consultative Conference because some three years ago we held a Political Consultative Conference with Chiang Kai-shek's Kuomintang. The results of that conference were sabotaged by Chiang Kai-shek's Kuomintang and its accomplices; nevertheless the conference left an indelible impression on the people. It showed that nothing in the interest of the people could be accomplished together with Chiang Kai-shek's Kuomintang, the running dog of imperialism, and its accomplices. Even when resolutions wree reluctantly adopted, it was of no avail, for as soon as the time was ripe, they tore them up and started a ruthless war against the people. The only gain from that conference was the profound lesson it taught the people that there is absolutely no room for compromise with Chiang Kai-shek's Kuomintang, the running dog of imperialism, and its accomplices -- overthrow these enemies or be oppressed and slaughtered by them, either one or the other, there is no other choice. In a little more than three years the Chinese people, led by the Chinese Communist Party, have quickly awakened and organized themselves into a nation-wide united front against imperialism, feudalism, bureaucrat-capitalism and their general representative, the reactionary Kuomintang government, supported the People's War of Liberation, basically defeated the reactionary Kuomintang government, overthrown the rule of imperialism in China and restored the Political Consultative Conference.

The present Chinese People's Political Consultative Conference is convened on an entirely new foundation; it is representative of the people of the whole country and enjoys their trust and support. Therefore, the conference proclaims that it will exercise the functions and powers of a National People's Congress. In accordance with its agenda, the conference will enact the Organic Law of the Chinese People's Political Consultative Conference, the Organic Law of the Central People's Government of the People's Republic of China and the Common Programme of the Chinese People's Political Consultative Conference; it will elect the National Committee of the Chinese People's Political Consultative Conference and the Central People's Government Council of the People's Republic of China; it will adopt the national flag and national emblem of the People's Republic of China; and it will decide on the seat of the capital of the People's Republic of China and adopt the chronological system in use in most countries of the world.

Fellow Delegates, we are all convinced that our work will go down in the history of mankind, demonstrating that the Chinese people, comprising one quarter of humanity, have now stood up. The Chinese have always been a great, courageous and industrious nation; it is only in modern times that they have fallen behind. And that was due entirely to oppression and exploitation by foreign imperialism and domestic reactionary governments. For over a century our forefathers never stopped waging unyielding struggles against domestic and foreign oppressors, including the Revolution of 1911 led by Dr. Sun Yat-sen, our great forerunner in the Chinese revolution. Our forefathers enjoined us to carry out their unfulfilled will. And we have acted accordingly. We have closed our ranks and defeated both domestic and foreign oppressors through the People' War of Liberation and the great people's revolution, and now we are proclaiming the founding of the People's Republic of China. From now on our nation will belong to the community of the peace-lowing and freedom-lowing nations of the world and work courageously and industriously to foster its own civilization and well-being and at the same time to promote world peace and freedom. Ours will no longer be a nation subject to insult and humiliation. We have stood up. Our revolution has won the sympathy and acclaim of the people of all countries. We have freinds all over the world.

Our revolutionary work is not completed, the People's War of Liberation and the people's revolutionary movement are still forging ahead and we must keep up our efforts. The imperialists and the domestic reactionaries will certainly not take their defeat lying down; they will fight to the last ditch. After there is peace and order throughout the country, they are sure to engage in sabotage and create disturbances by one means or another and every day and every minute they will try to stage a come-back. This is inevitable and beyond all doubt, and under no circumstances must we relax our vigilance.

Our state system, the people's democratic dictatorship, is a powerful weapon for safeguarding the fruits of victory of the people's revolution and for thwarting the plots of domestic and foreign enemies for restoration, and this weapon we must firmly grasp. Internationally, we must unite with all peace-lowing and freedom-lowing countries and peoples, and first of all with the Soviet Union and the New Democracies, so that we shall not stand alone in our struggle to safeguard these fruits of victory and to thwart the plots of domestic and foreign enemies for restoration. As long as we persist in the people's democratic dictatorship and unite with out foreign friends, we shall always be victorious.

The people's democratic dictatorship and solidarity with out foreign friends will enable us to accomplish our work of construction rapidly. We are already confronted with the task of nation-wide economic construction. We have very favourable conditions: a population of 475 million people and a territory of 9,600,000 square kilometres. There are indeed difficulties ahead, and a great many too. But we firmly believe that by heroic struggle the people of the country will surmount them all. The Chinese people have rich experience in overcoming difficulties. If our forefathers, and we also, could weather long years of extreme difficulty and defeat powerful domestic and foreign reactionaries, why can't we now, after victory, build a prosperous and flourishing country? As long as we keep to our style of plain living and hard struggle, as long as we stand united and as long as we persist in the people's democratic dictatorship and unite with our foreign friends, we shall be able to win speedy victory on the economic front.

An upsurge in economic construction is bound to be followed by an upsurge of construction in the cultural sphere. The era in which the Chinese people were regarded as uncivilized is now ended. We shall emerge in the world as a nation with an advanced culture.

Our national defence will be consolidated and no imperialists will ever again be allowed to invade our land. Our people's armed forces must be maintained and developed with the heroic and steeled People's Liberation Army as the foundation. We will have not only a powerful army but also a powerful air force and a powerful navy.

Let the domestic and foreign reactionaries tremble before us! Let them say we are no good at this and no good at that. By our own indomitable efforts we the Chinese people will unswervingly reach our goal.

The heroes of the people who laid down their lives in the People's War of Liberation and the people's revolution shall live for ever in our memory!

Hail the victory of the People's War of Liberation and the People's revolution!

Hail the founding of the People's Republic of China!

Hail the triumph of the Chinese People's Political Consultative Conference!

Source: *Selected Works of Mao Tsetung*, Volume 5, Foreign Languages Press, Peking: 1977.

P&D2   **PROCLAMATION OF THE PEOPLE'S REPUBLIC OF CHINA**

**Reds Proclaim a Republic
In China; Chou is Premier**

By Walter Sullivan

(Special to the New York Times)

SHANGHAI, October 1 -- Chou En-lai was today named in Peiping as Premier and consequently Foreign Minister of China's new People's (Communist) Republic. At the same time the new regime declared itself the sole legal Government of China and invited recognition by other nations.

This was announced in a proclamation read by Mao Tse-tung, head of the Chinese Communist party, before a crowd officially estimated at 200,000 that gathered in the newly cleared Square of the Gate of Heavenly Peace, Peking's equivalent of Red Square in Moscow.

Source: *New York Times*, October 2, 1949, p.1 (Excerpt).

P&D3   **Republic of China Presidential Decree**

                  SHIFT OF CAPITAL FROM NANKING TO TAIPEI

                       (Translation from Chinese document)

Date: December 7, 1949

Issued by: Acting President Li Zongren and Head of the Foreign Ministry Yan Xishan

Re: The Government will move to Taipei and supreme headquarters will be set
                  up in Xican to command the air force, the navy and the army, as well as to
                  conduct warfare on the mainland.

Source: ROC Archives, compilation of Presidential Decrees.

P&D4   **UNITED STATES GOVERNMENT CRITERIA CONCERNING
                  RECOGNITION OF GOVERNMENTS**

At his press and radio news conference on October 12, 1949, Secretary Acheson restated the main tests which the United States believed should be applied to the question on recognition of governments, as follows:

(1)   That it control the country that it claimed to control;

(2)   That it recognize its international obligations; and

(3)   That it rule with the acquiescence of the people who were ruled.

On that same day the Department of State in an instruction to 27 diplomatic and consular establishments abroad and to the United States delegation to the United Nations, restated the United States Government position of nonrecognition, for use should any foreign government first raise the question to any of our representatives or if any of them had reason to believe that the foreign government to which they were accredited might contemplate independent action to recognize without prior consultation.

On November 1, 1949, the British Government informed this Government of the views which were influencing it toward early reognition of the Chinese Communist regime and requested consultation with this Government on the basis of its appraisal of the situation. The British gave their own conclusion that recognition should be accorded.

Senator Brewster: What were the bases on which the Department decided against recognition, referring now to the three points you made?

Ambassador Jessup: On the three points? That you got a negative on each one, that the Communist Government did not control the whole country; it certainly did not recognize its international obligations; and it did not rule with the acquiescence of the people.

Senator Brewster: How many of those still prevail?

Ambassador Jessup: I think they all three prevail.

Senator Brewster: You consider the Soviet Government exercises an undue influence over the Chinese Government?

Ambassador Jessup: Absolutely; yes, sir.

Source: Jessup Hearings on the nomination of Philip Jessup before a subcommittee of the Senate Foreign Relations Committee, October 1951, pp. 615-616.

P&D5   U.S. SECRETARY OF STATE ACHESON'S STATEMENT REJECTING RECOGNITION OF PEOPLE'S REPUBLIC OF CHINA

Chairman Russell: Mr. Secretary, if you desire to make any statement now we will be glad to hear from you.

Secretary Acheson: Mr. Chairman, I should like to address myself to the question of this document. It deals with information to be given out over the Voice of America to minimize the damaging effects to the United States of the possible fall of Formosa.

Senator Wiley: We do not hear you, Mr. Secretary.

Secretary Acheson: I was just describing, Senator, what the document was about.

UNITED STATES POLICY TOWARD FORMOSA: OCTOBER 1948 TO JUNE 1950

In discussing the document which, obviously, relates to the policy of the United States, I have, first, to state what the policy of the United States was in regard to Formosa, and I should like to deal with the period from October 1948 to January 25, 1950.

Throughout that period there was one policy, and one policy only, which was adopted by the Government, with the exception of one point in that policy, which I shall describe later on, a point which arose on the 27th, 28th, and 29th of December 1949, this policy was unanimously recommended to the President of the United States by all the departments concerned, and was approved by him.

You see, therefore, that it originated during the administration of the State Department by my predecessor, and was carried on by me, so far as the State Department participation is concerned.

That policy was as follows: First of all, it was understood and agreed that Formosa had strategic importance so far as the United States was concerned.

The second point was that that strategic importance related to keeping Formosa out of the hands of a power which would be hostile to the United States, and did not concern occupying or using Formosa by the United States.

The third element of the policy, which never varied from October 1948 to January 25, 1950, was that, in the existing condition, and strength of the Armed Forces of the United States, it was not possible to commit or promise to commit any forces whatever, Armed Forces of the United States, to the defense of Formosa.

The next element of the policy was that the State Department should, to the best of its ability, by diplomatic and economic means try to keep Formosa from falling into hands which would be hostile to us.

Those are the main outlines of the policy.

I, in August 1949, as Secretary of State, reported that I could no longer guarantee that economic and diplomatic means would be successful in keeping Formosa out of the hands of a power which might be hostile to us, and I may say that this policy was reviewed very frequently during the whole time that I was there.

Senator Smith: Pardon me; what was that, Mr. Secretary?

Secretary Acheson: I was saying that this policy was reviewed frequently during the period.

Senator Smith: I thought you gave a date.

Secretary Acheson: I gave the wrong date, I am sorry to say. The period was October 1948 to June 25, 1950, when I reported that what I have just stated, that it was reviewed again.

BACKGROUND OF PREPARATION OF INSTRUCTIONS OF DECEMBER 1949

While we were in this condition which I have just described, the Department of the Army, which was represented on the interdepartmental group which coordinated the information policies, suggested to the Department of State, the suggestion coming from General Wedemeyer, who was Assistant Chief of Staff, to Assistant Secretary Allen, who is in charge of our Voice of America, that it might be very important to use the Voice of America and our international techniques to minimize any damage which might occur to us in event of the fall of Formosa.

The State Department said it was grateful for that suggestion and would go to work on the matter.

The Department did go to work on the matter.

First of all, there were two studies made, in September and October, as to the imminence and danger of this fall.

Those studies unanimously reported that the fall would occur, and would occur probably in the year 1950.

It was also unanimously reported that the fall would occur, and would occur probably in the year 1950.

It was also unanimously understood in these policies, and reported, that, without American military support, support by our own Armed Forces, the island could not be held by those on it against serious attack from the mainland.

In the light of those studies, and those conclusions of probable fact, this document which you have before you was prepared, and, as the heading indicates, the purpose of the document was to solve the problem, if possible, of formulating policy which would minimize damage to the United States prestige and others' morale by the possible fall of Formosa to the Chinese Communist forces.

Source: Hearings on the military situation in the Far East before the Senate Armed Services and Foreign Relations Committees, June 1951, pp. 1671-1672

P&D6   A REPORT TO THE PRESIDENT BY THE
                              NATIONAL SECURITY COUNCIL

                              Washington, December 30, 1949
NSC 48/2

THE POSITION OF THE UNITED STATES WITH RESPECT TO ASIA

CONCLUSIONS

Our basic security objectives with respect to Asia are:

a. Development of the nations and peoples of Asia on a stable and self-sustaining basis in conformity with the purposes and principles of the United Nations Charter.

b. Development of sufficient military power in selected non-Communist nations of Asia to maintain internal security and to prevent further encroachment by communism.

c. Gradual reduction and eventual elimination of the preponderant power and influence of the USSR in Asia to such a degree that the Soviet Union will not be capable of threatening from that area the security of the United States or its friends and that the Soviet Union would encounter serious obstacles should it attempt to threaten the peace, national independence and stablity of the Asiatic nations.

d. Prevention of power relationships in Asia which would enable any other nation or alliance to threaten the security of the United States from that area, or the peace, national independence and stability of the Asiatic nations.

2. In pursuit of these objectives, the United States should act to:

a. Support non-Communist forces in taking the initiative in Asia;

b. Exert an influence to advance its own national interests; and

c. Initiate action in such a manner as will appeal to the Asiatic nations as being compatible with their national interests and worthy of their support.

3. As the basis for realization of its objectives, the United States should pursue a policy toward Asia containing the following components:

a. The United States should make known its sympathy with the efforts of Asian leaders to form regional associations of non-Communist states of the various Asian areas, and if in due course associations eventuate, the United States should be prepared, if invited, to assist such associations to fulfill their purposes under conditions which would be to our interest. The following principles should guide our actions in this respect:

(1) Any association formed must be the result of genuine desire on the part of the participating nations to cooperate for mutual benefit in solving the political, economic, social and cultural problems of the areas.
(2) The United States must not take such an active part in the early stages of the formation of such an association that it will be subject to the charge of using the Asiatic nations to further United States ambitions.
(3) The association, if it is to be a constructive force, must operate on the basis of mutual aid and self-help in all fields so that a true partnership may exist based on equal rights and equal obligations.
(4) United States participation in any stage of the development of such an association should be with a view to accomplishing our basic objectives in Asia and to assuring that any association formed will be in accord with Chapter VIII of the Charter of the United Nations dealing with regional arrangements.

b. The United should act to develop and strengthen the security of the area from Communist external aggression or internal subversion. These steps should take into account any benefits to the security of Asia which may flow from the development of one or more regional groups. The United States on its own initiative should now:

(1) Improve the United States position with respect to Japan, the Ryukyus and the Philippines.
(2) Scrutinize closely the development of threats from Communist aggression, direct or indirect, and be prepared to help within our means to meet such threats by providing political, economic, and military assistance and advice

where clearly needed to supplement the resistance of the other governments in and out of the area which are more directly concerned.

(3) Develop cooperative measures through multilateral or bilateral arrangements to combat Communist internal subversion.

(4) Appraise the desirability and the means of developing in Asia some form of collective security arrangements, bearing in mind the following considerations:

> (a) The reluctance of India at this time to join in any anti-Communist security pact and the influence this will have among the other nations of Asia.
>
> (b) The necessity of assuming that any collective security arrangements which might be developed be based on the principle of mutual aid and on a demonstrated desire and ability to share in the burden by all the participating states.
>
> (c) The necessity of assuring that any such security arrangements would be consonant with the purposes of any regional association which may be formed in accordance with paragraph 3-a above.
>
> (d) The necessity of assuring that any such security arrangement would be in conformity with the provisions of Article 51 of the Charter relating to individual and collective self-defense.

c. The United States should encourage the creation of an atmosphere favorable to economic recovery and development in non-Communist Asia, and to the revival of trade along multilateral, non-discriminatory lines. The economic policies of the United States should be adapted to promote, where possible, economic conditions that will contribute to political stability in friendly countries of Asia, but the United States shold carefully avoid assuming responsibility for the economic welfare and development of that continent. Such policies might be projected along the following lines:

(1) Vigorous prosecution of the Point IV program in friendly countries of Asia, in an endeavor to assist them, by providing technical assistance, to make a start toward the solution of some of their long-range economic problems.

(2) Maintenance of a liberal United States trade policy with Asia and stimulation of imports from Asia. The special problems concerning trade with China are treated in paragraph 3-f-(4) below.

(3) Execution of a stockpiling program for strategic materials, based upon United States needs for strategic reserves and upon immediate and long-range economic effects in the supplying countries.

(4) Negotiation of treaties of friendship, commerce and navigation with non-Communist countries of Asia to define and establish conditions facilitating capital movements, trade and other economic relations between them and the United States.

(5) Encouragement of private United States investment in non-Communist countries and support of the early extension of credits by the International Bank and the Export-Import Bank for specific key economic projects of a self-

liquidating nature, especially those directed towards increasing production of food in this area.

(6) Efforts to obtain the adherence of Asiatic countries to the principles of multilateral, nondiscriminatory trade as embodied in the General Agreements on Tariffs and Trade, as a means of reducing trade barriers and expanding the international and intra-regional trade of the region of an economic basis. This would include, for example, further efforts to secure the benefits of most-favored-nation treatment for Japan.

d.   The question of a peace settlement with Japan, now receiving separate consideration, will be presented for the consideration of the National Security Council at a later date and policies with respect to Japan will be re-evaluated after the decision regarding a peace treaty has been made.

e.   (1) The United States should continue to provide for the extension of political support and economic, technical, military and other assistance to the democratically-elected Government of the Republic of Korea.

(2) The United States should therefore press forward with the implementation of the ECA, MDAP, USIE and related programs for Korea, and should continue to accord political support to the Republic of Korea, both within and without the framework of the United Nations.

f.   (1) The United States should continue to recognize the National Government of China until the situation is further clarified. The United States should avoid recognizing the Chinese Communist regime until it is clearly in the United States interest to do so. The United States should continue to express to friendly governments its own views concerning the dangers of hasty recognition of the Chinese Communist regime but should not take a stand which would engage the prestige of the United States in an attempt to prevent such recognition. In general, however, it should be realized that it would be inappropriate for the United States to adopt a posture more hostile or policies more harsh towards a Communist China than towards the USSR itself. It should also realize that the according of recognition by other friendly countries would affect the bargaining position of the United States in the absence of United States recognition and would affect United States private and national interests in CHina. In the event that recognition of the Chinese Communists is anticipated, appropriate steps should be taken to make it clear that recognition should not be construed as approval of the Chinese Communist regime, or abatement of our hostility to Soviet efforts to exercise control in China.

(2) The United States should continue the policies of avoiding military and political support of any non-Communist elements in China unless such elements are willing actively to resist Communism with or without United States aid and unless such support would mean resonable resistance to the Communists and contribute to the over-all national interests of the United States. In determining whether or in what manner any such assistance or encouragement should be given, consideration would have to be given to the protection which Chinese Communist authorities, as they become generally recognized by other governments, would be able to claim under international law and the Charter of the United Nations. The United States should maintain so far as feasible active contact with all elements in China and maintain our cultural and informational program at the most active feasible level.

(3)   The United States should exploit, through appropriate political, psychological and economic means, any rifts between the Chinese Communists and the USSR and between the Stalinists and other elements in China, while scrupulously avoiding the

appearance of intervention. Where appropriate, covert as well as overt means should be utilized to achieve these objectives.

(4) The United States should, as a security measure, seek to prevent the USSR, its European satellites, and North Korea from obtaining from abroad through China supplies of strategic materials and equipment which are currently denied them by the United States and its European allies through direct channels. The United States should also use every effort to prevent the Chinese Communists from obtaining from non-Soviet sources supplies of materials and equipment of direct military utility (1A items). The United States should, on the other hand, permit exports to China of 1B items within quantitative limits of normal civilian use and under controls which can be applied restrictively if it becomes necessary to do so in the national interest, and should place no obstacle in the way of trade with China in non-strategic commodities. The United States should seek the support and concurrence of its principal European allies in these policies. The United States should not extend governmental economic assistance to Communist China or encourage private investment in Communist China.

g.   (1) The United States should continue the policy set forth in NSC 37/2 and 37/5 of attempting to deny Formosa and the Pescadores to the Chinese Communists through diplomatic and economic means within the limitations imposed by the fact that successful achievement of this objective will primarily depend on prompt initiation and faithful implementation of essential measures of self-help by the non-Communist administration of the islands, and by the fact that freedom of U.S. diplomatic and economic action will be influenced, necessarily, by action taken by other countries.

(2) Since the United States may not be able to achieve its objectives through political and economic means, and in view of the opinion of the Joint Chiefs of Staff (reaffirmed in NSC 37/7 of August 22, 1949) that, while Formosa is strategically important to the United States, "the strategic importance of Formosa does not justify overt military action...so long as the present disparity between our military strength and our global obligations exists," the United States should make every effort to strengthen the over-all U.S. position with respect to the Philippines, the Ryukyus, and Japan. The United States should, for example, proceed apace with implementation of the policy set forth in regard to the Ryukyus in paragraph 5 of NSC 13/3.

h. The United States should continue to use its influence in Asia toward resolving the colonial-nationalist conflict in such a way as to satisfy the fundamental demands of the nationalist movement while at the same time minimizing the strain on the colonial powers who are our Western allies. Particular attention should be given to the problem of French Indo-China and action should be taken to bring home to the French the urgency of removing the barriers to the obtaining by Bao Dai or other non-Communist nationalist leaders of the support of a substantial proportion of the Vietnamese. With the successful conclusion of the Round Table Conference at The Hague the United States should give immediate consideration to the problems confronting the new Republic of United Indonesia and how best it can be aided in maintaining its freedom in the face of internal and external Communist pressures.

i. Active consideration should be given to means by which all members of the British Commonwealth may be induced to play a more active role in collaboration with the United States in Asia. Similar collaboration should be obtained to the extent possible from other non-Communist nations having interests in Asia.

j. Recognizing that the non-Communist governments of South Asia already constitute a bulwark against Communist expansion in Asia, the United States should exploit every opportunity to increase the present Western orientation of the area and to assist, within our capabilities, its governments in their efforts to meet the minimum aspirations of their people and to maintain internal security.

k. The United States should undertake an information program, both foreign and domestic, and publish United States policies and programs vis-a-vis Asia designed to gain maximum support both at home and abroad.

l. Nothing in this paper shall be construed as amending approved NSC papers unless a specific statement to that effect has been made on each point.

m. The sum of $75,000,000 for assistance to the general area of China, which was made available under Section 303 of the Mutual Defense Assistance Ac5t of 1949, should be programmed as a matter of urgency.

Source: *Foreign Relations of the United States*, 1949, Volume VII, Part 11, U.S. Government Printing Office, Washington, D.C., 1976, pp. 1215-1220.

P&D7   REPRESENTATION OF MEMBER STATES IN THE UNITED NATIONS

1. The Question of the Representation of China

a. Consideration by the Security Council

In a cablegram dated 18 November 1949 (A/1123) to the President of the General Assembly, the Foreign Minister of the Central People's Government of the People's Republic of China stated that his Government repudiated the legal status of the delegation under Mr. T.F. Tsiang and held that it could not represent China and had no right to speak on behalf of the Chinese people in the United Nations....

...At the 459th meeting of the Council on 10 January 1950, the representative of the USSR expressed his support for the position taken by the People's Republic of China in its communication of 8 January, and he insisted that the representative of the Kuomintang group should be excluded from the Council. If the Council did not take appropriate measures, the USSR delegation, he stated, would not take part in the work of the Council until the Kuomintang representative was excluded. He submitted a draft resolution (S/1443), by which the Council would decide not to recognize the credentials of the representative referred to in the statement by the Central People's Government of the Chinese People's Republic and to exclude him from the Security Council....

...The representative of China said that, when he had taken his seat in the Council, more than two years previously, his credentials had been duly certified to the Council as adequate. They had not been challenged until the USSR draft resolution had been presented. If the question before the Council was a matter of credentials. there could be no real question at all. Although the USSR draft resolution spoke of credentials, what it called into question was really the right of his Government to be represented at all. That was not a question of mere procedure but a political question of the utmost importance, and he would treat it as such....

...At 461st meeting, on 13 January 1950, the USSR draft resolution was put to the vote and was not adopted, having failed to obtain the affirmative votes of seven members. The vote was 6 to 3 (India, USSR, Yugoslavia) with 2 abstentions (Norway, United Kingdom).

The representative of the USSR declared that his delegation would not participate in the work of the Security Council until the representative of the Kuomintang group, who was illegally occupying a seat in that organ of the United Nations, had been removed from membership in the Council. His presence there was undermining the prestige and authority of the Security Council and of the United Nations as a whole. As a result, the Security Council was being transformed into an organ whose decisions could not be considered legal in those circumstances. Therefore, the USSR would not recognize as legal any decision of the Security Council adopted which the participation of the representative of the Kuomintang group and would not deem itself bound by such decisions. The representative of the USSR then left the Council chamber....

...A cablegram dated 20 January 1950, bearing the signature of the Minister of Foreign Affairs of the People's Republic of China, informed the Secretary-General and the Members of the United Nations and the Security Council that his Government had appointed Chang Wen Tien as Chairman of its delegation to attend the meetings and to participate in the work of the United Nations, including the meetings and work of the Security Council. He asked when the Kuomintang representative would be expelled from the United Nations and from the Security Council, and when the delegation of the People's Republic of China could participate in the work of the United Nations and the Security Council....

...During the month of February 1950, the Secretary-General requested the preparation of a confidential memorandum on the legal aspects of the problem of the representation of States in the United Nations. Some of the representatives on the Security Council asked to see the memorandum and references to it appeared in the Press. On 8 March, the Secretary-General informed the President of the Council that he felt it appropriate that the full text be made available to all members of the Council. Accordingly, he circulated the memorandum (S/1466) to all members and released it to the Press.

The memorandum stated that the primary difficulty in the current question of the representation of Member States in the United States in the United Nations was that the question of representation had been linked up with the question of recognition by Government of Member States. After arguing that the linkage was unfortunate from the practical standpoint, and wrong from the standpoint of legal theory, the memorandum concluded that the proper principle could be derived by analogy from Article 4 of the Charter. Article 4 required that an applicant for membership must be able and willing to carry out the obligations of membership. The obligations of membership could be carried out only by Governments which, in fact, possessed the power to do so. Where a revolutionary government presented itself as representing a State, in rivalry to an existing government, the question at issue should be which of these two governments in fact was in a position to employ the resources and direct the people of the State in the fulfillment of the obligations of membership. In essence, this meant an inquiry as to whether the new government exercised effective authority within the territory of the State and was habitually obeyed by the bulk of the population. If so, the memorandum stated, it would seem to be appropriate for the United Nations organs, through their collective action, to accord the new government the right to represent the State in the Organization, even though individual Members of the Organization refused, and might continue to refuse, to accord that government recognition as the lawful government for reasons which were valid under their national policies.

On 13 March, the representative of China lodged his Government's formal protest (S/1470) against the Secretary-General's memorandum (S/1466), which the representative of China considered to be an attack on China's United Nations front and would, in time, be recognized as an attack on the cause of freedom throughout the world. After analysing the political errors which he considered the document involved, he replied to the legal arguments it advanced and concluded that recognition and representation were based on similar considerations and that the linkage between the two was natural and inevitable.   If the Secretary-General wished to institute the inquiry to which he had referred, the only possible procedure consistent with the principles of the Charter was a fair and free election.   The communist regime did not have the support of the Chinese people, who regarded it as a puppet regime. The representative of China considered that the question of Chinese representation could not be held to "threaten the maintenance of international peace and security" within the meaning of Article 99 of the Charter, the only Article that assigned a sphere of political action to the Secretary-General.   For these reasons, he concluded that the Secretary-General had intervened against the interests of China on the basis of bad politics and bad law.

On 27 July, the permanent representative of the USSR at the United Nations informed the Secretary-General that, in accordance with established procedure, he was assuming the Presidency of the Security Council for August 1950. At the meeting on 1 August, the President ruled that the representative of the Kuomintang group did not represent China and therefore could not participate in the Council's meetings.

The representative of the United States considered that no President had the authority to rule by arbitrary fiat, upon the status of the representative of a country which was a Member of the United Nations. Accordingly he challenged the ruling.

After discussion during which the points of view previously expressed were maintained, the President's ruling was overruled by the Council by 8 votes to 3 (India, USSR, Yugoslavia). The representative of the USSR declared that this decision was illegal because the person concerned was the spokesman of a group which represented no one, and was not a representative of a State.

On 3 August, the Council rejected by 5 votes to 5 (China, Cuba, Ecuador, France, United States), with 1 abstention (Egypt), the proposal to include in the agenda the item "Recognition of the representative of the Central People's Government of the People's Republic of China as the representative of China" which had been placed on the Council's provisional agenda by the President (representative of the USSR).

b. Consideration by the General Assembly at its Fifth Session

In a cablegram (A/1364) dated 26 August 1950 to the Secretary-General, the Foreign Minister of the People's Republic of China recalled previous notes sent by his Government to the Secretary-General and to the General Assembly calling for the expulsion of the Kuomintang representatives from the United Nations organs.   The continued toleration of those representatives by the United Nations was, it was stated, a violation of the United Nations Charter and involved disregard of the rightful claims of the People's Republic of China. He requested that the necessary arrangements should be made for the delegation of the People's Republic of China to attend the fifth session of the General Assembly.

On 5 September, the Secretary-General replied that he would promptly make a request for the entry into the United States of the delegation of the People's Republic of China, on the General Assembly's acceptance of that delegation as representing the Republic of China, or on the invitation to it by the General Assembly to attend the session.

In a cablegram dated 18 September, the Foreign Minister of the Central People's Government of the People's Republic of China repeated the statements included in his previous message and declared that, should the fifth session of the General Assembly be held without the participation of his Government's delegation, all the resolutions of the General Assembly concerning China would be illegal, null and void....

...The representative of the USSR stated that the first point which the General Assembly ought to settle in connexion with the Indian draft resolution was whether the presence in the General Assembly of the representative of the Kuomintang group purporting to represent China was proper. He maintained that only a State Member of the United Nations was entitled to appoint its representatives to the Organization and to provide them with necessary credentials....

...The representative of China stated that he represented the only legal Government in China based on a constitution passed by the representatives of the Chinese people. After briefly outlining the achievements of that Government in the political and economic fields and its efforts in resisting Japan's aggression the representative of China analysed the origin and character of the Peking regime, which he said had been brought into power by the Soviet Union. He quoted General Chu The, the Communist Commander-in-Chief, to the effect that the victory of the Chinese democratic revolution was inseparable from Soviet aid. Mao Tse-tung had himself defined his policy on 1 July 1949 as alliance with the Soviet Union, with the new democratic countries of Europe and with the proletariat and masses of the people in other countries to form an international united front....

...The various proposals were then put to the vote. The Syrian proposal to postpone a decision was rejected by 21 votes to 16, with 13 abstentions. The Indian draft resolution (A/1365) was voted upon by roll-call and rejected by 33 votes to 16, with 10 abstentions....

Source: *Yearbook of the United Nations*, 1950, Columbia University Press in cooperation with the United Nations, New York, 1951, pp. 421-429.

P&D8   U.S. SECRETARY OF STATE ACHESON'S STATEMENT ON
              U.S. MILITARY INVOLVEMENT IN FORMOSA

There has been a great deal of amateur military strategy indulged in regard to this matter of Formosa. The underlying factors in the decision are not in that area. They have to do with the fundamental integrity of the United States and with maintaining in the world the belief that when the United States takes a position it sticks to that position and does not change it by reason of transitory expediency or advantage on its part. If we are going to maintain the free nations of the world as a great unit opposed to the encroachment of communism and other sorts of totalitarian aggression, the world must believe that we stand for principle and that we are honorable and decent people and that we do not put forward words, as propagandists do in other countries, to serve their advantage only to throw them overboard when some change in events makes the position difficult for us.

We believe in integrity in our foreign relations. We believe also in respect of the integrity of other countries. That is a view not held by some other countries. That is a view not held by some other countries with respect to China.

It is important that our position in regard to China should never be subject to the slightest doubt or the slightest question.

Now, what has that position been? In the middle of the war, the President of the United States, the Prime Minister of Great Britain, and the President of China agreed at Cairo that among the areas stolen from China by Japan was Formosa and Formosa should go back to China.

As the President pointed out this morning, that statement was incorporated in the declaration at Potsdam and that declaration at Potsdam was conveyed to the Japanese as one of the terms of their surrender and was accepted by them, and the surrender was made on that basis.

Shortly after that, the Island of Formorsa was turned over to the Chinese in accordance with the declarations made and with the conditions of the surrender.

The Chinese have administered Formosa for 4 years. Neither the United States nor any other ally ever questioned that authority and that occupation. When Formosa was made a province of China nobody raised any lawyers' doubts about that. That was regarded as in accordance with the commitments.

Now, in the opinion of some, the situation is changed. They believe that the forces now in control of the mainland of China, the forces which undoubtedly will soon be recognized by some other countries, are not friendly to us, and therefore they want to say, "Well, we have to wait for a treaty." We did not wait for a treaty on Korea. We did not wait for a treaty on the Kuriles. We did not wait for a treaty on the islands over which we have trusteeship.

Whatever may be the legal situation, the United States of America, Mr. Truman said this morning, is not going to quibble on any lawyers' words about the integrity of its position. That is where we stand.

Therefore, the President says, we are not going to use our forces in connection with the present situation in Formosa. We are not going to attempt to seize the Island. We are not going to get involved militarily in any way on the Island of Formosa. So far as I know, no responsible person in the Government, no military man has ever believed that we should involve our forces in the island.

I do not believe that is new policy. It would be new policy if we decided to do that. The President is affirming what so far as I know has been the view of his Administration, and the unquestioned view ever since I have known about it.

The President goes on to say that we do not intend to give military assistance or advice, that is materiel and military people, to the forces on Formosa, and he says why. He says that there are resources on that Island which are adequate to enable those on the island to obtain whatever necessary military supplies they believe they have to have.

Source: *U.S. Department of State Bulletin*, Volume 22, January 16, 1950, p. 80.

P&D9   UNITED STATES PROPOSALS FOR STRENGTHENING THE
            UNITED NATIONS SYSTEM IN ORDER TO MEET POSSIBLE
            FUTURE AGGRESSION: THE "UNITING FOR PEACE" RESOLUTION

330:1/7-2750: Telegram

THE UNITED STATES REPRESENTATIVE AT THE UNITED
NATIONS (AUSTIN) TO THE SECRETARY OF STATE

New York, July 27, 1950 - 7:02 p.m.

142. Reference Department's 54, July 24, we feel arguments set forth would apply with equal force to other possible conflict areas. In particular we agree, of course, with statement Deptel re desirability having Commissions similar UNCOK on duty in order to report immediately to SC outbreak aggression anywhere.

We are, however, inclined to feel any action such as proposed in reftel limited to one specific area of world such as Yugoslavia, Iran, Indochina or Formosa, would have two unfortunate effects:

First, impression would be created that particular area selected was believed to present most serious risk new outbreak aggression. Result would probably be jitters in area and increased political tensions, even among our friends, in regard to particular area.

Second, differences and complexities of political attitudes held by friendly nation with regard to particular areas would be highlighted and difficulties achieving purposes envisaged greatly increased if each possible conflict area were dealt with separately by SC.

Accordingly we feel that a general rather than a piecemeal approach in SC would deal more effectively with problem of preventing spread of conflict by new outbreaks of aggression by Soviet-inspired Communist forces in tender areas (such as Berlin, Yugoslavia, Iran, Burma, Indochina, Formosa).

We assume Department's objectives as follows:

1. Promptest possible halting of Korean aggression and, as minimum, restoration status quo without prejudice to military necessities or expendiency or achievement political objectives Korea by peaceful means after terminal hostilities.
2. Prevention spread elsewhere of conflict as a result new aggression or breach of peace.

3. In event objective number two not achieved, assurance that collective moreal, political and material weight of UN can be brought breach of peace wherever it may occur.

Since we cannot be sure where new Soviet-inspired thrust might take place we feel we must make every effort immediately (a) to deter by UN as well as by other practicable means any new Soviet adventures, and (b) to have UN prepared to deal as promptly and effectively as possible with outbreak of aggression anywhere.

Source: *American Foreign Relations*, 1950, Volume II, U.S. Government Printing Office, Washington, D.C., pp. 303-311 (Excerpts).

P&D10   **U.S. SECRETARY OF STATE ACHESON'S STATEMENT ON U.S. DEFENSE PERIMETER IN PACIFIC AREA**

Now let's in the light of that consider some of these policies. First of all, let's deal with the question of military security. I deal with it first because it is important and because, having stated our policy in that regard, we must clarly understand that the military menace is not the most immediate.

What is the situation in regard to the military security of the Pacific area, and what is our policy in regard to it?

In the first place, the defeat and the disarmament of Japan has place upon the United States the necessity of assuming the military defense of Japan so long as that is required, both in the interest of our security and in the interests of the security of the entire Pacific area and, in all honor, in the interest of Japanese security. We have American -- and there are Australian -- troops in Japan. I am not in a position to speak for the Australians, but I can assure you that there is no intention of any sort of abandoning or weakening the defenses of Japan and that whatever arrangements are to be made either through permanent settlement or otherwise, that defense must and shall be maintained.

This defensive perimeter runs along the Aleutians to Japan and then goes to the Ryukyus. We hold important defense positions in the Ryukyu Islands, and those we will continue to hold...

...The defensive perimeter runs from the Ryukyus to the Philippine Islands. Our relations, our defensive relations with the Philippines are contained in agreements between us...

...So far as the military security of other areas in the Pacific is concerned, it must be clear that no person can guarantee these areas against military attack...

...Should such an attack occur...the initial reliance must be on the people attacked to resist it and then upon the commitments of the entire civilized world under the Charter of the United Nations which so far has not proved a weak reed to lean on by any people who are determined to protect their independence against outside aggression. But it is a mistake, I think, in considering Pacific and Far Eastern problems to become obsessed with military considerations. Important as they are, there are other problems that press, and these other problems are not capable of solution through military means...

...Here, then, are the problems in these other areas which require some policy on our part, and I should like to point out two facts to you and then discuss in more detail some of these areas.

The first fact is the great difference between our responsibility and our opportunities in the northern part of the Pacific area and in the southern part of the Pacific area. In the north, we have direct responsibility in Japan and we have direct opportunity to act. The same thing to a lesser degree is true in Korea. There we had direct responsibility, and there we did act, and there we have a greater opportunity to be effective than we have in the more southerly part.

In the southerly part of the area, we are one of many nations who can do no more than help. The direct repsonsibility lies with the peoples concerned...

Source: *U.S. Department of State Bulletin*, Volume 22, January 23, 1950, pp. 115-116
                 (Excerpts).

P&D11   RESOLUTION CONCERNING THE INTERVENTION OF THE
               CENTRAL PEOPLE'S GOVERNMENT OF THE PEOPLE'S
               REPUBLIC OF CHINA IN KOREA, ADOPTED BY THE
               UNITED NATIONS GENERAL ASSEMBLY,
               FEBRUARY 1, 1959

The General Assembly,

Noting that the Security Council, because of lack of unanimity of the permanent members, has failed to exercise its primary responsibility for the maintenance of international peace and security in regard to Chinese Communist intervention in Korea,

Noting that the Central People's Government of the People's Republic of China has not accepted United Nations proposals to bring about a cessation of hostilities in Korea with a view to peaceful settlement, and that its armed forces continue their invasions of Korea and their large-scale attacks upon United Nations forces there,

1. Finds that the Central People's Government of the People's Republic of China, by giving direct aid and assistance to those who were already committing aggression in Korea and by engaging in hostilities against United Nations forces there, has itself engaged in aggression in Korea;

2. Calls upon the Central People's Government of the People's Republic of China to cause its forces and nationals in Korea to cease hostilities against the United Nations forces and to withdraw from Korea;

3. Affirms the determination of the United Nations to continue its action in Korea to meet the aggression;

4. Calls upon all States and authorities to continue to lend every assistance to the United Nations action in Korea;

5. Calls upon all States and authorities to refrain from giving any assistance to the aggressors in Korea;

6. Requests a Committee composed of the members of the Collective Measures Committee as a matter of urgency to consider additional measures to be employed to meet this aggression and to report thereon to the General Assembly, it being understood that the Committee is authorized to defer its report if the Good Offices Committee referred to in the following paragraph reports satisfactory progress in its efforts;

7. Affirms that it continues to be the policy of the United Nations to bring about a cessation of hostilities in Korea and the achievement of United Nations objectives in Korea by peaceful means, and requests the President of the General Assembly to designate forthwith two persons who would meet with him at any suitable opportunity to use their good offices to this end.

United Nations General Assembly, Document A/1771, February 1, 1951.

Source: *Documents on American Foreign Relations*, Volume XIII, 1951, U.S. Government Printing Office, Washington, D.C., pp. 451-453.

P&D12   RESOLUTION CONCERNING ADDITIONAL MEASURES TO BE EMPLOYED TO MEET THE AGGRESSION IN KOREA, ADOPTED BY THE UNITED NATIONS GENERAL ASSEMBLY, MAY 18, 1951

The General Assembly,

Noting the report of the Additional Measures Committee dated 14 May 1951, Recalling its resolution 498 (V) of 1 February 1951.

Noting that:

(a) The Additional Measures Committee established by that resolution has considered additional measures to be employed to meet the aggression in Korea,

(b) The Additional Measures Committee has reported that a number of States have already taken measures designed to deny contributions to the military strength of the forces opposing the United Nations in Korea,

(c) The Additional Measures Committee has also reported that certain economic measures designed further to deny such contributions would support and supplement the military action of the United Nations in Korea and would assist in putting an end to the aggression,

1.   Recommends that every State:

(a) Apply an embargo on the shipment to areas under the control of the Central People's Government of the People's Republic of China and of the North Korean authorities of arms, ammunition and implements of war, atomic energy materials, petroleum, [transportation materials of strategic value,] and items useful in the production of arms, ammunition and implements of war;

(b) Determine which commodities exported from its territory fall within the embargo, and apply controls to give effect to the embargo;

(c) Prevent by all means within its jurisdiction the circumvention of controls on shipments applied by other States pursuant to the present resolution;

(d) Co-operate with other States in carrying out the purposes of this embargo;

(e) Report to the Additional Measures Committee, within thirty days and thereafter at the request of the Committee, on the measures taken in accordance with the present resolution;

2.   Requests the Additional Measures Committee:

(a) To report to the General Assembly, with recommendations as appropriate, on the general effectiveness of the embargo and the desirability of continuing, extending or relaxing it;

(b) To continue its consideration of additional measures to be employed to meet the aggression in Korea, and to report thereon further to the General Assembly, it being understood that the Committee is authorized to defer its report if the Good Offices Committee reports satisfactory proegress in its efforts;

3.   Reaffirms that it continues to be the policy of the United Nations to bring about a cessation of hostilities in Korea, and the achievement of United Nations objectives in Korea by peaceful means, and requests the Good Offices Committee to continue its good offices.

United Nations General Assembly, Document A/1805, May 21, 1951.

Source: *Documents on American Foreign Relations*, Volume XIII, 1951, U.S. Government Printing Office, Washington, D.C., pp. 452-453.

P&D13   **PUBLIC LAW 195 - AUG. 5, 1953**   [67 Stat.]

Sec. III. It is the sense of the Congress that the Communist Chinese Government should not be admitted to membership in the United Nations as the representative of China.

This title may be cited as the "Department of State Appropriation Act, 1954".

Source: Department of State Appropriation Act, 1953, *U.S. Statutes at Large*, 83rd Congress, 1st Session, 1953, Volume 67, U.S. Government Printing Office, Washington, D.C., p. 372 (Excerpt).

P&D14

70 Stat.]   **PUBLIC LAW 853 - JULY 31, 1956**

Sec. 108. The Congress hereby reiterates its opposition to the seating in the United Nations of the Communist China regime as the representative of China, and it is hereby declared to be the continuing sense of the Congress that the Communist regime in China has not demonstrated its willingness to fulfill the obligations contained in the Charter of the United Nations and should not be recognized to represent China in the United Nations. In the event of the seating of representatives of the Chinese Communist regime in the Security Council or General Assembly of the United Nations, the President is requested to inform the Congress insofar as is compatible with the requirements of national security, of the implications of this action upon the foreign policy of the United States and our foreign relationships, including that created by membership in the United Nations, together with any recommendations which he may have with respect to the matter.

Sec. 109. This Act may be cited as the "Mutual Security Appropriation Act, 1957".

Approved July 31, 1956.

Source: Mutual Security Appropriation Act, 1957, *U.S. Statutes at Large*, 84th Congress, 2nd Session, 1956, Volume 70, U.S. Government Printing Office, Washington, D.C., p. 735 (Excerpt).

P&D15   STATEMENT BY SECRETARY OF STATE DULLES
                         SEPTEMBER 4, 1958 (EXCERPT)

I have reviewed in detail with the President the serious situation which has resulted from aggressive Chinese Communist military actions in the Taiwan (Formosa) Straits area. The President has authorized me to make the following statement.

1. Neither Taiwan (Formosa) nor the islands ofQuemoy and Matsu have ever been under the authority of the Chinese Communists. Since the end of the Second World War, a period of over 13 years, they have continuously been under the authority of Free China, that is, the Republic of China.

2. The United States is bound by treaty to help to defend Taiwan (Formosa) from armed attack and the President is authorized by Joint Resolution of the Congress to employ the armed forces of the United States for the securing and protecting of related positions such as Quemoy and Matsu.

3. Any attempt on the part of the Chinese Communists now to seize these positions or any of them would be a crude violation of the principles upon which world order is based, namely, that no country should use armed forces to seize new territory.

4. The Chinese Communists have, for about 2 weeks, been subjecting Quemoy to heavy artillery bombardment and, by artillery fire and use of small naval craft, they have been harassing the regular supply of the civilian and military population of the Quemoys, which totals some 125 thousand persons. The official Peiping radio repeatedly announces the purpose of these military operations to be to take by armed force Taiwan (Formosa), as well as Quemoy and Matsu. In virtually every Peiping broadcast Taiwan (Formosa) and the offshore islands are linked as the objective of what is called the "Chinese People's Liberation Army."

5. Despite, however, what the Chinese Communists say, and so far have done, it is not yet certain that their purpose is in fact to make an all-out effort to conquer by force Taiwan (Formosa) and the offshore islands. Neither is it apparent that such efforts as are being made, or may be made, cannot be contained by the courageous, and purely defensive, efforts of the forces of the Republic of China, with such substantial logistical support as the United States is providing.

7. The President and I earnestly hope that the Chinese Communist regime will not again, as in the case of Korea, defy the basic principle upon which world order depends, namely, that armed force should not be used to achieve territorial ambitions. And such naked use of force would pose an issue far transcending the offshore islands and even the security of Taiwan (Formosa). It would forecast a widespread use of force in the Far East which wold endanger vital free world positions and the security of the United States. Acquiescence therein would threaten peace everywhere. We believe that the civilized world community will never condone overt military conquest as a legitimate instrument of policy.

8. The United States has not, however, abandoned hope that Peiping will stop short of defying the will of mankind for peace. This would not require it to abandon its claims, however ill-founded we may deem them to be. I recall that in the extended negotiations which the representatives of the United States and Chinese Communist regime conducted at Geneva between 1955 and 1958, a sustained effort was made by the United States to secure, with particular reference to the Taiwan area, a declaration of mutual and reciprocal renunciation of force, except in self-defense, which, however, would be without prejudice to the pursuit of

policies by peaceful means. The Chinese Communists rejected any such declaration. We believe, however, that such a course of conduct constitutes the only civilized and acceptable procedure. The United States intends to follow that course, so far as it is concerned, unless and until the Chinese Communists, by their acts, leave us no choice but to react in defense of the principles to which all peace-loving governments are dedicated.

Source: *Department of State Bulletin*, September 22, 1958, pp. 445-446.

P&D16   **OCTOBER 24, 1958 JOINT ROC-U.S. COMMUNIQUE**
               IN WHICH CHIANG KAI-SHEK RENOUNCES
               USE OF FORCE TO RECOVER THE MAINLAND

President Chiang and Secretary Dulles Conclude
Three-Day Talks

Joint Communique Emphasizes Defense of
Offshore Islands

Taipei, October 24 (CNA): The Republic of China and the United States yesterday linked the defense of the offshore islands with the defense of Taiwan and Penghu islands and expressed hope for the peaceful liberation of the Communist held China mainland.

The above mentioned official remark was contained in a joint communique issued yesterday afternoon at the end of three days of talks between President Chiang Kai-shek and U.S. Secretary of State John Foster Dulles.

The joint Sino-U.S. communique declared that President Chiang and Mr. Dulles reaffirmed the solidarity of the two nations in the face of renewed Communist aggression--the new bombardment of Kinmen.

The communique said the three-day top-level Sino-American conferences "dealt largely with military aspects" because the Communists broke its self-imposed ceasefire on the eve of the arrival of Mr. Dulles in Taipei.

TEXT OF COMMUNIQUE

Following is the text of the joint Sino-U.S. communique:

Consultations have been taking place over the past three days between the Government of the United States and the Government of the Republic of China pursuant to Article IV of the Mutual Defense Treaty. These consultations had been invited by President Chiang Kai-shek. The following are among those who took part in the consultations:

For the Republic of China:

President Chiang Kai-shek
Vice President-Premier Chen Cheng
Secretary General to the President Chang Chun
Minister of Foreign Affairs Huang Shao-ku
Ambassador to the United States George K.C. Yeh

For the United States of America:

Secretary of State John Foster Dulles
Assistant Secretary of State Walter S. Robertson
Ambassador to the Republic of China Everett F. Drumright

The consultations had been arranged to be held during the two weeks when the Chinese Communists had declared they would cease fire upon Quemoy. It had been hoped that, under these circumstances, primary consideration could have been given to measures which would have contributed to stabilizing an actual situation of non-military. However, on the eve of the consultation, the Chinese Communists, in violation of their declaration, resumed artillery fire against the Quemoys. In the light of these developments, the consultations necessarily dealt largely with the military aspects of the situation. It was recognized that under the present conditions the defense of the Quemoys, together with the Matsus, is closely related to be the defense of Taiwan and Penghu.

The two governments recalled that their Mutual Defense Treaty had had the purpose of manifesting their unity "so that no potential aggressor could be under the illusion that either of them stands alone in the West Pacific area." The consultations provided a fresh occasion for demonstrating that unity.

The two governments reaffirmed their solidarity in the face of the new Chinese Communist aggression now manifesting itself in the bombardment of the Quemoys. This aggression and the accompanying Chinese Communist propaganda have not divided them, as the Communists have hoped. On the contrary, it has drawn them closer together. They believe that by unitedly opposing aggression they serve not only themselves but the cause of peace. As President Eisenhower said on September 11, the position of opposing aggression by force is the only position consistent with the peace of the World.

The two governments took note of the fact that the Chinese Communists, with the backing of the Soviet Union, avowedly seek to conquer Taiwan, to eliminate Free China and to expel the United States from the Wedtern Pacific generally, compelling the United States to abandon its collective security arrangements with free countries of that area. This policy cannot possibly succeed. It is hoped and believed that the Communists, faced by the proven unity resolution and strength of the government of the United States and the Republic of China, will not put their policy to the test of general war and that they will abandon the military steps which they have already taken to initiate their futile and dangerous policy.

In addition to dealing with the current military situation, the two governments considered the broad and long-range aspects of their relationship.

The United States, its Government and its people, have an abiding faith in the Chinese people and profound respect for the great contribution which they have made and will continue to make to a civilization that respects and honors the individual and his family life. The United

States recognized that the Republic of China is the authentic spokesman for Free China and of the hopes and aspirations entertained by the great mass of the Chinese people.

The Government of the Republic of China declared its purpose to be a worthy representative of the Chinese people and to strive to preserve these qualities and characteristics which have enabled the Chinese to contribute so much of benefit to humanity.

The two governments reaffirmed their dedication to the principles of the Charter of the United Nations. They recalled that the Treaty under which they are acting is defensive in character. The Government of the Republic of China considers that the restoration of freedom to its people on the Mainland is its sacred mission. It believes that the foundation of this mission resides in the minds and the hearts of the Chinese people and that the principal means of successfully achieving its mission is the implementation of Dr. Sun Yat-sen's Three People Principles (Nationalism, democracy and social well-being) and not the use of force.

The consultations which took place permitted a thorough study and reexamination of the pressing problems of mutual concern. As such they have proved to be of great value to both governments. It is believed that such consultations should continue to be held at appropriate intervals.

Source: News Item, Chinese News Agency, Taipei, October 24, 1958.

P&D17

74 Stat.]   **PUBLIC LAW 86-704 - SEPTEMBER 2, 1960**

Sec. 107. The Congress hereby reiterates its opposition to the seating in the United Nations of the Communist China regime as the representative of China, and it is hereby declared to be the continuing sense of the Congress that the Communist regime in China has not demonstrated its willingness to fulfill the obligations contained in the Charter of the United Nations. In the event of the seating of representatives of the Chinese Communist regime in the Security Council or General Assembly of the United Nations, the President is requested to inform the Congress insofar as is compatible with the requirements of national security of the implications of this action upon the foreign policy of the United States and our foreign relationships, including that created by membership in the United Nations, together with any recommendations which he may have with respect to the matter.

Source: *U.S. Statutes at Large*, 86th Congress, 2nd Session, 1960, Volume 74, U.S. Government Printing Office, Washington, D.C., p. 779 (Excerpt).

P&D18

79 Stat.]   **PUBLIC LAW 89-273 - OCTOBER 20, 1965**

Sec. 105. The Congress hereby reiterates its opposition to the seating in the United Nations of the Communist China regime as the representative of China, and it is hereby declared to be the continuing sense of Congress that the Communist regime in China has not demonstrated its willingness to fulfill the obligations contained in the Charter of the United Nations and should not be recognized to represent China in the United Nations.

Source: *U.S. Statutes at Large*, 89th Congress, 1st Session, 1965, Volume 79, U.S. Government Printing Office, Washington, D.C., p. 1003 (Excerpt).

P&D19

84 Stat.]   **PUBLIC LAW 91-472 - OCTOBER 21, 1970**

Sec. 105. It is the sense of the Congress that the Communist Chinese Government should not be admitted to membership in the United Nations as the representative of China.

This title may be cited as the "Department of State Appropriation Act, 1971."

Source: Department of State Appropriations Act, 1971, *U.S. Statutes at Large*, 91st Congress, 2nd Session, Volume 84, Part I, U.S. Government Printing Office, Washington, D.C., p. 1044 (Excerpt).

**P&D20   PRESIDENT NIXON'S ANNUAL REPORT TO THE CONGRESS
FEBRUARY 25, 1971 (Excerpt)**

We are prepared to establish a dialogue with Peking. We cannot accept its ideological precepts, or the notion Communist China must exercize hegemony over Asia. But neither do we wish to impose on China an international position that denies its legitimate national interests.

The evolution of our dialogue with Peking cannot be at the expense of international order or our own commitments. Our attitude is public and clear. We will continue to honor our treaty commitments to the security of our Asian allies. An honorable relationship with Peking cannot be constructed at their expense.

Among these allies is the Republic of China. We have been associated with that government since its inception in 1911, and with particular intimacy when we were World War II allies. These were among the considerations behind the American decision to assist the Government of the Republic of China on Taiwan with its defense and economic needs.

Out present commitment to the security of the Republic of China on Taiwan stems from our 1954 treaty. The purpose of the treaty is exclusively defensive, and it controls the entire range of our military relationship with the Republic of China.

Our economic assistance to the Republic of China has had gratifying results. Beginning in 1951, the U.S. provided $1.5 billion in economic assistance. Its effective and imaginative use by the Government of the Republic of China and the people of Taiwan made it possible for us to terminate the program in 1965.

I am recalling the record of friendship, assistance, and alliance between the United States and the Government of the Republic of China in order to make clear both the vitality of this relationshp and the nature of our defense relationship. I do not believe that this honorable and peaceful association need constitute an obstacle to the movement toward normal relations between the United States and the People's Republic of China. As I have tried to make clear since the beginning of my Administration, while I cannot foretell the ultimate resolution of the differences between Taipei and Peking, we believe these differences must be resolved by peaceful means.

In that connection, I wish to make it clear that the United States is prepared to see the People's Republic of China play a constructive role in the family of nations. The question of its place in the United Nations is not, however, merely a question of whether it should particpate. It is also a question of whether Peking should be permitted to dictate to the world the terms of its participation. For a number of years attempts have been made to deprive the Republic of China of its place as a member of the United Nations and its Specialized Agencies. We have opposed these attempts. We will continue to oppose them.

Source: *U.S. Foreign Policy for the 1970s: A Report to the Congress by Richard Nixon*,
            February 25, 1971, pp. 91, 107-108.

P&D21   PRESIDENT NIXON ANNOUNCES ACCEPTANCE OF
               INVITATION TO VISIT PEOPLE'S REPUBLIC OF CHINA
                              (July 15, 1971)

                     Statement by President Nixon

Good evening.

I have requested this television time tonight to announce a major development in our efforts to build a lasting peace in the world.

As I have pointed out on a number of occasions over the past 3 years, there can be no stable and enduring peace without the participation of the People's Republic of China and its 750 million people. That is why I have undertaken initiatives in several areas to open the door for more normal relations between our two countries.

In pursuance of that goal, I sent Dr. Kissinger, my Assistant for National Security Affairs, to Peking during his recent world tour for the purpose of having talks with Premier Chou En-Lai.

The announcement I shall now read is being issued simultaneously in Peking and in the United States:

> "Premier Chou En-Lai and Dr. Henry Kissinger, President Nixon's Assistant for National Security Affairs, held talks in Peking from July 9 to 11, 1971. Knowing of President Nixon's expressed desire to visit the People's Republic of China, Premier Chou En-Lai on behalf of the Government of the People's Republic of China has extended an invitation to President Nixon to visit China at an appropriate date before May, 1972.
>
> President Nixon has accepted the invitation with pleasure.
>
> The meeting between the leaders of China and the United States is to seek the normalization of relations between the two countries and also to exchange views on questions of concern to the two sides."

In the anticipation of the inevitable speculation which will follow this announcement, I want to put our policy in the clearest possible context. Our action in seeking a new relationship with the People's Republic of China will not be at the expense of our old friends.

It is not directed against any other nation. We seek friendly relations with all nations. Any nation can be our friend without being any other nation's enemy.

I have taken this action because of my profound conviction that all nations will gain from a reduction of tensions and a better relationship between the United States and the People's Republic of China.

It is in this spirit that I will undertake what I hope will become a journey for peace - - peace not just for our generation but for future generations on this earth we share together.

Thank you and good night.

Source: *U.S. Department of State Bulletin*, Volume 65, July-September 1971, p. 121.

P&D22   **THE POSITION OF THE UNITED STATES:**
POLICY STATEMENT BY SECRETARY OF STATE ROGERS,
AUGUST 2, 1971

The world is approaching the midpoint between the end of the World War II and the end of the 20th century. The United Nations, founded in the aftermath of the war, has passed its 25th anniversary.

President Nixon has been adapting American foreign policy with these facts in mind--forging policies directed to the future while taking fully into account the legacies of the past.

From its inception the United Nations was designed above all else to keep the peace shattered by two world wars within a generation. The first words of the United Nations Charter, adopted at San Francisco in 1945, express a common determination to "save succeeding generations from the scourge of war."

In October 1969 President Nixon said with regard to Latin America that "we must deal realistically with governments...as they are." Both in Asia and elsewhere in the world we are seeking to accommodate our role to the realities of the world today. Our objective is to contribute in practical terms to the building of a framework for a stable peace.

No question of Asian policy has so perplexed the world in the last 20 years as the China question--and the related question of representation in the United Nations. Basic to that question is the fact that each of two governments claims to be the sole government of China and representative of all of the people of China.

Representation in an international organization need not prejudice the claims or views of either government. Participation of both in the United Nations need not require that result.

Rather, it would provide governments with increased opportunities for contact and communication. It owuld also help promote cooperation on common problems which affect all of the member nations regardless of political differences.

The United States accordingly will support action at the General Assembly this fall calling for seating the People's Republic of China. At the same time the United States will oppose any action to expel the Republic of China or otherwise deprive it of representation in the United Nations.

Our consultations, which began several months ago, have indicated that the question of China's seat in the Security Council is a matter which many nations will wish to address. In the final analysis, of course, under the charter provision, the Security Council will make this decision. We, for our part, are prepared to have this question resolved on the basis of a decision of members of the United Nations.

Our consultations have also shown that any action to deprive the Republic of China of its representation would meet with strong opposition in the General Assembly. Certainly, as I have said, the United States will oppose it.

The Republic of China has played a loyal and conscientious role in the U.N. since the organization was founded. It has lived up to all of its charter obligations. Having made remarkable progress in developing its own economy, it has cooperated internationally by providing valuable technical assistance to a number of less developed countries, particularly in Africa.

The position of the United States is that if the United Nations is to succeed in its peacekeeping role, it must deal with the realities of the world in which we live. Thus, the United States will cooperate with those, who, whatever their views on the status of the relationship of the two governments, wish to continue to have the Republic of China represented in the United Nations.

The outcome, of course, will be decided by 127 members of the United Nations. For our part we believe that the decision we have taken is fully in accord with President Nixon's desire to normalize relations with the People's Republic of China in the interests of world peace and in accord with our conviction that the continued representation in the United Nations of the Republic of China will contribute to peace and stability in the world.

Source: *Department of State Bulletin*, August 1971.

P&D23   THE "ALBANIAN" RESOLUTION

                                          (Complete Text)

Albania, Algeria, Burma, Ceylon, Cuba, Equatorial Guinea, Guinea, Iraq, Mali, Mauritania, Nepal, Pakistan, People's Democratic Republic of Yemen, People's Republic of Congo, Romania, Sierra Leone, Somalia, Sudan, Syrian Arab Republic, United Republic of Tanzania, Yemen, Yugoslavia and Zambia: draft resolution

                                                                    (Original: French)
                                                                    (25 September 1971)
The General Assembly,

          Recalling the principles of the Charter of the United Nations,

          Considering that the restoration of the lawful rights of the People's Republic of China is essential both for the protection of the Charter of the United Nations and for the cause that the United Nations must serve under the Charter,

          Recognizing that the representatives of the Government of the People's Republic of China are the only lawful representatives of China to the United Nations and that the People's Republic of China is one of the five permanent members of the Security Council,

          Decides to restore all its rights to the People's Republic of China and to recognize the representatives of its Government as the only legitimate representatives of China to the United Nations, and to expel forthwith the representatives of Chiang Kai-shek from the place which they unlawfully occupy at the United Nations and in all the organizations related to it.

Source: U.N. document A/L.630 and Add. 1 and 2 in General Assembly, *Official Records: 26th Session Annexes*, Agenda item 93, pp. 3-4.

P&D24   **THE "IMPORTANT QUESTION" RESOLUTION**

(Complete Text)

Australia, Bolivia, Colombia, Costa Rica, Dominican Republic, El Salvador, Fiji, Gambia, Guatemala, Haiti, Honduras, Japan, Lesotho, Liberia, Mauritius, New Zealand, Nicaragua, Philippines, Swaziland, Thailand, United States of America and Uruguay: draft resolution

(Original: English)
(29 September 1971)

The General Assembly,

Recalling the provisions of the Charter of the United Nations,

Decides that any proposal in the General Assembly which would result in depriving the Republic of China of representation in the United Nations is an important question under Article 18 of the Charter.

Source: U.N. A/L.632 and Add. 1 and 2 in General Assembly *Official Records: 26th Session Annexes*, Agenda item 93, pp. 3-4.

P&D25   **THE "DUAL REPRESENTATION" RESOLUTION**

(Complete Text)

Australia, Bolivia, Chad, Costa Rica, Dominican Republic, Fiji, Gambia, Haiti, Honduras, Japan, Lesotho, Liberia, Mauritus, New Zealand, Philippines, Swaziland, Thailand, United States of America and Uruguay: draft resolution

(Original: English)
(29 September 1971)

The General Assembly,

Noting that since the founding of the United Nations fundamental changes have occurred in China,

Having regard for the existing factual situation,

Noting that the Republic of China has been continuously represented as a Member of the United Nations since 1945,

Believing that the People's Republic of China should be represented in the United Nations,

Recalling that Article 1, paragraph 4, of the Charter of the United Nations establishes the United Nations as a centre for harmonizing the actions of nations,

Believing that an equitable resolution of this problem should be sought in the light of the above-mentioned considerations and without prejudice to the eventual settlement of the conflicting claims involved,

1. Hereby affirms the right of representation of the People's Republic of China and recommends that it be seated as one of the five permanent members of the Security Council;

2. Affirms the continued right of representation of the Republic of China;

3. Recommends that all United Nations bodies and the specialized agencies take into account the provisions of this resolution in deciding the question of Chinese representation.

Source: U.N. document A/L.633 and Add. 1 and 2 in General Assembly *Official Records: 26th Session Annexes*, Agenda item 93, pp. 3-4.

P&D26   **ADDRESS BY SECRETARY OF STATE ROGERS**
TO THE GENERAL ASSEMBLY,
October 4, 1971

(Excerpt)

REPRESENTATION OF CHINA IN THE U.N.

This organization, during this session, faces a decision on the China question--a decision with major consequences for the United Nations.

In our interdependent world, no significant segment of the world's population and of the world's power should be isolated. It was this consideration which led President Nixon to alter the China policy of the United States. To pursue a policy which did not respond to present realities would risk the future for the sake of the past. On the other hand, to seek to improve relations with the People's Republic of China, and to contribute to its greater contact with the international community, could foster prospects for a stable peace in years to come.

Thus, President Nixon began over 2 years ago, unilaterally and at first without response, to improve bilateral relations. Recently he resolved to move decisively into a new era of relations by accepting an invitation to visit Peking before May 1, 1972. And he decided to support the seating of the People's Republic of China in the General Assembly and as a permanent member of the Security Council.

The United States wants to see the People's Republic of China come to this Assembly, take its seat, and participate. We want to see it assume as a permanent member of the Security Council the rights and responsibilities which go with that status. On the seating of the People's Republic of China there is widespread agreement in this body.

This assembly does, however, face a related and momentous issue. It could become the first Assembly in United Nations history to take action to expel a member, an action which would have the effect of expelling 14 million people from its councils. The path of explusion is perilous. To open it for one would be to open it for many.

So the United States and 16 other countries have introduced a draft resolution which would seat the People's Republic of China as a permanent member of the Security Council while providing representation both for it and for the Republic of China in the General Assembly. That resolution is based on political reality and on basic equity:

-It is only realistic to recognize a factual situation which has persisted for more than 20 years: that two governments now exercise authority over territory and over people who were given representation in the United Nations when China ratified the charter in 1945 as an original member.

-It is only realistic that all the Chinese people who were once represented here should again be represented, and represented by those who actually govern them.

-It is only realistic that the Security Council seat should be filled by the People's Republic of China, which exercises control over the largest number of people of all the world's governments.

-It would be unrealistic to expel from this body the Republic of China, which governs a population of Taiwan larger than the populations of two-thirds of the 130 United Nations members.

-Further, it would be unjust to expel a member which has participated for over 25 years in the work of this organization with unfailing devotion to the principles set forth in the charter.

-The proposal that both the People's Republic of China and the Republic of China should be represented in the United Nations should commend itself to member states of varying national policies.

-It would assure that the long-prevailing de facto situation in China is reflected in United Nations representation, but it does not ask member states to alter their recognition policies or their bilateral relations.

-It would provide representation for the people concerned by those who actually govern them, but it does not divide China into two separate states; after all, we all know Byelorussia and the Ukraine are not separate states.

-The dual representation resolution is founded on the reality of the current situation; but it does not seek to freeze that situation for the future, expressly providing that the present decision is without prejudice to a future settlement.

In short, the dual representation resolution asks simply, and only, that the United Nations take account of the situation as it exists today and give all the people of China representation in this organization. As the charter has accommodated practical solutions of other unusual situations in the past, so it is flexible enough to accommodate the realities of this one.

The other proposal before this Assembly, the draft resolution advanced by Albania and others, is punitive in substance and in intent. It does not seek to deal with facts, but to excoriate and condemn. Its essence is not to admit the People's Republic of China, but to expel the Republic of China and to expel it "forthwith."

That resolution would exacerbate, not harmonize, relations in Asia, and it would weaken, not strengthen, the moral and political fiber of this organization.

The issue, then, before this body is the issue of explusion. That is why we have proposed a draft resolution which we refer to as the "important question resolution" but which more properly should be referred to as the "non-explusion resolution." This draft resolution requires a two-thirds vote to expel a present member of the United Nations. It is consistent with the letter and the spirit of the charter.

Some members have argued that whatever the equities and realism of our proposal to maintain the representation of the Republic of China, it should not be supported because they feel that the People's Republic of China would refuse to take its seat. Such predictions are hazardous. Certainly the People's Republic of China may be expected to oppose the proposal so long as there is any possibility for a resolution that meets it maximum demands. But just as certainly, after a General Assembly decision providing the People's Republic of China with the status of a permanent member and a seat on the Security Council but not expelling the Republic of China, a new situation would exist. In any event, I submit, in deciding how to vote on this question we should look more to what the United Nations should do.

It is ironic that just as the sentiment for universality in the Assembly is growing, many of those who have long extolled it now seek to violate it. If the United Nations is to embrace universality, as some have suggested, then surely the admission of one member should not be accompanied by the expulstion of another.

Our task here, it seems to me, must be to make a decision that is reasonable, that accepts the realities of the existing situation, that does not prejudice the utlimate outcome, and that provides for representation of all the people concerned. Thereafter our efforts should be to convince those directly involved to take advantage of the decision we have made. The cause of peace has been greatly benefited in recent years by greater pragmatism in may capitals; it would be served by the same pragmatism on this issue.

As the United Nations becomes a more universal body it will be better able to deal with the lengthening list of global issues confronting it--in conciliating political differences, in reducing the world's armaments, in curbing the epidemic spread of narcotics addition, in protecting the environment, in assuring the exploitation of the oceans for the benefit of mankind.

In meeting those responsibilities, the United Nations must during this session deal with two important matters:

It must choose an outstanding successor to our most able and distinguished Secretary General U Thant, to whose dedication and idealism we all pay tribute. And as I pay respects to the Secretary General, I am sure my colleagues will understand if I also single out for special attention two American citizens who are now retiring: Paul Hoffman, who had devoted himself so effectively to the economic welfare of the developing countries, and Ralph Bunche, a Nobel Prize winner, who has contributed so markedly to the cause of peace.

The Assembly must also arrest the continuing deterioration of the United Nations financial position, which, as the Secretary General has pointed out, has eroded its fiscal credit and undermined confidence in its potential.

Responsibility for halting this decline rests primarily on those who fail to pay their share. Given assurances of adequate contributions by others, the United States will be prepared to assist toward an overall solution. Meanwhile we find it hard to understand why the membership should continue to recommend and approve budget increases beyond those necessary to meet inescapable cost increases.

Source: *Department of State Bulletin*, October 25, 1971, pp. 439-441.

P&D27   **"RESTORATION OF THE LAWFUL RIGHTS OF THE PEOPLE'S REPUBLIC OF CHINA IN THE UNITED NATIONS": GENERAL ASSEMBLY RESOLUTION 2758 (XXVI), ADOPTED OCTOBER 25, 1971**

(Complete Text)

The General Assembly,

Recalling the prinicples of the Charter of the United Nations,

Considering that the restoration of the lawful rights of the People's Republic of China is essential both for the protection of the Charter of the United Nations and for the cause that the United Nations must serve under the Charter,

Recognizing that the representatives of the Government of the People's Republic of China are the only lawful representatives of China to the United Nations and that the People's Republic of China is one of the five permanent members of the Security Council,

Decides to restore all its rights to the People's Republic of China and to recognize the representatives of its Government as the only legitimate representatives of China to the United Nations, and to expel forthwith the representatives of Chiang Kai-shek from the place which they unlawfully occupy at the United Nations and in all the organizations related to it.

Source: *General Assembly Official Records: 26th Session*, Supplement No. 29, (A/8429).

P&D28   IMPLICATIONS OF THE ASSEMBLY'S ACTION:
               NEWS CONFERENCE STATEMENT BY
               SECRETARY OF STATE ROGERS,
               OCTOBER 26, 1971

(Excerpt)

Last night's decision to admit the People's Republic of China as a member of the United Nations, of course, is consistent with the policy of the United States. President Nixon hopes that this action, which will bring into the United Nations representatives of more than 700 million people, will result in a reduction of tensions in the Pacific area.

At the same time, the United States deeply regrets the action taken by the United Nations to deprive the Republic of China of representation in that organization. We think that this precedent, which has the effect of expelling 14 million people on Taiwan from representation in the United Nations, is a most unfortunate one which will have many adverse effects in the future.

We and the cosponsors of our resolution made an all-out effort to prevent the expulsion of the Republic of China. We are particularly grateful to all of our cosponsors for the very dedicated and determined effort that was made to retain a place for the Republic of China in the United Nations.

The Republic of China, of course, continues to be a respected and valued member of the international community, and the ties between us remain unaffected by the action of the United Nations.

Although we believe that a mistake of major proportion has been made in expelling the Republic of China from the United Nations, the United States recognizes that the will of a majority of the members has been expressed. We, of course, accept that decision.

We hope that the United Nations will not have been weakened by what it has done. We continue to believe in its principles and purposes and hope that ways can be found to make it more effective in the pursuit of peace in the future.

Source: *Department of State Bulletin*, November 15, 1971, p. 541.

P&D29   SEATING OF DELEGATES FROM THE PEOPLE'S
                 REPUBLIC OF CHINA: STATEMENT BY
                 AMBASSADOR BUSH TO THE GENERAL ASSEMBLY,
                 NOVEMBER 15, 1971

(Complete Text)

The United States joins in welcoming to the United Nations the representatives of the People's Republic of China, Vice Foreign Minister Chiao [Kuan-hua], Ambassador Huang [Hua], and their colleagues.

Their presence here makes the United Nations more reflective of the world as it now exists, and we hope that it will contribute to the organization's potential for harmonizing the actions of nations. The issues of principle that divided the General Assembly in recent weeks were deeply felt and hard fought. Those differences should not obscure the proposition on which nearly all of us, including the United States, agreed: that the moment in history has arrived for the People's Republic of China to be in the United Nations.

The United States, whose people are linked by long ties of friendship with the great Chinese people, is confident that with renewed dedication to the principles of the charter we can move toward peace and justice in the world. We shall not cease to work here with all who share that hope and who wish to cooperate in its realization.

Source: *Department of State Bulletin*, December 20, 1971, pp. 715-716.

P&D30   JOINT COMMUNIQUE ISSUED AT SHANGHAI, 1972

President Richard Nixon of the United States of America visited the People's Republic of China at the invitation of Premier Chou En-lai of the People's Republic of China from February 21 to February 28, 1972. Accompanying the President were Mrs. Nixon, U.S. Secretary of State William Rogers, Assistant to the President Dr. Henry Kissinger, and other American officials.

President Nixon met with Chairman Mao Tse-tung of the Communist Party of China on February 21. The two leaders had a serious and frank exchange of views on Sino-US relations and world affairs.

During the visit, extensive, earnest and frank discussions were held between President Nixon and Premier Chou En-lai on the normalization of relations between the United States of America and the People's Republic of China, as well as on other matters of interest to both sides. In addition, Secretary of State William Rogers and Foreign Minister Chi Peng-fei held taks in the same spirit.

President Nixon and his party visited Peking and viewed cultural, industrial and agricultural sites, and they also toured Hangchow and Shanghai where, continuing discussions with Chinese leaders, they viewed similar places of interest.

The leaders of the People's Republic of China and the United States of America found it beneficial to have this opportunity, after so many years without contact, to present candidly to one another their views on a variety of issues. They reviewed the international situation in which important changes and great upheavals are taking place and expounded their respective positions and attitudes.

The U.S. side stated: Peace in Asia and peace in the world requires efforts both to reduce immediate tensions and to eliminate the basic causes of conflict. The United States will work for a just and secure peace: just, because if fulfills the aspirations of peoples and nations for freedom and progress; secure, because it removes the danger of foreign aggression. The United States supports individual freedom and social progress for all the peoples of the world, free of outside pressure or intervention. The United States believes that the effort to reduce tensions is served by improving communication between countries that have different ideologies so as to lessen the risks of confrontation through accident, miscalculation or misunderstanding. Countries should treat each other with mutual respect and be willing to compete peacefully, letting performance be the ultimate judge. No country should claim infallibility and each country should be prepared to re-examine its own attitudes for the common good. The United States stressed that the peoples of Indochina should be allowed to determine their destiny without outside intervention; its constant primary objective has been a negotiated solution; the eight-point proposal put forward by the Republic of Vietnam and the United States on January 27, 1972 represents a basis for the attainment of that objective; in the absence of a negotiated settlement the United States envisages the ultimate withdrawal of all US forces from the region consistent with the aim of self-determination for each country of Indochina. The United States will maintain its close ties with and support for the Republic of Korea; the United States will support efforts of the Republic of Korea to seek a relaxation of tension and increased communication in the Korean peninsula. The United States places the highest value on its friendly relations with Japan; it will continue to develop the existing close bonds. Consistent with the United Nations Security Council Resolution of December 21, 1971, the United States favors the continuation of the ceasefire between India and Pakistan and the withdrawal of all military forces to within their own territories and to their own sides of the ceasefire line in Jammu and Kashmir; the United States supports the right of the peoples of South Asia to shape their own future in peace, free of military threat, and without having the area become the subject of great power rivalry.

The Chinese side stated: Wherever there is oppression, there is resistance. Countries want independence, nations want liberation and the people want revolution--this has become the irresistible trend of history. All nations, big or small, should be equal; big nations should not bully the small and strong nations should not bully the weak. China will never be a superpower and it opposes hegemony and power politics of any kind. The Chinese side stated that it firmly supports the struggles of all the oppressed people and nations for freedom and liberation and that the people of all countries have the right to choose their social systems according to their own wishes and the right to safeguard the independence, sovereignty and territorial integrity of their own countries and oppose foreign aggression, interference, control and subversion. All foreign troops should be withdrawn to their own countries.

The Chinese side expressed its firm support to the peoples of Vietnam, Laos and Cambodia in their efforts for the attainment of their goal and its firm support to the seven-point proposal of the Provisional Revolutionary Government of the Republic of South Vietnam and the elaboration of February this year on the two key problems in the proposal, and to the

Joint Declaration of the Summit Conference of the Indochinese Peoples. It firmly supports the eight-point program for the peaceful unification of Korea put forward by the Government of the Democratic People's Republic of Korea on April 12, 1971, and the stand for the abolition of the "U.N. Commission for the Unification and Rehabilitation of Korea." It firmly opposes the revival and outward expansion of Japanese militarism and firmly supports the Japanese people's desire to build an independent, democratic, peaceful and neutral Japan. It firmly maintains that India and Pakistan should, in accordance with the United Nations resolutions on the India-Pakistan question, immediately withdraw all their forces to their respective territories and to their own sides of the ceasefire line in Jammu and Kashmir and firmly supports the Pakistan Government and people in their struggle to preserve their independence and sovereignty and the people of Jammu and Kashmir in their struggle for the right of self-determination.

There are essential differences between China and the United States in their social systems and foreign policies. However, the two sides agreed that countries, regardless of their social systems, should conduct their relations on the principles of respect for the sovereignty and territorial integrity of all states, non-aggression against other states, non-interference in the internal affairs of other states, equality and mutual benefit, and peaceful coexistence. International disputes hsould be settled on this basis, without resorting to the use or threat of force. The United States and the People's Republic of China are prepared to apply these principles to their mutual relations.

With these principles of international relations in mind the two sides stated that:

o   progress toward the normalization of relations between China and the United States is in the interests of all countries;

o   both wish to reduce the danger of international military conflict;

o   neither should seek hegemony in the Asia-Pacific region and each is opposed to efforts by any other country or group of countries to establish such hegemony; and

o   neither is prepared to negotiate on behalf of any third party or to enter into agreements or understandings with the other directed at other states.

Both sides are of the view that it would be against the interests of the peoples of the world for any major country to collude with another against other countries, or for major countries to divide up the world into spheres of interest.

The two sides reviewed the long-standing serious disputes between China and the United States. The Chinese side reaffirmed its position: The Taiwan question is the crucial question obstructing the normalization of relations between China and the United States; the Government of the People's Republic of China is the sole legal government of China: Taiwan is a province of China which has long been returned to the motherland; the liberation of Taiwan is China's internal affair in which no other country has the right to interfere; and all US forces and military installations must be withdrawn from Taiwan. The Chinese Government firmly opposes any activities which aim at the creation of "one China, or one Taiwan," "one China, two governments," "two Chinas," and "independent Taiwan," or advocate that "the status of Taiwan remains to be determined."

The US side declared: The United States acknowledges that all Chinese on either side of the Taiwan Strait maintain there is but one China and that Twian is a part of China. The United States Government does not challenge that position. It reaffirms its interest in a peaceful settlement of the Taiwan question by the Chinese themselves. With this prospect in mind, it affirms the ultimate objective of the withdrawal of all US forces and military installations from Taiwan. In the meantime, it will progressively reduce its forces and military installations on Taiwan as the tension in the area diminishes.

The two sides agreed that it is desirable to broaden the understanding between the two peoples. To this end, they discussed specific areas in such fields as science, technology, culture, sports and journalism, in which people-to-people contacts and exchanges would be mutually beneficial. Each side undertakes to facilitate the further development of such contacts and exchanges.

Both sides view bilateral trade as another area from which mutual benefit can be derived, and agreed that economic relations based on equality and mutual benefit are in the interest of the peoples of the two countries. They agree to facilitate the progressive development of trade between their two countries.

The two sides agreed that they will stay in contact through various channels, including the sending of a senior US representative to Peking from time to time for concrete consultations to further the normalization of relations between the two countries and continue to exhcnage views on issues of common interest.

The two sides expressed the hope that the gains achieved during this visit would open up new prospects for the relations between the two countries. They believe that the normalization of relations between the two countries is not only in the interest of the Chinese and American peoples but also contributes to the relaxation of tension in Asia and the world.

President Nixon, Mrs. Nixon and the American party expressed their appreciation for the gracious hospitality shown them by the Government and people of the People's Republic of China.

Source: *Public Papers of the Presidents of the United States: Richard Nixon, 1972,* U.S. Government Printing Office, Washington, DC, 1974. pp. 376-379.

P&D31

88 Stat.]   PUBLIC LAW 93-475 - OCTOBER 26, 1974

AN ACT

**To authorize appropriations for the Department of State and
the United States Information Agency, and for other purposes.**

Be it enacted by the Senate and House of Representatives of the United States of America in Congress assembled, That this Act may be cited as the "State Department/USIA Authorization Act, Fiscal Year 1975"...

...REPEAL OF THE FORMOSA RESOLUTION

Sec 3. The joint resolution entitled "Joint resolution authorizing the President to employ the Armed Forces of the United States for protecting the Security of Formosa, the Pescadores and related possessions and territories of that areas," approved January 29, 1955 (69 Stat. 7; Public Law 84-4), and known as the Formosa Resolution, is repealed.

Source: *U.S. Statutes at Large*, 93rd Congress, 1974, Volume 88, U.S. Government Printing Office, Washington, DC. p. 1955. (Excerpt)

CHAPTER SEVEN

MILITARY

A list of the important military documents for the period 1949-1978.

1. President Truman's statement on sending U.S. Fleet to Taiwan Strait - July 19, 1950. From *The Public Papers of the Presidents of the United States: Harry S. Truman -1950.* U.S. Government Printing Office, Washington, DC, 1965. p. 531.

2. Comments by the Joint Chiefs of Staff on Taiwan's offer to send troops to help U.N. forces in Korea--June 30, 1950. *Foreign Relations of the United States,* 1950, Volume VII, Korea, U.S. Government Printing Office, Washington, DC, 1976. p. 269.

3. Secretary of State to Chinese Ambassador re: Taiwan offer to furnish troops for service in Korea. *Foreign Relations of the United States*, 1950, Volume VII. p. 277.

4. 1951 China Mutual Defense Assistance Agreement. *U.S. Treaties and Other International Agreements*, Volume 2 -Part 2, 1951. U.S. Government Printing Office, Washington, DC, 1952. pp. 1498-1507.

5. 1952 China Mutual Security. *U.S. Treaties and Other International Agreements*, Volume 3 - Part 4, 1952. U.S. Government Printing Office, Washington, DC, 1955. pp.4543-4553.

6. 1954 Mutual Defense Treaty Between the U.S. and the ROC. *U.S. Treaties and Other International Agreements*, Volume 3 - Part 4, 1952. U.S. Government Printing Office, Washington, DC, 1955. pp. 433-454.

7. 1955 Establishment of U.S. Navy Medical Research Center at Taipei, Taiwan. *U.S. Treaties and Other International Agreements*, 1955. U.S. Government Printing Office, Washington, DC. pp. 173-181.

8. Joint Resolution Authorizing President of the U.S. to Protect the Security of Formosa-January 29, 1955, H.J. Resolution 159. *U.S. Statutes at Large*, 84th Congress, 1st Session, 1955, Volume 69. U.S. Government Printing Office, Washington, DC 1955. Public Law 4. p. 7.

9. 1956 Mutual Defense Assistance Agreement: Construction of Military Installations and Facilities. *U.S. Treaties and Other International Agreements*, Volume 7, Part 3, 1956. U.S. Government Printing Office, Washington, DC, 1957. pp. 3411-3415.

10. Statement of U.S. commitment to the defense of Taiwan and the Pescadores. *U.S. Security Agreements and Commitments Abroad*, Volume 1, Part 4, 1969-1970. U.S. Government Printing Office, Washington, DC, 1971. pp. 1114-1125.

11. The Situation in the Taiwan Strait: Statement by President Kennedy, June 27, 1962. Text in the *New York Times*, June 28, 1962.

12. 1965 Combined Military Exercises. *U.S. Treaties and Other International Agreements*, Volume 15, Part 2, 1964. U.S. Government Printing Office, Washington, DC, 1964. pp. 2390-2392.

13.   1965 Defense: Status of U.S. Armed Forces in the Republic of China. *U.S. Treaties and Other International Agreements*, Volume 17, Part I, 1966. U.S. Government Printing Office, Washington, DC, 1967. pp. 373-449. (Excerpts)

14.   1969 Extension of Loan of Vessels: U.S.S. Benson, U.S.S. Hilary P. Jones and U.S.S. Plunkett. *U.S. Treaties and Other International Agreements*, U.S. Government Printing Office, Washington, DC, 1969. pp. 2647-2649.

15.   1971 Extension of Loan of Vessels: U.S.S. Pecatonica and U.S.S. Whitemarsh. *U.S. Treaties and Other International Agreements*, Volume 22, Part I, 1971. U.S. Government Printing Office, Washington, DC, 1971. pp. 802-803.

16.   1972 Military Assistance: Deposits Under Foreign Assistance Act of 1971. *U.S. Treaties and Other International Agreements*, Volume 23, Part 1, 1972. U.S. Government Printing Office, Washington, DC, 1972. pp. 630-33.

17.   1976 Approval of Sale of Naval Vessels to the Republic of China. Public Law 94-457, October 5, 1976. *U.S. Statutes at Large*, 94th Congress, 2nd Session, Volume 90. U.S. Government Printing Office, Washington, DC. p. 1938.

M1   PRESIDENT TRUMAN'S STATEMENT ON SENDING
                      U.S. FLEET TO TAIWAN STRAITS
                              JULY 19, 1950

...In addition to the direct military effort we and other members of the United Nations are making in Korea, the outbreak of aggression there requires us to consider its implications for peace throughout the world. The attack upon the Republic of Korea makes it plain beyond all doubt that the international communist movement is prepared to use armed invasion to conquer independent nations. We must therefore recognize the possibility that armed aggression may take place in other areas.

In view of this, I have already directed that United States forces in support of the Philippines be strengthened, and that military assistance by speeded up to the Philippine Government and to the Associated States of Indo-China and to the forces of France in Indo-China. I have also ordered the United States Seventh Fleet to prevent any attack upon Formosa, and I have requested the Chinese Government on Formosa to cease all air and sea operations against the mainland. These steps were at once reported to the United Nations Security Council.

Our action in regard to Formosa was a matter of elementary security. The peace and stability of the Pacific area had been violently disturbed by the attack on Korea.

Attacks elsewhere in the Pacific area would have enlarged the Korean crisis, thereby rendering much more difficult the carrying out of our obligations to the United Nations in Korea.

In order that there may be no doubt in any quarter about our intentions regarding Formosa, I wish to state that the United States has no territorial ambitions whatever concerning that island, nor do we seek for ourselves any special position or privilege on Formosa. The present military neutralization of Formosa is without prejudice to political questions affecting that island...

Source: *The Public Papers of the Presidents of the United States: Harry S. Truman - 1950.* U.S. Government Printing Office, Washington, DC, 1965. p. 531 (Excerpt).

M2
795.00/S-2550   THE JOINT CHIEFS OF STAFF TO THE
                           COMMANDER IN CHIEF, FAR EAST
                                  (MACARTHUR)

TOP SECRET   WASHINGTON, June 30, 1950--3:56 p.m.
OPERATIONAL IMMEDIATE

JCS 84737. Joint Chiefs of Staff consider that the decision whether to accept or reject the proffer of military aid by foreign governments should properly be made at highest levels in

Washington. The Secretary of State has been advised that any proffer of troops made by Generalissimo Chiang Kai Shek should be declined at present.[1] In the event any such proffer is made by the Generalissimo to you, he should be advised to refer it to Department of State.

[1]See the aide-memoire from the Secretary of State to the Chinese Ambassador, July 1, p. 276.

Source: *Foreign Relations of the United States*, 1950,   Volume VII, Korea, U.S. Government Printing Office, Washington, D.C., 1976, p. 269.

M3

795B.5/6-2950

THE SECRETARY OF STATE TO THE
CHINESE AMBASSADOR (KOO)[2]
AIDE-MEMOIRE

In response to the request contained in the Chinese Embassy's Aide-Memoire of June 29,1950,[3] the appropriate authorities of the Government of the United States have given consideration to the expression of willingness on the part of the Government of the Republic of China to furnish ground fources for service in Korea in support of the United Nations.

The Secretary of State desires to inform His Excellency the Ambassador of the Republic of China of the deep appreciation of the United States Government for this prompt and substantial demonstration of support for the United Nations on the part of the Government of the Republic of China. In light, however, of the threat of invasion of Taiwan by Communist forces from the mainland, a threat repeated in the last day or so by spokesmen for the Chinese Communist regime in Peiping, it is the view of the Government of the United States of America that it would be desirable for representatives of General MacArthur's Headquarters to hold discussions with the Chinese military authorities on Taiwan concerning the plans for the defense of the island against invasion prior to any final decision on the wisdom of reducing the defense forces on Taiwan by transfer of troops to Korea. It is understood that Gernal MacArthur's Headquarters will be in communication with the appropriate Chinese military authorities on Taiwan with a view to the dispatch from Toyko of representatives of General MacArthur's Headquarters for this purpose.[4]

WASHINGTON, July 1, 1950.

[2]A manuscript note in the source text by the Deputy Assistant Secretary of State for Far Eastern Affairs (Merchant) indicated that this note was approved in substance by Secretary of Defense Johnson and directly by General Bradley for the JCS, incorporating changes Bradley suggested, after which it was initiated by Mr. Acheson at 5:50 p.m.

[3]See the memorandum by Mr. Merchant, June 29, p. 239, and also the memorandum of conversation by Mr. Freeman, June 30, with the annexed aide-memoire from the Chinese Embassy, p. 262.

[4]For related documentation, see vol. vi, pp. 256 ff.

Source: *Foreign Relations of the United States*, 1950, Volume VII, Korea, U.S.
                Government Printing Office, Washington, D.C., 1976, p. 276-277.

M4   CHINA MUTUAL DEFENSE ASSISTANCE

                Agreement effected by exchange of notes signed at Taipei
              January 30 and February 9, 1951; entered into force February 9, 1951

                      The American Charge d'Affaires ad interim to the
                             Chinese Minister of Foreign Affairs

                                                        AMERICAN EMBASSY,
No. 13   Taipei, January 30, 1951.

EXCELLENCY:

        Pursuant to instructions from my Government, I have the honor to deliver the following
statement:

        "The Government of the United States is prepared to make available to the Republic
of China under the terms of P.L. 329, 81st Congress, as amended, certain military material for
the defense of Taiwan against possible attack.

        "This material, and any other furnished under the authority of the law referred to, is
transferred on the understanding that it will be used and disposed of pursuant to the following
undertakings and that failure to do so by the Chinese Government will be contrary to the
understanding of the United States Government, and may be considered by the United States
to be cause for the cessation of further deliveries (it being understood that the undertakings
contained in the first three paragraphs below apply as well to the material transferred to the
Chinese Government under that law since June 27, 1950);

        "1. The Chines Government will use the material to maintain its internal security or
its legitimate self-defense.

        "2. The Chinese Government will take such security measures as may be agreed in
each case between the United States Government and the Chinese Government in order to
prevent the disclosure and compromise of classified military articles, services or information
furnished by the United States Government.

        "3. The Chinese Government agrees to receive personnel of the United States
Government who will discharge in the territory under the control of the Chinese Government
the responsibilities of the United States Government under this agreement and who will be
accorded adequate facilities to observe the progress of the assistance furnished, to confirm that
the material furnished is being used for the purpose for which it is provided, and to carry out
such other operations or arrangements as shall be mutually agreed pursuant to this agreement.

Such personnel, including personnel temporarily assigned, will, in their relations with the Chinese Government, operate as a part of the United States Embassy, under the direction and control of the Chief of the United States Diplomatic Mission.

"4. The Chinese Government will not transfer, sell, or otherwise dispose of the material provided pursuant to the above undertakings, or any other equipment susceptible of military use, without regard to its source, or the time or manner of its acquisition, without first obtaining the assurance of the United States Government that such equipment or material is not required by the United States for its own use or required to support programs of military assistance undertaken by the United States.

"The United States Government would appreciate a written assurance from the Chinese Government of its acceptance of the undertakings in this note."

Accept, Excellency, the assurances of my highest consideration.

K.L. RANKIN

His Excellency
 Dr. George K.C. Yeh,
  Minister of Foreign Affairs,
   Taipei.

Source: *U.S. Treaties and Other International Agreements*, Volume 2, Part 2, 1951, U.S. Government Printing Office, Washington, D.C., 1952, pp. 1498-1507.

M5   CHINA MUTUAL SECURITY

Agreement effected by exchange of notes signed at Taipei
December 29, 1951, and January 2, 1952; entered into
force January 2, 1952.

The American Charge d'Affaires ad interim to the
Chinese Minister of Foreign Affairs

AMERICAN EMBASSY
Taipei, December 29, 1951

No. 114

EXCELLENCY:

  I have the honor to refer to the conversations which have recently taken place between representatives of our Governments relating to the effect of the enactment by the Congress of the Mutual Security Act of 1951 (P.L. 165, 82nd Congress) upon furnishing assistance under the Economic Aid Agreement signed on July 3, 1948, as heretofore amended, and the exchange of notes dated January 30 and February 9, 1951 respectively, between the American Charge d'Affaires, ad interim, and the Minister of Foreign Affairs of the Republic of China, regarding the extension of military aid to China by the United States. I also have the honor to confirm the understandings reached as a result of these conversations, as follows:

1. The Government of the Republic of China hereby confirms that it has agreed to:

    (1) join in promoting international understanding and good will, and maintaining world peace;

    (2) take such action as may be mutually agreed upon to eliminate causes of international tension;

    (3) fulfill the military obligations which it has assumed under multilateral or bilateral agreements or treaties to which the United States is a party;

    (4) make, consistent with its political and economic stability, the full contribution permitted by its manpower, resources, facilities, and general economic condition to the development and maintenance of its own defensive strength and the defensive strength of the free world;

    (5) take all reasonable measures which may be needed to develop its defense capacities; and

    (6) take appropriate steps to insure the effective utilization of the economic and military assistance provided by the United States.

2. The two Governments will establish procedures to ensure that equipment and materials furnished by the Government of the United States under the Mutual Defense Assistance Act of 1949, as amended, or by either Government under the Mutual Defense Assistance Agreement of 1951, other than equipment or materials furnished under terms requiring reimbursement, and no longer required for the purposes for which originally made available will be offered for return to the Government which furnished such assistance for appropriate disposition.

3. The two Governments will establish procedures whereby the Government of the Republic of China will so deposit, segregate, or assure title to all funds allocated to or derived from any program of assistance undertaken by the Government of the United States to ensure that such funds shall not be subject to garnishment, attachment, seizure or other legal process by any person, firm, agency, corporation, organization or Government, when in the opinion of the Government of the United States any such legal process would interfere with the attainment of the objectives of the said program of assistance.

4. Paragraph 5 of Article V of the Economic Aid Agreement of July 3, 1948, shall include expenditures for military production, construction, equipment and materiel.

5. Whenever reference is made in the Economic Aid Agreement to the China Aid Act of 1948, such reference shall be construed as meaning also the Mutual Security Act of 1951 and the applicable provisions of the Economic Cooperation Act of 1948, as amended.

Upon receipt of a Note from your Government indicating that the foregoing provisions are acceptable to the Government of the Republic of China the Government of the United States of America will consider that this Note and your reply thereto constitute an agreement between the two Governments on this subject which shall enter into force on the date of your Note in reply.

Accept, Excellency, the renewed assurances of my most distinguished consideration.

                                                                           K.L. RANKIN
His Excellency
    George K.C. Yeh,
        Minister of Foreign Affairs,
            Republic of China

Source: *U.S. Treaties and Other International Agreements*, Volume 3, Part 4, 1952, U.S.
               Government Printing Office, Washington, D.C., 1955, pp. 4543-4553.

M6   CHINA MUTUAL DEFENSE

Treaty signed at Washington December 2, 1954;
Ratification advised by the Senate of the United States
    of America February 9, 1955;
Ratified by the President of the United States of America
    February 11, 1955;
Ratified by the Republic of China February 15, 1955;
Ratifications exchanged at Taipei March 3, 1955;
Proclaimed by the President of the United States of America
    April 1, 1955;
Entered into force March 3, 1955.
And exchange of notes
Signed at Washington December 10, 1954.

BY THE PRESIDENT OF THE UNITED STATES OF AMERICA

A PROCLAMATION

        Whereas the Mutual Defense Treaty between the United States of America and the
Republic of China was signed at Washington on December 2, 1954 by their respective
plenipotentiaries, the original of which Treaty in the English and Chinese languages is word for
word as follows:

MUTUAL DEFENSE TREATY
BETWEEN
THE UNITED STATES OF AMERICA
AND
THE REPUBLIC OF CHINA

        The Parties to this Treaty,
        Reaffirming their faith in the purposes and principles of the Charter of the United
Nations and their desire to live in peace with all peoples and all Governments, and desiring to
strengthen the fabric of peace in the West Pacific Area,

Recalling with mutual pride the relationship which brought their two peoples together in a common bond of sympathy and mutual ideals to fight side by side against imperialist aggression during the last war,

Desiring to declare publicly and formally their sense of unity and their common determination to defend themselves against external armed attack, so that no potential aggressor could be under the illusion that either of them stands alone in the West Pacific Area, and

Desiring further to strengthen their present efforts for collective defense for the preservation of peace and security pending the development of a more comprehensive system of regional security in the West Pacific Area,

Have agreed as follows:

ARTICLE I

The Parties undertake, as set forth in the Charter of the United Nations, to settle any international dispute in which they may be involved by peaceful means in such a manner that international peace, security and justice are not endangered and to refrain in their international relations from the threat or use of force in any manner inconsistent with the purposes of the United Nations.

ARTICLE II

In order more effectively to achieve the objective of this Treaty, the Parties separately and jointly by self-help and mutual aid will maintain and develop their individual and collective capacity to resist armed attack and communist subversive activities directed from without against their territorial integrity and political stability.

ARTICLE III

The Parties undertake to strengthen their free institutions and to cooperate with each other in the development of economic progress and social well-being and to further their individual and collective efforts toward these ends.

ARTICLE IV

The Parties, through their Foreign Ministers or their deputies, will consult together from time to time regarding the implementation of this Treaty.

ARTICLE V

Each Party recognizes that an armed attack in the West Pacific Area directed against the territories of either of the Parties would be dangerous to its own peace and safety and declares that it would act to meet the common danger in accordance with its constitutional processes.

Any such armed attack and all measures taken as a result thereof shall be immediately reported to the Security Council of the United Nations. Such measures shall be terminated when the Security Council has taken the measures necessary to restore and maintain international peace and security.

ARTICLE VI

For the purposes of Articles II and V, the terms "territorial" and "territories" shall mean in respect of the Republic of China, Taiwan and the Pescadores; and in respect of the United

States of America, the island territories in the West Pacific under its jurisdiction. The provisions of Articles II and V will be applicable to such other territories as may be determined by mutual agreement.

ARTICLE VII

The Government of the Republic of China grants, and the Government of the United States of America accepts, the right to dispose such United States land, air and sea forces in and about Taiwan and the Pescadores as may be required for their defense, as determined by mutual agreement.

ARTICLE VIII

This Treaty does not affect and shall not be interpreted as affecting in any way the rights and obligations of the Parties under the Charter of the United Nations or the responsibility of the United Nations for the maintenance of international peace and security.

ARTICLE IX

This Treaty shall be ratified by the United States of America and the Republic of China in accordance with their respective constitutional processes and will come into force when instruments of ratification thereof have been exchanged by them at Taipei.

ARTICLE X

This Treaty shall remain in force indefinitely. Either Party may terminate it one year after notice has been given to the other Party.

IN WITNESS WHEREOF the undersigned Plenipotentiaries have signed this Treaty.

DONE in duplicate, in the English and Chinese languages, at Washington on this second day of December of the Year One Thousand Nin Hundred and Fifty-four, corresponding to the second day of the twelfth month of the Forty-third year of the Republic of China.

FOR THE UNITED STATES OF AMERICA:

John Foster Dulles [s]

FOR THE REPUBLIC OF CHINA:

George K. C. Yeh [s]

WHEREAS the Senate of the United States of America by their resolution of February 9, 1955, two-thirds of the Senators present concurring therein, did advise and consent to the ratification of the said Treaty;

WHEREAS the said Treaty was ratified by the President of the United States of America on February 11, 1955, in pursuance of the aforesaid advice and consent of the Senate, and was duly ratified also on the part of the Republic of China on February 15, 1955;

WHEREAS it is provided in Article IX of the said Treaty that the Treaty will come into force when instruments of ratification thereof have been exchanged at Taipei;

WHEREAS the respective instruments of ratification of the said Treaty were duly exchanged at Taipei on March 3, 1955, and a protocol of exchange of instruments of ratification was signed on that date by the respective plenipotentiaries of the United States of America and the Republic of China;

AND WHEREAS, pursuant to the aforesaid provisions of Article IX of the said Treaty, the Treaty came into force on March 3, 1955;

NOW THEREFORE, be it known that I, Dwight D. Eisenhower, President of the United States of America, do hereby proclaim and make public the said Mutual Defense Treaty between the United States of America and the Republic of China to the end that the same and every article and clause thereof shall be observed and fulfilled with good faith, on and after March 3, 1955, by the United States of America and by the citizens of the United States of America and all other persons subject to the jurisdiction thereof.

IN TESTIMONY WHEREOF, I have hereunto set my hand and caused the Seal of the United States of America to be affixed.

DONE at the city of Washington this first day of April in the year of our Lord one thousand nine hundred fifty-five and of the Independence of the United States of America the one hundred seventy-ninth.

DWIGHT D. EISENHOWER

By the President:
JOHN FOSTER DULLES
Secretary of State

DECEMBER 10, 1954

EXCELLENCY:

I have the honor to acknowledge the receipt of your Excellency's Note of today's date, which reads as follows:

"I have the honor to refer to recent conversations between representatives of our two Governments and to confirm the understandings reached as a result of those conversations, as follows:

"The Republic of China effectively controls both the territory described in Article VI of the Treaty of Mutual Defense between the Republic of China and the United States of America signed on December 2, 1954, at Washington and other territory. It possesses with respect to all territory now and hereafter under its control the inherent right of self-defense. In view of the obligations of the two Parties under the said Treaty and of the fact that the use of force from either of these areas by either of the Parties affects the other, it is agreed that such use of force will be a matter of joint agreement, subject to action of an emergency character which is clearly an exercise of the inherent right of self-defense. Military elements which are a product of joint effort and contribution by the two Parties will not be removed from the territories described in Article VI to a degree which would substantially diminish the defensibility of such territories without mutual agreement."

I have the honor to confirm, on behalf of my Government, the understanding set forth in Your Excellency's Note under reply.

I avail myself of this opportunity to convey to Your Excellency the assurances of my highest consideration.

GEORGE K.C. YEH
Minister for Foreign Affairs of
the Republic of China

His Excellency
JOHN FOSTER DULLES
Secretary of State of
the United States of America

Source: *U.S. Treaties and Other International Agreements*, Volume 3, Part 4, 1952, U.S. Government Printing Office, Washington, D.C., 1955, pp. 433-454.

M7   CHINA
ESTABLISHMENT OF U.S. NAVY MEDICAL RESEARCH CENTER
AT TAIPEI, TAIWAN

Agreement effected by exchanges of notes
Dated at Taipei March 30, April 26, and October 14, 1955;
Entered into force October 14, 1955.

The American Ambassador to the Chinese
Minister of Foreign Affairs

The Foreign Service
of the
United States of America

No. 20

The Ambassador of the United States of America presents his compliments to the Minister of Foreign Affairs of the Republic of China and has the honor to refer to the subject of arrangements for the establishment of a United States Navy Medical Research Center at Taipei, Taiwan.

It is the understanding of the Government of the United States that the Government of the Republic of China is agreeable to the stationing of a United States Navy Medical Research Unit in Taipei for the purpose of conducting study and research on a long range basis in the field of diseases endemic and epidemic in the Far East.   The Ambassador is informed that conversations to this effect have been held by Commander Robert A. Phillips, Medical Corps, United States Navy, and members of his staff with representatives of the Government of the Republic of China and Taiwan National University, particularly Dr. S. L. Chien, President of the University.

It is contemplated that, for the time being and until more permanent arrangements can be made between the two governments, the Navy Medical Research unit will operate as part of the Military Assistance Advisory Group, and it is requested that this unit and its personnel be accorded the same rights, privileges and immunities as are granted to other components of the Military Assistance Advisory Group by the Government of the Republic of China. The initial complement of the United States Navy Medical Research Unit will consist of two officers, two enlisted men and their families, who are expected to arrive in Taiwan the latter part of May 1955. It is planned to expand this group to a total of approximately twelve scientists and technicians when the research center reaches full operating status.

The Ambassador is pleased to inform the Minister that Lt. Commander John Richey, United States Navy, has been authorized to act on behalf of the Government of the United States in making arrangements with representatives of the Government of the Republic of China for the leasing of facilities and areas necessary for the operation of the medical research center. The assistance of the Ministry is requested in enabling Commander Richey to make such arrangements with the appropriate officials of the Government of the Republic of China at the earliest opportunity.

It would be appreciated if the Minister would confirm the understanding of the AMbassador as to the matters set forth above and inform the Embassy of the name of the official authorized by the Government of the Republic of China to effect the detailed arrangements and to execute documents for the leasing of facilities and areas necessary for the operation of the medical research center.

AMERICAN EMBASSY,
Taipei, March 30, 1955.

TRANSLATION

No. Wal(44)MEI/I-003937

MEMORANDUM

The Ministry of Foreign Affairs of the Republic of China presents its compliments to the United States Embassy and, referring to the Embassy's Memorandum No. 20 dated March 30, 1955, has the honor to state that the Chinese Government agrees, as requested by the United States Government, to the stationing in Taipei of a United States Navy Medical Research Unit consisting of not more than twelve officers and men for the purpose of establishing a United States Navy Medical Research Center to conduct study and research on a long range basis in the field of diseases endemic and epidemic in the Far East.

In agreeing to the request referred to above, the Chinese Government wishes also to confirm the understanding that a formal agreement on the detailed arrangements, similar to those made by the United States Government with governments of other countries where similar medical research units of the United States Navy operate, will be negotiated and concluded between the two Governments as soon as possible and that, pending the conclusion of and without prejudice to such an agreement, the said Unit will be considered provisionally as a part of the United States Miliary Assistance Advisory Group and its personnel as components of the MAAG.

The Chinese Government has designated Dr. S.L. Chien, President of the National Taiwan University, as its represtnative to negotiate for the aforesaid formal agreement.

The Embassy is also requested to notify the Ministry as far in advance as possible the actual date of arrival in Taipei of the personnel of the United.

MINISTRY OF FOREIGN AFFAIRS
Taipei, April 26, 1955

Source: *U.S. Treaties and Other International Agreements*, 1955, U.S. Government
                 Printing Office, Washington, D.C., pp. 173-181.

M8

PUBLIC LAW 4   CHAPTER 4

JOINT RESOLUTION

Authorizing the President to employ the Armed Forces of the United States for protecting the security of Formosa, the Pescadores and related positions and territories of that area.

Whereas the primary purpose of the United States, in its relations with all other nations, is to develop and sustain a just and enduring peace for all; and

Whereas certain territories in the West Pacific under th jurisdiction of the Republic of China are now under armed attack, and threats and declarations have been and are being made by the Chinese Communists that such armed attack is in aid of and in preparation for armed attack on Formosa and the Pescadores,

Whereas such armed attack if continued would gravely endanger the peace and security of the West Pacific Area and particularly of Formosa and the Pescadores; and

Whereas the secure possession by friendly governments of the Western Pacific Island chain, of which Formosa is a part, is essential to the vital interests of the United States and all friendly nations in or bordering upon the Pacific Ocean; and

Whereas the President of the United States on January 6, 1955, submitted to the Senate for its advice and consent to ratification a Mutual Defense Treaty between the United States of America and the Republic of China, which recognizes that an armed attack in the West Pacific area directed against territories, therein described, in the region of Formosa and the Pescadores, would be dangerous to the peace and safety of the parties to the treaty: Therefore be it

Resolved by the Senate and House of Representatives of the United States of America in Congress assembled, That the President of the United States be and he hereby is authorized to employ the Armed Forces of the United States as he deems necessary for the specific purpose of securing and protecting Formosa and the Pescadores against armed attack, this authority to include the securing and protection of such related positions and territories of that area now in friendly hands and the taking of such other measures as he judges to be required or appropriate in assuring the defense of Formosa and the Pescadores.

This resolution shall expire when the President shall determine that the peace and security of the area is reasonably assured by international conditions created by action of the United Nations or otherwise, and shall so report to the Congress.

Approved January 29, 1955, 8:42 a.m.

Source: *U.S. Statutes at Large*, 84th Congress, 1st Session, 1955, Volume 69, U.S. Government Printing Office, Washington, DC, 1955, Public Law 4. p. 7.

M9

CHINA
MUTUAL DEFENSE ASSISTANCE: CONSTRUCTION OF MILITARY INSTALLATIONS AND FACILITIES

Agreement effected by exchange of notes
Signed at Taipei November 21, 1956;
Entered into force November 21, 1956.

The American Ambassador to the Chinese
Minister of Foreign Affairs

AMERICAN EMBASSY,
No. 31.   Taipei, November 21, 1956.

EXCELLENCY:

I have the honor to refer to the Mutual Defense Assistance Agreement between the United States of America and the Republic of China, embodied in the Exchanges of Notes at Taipei on January 30 and February 9, 1951, and on October 23 and November 1, 1952, and to propose the following understandings between our two Governments in order to facilitate the provision by the Government of the United States of assistance to the Government of the Republic of China under the terms of the aforesaid Agreement, in connection with the construction in Taiwan of military installations and facilities for the use of the Armed Forces of the Republic of China or for their joint use with the Armed Forces of the United States of America, financed wholly or in part by the Government of the United States, and in particular for the construction of the facility known as Kung Kuan Airfield and the Chinese Navy projects for the development of Tsoying Harbor and construction and development work at existing Chinese naval facilities in Kaohsiung, Keelung and Makung:

1. For purposes of the orderly and economical prosecution of work contemplated by these understandings, and for other projects as may be mutually agreed between the two Governments, the United States Military Assistance Advisory Group (MAAG), Taiwan, shall have attached or assigned to it as part of the MAAG, military and United States civilian personnel of the Okinawa Engineer District Corps of Engineers, United States Army, and of the Bureau of Yards and Docks, United States Navy, who, for purposes of this agreement, shall be treated as "Members of the MAAG."

2. The Government of the Republic of China, at times appropriate to the orderly and economical prosecution of the agreed construction work, and without cost to the United States Government, its Contractors or sub-contractors, will, on request, place at the disposal of the Chief, MAAG, areas necessary for carrying out the construction and related work contemplated by these understandings. The term "necessary areas" shall be understood to include, in addition to the real estate on which construction will be performed, rights to use of water available, rights of entry for purposes of survey, and such borrow areas, spoil areas, quarry sites and aggregate production sites in streams or elsewhere as may be necessary, together with rights of ingress and egress and rights to remove such materials or deposit excess materials as may be necessary to the agreed construction work. Such "necessary areas" shall cease to be at the disposal of the Chief, MAAG, upon completion of the construction work contemplated by these understandings.

3. The Government of the Republic of China will hold the Government of the United States, its Contractors and their subcontractors harmless for such destruction of any buildings, streets, roads, public utilities and improvements of any kind on real property placed at the disposal of the Chief, MAAG, as necessary to the construction work contemplated by these understandings. Should any relocation of facilities be required or resettlement costs be involved, relocation and resettlement shall be accomplished by the Government of the Republic of China at its own expense and at such time as not to interfere with the orderly and economical prosecution of the work.

4. The Chief, MAAG, or his representatives shall have the right to select and engage such individual persons, corporations, companies, and partnerships of United States nationality, herein referred to as "Contractors" as he may deem necessary for purposes of carrying out the functions contemplated in these understandings. It is, of course, understood that the Chief, MAAG, undertakes that local unskilled laborers will be used exclusively and he will engage local Contractors to the maximum practicable extent. Such of the Contractors and their sub-contractors as must be brought into Taiwan shall not be required to hold license or to register in order to perform in Taiwan the work contemplated by these understandings, nor to maintain a resident representative after completion of their contract and after fulfillment of their contractual obligations assumed in their dealings with residents of Taiwan or government agencies of the Republic of China. Terms and conditions of employment of Contractor personnel brought into Taiwan by the Chief, MAAG, or his representatives shall be exempt from the application of laws and regulations of the Government of the Republic of China. It is of course understood that terms and conditions of employment of residents of Taiwan will be subject to Chinese law. When notified by the Chief, MAAG, that it is essential to the prosecution of the agreed construction and that necessary U.S. security clearance has been granted in each case, the Government of the Republic of China will receive employees (together with their dependents) of the Okinawa Engineer District and the Bureau of Yards and Docks who are not United States nationals and of Contractors and sub-contractors, selected or approved and brought into Taiwan by the Chief, or his representative. Such employees, unless United States nationals, will be received only with prior approval of the Government of the Republic of China in each case. No fee or charge shall be made by the Government of the Republic of China for the entry or exit of such employees and their dependents or for

quarantine, work permits or residence permits. Administrative procedures will be devised to expedite entry into or exit from Taiwan.

5. All property, materials, equipment and supplies imported into or re-exported from Taiwan by the Government of the United States or by its Contractors or their sub-contractors brought into Taiwan, in connection with the agreed construction or work related thereto and certified to as such by the Chief, MAAG, shall be accorded the same customs and tax exemptions as are accorded MAAG under the Mutual Defense Assistance Agreement. Such property, materials equipment and supplies, if procured in Taiwan, and services procured in Taiwan, shall be exempt from Commodity Tax, Salt Tax and other readily detectable taxes. In the event that problems arise in effectuating such tax exemptions, the Government of the Republic of China and the Government of the United States shall remain the property of the Government of the United States or its Contractors or sub-contractors brought into Taiwan, and may be removed from Taiwan at any time or may be disposed of in Taiwan by such owners in accordance with measures to be agreed upon by the two governments and, in the case of Contractors and sub-contractors brought into Taiwan, subject to claims resulting from contractual obligations assumed in dealings with residents of Taiwan or the Government of the Republic of China. In event of disposal in Taiwan, any applicable customs duty or tax will be paid by the purchaser in accordance with the laws and regulations of the Republic of China. The Government of the Republic of China will take all reasonable steps within the framework of its laws to prevent any unwarranted increases in the prices of either materials or services, including transportation, and in fees for port facilities, purchased or utilized by the Chief, MAAG, or by his Contractors or their sub-contractors to carry out the functions contemplated by these understandings.

6. All vehicles and equipment imported into Taiwan by the Government of the United States or by its Contractors and sub-contractors brought into Taiwan, to carry out the functions contemplated by these understandings, when certified as such by the Chief, MAAG, shall bear license tags or markings of the same kind as are assigned to MAAG vehicles and equipment of similar types, and such vehicles and equipment shall not be subject to taxes or fees relating to their registration or licensing in Taiwan. Operators of such vehicles and equipment shall carry at all times a valid operator's permit as may be required by the Chinese Government, which, except in the case of residents of Taiwan, shall be issued without charge. Prior consultation with the appropriate authorities of the Republic of China shall be required in regard to movements on land or water of such vehicles and equipment which are necessary to the completion of the work contemplated by these understandings but are in conflict with existing laws or regulations limiting the use of roads or waterways to certain types of vehicles.

7. Employees of the United States Government and their dependents, as well as Contractors and sub-contractors and their employees and dependents, who enter Taiwan to carry out the functions contemplated by these understandings shall be granted the same personal customs and tax exemptions as are granted members of MAAG under the Mutual Defense Assistance Agreement. Not more than one motor vehicle per family may be imported duty free for personal use, with the understanding that such vehicles may not be disposed of in Taiwan, but must be exported upon departure of the owner.

8. Contractors selected by the Chief, MAAG, shall have the right, subject to his approval, to select such sub-contractors, from either within or outside Taiwan, as may be necessary for the performance of the contemplated construction work and the discharge of their contractual obligations to MAAG, again with the understanding that local sub-contractors will be used to the maximum practicable extent and provided that such sub-contractors as must be brought into Taiwan, unless of U.S. nationality, shall be engaged only with prior approval of the Government of the Republic of China.

On behalf of the Government of the United States, I would appreciate a written assurance from the Government of the Republic of China of its acceptance of the understandings expressed above. This note, together with your Excellency's note in reply, shall be considered as constituting an agreement between the two Governments on the understandings.

Accept, Excellency, the renewed assurances of my most distinguished consideration.

K. L. RANKIN

His Excellency
    GEORGE K. C. YEH,
        Minister of Foreign Affairs,
        Republic of China,
        Taipei

Source: *U.S. Treaties and Other International Agreements*, Volume 7, Part 3, 1956, U.S. Government Printing Office, Washington, D.C., 1957, pp. 3411-3415.

M10   **APPENDIX**

STATEMENT ON UNITED STATES-REPUBLIC OF CHINA SECURITY RELATIONS, PRESENTED BY AMBASSADOR WALTER P. McCONAUGHY

I. U.S. COMMITMENT TO THE DEFENSE OF TAIWAN AND THE PESCADORES

A.   Circumstances Leading Up to the 1954 Mutual Defense Treaty

The present U.S. defense commitment to the Government of the Republic of China (GRC), which is embodied in the 1954 Mutual Defense Treaty, had its antecedent in the Truman Declaration of June 27, 1950, made just three days after the outbreak of the Korean War. This declaration reversed the earlier U.S. decision neither to use U.S. forces to prevent the Chinese Communist occupation of Taiwan nor to extend military assistance to the Republic of China (ROC), a policy enunciated by President Truman on January 5, 1950. The June Declaration postulated that Chinese Communist possession of Taiwan "would be a direct threat to the security of the Pacific area and to United States forces" there, and therefore announced the interposition of the Seventh Fleet in the Taiwan Strait. As a corollary, the GRC was asked to cease air and sea operations against the mainland.

The decision embodied in that Declaration was based on the military judgment that, with the U.S. involved in hostilities in Asia, Taiwan formed an integral part of the defense littoral extending from the Aleutians to the Philippines from which a decisive degree of control of military operations along the periphery of East Asia could be exercised. In unfriendly hands, Taiwan would pose a substantial danger to the other parts of the southern half of this littoral--the Ryukyus and the Philippines. To strengthen the Republic of China's ability to contribute to the defense of Taiwan, the United States six months later instituted a military assistance program with the GRC.

President Eisenhower, soon after taking office in 1953, altered the Seventh Fleet's mission in the Taiwan Strait so that it would "no longer be employed to shield Communist China..." There was no change in its mission of defending Taiwan [deleted]. The aim of the alteration of the Seventh Fleet's mission was principally to make the Korean War less attractive to Communist China without assuming undue risks.

The U.S. decision to convert its defense undertaking into a formal treaty patterned on those already concluded with Japan, the Philippines, and the Republic of Korea was taken shortly after the outbreak of the Offshore Island crisis in September 1954. In hearings before the Senate Foreign Relations Committee, Secretary Dulles stated that the Treaty would serve two purposes:

> (1) "It would give the Chinese Communists notice, beyond any possibility of misinterpretation, that the United States would regard an armed attack directed against Taiwan (Formosa) and the Pescadores as a danger to its own peace and safety and would act to meet the danger--such action to be in accordance with our constitutional processes."

> (2) "It would provide firm reassurance to the Republic of China and to the world that Taiwan (Formosa) and the Pescadores are not a subject for barter as part of some Far Eastern 'deal' with the Chinese Communists."

The treaty was negotiated in Washington beginning in October 1954 and was signed December 2, followed on December 10 by a corollary exchange of notes requiring GRC consultation on any offensive action against the mainland.

B.   Basic Provisions of the Tready

Under the central provision of the Treaty (Article V):

> "Each Party recognizes that an armed attack in the West Pacific Area directed against the territories of either the Parties would be dangerous to its own peace and safety and declares that it would act to meet the common danger in accordance with its constitutional processes."

Territories encompassed by the Treaty in the case of the GRC are specifically defined as Taiwan and the Pescadores, and "such other territories as may be determined by mutual agreement" (Article VI). The Parties are obliged "separately and jointly by self-help and mutual aid [to] maintain and develop their individual and collective capacity to resist armed attack and communist subversive activities directed from without against their territorial integrity and political stability" (Article II). The U.S. obtained 'the right to dispose such United States land, air and sea forces in and about Taiwan and the Pescadores as may be required for their defense, as determined by mutual agreement" (Article VII).

An exchange of diplomatic notes accompanying the Treaty bound the GRC to consult before taking offensive action: "In view of the obligations of the two Parties under the said Treaty and of the fact that the use of force from either of these areas (i.e., the territory described in the Treaty and other territory controlled by the Republic of China) by either of the Parties affects the other, it is agreed that such use of force will be a matter of joint agreement, subject to action of an emergency character which is clearly an exercise of the inherent right of self-defense."

The Treaty's central provision quoted above employed the Monroe Doctrine formula, which also has been used in mutual defense treaties with the Philippines, Korea, and Japan, the ANZUS Pact, and the SEATO Treaty. In the Monroe Doctrine formula an attack is regarded as "dangerous to the peace and safety" of the Parties, and they are committed only to resond "in accordance with their constitutional procedures."

Other explicit or implicit limitations of the Treaty include the following:

--the U.S. has no obligation to station forces on Taiwan or the Pescadores.
--the Treaty does not affect the existing legal status of Taiwan or the Pescadores.
--the U.S. has no commitment to defend the Offshore Islands, and any extension of the Treaty to other territories as provided in Article VI (defining the territorial scope of the agreement) requires the advice and consent of the Senate.

In addition, the U.S. has no obligation to come to the defense of Taiwan and the Pescadores in the event of an external attack which is the result of GRC offensive actions undertaken without prior U.S. agreement. This interpretation of the Treaty is known to the Government of the Republic of China [deleted.]

C.   The Current Security Threat

Communist China constitutes an extremely powerful threat to Taiwan. The Chinese Communists continue to assert their intentions to occupy Taiwan and to destroy the GRC. There appears to be no change to Peking's ultimate objective in this respect, despite the turmoil caused by the Cultural Revolution and the deterioration of relations with the USSR. The theme "liberate Taiwan" routinely appears in domestic and international broadcasts but has not been stressed for the past few years. However, it is possible that the Taiwan problem once again will be highlighted if and when Peking successfully solves its pressing domestic matters and the Soviet problem.

The Communist Chinese armed forces are comprised of a large Army, a jet-fighter equipped Air Force and a growing Navy. The Chinese Army has an estimated 2.4 million troops with 164 tactical divisions. The inventory of the Chicom Air Force and the Chicom Naval air force includes more than 3,000 combat aircraft. The Communist Navy with 47 major ships [deleted] is essentially a coastal defense force. However, it is growing both in number of ships, quality of personnel and training, and therefore in its operational capabilities.

The Chinese Communists continue to be deterred from extensive military action against the GRC by their own limited military sealift capability. [Deleted.]

II. THE OFFSHORE ISLANDS

The United States is not committed to assist the Government of the Republic of China in the event of an attack on the Offshore Islands of Quemoy and Matsu. As already noted, Article 6 of the Mutual Defense Treaty specifies that the territories of the Republic of China to which the Treaty applies are "Taiwan and the Pescadores." The Joint Congressional Resolution approved on January 29, 1955 (Public Lsw 4--84th Congress), however, authorizes the President "to employ the Armed Forces of the United States as he deems necessary for the specific purpose of securing and protecting Formosa and the Pescadores against armed attack, this authority to include the securing and protection of such related positions and territories of that area [Formose and the Pescadores] now in friendly hands and the taking of such other measures as he judges to be required or appropriate in assuring the defense of Formosa and the Pescadores." The Government of the Republic of China recognizes the basic distinction between our commitment to the defense of Taiwan and the Pescadores as provided in the Mutual Defense Treaty and the authority vested by Congress in the President to determine unilaterally whether an attack against the Offshore Islands relates to the defense of Taiwan and the Pescadores and, if so, what action is appropriate to meet that threat.

In the case of a Chinese Communist attack against the Offshores, we would take into account whether such attack was retaliatory in response to military action by the Republic of China to which we had not agreed in advance. In view of the possibility contemplated in the Joint Resolution, that an attack against the Offshore Islands might be directed against Taiwan and the Pescadores, the Commander, United States Taiwan Defense Command (COMUSTDC) is responsible to be prepared to assist the GRC in the defense of the principal Offshore Islands of Quemoy and Matsu, if directed by Presidential authority. [Deleted.]

III. THE CONTINUING CIVIL WAR

Both Taipei and Peking insist that the struggle for the control of China continues. Although neither side has risked large-scale hostilities since the Taiwan Strait crisis of 1958, both have continued limited military actions against each other's territory.

A.   Chinese Communist Incursions into GRC Territory

Since 1964, the Chinese Communists have continued alternate-day firing of propaganda leaflet shells on to the Offshore Islands of Quemoy and Matsu, occasionally causing some property damage and injury to persons. During this period, several instances of minor intelligence raids on the Offshore Islands, intrusion into GRC air or water space, detainment of GRC fishermen and the like have been reported. Many of these reports, however, have been vague, incomplete and often delayed and, for the most part, have not been confirmed by the Republic of China.

[Deleted.}

We have been able to confirm only two such reports. [Deleted.]

January 8-9, 1966: A GRC HU-16 aircraft transport, the Chinese Communist crew of an LSM which had defected to Matsu was attacked and shot down by Chinese Communist fighters as it was proceeding to Taipei. All personnel were lost.

February 28, 1968: [Deleted.]

B.   GRC Incursions into Chinese Communist Territory

The GRC over the past five years has been much more active than Communist China in conducting continued low-level small-scale military actions against mainland China for both military and political reasons. These actions have consisted of reconnaissance flights, maritime raids and propaganda shelling.

[Deleted}

As regards propaganda shelling, the GRC from its position on Kinmen and Matsu Keeps up its half of the alternate-day exchange with the Chicoms. (High explosive shells were last used in these exchanges in 1964.) The GRC also uses Kinmen and other locations to launch propaganda ballons against the mainland.

C.   The U.S. Role

It has been and remains the position of the United States that whatever the ultimate resolution of the dispute between the Republic of China on Taiwan and the People's Republic of China on the mainland, it should be by peaceful means. We have attempted, therefore, to discourage the use of force by either the ROC or Communist China in the Taiwan Strait area.

We have used the Warsaw talks over the years to try to gain Peking's agreement to a formal renunciation of force in the Taiwan Strait. Serious discussion between the two sides took place in the latter part of 1955 and early 1956 and a measure of agreement was reached. Peking, however, refused to include a reference to self-defense in the operative part of the proposed statement, "The PRC and USA are determined that they will settle disputes between them through peaceful negotiations, and that, without prejudice to the inherent right of individual and collective self-defense, they will not resort to the threat or use of force in the Taiwan area or elsewhere." The Communist Chinese held that the reference to the right of self-defense as applied to Taiwan implied such a right for the U.S. or Nationalist Chinese as regards Taiwan, which would constitute for Peking an unacceptable interference in its internal affairs, Some discussion of the question was continued in subsequent meetings, but without result.

The U.S. is opposed to the use of force in the Taiwan Strait area. The Government of the Republic of China is fully aware that the United States is opposed to any large-scale military operations against the mainland or the mounting of a "counter-attack." [Deleted] the 1954 Dulles-Yeh exchange of notes, undertaken at the time of the conclusion of the Mutual Defense Treaty, requires that the use of force from within the territory controlled by the Republic of China "will be a matter of joint agreement, subject to action of an emergency character which is clearly an exercise of the inherent right of self-defense." In addition, on October 23, 1958, President Chiang and Secretary Dulles, following their meeting in Taipei, issued a joint communique in which the Government of the Republic of China declared that the principal means of achieving its mission of restoring freedom to the Chinese people on the mainland "is the implementation of Dr. Sun Yat-sen's three principles (nationalism, democracy and social well-being) and not the use of force." [Deleted} the Government of the Republic of China is aware that we would not consider ourselves bound by the obligations of the Mutual Defense Treaty in the event of a Chinese Communist attack on Taiwan and the Pescadores provoked by GRC offensive action against the mainland to which we had not agreed.

D.   Consultations With the GRC on Actions Against the Mainland

[Deleted]

U.S. forces have not launched any combat missions against the mainland from Taiwan. The 327th Air Division does participate in the "Peacetime Aerial Reconnaissance Program" (PARPRO), including "Beggar Watch," a Navy P-3A ocean surveillance air patrol (OSAP) mission [deleted].

E.   The July 2, 1969, Min River Estuary Incident

As the Vietnam war intensified, we became increasingly concerned for the possibility that even small-scale GRC raids against the mainland might lead to Chinese Communist provocation [deleted.]

At the time of the clash of ROC forces and the Chinese Communist vessels in the area of the Minh River Estuary on the night of July 2, 1969 [deleted.] No U.S. official had been informed of the July 2, 1969 action in advance, and the first word received was through wire service reports on July 3 citing an official Chinese Central News Agency release that "seaborne commandos of the Anti'Communist National Salvation Corps destroyed two Communist supply ships and one gunboart Wednesday night [July 2] in two surprise attachs off the China mainland coast...near the estuary of the Min River of Fukien Province." Some delay was encountered in obtaining confirmation of this report through GRC authorities, but by July 7 it had been determined that a small-scale encounter, [deleted] had occurred in which [deleted] ROC [deleted] small craft attacked several Chinese Communist vessels in an area about 15 miles to the northeast of the Min River estuary. We were unable to obtain any details on the Chinese Communist craft, although available information indicated they also were of small-size. It was confirmed that no "warships" were involved on either side, contrary to reports in the American press.

On July 3 the Department of State spokesman issued a statement expressing the concern of the United States Government for "any action by either side which might create tensions in the Taiwan Strait." The spokesman subsequently stated that this view had been conveyed to the Government of the Republic of China.

[Deleted.]

IV. U.S.--GRC MILITARY COOPERATION

A.   The Military Assistance Program

Basic Provisions of the Military Assistance Agreement.--U.S. military assistance is provided to the Republic of China under a formal agreement, supplemented by several understandings. The formal agreement consists of two exchanges of notes. The first, an exchange of notes dated January 30 and February 9, 1951, established the framework for the military assistance program:

> The Government of the United States is prepared to make available to the Republic of China...certain military material for the defense of Taiwan against possible attack.
>
> This material, and any other furnished under the authority of the law referred to, is transferred on the understanding that it will be used and disposed of pursuant to the following undertakings and that failure to do so by the Chinese Government will be contrary to the understanding of the United States Government, and may be considered by the United States to be cause for the cessation of further deliveries...;
>
> 1.   The Chinese Government will use the material to maintain its internal security or its legitimate self-defense.

The second exchange of notes, dated October 23 and November 1, 1952, and popularly referred to as the Military Assistance Advisory Group (MAAG) Administrative Agreement, defines certain terms in the original notes along with privileges and exemptions both for MAAG as an organization and for its personnel and their dependents as individuals.

Three other understandings supplement the MAAG Agreement: (1) an exchange of notes dated December 29, 1951 and January 2, 1952 confirmed the understandings of the two governments on, among other things, effective utilization of economic and military assistance provided by the U.S.; (2) an exchange of notes dated April 3, 1956 established procedures for the disposition of grant aid equipment and materials; and (3) an exchange of notes dated June 3, 1964 amended that of April 3, 1956 to provide for the use of proceeds from the disposition of grant aid equipment and materials not returned to the U.S.

Amount of MAP Assistance.--During the past five years, Military Assistance Programs provided $61.5 million in FY 1965, $86 million in FY 1966, $90.5 million in FY 1967, $67.4 million in FY 1968, and $36 million in FY 1969.

Major Weapons Systems and Components.--MAP has provided [deleted] F-5 aircraft the period Fiscal Years 1965-1969; [deleted] additional F-5s have been purchased by the ROC. The mission of these aircraft is air defense, counter air operations, close air support, patrol and armed reconnaissance. The Chinese Communist Air Force has sufficient fighter and light bomber strength for limited planned strikes against Taiwan, the offshore islands and other neighboring non-Communist countries. The Chinese Communist Air Force light bomber units are untested in combat, but probably represent the most proficient portion of Communist China's tactical air force. [Deleted.] Although the Chinese Communist light jet bombers are obsolescent by western standards, they could pose a threat against selected targets, or any target in the ROC, should sufficient fighter escort be provided.

The U.S. has provided on a loan basis in the period Fiscal Years 1965-1969, one destroyer and one destroyer escort. These ships have the mission of extended anti-submarine and anti-surface warfare, limited air defense and gunfire support. They screen and escort support forces, amphibious forces and convoys and conduct surveillance of and patrol the Taiwan straits. The Chinese Communist Navy has increased the construction of almost every type ship in its inventory. New fleet additions since mid-1968 were highlighted by the appearance of one Kiangnan class destroyer escort, [deleted] guided missile patrol boats, and [deleted] Romeo class submarines. [Deleted.}

The ROC has been supplied with [deleted] surplus [deleted] tanks. [Deleted] were rehabilitated at MAP expense in Fiscal Year 1965, and the remainder were provided with the cost of transportation and rehabilitation funded by the GRC in Fiscal Years 1968 and 1969. The tanks [deleted] have improved the mobile defense capability of the ROC army. The tanks could be used to defense against invading enemy armor and infantry forces.

[Deleted] howitzers were programmed in FY 1967. [Deleted.] The howitzers serve to increase the capability of the ROC army to defend against an invading force.

Budget Support and Level of GRC Defense Expenditures.--For the period FY 1965 through FY 1969, the U.S. Military Assistance contributions in relationship to the Republic of China defense budget amounted to [deleted] of the Chinese defense budget in FY 1965, [deleted] in FY 1966, [deleted] in FY 1967, [deleted] in FY 1968, and [deleted] in FY 1969.

[Deleted.]

Excess Military Equipment From the U.S.--Major items of excess U.S. military equipment provided the Republic of China Armed Forces during the past five years are shown in a classified table provided to the Committee. The value assigned in each case represents acquisition cost, although the utility value may actually be considerably less. Extensive repair and rehabilitation is often required to restore equipment to a useable status. Life expectancy, however, is considerably less than that of a new item. In certain instances, it is more economical to utilize the equipment as a source of spare parts rather than to expend repair and rehabilitation funds.

Purchases of U.S. Military Equipment.--Major items of U.S. equipment purchased by the Republic of China during the past five years and the source of funding are shown in a classified table provided the Committee. Both credit and cash sales are paid for by the ROC. In addition, the ROC purchases relatively small quantities of supplies for its military establishment through regular commercial channels. A detailed breakdown of commercial sales is not available but they consist largely of operating and maintenance type items. Estimated commercial purchases by fiscal years are as follows: Fiscal Year 1965, $.6 million; Fiscal Year 1966, $.7 million; Fiscal Year 1967, $.7 million; Fiscal Year 1968, $1.2 million and Fiscal Year 1969, $1.9 million.

Republic of China Force Level Support Goals.--[Deleted.]

Economic Impact of GRC Defense Expenditures.--GRC defense expenditures, now running at a rate of approximately 9-10% of GNP and more than 50% of the combined central and local government combined budget, are high compared with most other countries. By definition, such expenditures deprive the civilian economy of resources which otherwise could be used for investment in infrastructure improvements required for continued economic growth, as well as for such programs as public housing, health and education which are directly related to an improvement in the quality of life. As in any government, the allocation of resources between defense and the needs of the civilian economy reflects a deliberate assignment of relative priorities. In the case of the Republic of China, however, given the level of capabilities required for its forces to make an effective contribution within the terms of the Mutual Defense Treaty, as well as to defend its position on the Offshore Islands, and the sharp and sudden cut in grant MAP support, it probably is unavoidable that its defense expenditures will remain at least at the present rate for the foreseeable future.

Even at that rate, however, the projected levels of economic growth and government consumption, including military expenditures, should permit private consumption to continue to grow at rates approximating those of the past, while at the same time permitting a satisfactory rate of growth in domestic capital formation. Any substantial increase in future exports, direct foreign investment, foreign loans or domestic investment above the conservative levels projected, of course, will ease the ability of the Taiwan economy to sustain both a health rate of economic growth and a large military force.

On the other hand, expensive new military programs, if not offset by reductions in other military areas, could compete with investment in badly needed infrastructure projects. To the extent that such new programs are required to prevent obsolescence and maintain a reasonable measure of modernization, GRC policymakers--both military and civilian-- increasingly will be faced by the need for adhering to a total resource approach in the allocation of available resources between economic and military needs.

Organization of the ROC Army.--The primary mission of the ROC Army is to organize, equip, train and employ army forces for the ground defense of the territory of the Government of ROC. It provides troops and combat service support for ground defense of the offshore islands and security for navy and air force logistic bases, installations and important administrative establishments. It assists the primary internal security forces in the maintenance of internal security as needed.

Comparative Size of the ROC Army.--The armed forces of ROC total 592,200 of which Army strength is 376,500. The population of Taiwan is estimated at 14,000,000. The armed forces thus account for 4.2% of the total population. The following chart shows for selected Asian countries the size of the armed forces, army strength, total population, and percentage of armed forces to the total population:

Country	Forces	Armed Army	Population	Total Population	Percent of
Indonesia		357,600	256,000	116,000,000	0.3
Japan		230,000	155,800	101,500,000	0.2
Korea		626,530	547,500	30,800,000	2.0
Philippines*		35,200	15,900	36,500,000	0.1

*   Excludes Philippine constabulary.

Force Reduction and Reorganization.--[Deleted.] Within MND, planning to reduce and modernize the forces was initiated last June. The Country Team has cooperated to the extent possible in providing advice and assistance to the MND in such planning, [deleted].

The Ministry of National Defense considers that modernization of the forces is a sine qua non for force reduction. The MAAG has developed four programs to assist in improving the quality of the forces and reducing their size. These programs are: a) selling the ROC under FMS cash and credit at greatly reduced cost surplus U.S. military equipment needed for force modernization; b) increasing ROC self sufficiency so that in-country production capabilities can meet almost all armed forces requirements for individual clothing and equipment, small arms, ammunition, field tactical communications equipment, military maps and certain transport vehicles and spare parts; c) rebuilding by the ROC of U.S. battle-damaged and worn equipment becoming available in the Far East for inclusion in its armed forces inventory; and d) initiation of co-production programs such as those for vehicles and helicopters.

Composition of the ROC Army.--The conscription law of the ROC provides for the registering of all males at age 19, and for a minimum age of 20 for induction. Enlistments are permitted at age 18. Terms of service in the Army are two years except for those serving in the technical service branches who serve three years. Approximately [deleted] enter the military service each year principally as replacements for the Army. Taiwanese make up the bulk of conscriptees whereas the senior NCOs and officers are largely Chinese who came to Taiwan at the time of evacuation from the mainland.

Leadership of the ROC Army.--Chinese Army commanders from the commander-in-chief to the combat battalion command level consistently perform in a highly professional manner and are extremely dedicated to duty. The corps and field army commanders have not had real combat experience above division level. Combat experience was gained during World War II against the relatively inactive Japanese Field Force on the Mainland, and during the postwar conflict with the Chinese Communists when actual combat engagements were of limited scope and duration and did not employ complex modern equipment for ground warfare [Deleted.]

The Anti-Communist National Salvation Force.--The Anti-Communist National Salvation Force (ACNSC) is a [deleted] man organization which garrisons the island of Tung Yin in the Matsu Group of Offshore Islands and the Island of Wu Chiu. [Deleted.]

The ACNSC receives no MAP assistance of any type.

MAAG Presence on the Offshore Islands.--One MAAG army officer is on Matsu; three MAAG army officers are on Quemoy. The MAAG advisors provide advice and assistance on organization, training, administration and logistics to the local ROC commanders.

[Deleted.]

Special Forces Training.--Initial provision of special forces advisory effort to the ROC began in 1957 when a U.S. mobile training team was assigned for a limited period to Taiwan. A two-man special advisory team was permanently assigned to the MAAG the next year, and in 1960 was increased to nine men. Gradually this team has been reduced to one officer who carries on the special forces advisory function.

The mission of the ROC special forces is to conduct, during hostilities, unconventional warfare in support of military operations to include: psychological, political and economic warfare; sabotage and countersabotage; evacuation; evasion and escape; subversion against hostile states; assisting indigenous resistance groups; and organizing, training and conducting guerrilla warfare.

B.   U.S. Forces, Missions and Operations

Taiwan Defense Command.--In September of 1952, the Formosa Defense Command was activated under Vice Admiral Clark who was concurrently Commander U.S. Seventh Fleet. In October 1954, Admiral Clark established a Liaison Center ashore in Taipei which became known as the Formosa Liaison Center. The Chief MAAG was the director of the center as a collateral duty. In April 1955, it was announced that the Formosa Defense Command was moving ashore as a separate command. On November 1, 1955, the name of the headquarters was changed to Taiwan Defense Command (TDC). In December of that sam eyear, Vice Admiral Ingersoll became Commander of U.S. Seventh Fleet and concurrently the Commander U.S. Taiwan Defense Command. In January 1957, Admiral Ingersoll relinquished command of Seventh Fleet and became the first full-time commander of USTDC, which then became, and still is, a subordinate Unified Command directly under Commander in Chief, Pacific.

The Commander, United States Taiwan Defense Command (COMUSTDC) has a primary mission of planning the defense of Taiwan, the Pescadores, and the Offshore Islands in support of the Mutual Defense Treaty of 1954 and the Joint Congressional REsolution of 1955. A secondary mission is to be prepared to conduct any operations as directed by the Commander-in-Chief, Pacific Forces (CINCPAC).

All TDC personnel are located in the Taipei area. The personnel strength over the past three years has been:

	Officers	Enlisted	Civilian	Local Nationals	Dependents
July 1, 1967 (FY 1968)	57	138	5	9	280
July 1, 1968 (FY 1969)	56	113	8	9	290
July 1, 1969 (FY 1970)	63	121	8	0	303

Operating costs, including military pay, were $1,655,888 in FY67, $1,982,351 in FY68, and $2,083503 in FY69. The TDC personnel are organized into the usual staff sections of Personnel (J-1), Intelligence (J-2), Operations (J-3), Logistics (J-4), and Communications (J-6). These staff sections maintain the common staff and planning relationships with their counterpart staff sections in the GRC Ministry of National Defense. There are no U.S. military units under TDC control.

The Military Assistance Advisory Group.--(MAAG) MAAG China was established in Taipei on May 1, 1951, soon after the conclusion of the Military Assistance Agreement. The mission of the Military Assistance Advisory Group is to assist and advise the Armed Forces of the Republic of China in organization, equippage and training.

In 1967, the MAAG operated in support of this mission with an authorized strength of 727 personnel, consisting of 312 officers, 264 enlisted men, 57 U.S. civilians, and 94 local nationals. This strength remained unchanged in 1968. In 1969, the strength of the MAAG was reduced to 487, which consisted of 221 officers, 171 enlisted men, 37 U.S. civilians, and 58 local nationals.

The cost to the U.S. Government, including military pay, of maintaining this organization were $10.6 million in FY 1967, $9.1 million in FY 1968, and $8.7 million in FY 1969. In addition to these U.S. costs, the Government of the Republic of China, pursuant to the Military Assistance Agreement, as amended, contributed facilities, and utilities, and personnel services, such as guards, drivers, and typists, valued at $884,000 in FY 1967, $865,000 in FY 1968, and $800,000 in FY 1969. In carrying out its mission, MAAG personnel are stationed in eleven different locations throughout the island of Taiwan and on the islands of Quemoy and Matsu.

Specifically, the MAAG is a joint staff organization, with four major subordinate elements. The headquarters is located in Taipei and is primarily charged with advising the Ministry of National Defense on matters relating to the entire spectrum of military defense. The four subordinate elements consist of Army, Navy, Air Force, and Combined Service Force sections. The Combined Service Force section advises a Chinese military organization responsible for military production facilities in support of all Chinese military forces. The primary mission of all four MAAG service sections is to carry out the everyday operation, training, and logistic advisory functions to the four individual Chinese military services--Army, Navy, Air Force, and Combined Service Forces. While the headquarters of each of these MAAG service sections are located in Taipei, they have subordinate elements advising major Chinese Armed Forces units and activities throughout Taiwan and on the Offshore Islands.

Separation of TDC and MAAG.--The two commands were merged for a very short interval. The Formosa Liaison Center was ashore in Taiwan in 1953 representing the Commander Formosa Defense Command, who was afloat and concurrently Commander Seventh Fleet. At that time, Chief MAAG was the director of the liaison center. The title Formosa Liaison Center remained in use until NOvember 1, 1955 when the command officially became known as the United States Taiwan Defense Command. On March 14, 1958, the designation of the command was changed to United States Taiwan Defense Command and Military Assistance Advisory Group. On August 6, 1959, the command relationship between USTDC and MAAG Taiwan reverted to the status which existed before the partial merger of March 1958.

U.S.-GRC Military Coordination.--Coordination of military-related questions with the GRC is normally accomplished by various formal and informal committee meetings as necessary to discuss areas of common U.S.-ROC military interests. Examples are meetings to discuss planning, logistics, and status of forces. The U.S. representative on committees are guided by guidelines established by COMUSTDC, the Country Team, CINCPAC or higher U.S. authority. Major decisions or requests for additional guidance would be cleared through the appropriate military or State channel. Thus, a major proposal which might possibly deviate from stated U.S. military planning guidance would be cleared with CINCPAC. When appropriate, the Country Team is consulted for guidance.

Illustrative of the coordination process is the U.S.-ROC Joint Committee, composed of one U.S. and one GRC representative, in existence to consult on implementing the U.S.-GRC Status of Forces Agreement. That Agreement, in general terms, governs the presence and operation of U.S. military forces in the Republic of China. The committee is composed of the Chief of Staff USTDC, as U.S. representative, and a Chinese diplomat (ordinarily the Director, North American Affairs Department, Ministry of Foreign Affairs) as the Chinese representative. The Joint Committee meets on call of either representative, not on a fixed schedule. Twelve formal plenary sessions have been held since the Agreement came into force on April 12, 1966. A substantial portion of business is disposed of by Memoranda of Understanding. The decision of this Joint Committee are reported in the form of joint minutes to the respective governments. The substance of agreements deal basically with "housekeeping" matters as distinguished from military operational or planning matters. In the formulation process, decisions or proposals on the U.S. side are staffed within the U.S. military structure as appropriate and, when necessary, with the American Embassy, CINCPAC, JCS, DOD and Department of State as required.

MAJOR U.S. OPERATING FORCES--327TH AIR DIVISION

Within the Pacific Air Forces Command structure, the 327th Air Division is subordinate to Thirteenth Air Force, located at Clark AB, Philippines. The mission of the 327th Air Division is to discharge Air Force responsibilities for the employment and/or service support of Air Force units on or deployed throughout the Taiwan area; to provide logistic and administrative support for military and U.S. government agencies on Taiwan as directed by the Commander, 13th Air Force; to coordinate air operations with the Chinese Air Force; and to maintain assigned airlift capability to provide intratheatre airlift for elements of the Pacific Command.

The Commander of the division has three other major responsibilities. He is designated as Commander of the Taiwan Air Defense sector. As such, he is responsible for Air Defense of Pacific land areas.

[Deleted.]

The Commander is also Chief, Air Force section, MAAG China. This MAAG responsibility necessitates a separate staff which is located at Chinese Air Force Headquarters in Taipei. In this position the Division Commander reports directly to the Chief, MAAG China. Finally, the Commander is designated Air Component Commander for the United States Taiwan Defense Command (TDC).

For the past three fiscal years there has been only minor change in the major USAF units stationed on Taiwan. The 327th Air Division, 314th Tactical Airlift Wing, [deleted.] Task Force and Detachment One of the 405th Fighter Wing have all been in position during this period. The air base groups at CCK and Tainan have also been in existence during this period.

In January 1968, the 4220 Air Refueling Squadron was assigned to CCK.

In November 1968, the mission of the 327th Air Division was expanded when it was assigned the 314th Tactical Airlift Wing. There are attached a summary of mission statements (Annex 8), personnel figures (Annex 6), and operating costs (Annex 5).

In June 1969, Detachment Two of the 405th Fighter Wing was formed at Tainan [deleted.]

Headquarters Support Activity (HSA).--Provides administrative and logistic support to the Headquarters U.S. Taiwan Defense Command, the Military Assistance Advisory Group, Fleet Units and units as designated by the Chief of Naval Operations. Agreements are currently in effect between HSA and the Republic of China that provide for Chinese military drivers for U.S. owned vehicles on a reimbursable basis; Chinese hostel accommodations for military personnel in Taiwan; off-load of U.S. military cargo entering and leaving Taiwan on a reimbursable basis; assignment of 17 Chinese Foreign Affairs policemen to the Provost Marshal's Office; assignment, at no cost to the U.S. Government of a 13-man fire brigade to operate U.S. owned fire fighting equipment.

STRATCOM.--Establish, engineer, install, operate and maintain the Army portion of the Defense Communication System and non-DCS Army facilities as assigned on Taiwan. Sites on Taiwan were established under the provisions of the Status of Forces Agreement between the U.S. and the Government of the Republic of China. Land Use Certificates are on file at COMUSTDC (J-4).

(NAVHOPS) Navy Hospital.--Provides general clinical and hospitalization services for active duty U.S. military personnel, dependents of active duty personnel and other authorized persons as outlined in current directives; and to cooperate with military and civil authorities in matters pertaining to health, sanitation, local disasters and other emergencies. There are no official relationships with the Ministry of National Defense or ROC military units.

Naval Medical Research Unit Number 2 (NAMRU-2).--Conducts basic research in the biomedical sciences, provide essential information on disease and medical problems of military significance, recommend control measures for communicable disease that are endemic or epidemic to specific areas world-wide and, as required, provide training in research techniques. There is no specific relationship with Ministry of National Defense or ROC military units.

Taiwan Field Office (TAIFO).--Negotiates, executes and administers contracts on Taiwan for requirements submitted by USARJ, Director of Procurement and U.S. Forces in Western Pacific. This includes monitoring and contracting for the ROC overhaul program for equipment evacuated from Vietnam. There is no specific relationship with Ministry of National Defense or ROC military units.

Military Sea Transport Service (MSTS).--Exercises local operational control of MSTS vessels and MSTS controlled vessels while in port. Maintain liaison and coordinate with Receiving of Aid and Material, Combined Service Forces of the ROC and the various Harbor Bureaus on berth, tug, and piloting at ports concerned.

Commissary and Stores Office (COMYSTO).--Provides a convenient and reliable source from which authorized patrons may obtain foodstuffs and other authorized items at the lowest practicable costs. The support of all troop messes, clubs and hostels on Taiwan. This includes the procurring, receiving and issuing of subsistence items required in the support of all military dependents, American civilian personnel of all U.S. Government agencies and their dependents on Taiwan. The only direct relationship this activity has with MND or ROC military unit is that key members of all Foreign Embassies and Diplomatic Missions are given commissary privileges.

Taipei Area Office, U.S. Army Engineer District, Okinawa.--Is the construction agency representing all U.S. military forces on Taiwan, with exception of MAAG, Coordinates administrative effort including arrangements for purchase of tax-exempt commodities for locally manufactured items, with Ministry of National Defense.

Personnel strengths, operating costs and foreign exchange expenditures for these activities are at Annex 9.

Pre-Tonkin Gulf Incident Level of U.S. Forces on Taiwan.--Prior to the Tonkin Gulf incident in August, 1964, there were 3,700 U.S. military personnel on Taiwan, including 1,127 TDC and MAAG personnel. The only USAF combat unit on Taiwan prior to that date was the detachment of the 405th Fighter Wing at Tainan Air Base. A support squadron was at Tainan Air Base to service the 405th FW Detachment.

POL Handling Charges and Other Fees Charged U.S. Forces--POL.--Requests for Navy Special and JP 5 delivered as Bunkers into government ships are provided under terms of Contract No. DSA 600-69-D-1621 and into plane AvGas under Contract No. DSA 600-69-D-2450, both issued by the Defense Fuel Supply Center at a single unit price. These contracts do not use a unit price breakdown between basic commodity, services, taxes, or other fees. Direct taxes or fees do not appear to be included.

There are joint U.S.-GRC POL agreements which provide for CAF handling of USAF owned petroleum. Agreements provide for CAF receipt, storage and delivery of USAF owned product to USAF activities on Taiwan and agreements are necessary to provide additional storage plus inter-island distribution of USAF owned fuel from Taiwan ports and terminal storage areas to USAF installations, primarily CCK and Tainan Air Base. USAF pays CAF in fuel rather than dollars (repayment in kind) for this support according to following terms: for all USAF owned fuel input into the CAF system: 0.5% surcharge to cover port handling and input fees (effective since October 1, 1964). For all USAF owned fuel stored in the CAF system: 0.5% surcharge to cover storage fees (effective since October 1, 1964). For all USAF owned fuel delivered into USAF owned equipment and storage tanks by CAF owned or operated pipeline, tank cars, or tank trucks: 2% surcharge to cover transportation and handling fees (effective since January 1, 1967). For all USAF owned fuel issued into U.S. military aircraft by CAF owned equipment: 3.5% surcharge to cover transportation and servicing fees (effective since January 1, 1967).

Above surcharges are jointly computed and reconciled by USAF/CAF once each month and fuel inventories adjusted accordingly. Accounting procedures are adequate to assure proper safeguard and control of government owned fuel as confirmed by a GAO audit completed in September 1969. Actual cost to the U.S. for CAF POL support is nominal. Total monthly repayment in kind equivalent dollar cost is usually in the $15,000-$20,000 range.

Harbor Fees.--No Harbor or Mooring fees are currently assessed against ships of the U.S. Navy operating forces (USS, USNS). We pay no taxes or fees as such. We do pay for services furnished to our ships such as pilot, tug, water, or POL.

Landing Fees.--U.S. military aircraft are not assessed landing fees for use of commercial or military air fields. However, beginning in August 1969, commercial aircraft under contract to the Military Airlift Command (MAC) as Category "B" have paid landing fees of $300 per landing. This has occurred at the rate of about 3 per week since August.

Source: *U.S. Security Agreements and Commitments Abroad*, Volume 1, Part 4, 1969-
               1970. U.S. Government Printing Office, Washington, DC, 1971. pp. 1114-
               1115.

M11
THE SITUATION IN THE TAIWAN STRAIT:
STATEMENT BY PRESIDENT KENNEDY, JUNE 17, 1962

The situation in the area of the Taiwan Strait is a matter of serious concern to this Government.

Very large movements of Chinese Communist forces into this area have taken place. The purpose of these moves is not clear. It seems important in these circumstances that the position of the United States Government be clearly understood.

Our basic position has always been that we are opposed to the use of force in this area. In earlier years, President Eisenhower made repeated efforts to secure the agreement of Communist China to the mutual renunciation of the use of force in the Taiwan area. And our support for this policy continues.

One possibility is that there might be aggressive action against the offshore islands of Matsu and Quemoy. In that event the policy of this country will be that established seven years ago under the Formosa resolution. The United States will take the action necessary to assure the defense of Formosa and the Pescadores.

In the last crisis in the Taiwan area in 1958, President Eisenhowever made it clear that the United States would not remain inactive in the face of any aggressive action against the offshore islands which might threaten Formosa. In my own discussion of this issue, in the campaign of 1960, I made it quite clear that I was in agreement with President Eisenhower's position on this matter. I stated this position very plainly, for example, on October 16, 1960, and I quote:

> "The position of the Administration has been that we would
> defend Quemoy and Matsu if there were an attack which was

part of an attack on Formosa and the Pescadores. I don't want the Chinese Communists to be under any missapprehension.

I support the Administration policy towards Quemoy and Matsu over the last five years."

Under this policy, sustained continuously by the United States Government since 1954, it is clear that any threat to the offshore islands must be judged in relation to its wider meaning for the safety of Formosa and the peace of the area.

Exactly what action would be necessary in the event of any such act of force would depend on the situation as it developed. But there must be no doubt that our policy, specifically including our readiness to take necessary action in the face of force, remains just what it has been on this matter since 1955.

It is important to have it understood that on this point the United States speaks with one voice. But I repeat that the purposes of the United States in this area are peaceful and defensive.

As Secretary Dulles said in 1955, and I quote: "The treaty arrangements which we have with the Republic of China make it quite clear that it is in our mutual contemplation that force shall not be used. The whole character of that treaty is defensive."

This continues to be the character of our whole policy in this area now.

Source: Text in the *New York Times*, June 28, 1962.

M12   CHINA
                      COMBINED MILITARY EXERCISES, 1965

Agreement effected by exchange of letters
Signed at Taipei December 10 and 19, 1964;
Entered into force December 19, 1964.

The American Ambassador to the Chinese Minister of Foreign Affairs

American Embassy,
Taipei, Taiwan,
December 10, 1964.

Dear Mr. Minister:

Combined U.S.-Chinese military exercises to be held in Taiwan during 1965 are now being scheduled by the Taiwan Defense Command and the Ministry of National Defense. In connection with these exercises, it is requested that the Government of the Republic of China extend to the participating United States forces, their members, naval vessels, aircraft, and equipment, to the extent applicable, the same rights, privileges, assistance, immunities, and exemptions as are extended to the Military Assistance Advisory Group, or its members, Republic of China, under the Military Assistance Agreement between the United States and China, concluded by exchange of notes of January 30, 1951 and February 9, 1951, as amended by the Mutual Defense Assistance Agreement, concluded by exchange of notes of October 23, 1952 and November 1, 1952.

In amplification of the above it is also requested that it be understood between our two Governments that each Government agrees to waive all claims aginst the other Government for damages to any property owned by it and used by its land, sea or air armed forces if such damage:

(a)   was caused by a member or an employee of the armed forces of the other Government in the execution of his duties; or

(b)   arose from the use of any vehicle, vessel or aircraft owned by the other Government and used by its armed forces, provided either that the vehicle, vessel or aircraft causing the damage was being used for official purposes, or that the damage was caused to property being so used.

Claims for maritime salvage by one Government against the other Government shall be waived, provided that the vessel or cargo salvaged was owned by one of the Government and being used by its armed forces for official purposes.

Sincerely yours,

JERAULD WRIGHT
Ambassador

His Excellency
SHEN CHANG-HUAN,
Minister of Foreign Affairs
of the Republic of China,
Taipei, Taiwan

The Chinese Acting Minister of Foreign Affairs
to the American Ambassador

Ministry of Foreign Affairs
Republic of China

December 19, 1964

Dear Mr. Ambassador:

Reference is made to your letter of December 10, 1964 addressed to Minister Shen concerning Sino-American combined military exercises to be held in Taiwan during 1965 now being scheduled by the US Taiwan Defense Command and the Ministry of National Defense.

In reply, I wish to signify on behalf of the Government and the Republic of China its concurrence in your request that the same rights, privileges, assistance, immunities, and exemptions extended to the United States Government for the official use of the Military Assistance Advisory Group, Republic of China, or its members, under the Military Assistance Agreement between the United States and China, concluded by exchange of notes on January 30, 1951 and February 9, 1951, as clarified and confirmed by the MAAG Agreement, concluded by exchange of notes of October 23, 1951 and November 1, 1952, will be extended to the United States forces, their members, naval vessels, aircraft, and equipment, participating in the combined military exercises under reference.

I wish also to concur in the understanding that each Government agrees to waive all claims against the other Government for damages to any property owned by it and used by its land, sea or air armed forces if such damage:

(a)   was caused by a member or an employee of the armed forces of the other Government in the execution of his duties; or

(b)   arose from the use of any vehicle, vessel or aircraft owned by the other Government and used by its armed forces, provided either that the vehicle, vessel or aircraft causing the damage was being used for official purposes, or that the damage was caused to property being so used.

Claims for maritime salvage by one Government against the other Government shall be waived, provided that the vessel or cargo salvaged was owned by one of the Government and being used by its armed forces for official purposes.

Sincerely yours,

CHU FU SUNG
Acting Minister of Foreign Affairs

His Excellency
JERAULD WRIGHT,
Ambassador of the United
States of America,
Taipei

Source: *U.S. Treaties and Other International Agreements*, Volume 15, Part 2, 1964, U.S. Government Printing Office, Washington, D.C., 1964, pp. 2390-2392.

M13
REPUBLIC OF CHINA
DEFENSE: STATUS OF UNITED STATES ARMED FORCES IN THE REPUBLIC OF CHINA

Agreement, incorporating agreed minutes,
Signed at Taipei August 31, 1965;
Entered into force April 12, 1966.
With exchanges of notes.

AGREEMENT BETWEEN THE UNITED STATES OF AMERICA AND THE REPUBLIC OF CHINA ON THE STATUS OF UNITED STATES ARMED FORCES IN THE REPUBLIC OF CHINA

Whereas the United States of America and the Republic of China on December 2, 1954, signed a Mutual Defense Treaty[5] which contains in Article VII[6] provisions for the disposition of United States land, air and sea forces in and about Taiwan and Penghu (the Pescadores); and

Whereas, in implementing the aforementioned treaty provisions the United States of America and the Republic of China are desirous of defining the status of such United States armed forces as are now or may be, by mutual agreement, in and about Taiwan and Penghu (the Pescadores) except for the United States Military Assistance Advisory Group, for which status has otherwise been provided;

Therefore the United States of America and the Republic of China have entered into this Agreement in the terms set forth below:

ARTICLE I

1.   In this Agreement, the expression

   (a)   "Agreement Area" means the area in and about Taiwan and Penghu (the Pescadores);

   (b)   "members of the United States armed forces: means the military personnel on active duty belonging to the land, sea or air armed services of the United States of America when in the Agreement Area, except members of the United States Military Assistance Advisory Group;

   (c)   "members of the civilian component," means the civilian personnel who are in the employ of, serving with or accompanying the United States armed forces in the Agreement Area, except members of the United States Miliary Assistance Advisory Group and persons who are nationals of China or who are ordinarily resident in the Agreement Area or who are mentioned in paragraph 1 of Article XII of this Agreement;

(d) "dependents" means (i) spouse, and children under 21, and (ii) children over 21 and close relatives, if dependent for over half of their support upon a member of the armed forces or civilian component.

2. For the purpose of this Agreement, persons with dual United States-Chinese nationality or dual United States and third country nationality, who are brought into the Agreement Area by the United States Government shall be considered as United States nationals. The foregoing shall apply also to dependent children who are dual nationals and who are born in the Agreement Area of parents at least one of whom was brought into the Agreement Area by the United States Government.

ARTICLE II

1. The United States armed forces may conduct all activities and operations necessary for the accomplishment of their mission under the Mutual Defense Treaty of 1954 and shall act in the closest collaboration with the appropriate Chines4e authorities through channels mutually agreed upon.

2. The appropriate Chinese authorities shall cooperate fully with the United States armed forces to facilitate the accomplishment of such mission.

ARTICLE III

1. The Government of the Republic of China undertakes, without prejudice to the minimum requirement of its own military activities and operations, to furnish to the United States, free of charge and without present or future liability, including claims incident to the use thereof, such areas and existing facilities, including utility connections, access roads, water rights, and, subject to mutual agreement, such other rights of use as are required by the United States armed forces for their mission under the Mutual Defense Treaty of 1954. To the extent not already accomplished, the exact location of such areas and facilities shall be determined by the appropriate United States and Chinese authorities through mutual consultation.

2. Expenses involved in the development of such areas and facilities for the exclusive use of the United States armed forces shall be borne by the United States. Where such areas or facilities are, by agreement, to be developed for joint use, the cost of such development shall be shared by the two Governments on the basis of proportionate usage, unless agreed otherwise by the appropriate authorities of the two Governments.

3. The United States armed forces may carry out, through such means as they may adopt, including the use of United States contractors and military construction units, such construction, development, maintenance and improvement as may be required withint the a5reas and facilities made available for their use by the Government of the Republic of China. The Chinese military authorities will be consulted prior to any major alterations in existing buildings, and prior to any new construction or development which may affect military security, public safety or public health in the Agreement Area. It is further agreed that Chinese contractors shalll be used to the maximum practicable extent for such purposes; the decision as to their use is left to the discretion of the United States military authorities.

4.   The cost of maintaining the areas and facilities jointly used by the United States and the Republic of China under this Agreement shall be shared by the two Governments on the basis of proportionate usage, unless otherwise agreed by the appropriate authorities of the two Government.

5.   Military agreements for the implementation of this Article shall be negotiated and signed by the military authorities of the two Governments.

6.   The Government of the United States and the Government of the Republic of China will cooperate in taking such steps as may from time to time be ncesssary to ensure: (a) the security of the United States armed forces, the members thereof and of the civilian component, their dependents, and their property; (b) the security of installations, equipment, property, records, and official information of the United States; and (c) the punishment of offenders under the applicable laws of the Republic of China.

Agreed Minutes to Article III

1.   Within the areas and facilities made available under this Agreement the United States military authorities may designate areas into which only personnel authorized by the local United States Commander may enter.   The United States military authorities will be responsible for the internal security of these areas.

2.   Members of the United States armed forces and civilian component may carry arms while entering, leaving or within the Agreement Area when their official duties require them to do so.   However, they shall observe the pertinent regulations on civil aviation of the Government of the Republic of China.

3.   The Chinese military authorities shall be informed prior to any major alteration in existing buildings, and prior to any new construction or development.   Major alterations to buildings furnished by the Government of the Republic of China shall be accomplished with the consent of Chinese military authorities...

. . .

ARTICLE XIV

1.   Subject to the provisions of this Article,

(a)   the military authorities of the United States shall have the right to exercise with respect to offenses committed within the Agreement Area all criminal and disciplinary jurisdiction conferred on them by the law of the United States over all persons subject to the military law of the United States;

(b)   the authorities of the Republic of China shall have jurisdiction over the members of the United States armed forces or civilian component, and their dependents, with respect to offenses committed withing the Agreement Area and punishable by the law of the Repbulic of China.

2.   (a)   The military authorities of the United States shall have the right to exercise exclusive jurisdiction over persons subject to the military law of the United States with respect to offenses, including offenses relating to its security, punishable by the law of the United States, but not by the law of the Republic of China.

(b)   The authorities of the Republic of China shall have the right to exercise exclusive jurisdiction over members of the United States armed forces or civilian component, and their dependents, with respect to offenses, including offenses relating to the security of the Republic of China, punishable by its law but not by the law of the United States.

(c)   For the purposes of this paragraph and of paragraph 3 of this Article a security offense against a State shall include:

(i)   treason against the State;
(ii)   sabotage, espionage or violation of any law relating to official secrets of that State, or secrets relating to the national defense of that State.

3.   In the cases where the right to exercise jurisdiction is concurrent the following rules shall apply:

(a)   The military authorities of the United States shall have the primary right to exercise jurisdiction over all ersons subject to the military law of the United States, in relation to:

(i)   offenses solely aginst the property or security of the United States, or offenses solely against the person or property of a member of the United States armed forces or civilian component, or a dependent;
(ii)   offenses arising out of any act or omission done in the performance of official duty.

(b)   In the case of any other offense, the authorities of the Republic of China shall have the primary right to exercise jurisdiction.

(c)   If the State having the primary right decides not to exercise jurisdiction, it shall notify the authorities of the other State as soon as practicable. The authorities of the State having the primary right shall give sympathetic consideration to a request from the authorities of the other State for a waiver of its right in cases where that other State considers such waiver to be of particular importance.

4.   The foregoing provisions of this Article shall not imply any right for the military authorities of the United States to exercise jurisdiction over persons who are nationals of or ordinarily resident in the Republic of China, unless they are members of the United States armed forces.

5.   (a)   The appropriate authorities of the United States and the authorities of the Republic of China will undertake, within the limites of their authority, to assist each other in the arrest of members of the United States armed forces or civilian component, and their dependents, in the Agreement Area and in handing them over to the authority which is to have custody in accordance with the provisions of this Article.

(b)   The authorities of the Republic of China shall notify promptly the appropriate authorities of the United States of the arrest of any member of the United States armed forces or civilian component, or a dependent.

(c)   The custody of an accused member of the United States armed forces or civilian component, or a dependent, shall be promptly entrusted to the military authorities of the United States pending conclusion of all judicial proceedings. The United States military authorities will make any member of the United States armed forces or civilian component, and their dependents, over whom the Republic of China is to exercise jurisdiction immediately available to the authorities of the Republic of China upon their request for purpose of investigation and trial.

(d)   The United States military authorities shall notify promptly the authorities of the Republic of China of the arrest of any person subject to the military law of the United States in cases in which the Republic of China has the primary right to exercise jurisdiction.

6.   (a)   The appropriate authorities of the United States and the authorities of the Republic of China shall assist each other in the carrying out of all necessary investigations into offenses, and in the collection and production of evidence, including the seizure and, in proper cases, the handing over of objects connected with an offense. The handing over of such objects may, however, be made subject to their return within the time specified by the authority delivering them.

(b)   The military authorities of the United States and the authorities of the Republic of China shall notify one another of the disposition of all cases in which there are concurrent rights to exercise jurisdiction.

7.   (a)   A death sentence shall not be carried out in the Agreement Area by the military authorities of the United States if the legislation of the Republic of China does not provide for such punishment in a similar case.

(b)   The authorities of the Republic of China shall give sympathetic consideration to a request from the military authorities of the United States for assistance in carrying out a sentence of imprisonment pronounced by the military authorities of the United States under the provisions of this Article within the Agreement Area.

8.   Where an accused person has been tried in accordance with the provisions of this Article either by the military authorities of the United States or by the authorities of the Republic of China and has been acquitted, or has been convicted and is serving, or has served, his sentence, or has had his sentence suspended, or has been pardoned, he may not be tried again for the same offense within the Agreement Area by the authorities of the other State. However, nothing in this paragraph shall prevent the military authorities of the United States from trying a member of its armed forces for any violation of rules of discipline arising from an act or omission which constituted an offense for which he was tried by the authorities of the Republic of China.

9.   Whenever a member of the United States armed forces or civilian component, or a dependent, is prosecuted under the jurisdiction of the Republic of China, he shall be entitled:

(a)   to a prompt and speedy trial;

(b)   to be informed, in advance of trial, of the specific charge or charges made against him;

(c)   to be confronted with the witnesses against him;

(d)   to have compulsory process for obtaining witnesses in his favor, if they are within the jurisdiction of the Republic of China;

(e)   to have legal representation of his own choice for his defense or to have free or assisted legal representation under the conditions prevailing for the time being in the Republic of China;

(f)   if he considers it necessary, to have the service of a competent interpreter; and

(g)   to communicate with a representative of the United States Government, and to have such a representative present at his trial.

10.   (a)   Regularly constitued military units or formation of the United States armed forces shall have the right to police any areas or facilities which they use under Article III of this Agreement. The military policy of such forces may take all appropriate measures to ensure the maintenance of order and security within such areas and facilities.

(b)   Outside these areas and facilities, such military police shall be employed only subject to arrangements with the authorities of the Republic of China and in liaison with those authorities, and insofar as such employment is necessary to maintain discipline and order among the members of the United States armed forces, or ensure their security.

11.   In the event of hostilities the provisions of this Article shall be suspended immediately upon notice given by either Party. In such a case the two Government shall immediately consult with a view to agreeing on suitable provisions to replace the provisions suspended, Pending such agreement the United States military authorities shall have the primary right to exercise jurisdiction over all offenses which may be committed by persons subject to the military law of the United States in the Agreement Area.

ARTICLE XIX

1.   This Agreement shall be approved by the United States and the Republic of China in accordance with their respective constitutional procedures; notes indicating such approval shall be exchanged and this Agreement shall enter into force from the date of the exchange of notes.[3]

2.   The two Governments undertake to seek from their respective legislatures necessary legislative action with respect to any provision of the Agreement which requires such action for its execution.
3.   Either Party may at any time request the revision of any Article of this Agreement, in which case the two Governments shall enter into negotiations through normal diplomatic channels.

ARTICLE XX

This Agreement, and agreed revisions thereof, shall remain in force while the Mutual Defense Treaty between the United States of America and the Republic of China, signed on December 2, 1954, remains in force, unless terminated earlier by agreement between the two Governments.

In Witness Whereof, the undersigned representatives of the two Governments, duly authorized for the purpose, have signed this Agreement.

Done in duplicate, in the English and Chinese languages, both texts authentic, at Taipei, on this 31st day of August of the Year One Thousnad Nine Hundred and Sixty-five, corresponding to the 31st day of the eighth month of the Fifty-fourth Year of the Republic of China.

FOR THE GOVERNMENT OF THE   FOR THE GOVERNMENT OF THE
UNITED STATES OF AMERICA   REPUBLIC OF CHINA

RALPH N. CLOUGH   SHEN CHANG-HUAN

[5]TIAS 3178; 6 UST 433, 437.

[6]Ibid.

[7]April 12, 1966.

Source: *U.S. Treaties and Other International Agreements*, Volume 17, Part I, 1966, U.S. Government Printing Office, Washington, D.C., 1967,   pp. 373-449. (Excerpts).

M14   REPUBLIC OF CHINA

EXTENSION OF LOAN OF VESSELS: U.S.S. BENSON,
U.S.S. HILARY P. JONES, AND U.S.S. PLUNKETT

Agreement effect by exchange of notes
Signed at Taipei June 11 and 18, 1969;
Entered into force June 18, 1969.

The American Ambassador to the Minister of Foreign
Affairs of the Republic of China

No. 9   Taipei, June 11, 1969.

EXCELLENCY:

I have the honor to refer to the Ministry's letter of January 31, 1969 regarding the extensions of the loans of certain naval vessels discussed below.

(1) U.S.S. Benson (DD-421) and U.S.S. Hilary P. Jones (DD-427).

The loans of these two destroyers were made pursuant to the agreement between the Government of the United States of America and the Government of the Republic of China, effected by an exchange of notes signed at Taipei on January 13, 1954, as extended by the exchange of notes signed at Taipei on February 23, 1965.[8] The loans of these two destroyers were shceduled to expire on February 26, 1969.

(2) U.S.S. Plunkett (DD-431).

The loan of this destroyer was made pursuant to the agreement between the Government of the United States of America and the Government of the Republic of China, effected by an exchange of notes signed at Taipei February 7, 1959,[9] as extended by the exchange of notes signed at Taipei on February 23, 1965. The loan of this destroyer was scheduled to expire on February 16, 1969.

I now have the honor to inform Your Excellency that in response to the request of the Government of the Republic of China, the Government of the United States agrees to extend further the loans of the three destroyers in question for an additional period of five years from the original dates of their respective delivery under the same terms and conditions of the agreements pertaining to them referred to above. Accordingly, the new expiration dates for these destroyers will be as follows:

NAME OF VESSEL	NO. OF VESSEL	EXPIRATION DATE
USS Bension	DD-421	February 26, 1974
USS Hilary P. Jones	DD-427	February 26, 1974
USS Plunkett	DD-431	February 16, 1974

If the foregoing is acceptable to the Government of the Republic of China, I have the further honor to propose that Your Excellency's reply to that effect and my note shall constitute an agreement for the extensions of the loans of the three destroyers concerned, which shall enter into force on the date of Your Excellency's reply.

Accept, Excellency, the renewed assurances of my highest consideration.

WALTER P. MCCONAUGHY

His Excellency
WEI TAO-MING
Minister of Foreign Affairs,
Taipei

[8]TIAS 2916, 4340, 5771; 5 UST 207; 10 UST 1819; 16 UST 126.

[9]TIAS 4180: 10 UST 177.

Source: *U.S. Treaties and Other International Agreements*, Volume 22, Part I, 1971, U.S. Government Printing Office, Washington, D.C., 1971, pp. 802-803.

M15   REPUBLIC OF CHINA

EXTENSION OF LOAN OF VESSELS: U.S.S. PECATONICA
AND U.S.S. WHITEMARSH

Agreement effected by exchange of notes
Signed at Taipei May 17 and June 16, 1971;
Entered into force June 16, 1971.

The American Charge d'Affaires ad interim to
the Chinese Minister of Foreign Affairs

No. 12   Taipei, May 17, 1971.

EXCELLENCY:

I have the honor to refer to the Note from the Ministry of Foreign Affairs dated March 21, 1970[10] and to subsequent discussions between representatives of our two Governments regarding the extensions of the loans of the naval vessels ex-USS Pecatonica (AOG-57) and ex-USS Whitemarsh (LSD-8).

The loans of these two vessels were made pursuant to agreements between the Government of the United States and the Government of the Republic of China, effected by the exchange of notes signed on January 18, 1961, the exchange of notes signed on June 8, 1961, the exchange of notes signed on February 7, 1959, and the exchange of notes signed on January 16 and March 6, 1967.[11]

I now have the honor to inform Your Excellency that, in response to the request of the Government of the Republic of China, the Government of the United States agrees to extend the loans of these vessels for an additional period of five years commencing from their respective expiration dates under the same terms and conditions of the agreements pertaining to these vessels referred to above. The five-year extension of the loans of these vessels is in addition to the periods previously agreed as computed from the respective dates of delivery of these vessels. Accordingly, the new expiration dates of these vessels will be as follows:

NAME OF VESSEL	EXPIRATION DATE
ex-USS Whitemarsh (LSD-8)	November 17, 1975
ex-USS Pecatonica (AOG-57)	April 22, 1976

If the foregoing is acceptable to the Government of the Republic of China, I have the honor further to propose that Your Excellency's reply to that effect and my note shall together constitute an agreement between our two Governments regarding this matter, which shall enter into force on the date of Your Excellency's reply.

Accept, Excellency, the renewed assurances of my highest consideration.

WILLIAM N. MORELL, JR.
Charge d'Affaires ad interim

His Excellency,
CHOU SHU-K'AI
Minister of Foreign Affairs,
Taipei.

[10]Not printed.

[11]TIAS 4676, 4828, 4180, 6283; 12 UST 78, 1164; 10 UST 177; 18 UST 1281.

Source: *U.S. Treaties and Other International Agreements*, Volume 22, Part I, 1971,
            U.S. Government Printing Office, Washington, D.C., 1971, pp. 802-803.

M16   REPUBLIC OF CHINA
             MILITARY ASSISTANCE: DEPOSITS UNDER FOREIGN
                         ASSISTANCE ACT OF 1971

Agreement effected by exchange of notes
Signed at Taipei April 18, 1972;
Entered into force April 18, 1972;
Effective February 7, 1972.

                        The American Ambassador to the
                        Chinese Minister of Foreign Affairs

No. 8   Taipei, April 18, 1972.

EXCELLENCY:

I have the honor to refer ro recent discussions regarding the United States Foreign
Assistance Act of 1961, as amended,[12] which includes a provision requiring payment to the
United States Government in New Taiwan Dollars of ten percent of the value of Grant Military
Assistance and Excess Defense Articles provided by the United States to the Government of
the Republic of China.

In accordance with that provision, it is proposed that the Government of the Republic
of China will deposit in an account, subject to withdrawal on demand, at the Central Bank of
China in favor of the United States Government, at a rate of exchange which is not less
favorable to the United States Government than the best legal rate at which United States
dollars are sold by authorized dealers in the country of the Republic of China for New Taiwan
Dollars on the date deposits are made, the following amounts in New Taiwan Dollars:

(A) In the case of any Excess Defense Article given to the Government of the
Republic of China, an amount equal to ten percent of the fair value of that article, as
determined by the United States Government, and

(B) In the case of a Grant of Military Assistance to the Government of the Republic
of China, an amount equal to ten percent of each such grant. The Government of the
Republic of China will be notified quarterly of deliveries of Defense Articles and rendering of
defense services and the values thereof. Deposits to the account of the United States
Government will be due and payable upon request by the United States Government, which
request shall be made, if at all, within one year following the aforesaid notification of deliveries.

No more than US$20 million dollars in New Taiwan Dollars will be required to be deposited for deliveries in any one United States fiscal year.

It is further proposed that the amounts to be deposited may be used to pay all official costs of the United States Government payable in New Taiwan Dollars, including but not limited to all costs relating to the financing of international educational and cultural exchange activities under programs authorized by the United States Mutual Education and Cultural Exchange Act of 1961.[13]

It is finally proposed that Your Excellency's reply stating that the foregoing is acceptable to the Government of the Republic of China shall, together with this note, constitute an agreement between our governments on this subject effective from and after February 7, 1972 and applicable to deliveries of defense articles and rendering of defense services funded or agreed to and delivered or rendered on or subsequent to that date.

Accept, Excellency, the renewed assurance of my highest consideration.

WALTER P. MCCONAUGHY

Enclosure: Section 514 of the Foreign Assistance Act of 1961, as amended.

His Excellency
       CHOW SHU-KAI,
              Minister of Foreign Affairs,
                     Taipei

SECTION 514

(A) Unless provided elsewhere in this section, defense articles may not be given nor a military assistance grant be made to a foreign country unless it agrees:

(1) to deposit in a special account, as established by the Government of the United States, its own currency in the following amount:

(a) for any excess defense article to be given, an amount equivalent to ten percent of the article's fair value, to be determined by the Secretary of State, when the agreement to give the article is made; and
(b) for a military assistance grant, an amount equivalent to ten percent of the grant; and

(2) to permit the Government of the United States to utilize these funds from the special account as determined over time by the President as necessary for payment of all of the official costs of the United States Government payable in the currency of that country, including all costs relating to financing the international educational and cultural exchange programs participated in by that country as authorized by the Mutual Educational and Cultural Exchange Act of 1961.

(B) Any amount of currency of a foreign country which is required to be deposited under Subsection (A)(1) of this Section may be waived by the President if he determines that the Government of the United States will be in a position to pay all its official costs, payable in that currency, enumerated under Subsection (A)(2) without the deposit of such amounts and without the necessity of expending U.S. dollars for the purchase of the currency of that country to pay such costs.

(C) Provisions of this Section do not apply in cases where an excess defense article is given or a military assistance grant is made:

(1) to a foreign country under a bilateral agreement wwhich permits the United States Government to operation a military or other similar base there in exchange for excess article or grant; and
(2) Laos, South Vietnam and Cambodia.

(D) No foreign state will be required under this Section to make deposits in the special account which exceed in the aggregate more than US$20 million in any one year.

[12]86 Stat. 26; 22 U.S.C. 2821 g.

[13]75 Stat. 527; 22 U.S.C. 2451 note.

Source: *U.S. Treaties and Other International Agreements*, Volume 23, Part 1, 1972, U.S. Government Printing Office, Washington, D.C., 1972, pp. 630-633.

M17

PUBLIC LAW 94-457
94TH CONGRESS
OCTOBER 5, 1976

90 Stat. 1938

AN ACT

To approve the sale of certain naval vessels, and for other purposes.

Be it enacted by the Senate and House of Representatives of the United States of America in Congress assembled, That (a) the President may sell, subject to such terms and conditions as he may determine and at a price not less than the value thereof in United States dollars, three destroyers to the Government of Argentina; two landing ships dock and one auxiliary repair dry dock to the Government of the Republic of China; one destroyer to the Government of Colombia; four destroyers to the Government of the Federal Republic of Germany; seven destroyers and two tank landing ships to the Government of Greece; one repair ship and one auxiliary repair dry dock to the Government of Iran; seven destroyers and one landing craft repair ship to the Government of the Republic of Korea; two destroyers to the Government of Pakistan; one landing craft repair ship and one inshore patrol craft to the Government of the Philippines; five destroyers and three tank landing ships to the Government of Spain; one landing craft repair ship, one tank landing ship, and one auxiliary repair dry dock to the Government of Venezuela.

(b) All expenses involved in the sales authorized by this Act shall be charged to funds provided by the recipient government. The authority of the President to sell vessels under this Act shall terminate two years after the date of enactment of this Act.

SEC. 2. Subsection (b)(1) of section 7307 of title 10, United States Code, is amended by striking out "2,000" and inserting in lieu thereof "3,000".

Aproved October 5, 1976.

LEGISLATIVE HISTORY:

HOUSE REPORT No. 94-1646 (Comm. on Armed Services).
SENATE REPORT No. 94-1123 (Comm. on Armed Services).
CONGRESSIONAL RECORD, Vol. 122 (1976):
 Aug. 25, considered and passed Senate.
 Sept. 27, considered and passed House.

Source: *U.S. Statutes at Large, 94th Congress, 2nd Session*, Volume 90. U.S. Government Printing Office, Washington, D.C., p. 1938.

CHAPTER EIGHT

ECONOMIC AND TECHNOLOGICAL

A list of the important economic and technological documents for the period 1949-1978.

1. 1950 U.S. - ROC Air Transport Services Agreement, *U.S. Treaties and Other International Agreements*, Volume 2 - Part I, 1951. U.S. Government Printing Office, Washington, DC, 1952. pp. 421-423.

2. 1955 U.S. - ROC Atomic Energy Agreement: Cooperation for Civil Uses, *U.S. Treaties and Other International Agreements*, Volume 6, Part 2, 1955. U.S. Government Printing Office, Washington, DC, 1956. pp. 2617-2622.

3. 1956 U.S. - ROC Surplus Agricultural Commodities. *U.S. Treaties and Other International Agreements*, Volume 7, Part 3, 1956. U.S. Government Printing Office, Washington, DC 1956. pp. 2843-2849.

4. 1958 U.S. - ROC Development Loan Fund: Use of Chinese Currency Repayments, *U.S. Treaties and Other International Agreements*, Volume 10, Part 1, 1959. U.S. Government Printing Office, Washington, DC, 1959. pp. 16-17.

5. 1962 U.S. - ROC Agricultural Trade Agreement, *U.S. Treaties and Other International Agreements*, Volume 13, Part 1, 1962. U.S. Government Printing office, Washington, DC, 1962. pp. 398-400.

6. 1963 U.S. - ROC Trade in Cotton Textiles, *U.S. Treaties and Other International Agreements*, Volume 14, Part 2, 1963. U.S. Government Printing Office, Washington, DC, 1963. pp. 1741-1753.

7. 1963 U.S. - ROC Investment Guaranties, *U.S. Treaties and Other International Agreements*, Volume 14, Part 2, 1963. U.S. Government Printing Office, Washington, DC, 1963. pp. 2222-2223.

8. 1965 U.S. - ROC Economic and Social Development: Sino-American Fund. *U.S. Treaties and Other International Agreements*, Volume 16, Part 1, 1965. U.S. Government Printing Office, Washington, DC, 1965. pp. 583-595.

9. 1965 U.S. - ROC Economic Aid, *U.S. Treaties and Other International Agreements*, Volume 16, Part 2, 1965. U.S. Government Printing Office, Washington, DC, 1965. pp. 1650-1651.

10. 1971 Trade in Wool and Man-made Fiber Textile Products. *U.S. Treaties and Other International Agreements*, Volume 23, 1972, Part 4. U.S. Government Printing Office, Washington, DC, 1972. pp. 3197-3201.

11. 1975 Trade in Cotton, Wool and Man-made Fiber Textiles. *U.S. Treaties and Other International Agreements*, Volume 26, Part 1, 1975. U.S. Government Printing Office, Washington, DC, 1975. pp. 281-301.

12. Table 4-1. Taiwan's Trade with the United States.

CHINA

AIR TRANSPORT SERVICES

Agreement extending and amending agreement of December 20, 1946.
Effected by exchange of notes dated at Washington December 1 and 19, 1950;
Entered into force December 20, 1950.

The Secretary of State to the Chinese Ambassador

The Secretary of State presents his compliments to his Excellency the Chinese Ambassador and has the honor to refer to the Air Transport Agreement between the two Governments signed on December 20, 1946 and by its terms to continue in force for a period of four years. The United States Government desires to renew the Agreement upon its expiration on December 20, 1950 through the exchange of diplomatic notes as provided for in Article 12. The Department of State understands that such is the desire also of the Chinese Government and in addition that it proposes amending Article 9 of the Agreement to provide, through means other than the International Civil Aviation Organization, an arrangement for the settlement of disputes which cannot be resolved through consultation between the two Governments.

An examination of the Agreement and the route Annex, considered in the light of developments since the Agreement was signed, discloses certain provosions which the United States Government would normally desire to amend in order to modernize the language of the Agreement. It is believed, however, in as much as the Agreement and the Annex in their present form are causing no undue dissatisfaction to either Government, that it would be preferable to minimize amendments to those required to meet immediate circumstances. With respect to the Chinese Government's proposal to amend Article 9, it is hoped that upon reconsideration the Chinese Government will be willing to forego making such a change in view of both Governments' strong desire to utilize agencies of the United Nations Organization for the settlement of disagreements which may arise. It is proposed, therefore, that the Agreement be renewed without change of its present text except to provide that;

a.   The Agreement shall be considered to extend for an indefinite period and subject to the provisions of the termination clause contained in Article 12.

b.   The exercise by United States airlines of traffic rights at Taipei, Taiwan shall continue indefinitely unless otherwise agreed to by the two Governments. The United States carrier presently designated to serve this point is Northwest Airlines.

It is further proposed that, at such time as the implementation of the Chinese mainland routes granted to the United States under the route Annex may become possible, the two Governments will consult with a view to revising the text of the Agreement and Annex to incorporate modern language and provision.

If the Chinese Government concurs in the foregoing it is proposed that the Ambassador's reply in that sense, together with this note, be considered as constituting the exchange of diplomatic notes accomplishing a renewal of the Agreement effective December 20, 1950.

OEC

DEPARTMENT OF STATE,
Washington, December 1, 1950.

The Chinese Ambassador to the Secretary of State

Chinese Embassy
Washington
December 19, 1950

Sir:

I have the honor to acknowledge the receipt of your note of December 1, 1950, concerning the Air Transport Agreement between China and the United States which the United States Government desires to renew upon its expiration on December 20, 1950, through the exchange of diplomatic notes as provided under Article 12. The United States Government has proposed that the Agreement be renewed without change of its present text except to provide that:

a.   The Agreement shall be considered to extend for an indefinite period and subject to the provisions of the termination clause contained in Article 12;

b.   The exercise by United States airlines of traffic rights at Taipeh, Taiwan, shall continue indefinitely unless otherwise agreed to by the two Governments. The United States carrier presently designated to serve this point is Northwest Airlines.

The United States Government also proposes that, at such time as the implementation of the Chinese mainland routes granted to the United States under the route Annex may become possible, the two Governments will consult with a view to revising the text of the Agreement and Annex to incorporate modern language and provisions.

I beg to inform you, pursuant to instructions of my Government, that it concurs in the foregoing proposals. This reply and your note of December 1, 1950, together are considered to constitute an exchange of diplomatic notes consummating the renewal of the Agreement effective from December 20, 1950.

Accept, Sir, the renewed assurances of my highest consideration.

V.K. WELLINGTON KOO

THE HONORABLE DEAN ACHESON,
Secretary of State

Source: *U.S. treaties and Other International Agreements*, Volume 2, Part I, 1951. U.S. Government Printing Office, Washington, DC. pp. 421-423.

E&T2   CHINA
                                  ATOMIC ENERGY

Agreement signed at Washington July 18, 1955;
Entered into forced July 18, 1955.

AGREEMENT FOR COOPERATION BETWEEN THE GOVERNMENT
OF THE UNITED STATES OF AMERICA AND
THE GOVERNMENT OF THE REPUBLIC OF CHINA
CONCERNING CIVIL USES OF ATOMIC ENERGY

Whereas the peaceful uses of atomic energy hold great promise for all mankind; and

Whereas the Government of the United States of America and the Government of the Republic of China desire to cooperate with each other in the development of such peaceful uses of atomic energy; and

Whereas there is well advanced the design and development of several types of research reactors (as defined in Article X of this Agreement); and

Whereas research reactors are useful in the production of research quantities of radioisotopes, in medical therapy and in numerous other research activities and at the same time are a means of affording valuable training and experience in nuclear science and engineering useful in the development of other peaceful uses of atomic energy including civilian nuclear power; and

Whereas the Government of the Republic of China desires to pursue a research and development program looking toward the realization of the peaceful and humanitarian uses of atomic energy and desires to obtain assistance from the Government of the United States of America and United States industry with respect to this program; and

Whereas, the Government of the United States of America, represented by the United States Atomic Energy Commission (hereinafter referred to as the "Commission"), desires to assist the Government of the Republic of China in such a program;

The Parties therefore agree as follows:

ARTICLE I

Subject to the limitations of Article V, the Parties hereto will exchange information in the following fields:

A. Design, construction and operation of research reactors and their use as research, development, and engineering tools and in medical therapy.

B. Health and safety problems related to the operation and use of research reactors.

C. The use of radioactive isotopes in physical and biological research, medical therapy, agriculture, and industry.

ARTICLE II

A. The Commission will lease to the Government of the Republic of China uranium enriched in the isotope U-235, subject to the terms and conditions provided herein, as may be required as initial and replacement fuel in the operation of research reactors which the Government of the Republic of China, in consultation with the Commission, decides to construct and as required in agreed experiments related thereto. Also, the Commission will lease to the Government of the Republic of China uranium enriched in the isotope U-235, subject to the terms and conditions provided herein, as may be required as initial and replacement fuel in the operation of such research reactors as the Government of the Republic of China may, in consultation with the Commission, decide to authorize private individuals or private organizations under its jurisdiction to construct and operate, provided the Government of the Republic of China shall at all times maintain sufficient control of the material and the operation of the reactor to enable the Government of the Republic of China to comply with the provisions of this Agreement and the applicable provisions of the lease arrangement.

B. The quantity of uranium enriched in the isotope U-235 transferred by the Commission and in the custody of the Government of the Republic of China shall not at any time be in excess of six (6) kilograms of contained U-235 in uranium enriched up to a maximum of twenty percent (20%) U-235, plus such additional quantity as, in the opinion of the Commission, is necessary to permit the efficient and continuous operation of the reactor or reactors while replaced fuel elements are radioactively cooling in China or while fuel elements are in transit, it being the intent of the Commission to make possible the maximum usefulness of the six (6) kilograms of said material.

C. When any fuel elements containing U-235 leased by the Commission require replacement, they shall be returned to the Commission and, except as may be agreed, the form and content of the irradiated fuel elements shall not be altered after their removal from the reactor and prior to delivery to the Commission.

D. The lease of uranium enriched in the isotope U-235 under this Article shall be at such charges and on such terms and conditions with respect to shipment and delivery as may be mutually agreed and under the conditions stated in Articles VI and VII.

ARTICLE III

Subject to the availability of supply and as may be mutually agreed, the Commission will sell or lease through such means as it deems appropriate, to the Government of the Republic of China or authorized persons under its jurisdiction such reactor materials, other than special nuclear materials, as are not obtainable on the commercial market and which are required in the construction and operation of research reactors in China. The sale or lease of these materials shall be on such terms as may be agreed.

ARTICLE IV

It is contemplated that, as provided in this Article, private individuals and private organizations in either the United States or China may deal directly with private individuals and private organizations in the other country. Accordingly, with respect to the subjects of agreed exchange of information as provided in Article I, the Government of the United States will permit persons under its jurisdiction to transfer and export materials, including equipment and devices, to, and perform services for, the Government of the Republic of China and such persons under its jurisdiction as are authorized by the Government of the Republic of China to receive and possess such materials and utilize such services, subject to:

A.   Limitations in Article V.

B.   Applicable laws, regulations and license requirements of the Government of the United States, and the Government of the Republic of China.

ARTICLE V

Restricted Data shall not be communicated under this Agreement, and no materials or equipment and devices shall be transferred and no services shall be furnished under this Agreement to the Government of the Republic of China or authorized persons under its jurisdiction if the transfer of any such materials or equipment and devices or the furnishing of any such services involves the communication of Restricted Data.

ARTICLE VI

A. The Government of the Republic of China agrees to maintain such safeguards as are necessary to assure that the uranium enriched in the isotope U-235 leased from the Commission shall be used solely for the purpose agreed in accordance with this Agreement and to assure the safekeeping of this material.

B. The Government of the Republic of China agrees to maintain such safeguards as are necessary to assure that all other reactor materials, including equipment and devices, purchased in the United States under this Agreement by the Government of the Republic of China or authorized persons under its jurisdiction, shall be used solely for the design, construction, and operation of research reactors which the Government of the Republic of China decides to construct and operate and for research in connection therewith, except as may otherwise be agreed.

C. In regard to research reactors constructed pursuant to this Agreement the Government of the Republic of China agrees to maintain records relating to power levels of operation and burn-up of reactor fuels and to make annual reports to the Commission on these subjects. If the Commission requests, the Government of the Republic of China will permit Commission representatives to observe from time to time the condition and use of any leased material and to observe the performance of the reactor in which the material is used.

ARTICLE VII

Guaranties Prescribed by the United States
Atomic Energy Act of 1954

The Government of the Republic of China guarantees that:

A. Safeguards provided in Article VI shall be maintained.

B. No material, including equipment and devices, transferred to the Government of the Republic of China or authorized persons under its jurisdiction, pursuant to this Agreement, by lease, sale, or otherwise will be used for atomic weapons or for research on or development of atomic weapons or for research on or development of atomic weapons or for any other military purposes, and that no such material, including equipment and devices, will be transferred to unauthorized persons or beyond the jurisdiction of the Government of the Republic of China except as the Commission may agree to such transfer to another nation and then only if in the opinion of the Commission such transfer falls within the scope of an agreement for cooperation between the United States and the other nation.

ARTICLE VIII

This Agreement shall enter into force on July 18, 1955 and remain in force until July 17, 1960, inclusively, and shall be subject to renewal as may be mutually agreed.

At the expiration of this Agreement or an extension thereof the Government of the Republic of China shall deliver to the United States all fuel elements containing reactor fuels leased by the Commission and any other fuel material leased by the Commission. Such fuel elements and such fuel materials shall be delivered to the Commission at a site in the United States designated by the Commission at the expense of the Government of the Republic of China, and such delivery shall be made under appropriate safeguards against radiation hazards while in transit.

ARTICLE IX

It is the hope and expectation of the Parties that this initial Agreement for Cooperation will lead to consideration of further cooperation extending to the design, construction, and operation of power producing reactors. Accordingly, the Parties will consult with each other from time to time concerning the feasibility of an additional agreement for cooperation with respect to the production of power from atomic energy in China.

ARTICLE X

For purposes of this Agreement:

A. "Commission" means the United States Atomic Energy Commission or its duly authorized representatives.

B. "Equipment and devices" means any instrument or apparatus, and includes research reactors, as defined herein, and their component parts.

C. "Research reactor" means a reactor which is designed for the production of neutrons and other radiations for general research and development purposes, medical therapy, or training in nuclear science and engineering. The term does not cover power reactors, power demonstration reactors, or reactors designed primarily for the production of special nuclear materials.

D. The terms "Restricted Data," "atomic weapon," and "special nuclear material" are used in this Agreement as defined in the United States Atomic Energy Act of 1954.
IN WITNESS WHEREOF, the Parties hereto have cuased this Agreement to be executed pursuant to duly constituted authority.

DONE at Washington in duplicate this eighteenth day of July, 1955.

FOR THE GOVERNMENT OF THE UNITED STATES OF AMERICA:

WALTER S. ROBERTSON
Assistant Secretary of State for
Far Eastern Affairs

LEWIS L. STRAUSS
Chairman, United States
Atomic Energy Commission

FOR THE GOVERNMENT OF THE REPUBLIC OF CHINA

V. K. WELLINGTON KOO
Ambassador of China

Source: *U.S. Treaties and Other International Agreements*, Volume 6, Part 2, 1955. U.S.
               Government Printing Office, Washington, DC. pp. 2617-2622.

E&T3   CHINA
                                       SURPLUS AGRICULTURAL COMMODITIES

Agreement and exchange of notes
Signed at Taipei August 14, 1956;
Entered into force August 14, 1956.

AGRICULTURAL COMMODITIES AGREEMENT
BETWEEN
THE UNITED STATE OF AMERICA AND THE REPUBLIC OF CHINA
UNDER TITLE I OF
THE AGRICULTURAL TRADE DEVELOPMENT AND ASSISTANCE ACT

        The Government of the United States of America and the Government of the Republic
of China,

        Recognizing the desirability of expanding trade in agricultural commodities between
their two countries and with other friendly nations in a manner which would not displace usual
marketings of the United States in these commodities, or unduly disrupt world prices of
agricultural commodities;

        Considering that the New Taiwan Dollars from such purchases will be utilized in a
manner beneficial to both countries;

        Desiring to set forth the understandings which will govern the sales of surplus
agricultural commodities to the Republic of China pursuant to Title I of the Agricultural Trade
Development and Assistance Act of 1954, as amended, and the measures which the two
governments will take individually and collectively in furthering the expansion of trade in such
commodities;

Have agreed as follows:

ARTICLE I

Sales for New Taiwan Dollars

1. Subject to the issuance and acceptance of the purchase authorizations referred to in paragraph 2 of this Article, the Government of the United States of America undertakes to finance on or before August 31, 1956, the sale for New Taiwan Dollars of certain agricultural commodities determined to be surplus pursuant to the Agricultural Trade Development and Assistance Act of 1954, as amended, to the Government of the Republic of China.

2. The United States Government will issue, within the terms of this Agreement, purchase authorizations which shall include provisions relating to the sale and delivery of commodities, the time and circumstances of deposit of the New Taiwan Dollars accruing from such sales and other relevant matters, and which shall be subject to acceptance by the Government of the Republic of China. Certain commodities and amounts with respect to which tentative agreement has been reached by the two governments are listed in paragraph 3 of this Article.

3. The United States Government undertakes to finance the sale to the Republic of China of the following commodities, in the amounts and approximate quantities indicated, during the United States fiscal year 1956, [should read "1957"], under the terms of Title I of the said Act and of this Agreement.

Commodity	Export Market Value (Millions of United States Dollars)
Cotton (about 30,000 bales)	5.0
Dairy Products (about 5,070 metric tons)	1.5
Tobacco (about 750 metric tons)	1.7
Inedible Tallow (about 4,400 metric tons)	1.0
Ocean Transportation (estimated 50% of cost)	.6
	9.8

ARTICLE II

Uses of New Taiwan Dollars

1. The two governments agree that the New Taiwan Dollars accruing to the United States of America as a consequence of sales made pursuant to this Agreement will be used by the Government of the United States for the following purposes in the amounts shown:

(a)   To help develop new markets for United States agricultural commodities, to finance international educational exchange activities in the Republic of China, and for other United States expenditures in the Republic of China under subsections (a), (f), and (h) of Section 104 of the Act, the New Taiwan Dollars equivalent of US$4.9 million.

(b)   To procure military equipment, materials, facilities and services for the common defense in accordance with sub-section (c) of Section 104 of the Act, the New Taiwan Dollar equivalent of US$4.9 million, subject to supplemental agreement between the two governments.

2. The New Taiwan Dollars accruing under this Agreement shall be expended by the Government of the United States for the purposes stated in paragraph 1 of this Article, in such manner and order or priority as the Government of the United States shall determine.

ARTICLE III

Deposit of New Taiwan Dollars and Rate of Exchange

The deposit of New Taiwan Dollars in payment for the commodities and for ocean freight costs financed by the United States (except excess costs resulting from the requirement that United States flag vessels be used) shall be made at the rate of exchange for United States dollars generally applicable to import transactions (excluding imports granted a preferential rate) in effect on the date of United States dollar disbursement by United States banks or by the United States as provided in the purchase authorizations.

ARTICLE IV

General Undertakings

1. The Government of the Republic of China agrees that it will take all possible measures to prevent the resale or transshipment to other countries or use for other than domestic purposes (except where such resale, transshipment or use is specifically approved by the Government of the United States) of surplus agricultural commodities purchased pursuant to the provisions of the Agricultural Trade Development and Assistance Act of 1954, as amended, and to assure that its purchase of such commodities does not result in increased avilability of those or like commodities to nations unfriendly to the United States.

2. The two governments agree that they will take reasonable precautions to assure that all sales of surplus agricultural commodities pursuant to the Agricultural Trade Development and Assistance Act of 1954 will not unduly distupt world prices of agricultural commodities, or materially impair trade relations among the countries of the free world.

3. In carrying out this Agreement that two governments will seek to assure conditions of commerce permitting private traders to function effectively and will use their best endeavours to develop and expand continusou market demand for agricultural commodities.

4. The Government of the Republic of China agrees to furnish, upon request of the Government of the United States, information on the progress of the program, particularly with respect to arrivals and condition of commodities and the provisioins for the maintenance of usual marketings, and information relating to exports of the same and like commodities.

ARTICLE V

Consultation

The two governments will, upon the request of either of them, consult regarding any matter relating to the application of this Agreement or to the operation of arrangements carried out pursuant to this Agreement.

This Agreement shall enter into force upon signature.

IN WITNESS WHEREOF, the respective representatives, duly authorized for the purpose, have signed the present Agreement.

DONE in duplicate, in the English and Chinese languages, at Taipei, this Fourteenth day of August, 1956, corresponding to the Fourteenth day of the Eighth month of the Forty-Fifth year of the Republic of China.

FOR THE UNITED STATES OF AMERICA: FOR THE REPUBLIC OF CHINA:

K. L. RANKIN   SHEN CHANG-HUAN

Source: *U.S. Treaties and Other International Agreements*, Volume 7, Part 3, 1956. U.S. Government Printing Office, Washington, DC, 1956. pp. 2843-2849.

E&T4   **CHINA**
                           DEVELOPMENT LOAN FUND: USE OF CHINESE
                                       CURRENCY REPAYMENTS

Agreement effected by exchange of notes
Dated at Taipei December 24, 1958;
Entered into force December 24, 1958.

The American Embassy to the Chinese
Ministry of Foreign Affairs

No. 9

The Embassy of the United States of America presents its compliments to the Ministry of Foreign Affairs of the Republic of China and has the honor to request the concurrence of the Government of the Republic of China in the following understanding in regard to currency of China paid to the Development Loan Fund:

The Government of the Republic of China agrees that any currency of China paid to the Development Loan Fund, an agency of the Government of the United States of America, pursuant to any transaction entered into by the Development Loan Fund under the authority provided in the Mutual Security Act of 1954 as it is or may hereafter from time to time be amended,[1] shall be recognized as property of the Development Loan Fund. The Government of the Republic of China further agrees that such currency may be used by the Development Loan Fund or by any agency of the Government of the United States of America for any expenditures of or payments by the Development Loan Fund or any such agency, including any expenditures of or payments by the development Loan Fund for purposes of transactions authorized by the Mutual Security Act of 1954, as it is or may hereafter from time to time be amended. Unless agreed to in advance by the Government of the Republic of China, such currency shall not be used by the Development Loan Fund or any other agency of the

Government of the United States to finance exports from China or its territories nor shall it be sold for other currencies to entities other than agencies of the Government of the United States. The Government of the United States agrees that it and the Development Loan Fund will take into account the economic position of China in any contemplated use of currency of China received by the Development Loan Fund.

JY

EMBASSY OF THE UNITED STATES OF AMERICA,
Taipei, December 24, 1958.

---

[1] 68 Stat. 832; 71 Stat. 357; 22 U.S.C. 1751, 1871-1876.

Source: *U.S. Treaties and Other International Agreements*, Volume 10, Part 1, 1959.
                 U.S. Government Printing Office, Washington, DC, 1959. pp. 16-17.

E&T5   REPUBLIC OF CHINA

AGRICULTURAL TRADE

Agreement signed at Washington April 16, 1962;
Entered into force April 16, 1962.

AGRICULTRUAL TRADE AGREEMENT BETWEEN THE
GOVERNMENT OF THE UNITED STATES OF AMERICA AND
THE GOVERNMENT OF THE REPUBLIC OF CHINA

The Government of the United States of America and the Government of the Republic of China,

Recognizing the desirability of expanding trade in agricultural commodities between their two countries;

Considering an announcement by the Department of Agriculture of the Government of the United States of America on February 12, 1962, relating to the exchange of raw sugar import allocations for purchases of United States agricultural commodities and a proposal relating to that announcement submitted by the Government of the Republic of China through the Taiwan Sugar Corporation, New York City, dated March 8, 1962;

Desiring to set forth the understandings reached in conversations between representatives of their two Governments and the measures which the two Governments will take individually and collectively in furthering the expansion of trade in such commodities;

Have agreed as follows:

ARTICLE I

1. The Government of the United States of America will authorize the importation into the United States of America of 29,000 short tons of raw non-quota sugar from the Republic of China during the period from the date of entry into force of this agreement through June 30, 1962. The Government of China assures the Government of the United States of America that this quantity of raw sugar is available for shipment to the United States of America and will make necessary arrangements for its delivery to continental ports of the United States of America on or before June 30, 1962.

2. The Government of the Republic of China will purchase, or cause to be purchased, 29,000 bales (500 pounds equivalent) of cotton and 333,000 pounds of 1961 or earlier crop flue cured tobacco through normal trade channels within the United States of America for importation by the Republic of China during the period January 1, 1962 through December 31, 1962.

3. The Government of the Republic of China assures the Government of the United States of America that the tobacco purchased by the Republic of China pursuant to paragraph 2 above shall be over and above usual commercial imports from the United States of America of a minimum of $800,000 worth of tabacco and from free world sources (including the United States of America) of a minimum of $1,000,000 worth of tobacco and from free world sources (including the United States of America) of a minimum of $1,000,000 worth of tobacco during the period July 1, 1961 through June 30, 1962 and further assures that such purchases will not result in any reduction of usual commercial imports from the United States of America (of tobacco) and from free world sources (of tobacco and cotton) during the period July 1, 1962 through June 30, 1963.

4. The cotton and tobacco specified in paragraph 2 above and any increase in such quantity of cotton that may be made pursuant to Article II of this agreement shall be in addition to any cotton and tobacco purchased by the Republic of China under Section 303 of United States Public Law 480^I (barter for strategic materials), the Commodity Credit Corporation's credit sales program, or other programs involving financing of the purchase of such commodities by the Government of the United States of America (including quantities of cotton purchased by the Republic of China to replace the cotton content of textiles exported by the Republic of China as required under surplus agricultural commodity agreements between the two Governments authorized by Public Law 480).

5. The Republic of China will not export any cotton in calendar years 1962 and 1963.

6. The cotton and tobacco imported by the Republic of China pursuant to this agreement will be consumed in the Republic of China.

ARTICLE II

If the Government of the United States of America should authorize importation of raw non-quota sugar from the Republic of China during the period from the date of entry into force of this agreement through June 30, 1962 in addition to the 29,000 short tons stipulated in Artile I of this agreement and any raw sugar authorized prior thereto, the Government of the Republic of China agrees that it will purchase, or cause to be purchased, additional cotton through normal trade channels within the United States of America for importation by the Republic of China from January 1, 1962 through December 31, 1962 at the rate of 1,000 bales (500 pounds equivalent) of cotton for each 1,000 short ton increase in raw sugar import authorization.

ARTICLE III

The Government of the Republic of China will furnish, upon the request of the Government of the United States of America, information on the progress of the program, particularly, with respect to the purchase and arrival of the cotton and tobacco, the provision for the maintenance of usual commercial imports and information relating to the exports of same or like commodities.

ARTICLE IV

The two Governments will, upon request of either of them, consult regarding any matter relating to the application of this agreement or to the operation of arrangements entered into pursuant to this agreement.

ARTICLE V

This agreement shall enter into force upon signature.

IN WITHNESS WHEREOF, the respective representatives, duly authorized for the purpose, have signed the present Agreement.

DONE at Washington this sixteenth day of April, 1962.

FOR THE GOVERNMENT OF THE UNITED STATES OF AMERICA:

PHILIP H. TREZISE

FOR THE GOVERNMENT OF THE REPUBLIC OF CHINA

SANDYS BAO

---

[1] 68 Stat. 459; 7 U.S.C. 1692.

Source: U.S. Treaties and Other International Agreements, Volume 13, Part 1, 1962. U.S. Government Printing Office, Washington, DC, 1062. pp. 398-400.

E&T6   CHINA

TRADE IN COTTON TEXTILES

Agreement effected by exchange of notes
Signed at Taipei October 19, 1963;
Entered into force October 19, 1963.
With exchange of letters
Signed at Taipei October 21, 1963.

The American Ambassador the the
Chinese Minister of Foreign Affairs

No. 36   Taipei, October 19, 1963.

EXCELLENCY:

I have the honor to refer to recent discussions in Taipei between representatives of the Government of the United States of America and the Government of the Republic of China concerning exports of cotton textiles from the Republic of China to the United States.

As a result of these discussions, I have the honor to propose the following agreement relating to trade in cotton textiles between the Republic of China and the United States:

(1) The Government of the Republic of China shall limit its exports to the United States in all categories of cotton textiles for the twelve-month period beginning October 1, 1963 to an aggregate limit of 53 million square years equivalent.

(2) Within this overall ceiling, the following group ceilings shall apply:

(a)	Apparel categories (Categories 39-63)	19.7 million syds.
(b)	All other categories (Categories 1-38 and 64)	33.3 million syds.

If these proposals are acceptable to the Government of the Republic of China, this note and Your Excellency's note of acceptance on behalf of the Government of the Republic of China shall constitute an agreement between our Governments.

Accept, Excellency, the renewed assurances of my highest consideration.

JERAULD WRIGHT

His Excellency
SHEN CHANG-HUAN
Minister of Foreign Affairs, Taipei.

The Chinese Minister of Foreign Affairs
to the American Ambassadory

Ministry of Foreign Affairs
Republic of China

Source: *U.S. Treaties and Other International Agreements*, Volume 14, Part 2, 1963.
               U.S. Government Printing Office, Washington, DC, 1963. pp. 1741-1753.

E&T7   CHINA

                        INVESTMENT GUARANTIES

Agreement relating to the agreement of June 25, 1952, as amended.
Effected by exchange of notes
Signed at Taipei December 30, 1963;
Entered into force December 30, 1963.

                   The American Ambassdor to the
                   Chinese Minister of Foreign Affairs

No. 42   Taipei, December 30, 1963.

EXCELLENCY:

      I have the honor to refer to the Agreement effected by the exchange of notes of June
25, 1952[1] as amended by the agreement effected by the exchange of notes of May 3, 1957,[2]
between our two Governments relating to investment guaranties which may be issued by the
Government of the United States of America for American investments in activities in Taiwan.
After the conclusion of these Agreements, legislation has been enacted in the United States of
America modifying and augmenting the coverage to be provided investors by investment
guaranties that may be issued by the Government of the United States of America.

      In the interest of facilitating and increasing the participation of private enterprise in
furthering economic development in Taiwan, the Government of the United States of America
is prepared to issue investment guaranties providing such coverage as may be authorized by the
applicable United States legislation for appropriate investments in activities approved by your
Government provided that your Government agrees that the undertakings betwen our respective
Governments contained in Agreement effected by the exchange of notes on June 25, 1952 will
be applicable to such guaranties including, but not limited to, those issued under the Mutual
Security Act of 1954,[3] as amended, and the Act for International Development of 1961,[4] as
amended.

      I have the honor to propose further that the above-mentioned Agreement effected by
exchange of notes of May 3, 1957 will terminate upon the entry into force of the present
Agreement.

Upon receipt of a note from Your Excellency indicating that the foregoing is acceptable to the Government of the Republic of China and that such undertakings shall apply, the Government of the United States of America will consider that this note and your reply thereto constitute an Agreement between our two Governments on this subject, the Agreement to enter into force on the date of your note in reply.

Accept, Excellency, the renewed assurances of my highest consideration.

JERAULD WRIGHT

His Excellency
     SHEN CHANG-HUAN
          Minister of Foreign Affairs,
               Taipei.

---

[1] TIAS 2657; 3 UST (pt. 4) 4846.

[2] TIAS 3831; 8 UST 753.

[3] 68 Stat. 846; 22 U.S.C. 1933, 1958 ed.

[4] 75 Stat. 429; 22 U.S.C. 2181 et seq.

Source: *U.S. Treaties and Other International Agreements*, Volume 14, Part 2, 1963.
           U.S. Government Printing Office, Washington, DC, 1963. pp. 2222-2223.

E&T8   CHINA

                    ECONOMIC AND SOCIAL DEVELOPMENT:
                         SINO-AMERICAN FUND

Agreement effected by exchange of notes
Signed at Taipei April 9, 1965;
Date of entry into force July 1, 1965.

                    The American Ambassador to the
                    Chinese Minister of Foreign Affairs

No. 60   Taipei, April 9, 1965.

EXCELLENCY:

     I have the honor to refer to the Economic Aid Agreement between the Government of the United States of America and the Government of the Republic of China, dated July 3, 1948,[1] as amended, and to the exchange of notes dated August 5, 1948,[2] as amended, providing for the establishment of a Sino-American Joint Commission on Rural Reconstruction. I refer also to discussions which have recently taken place between representatives of our two Governments concerning arrangements with respect to the utilization of the New Taiwan dollars generated as a consequence of assistance furnished by the Government of the United States of America to the Government of the Republic of China.

Article V of the Economic Aid Agreement stipulates, following the provisions on specific uses of such funds, that the balance thereof shall be disposed of by the Government of the Republic of China only for such purposes as may be agreed upon from time to time with the Government of the United States of America. The Government of the United States of America has heretofore expressed its agreement in this regard through the United States Aid Mission to China. With the closing of that Mission on June 30, 1965, I have the honor to propose that the remaining balances of such funds held by the Government of the Republic of China as of July 1, 1965, and all such funds to be received thereafter, be transferred to and consolidated in a single fund to be designed the Sino-American Fund for Economic and Social Development (hereinafter called "Sino-American Development Fund") and to be made available for the economic and social development of the Republic of China in accordance with the arrangements set forth hereunder. In consideration of these arrangements, no further approval by the Government of the United States of America with respect to the use of these funds will be required after July 1, 1965...

...Upon receipt of a note from your Excellency confirming the foregoing and indicating that the arrangements et forth herein are acceptable to the Government of the Republic of China, the Government of the United States of America will consider that this note and your Excellency's reply constitute an agreement by our two Governments concerning the disposition of the New Taiwan dollars generated as a consequence of assistance furnished under the Economic Aid Agreement, in pursuance of Article V Paragraph 5 thereof, to be effective from July 1, 1965 through June 30, 1970. These arrangements will be reviewed by our two Governments on or about July 1, 1970, or at any earlier time on thirty days notice by either Government.

Accept, Excellency, the renewed assurances of my highest consideration.

JERAULD WRIGHT

His Excellency
SHEN CHANG-HUAN,
Minister of Foreign Affairs
Taipei.

---

[1] TIAS 1837, 1848; 62 Stat. (pt. 3) 2945, 3139.

[2] Ibid.

Source: *U.S. Treaties and Other International Agreements*, Volume 16, Part 1, 1965. U.S. Government Printing Office, Washington, DC, 1965. pp. 583-595.

E&T9   CHINA

                                  ECONOMIC AID

Agreement amending the agreement of July 3, 1948, amended.
Effected by exchange of notes
Signed at Taipei August 11, 1965;
Entered into force August 11, 1965; effective August 26, 1954.
With related notes.

                   The American Charge d'Affaires ad interim to
                        the Chinese Minister of Foreign Affairs

No. 2   Taipei, August 11, 1965.

EXCELLENCY:

        I have the honor to refer to recent conversations between representatives of our two
Governments concerning the Economic Aid Agreement between the Government of the United
States of America and the Government of the Republic of China signed at Nanking on July 3,
1948, as amended,[1] and to propose that the Agreement, as amended, be further amended as
follows:

        1. For subparagraph 2(c) of Article V substitute the following:

        "The amount of currency of the Government of the Republic of China equivalent to
the proceeds accruing to the Government of the Republic of China from the import or sale of
commodities or services furnished to the Government of the Republic of China on a grant basis
under this Agreement. The Government of the Republic of China shall deposit such amounts
of Chinese currency, as mentioned above, promptly into the special account and may at any
time make advance deposits in the account which shall be applied against subsequent deposit
obligations."

        2. In paragraph 3 of Article V substitute "Chinese currency" for "administrative
expenditures in Chinese currency within China incident to operations under the China Aid Act
of 1948."[2]

        3. Delete paragraph 6 of Article V and renumber paragraph 7 thereof as paragraph
6.

        4. Wherever reference is made in the Economic Aid Agreement of July 3, 1948, as
amended, to the China Aid Act of 1948, such reference shall, as appropriate, be deemed to
include also the Mutual Security Act of 1954,[3] as amended, and the Foreign Assistance Act of
1961,[4].

        5. For paragraph 7 of Article V substitute the following:

        "Any unencumbered balances of funds which, upon termination of assistance to the
Government of the Republic of China under the Mutual Security Act of 1951,[5] Mutual Security
Act of 1954, Foreign Assistance Act of 1961, or any act amendatory of supplementary thereto,
remain in or payable into the special account or any similar account representing counterpart
of proceeds of assistance hereunder shall be disposed of for such purposes as may be agreed

upon by the Governments of the United States of American and of the Republic of China, it being understood that the agreement of the United States shall be subject to approval by Act of the Congress of the United States."

I have also the honor to propose that, if the foregoing proposals are acceptable to the Government of the Republic of China, this note and your Excellency's reply to that effect shall constitute an agreement between our Governments which shall enter into force on the date of your note and shall be deemed to be effective as of August 26, 1954, the date of the enactment of the Mutual Security Act of 1954.

Accept, Excellency, the renewed assurances of my highest consideration.

RALPH N.CLOUGH
Charge d'Affaires ad interim

His Excellency
SHEN CHANG-HUAN
Minister of Foreign Affairs.
Taipei.

---

[1] TIAS 1837, 1923, 3077; 62 Stat. (pt. 3) 2945; 63 Stat. (pt. 3) 2425; 5 UST (pt. 3) 2154.

[2] 62 Stat. 158; 22 U.S.C. 1541 note.

[3] 68 Stat. 832; 22 U.S.C. 1751 note.

[4] 75 Stat. 424; 22 U.S.C. 2151 note.

[5] 65 Stat. 373; 22 U.S.C. 1651 note.

Source: *U.S. Treaties and Other International Agreements*, Volume 23, Part 4, 1972. U.S. Government Printing Office, Washington, DC, p. 1650.

E&T10   **REPUBLIC OF CHINA**

TRADE IN WOOL AND MAN-MADE FIBER TEXTILE PRODUCTS

Agreement effected by exchange of notes
Signed at Washington December 30, 1971;
Entered into force December 30, 1971;
Effective October 1, 1971.
And amending agreements
Effected by exchange of notes
Signed at Washington September 20, 1972;
Entered into force September 20, 1972.
And exchange of notes
Signed at Washington November 16, 1972;
Entered into force November 16, 1972.

The American Ambassador at Large to the Chinese
Director General, Board of Foreign Trade

DEPARTMENT OF STATE
WASHINGTON

December 30, 1971

EXCELLENCY:

I refer to recent discussions between our two governments concerning exports of wool and man-made fiber textile products from the Republic of China to the United States of America. As a result of those discussions, I propose the following Agreement.

1. The Republic of China shall limit exports of wool and man-made fiber textile products to the United States of America for the five agreement years beginning October 1, 1971, and extending through September 30, 1976, to the annual aggregate, group and specific limits set forth in Annex A, and in accordance with the provisions of this Agreement.

2.   (a) Within the applicable aggregate and group limits shown in Annex A [not included here], for wool and man-made fiber textiles, the following specific limits shall apply for the first agreement year.

Wool Textile Products

Category	Millions Square Yards Equivalent
116	1.6
117	1.0

Man-made Fiber Textile Products

Category	Millions Square Yards Equivalent
211	5.0
213	50.0
216	25.0
219	78.0
221	110.0
222	50.0
228	5.0
232	25.0
234	20.0
235	32.0

(b) Within the annual aggregate and group limits set forth in Annex A, the specific limits set forth in (a) of this paragraph for man-made fiber textile products shall be increased over the preceding agreement year by 9.5 percent and 9 percent for the second and third agreement years respectively. During the third year, the two governments shall consult to determine the growth rates appropriate for man-made fiber textiles to distribute between the fourth and fifth year the balance remaining of the five-year aggregate limit shown in Annex A after deduction of the aggregate limits provided for the first three years. The growth rates determined in such consultations shall also be applied to the group and specific limits provided for herein.

(c) The specific limits for wool textile products set forth in (a) of this paragraph shall be increased beginning with the second agreement year by 1 percent for each agreement year over the preceding agreement year.

3. The following procedures shall apply during each agreement year with respect to all exports in that year in each category of man-made fiber and wool textile products not subject to a specific limit under paragraph 2 above:

(a) By August 15 of each agreement year the two Governments shall consult regarding anticipated exports in each such category during the succeeding agreement years. The Government of the Republic of China, in such consultations, shall notify the Government of the United States of America of its anticipated exports by category. Following receipt of such notice, the Government of the United States of America shall have 30 days in which to request consultations with respect to any category.

(b) When the Government of the United States of America requests consultations, the Government of the Republic of China shall meet promptly with the Government of the United States of Amercia to work out a mutually satisfactory solution to such problems as may exist with respect to the anticipated exports referred to under (a) of this paragraph. The consultations shall be concluded within 30 days, unless the two governments agree otherwise. In the event that such consultations do not result in a mutually acceptable solution, the Government of the Republic of China shall limit its exports in any category in question during the agreement year in question to the level requested by the Government of the United States of America at the conclusion of such consultations.

(c) If no consultations are requested by the Government of the United States of America, the Government of the Republic of China shall not permit exports to exceed the level stated by the Government of the Republic of China under (a) of this paragraph without the specific concurrence of the Government of the United States of America to such additional exports. The Government of the Republic of China may request such agreement at any time it believes appropriate. The Government of the United States of America shall give due consideration to such request and shall respond promptly thereto.

4. The Following shall be applied separately to the wool textile aggregate, group and specific limits and to the man-made fiber textile aggregate, group and specific limits:

(a) For any agreement year subsequent to the first agreement year and immediately following a year of a shortfall (i.e., a year in which textile exports from the Republic of China were below the aggregate limit and any group and specific limits applicable to the category concerned) the Government of the Republic of China may permit exports to exceed these limits by carryover in the following amounts and manner:

(i) The carryover shall not exceed the amount of shortfall in either the aggregate limit or any applicable group or specific limit and shall not exceed either five percent of the aggregate limit or five percent of the applicable group limit in the year of the shortfall, and

(ii) in the case of shortfalls in the categories subject to specific limits the carryover shall be used in the same category in which the shortfall occurred, and shall not exceed five percent of the specific limit in the year of the shortfall, and

(iii) in the case of shortfalls not attributable to categories subject to specific limits, the carryover shall be used in the same group in which the shortfall occurred and shall not be used to exceed any applicable specific limit except in accordance with the provisions of paragraph 7 and shall be subject to the provisions of paragraph 3 of this Agreement.

(b) The limits referred to in subparagraph (a) of this paragraph are without any adjustments under this paragraph or paragraphs 5, 6, or 7.

(c) The carryover shall be in addition to the exports permitted in paragraphs 5, 6, and 7 of this Agreement.

5. In addition to the amounts provided for under paragraphs 2 and 4, aggregate exports of man-made fiber textiles may be increased by an amount equal to 5 percent of the aggregate limit, and within that amount, exports in any group or category may be exceeded by 5 percent of the applicable group and category limits, provided that exports under the bilateral cotton textile agreement for the corresponding year ending December 31, are below the aggregate limit and the comparable group and category limits established therein by an equivalent square yard amount. In applying this paragraph only, the maximum allowable exports under the bilateral cotton textile agreement shall be deemed the "limits."

6. Within the applicable aggregate limits, as they may be adjusted under paragraphs 4 and 5, exports in the apparel groups for man-made fiber textiles and for wool textiles may exceed the applicable group limits as adjusted pursuant to paragraph 5 by 5 percent of such adjusted limits in each year and exports in the other groups may exceed the group limits applicable thereto as adjusted pursuant to paragraph 5 by 10 percent.

7. Within the applicable aggregate and group limits as adjusted pursuant to paragraphs 4, 5, and 6, exports in any category given a specific limit may exceed that limit by not more than 5 percent in addition to the amount authorized under paragraph 4; provided, however, that the total of exports authorized for any category under this paragraph and paragraph 5 shall not exceed 5 percent of the unadjusted category limit for the year in question.

8. The Government of the Republic of China shall use its best efforts to space exports to the United States of America as evenly as practicable taking into account seasonal factors.

9. If the Government of the Republic of China considers that as a result of limits specified in this Agreement the Republic of China is being placed in an inequitable position vis-a-vis a third country, the Government of the Republic of China may request consultations with a view to taking appropriate remedial action such as a reasonable modification of this Agreement.

10. Each government agrees to supply promptly any relevant available statistical data requested by the other government. In particular, the governments agree to exchange monthly data on exports and imports of wool and man-made fiber textiles from the Republic of China to the United States of America.

11.   (a) For the purpose of this Agreement the schedules of categories and conversion factors attached hereto as Annex B [not included here] shall apply.

(b)   (i) Any textile product which is wholly or in part of wool and/or man-made fiber, but is not in chief value cotton, shall be subject to the terms of this Agreement.

(ii) For purpose of this Agreement a product covered under (b) (i) shall be treated as a wool textile product if in chief value wool or if, (a) it is 17 percent or more by weight of wool, or, (b) the weight of the wool component is not less than the weight of the man-made fiber content, or (c) the product contains no man-made fiber. All other textile products provided for under (b) (i) shall be considered man-made fiber textile products.

(c) Both governments agree to take such measures as may be appropriate to prevent the evasion of this Agreement by substitution, transshipment, or other means.

12.   (a) The governments agree to consult on any question arising in the implementation of this Agreement. Mutually satisfactory administrative arrangements or adjustments may be made to resolve minor problems arising in the implementation of this Agreement including differences in points of procedure or operation.

(b) Experts of the two governments shall meet to consider hardship situations which may exist at the outset of the present Agreement. The experts may make recommendations to the two governments for appropriate solutions. In considering these situations, conditions in both countries shall be taken into account.

13. The Government of the Republic of China shall administer its export control system under this Agreement. The Government of the United States of America may assist the Government of the Republic of China in implementing the limitations of this Agreement.

14. A Schedule of handicraft and art articles which shall be exempt from the limitations of this Agreement shall be developed by the two governments and incorporated into this Agreement as Annex C.

15. Either government may terminate this Agreement effective at the end of an agreement year by written notice to the other government to be given at least 90 days prior to the end of such agreement year. Either government may at any time propose revisions in the terms of this Agreement.

If this proposal is acceptable to the Government of the Republic of China, this note and your note of confirmation on behalf of the Government of the Republic of China shall constitute an Agreement between the Government of the United States of America and the Government of the Republic of China.

Accept, Excellency, the assurances of my highest consideration.

For the Secretary of State:
DAVID M. KENNEDY
Ambassador at Large
of the United States of America

His Excellency
    Y. T. WONG
        Director General,
           Board of Foreign Trade,
           Republic of China.

Source: *U.S. Treaties and Other International Agreements*, Volume 23, Part 4, 1972. U.S. Government Printing Office, Washington, DC. pp. 3197-3201.

ET11   REPUBLIC OF CHINA

TRADE IN COTTON, WOOL AND MAN-MADE FIBER TEXTILES

**Agreement effected by exchange of notes
Signed at Washington May 21, 1975;
Entered into force May 21, 1975;
Effective January 1, 1975.**

The Secretary of State to the Chinese Ambassador

Department of State
Washington

May 21, 1975

EXCELLENCY:

I refer to the Arrangement Regarding International Trade in Textiles done at Geneva on December 20, 1973,[1] hereinafter referred to as the Arrangement. I also refer to recent discussions between Representatives of our two Governments concerning exports of cotton, wool and man-made fiber textiles and textile products from the Republic of China to the United States. As a result of those discussions, I wish to propose the following agreement relating to trade in cotton, wool, and man-made fiber textiles and apparel products between the Republic of China and the United States, to replace and supersede, effective Janaury 1, 1975, the existing Cotton Textile[2] and Wool and Man-Made Fiber Textile Agreements of December 30, 1971, as amended.[3]

1. The term of this Agreement shall be from January 1, 1975 through December 31, 1977. During such term, the Government of the Republic of China will limit annual exports of cotton, wool and man-made fiber textiles and textile products from the Republic of China to the United States to aggregate, group, and specific limits at the levels specified in the following paragraphs...

His Excellency
JAMES C.H. SHEN,
    Ambassador of Republic of China.

If this proposal is acceptable to the Government of the Republic of China, this note and your note of confirmation on behalf of the Government of the Republic of China shall constitute an Agreement between the Government of the Republic of China and the Government of the United States of America.

Accept, Excellency, the renewed assurances of my highest consideration.

For the Secretary of State:

JULIUS L. KATZ

The Chinese Ambassador to the Secretary of State

Embassy of the Republic of China
Washington, DC 20008

May 21, 1975

EXCELLENCY:

I have the honor to acknowledge receipt of Your Excellency's note of today's date, containing a proposed agreement on the exports of cotton, wool, and man-made fiber textiles from the Republic of China to the United States of America, to replace and supersede, effective January 1, 1975, the existing Cotton Textile and Wool and Man-Made Fiber Textile Agreements signed on December 30, 1971, as amended.

I wish to confirm, pursuant to instructions, that the Government of the Republic of China accepts the proposed agreement contained in your note mentioned above and agrees that your note and this note of confirmation shall constitute an Agreement between our two Governments.

I renew to Your Excellence the assurances of my highest consideration.

JAMES C. H. SHEN
Ambassador of the Republic of China

THE HONORABLE HENRY A. KISSINGER
   Secretary of State
      Department of State,
         Washington, DC

---

1   TIAS 7840; 25 UST 1001.

2   TIAS 7249, 7468, 7590; 22 UST 2084; 23 UST 2807; 24 UST 863.

3   TIAS 7498, 7591; 23 UST 3197, 3205, 3207; 24 UST 866.

Source: *U.S. Treaties and Other International Agreements*, Volume 26, Part 1, 1975.
                 U.S. Government Printing Office, Washington, DC, 1975. pp. 281-301.

E&T12   TABLE 4-1

                         TAIWAN'S TRADE WITH THE UNITED STATES

                                                                   Unit: US $ millions

Year	Amount	% of Total Export	Amount	% of Total Import	Amount	% of Total Trade	Surplus or Deficit
1976	3,038.7	37.2	1,797.6	23.7	4,836.3	30.7	+ 1,241.1
1977	3,636.3	38.9	1,963.8	23.1	5,600.1	31.3	+ 1,672.5
1978	5,010.4	39.5	2,376.1	21.5	7,386.5	31.1	+ 2,634.3
1979	5,652.3	35.1	3,380.8	22.9	9,033.1	29.3	+ 2,271.5
1980	6,760.3	34.1	4.673.5	23.7	11,433.8	28.9	+ 2,086.8
1981	8,163.1	36.1	4,765.7	22.5	12,928.8	29.5	+ 3,397.4
1982	8,758.9	39.4	4,563.2	24.2	13,322.1	32.4	+ 4,195.7
1983	11,333.7	45.1	4,646.4	22.9	15,980.1	35.2	+ 6,687.3
1984	14,867.7	48.8	5,041.6	23.0	19,909.3	38.0	+ 9,826.1
1985	14,770.3	48.1	4,746.5	23.6	19,516.8	38.4	+10,023.8
1986	18,994.4	47.8	5,416.3	22.4	24,410.7	38.2	+13,578.1
1987	23,637.1	44.2	7,628.3	22.1	31,265.4	35.5	+16,008.7

Source: Taiwan's Customs Statistics, furnished by the Coordination Council for North American
   Affairs. Because of different accounting methods, U.S. calculations show the U.S. trade
   deficit as somewhat larger. The 1986 U.S. trade deficit with Taiwan was $15.7 billion
   and the 1987 deficit was $19.0 billion according to the U.S. Department of Commerce.

Part III

Documents: 1979-1988

CHAPTER NINE

TAIWAN RELATIONS ACT AND ITS FUTURE

A list of the important political, military, economic and technological documents for the period 1979-1988.

1. December 15, 1978 Joint Communique on the Establishment of diplomatic Relations Between the United States and the People's Republic of China. *Public Papers of the Presidents of the United States: Jimmy Carter 1978*, Volume II. U.S. Government Printing Office, Washington, DC. pp. 2264-2266.

2. December 15, 1978 U.S. Statement on Diplomatic Relations Between the U.S. and the PRC. *Public Papers of the Presidents of the United States: Jimmy Carter 1978*, Volume II, U.S. Government Printing Office, Washington, DC. pp. 2266.

3. December 15, 1978 President Carter's Remarks at a White House Briefing. *Public Papers of the Presidents of the United States: Jimmy Carter 1978*, Volume II. U.S. Government Printing Office, Washington, DC. p. 2266-2268.

4. December 16, 1978 PRC Statement on Establishment of U.S. - PRC Diplomatic Relations, January 1, 1979. Text from the *New York Times*, Dec. 17, 1978.

5. December 19, 1978 Letter to the President from Chairman Clement J. Zablocki and Hon. Lester L. Wolff. Reprinted in "Implementation of Taiwan Relations Act: Issues and Concerns". Hearings Before the Subcommittee on Asian and Pacific Affairs of the Committee on Foreign Affairs, House of Representatives, 96th Congress, 1st Session, February 14-15, 1979. p. 135.

6. December 29, 1978 President Chiang Ching-kuo's Five Principles on U.S. - ROC Relations in the Postnormalization Period. As reprinted in Martin Lasater's *Taiwan Facing Mounting Threats*, Asian Studies Monograph, Heritage Foundation, 1984. pp. 62-64.

7. February 5, 1979 Taiwan Security Considerations. Hearings on S.245 before the Committee on Foreign Relations, U.S. Senate, 96th Congress, 1st Session on S. 245. pp.1-3.

8. February 5-22, 1979 Statement of Defense Secretary Harold Brown on Normalization with PRC and Security of Taiwan. Hearings Before Committee on Foreign Relations, U.S. Senate. pp. 35-38.

9. February 14, 1979 Letter to Hon. Lester L. Wolff from Former President Nixon. Reprinted in "Implementation of Taiwan Relations Act: Issues and Concerns". Hearings Before the Subcommittee on Asian and Pacific Affairs of the Committee on Foreign Affairs, House of Representatives, 96th Congress, 1st Session, February 14-15, 1979. p. 136.

10. March 1, 1979 Comments of Senator Jesse Helms on President Carter's Taiwan Policy, Report of the Committee on Foreign Relations, pp. 46-60.

11.   April 10, 1979 "Taiwan Relations Act" PL 96-98. *United States Statutes at Large*, 96th Congress, 1st Session, Volume 93. Government Printing Office, Washington, DC, 1981.

12.   June 4, 1979 Agreement for the Finance of Certain Educational and Cultural Exchange Programs. American Institute in Taiwan, Arlington, Virginia.

13.   November 15, 1979 *Oversight of Taiwan Relations Act*. Hearings before the Subcommittee on East Asia and Pacific Affairs of the Committee of Foreign Relations United States Senate, pp. 1-3.

14.   October 24, 1979 U.S. - ROC Bilateral Trade Agreement: Tariff Concessions. American Institute in Taiwan, Arlington, Virginia.

15.   December 31, 1979 Agreement between the American Institute in Taiwan and the Coordination Council for North American Affairs concerning Privileges, Exemptions and Immunities. American Institute in Taiwan, Arlington, Virginia.

16.   March 1979. Excerpts from the *Congressional Record*. House, March 5, 13, 1979. Senate, March 7, 29, 1979. Hearings on the Taiwan Relations Act.

17.   March 5, 1980 Air Transport Agreement between the American Institute in Taiwan and the Coordination Council for North American Affairs. American Institute in Taiwan, Arlington, Virginia. (Excerpts)

18.   March 7, 1980 Statement by James Lilley, Security Considerations in Taiwan's Future. *Taiwan: One Year After United States-China Normalization*, Committee on Foreign Relations, U.S. Senate and Congressional Research Service, Library of Congress, U.S. Government Printing Office, Washington, DC, 1980. pp. 140-144.

19.   June 30, 1980 American Institute on Taiwan - Problems. *Implementation of the Taiwan Relations Act: The First Year*, Committee on Foreign Relations, U.S. Senate. U.S. Government Printing Office, Washington, DC, 1980. pp. 8-13.

20.   August 1980 Republican Platform Statement Regarding Taiwan. Furnished by the Republican National Committee, Washington, DC.

21.   August 25, 1980 Candidate Ronald Reagan's Statement on Taiwan (Excerpt), Reagan Campaign Press Release.

22.   September 4, 1980 Agreement between the American Institute in Taiwan and the Coordination Council for North American Affairs concerning Scientific and Scholarly Cooperation. American Institute in Taiwan, Arlington, Virginia.

23.   October 2, 1980 Agreement between the American Institute in Taiwan and the Coordination Council for North American Affairs concerning Privileges, Exemptions and Immunities. American Institute in Taiwan, Arlington, Virginia.

24.   December 31, 1981 PRC Statement of Opposition to Foreign Arms Sales to Taiwan. *Renmin Ribao*, December 31, 1981, in *FBIS-China*, December 31, 1981. p. B1.

25.   July 6, 1981 White House Press Briefing regarding "Unofficial Relations with Taiwan" *American Foreign Policy Current Documents*, 1981. Department of State Publication, U.S. Government Printing Office, 1984. Document 496, pp. 958-959.

26.	July 16, 1981	Statement by Ambassador Holdridge regarding U.S. Relations with China. *U.S. Department of State Bulletin*, Volume 81, July-December, 1981, pp. 38-40.

27.	September 30, 1981 PRC Nine-Point Proposal for Reunification. China Mainland Affairs Research Center, Taipei, Taiwan, May 1982.

28.	October 22, 1981 Statement by Secretary of State Alexander Haig regarding Chinese Concern with the U.S. Relationship with Taiwan. *American Foreign Policy Current Documents*, 1981. Department of State Publication, U.S. Government Printing Office, 1984. Document 499, pp.964-965.

29.	November 12, 1981 Secretary of State Haig's Statements on Proposed Sale of Aircraft to Taiwan and U.S.-China Differences Concerning Taiwan. *American Foreign Policy Current Documents*, 1981. Department of State Publication, U.S. Government Printing Office, 1984. Documents 501-2, p. 966.

30.	January 11, 1982 Statement by Department of State on No Sale of Advanced Fighter Aircraft to Taiwan. *American Foreign Policy Current Documents*, 1982. Department of State Publication 9415, U.S. Government Printing Office, Washington, DC, 1985. Documents 483-4, pp. 1025-1026.

31.	February 28, 1982 Exchange of letters between President Reagan and Chinese Premier Zhao regarding Tenth Anniversary of the Shanghai Communique. *American Foreign Policy Current Documents*, 1982. Department of State Publication, U.S. Government Printing Office, Washington, DC, 1985. Document 485, pp. 1027.

32.	April 5, 1982 Letter from President Reagan to the Vice Chairman of the Chinese Communist Party concerning U.S. Interest in Resolving U.S. - Chinese Differences. *American Foreign Policy Current Documents*, 1982. Department of State Publication, U.S. Government Printing Office, Washington, DC, 1985. Document 486, p. 1028.

33.	April 5, 1982 Letter from President Reagan to Chinese Premier Zhao regarding Arms Sales to Taiwan. *American Foreign Policy Current Documents*, 1982. Department of State Publication, U.S. Government Printing Office, Washington, DC, 1985. Document 487, p. 1029.

34.	May 3, 1982 Letter from President Reagan to the Chairman of the Chinese Communist Party regarding Arms Sales to Taiwan. *American Foreign Policy Current Documents*, Department of State Publication, U.S. Government Printing Office, Washington, DC, 1985. Document 489, p. 1030.

35.	May 28, 1982 Chinese Eligibility for U.S. Assistance Programs. *American Foreign Policy Current Documents*, 1982. Department of State Publication, U.S. Government Printing Office, Washington, DC, 1985. Document 492, pp. 1032-1033.

36.	June 7, 1982 Agreement Between American Institute in Taiwan and the Coordination Council for North American Affairs concerning Fisheries off the Coasts of the U.S. American Institute in Taiwan, Arlington, Virginia.

37.	August 17, 1982 American Institute in Taiwan and the Coordination Council for North American Affairs Agreement on Maritime trade and the Safety of Life at Sea. American Institute in Taiwan, Arlington, Virginia.

38.   August 17, 1982 President Reagan's Statement on the Joint Communique. *American Foreign Policy Current Documents*, 1982. Department of State Publication, U.S. Government Printing Office, Washington, DC, 1985. Document 496, p. 1040.

39.   August 17, 1982 Chinese Statement on the Joint Communique. *American Foreign Policy Current Documents*, 1982. Department of State Publication, U.S. Government Printing Office, Washington, DC, 1985. Document 497, pp. 1040-1042.

40.   August 17, 1982 U.S. - China Joint Communique accompanied by Statement by Assistant Secretary of State John H. Holdridge on August 18, 1982 before the House Foreign Affairs Committee. Text from *Weekly Compilation of Presidential Documents*, August 23, 1982, p. 20.

41.   August 17, 1982 Statements by Members of the Senate Foreign Relations Committee and by the Assistant Secretary of State John H. Holdridge. *American Foreign Policy Current Documents*, 1982. Department of State Publication, U.S. Government Printing Office, Washington, DC, 1985. Document 498, pp. 1042-1050.

42.   August 17, 1982 ROC Statement on August 17 Communique. Furnished by the Coordination Council of North American Affairs, Washington, DC.

43.   August 17, 1982 Discussion by Senator John Glenn regarding the August 17, 1982 U.S.-PRC Joint Communique. Hearings before the Committee on Foreign Relations, U.S. Senate, 97th Congress, Second Session. U.S. Government Printing Office, Washington, DC, 1982. pp. 2-4.

44.   August 18, 1982 Questions Raised by the Joint Communique. *American Foreign Policy Current Documents*, 1982. Department of State Publication, U.S. Government Printing Office, Washington, DC. Document 499, pp. 1051-1053.

45.   August 18, 1982 China-Taiwan: United States Policy. Hearings before the Committee on Foreign Affairs, U.S. House of Representatives, 97th Congress, 2nd Session. U.S. Government Printing Office, Washington, DC, 1982. pp. 1-8.

46.   June, 1983 Taiwan Communique and Separation of Powers. Report on the Taiwan Relations Act and the Joint Communique. Committee on the Judiciary, U.S. Senate, U.S. Government Printing Office, Washington, D.C., June 1983. pp. 1-20.

47.   November 18, 1982 American Institute in Taiwan and the Coordination Council for North American Affairs on Trade in Cotton, Wool and Man-made Fiber Textiles and Textile Products. American Institute in Taiwan, Arlington, Virginia.

48.   February 3, 1983 American Institute in Taiwan and the Coordination Council for North American Affairs Agreement concerning the Taipei American School. American Institute in Taiwan, Arlington, Virginia.

49.   February 23, 1983 Senate Resolution 74, Expressing the Sense of the Senate concerning the Future of the People on Taiwan. 98th Congress, 1st Session. U.S. Government Printing Office, Washington, DC, 1983.

50.   February 28, 1983 U.S. - China Relations 11 Years After the Shanghai Communique. *American Foreign Policy Current Documents*. Department of State Publication 9441, Washington, DC, 1985. Document 467, pp. 996-1000.

51.   March 21, 1983 Press Briefing Concerning the Sale of Arms to Taiwan. *American Foreign Policy Current Documents*. Department of State Publication, U.S. Government Printing Office, Washington, DC, 1983. Document 468, pp. 1000-1002.

52.   November 9, 1983 Proposed Senate Resolution on the Future of Taiwan. *American Foreign Policy Current Documents*, 1983. Department of State Publication, U.S. Government Printing Office, Washington, DC, 1983. Document 475, pp. 1010-1011.

53.   November 30, 1983 Response by President Reagan Regarding U.S. Policy Toward China. *American Foreign Policy Current Documents*, 1983. Department of State Publication, U.S. Government Printing Office, Washington, DC. Document 478, p. 1013.

54.   Asian Development Bank. ROC a Charter Member. *U.S. Statutes at Large*, 98th Congress, 1st Session, 1983, Vol. 97, p. 1285.

55.   March 1, 1984 American Institute in Taiwan and the Coordination Council for North American Affairs Agreement concerning Exports of Rice from Taiwan. American Institute in Taiwan, Arlington, Virginia.

56.   November 7, 1984 American Institute in Taiwan and the Coordination Council for North American Affairs Agreement on Probabilistic Risk Analysis. American Institute in Taiwan, Arlington, Virginia.

57.   January 22, 1985 American Institute in Taiwan and the Coordination Council for North American Affairs Agreement on Maritime Trade and the Prevention of Pollution from Ships. American Institute in Taiwan, Arlington, Virginia.

58.   February 14, 1985 American Institute in Taiwan and the Coordination Council for North American Affairs Agreement on Bilateral Cooperation on Expansion of the PRA Agreement. American Institute in Taiwan, Arlington, Virginia.

59.   June 3, 1985 Interview with PRC General Secretary Hu Yaobang regarding use of force against Taiwan. See *Pai Hsing*, June 1, 1985 in *FBIS-China*, June 3, 1985, pp. W1-11.

60.   April 29, 1986 Department of State Statement on Proposed Sale of Aircraft Avionics Components to China. *U.S. Department of State Bulletin*, Volume 86. July-December 1986.

61.   May 12, 1986 American Institute in Taiwan and the Coordination Council for North American Affairs Guidelines for a Cooperative Program in Labor Affairs. American Institute in Taiwan, Arlington, Virginia.

62.   July 28, 1986 American Institute in Taiwan and the Coordination Council for North American Affairs Agreement to Revise the Air Transport Agreement of March 5, 1980. American Institute in Taiwan, Arlington, Virginia.

63.   October 22, 1986 American Institute in Taiwan and the Coordination Council for North American Affairs Agreement to Amend the Trade Agreement of July 1986 regarding Trade in Cotton, Wool, Man-made Fiber, Silk Blend and other Vegetable Fiber Textiles and Textile Products. American Institute in Taiwan, Arlington, Virginia.

64.   December 12, 1986 American Institute in Taiwan and the Coordination Council for North American Affairs Agreement regarding Guidelines for the Importation, Distribution and Sale within Taiwan of Beer, Wine and Cigarettes. American Institute in Taiwan, Arlington, Virginia.

65.   December 15, 1986 American Institute in Taiwan and the Coordination Council for North American Affairs Agreement concerning Trade in Machine Tools. American Institute in Taiwan, Arlington, Virginia.

66.   March 10, 1987 American Institute in Taiwan and the Coordination Council for North American Affairs Renewal and Extension of the Cooperative Science Agreement of 1980. American Institute in Taiwan, Arlington, Virginia.

67.   May 4, 1987 American Institute in Taiwan and the Coordination Council for North American Affairs Guidelines for a Cooperative Program in Atmospheric Research. American Institute in Taiwan, Arlington, Virginia.

68.   July 14, 1987 Lifting the Emergency Decree in the Taiwan Area. Government Information Office, Executive Yuan, ROC.

69.   July 21, 1987 Remarks by Vincent Siew, Director General of the Board of Foreign Trade, ROC, Concerning ROC Purchasing Commission sent to the U.S.

70.   November 17, 1987 American Institute in Taiwan and the Coordination Council for North American Affairs Agreement for a Cooperative Program in the Sale and Exchange of Technical, Scientific, and Engineering Information. American Institute in Taiwan, Arlington, Virginia.

TRA1   DIPLOMATIC RELATIONS BETWEEN
                        THE UNITED STATES AND THE
                        PEOPLE'S REPUBLIC OF CHINA
                    ADDRESS TO THE NATION. DECEMBER 15,1978

Good Evening.

I would like to read a joint communique which is being simultaneously issued in Peking at this very moment by the leaders of the People's Republic of China:

(At this point, the President read the text of the joint communique, which reads as follows:)

JOINT COMMUNIQUE ON THE ESTABLISHMENT
OF DIPLOMATIC RELATIONS BETWEEN THE
UNITED STATES OF AMERICA AND THE
PEOPLE'S REPUBLIC OF CHINA
January 1, 1979

The United States of America and the People's Republic of China have agreed to recognize each other and to establish diplomatic relations as of January 1, 1979.

The United States of America recognizes the Government of the People's Republic of China as the sole legal Government of China. Within this context, the people of the United States will maintain cultural, commercial, and other unofficial relations with the people of Taiwan.

The United States of America and the People's Republic of China reaffirm the principles agreed on by the two sides in the Shanghai Communique and emphasize once again that:

-Both wish to reduce the danger of international military conflict.

-Neither should seek hegemony in the Asia-Pacific region or in any other region of the world and each is opposed to efforts by any other country or group of countries to establish such hegemony.

-Neither is prepared to negotiate on behalf of any third party or to enter into agreements or understandings with the other directed at other states.

-The Government of the United States of America acknowledges the Chinese position that there is but one China and Taiwan is part of China.

-Both believe that normalization of Sino-American relations is not only in the interest of the Chinese and American peoples but also contributes to the cause of peace in Asia and the world.

The United States Of America and the People's Republic of China will exchange Ambassadors and establish Embassies on March 1, 1979.

Yesterday, our country and the People's Republic of China reached this final historic agreement. On January 1, 1979, a little more than 2 weeks from now, our two Governments will implement full normalization of diplomatic relations.

As a nation of gifted people who comprise about one-fourth of the total population of the Earth, China plays, already, a role that can only grow more important in the years ahead.

We do not undertake this important step for transient tactical or expedient reasons. In recognizing the People's Republic of China, that it is the single Government of China, we are recognizing simple reality. But far more is involved in this decision than just the recognition of a fact.

Before the estrangement of recent decades, the American and the Chinese people had a long history of friendship. We've already begun to rebuild some of those previous ties. Now our rapidly expanding relationship requires the kind of structure that only full diplomatic relations will make possible.

The change that I'm announcing tonight will be of great long-term benefit to the peoples of both our country and China--and, I believe, to all the peoples of the world. Normalization--and the expanded commercial and cultural relations that it will bring--will contribute to the well-being of our own Nation, to our own national interest, and it will also enhance the stability of Asia. These more positive relations with China can beneficially affect the world in which we live and the world in which our children will live.

We have already begun to inform our allies and other nations and the Members of the Congress of the details of our intended action. But I wish also tonight to convey a special message to the people of Taiwan--I have already communicated with the leaders in Taiwan-- with whom the American people have had and will have extensive, close, and friendly relations. This is important between our two peoples.

As the United States asserted in the Shanghai Communique of 1972, issued on President Nixon's historic visit, we will continue to have an interest in the peaceful resolution of the Taiwan issue. I have paid special attention to ensuring that normalization of relations between our country and the People's Republic will not jeopardize the well-being of the people of Taiwan. The people of our country will maintain our current commercial, cultural, trade, and other relations with Taiwan through nongovernmental means. Many other countries in the world are already successfully doing this.

These decisions and these actions open a new and important chapter in our country's history and also in world affairs.

To strengthen and to expedite the benefits of this new relationship between China and the United States, I am pleased to announce that Vice Premier Teng has accepted my invitation and will visit Washington at the end of January. His visit will give our Governments the opportunity to consult with each other on global issues and to begin working together to enhance the cause of world peace.

These events are the final result of long and serious negotiations begun by President Nixon in 1972, and continued under the leadership of President Ford. The results bear witness to the steady, determined, bipartisan effort of our own country to build a world in which peace will be the goal and the responsibility of all nations.

The normalization of relations between the United States and China has no other purpose than this: the advancement of peace. It is in this spirit, at this season of peace, that I take special pride in sharing this good news with you tonight.

Thank you very much.

Note: The President spoke at 9 p.m. from the Oval Office at the White House. The address was broadcast live on radio and television.

Source:		*Public Papers of the Presidents of the United States: Jimmy Carter 1978,* Volume II, U.S. Government Printing Office, Washington, D.C., pp. 2264-2266.

TRA2				DIPLOMATIC RELATIONS BETWEEN THE
					UNITED STATES AND THE PEOPLE'S
					REPUBLIC OF CHINA
					UNITED STATES STATEMENT. DECEMBER 15,1978

As of January 1, 1979, the United States of America recognizes the People's Republic of China as the sole legal government of China. On the same date, the People's Republic of China accords similar recognition to the United States of America. The United States thereby establishes diplomatic relations with the People's Republic of China.

On that same date, January 1, 1979, the United States of America will notify Taiwan that it is terminating diplomatic relations and that the Mutual Defense Treaty between the United States and the Republic of China is being terminated in accordance with the provisions of the Treaty. The United States also states that it will be withdrawing its remaining military personnel from Taiwan within four months.

In the future, the American people and the people of Taiwan will maintain commercial, cultural, and other relations without official government representation and without diplomatic relations.

The Administration will seek adjustments to our laws and regulations to permit the maintenance of commercial, cultural, and other non-governmental relationships in the new circumstances that will exist after normalization.

The United States is confident that the people of Taiwan face a peaceful and prosperous future. The United States continues to have an interest in the peaceful resolution of the Taiwan issue and expects that the Taiwan issue will be settled peacefully by the Chinese themselves.

The United States believes that the establishment of diplomatic relations with the People's Republic will contribute to the welfare of the American people, to the stability of Asia where the United States has a major security and economic interest, and to the peace of the entire world.

Source:		*Public Papers of the Presidents of the United States: Jimmy Carter 1978,* Volume II, U.S. Government Printing Office, Washington, DC. p. 2266.

TRA3

DIPLOMATIC RELATIONS BETWEEN THE
UNITED STATES AND THE
PEOPLE'S REPUBLIC OF CHINA

REMARKS AT A WHITE HOUSE BRIEFING
FOLLOWING THE ADDRESS
TO THE NATION. DECEMBER 15,1978

THE PRESIDENT. Well, I wanted to come by and let you know that I believe this to be an extremely important moment in the history of our Nation. It's something that I and my two predecessors have sought avidly. We have maintained our own United States position firmly, and only since the last few weeks has there been an increasing demonstration to us that Premier Hua and Vice Premier Deng have been ready to normalize relations. I think the interests of Taiwan have been adequately protected. One of the briefers will explain the details to you.

Our Ambassador there, Leonard Woodcock, has done a superb job in presenting our own views strongly and clearly to the officials of the People's Republic of China. I will be preparing myself adequately for the visit of Vice Premier Teng. We invited him on one day, he accepted the next, without delay, and I think he's looking forward to this trip with a great deal of anticipation and pleasure.

I have talked personally this evening to Prime Minister Ohira (of Japan). Early this morning we notified the officials in Taiwan, and we have also notified many of the leaders around the world of this long-awaited development in international diplomacy.

I think that one of the greatest benefits that will be derived from this is the continuation of strong trade, cultural relationships with Taiwan, the people of Taiwan, and a new vista for prosperous trade relationships with almost a billion people in the People's Republic of China. This is also, of course, enhanced by the new opportunities for us to understand the people of China, and to work avidly for peace in that region and for world peace.

This afternoon the Soviet Union officials were notified through their Ambassador here, Mr. Dobrynin. And I think the Soviets were familiar with the fact that we were anticipating normalization whenever the Chinese were willing to meet our reasonable terms, and they were not surprised. As you well know, the Soviet Union and People's Republic of China have diplomatic relations between themselves.

My own assessment is that this will be well received in almost every nation of the world, perhaps all of them, because it will add to stability. And the Soviets and others know full well, because of our own private explanations to them, not just recently but in months gone by, that we have no desire whatsoever to use our new relationships with China to the disadvantage of the Soviets or anyone else. We believe this will enhance stability and not cause instability in Asia and the rest of the world.

I'm very pleased with it. And I obviously have to give a major part of the credit to President Nixon and to President Ford, who laid the groundwork for this successful negotiation. And most of the premises that were spelled out in the Shanghai Communique 6 years ago or more have been implemented now.

You can tell that I'm pleased, and I know that the world is waiting for your accurate explanation of the results.

Q. How did the congressional leaders take it?

THE PRESIDENT. With mixed response. Some of the congressional leaders who were there have long been very strong personal friends of the officials in Taiwan. They are not as thoroughly familiar with the officials in the People's Republic of China.

One of the most long debated issues was whether or not we would peremptorily terminate our defense treaty with Taiwan, or whether we would terminate that treaty in accordance with its own provisions. And the People's Republic officials agreed with our position that we would give Taiwan a 1-year notice and that the defense treaty would prevail throughout 1979. I think that alleviated some of the concerns among the Senators.

And another concern expressed by them was whether or not we could continue cultural relationships, trade relationships with the people of Taiwan. I assured them that we could, that the Chinese knew this. And we will ask the Congress for special legislation quite early in the session to permit this kind of exchange with the people of Taiwan. This would include authorization for the Eximbank and OPEC to guarantee and to help with specific trade negotiations.

I think that many of their concerns have been alleviated, although there certainly will be some Members of the Congress who feel that we should have maintained the status quo.

I'll take just one question.

Q. Mr. President, you said the response to your speech would be "massive applause throughout the Nation." What do you think the response to your speech will be in Taiwan?

THE PRESIDENT. I doubt if there will be massive applause in Taiwan, but we are going to do everything we can to assure the Taiwanese that we put at top-as one of the top priorities in our own relationships with the People's Republic and them-that the well-being of the people of Taiwan will not be damaged.

To answer the other question, I don't think this will have any adverse effect at all on the SALT negotiations as an independent matter. And I think that the Soviets, as I said earlier, have been expecting this development. They were not surprised, and we have kept them informed recently. Their reaction has not been adverse, and we will proceed aggressively as we have in recent months, in fact throughout my own administration, to conclude a successful SALT agreement.

Good night.

Note: The President spoke at approximately 9:30 p.m. to reporters assembled in the Briefing Room at the White House. Following his remarks, administration officials held the background briefing on the announcement.

Source: *Public Papers of the Presidents of the United States: Jimmy Carter 1978*, Volume II, U.S. Government Printing Office, Washington, D.C., pp. 2266-2268.

TRA4

STATEMENT BY THE GOVERNMENT
OF THE PEOPLE'S REPUBLIC
OF CHINA.

As of Jan. 1, 1979, the People's Republic of China and the United States of America recognize each other and establish diplomatic relations, thereby ending the prolonged abnormal relationship between them. This is an historic event in Sino-United States relations.

As is known to all, the Government of the People's Republic of China is the sole legal Government of China and Taiwan is part of China. The question of Taiwan was the crucial issue obstructing the normalization of relations between China and the United States. It has now been resolved between the two countries in the spirit of the Shanghai Communique and through their joint efforts, thus enabling the normalization of relations so ardently desired by the people of the two countries.

As for the way of bringing Taiwan back to the embrace of the motherland and reunifying the country, it's entirely China's internal affair.

At the invitation of the U.S. Government, Teng Hsiao-ping, Deputy Prime Minister of the State Council of the People's Republic of China, will pay an official visit to the United States in January 1979, with a view to further promoting the friendship between the two peoples and good relations between the two countries.

Source: Text from the *New York Times*, December 17, 1978.

TRA5   LETTER TO THE PRESIDENT FROM
                        CHAIRMAN CLEMENT J. ZABLOCKI AND
                        HON. LESTER L. WOLFF

                        CONGRESS OF THE UNITED STATES,
                        COMMITTEE ON INTERNATIONAL RELATIONS,
                        HOUSE OF REPRESENTATIVES,
                        WASHINGTON, D.C., DECEMBER 19,1978.

HON. JIMMY CARTER,
THE PRESIDENT,
THE WHITE HOUSE, WASHINGTON, D.C.

Dear Mr. President: The implications of your December 15 announcement regarding normalization of relations with the People's Republic of China are more far-reaching than any of us can comprehend at this time. While some of us may have reservations regarding the timing, method and substance of your decision, our purpose in writing now is not to take issue with those aspects of the question, important and serious as they might be.

Rather, in the strongest possible terms, we wish to register our concern, displeasure and dismay over the cavalier way in which this decision was conveyed to the Congress. In particular, we object tot the fact that the only information available to the Congress on this matter came from representatives of the media hours before you briefed members of the Congress at 6:15 p.m. only two hours and 45 minutes before you were scheduled to make the public announcement.

In particular, we object most to the fact that the provisions of Section 26 of the International Security Assistance Act of 1978, (P.L. 95-384), which became law on September 26, 1978 were not complied with. As you know, subsection (b) of Section 26 states that "It is the sense of the Congress that there should be prior consultation between the Congress and the executive branch on any proposed policy changes affecting the continuation in force of the Mutual Defense Treaty of 1954."

Mr. President, we have long believed that for consultation to be truly meaningful and effective it must be timely enough for Congressional views to be taken into consideration. Further, we have repeatedly stressed that merely informing Congress of decisions already taken does not constitute adequate consultation. Certainly, being informed of a decision of such consequence less than three hours before a public announcement cannot in any way be construed as consultation.

We have been pleased with your policy regarding prior consultation with Congress to which you have committed your Administration and which you have, with few exceptions, practiced up to now. Unfortunately, this step contradicts that record.

As we have indicated on several occasions we are prepared to support your policies wherever and whenever we are able. To do so, however, we must know what those policies are going to be in sufficient time to work out any problems that some, or all, of us may have, with respect to a particular decision.

In closing, we would like to point out that we recognize that diplomacy cannot always be conducted in public and that there may be a need for secrecy. Nevertheless we feel that we are patriotic enough and responsible enough to be consulted during the decision-making process instead of being confronted with a fait accompli.

Mr. President, we would hope that you will accept this letter in the spirit in which it is written. We want to support you. To do this you must have the confidence in us that you expect us to have in you.

In closing, we wish to take this opportunity to wish you and yours a happy, Merry Christmas, and the happiest of New years.

With best wishes.

Sincerely yours,

CLEMENT J. ZABLOCKI, M.C.
LESTER L. WOLFF, M.C.

Source: Reprinted in "Implementation of Taiwan Relations Act: Issues and Concerns." Hearings before the Subcommittee on Asian and Pacific Affairs of the Committee on Foreign Affairs, House of Representatives, 96th Congress, 1st Session, February 14-15, 1979. p. 135.

PRESIDENT CHIANG CHING-KUO'S
FIVE PRINCIPLES ON U.S.-ROC RELATIONS
IN THE POSTNORMALIZATION PERIOD,
DECEMBER 29, 1978

(President Chiang Ching-kuo informed Deputy Secretary of State Christopher that future ties between the Republic of China and the United States must rest on five underlying principles--reality, continuity, security, legality, and governmentality. The President's statement is summarized by Dr. James Soong, Deputy-Director of the Government Information Office, as follows:)

The Republic of China is an independent sovereign state with a legitimately established government based on the Constitution of the Republic of China. It is an effective government, which has the wholehearted support of her people. The international status and personality of the Republic of China cannot be changed merely because of the recognition of the Chinese Communist regime by any country of the world. The legal status and international personality of the Republic of China is a simple reality which the United States must recognize and respect.

The United States has expressed its intention that it will continue to maintain cultural, economic, trade, scientific, technological, and travel relations with the Republic of China. The ties that bound our two countries and people together in the past, however, include much more than these. The Republic of China is ready and willing to continue these traditional ties. The United States, on the other hand, must also realize the importance of the continuity of these ties, not only in their present scope, but also on an expanded scale to meet future needs.

The security of the Asian-Pacific region is also of utmost importance to the well-being and livelihood of the 17 million people on Taiwan, as well as American interests in the area.

The Sino-U.S. Mutual Defense Treaty signed in 1954 was designed to be a vital link in the chain of the collective defense system of free countries in the West Pacific. The situation in this region has not changed. It is still unstable and insecure. The threat of invasion and subversion by Communist forces to the free nations of Asia, particularly after the fall of Vietnam, is even more serious than before.

Hence, the U.S. unilateral action to terminate the Sino-U.S. Mutual Defense Treaty will further destabilize this region and might create a new crisis of war. Thus, in order to ensure the peace and security of the West Pacific, which includes that of the Republic of China, it is imperative that the United States take concrete and effective measures to renew its assurances to countries in this region.

We are ready and determined to continue to do our share in securing stability and peace in the West Pacific. But in order to do this, we must have sufficient capabilities to defend ourselves, and thereby protect our neighbors. President Carter has indicated that he is still concerned about the peace, security, and prosperity of this region after the termination of the Sino-U.S. Mutual Defense Treaty, and will continue to supply the Republic of China with defense weapons. The U.S. must give us assurances of a legal nature which would ensure the fulfillment of this commitment.

We are at present faced with the pragmatic problems involved in continuing and maintaining 59 treaties and agreements, as well as other arrangements, between our two countries. Since both the Republic of China and the United States are governed by law, the private interests of both Chinese and American citizens require the protection of definite legal provisions. Appropriate legislative measures in both countries must therefore be taken to provide legal basis on which these security, commercial, and cultural treaties and agreements can continue to remain in full force and effect.

The complex nature of the activities of mutual interest to our two countries makes it impossible for them to be carried out by any private organization or individual. To facilitate the continuation and expansion of all relations between our two countries, it is necessary that government-to-government level mechanisms be set up in Taipei and Washington. This model alone can serve as the framework on which the future relationship of our two countries can be constructed.

Source: As reprinted in Martin Lasater, *Taiwan Facing Mounting Threats*, Washington, D.C., Heritage Foundation, 1984, pp. 62-64.

TRA7   TAIWAN

MONDAY, FEBRUARY 5, 1979
UNITED STATES SENATE,
COMMITTEE ON FOREIGN RELATIONS,
WASHINGTON, D.C.

The committee met, pursuant to notice, at 10:10 a.m., in room 4221, Dirksen Senate Office Building, Hon. Frank Church (chairman of the committee) presiding.

Present: Senators Church, Biden, Glenn, Stone, Sarbanes, Muskie, Zorinsky, Javits, Percy, Helms, Hayakawa, and Lugar.

The **CHAIRMAN**. The hearing will please come to order.

OPENING STATEMENT

President Carter's action in extending U.S. diplomatic recognition to the People's Republic as the legal government of China gives long overdue acknowledgment of one of the central realities of Asian affairs, the existence of the government which actually exercises jurisdiction over the most populous and second largest nation on Earth.

It is no wonder that the President's decision has been applauded by all our friends and allies in Asia, from New Zealand to Japan. Recognition of the People's Republic also gives the United States an opportunity unique in modern times: The opportunity to have cordial and cooperative relations with both China and Japan.

TAIWAN SECURITY CONSIDERATIONS

However, we must also face another reality: The importance the United States must attach to the future security and well-being of the people of Taiwan. Our long alliance with Taiwan demands that this be given careful attention.

The people of Taiwan, with whom we have cooperated for so many years, are understandably uncertain and concerned about their future. They have demonstrated extraordinary diligence in developing one of the world's fastest growing economies. Equally impressive has been their record in reducing the gap in living standards between the rich and the poor on the island itself. Such achievements are all too rare in today's world and the American policy should be to encourage continued economic progress on Taiwan.

Taiwan's prosperity has been built upon foreign trade, and the United States is its largest trading partner. We must take the steps necessary to facilitate the continued growth of this trade as well as to enable Taiwan to secure continued American loans and attract further American private investment. Our success in doing this will encourage the Japanese, Taiwan's other major source of trade and investment, to continue to expand their economic relations with Taiwan, as they have done since they shifted diplomatic recognition from Taipei to Peking 7 years ago.

We must also be concerned about Taiwan's security in the light of President Carter's announcement that the mutual security treaty will be terminated on January 1, 1980. It is not for us to decide Taiwan's ultimate destiny. However, the United States does have an important interest that this issue be resolved peacefully and in a manner that takes into account the will of the people of Taiwan.

It is very encouraging that the People's Republic of China has adopted a flexible approach to this issue in recent months. We should do nothing to discourage the Chinese leaders from continuing along this course.

At the same time, it is important that the People's Republic of China understand the deep interest of the United States in a peaceful resolution of this question and that the people on Taiwan be assured that we are not abandoning them. In this regard, I hope the committee will recommend appropriate language to the Senate expressing the American view.

We should also give substance to that view by making possible the continued supply of defensive arms to Taiwan in a manner consistent with the President's pledge to the People's Republic of China.

CONSIDERATION OF LEGISLATION

The committee meets this morning to consider legislation designed to promote and to protect the well-being of the people of Taiwan and to bolster their capacity for self-defense in the years to come.

[Text of S.245 follows:]

96TH CONGRESS
1ST SESSION
S.245

To promote the foreign policy of the United States through the maintenance of commercial, cultural, and other relations with the people of Taiwan on an unofficial basis, and for other purposes.

IN THE SENATE OF THE UNITED STATES

January 29 (legislative day, January 15), 1979

Mr. Church (by request) introduced the following bill; which was read twice and referred to the Committee on Foreign Relations

A BILL

To promote the foreign policy of the United States through the maintenance of commercial, cultural, and other relations with the people of Taiwan on an unofficial basis, and for other purposes.

Be it enacted by the Senate and House of Representatives of the United States of America in Congress assembled,

TITLE I

SEC. 101. No requirement for maintenance of diplomatic relations with the United States, or for recognition of a government by the United States, as a condition of eligibility for participation in programs, transactions, or other relations authorized by or pursuant to United States law shall apply with respect to the people on Taiwan.

SEC. 101. Whenever any law, regulation, or order of the United States refers or relates to a foreign country, nation, state, government, or similar entity, such terms shall include, and such law, regulation, or order shall apply with respect to, the people on Taiwan.

SEC. 103. Whenever authorized or required by or pursuant to United States law to conduct or carry out programs, transactions, or other relations with respect to a foreign country, nation, state, government, or similar entity, the President or any department or agency of the United States Government is authorized to conduct and carry out such programs, transactions, and other relations with respect to the people on Taiwan, in accordance with applicable laws of the United States.

SEC. 104. Programs, transactions, and other relations conducted or carried out by the President or any department or agency of the United States Government with respect to the people on Taiwan shall, as the President may direct, be conducted and carried out by or through the American Institute in Taiwan, a nonprofit corporation incorporated under the laws of the District of Columbia (hereinafter "the Institute").

SEC. 105. Whenever the President or any department or agency of the United States Government is authorized or required by or pursuant to United States law to enter into, perform, enforce, or have in force an agreement or arrangement relative to the people on Taiwan, such agreement or arrangement shall be entered into, or performed and enforced, as the President may direct, by or through the Institute.

SEC. 106. Whenever the President or any department or agency of the United States Government is authorized or required by or pursuant to United States law to render or provide to, or to receive or accept from, the people on Taiwan any performance, communication, assurance, undertaking, or other action, such action shall, as the President may direct, be rendered or provided to, or received or accepted from, an instrumentality established by the people on Taiwan shall be considered foreign law for that purpose.

TITLE II

SEC. 201. Any department or agency of the United States Government is authorized to sell, loan, or lease property, including interests therein, to, and to perform administrative and technical support functions and services for the operations of, the Institute upon such terms and conditions as the President may direct. Reimbursements to departments and agencies under this section shall be credited to the current applicable appropriate of the department or agency concerned.

SEC. 202. Any department or agency of the United States Government is authorized to acquire and accept services from the Institute upon such terms and conditions as the President may direct, without regard to the laws and regulations normally applicable to the acquisition of services by such department or agency.

SEC. 203. Any department or agency of the United States Government employing alien personnel in Taiwan is authorized to transfer such personnel, with accrued allowances, benefits, and rights, to the Institute without a break in service for purposes of retirement and other benefits, including continued participation in any system established by law or regulation for the retirement of employees, under which such personnel were covered prior to the transfer to the Institute: **Provided,** That employee deductions and employer contributions, as required, in payment for such participation for the period of employment with the Institute, are currently deposited in the system's fund or depository.

SEC. 204. (a) Under such terms and conditions as the President may direct, any department or agency of the United States Government is authorized to separate from Government service for a specific period any officer or employee of that department or agency who accepts employment with the Institute.

(b) An officer or employee separated under subsection (a) of this section shall be entitled upon termination of such employment with the Institute to reemployment or reinstatement with that department or agency or a successor agency in an appropriate position with attendant rights, privileges, and benefits which the officer or employee would have had or acquired had he or she not been so separated, subject to such time period and other conditions as the President may prescribe.

(c) An officer or employee entitled to reemployment or reinstatement rights under subsection (b) of this section shall, while continuously employed by the Institute with no break in continuity of service, continue to participate in any benefit program in which such officer or employee was covered prior to employment by the Institute, including programs for compensation for job-related death, injury or illness; for health and life insurance; for annual, sick and other statutory leave; and for retirement under any system established by law or regulation: **Provided,** That employee deductions and employer contributions, as required, in payment for such participation for the period of employment with the Institute, must be currently deposited in the program's or system's fund or depository. Death or retirement of any such officer or employee during approved service with the Institute and prior to reemployment or reinstatement shall be considered a death in service or retirement from the service for the purposes of any employee or survivor benefits acquired by reason of service with a department or agency of the United States Government.

(d) Any employee of a department or agency of the United States Government who entered into service with the Institute on approved leave of absence without pay prior to the enactment of this Act shall receive the benefits of this title for the period of such service.

SEC. 205. The Institute shall be treated as a tax exempt organization described in section 501(c)(3) of the Internal Revenue Code of 1954, and shall not be an agency or instrumentality of the United States. Employees of the Institute shall not be employees of the United States and, in representing the Institute, shall be exempt from section 207 of Title 18, United States Code. The salaries and allowances paid to employees of the Institute shall be treated in the same way for tax purposes, under sections 911, 912, and 913 of the Internal Revenue Code of 1954, as salaries and equivalent allowances paid by departments and agencies of the United States Government.

TITLE III

SEC. 301. In addition to funds otherwise available for the purposes of this Act, there are authorized to be appropriated to the Secretary of State from time to time such funds as may be necessary to carry out such purposes. Such funds are authorized to remain available until expended.

SEC. 302. The Secretary of State is authorized to use funds made available to carry out this Act to further the maintenance of commercial, cultural and other relations with the people on Taiwan on an unofficial basis. The Secretary may provide such funds to the Institute for expenses directly related to the purposes of this Act, including:

(1) payment of salaries and benefits to Institute employees;

(2) acquisition and maintenance of buildings and facilities necessary to the conduct of Institute business;

(3) maintenance of adequate security for Institute employees and facilities; and

(4) such other expenses as may be necessary for the effective functioning of the Institute.

SEC. 303. Any department or agency of the United States Government making funds available to the Institute in accordance with this Act shall make arrangements with the Institute for the Comptroller General of the United States to have access to the books and records of the Institute and the opportunity to audit the operations of the Institute.

SEC. 304. The programs, transactions, and other relations carried out by the President or any department or agency of the United States Government with respect to the people on Taiwan since January 1, 1979, are approved and confirmed.

SEC. 305. The President is authorized to prescribe such rules and regulations as he may deem appropriate to carry out the purposes of this Act.

Source: Hearings before the Committee on Foreign Relations, U.S. Senate, 96th Congress, 1st Session on S. 245. pp. 1-3.

TRA8

SECRETARY OF DEFENSE HAROLD BROWN:
STATEMENT OF NORMALIZATION WITH PRC AND SECURITY OF TAIWAN

Mr. Chairman, I am pleased to participate in this Committee's hearings on the normalization of U.S. diplomatic relations with the People's Republic of China and the Taiwan Omnibus legislation. In my opening statement, I will address two issues which I know are of concern to many members of this committee.

--What are security implications for the U.S. of normalization?

--Have adequate provisions been made for the future security of Taiwan?

SECURITY IMPLICATIONS

I would like to start by noting two important realities. First, China is an emerging power which will exercise increasing influence on world events. This is a fact, not a consequence of normalization. But the Administration's decision to complete the process begun in 1971 was designed to take this fact into account. Second, we now confront an Asia much less menacing to the U.S. than it appeared--and was--in the 1950s when the Russians and Chinese acted in concert.

As a result of the deepening Sino-Soviet rivalry, the USSR has had to deal with the challenge to Soviet security from the PRC. Moscow has now deployed 20 to 25 percent of its ground and tactical aviation forces along the Sino-Soviet border.

We did not precipitate the split between Moscow and Peking, and have no desire to see the present level of Sino-Soviet differences intensify. The accompanying change in China's orientation, however, does effect--and improve--our security by relieving us of the requirement we perceived in the past, of confronting two major adversaries on different fronts. Military resources have been freed for other purposes, thereby importing greater global flexibility to our military (particularly general purposes) forces. The Soviets, on the other hand, now have to plan for what they view as a two-front security problem.

Moreover, Peking, in its desire for expanded ties with the U.S. has acquired additional incentives for restraint on the Taiwan issue and for the pursuit of moderate policies elsewhere. For example, the People's Republic supports a strong NATO, endorses the preservation of the U.S.-Japanese defense relationship, applauds our presence in the Western Pacific, actively encourages the growing cohesion of ASEAN, and shares our stake in avoiding a renewal of war on the Korean peninsula. This is beneficial to the security of many of our allies as well as to our own security.

To be sure, China's foreign policy goals and actions do not fully coincide with American interests and policies. Nor can we expect the Chinese to neglect their own national interests in pursuit of improved Sino-American relations any more than we are willing to subordinate our interests to theirs. What is significant, however, is the substantial parallelism of U.S.-PRC interests which permits us to maintain compatible approaches to many issues around the globe that affect our national security in various dimensions.

Some of these benefits, of course, are not directly attributable to improvements in Sino-American relations. The Sino-Soviet split would have persisted even without full normalization, as would some convergence of U.S. and Chinese security interests. However, completion of the normalization process serves to reduce the future possibility that we might slip back into a confrontation with the Chinese. It provides a framework for the further reduction of tensions in the region. And it lays the groundwork for a major expansion in Sino-American cooperation. While the future contours of our relationship are yet to be charted, I see no reason to expect that the interests which have led Chinese leaders to seek normal relations with the U.S. will change in the foreseeable future.

Finally, I would like to emphasize that establishment of U.S.-PRC diplomatic relations and the removal of our military personnel from Taiwan will not significantly affect our regional military posture. As the Committee well knows, our last combat forces were withdrawn from Taiwan four years ago.

THE MILITARY THREAT OF TAIWAN

Many individuals have asked why the U.S. did not insist on an explicit PRC renunciation of the use of force against Taiwan. The answer rests essentially on an assessment of what was diplomatically feasible and a judgement of the present and anticipated military threat to Taiwan's security. The State Department can best address the negotiating issue. For my part I want to emphasize my belief that for a variety of reasons PRC military action against Taiwan is extremely unlikely for the foreseeable future.

Militarily, China is not now capable of mounting a successful combined air and sea invasion of Taiwan. Peking is now primarily concerned about the threat from the Soviet Union, which requires that it maintain large forces along its northern border. Nor can it ignore Soviet-supported Vietnam on its southern border. Any serious PRC effort to mount an attack on Taiwan would require seriously weakening China's border defenses. Though Peking could use its air and naval assets to degrade Taiwan's air force or attempt to blockade the island, such action could not be undertaken without great risk given the condition of China's air and naval forces, Taiwan's defense capabilities, and the likely international response to such actions. The PRC could thus have no confidence even in the outcome of these lesser attempts to harass Taiwan.

Let me turn in more detail to these military considerations. Although China has a large number of combat aircraft, many are obsolescent fighters based on Soviet technology of the early 1950s, which are limited in range and payload. Few are equipped with air-to-air missiles; and pilot proficiency is well below Taiwan's standards. Although China has a large diesel submarine fleet, its Navy is primarily a coastal defense force, and the PRC lacks the amphibious shipping necessary to mount a successful invasion of Taiwan. Nor can Peking expect to develop substantial amphibious forces before the mid-1980s even if they began a concentrated effort now.

For its part Taiwan possesses impressive deterrent capabilities of its own. The island's army numbers about 335,000 men; its air force 75,000; and its navy 70,000. Taiwan's air defense capability rests upon a mixture of surface-to-air missile battalions (Improved Hawk and Nike-Hercules), and an interceptor fleet of 300 aircraft (F-100s, F-104s and F-5Es). The latter are fitted with late model air-to-air missiles (AIM9-J) which are more sophisticated than anything PRC can deploy. Taiwan has recently installed a semi-automated air defense radar system, augmented by mobile radars for extra insurance against surprise attack. Its command-and-control system is far more advanced than the PRC's as are its electronic counter-measures capabilities.

Beyond these military factors, there are a number of political constraints that will continue to make a PRC attack of Taiwan extremely unlikely. China has embarked on a massive effort to modernize its economy at a rapid pace. The efficacy of this undertaking depends heavily upon cooperative relations with the industrial democracies. Those relations would be jeopardized--indeed very probably ruptured--by an attack on Taiwan. Similarly, the Chinese are concerned with Moscow's growing influence in Vietnam and elsewhere in East Asia. That concern enhances Peking's stake in cultivating closer state-to-state relations with the ASEAN countries, which remain extremely sensitive to Taiwan's fate. Peking also must consider the possibility that any attack on Taiwan will evoke Japanese anxieties and precipitate a major reorientation of Japan's security policies with anti-Chinese overtones. Nor, I might add, can the Chinese discount the possibility of a U.S. military response.

The Administration has consistently affirmed a continuing U.S. interest in the future security and well-being of the people of Taiwan and its expectation--not hope, but expectation --that the Taiwan issue will be resolved peacefully. It is important to note that Peking has not challenged these statements. On the contrary, PRC spokesman no longer talk of "liberating" Taiwan. Vice-Premier Teng and others have repeatedly stated that reunification is not an immediate issue; and they have shown considerable flexibility in discussing the future status of Taiwan including an expressed willingness to see Taiwan retain some armed forces of its own as well as its economic and social system. To be sure, they have resisted any explicit commitment not to use force, which they regard ultimately as a matter of sovereignty. But Peking has decided to pursue the development of normal U.S.-PRC relations despite the President's intention, publicly expressed, to assist the people of Taiwan in maintaining their defenses through sales of selected weapons of a defensive character.

THE NORMALIZATION AGREEMENT

Let me now review in more detail the basic elements of our normalization policy as they apply to our future security relations with Taiwan.

First, as I have just noted, the U.S. has and will retain an interest in what we expressly expect to be the peaceful resolution of the Taiwan issue by the parties directly concerned. This position is clearly known to Peking.

Second, in the recent normalization negotiations with the PRC, we insisted that termination of the Mutual Defense Treaty must be accomplished in accordance with its provisions, rather than abrogated as Peking proposed.

Third, despite the PRC'S disagreement, we have expressed our intention to extend to Taiwan access to selected items of defense equipment, including follow-on support for weapons systems previously supplied.

All arms we have agreed to sell to Taiwan, and which are now in the pipeline--and these amount to more than $50 million--will be delivered. No new commitments will be made during calendar year 1979, but thereafter we will resume sales of selected defensive arms taking into account the situation in the Taiwan Straits. The legal authority for future arms sales to Taiwan is provided for in the Omnibus Legislation currently before this committee.

Let me comment briefly on some of the reasons why we felt we could agree not to make any new commitments for arms sales to Taiwan during 1979. First, we did not wish to create an impression that we were loading Taiwan up with additional arms as an offset to normal relations to Peking. Such action would have implied an urgent need to shore up Taiwan's forces --a judgement at odds with our appraisal of Taiwan's current strength. Moreover, we had already approved an extensive arms sales program for FY 1979 which includes ongoing deliveries that will not be completed until 1983. Hence, there was no pressing need for new sales to Taiwan during 1979.

Second, during CY 1979 we will be establishing a new legal basis for future arms sales to Taiwan through the passage of the Omnibus legislation, as well as establishing procedures for processing these sales in a manner compatible with the unofficial relations we shall conduct with the people of Taiwan.

THE FUTURE SECURITY OF TAIWAN

In closing, let me emphasize that we will sustain our concern for the security and well-being of the people on Taiwan. And there are positive steps that we can and will take to express that concern in a tangible way. Of primary importance to Taiwan's security has been the island's ability to maintain modern military forces adequate for its self-defense. Over the years, the U.S. has given Taiwan access, through Foreign Military Sales (FMS) and commercial channels to selected defensive equipment, with particular emphasis on air and naval defenses. We will continue to do so.

We are also completing processing formalities, including the requisite notification of Congress, for the sale to Taiwan of those major items of military equipment approved late in 1978, including additional F-5E interceptor aircraft with improved weaponry such as precision-guided-munitions and Maverick missiles.

In sum, the U.S. is not "abandoning" Taiwan. Our interest in the future security of the people of the island and the peaceful resolution of the Taiwan issue by the Chinese themselves will continue.

Source: "Taiwan" Hearings Before the Committee on Foreign Relations, U.S. Senate, February 5-22, 1979. pp. 35-38.

TRA9

LETTER TO HON. LESTER L. WOLFF FROM FORMER PRESIDENT NIXON

RICHARD NIXON
LA CASA, PACIFICA.
San Clemente, Calif., February 14, 1979.

HON. LESTER L. WOLFF,
Chairman, Subcommittee on Asian and Pacific Affairs,
House of Representatives, Washington, D.C.

Dear Mr. Chairman: With regard to your letter of February 2, I must respectfully decline your invitation to testify before your committee. I see no useful purpose to be served by my trying to second-guess President Carter's P.R.C. normalization decision. Any one of us might have handled the situation differently, but now the decision has been made we should look to the future and not to the past.

With regard to the questions you raised in your letter, Dr. Kissinger and I had extensive discussions with Chairman Mao and Premier Chou En-lai on the Taiwan issue in 1972. We could not reach an agreement and consequently stated our positions separately in the Shanghai Communique. In that document the U.S. "reaffirmed" its support of a peaceful resolution of the Taiwan issue. I consider that to be an unequivocal moral commitment. In my view U.S. policies toward the P.R.C. and Taiwan in the future should be formulated in a way to honor or that commitment.

Normalization of U.S. relations with the P.R.C. is indispensable in furthering our goal of building a structure of peace in Asia and in the world. But at a time when U.S. credibility as a dependable ally and friend is being questioned in a number of countries, it is also vitally important that the Taiwan issue be handled in a way which will reassure other nations-- whether old friends, new friends, potential friends or wavering friends--that it is safe to rely on America's word and to be America's friend.

Sincerely,

RICHARD NIXON

Source: Reprinted in "Implementation of Taiwan Relations Act: Issues and Concerns." Hearings before the Subcommittee on Asian and Pacific Affairs of the Committee on Foreign Affairs, House of Representatives 96th Congress, 1st Session, February 14-15, 1979. p. 136.

TRA10

SENATOR JESSE HELMS: COMMENTS ON
PRESIDENT CARTER'S TAIWAN POLICY (Excerpts)

The whole question of the future security of Taiwan is cast into a deep shade by the failure of the Administration to secure commitments and practical arrangements that would guarantee Taiwan's freedom of action. More deeply disturbing is not simply the failure to obtain such guarantees; the most damaging blow is the admission that Taiwan's future was conceded in advance to the will of Peking. The testimony of Ambassador Woodcock before this Committee was startling in its revelation of the abject capitulation of the United States before the rulers of Peking.

It had been the American position that we were seeking a guarantee of the nonuse of force in the settlement of the Taiwan question. I personally came to the conclusion --and I am now speaking in personal terms--that to insist upon that would be to run into a roadblock because it was, in essence, the negotiation of sovereignty. It isn't a question of who we look upon in the situation. The Chinese in Peking and The Chinese in Taipei both insisted that there was one China. It was a question of trying to negotiate directly a guarantee of the nonuse of force by a sovereign government against what in the mind of that government is its own province. So central to our negotiations beginning in the period of July, 1978, was our insistence and our expectancy that it would be settled on a peaceful basis, but recognizing the roadblock of the sovereignty issue, which would have led the negotiations nowhere.

The CHAIRMAN. At any time during the negotiations over the period that you were in Peking, was the matter of an express commitment by Peking against the use of force in settling the Taiwan question posed?

Ambassador WOODCOCK. Not by me, sir. No.

Keeping in mind that the Ambassador was the sole channel for the negotiations which led to "normalization", we must conclude the following:

1. Peking considers that it has sovereign authority over Taiwan.
2. The use of force is the ultimate determinate of sovereignty.
3. Peking's ultimate sovereignty over Taiwan was a nonnegotiable item for Peking.
4. The United States view of Peking's sovereignty over Taiwan is irrelevant to Peking's intention to assert that sovereignty.
5. The United States, in refusing even to attempt to negotiate the question, conceded the ultimate disposition of Taiwan to Peking's authority.
6. The United States encourages the incorporation of Taiwan into the People's Republic of China by peaceful means.
7. The United States would be displeased if force were used to bring about unification, but we expect that "unification" by some means would be the "settlement" of the Taiwan question.

A "DECENT INTERVAL" FOR TAIWAN

These conclusions, which flow indisputably from Ambassador Woodcock's testimony, can leave no particle of doubt that the New China Policy has already surrendered the legal and moral status of Taiwan to the Communist rulers of Peking. All that is retained is a pragmatic, under-the-table relationship, designed to provide a temporary umbrella, a "decent interval," as it were, to shield the people on Taiwan from an immediate blow, to give time to phase our American Capital investment there if necessary, and to bamboozle the American people.

The impact of the new China policy is that both Peking and the United States agree that Taiwan has only one option: To come under Communist hegemony, to use the word that Peking always applies to the Soviet Union. The only question remaining for Taiwan is a question of timing. We are saying that Taiwan has no right to refuse indefinitely. And to help Taiwan to negotiate quickly, both the PRC and the United States hold the ultimate levers: the PRC retaining the right to use force, and the United States retaining the right to supply defensive weapons. Our right to supply weapons conceivably could be continued at such a level as to force the PRC into a better deal for Taiwan and for American investment there; but it could also be withheld if Taiwan were recalcitrant and refused to be absorbed into the Communist system. The execution of the New China Policy so far ought to be a warning to the people on Taiwan that the present leadership of the United States is willing to subordinate the human rights and dignity of the people of Taiwan to other considerations.

It is for this reason that I have found a widespread concern among my colleagues over the exact nature of the security guarantees to Taiwan. The questions turns upon whether the policy of the United States is to support the indefinite autonomy of the people on Taiwan, or whether our security assistance is to support the interests of the New China Policy. The information, at first suppressed, that no new weapons would be supplied under the Mutual Defense Treaty during the last year of its existence is further evidence that the architects of the New China Policy are seeking to avoid any real test of our true intentions.

The notion that Taiwan's social, economic, and political autonomy could be preserved within the sovereignty of the PRC will hardly bear the least examination. The notorious example of Tibet, which concluded a written agreement with Peking guaranteeing its religious, social, and political systems, demonstrates the extent to which Peking will perpetuate cultural genocide.

TWO GOVERNMENTS IN ONE CHINA

The New China Policy is predicated upon the expectation that Taiwan will eventually come under the domination of the Communist government in Peking. The Institute provides a restraining mechanism for slowing down that process; if strengthened, it could help thwart that process completely.

Hopefully, the Institute can provide a bridge to a more realistic China policy. The reality is that China has two governments which each effectively control different parts of Chinese territory. A realistic policy would recognize each government as competent in the territory it controls. There is no need to recognize the claim which each makes to the territory controlled by the other, nor is there any need to deny such claims. Above all, the United States should refrain from actions which would tend to coerce "unification."

The New China Policy is despicable not because it tries to deal with mainland China, but because its aim is to consign the people on Taiwan to a fate which they would not freely choose. It attempts to retain the substance of sovereignty for Taiwan while conceding the juridical basis for sovereignty to the Communist rulers of Peking. Insofar as the Institute retains the substance of a relationship with a sovereign power, the Institute should be encouraged and strengthened. For the decision of the President of the United States is not determinative *de jure* of the existence of a sovereign state. The Republic of China remains a sovereign state as long as it effectively controls its own territory. As long as a small nation retains the help of allies who will back up its sovereign powers with a defensive capability, it can retain its independence. The Institute, for the time being, can perform that function.

Congress must keep a close oversight on the Institute to ensure that it is used to preserve Taiwan's independent options, not to destroy them. Congress must avoid complicity in the New China Policy.

THREE MAJOR ISSUES

Three major issues were raised by the President's actions of December 15, 1978.

First, the President derecognized a long-time ally and friend, the Republic of China. This precipitate action not only was unnecessary, it came at the worst possible time. As the world looked to the United States for a demonstration of resolve and fidelity after a period of growing setbacks for American interests, the world saw instead vacillation, weakness and betrayal of friendship in the derecognition of the Republic of China.

It is not up to the Congress to change that action. The President may choose the nations he wishes to recognize, and which he does not. The issue of derecognition may well be a matter to be dealt with in the 1980 Presidential elections. That is a more proper forum for settlement of that issue.

The second issue raised by the President's actions of December 15, 1978, is the termination of a mutual defense treaty with an ally in time of peace.

Needless to say, this unprecedented action has not gone without notice by allies and opponents alike around the world. Despite Administration protestations to the contrary, many of our allies rightfully question the value of the United States' mutual security commitments. Newspaper reports that the Ambassador the United States from one nation bordering the Indian Ocean littoral has sought to be moved to Moscow because "that is where the power is" cannot be brushed aside as reportage of a mere diplomatic aberration. How much the Presidential decision to abandon the people on Taiwan affected the Ambassador's decision one only can speculate; but it is difficult to believe that it had no effect.

The Congress may not be the proper forum to deal with the specific issue of termination of the treaty, *per se*; although Congress certainly must deal with the broader issue of the defense of the people on Taiwan. Already, a court suit has been undertaken to deal with the President's power to terminate a treaty with an ally, unilaterally and without prior consultation with and approval by the Congress. At a time when the American public is wary of overextension of Executive power, a proper resolution of the issues raised in the suit will do much to define the limits of Executive power.

The final issue raised by the President's actions of December 15, 1978, is the protection of the interests of the people of the United States in Taiwan, and the concurrent protection of the legitimate interests of our friends and allies, the people of the Republic of China on Taiwan....

In spite of this legislation, there are many issues which need to be addressed by the Congress, so as not to jeopardize our valuable relations with the people on Taiwan. Foremost is the continuing interest of the people of the United States in the security and defense of the people on Taiwan. Nor should the value of Taiwan to legitimate U.S. and allied security interests in the Pacific be overlooked. Close scrutiny should be made of the People's Republic of China, not only in terms of what good can come of the new United States relations with that nation, but also what pitfalls exist for U.S. policymakers.

TAIWAN, AN ALLY AND LONGSTANDING FRIEND

As America's eighth largest trading partner, the Republic of China remains an important economic asset of the United States. One expert has told me that withdrawal of Taiwan's funds from the banks in New York would precipitate a severe economic situation, forcing some banks to face possible bankruptcy as a result. Thus, many would not want to antagonize Taiwan too harshly.

Strategically, Taiwan serves as an important intelligence resource for the United States off the coast of mainland China. While some may contend that a larger U.S. presence in the PRC will facilitate intelligence gathering and obviate, somewhat, Taiwan's importance, many do not agree with conclusion. One need only consider the restrictions on movement in the Soviet Union to see how the other major totalitarian state in the region deals with human intelligence gathering. The Taiwan post is so important for the United States, and will remain so. Nor should anyone be deluded into believing that such intelligence gathering is unnecessary, now that the United States has opened up full relations with Peking.

We must not forget that Peking views any relationship with the United States as only a matter of necessity--again, playing off the far barbarian against the near one. Peking's relationship with the United States will remain an adversary one over the long haul, as even top China hands in the Carter Administration are quick to admit.

With rumored new missile capability under development, with a missile possibly able to reach the United States said to be part of the Chinese strategic nuclear delivery program, the United States has every need to be wary of Peking's long-term intentions. Thus, the need continues for a Taiwan base, not only for intelligence gathering, but as an advance-base for U.S. forces in any emergency, either on the mainland, or in Japan or Korea.

Thus, the United States continues to have important and strategic interests in Taiwan.

Source: "Taiwan Enabling Act." Report of the Committee on Foreign Relations, March 1, 1979. pp. 46-60.

TRA11

PUBLIC LAW 96-8 APRIL 10, 1979

96TH CONGRESS

AN ACT

To help maintain peace, security, and stability in the Western Pacific and to promote the foreign policy of the United States by authorizing the continuation of commercial, cultural, and other relations between the people of the United States and the people on Taiwan, and for other purposes.

Be it enacted by the Senate and House of Representatives of the United States of America in Congress assembled,

SHORT TITLE

SECTION 1. This Act may be cited as the "Taiwan Relations Act."

FINDINGS AND DECLARATION OF POLICY

SEC. 2 (a) The President having terminated governmental relations between the United States and the governing authorities on Taiwan recognized by the United States as the Republic of China prior to January 1, 1979, the Congress finds that the enactment of this Act is necessary--

(1) to help maintain peace, security, and stability in Western Pacific; and

(2) to promote the foreign policy of the United States by authorizing the continuation of commercial, cultural, and other relations between the people of the United States and the people on Taiwan.

(b) It is the policy of the United States--

(1) to preserve and promote extensive, close, and friendly commercial, cultural, and other relations between the people of the United States and the people on Taiwan, as well as the people on the China mainland and all other peoples of the Western Pacific area;

(2) to declare that peace and stability in the area are in the political, security, and economic interests of the United States, and are matters of international concern;

(3) to make clear that the United States decision to establish diplomatic relations with the People's Republic of China rests upon the expectation that the future of Taiwan will be determined by peaceful means;

(4) to consider any effort to determine the future of Taiwan by other than peaceful means, including by boycotts or embargoes, a threat to the peace and security of the Western Pacific area and of grave concern to the United States;

(5) to provide Taiwan with arms of a defensive character, and

(6) to maintain the capacity of the United States to resist any resort to force or other forms of coercion that would jeopardize the security, or the social or economic system, of the people on Taiwan.

(c) Nothing contained in this Act shall contravene the interest of the United States in human rights, especially with respect to the human rights of all the approximately eighteen million inhabitants of Taiwan. The preservation and enhancement of the human rights of all the people on Taiwan are hereby reaffirmed as objectives of the United States.

IMPLEMENTATION OF UNITED STATES POLICY WITH REGARD TO TAIWAN

SEC. 3. (a) In furtherance of the policy set forth in section 2 of this Act, the United States will make available to Taiwan such defense articles and defense services in such quantity as may be necessary to enable Taiwan to maintain a sufficient self-defense capability.

(b) The President and the Congress shall determine the nature and quantity of such defense articles and services based solely upon their judgment of the needs of Taiwan, in accordance with procedures established by law. Such determination of Taiwan's defense needs shall include review by United States military authorities in connection with recommendations to the President and the Congress.

(c) The President is directed to inform the Congress promptly of any threat to the security or the social or economic system of the people on Taiwan and any danger to the interests of the United States arising therefrom. The President and the Congress shall determine, in accordance with constitutional processes, appropriate action by the United States in response to any such danger.

APPLICATION OF LAWS; INTERNATIONAL AGREEMENTS

SEC. 4. (a) The absence of diplomatic relations or recognition shall not affect the application of the laws of the United States with respect to Taiwan prior to January 1, 1979.

(b) The application of subsection (a) of this section shall include, but shall not be limited to, the following:

(1)   Whenever the laws of the United States refer or relate to foreign countries, nations, states, governments, or similar entities, such terms shall include and such laws shall apply with respect to Taiwan.

(2)   Whenever authorized by or pursuant to the laws of the United States to conduct or carry out programs, transactions, or other relations with respect to foreign countries, nations, states, governments, or similar entities, the President or any agency of the United States Government is authorized to conduct and carry out, in accordance with section 6 of this Act, such programs, transactions, and other relations with respect to Taiwan (including, but not limited to, the performance of services for the United States through contracts with commercial entities on Taiwan), in accordance with the applicable laws of the United States.

(3)(A)   The absence of diplomatic relations and recognition with respect to Taiwan shall not abrogate, infringe, modify, deny, or otherwise affect in any way any rights or obligations (including but not limited to those involving contracts, debts, or property interests of any kind) under the laws of the United States heretofore or hereafter acquired by or with respect to Taiwan.

(B)   For all purposes under the laws of the United States, including actions in any court in the United States, recognition of the People's Republic of China shall not affect in any way the ownership of or other rights or interests in properties, tangible and intangible, and other things of value, owned or held on or prior to December 31, 1978, or thereafter acquired or earned by the government authorities on Taiwan.

(4)   Whenever the application of the laws of the United States depends upon the law that is or was applicable on Taiwan or compliance therewith, the law applied by the people on Taiwan shall be considered the applicable law for that purpose.

(5)   Nothing in this Act, nor the facts of the President's action in extending diplomatic recognition to the People's Republic of China, the absence of diplomatic relations between the people on Taiwan and the United States, or the lack of recognition by the United States, and attendant circumstances thereto, shall be construed in any administrative or judicial proceeding as a basis for any United States Government agency, commission, or department to make a finding of fact or determination of law, under the Atomic Energy Act of 1954 and the Nuclear Non-Proliferation Act of 1978, to deny an export license application or to revoke an existing export license for nuclear exports to Taiwan.

(6)   For purposes of the Immigration and Nationality Act, Taiwan may be treated in the manner specified in the first sentence of section 202(b) of that Act.

(7)   The capacity of Taiwan to sue and be sued in courts in the United States, in accordance with the laws of the United States, shall not be abrogated, infringed, modified, denied, or otherwise affected in any way by the absence of diplomatic relations or recognition.

(8)   No requirement, whether expressed or implied, under the laws of the United States with respect to maintenance of diplomatic relations or recognition shall be applicable with respect to Taiwan.

(c)   For all purposes, including actions in any court in the United States, the Congress approves the continuation in force of all treaties and other international agreements, including multilateral conventions, entered into by the United States and the governing authorities on Taiwan recognized by the United States as the Republic of China prior to January 1, 1979, and in force between then on December 31, 1978, unless and until terminated in accordance with law.

(d) Nothing in this Act may be construed as a basis for supporting the exclusion or expulsion of Taiwan from continued membership in any international financial institution or any other international organization.

OVERSEAS PRIVATE INVESTMENT CORPORATION

SEC. 5. (A) During the three-year period beginning on the date of enactment of this Act, the $1,000 per capita income restriction in clause (2) of the second undesignated paragraph of section 231 of the Foreign Assistance Act of 1961 shall not restrict the activities of the Overseas Private Investment Corporation in determining whether to provide any insurance, reinsurance, loans, or guaranties with respect to investment projects on Taiwan.

(b) Except as provided in subsection (a) of this section, in issuing insurance, reinsurance, loans, or guaranties with respect to investment projects on Taiwan, the Overseas Private Insurance Corporation shall apply the same criteria as those applicable in other parts of the world.

THE AMERICAN INSTITUTE OF TAIWAN

SEC. 6 (a) Programs, transactions and other relations conducted or carried out by the President or any agency of the United States Government with respect to Taiwan shall, in manner and to the extent directed by the President, be conducted and carried out by or through--

(1) The American Institute in Taiwan, a nonprofit corporation incorporated under the laws of the District of Columbia, or

(2) such comparable successor nongovernmental entity as the President may designate, (hereafter in this Act referred to as the "Institute").

(b) Whenever the President or any agency of the United States Government is authorized or required by or pursuant to the laws of the United States to enter into, perform, enforce, or have in force an agreement or transaction relative to Taiwan, such agreement or transaction shall be entered into, performed, and enforced, in the manner and to the extent directed by the President, by or through the Institute.

(c) To the extent that any law, rule, regulation, or ordinance of the District of Columbia, or of any State or political subdivision thereof in which the Institute is incorporated or doing business, impedes or otherwise interferes with the performance of the functions of the Institute pursuant to this Act, such law, rule, regulation, or ordinance shall be deemed to be preempted by this Act.

SERVICES BY THE INSTITUTE TO UNITED STATES CITIZENS ON TAIWAN

SEC. 7. (a) The Institute may authorize any of its employees on Taiwan--

(1) to administer to or take from any person an oath, affirmation, affidavit, or deposition, and to perform any notarial act which any notary public is required or authorized by law to perform within the United States;

(2) To act as provisional conservator of the personal estates of deceased United States citizens; and

(3) to assist and protect the interest of United States persons by performing other acts such as are authorized to be performed outside the United States for consular purposes by such laws of the United States as the President may specify.

(b) Acts performed by authorized employees of the Institute under this section shall be valid, and of like force and effect within the United States, as if performed by any other person authorized under the laws of the United States to perform such acts.

TAX EXEMPT STATUS OF THE INSTITUTE

SEC. 8. (a) The Institute, its property, and its income are exempt from all taxation now or hereafter imposed by the United States (except to the extent that section 11(a)(3) of this Act requires the imposition of taxes imposed under chapter 21 of the Internal Revenue Code of 1954, relating to the Federal Insurance Contributions Act) or by any State or local taxing authority of the United States.

(b) For purposes of the Internal Revenue Code of 1954, the Institute shall be treated as an organization described in sections 170(b)(1)(A), 170(c), 2055(a), 2106(a)(2)(A), 2522(a), and 2522(b).

FURNISHING PROPERTY AND SERVICES TO
AND OBTAINING SERVICES FROM THE INSTITUTE

SEC. 9. (a) Any agency of the United States Government is authorized to sell, loan, or lease property (including interests therein) to, and to perform administrative and technical support functions and services for the operations of, the Institute upon such terms and conditions as the President may direct. Reimbursements to agencies under this subsection shall be credited to the current applicable appropriation of the agency concerned.

(b) Any agency of the United States Government is authorized to acquire and accept services from the Institute upon such terms and conditions as the President may direct. Whenever the President determines it to be in furtherance of the purposes of this Act, the procurement of services by such agencies from the Institute may be effected without regard to such laws of the United States normally applicable to the acquisition of services by such agencies as the President may specify by Executive order.

(c) Any agency of the United States Government making funds available to the Institute in accordance with this Act shall make arrangements with the Institute for the Comptroller General of the United States to have access to the books and records of the Institute and the opportunity to audit the operations of the Institute.

TAIWAN INSTRUMENTALITY

SEC. 10 (a) Whenever the President or any agency of the United States Government is authorized or required by or pursuant to the laws of the United States to render or provide to or to receive or accept from Taiwan, any performance, communication, assurance, undertaking, or other action, such action shall, in the manner and to the extent directed by the President, be rendered or provided to, or received or accepted from, an instrumentality established by Taiwan which the President determines has the necessary authority under the laws applied by the people on Taiwan to provide assurances and take other actions on behalf of Taiwan in accordance with this Act.

(b) The President is requested to extend to the instrumentality established by Taiwan the same number of offices and complement of personnel as were previously operated in the United States by the governing authorities on Taiwan recognized as the Republic of China prior to January 1, 1979.

(c) Upon the granting by Taiwan of comparable privileges and immunities with respect to the Institute and its appropriate personnel, the President is authorized to extend with respect to the Taiwan instrumentality and its appropriate personnel, such privileges and immunities (subject to appropriate conditions and obligations) as may be necessary for the effective performance of their functions.

SEPARATION OF GOVERNMENT PERSONNEL
FOR EMPLOYMENT WITH THE INSTITUTE

SEC. 11. (a)(1) Under such terms and conditions as the President may direct, any agency of the United States Government may separate from Government service for a specified period any officer or employee of that agency who accepts employment with the Institute.

(2) An officer or employee separated by an agency under paragraph (1) of this subsection for employment with the Institute shall be entitled upon termination of such employment to reemployment or reinstatement with such agency (or a successor agency) in an appropriate position with the attendant rights, privileges, and benefits with the officer or employee would have had or acquired had he or she not been so separated, subject to such time period and other conditions as the President may prescribe.

(3) An officer or employee entitled to reemployment or reinstatement rights under paragraph (2) of this subsection shall, while continuously employed by the Institute with no break in continuity of service, continue to participate in any benefit program in which such officer or employee was participating prior to employment by the Institute, including programs for compensation for job-related death, injury, or illness; programs for health and life insurance; programs for annual, sick, and other statutory leave; and programs for retirement under any system established by the laws of the United States; except that employment with the Institute shall be the basis for participation in such programs only to the extent that employee deductions and employer contributions, as required, in payment for such participation for the period of employment with the Institute, are currently deposited in the program's or system's fund or depository. Death or retirement of any such officer or employee during approved service with the Institute and prior to reemployment or reinstatement shall be considered a death in or retirement from Government service for purposes of any employee or survivor benefits acquired by reason of service with an agency of the United States Government.

(4) Any officer or employee of an agency of the United States Government who entered into service with the Institute on approved leave of absence without pay prior to the enactment of this Act shall receive the benefits of this section for the period of such service.

(b) Any agency of the United States Government employing alien personnel on Taiwan may transfer such personnel, with accrued allowances, benefits, and rights, to the Institute without a break in service for purposes of retirement and other benefits, including continued participation in any system established by the laws of the United States for the retirement of employees in which the alien was participating prior to the transfer to the Institute, except that employment with the Institute shall be creditable for retirement purposes only to the extent that employee deductions and employer contributions, as required, in payment for such participation for the period of employment with the Institute, are currently deposited in the system's fund or depository.

(c) Employees of the Institute shall not be employees of the United States and, in representing the Institute, shall be exempt from section 207 of title 18, United States Code.

(d)(1) For purposes of sections 911 and 913 of the Internal Revenue Code of 1954, amounts paid by the Institute to its employees shall not be treated as earned income. Amounts received by employees of the Institute shall not be included in gross income, and shall be exempt from taxation, to the extent that they are equivalent to amounts received by civilian officers and employees of the Government of the United States as allowances and benefits which are exempt from taxation under section 912 of such Code.

(2) Except to the extent required by subsection (a)(3) of this section, service performed in the employ of the Institute shall not constitute employment for purposes of chapter 21 of such Code and title II of the Social Security Act.

REPORTING REQUIREMENT

SEC. 12. (a) The Secretary of State shall transmit to the Congress the text of any agreement to which the Institute is a party. However, any such agreement the immediate public disclosure of which would, in the opinion of the President, be prejudicial to the national security of the United States shall not be so transmitted to the Congress but shall be transmitted to the Committee on Foreign Relations of the Senate and the Committee on Foreign Affairs of the House of Representatives under an appropriate injunction of secrecy to be removed only upon due notice from the President.

(b) For purposes of subsection (a), the term "agreement" includes--

(1) any agreement entered into between the Institute and the governing authorities on Taiwan or the instrumentality established by Taiwan; and
(2) any agreement entered into between the Institute and an agency of the United States Government.

(c) Agreements and transactions made or to be made by or through the Institute shall be subject to the same congressional notification, review, and approval requirements and procedures as if such agreements and transactions were made by or through the agency of the United States Government on behalf of which the Institute is acting.

(d) During the two-year period beginning on the effective date of this Act, the Secretary of State shall transmit to the Speaker of the House of Representatives and the Committee on Foreign Relations of the Senate, every six months, a report describing and reviewing economic relations between the United States and Taiwan, noting any interference with normal commercial relations.

RULES AND REGULATIONS

SEC. 13. The President is authorized to prescribe such rules and regulations as he may deem appropriate to carry out the purposes of this Act. During the three-year period beginning on the effective date of this Act, such rules and regulations shall be transmitted promptly to the Speaker of the House of Representatives and to the Committee on Foreign Relations of the

Senate. Such action shall not, however, relieve the Institute of the responsibilities placed upon it by this Act.

CONGRESSIONAL OVERSIGHT

SEC. 14. (a) The Committee on Foreign Affairs of the House of Representatives, the Committee on Foreign Relations of the Senate, and other appropriate committees of the Congress shall monitor--

(1) the implementation of the provisions of this Act;
(2) the operation and procedures of the Institute;
(3) the legal and technical aspects of the continuing relationship between the United States and Taiwan; and
(4) the implementation of the policies of the United States concerning security and cooperation in East Asia.

(b) Such committees shall report, as appropriate, to their respective Houses on the results of their monitoring.

DEFINITIONS

SEC. 15. For purposes of this Act--

(1) the term "laws of the United States" includes any statute, rule, regulation, ordinance, order, or judicial rule of decision of the United States or any political subdivision thereof; and
(2) the term "Taiwan" includes, as the context may require, the islands of Taiwan and the Pescadores, the people on those islands, corporations and other entities and associations created or organized under the laws applied on those islands, and the governing authorities on Taiwan recognized by the United States as the Republic of China prior to January 1, 1979, and any successor governing authorities (including political subdivision, agencies, and instrumentalities thereof).

AUTHORIZATION OF APPROPRIATIONS

SEC. 16. In addition to funds otherwise available to carry out the provisions of this Act, there are authorized to be appropriated to the Secretary of State for the fiscal year 1980 such funds as may be necessary to carry out such provisions. Such funds are authorized to remain available until expended.

SEVERABILITY OF PROVISIONS

SEC. 17. If any provision of this Act or the application thereof to any person or circumstance is held invalid, the remainder of the Act and the application of such provision to any other person or circumstance shall not be affected thereby.

EFFECTIVE DATE

SEC. 18. This Act shall be effective as of January 1, 1979.

Approved April 10, 1979.

LEGISLATIVE HISTORY:

HOUSE REPORTS: No. 96-26 (Comm. on Foreign Affairs) and No. 96-71 (Comm. of   Conference).
SENATE REPORT: No. 96-7 accompanying S. 245 (Comm. on Foreign Relations).
CONGRESSIONAL RECORD, Vol. 125 (1979):
    Mar. 8, 13, considered and passed House.
    Mar. 5, 7, 8, 12, 13, S. 245 considered and passed Senate.
    Mar. 14, proceedings vitiated; H.R. 2479, amended, passed in lieu.
    Mar. 28, House agreed to conference report.
    Mar. 29, Senate agreed to conference report.
WEEKLY COMPILATION OF PRESIDENTIAL DOCUMENTS, Vol. 15, No. 15:
    Apr. 10, Presidential statement.

Source: *United States Statutes at Large*, 96th Congress, 1st Session, Volume 93. U.S.
                 Government Printing Office, Washington, DC, 1981.

TRA12
Ref No: (68) WEIFA 0228

                           Coordination Council for North American Affairs
                           133 Po Ai Road, Taipei, Taiwan
                           Republic of China
                           Tel 312-0888

                           June 4, 1979

Communications Programs Office
American Institute in Taiwan
Attention: Mr. William A. Brown
7, Lane 134, Hsin Yi Rd., Sec. 3
Taipei, Taiwan

Dear Mr. Brown:

Your letter of April 14, 1979 concerning the Foundation of Scholarly Exchange, addressed to
Dr. Tsai Weiping, Chairman of the Coordination Council for North American Affairs, has
been brought to my attention.

In reply, I wish to inform you that the points made in your letter are acceptable, and we will
proceed our contacts on this basis, with the understanding that the incumbent board members
of the Chinese side will remain unchanged. This letter, together with your letter, will constitute
an agreement between us. The CCNAA has been given the responsibility to deal with the AID
on matters relating to this agreement.

                           Sincerely,

                           Paul S.K. Tso
                           Secretary-General

April 14, 1979

Dr. Ts'ai Wei-p'ing
Chairman
Coordination Council for
  North American Affairs
133 Po Ai Road
Taipei

Dear Dr. Ts'ai:

Please be advised that this Institute desires to comply with the provisions of the Agreement of April 23, 1964, which provides for the finance of certain educational and cultural exchange programs. To that end, we propose that the foundation established by Article 1 of the Agreement be continued as the Foundation for Scholarly Exchange and, unless we are advised otherwise by you, the Chairman of the Board of Trustees of the Institute (currently David Dean) will assume the responsibilities and functions formerly assigned to the Secretary of State by Article 2, 3, 7, 10 and 12 of that Agreement. In like manner, the Director of the AIT Taipei Office shall perform the responsibilities and functions formerly assigned to the Chief of Mission and at least three other employees of the Institute shall be considered qualified pursuant to Article 5 for appointment to the Board of Directors of the Foundation. We assume your organization will take on the responsibilities and perform the functions formerly assigned to your government and to the Ministries of Education and Foreign Affairs. (The total number of Board of Directors, five from each side, shall remain as ten as provided in Article 5.)

In all, other respects we propose to continue the provisions of the Agreement in the hope that the educational and cultural exchanges may be continued without disruption.

> William A. Brown
> Acting Director
> American Institute
>   in Taiwan
> Taipei Office

Source: American Institute in Taiwan, Arlington, Virginia.

TRA13   OVERSIGHT OF TAIWAN RELATIONS ACT

THURSDAY, NOVEMBER 15, 1979

UNITED STATES SENATE,
SUBCOMMITTEE ON EAST ASIAN AND PACIFIC AFFAIRS
OF THE COMMITTEE ON FOREIGN RELATIONS,
WASHINGTON, D.C.

The subcommittee met, pursuant to notice, at 2:06 p.m., in room 4221, Dirksen Senate Office Building, Hon. John Glenn (chairman of the subcommittee) presiding.
Present: Senators Glenn, Stone, Javits, and Helms.
The CHAIRMAN. The hearing will come to order.

OPENING STATEMENT

The hearing today will consider the Taiwan Relations Act (TRA). We are performing the oversight hearing function of the Foreign Relations Committee, this being the Subcommittee on East Asian and Pacific Affairs.

Secretary Christopher, I welcome you here today and hope you will be able to enlighten us on the intentions of the administration regarding the treaties and agreements that we have with Taiwan.

I particularly am concerned about the air transport agreement which I understand the administration plans to terminate.

It was my understanding throughout the Taiwan Relations Act debate, and I am sure other Senators would agree with me, that, except for the mutual defense Treaty and related military agreements our treaties and agreements with Taiwan would remain in force.

You and others in the administration repeatedly presented this view, and frankly, I was somewhat shocked to discover that this was not the intention by what we have seen from subsequent events.

Clearly, terminating the air transport agreement goes beyond anything I contemplated when we voted to establish our new and unofficial relationship with Taiwan. Replacing it with an " arrangement" does not really change that fact.

I also am somewhat disappointed there was not more consultation on this once you had discovered there was a problem. I would have thought the administration had learned its lesson when it failed to consult adequately with us concerning normalization. In large measure,that is what the TRA was all about in the debate and discussion we had on the Senate floor in regard to it.

We in the Congress wanted to insure that there were no more surprises and that we would play an active role in maintaining our unofficial, but extremely important, relationship with Taiwan.

Despite the lack of consultation, I approve normalizing our relationship with mainland China. I want to see that relationship improve. For too long we have closed our eyes to the reality of PRC (People's Republic of China) control of the mainland and one-quarter of the total world population. I also do not want to turn back the clock on Taiwan, as some might desire. But I also do not think it is necessary to walk constantly on egg shells for fear of upsetting the PRC. It is high time they understand that we intend to maintain close, friendly, but unofficial, relations with Taiwan, the details of which are our business and not theirs. We met their conditions when we normalized--period.

If they cannot accept this or are unhappy with the details of that relationship, so be it. I, for one, do not believe we can afford to make further concessions regarding Taiwan.

Having said this, I think it is important now that we realize there is going to be a problem with treaties and agreements, that we approach each one on a case-by-case basis. In most instances, I do not think it should be necessary to terminate the existing arrangements. We should be able to amend or extend most of them through the respective institutes as circumstances and the passage of time require.

However, there may be cases where termination is most appropriate. In fact, the air transport agreement may be such a case. But I think it is up to the administration to prove this, and PRC threats or demands should not be the sole determining factor of our policy.

Before we proceed, I also would like to announce that I intend this session today to be the first in a series. I consider oversight of the TRA an extremely important matter and will give it my close attention in the coming months. I already anticipate that we will need to examine the question of arms sales to Taiwan, for example, as we will other issues.

In any event, soon after the first of the year, probably in the early spring, to coincide with the first anniversary of the act, I plan to conduct comprehensive hearings and look closely at the overall implementation of the TRA. In this regard, I have requested GAO (General Accounting Office) assistance.

I would be lad to give you a copy of the letter I have sent to them so you will know the details of our request.

(The letter referred to follows:)

U.S.SENATE
COMMITTEE ON FOREIGN RELATIONS
WASHINGTON, D.C., NOVEMBER 6, 1979.

Hon. Elmer B. Staats,
Comptroller General of the United States,
Washington, D.C.

Dear Mr. Staats: I am writing to request that the General Accounting Office conduct an investigation of the operation of the "American Institute in Taiwan," which, as you know, is an organization that was established by the Taiwan Relations Act of 1979 to carry out U.S. Government "Programs, transactions, and other relations...with respect to the people on Taiwan." Such a study would be a central piece of evidence tabled at oversight hearings I plan to hold in the spring regarding the implementation of this Act.

I have in mind an investigation that examines the Institute's problems and successes during the first year, both here in Washington and on Taiwan, and includes an examination of the Taiwan Defense Command's operations since moving to Hawaii. The status of military equipment deliveries planned and scheduled for Taiwan is another area of interest to me.

Obviously, these are very complicated matters involving not only the letter of the Act itself, but also congressional intent, and matters I do not want to make more difficult by dictating too precisely how you should proceed with your investigation. Instead, I suggest that members of your staff contact Carl Ford of the Committee on Foreign Relations staff, who is assisting me with this matter, to work out the details. This procedure has worked well in the past, due primarily, I believe, to the excellent input of your experienced and highly-motivated staff. I think it is the wise course to follow on this occasion.

Best regards.

Sincerely,

JOHN GLENN,
Chairman, Subcommittee on East
Asian and Pacific Affairs.

THE CHAIRMAN. Other studies are planned, and I intend to dispatch staff to Taiwan to view the situation firsthand and report back to the committee in preparation for the oversight hearings which will follow.

Today we will hear from the Honorable Warren Christopher , Deputy Secretary of State. After Secretary Christopher's testimony, we will hear from a panel comprised of Mr. Robert P. Parker, president of the American Chamber of Commerce in Taiwan, William N. Morell, president of the USA-ROC Economic Council; and Victor Li of the Stanford University School of Law.

Mr. Secretary, we welcome you here today. We look forward to your statement and testimony, either in summarized version or its entirety, as you may choose.

Senator Stone, Senator Javits, Senator Percy, and Senator Helms have indicated they will try to attend this meeting. I know Senator Stone plans to be here because I talked with him just a few minutes ago. I presume other Senators will be joining us shortly.

We await your statement.

Source: Hearings before the Subcommittee on East Asia and Pacific Affairs of the Committee of Foreign Relations, United States Senate, pp. 1-3.

TRA14

October 24, 1979

Konsin C. Shah, Representative
Coordination Council for North
 American Affairs
5161 River Road
Washington, DC 20016

Dear Mr. Shah:

I have the honor to refer to recent discussions concerning our bilateral trade. During those discussions, it was noted that as a result of the Tokyo Round trade negotiations, reductions in United States tariffs are expected that will benefit exports from Taiwan, and it was agreed that in consideration of these concessions, measures will be implemented in Taiwan that will benefit exports from the United States. This letter describes these reciprocal actions more fully.

It is understood that among the Tokyo Round concessions to be made by the United States and to be implemented domestically on a non-discriminatory basis will be included certain tariff concessions which have been discussed among us and which are included in the

United States' Schedule XX deposited with the GATT, a copy of which has been furnished to your delegation. Those tariff concessions enumerated in Annex I to this letter will also be implemented in the United States on a non-discriminatory basis. We understand that those items contained in the U.S.Schedule XX for which exports from Taiwan constituted ten percent or more of total U.S. imports in 1976, as well as all articles described in Annex I to this letter, have been considered in establishing their initial bilateral balance. It is further understood that the implementation in the United States of tariff concessions referred to in this letter will begin on January 1, 1980, in accordance with the staging schedules enumerated in Annex I to this letter.

In consideration of the implementation of the above action, we understand that all tariff and non-tariff measure concessions previously offered affecting trade with the United States will continue in effect in Taiwan, and any concessions not yet implemented, with the exception of those items subject to deferred staging as enumerated in Annex II, will be implemented as of January 1, 1980 in Taiwan. We note with satisfaction that the concessions concerning apples and automobiles have already been implemented.

With regard to tariff measures referred to in this letter, both sides shall have the same rights a GATT Contracting Party would have with respect to articles bound in the GATT for which it becomes or ceases to be a principal or substantial supplier.

We are confident that amicable adjustments will be made if necessary to ensure that the bilateral undertakings described in this exchange of letters remain appropriately balanced.

Every effort will be made to consult through appropriate channels on any trade matters, including those covered by this letter.

It is further understood that both sides will consider favorably incorporating matters covered by this letter into other arrangements at an appropriate time.

Sincerely,

David Dean
Chairman of the Board
and Managing Director
October 24, 1979

Mr. David Dean
Chairman of the Board and
  Managing Director
American Institute in Taiwan
1700 North Moore Street
Arlington, Virginia 22209

Dear Mr. Dean:

I have the honor to acknowledge receipt of your letter of today's date...

'We are confident that amicable adjustments will be made if necessary to ensure that the bilateral undertakings described in this exchange of letters remain appropriately balanced. Every effort will be made to consult through appropriate channels on any trade matters, including those covered by this letter. It is further understood that both sides will consider favorably incorporating matters covered by this letter into other arrangements at an appropriate time.'

Sincerely

(signed)
David Dean'"

I have the honor to inform you that the concessions and measures described in your letter with its Annexes will be implemented in Taiwan.

Accordingly, your letter correctly reflects the understandings reached during the course of recent discussions concerning our bilateral trade.

Sincerely,

(signed)
Konsin C. Shah
Representative

Source: American Institute in Taiwan, Arlington, Virginia.

TRA15

COORDINATION COUNCIL FOR NORTH AMERICAN AFFAIRS
OFFICE IN U.S.A.
5161 River Road, Washington, D.C. 20016

December 31, 1979
SI-68031

Mr. David Dean
Chairman of the Board
and Managing Director
American Institute in Taiwan
1700 North Moore Street (17th Floor)
Arlington, VA 22209

Dear Mr. Dean:

In pursuance of our conversation of December 21, 1979 and in view of the urgent need for both parties to implement the proposed courier system, I would like to suggest that Article (4) of your draft of the "AIT-CCNAA Agreement on Privileges, Exemptions and Immunities" be put into effect immediately. This Article reads as follows:

1.   The sending counterpart organization shall be entitled to free communication for all purposes related to the performance of its functions, as well as inviolability for all correspondence related to its functions.

2.   The bag carrying the correspondence referred to in the preceding paragraph and other articles related to the performance of the counterpart organization's functions shall not be opened or detained.

3.   The packages constituting such a bag must bear visible external specified marks of their character and may contain only documents or articles intended for the performance of the organization's designated functions.

4.   The designated carriers of such bags, who shall be provided with a document indicating their status and the number of packages constituting such bags, shall be protected in the performance of their functions. The designated carrier shall enjoy personal inviolability and shall not be liable to any form of arrest or detention.

5.   The sending counterpart organization may designate such carriers ad hoc.

6.   Bags carrying such correspondence and articles may be entrusted to the captain of a commercial aircraft scheduled to land at an authorized post-of-entry. The captain shall be provided with a document indicating the number of packages constituting the bag but the captain shall not be considered to be a designated carrier of such bags. The sending counterpart organization may send one of its members to take possession of such a bag directly and freely from the captain of the aircraft.

Enclosed please find a specimen of a letter to be issued by CCNAA and to be used as a formal certificate for its designated courier. It is requested that the said letter be verified by the U.S. authorities concerned and thus appropriate protection and immunities as agreed upon between the two parties could be accorded t o the designated courier during the performance of his (or her) duty within the U.S. territory.

It is also understood that should there be any further modification of the terms of the said courier system in the final Agreement between the two parties on privileges, exemptions and immunities, the modifications shall supersede the terms agreed to in this letter.

I shall appreciate your prompt attention to this letter and your approval of it shall constitute an agreement between us on this matter.

Sincerely,

Konsin C. Shah
Representative

Enclosure

Source: American Institute in Taiwan, Arlington, Virginia.

CONGRESSIONAL RECORD--HOUSE
                                            MARCH 5, 1979

                              THE U.S. SECURITY RELATIONSHIP
                                       WITH TAIWAN

The SPEAKER pro tempore. Under a previous order of the House, the gentleman
from New York (Mr. Bingham) is recognized for 10 minutes.

MR. BINGHAM. Mr. Speaker, at various times in our debate over normalization of
U.S. relations with the People's Republic of China, the termination of the United States-
Republic of China Mutual Defense Treaty, and the establishment of a basis for continuing
relations between the people of the United States and the people on Taiwan, I have noticed a
tendency on the part of some Members to describe the past U.S. security commitment to
Taiwan in very sweeping, almost absolute terms. I do not believe that this approach is either
helpful to our discussion or historically accurate, and I believe that a good deal of unnecessary
confusion could be avoided if we would keep in mind some of the basic historical realities of
this relationship.

The following points seem to me to be particularly relevant:

First. There was no formal security relationship between the United States and the
Republic of China during its first 5 years on Taiwan.

The decision of the Chinese nationalist leaders in 1949 to evacuate to Taiwan and
reconstitute and continue their operations on the islands was a decision reached entirely on
their own in the aftermath of the collapse of their authority on the mainland and the
consolidation of control there by the Communist side. The U.S. Government played no part
in this decision and no role in the transfer of the nationalist forces and administration to
Taiwan. Secretary Acheson in his controversial but nonetheless authoritative statement of early
1950 which placed Korea outside the basic U.S. defense perimeter, put Taiwan in the same
category. Shortly after the onset of the Korean war, this policy vis-a-vis Taiwan was modified
by President Truman's announcement that Taiwan would come under the protection of the 7th
Fleet. Nevertheless, despite continuing and active interest in the evolving security situation in
the region, there was no formal or mutually agreed security relationship between the United
States and the Republic of China Government on Taiwan until the end of 1954.

Second. The U.S. decision in 1954 to enter into a mutual defense treaty with the ROC
was based primarily on overall U.S. security and political interests rather than bilateral
considerations.

The conclusion of the treaty in December 1954 was the result of a general U.S.
reappraisal of our security posture in the aftermath of the Korean war. It was the last of the
series of mutual security treaties pushed through by Secretary Dulles in the Asian region during
this period--treaties with Japan, Korea, the Philippines, and Australia/New Zealand as well as
the Southeast Asia Collective Defense Treaty (SEATO) completed in September 1954. The
United States-Republic of China treaty thus became one link in the whole chain of treaties with
states on the periphery of the Sino-Soviet region.

It should also be remembered that the treaty was concluded during a period of open
military confrontation in the region. The Korean war had involved direct conflict between
mainland Chinese and American troops. Communist Chinese military operations were actively
being mounted against nationalist-held islands in the Formosa Strait, a campaign which

triggered the introduction and passage of the "Formosa Resolution" in the Congress in January 1955. And the belligerence on the part of the Communist Chinese reflected in these actions was generally considered in the United States to be part of an overall Sino-Soviet strategy directed at bringing down the Western world. The underlying purpose of the whole series of defense treaties was to deter what was seen as worldwide Sino-Soviet adventurism.

It is also worth noting in this context that the conclusion of a United States-Republic of China treaty at this time was one means of explicitly erasing the uncertainty caused by Acheson's 1950 statement placing Taiwan outside the U.S. security perimeter. Had the post-Korean war defense pacts excluded Taiwan, this could well have further tempted the militant mainland leadership to think that the United States would have been indifferent in the fact of an attack on Taiwan.

Third. The mutual defense treaty did not constitute an unqualified or immutable U.S. military commitment to the Republic of China.

The extent of the U.S. commitment and the degree of identity of purpose between the United States and the Republic of China reflected in the treaty were clearly limited. The language of the treaty carefully avoided any implication of U.S. endorsement of the nationalists' declared objective of regaining the mainland by force. U.S. concern lest the defensive guarantees in the treaty embolden the Republic of China to move against the mainland also is evident in the exchange of notes which accompanied the treaty, in which the Republic of China undertook not to use force outside the areas already under its control without advance U.S. agreement.

It is indisputably clear that the commitments undertaken in the treaty were not irrevocable. The termination clause built into the treaty provided that either party could withdraw on 1 year's notice. Further, this action could be taken at the absolute discretion of the withdrawing party; no other conditions were specified. The present U.S. action terminating the treaty is thus in complete conformity with the terms of the treaty.

Fourth. The present situation is dramatically different from that which prevailed when the mutual defense treaty was concluded.

The "Sino-Soviet bloc" has long since been superseded by the Sino-Soviet conflict; the most immediate danger to international peace now posed by the relationship between these two states is that of conflict between them rather than any combined threat against the non-Communist world. The present leaders of Communist China are actively pursuing improved relations and expanded economic ties with the West, a far cry from the armed confrontation of the Korean war period. And Chinese military activity in the Formosa Strait has moderated over time and, with the establishment of normalized relations with the United States, has given way to expressions of People's Republic of China interest in a negotiated reunification involving a remarkable degree of autonomy for Taiwan.

At the same time, Taiwan is now economically stronger, politically more mature, and militarily far better able to defend itself than was the case in the early 1950s. Further, the U.S. stress on the Taiwan issue throughout the prolonged negotiations with the People's Republic of China over normalization, including our explicit intention to continue providing arms to Taiwan, has left the People's Republic of China in no doubt as to our continuing interest in Taiwan's security even after termination of the defense treaty. Thus the termination of the treaty now does not carry with it overtones of again appearing to exclude Taiwan from the area of U.S. security concern in the Pacific.

There is obviously room for honorable men to disagree on various aspects of the U.S. relationship and policy with regard to China. However, I would hope that to the maximum extent possible our discussion could be based on mutual agreement as to the factual background. I hope that these remarks will make a contribution to such an understanding.

CONGRESSIONAL RECORD--SENATE
MARCH 7, 1979

TAIWAN ENABLING ACT

The PRESIDING OFFICER. Under the previous order, the Senate will now resume consideration of the pending business, S. 245, which will be stated by title.

The assistant legislative clerk read as follows:

A bill (S. 245) to promote the foreign policy of the United States through the maintenance of commercial, cultural, and other relations with the people of Taiwan on an unofficial basis, and for other purposes.

Mr. Glenn. Mr President, the bill we take up today, S. 245, the Taiwan enabling legislation, has been significantly modified by the Foreign Relations Committee to correct deficiencies in the original administration proposal. The revised bill clarifies many ambiguities regarding trade, legal, and economic issues, in addition to inserting a specific security clause designed to reassure the people on Taiwan and alert the PRC to our expectations concerning the future.

Many Members share my dissatisfaction with the President's presentation of a fait accompli to Congress, and of the failure to better provide for the security of Taiwan despite an April 1977 Presidential review memorandum (No. 24) which reportedly set a goal of obtaining a specific commitment from the PRC that there would be no use of force against Taiwan.

I want to emphasize that this is a committee-drafted measure, not the administration bill. Taiwan's future is not some vague abstraction; rather, it is the reality of 17 million people with the second highest standard of living in Asia. The Committee, while agreeing upon importance of normalization with the PRC, nevertheless felt these legislative changes were necessary to chart a safer course for Taiwan.

The immediate issue before the committee and the Senate is how to maintain an informal relationship with Taiwan in the absence of formal diplomatic ties. I believe that S. 245 will allow us to retain close and cordial ties with Taiwan, to continue mutually beneficial trade and investment, and to insure the freedom of the people of Taiwan to choose their own destiny.

The instability and violence of Asia during our lifetime has been intertwined with China's inability to rule itself. Since World War II, the festering Chinese civil war and the "one China" claims of both Taiwan and Peking has bedeviled American foreign policy. With the President's announcement of December 15, 1978, the United States opted out of supporting the continuation of that civil war and recognized the People's Republic of China, the Government ruling the mainland of China.

The United States has struggled for four decades to develop and implement an East Asian policy that would protect American interests and contribute to people and stability in the western Pacific. This effort has been carried out at great cost in blood and treasure and with traumatic divisions among our people as to whether the right course was being followed.

The task will not be simple, it will not be easy, but the United States must develop a sound and mutually beneficial relationship with China. Its central geographic position, 1 billion people, untapped resources, and cultural heritage make China the key nation in East Asia. Hostility between China and the United States has led, in part, to two wars. Cooperation between our two nations, even if limited, could benefit us all.

Yet such cooperation can only begin if each nation understands and respects the interests and views of the other. American and Chinese interests and policies coincide in some respects and differ in others, and it is crucial that we can differentiate one from the other. For example, the Sino-Vietnamese border conflict illustrates differing policies. We must remember that those in power today in Peking are essentially the same group that "punished" India in 1962, and may have a greater inclination toward the use of coercion in foreign policy. Americans have tended either to idolize or to disdain the Chinese, and we have frequently exaggerated or under-estimated China's strength. No sound policy can be based upon such distorted perspectives.

Although this legislation deals only with Taiwan, it cannot be viewed in isolation. American policy toward Taiwan must be considered in the context of U.S. policy toward East Asia as a whole. This involves our relations with the People's Republic of China, the Soviet Union, Japan, the Republic of Korea, Australia and New Zealand, and members of the Association of Southeast Asian Nations (ASEAN)--Indonesia, Malaysia, the Philippines, Singapore, and Thailand. Their judgment of our political will and our wisdom will be significantly influenced by our ability to forge a new relationship with the PRC while continuing to conduct mutually beneficial relations with Taiwan. Indeed, the final judgment by Asian leaders on whether we are disengaging from Asia will be directly tied to how we deal with China and Taiwan in the next few year.

The importance of East Asia can hardly be exaggerated. The United States has fought three wars in the past four decades in the Western Pacific region. Even today military conflicts continue to rage in Vietnam and Cambodia. Since 1972, American trade with East Asia surpasses our trade with Western Europe. The natural resources, a third of the world's population, and the future evolution of international trade suggest that a part of our destiny is in East Asia.

The key to a stable East lies in the search for a less hostile relationship between China and the United States. This quest began in the late 1960s, when China's growing fear of the Soviet Union led it to fear the USSR more than the United States. America's bitter experience in the Vietnam war, undertaken in large part to contain China, led the United States to conclude that it was overextended in Asia. A reappraisal of our China policy was thus essential.

BILATERAL RELATIONS

As a result of that reappraisal, the Shanghai Communique, signed during President Nixon's visit to China in 1972, pledged both nations to normalize their relationships. Progress during most of the past 7 years was slow and uneven, despite the commitment of the Nixon, Ford, and Carter administrations to this goal.

The PRC continued to insist that diplomatic relations could only be established after the United States withdrew recognition from the Republic of China, withdrew all U.S. troops from the island, and ended the Mutual Security Treaty. Indeed, in 1977 the PRC added a fourth demand--that no arms sales be made to Taiwan after normalization.

In mid-1978, however, the prospects began to improve. The PRC had begun to place top priority on economic development and its four modernizations--industry, agriculture, science and defense. This forced it to look to the West and Japan for capital goods, technology and financial support. In these circumstances, any military move against Taiwan would risk rupturing its relations with the United States and Japan--thus destroying its "four modernizations" and its hope to become strong enough to face its major adversary, the Soviet Union. Hence, the PRC began to demonstrate greater flexibility on Taiwan.

The PRC began to speak of "reunification," rather than "liberation" regarding Taiwan. Vice Premier Teng Hsiao-ping and other Chinese leaders said that after reunification Taiwan would be allowed to retain its higher living standards, its economic and social system, and even its armed forces. Declaratory policies can change, of course, but nonetheless, these are encouraging sings.

Events moved rapidly late in 1978, and on December 15, President Carter announced that the United States would recognize the PRC and withdraw recognition from the Republic of China on January 1, 1979. Unfortunately, during the negotiations the administration, from my perspective, and I believe that of many other Members, made no effort to obtain a PRC pledge not to use force against Taiwan. It apparently believed that no Chinese Government could pledge itself not to use force against what it claimed was one of its own provinces. Yet, the administration states that it has made clear to the PRC that U.S. recognition was based upon the expectation that the issue would be resolved peacefully. The United States also insisted that the Mutual Security Treaty not be abruptly abrogated, as the PRC had previously demanded, but by being terminated after 1 year's notice as fully provided for in the treaty itself.

Finally, the United States insisted that it would continue to sell selected defensive arms to Taiwan after normalization of relations with the PRC, although it would agree not to make any new sales during 1979. The PRC objected to such arms sales; but agreed to normalization despite the U.S. position. On the basis of these understandings, the United States agreed to the PRC's original three conditions.

CONGRESSIONAL CONSULTATION

Unfortunately, the administration acted with such speed and secrecy that the Congress was not consulted. Let there be no doubt: informing some of us 2 hours before the public announcement cannot be considered consultation. This failure was particularly serious since the Congress had specifically directed the President in the International SEcurity Act of 1978 to consult with Congress before making any move which could affect the Mutual Security Treaty.

Regrettably, the administration's failure to consult Congress on important issues has become, I am afraid, too much of a pattern, one which harms both the administration regarding our new relationship with Taiwan. Congress could well have provided useful advice to the President on how to normalize relations with the PRC while providing for Taiwan's security and economic progress.

TAIWAN-UNITED STATES RELATIONS

The Sino-American rapprochement in the early 1970s was a bitter disappointment for the Republic of China, which feared that it was being abandoned. Its fears increased when Japan shifted its diplomatic recognition from the Republic of China to the PRC in 1972. Nonetheless, Taiwan reacted with imagination and fortitude. It found ways to maintain the de facto status quo on an unofficial basis with Japan, and with other nations which had recognized the PRC. Taiwan's economy and foreign trade continued to expand rapidly--tripling, as a matter of act. More native Taiwanese were brought into important government positions by the mainlanders who control the island, and the two groups have drawn closer together in the face of a common danger. The United States continued to provide arms to Taiwan, and its military capabilities remain sufficient to defend itself against any foreseen PRC threat.

Yet the December 1978 decision of the United States to shift diplomatic recognition from the Republic of China to the People's Republic of China created anger and anxiety on Taiwan. Taiwan had long feared and expected such moves, but their impact was made more severe by the failure of the Administration to consult a long-time ally--or even to inform it of the impending change until the last moment. Nonetheless, Taiwan has once again demonstrated its fortitude and its resilience. Economic activity continues at a fast pace, and despite their worries the people on Taiwan are adapting to their new situation.

American interests and our moral obligation demand that we assist Taiwan in adapting to these changed conditions. Our trade with Taiwan was $7.2 billion in 1978, and is expected to reach $9-$10 billion in 1979. We should make sure that trade can continue to grow. We have more than $500 million in direct private investments in Taiwan, $3 billion in loans from U.S. private institutions, and almost $2 billion from the Export-Import Bank. The island's continued access to both public and private American capital should therefore be assured. Taiwan is one of the few places in the world which has undergone rapid economic growth while reducing income disparities. Such a rare achievement should be encouraged by our policies.

MR. JAVITS. Mr. President, will the Senator yield at that point?

MR. GLENN. Yes.

MR. JAVITS. I think what the Senator has said about trade is so important that it ought to be highlighted and juxtaposed with the expected trade with the People's Republic of China.

Let us remember that the much-applauded Japanese trade deal with the People's Republic is $2 billion a year for 10 years. That is approximately two and half times that which we do with Taiwan right now.

MR. GLENN. I thank the Senator for his remarks.

With less than one-fiftieth the PRC population, Taiwan does seven times as much trade with the U.S. as does the PRC. For the immediate future at least, Taiwan will remain a far more important economic partner.

Finally, there is substantial public support for the maintenance of close relations with Taiwan. Public opinion polls, both before and after President Carter's announcement confirm this fact. Thus, S. 245 provides a legal mechanism to insure the continuity of ties between the people of Taiwan and the people of the United States.

COMMITTEE ACTION

In considering this legislation, the committee heard a balanced and large number of witnesses. These included administration witnesses, such as the Secretary of Defense and the Deputy Secretary of State, a number of Members of the Senate, and public witnesses representing a wide variety of views. We also heard testimony in executive session in dealing with Taiwan's security from the Chairman of the Joint Chiefs of Staff and other senior Defense Department officials. We also consulted many specialists in the fields of trade, banking and law. Their assistance was invaluable to us in dealing with the unique situation we faced.

When the administration recognized the People's Republic of China as the sole legal government of China, it also acknowledged the Chinese position that Taiwan is a part of China. However, the United States has not itself agreed to the PRC position, nor has the United States contested it. Neither the bill submitted by the administration nor the amended bill as approved by the committee takes a position on the extremely complex issue of Taiwan's status under international law. No such determination is necessary. For the bill treats Taiwan as a country for purposes of U.S. domestic law. It is based on the view that any benefits the United States decides to confer on Taiwan by statute can be conferred without regard to Taiwan's international legal identity. The committee consulted several eminent legal scholars, and they supported this view. Thus the bill sets forth the specific manner in which relations between the United States and Taiwan will be maintained.

The bill submitted by the administration provides for U.S. relations with the people on Taiwan to be conducted through the American Institute in Taiwan, a private organization which is funded by the U.S. Government and whose trustees are appointed by the Secretary of State. This is a unique approach for the United States, but one that has worked successfully for Japan since it normalized relations with the PRC.

The administration's bill, while sound in its basic structure and approach, was deficient in several important respects. The committee added a substantial number of amendments to remedy these shortcomings. I do not intend to describe in detail all the changes we made, for these are spelled out in the committee report, which I commend to all Senators and their staff. However, I do want to point out those changes that involve major policy issues.

One central difference between the bill submitted by the administration and the bill approved by the committee concerns the matter of specificity. Many matters in the administration's bill were dealt with implicitly or in very general terms--if they were dealt with at all. The administration apparently believed that the intent of the various sections of the bill was clear enough so that a combination of administrative regulations and court decisions would provide an adequate framework for continued relations with Taiwan. The committee regarded such an approach as risky at best. Trade and investment do not flourish in an unknown and unpredictable environment. Billions of dollars in trade and financial assets are involved, and the laws that govern commercial activity between the United States and Taiwan must be clear.

Likewise, legal issues must be recognized and dealt with to insure minimal disruption. The committee was convinced that a definition of the phrase "the people on Taiwan" which appears throughout the bill was required. One was added, and the meaning of the phrase as defined includes the governing authority as well as the people governed by it. The continued validity of treaties and other international agreements made while the United States still had diplomatic relations with the Republic of China was thus affirmed. Matters involving the legal standing of the people on Taiwan to sue and be sued in U.S. courts, and the protection of the property rights of organizations and persons in both countries were dealt with through other amendments.

The bill as amended authorizes the President, on a reciprocal basis, to extend extensive privileges and immunities to the appropriate members of the organization established by the people on Taiwan to conduct their relations with the United States. The premises and organization itself will be accorded the same privileges and immunities as are accorded to foreign missions, and the privileges and immunities accorded the employers will be complete for all actions taken in the performance of their duties, but will not be as absolute as those granted diplomats. Anything less would seriously limit the effectiveness of the instrumentality. Anything more would have involved treating it as if it were an official government organization.

TAIWAN'S SECURITY

Finally, the bill as submitted by the administration contained no reference to Taiwan security or to the need to provide defensive arms to the people on Taiwan. The committee was determined to correct this weakness, and Members carried out extensive discussions on this matter. Some form of a tangible security clause of an indefinite future was deemed mandatory. I would like to read you the section in the bill that the committee adopted:

(1) to maintain extensive, close and friendly relations with the people on Taiwan;
(2) to make clear that the United States' decision to establish diplomatic relations with the People's Republic of China rests on the expectations that any resolution of the Taiwan issue will be by peaceful means;
(3) to consider any effort to resolve the Taiwan issue by other than peaceful means a threat to the peace and security of the Western Pacific area and of grave concern to the United States; and
(4) to provide the people on Taiwan with arms of a defensive character.
(b) In order to achieve the objectives of this section--
(1) the United States will maintain its capacity to resist any resort to force or other forms of coercion that would jeopardize the security, or the social or economic system, of the people on Taiwan;
(2) the United States will assist the people on Taiwan to maintain a sufficient self-defense capability through the provision of arms of a defensive character;
(3) the President is directed to inform the Congress promptly of any threat to the security of Taiwan and any danger to the interests of the United States arising therefrom; and
(4) the United States will act to meet any danger described in paragraph (3) of this subsection in accordance with constitutional processes and procedures established by law.

I want to make several points about this section of the bill, and the problem it is designed to deal with. First, the provisions should be read as a unit in order to be aware of their full force. Second, there were members of the committee who would have liked somewhat different language, on one point or another, but the committee believed it was important to have as broad a consensus as possible on this central issue. The same is true regarding the Senate as a whole. I believe that both China and Taiwan will be more impressed with a statement that has extensive support, rather than one that is approved by a small majority.

Finally, we must keep in mind the actual military balance in the area today, which is likely to prevail some years hence. The military forces on Taiwan are well-equipped, well-trained, and strongly motivated. U.S. sales of defensive arms can assure that these capabilities remain intact. The PRC has no amphibious capacity, nor it is moving to develop one, and such developments would be detectable well before any invasion could be mounted. It has a major adversary on its northern frontier, and it has recently acquired a small but powerful enemy on its southern border. In these circumstances its ability and inclination to move militarily against Taiwan will be quite limited.

But in this section of the bill, we have also addressed external coercion directed against the island's economic or social system. Thus the United States will maintain its capacity to resist any boycotts or blockades directed against Taiwan.

In conclusion, the committee has expressed in strong terms the U.S. interest in the peaceful resolution of the Taiwan issue.

The committee believes that the provisions we have added to the bill will reassure Taiwan without undermining the new relationship between the United States and the People's Republic of China. Based upon this conviction, we urge the Senate to approve this bill. Prompt passage will provide the continuity crucial in existing laws, treaties, and agreements.

Indeed, rapid passage is crucial for an additional reason--by passing a congressionally refined bill, we can symbolically manifest the American commitment to old friends and reassure out allies in East Asia.

MR. LAXALT. Mr. President, although I intend to support strengthening amendments. I will not oppose S. 245, the Taiwan Enabling Act. It seems to me that it is essential that we provide some mechanism for continuing relations with Taiwan and clearly state our ongoing security commitment to that island nation.

But I deplore the sequence of events which has made the bill necessary, a sequence which to my mind is part and parcel of an overall foreign policy which quite frankly frightens me. With this in mind, I will leave it to my distinguished colleagues to debate the finer points of S. 245, while confining my observations to the deplorable decision to jettison Taiwan, which made this bill necessary.

THE DECISION

Few in this body seriously object to extending diplomatic recognition to the People's Republic of China (PRC). I think most of us felt that this was a decision bound to come and even to a certain extent overdue.

But I do object, and I believe many of my colleagues object, to the manner in which the announcement was made, to the absence of consultation with the Congress, and to the extremely poor nature of the bargain struck.

Quite literally in the deal of night and right in the middle of the holiday season with Congress out of town and the Nation preoccupied with other matters, President Carter presented us with a secretly negotiated, fait accompli. As I under it, our allies of some 30 years standing were cut loose with less than 1 hour's notice. This was a bit much from an administration which had made a campaign issue of the secretive nature of its predecessor's "Lone Ranger" methods and fancied itself to be in the Wilsonian tradition of "open covenants openly arrived at."

Yet, bad as it was to not consult with our allies, neglecting "prior consultation" with the Congress in clear violation of the Dole-Stone amendment to the International Security Assistance Act of 1978 was even worse. Although the administration did claim to have consulted with some Senators, this apparently consisted of at best a few hours' notice prior to the President's appearance on national television. As a cosponsor of the Dole-Stone amendment, this was certainly not my idea of "prior consultation" and I doubt whether it will satisfy any of the other 93 of my colleagues who approved the amendment in a unanimous vote.

In fact, the suddenness of the decision made in extreme secrecy at a time when Congress was not in session could certainly lead one to believe that the administration intentionally chose to evade the provisions of the Dole-Stone amendment. This is particularly disturbing from an administration which had chided its predecessor for not working well with Congress on foreign policy and which had pledged to the electorate in 1976 to do better.

But it is the substance of the China decision that I object to most. The People's Republic of China got everything it has asked for and then some. The United States was left with scarcely a fig leaf to cover what I consider a disastrous retreat. And Taiwan, of course, got nothing at all.

President Nixon could have secured the same terms in 1972 at the time of the Shanghai Communique. President Ford could certainly have secured them during his term of office. Indeed, it is fair to say that the terms offered by Teng Hsiao-ping and accepted by President Carter are little different than those offered to and rejected by five Presidents over the last 20 years.

The substance of the People's Republic of China demands has been known for a long time. The People's Republic of China has insisted: First, that diplomatic relations with Taiwan had to be determined; second, that all U.S. military forces and installations had to be removed from the island; and third, that the United States-Republic of China Mutual Security Treaty had to be terminated.

Mr. President, the People's Republic of China achieved each and every one of these objectives. They also got a 1-year moratorium on new arms sales commitments by the United States to Taiwan.

In exchange for what? We can now call our mission in Peking an embassy rather than a liaison office. But, as the Foreign Relations Committee noted in its committee report on S. 245, the liaison office already was an embassy in all but name. The People's Republic of China has promised to be somewhat more sympathetic to economic offers tendered by our businessmen. But then again, the present political climate is very volatile: It could change, leaving our businessmen right back where they started. Finally, the People's Republic of China might even look the other way if we were to sell Taiwan arms of a defensive nature after the end of the year. But as the committee hearings show, even this is far from certain.

What about the use of force? Would the People's Republic of China pledge not to use force in resolving the Taiwan issue? Teng Hsiao-ping made it clear while in this country that it would not. Although the Foreign Relations Committee has gone to some length to express our concern that the Taiwan situation be resolved peacefully, the fact is the administration proceeded to recognize Peking without any commitment at all from the People's Republic of China on this score.

In exchange for tangible concessions of a concrete nature, then, we have secured ambiguous assurances from a 74-year-old leader of a highly explosive country, and nothing at all about the renunciation of the use of force. If Mr. Teng is in control in the People's Republic of China today, he may not be tomorrow, and there is no way for anyone to be certain just what will happen to President Carter's new China policy once Teng passes from the scene.

ITS CONSEQUENCES

Mr. President, I strongly believe that this new China policy is built on sand. I also believe that it is morally reprehensible in that we are abandoning a tried and trusted friend without cause and taking up with that friend's mortal enemy.

CONGRESSIONAL RECORD--HOUSE
MARCH 13, 1979

MR. WRIGHT: Mr. Chairman, I move to strike the requisite number of words.

Mr. Chairman, let me say something now with regard to the amendment presently before us. I think it suffers two deficiencies.

First, it is unnecessary. It would accomplish nothing beyond what is accomplished in the bill. Secondly, it probably would subject the bill to a veto on the grounds of an unwarranted invasion of Executive power.

Let me point out to those who have not focused carefully upon the strong language already contained in this legislation. First, looking to section 204 as it appears at page 9 of the bill, we see that the designated entity is fully empowered to perform those services normally performed by a consulate of the United States.

Let me attract our attention next to the language appearing on page 5 beginning on line 17. This is language which would be stricken from the bill by adoption of the amendment.

The laws of the United States which apply with respect to agencies of the United States Government shall, to the extent the President may specify, apply with respect to the designated entity as if the designated entity were an agency of the United States Government.

Finally on page 10 in definitions of what is meant in our reference to the laws of the United States, we find the definition:

(1) the term "laws of the United States" includes any statute, rule, regulation, ordinance, order, or judicial rule of decision of the United States or any political subdivision thereof:

The definition could hardly be broader.

So what we have for all practical intents and purposes is a consulate. It serves every conceivable purpose a consulate could serve. We have arranged a unique entity in the exercise of the congressional prerogative. The bill creates a continuing relationship with our friends in Taiwan. We are empowered to deal with them, for every practical purpose precisely as we have dealt with them in the past.

Now, the language which is continued in this bill is strong language. It asserts the emphatic desire of the United States to protect our friendship with Taiwan. It asserts that the future of Taiwan must be determined through peaceful means without prejudice to the well-being of the people on Taiwan.

It declares that any armed attacked against Taiwan or any use of force. Boycott, or embargo to prevent Taiwan from engaging in trade with other nations would be a threat to the peace and stability of the Western Pacific area and of grave concern to the United States.

It declares that the United States will make available to Taiwan defense articles and defense services for its defense against armed attack.

I do not know what more the gentleman wishes. Those representatives of the Government of Taiwan who have discussed the matter with me have declared that they desire for this bill to be passed, for this entity to be created, and for it to be done as soon as possible. That purpose, I think, will not be served by creating a direct conflict which would provoke a confrontation with the executive branch of Government, invite a veto, and delay and leave further in limbo the important relations which we as a people desire to maintain with the people of Taiwan.

CONGRESSIONAL RECORD--SENATE
MARCH 29, 1979

TAIWAN RELATIONS ACT--
CONFERENCE REPORT

MR. CHURCH. Mr President, I submit a report of the committee of conference on H.R. 2479 and ask for its immediate consideration.

The Presiding Officer. The Report will be stated.

The legislative clear read as follows:

The committee of conference on the disagreeing votes of the two House on the amendments of the Senate to the bill (H.R. 2479) to help maintain peace, security, and stability in the Western Pacific and to promote continued extensive, close, and friendly relations between the people of the United States and the people on Taiwan, having met, after full and free conference, have agreed to recommend and do recommend to their respective Houses this report, signed by all of the conferees.

The Presiding Officer. Without objection, the Senate will proceed to the consideration of the conference report.

(The conference report is printed in the House proceedings of the Record of March 24, 1979.)

MR. CHURCH. Mr. President, this conference report is a vast improvement over the legislation initially proposed by the administration. The measure as it now stands clarified many uncertainties and ambiguities concerning trade, legal and economic issues. It includes a security clause designed to reassure Taiwan. And it provides for comprehensive congressional oversight of U.S. relations with Taiwan. The test we applied in deciding each of the many complex and difficult decisions before us was not the views of Taiwan or the People's Republic, but the national interest of the United States. I believe that this measure advances our national interest.

Mr. President, I acknowledge the presence of the ranking Republican member on the committee, the able Senator from New York, Mr. Javits. His work in drafting this legislation was indispensable. I think he shares with me a general sense of satisfaction with the compromise we were able to hammer out in conference with the Representatives of the House of Representatives.

The purpose of this legislation, Mr. President, is to authorize unofficial, nongovernmental relations with Taiwan. It is simply an adjustment to our laws to permit the maintenance of commercial, cultural, and other nongovernmental relationships in the new circumstances that exist after normalization. I intend to describe the principal features of this measure in a moment, but before doing so, I believe that this point needs to be reiterated: the relationship provided for in this bill--however extensive, however close, and however friendly--is not a government-to-government relationship. It is a relationship between two private entities--the American Institute in Taiwan and the corresponding Taiwan instrumentality--which will deal with each other in a manner reflecting the unofficial ties between the people of the United States and the people on Taiwan. The unofficial nature of this relationship is evident throughout the act--beginning with the title, which states that the purpose of the act is to promote people-to-people relations.

The central provision in this regard is subsection (a) of section 2. It recognizes that official, governmental relations between the United States and the governing authorities on Taiwan have been terminated. It is upon this premise--stated at the outset so that there can be no mistake as to its importance--that the rest of the act is based; all other provisions in the act must be interpreted in its light. I refer, in particular, to use of the term "Taiwan." The Senate version referred throughout the bill to the "people on Taiwan" to make clear that it was the people--and not the governing authorities--with whom relations were being continued, and to make clear as well that the bill did not address the issue of Taiwan's international legal identity.

These same purposes are carried out by section 2(a) of the conference report, which leaves no doubt concerning the termination of official relations with the governing authorities on Taiwan. I would point out also that nowhere does the conference report address the question of whether Taiwan is a country or nation under international law. Although the term "Republic of China" does appear several times--most notably in the definition of Taiwan--each such use contains a reference to past U.S. recognition, and none implies current governmental relations. I will elaborate on this point in a moment, but before doing so, I would point out that several other provisions must also be viewed in the same perspective.

Section 4(b)(1), for example, treats Taiwan as a "country" for purposes of U.S. law. This is a technical drafting matter, really; certain statutory authorities needed to be extended to continue the program eligibility of Taiwan, and the simplest and cleanest way of doing that was to treat Taiwan as a country under those statues. There is absolutely no indication in this provision that the United States views Taiwan as a separate country; if anything, it could be argued that the need to include a provision such as this implies exactly the opposite. But that question, as I stated, is one that is not addressed in this legislation.

Section 4(b)(4) is also a somewhat technical legal provision relating to the question of which law is to be applied in U.S. courts. It provides that, when the circumstances require, that law is to be the law applied by the people on Taiwan. This provision, like other provisions, in no way constitutes recognition of any government and in no way implies official relations. It simply takes cognizance of the undisputed reality that there is a law applied on Taiwan. It does not freeze the United States into the position, obviously, of forever applying in its own courts the law now applied on Taiwan; if the law applied on Taiwan were to change, a different law would then be applied by the United States.

Nor is recognition implied in the "security" language appearing in section 2 and 3 of this measure. The conference committee intended that this carefully drafted language support the President's statement of December 15, 1978, that the United States retains an interest in the peaceful settlement of the Taiwan issue by the Chinese themselves. Nothing in these provisions was intended to be inconsistent with the mutually agreed terms of normalization.

The cornerstone of our new unofficial relations with Taiwan is the American Institute in Taiwan. This is a private, nonprofit corporation whose employees are not employees of the U.S. Government. This is an extremely important principle, and is made explicit in section 11(c) of the conference report. Relations with Taiwan will be conducted through the Institute, and references to it thus appear throughout the bill.

Section 7(a)(3) of the conference report, for example, authorizes Institute employees to perform certain acts "such as are authorized" to be performed for consular purposes. Those words are critically important: They make clear that the functions being carried out are not those of official governmental representatives. Similarly, section 10 requests that the President extend to the Taiwan instrumentality the same number of offices and complement of personnel as were operated previously. Two points bear emphasis: that these are private offices, not consulates, and that they are manned by "personnel," not diplomats or governmental officials of any sort.

Likewise, the immunity that the Congress requests be extended in this section is not absolute immunity--not the full and complete immunity extended official diplomats--functional immunity, which would extend only to acts performed in the course of one's duties.

Finally, there is the definition. Section 15(a) refers to the "governing authorities on Taiwan recognized by the United States as the Republic of China prior to January 1, 1979. ..."This is an historical reference with which no one can argue: It merely acknowledges--for purposes of legal clarity in identifying the authorities to which the section refers--that the United States recognized the Republic of China prior to January 1, 1979. It does not suggest that that recognition continues--indeed, the definition expressly notes that recognition terminated on January 1, 1979. The reference is thus comparable to other references to the Republic of China appearing in the conference report, such as that contained in section 4(c), which relates to international agreements. There, as elsewhere, the reference appears only to make clear, legally, which governing authorities are being referred to; there is absolutely no intent to suggest--in section 4(c) or anywhere else in the bill--that the United States continues to maintain official relations with the people on Taiwan.

Mr. President, I have described these particular provisions of the conference report at some length because it is vitally important that everyone understand that this legislation is entirely consistent with the joint statement issued December 15 by the United States and China. In that statement the President agreed to recognize the Peking government as the sole legal government of China. This was his prerogative under our constitutional system, and it is not within the power of the Congress to overturn that decision. The Congress does not have the authority--constitutionally--to recognize a given government or to establish government-to-government relations with a given country after the President has terminated those relations. The Congress cannot do so, and the Congress will not have done so in enacting this legislation. It will simply have authorized the maintenance of commercial, cultural and other relations without official Government representation and without diplomatic relations.

I should like to turn now, Mr. President, to a summary of the contents of this conference report. The main provisions of the conference report deal with, first, peace and security in the western Pacific; second, the continued applicability of U.S. laws with respect to Taiwan despite the absence of diplomatic relations and recognition; third, the continuation in force of all treaties and agreements not specifically terminated according to law; fourth, legal rights, such as the capacity of Taiwan, its people, and entities established by their law to sue and be sued in U.S. courts; fifth, trade and economic relations between the United States and Taiwan, and property rights of Taiwan; sixth, the staffing, authority and responsibilities of the American Institute in Taiwan to conduct relations with the people on Taiwan as well as the status of its unofficial Taiwan counterpart; and seventh, congressional oversight regarding these relations in general, and of the activities of the American Institute in Taiwan in particular.

It is not necessary to go into all of these matters in detail, although I do want to discuss a few. However, I want to emphasize that both the Senate and the House have been exceedingly thorough and careful in their consideration of all of the issues involved, in view of the great importance of this legislation and the unique situation it addresses. We have combined clear statements of principle with detailed provisions on important matters, and have done so in a way that provides firm policy guidance combined with operational flexibility.

One of the issues that received extensive consideration was Taiwan's security. The provisions dealing with this matter in the conference report represent a constructive compromise between the language of the acts passed by the Senate and the House. The conference report spells out that peace and stability in the area are in the political, security, and economic interest of the United States; that any effort to determine the future of Taiwan by other than peaceful means, including boycotts or embargoes, would be a threat to the peace and security of the western Pacific and of grave concern to the United States; that the United States will maintain its capacity to resist any resort to force or other forms of coercion that would jeopardize the security, or the social or economic system, of the people on Taiwan; and that the United States will make available to Taiwan defense articles and services in such quantity as may be necessary to enable Taiwan to maintain a sufficient self-defense capability.

This should be very reassuring indeed to the people on Taiwan, for it specifies that the United States will oppose any form of external coercion directed against Taiwan. And it provides that we will assist Taiwan to maintain its own defense capability, which the Israelites have demonstrated is the best assurance of any nation's security. These provisions, together with the President's December 15, 1978, statement, our improved communications with the PRC resulting from normalization, the lack of any significant amphibious capacity on the part of the People's Republic, and the fact that any PRC threat directed against Taiwan would dash its hopes for better relations with the United States, Japan and Western Europe--all these elements combined to make it clear that Taiwan's security is not endangered.

The conference report also clearly provides for Congressional oversight of these relations and of the operations of the American Institute in Taiwan. The Institute has the authority and the responsibility to help American citizens carry out their many kinds of dealings with Taiwan, which will enable our commercial and cultural relations to continue to expand. The legislation provides that agreements and transactions made by or through the Institute shall be subject to the same congressional notification, review, and approval requirements and procedures as would normally apply. The conference report also places on the President and the Secretary of State specific reporting requirements concerning the Institute's operations and economic relations between the United States and Taiwan. These provisions were taken from the act passed by the Senate. They will enable the appropriate committees of the Senate and House of Representatives to carry out the responsibilities assigned them in the Act passed by the House--the responsibility to monitor the implementation of this legislation, and to monitor developments in U.S. relations with Taiwan under these unique arrangements.

In connection with these oversight provisions, Mr. President, I submit for the Record a letter from the Department of State concerning arms exports to the People's Republic of China and I ask unanimous consent that it be printed in the Record at this point.

DEPARTMENT OF STATE
Washington, D.C., March 19, 1979

HON. FRANK CHURCH
Chairman, Senate Foreign Relations
  Committee

Dear Mr. Chairman: In today's proceeding of the committee of conference on H.R. 2479, the question was raised as to whether the Congress would be informed at least thirty days in advance of the issuance of any license for significant arms export to the People's Republic of China.

It is the policy of the United States, as reflected in section 126.01 of the International Traffic in Arms Regulations, not to license arms exports to the People's Republic of China.

We do not contemplate any change in this policy. In view of the concerns expressed by the conference committee, however, I can assure you that the Department of State would not license significant arms exports to the People's Republic of China without providing the Congress at least thirty days' prior notice. This assurance is in addition to the reporting requirements of existing law, which requires thirty days' prior notice to the Congress of the proposed issuance of licenses for the export of major defense equipment sold for $7 million or more, or other defense articles or services sold for $25 million or more.

I trust that the foregoing assurance meets the concerns expressed in today's meeting of the conference committee.

Sincerely,

DOUGLAS J. BENNET, JR.,
    Assistant Secretary for
    Congressional Relations.

MR. CHURCH. It is not for the United States to determine Taiwan's destiny, However, we do have an important interest that this issue be resolved peacefully and in a manner that takes into account the will of the people on Taiwan. It is encouraging that the People's Republic of China has adopted a flexible approach toward this issue in recent months. We should do nothing to discourage the Chinese leaders from continuing along this course.

Mr. President, this measure makes clear to the People's Republic of China that the United States has a deep interest in a peaceful resolution of the Taiwan issue. It also makes clear to the people on Taiwan that we are not abandoning them by providing for the continued supply of defense articles and services, and by establishing a sound legal and economic basis for continued relations between the United States and Taiwan.

I believe that this conference report will enable the United States to continue a close and friendly relationship with the people on Taiwan while simultaneously developing a mutually beneficial relationship with the People's Republic of China. I therefore urge the Senate to approve the conference report.

MR. JAVITS. Mr. President, the legislation crafted by the conference committee is, in fact, much better for having had to go through this "buffeting" of the American political process. It is more careful and more thorough than the bill which the administration originally proposed. By protecting the commercial, cultural, and other relations of the United States with the 17 1/2 million people on Taiwan, it provides a firmer political foundation in this country for the improvement of relations with the People's Republic. I think that the leaders of the PRC will come to recognize this fact--that having dealt fairly with our friends on Taiwan, we are in a better position to continue the process or normalization with the People's Republic.

The majority of the Member of Congress, in my judgment, strongly favor the normalization of relations with the People's Republic of China and, in this legislation, sought only to fulfill our basic moral commitments to the people on Taiwan, in a way which is compatible with the goals and conditions for normalization of relations with the People's Republic.

Now, Mr. President, this matter has been very much debated, and I will not reiterate the arguments about it or the meanings of the words which are used. However, I do wish to emphasize two things: First, under section 2(b)(3) we make it very clear that when we sought to normalize relations with the PRC, that policy "rests upon the expectation that the future of Taiwan will be determined by peaceful means."

We mean it. I hope when the President signs this bill, as I hope he will, that the implications of that paragraph will be crystal clear.

And I might say, Mr. President, that is no different from the fact that the PRC normalized relations with us upon the expectation that we would no longer maintain official diplomatic relations with the Republic of China on Taiwan. We have honored our commitment.

Second, Mr. President, when we speak of the future of Taiwan and the fact that is shall only be changed by peaceful means, we also include--and this is, in my judgment, very, very important--the way in which they run their society and their right to determine how they shall run their society. That, Mr. President, is a very important element in our consideration because we say in section 2(b)(6), "to maintain the capacity of the United States to resist any resort to force or other forms of coercion" and these are the pertinent words "that would jeopardize the security or the social or economic system of the people on Taiwan." That means not only their security but the social or economic system that they choose. I wish to make that crystal clear.

Here, too, I refer the Government of the People's Republic of China to section 2(b)(1) which makes it very clear that we want the same close, friendly, and commercial relations with the PRC, itself. We have wrapped that into this very same security clause so there can be no doubt about our good faith in undertaking a normalization of relations with the People;s Republic of China, just as there can be no doubt about our good faith as far as the people on Taiwan are concerned.

Mr. President, the other matter to which I wish to call attention, which relates to laws of the United States, is that we have been very careful to preserve property and other comparable rights without trying to decide the issue of the diplomatic installations which are here, especially the embassy property in Washington. Generally speaking, we have been very protective of property rights, etc, respecting the people on Taiwan and what they have created in this country, in the United States.

In that respect, I wish to emphasize, because it is very important to lawyers, the preemption clause which makes this measure, if signed by the President into law, the governing law, if there is any conflict with other law of the United States or of the District of Columbia where this institute which is provided for is incorporated, or with the law of any State or political subdivision which "impedes or otherwise interferes with the performance of the functions of the institute pursuant to that act."

That is a very important clause, Mr. President, certainly, to the courts, to lawyers, and to people who are engaged in any litigation respecting property rights, and I call special attention to it.

Finally, Mr. President, the definition. We worked on this definition very ardently and with great concern. I believe it spells out precisely what we mean when we use the term Taiwan. It refers not only to corporations and other entities and associations which are private, but also to the public authorities on Taiwan as recognized by the United State prior to January 1, 1979, as well as any successor governing authority there.

I believe we have sought, as far as human beings can, to anticipate all of our problems and we have dealt with them in the text of this legislation.

Mr. President, I hope that we will also now arrive at a relationship with the People's Republic of China which will move on satisfactorily, satisfactorily to them and satisfactorily to us, the ground rules having been laid down so very carefully and so very precisely. Though it has been an arduous task, this represents one of the great decisions in our postwar history. I think it has been made well and wisely. I take great pleasure and deep gratification in the fact that the Congress will have, when this bill is made into law, contributed an affirmative and a very constructive element to this relationship. Congress has demonstrated its ability carefully to architect a piece of legislation which will do what needs to be done in terms of the national interest and the moral interest of the United States as far as the people on Taiwan were concerned. It does so without in any way transgressing any obligation undertaken by the United States, in the joint communique or otherwise, toward the People's Republic of China, or in any way complicating or nullifying the relationship which we have now agreed it is the high policy of the United States to establish with the People's Republic of China.

Mr. President, I commend this conference report to my colleagues. I commend to them also a careful examination of its craftsmanship in legal terms. I hope very much that the Senate will see fit today, as the other body has largely done, to approve this conference report.

* * * * *

MR. PERCY. Mr President, I wish to associate myself with the comments of my distinguished colleague from Arizona. There is no abandonment by any means, implied or expressed, in this legislation. In fact, my opening comments were to the effect that I think the bill before us represents the will of the majority in this Chamber because it expresses the concern of the American people that the future of Taiwan and the Pescadores be resolved on a peaceful basis, and we reaffirm this.

And I do look forward to a constructive unofficial relationship with the people of Taiwan.

We also look forward to an expanding cooperative relationship with the People's Republic of China, the most populous nation on Earth.

I am personally satisfied that this bill allows us to maintain unofficial contacts with Taiwan as we move toward closer and mutually beneficial official relations with China.

Mr. President, because this has been an extraordinarily complicated matter, and it is a matter that is so significant to the interests of this country, it is important that we have an overwhelming vote in the House and the Senate. This is not the kind of an issue we would want resolved by one or two votes on either side. We should have a mandate from the Congress of the United States that we stand together with the executive branch of Government in taking this momentous step forward.

For that reason, I wish particularly to commend my colleagues, the managers of the bill, Senator Church, the chairman of the Committee on Foreign Relations, and Senator Javits, the ranking minority member, for an extraordinary job.

Although I have disagreed on a few matters, that does not in any way detract from my great admiration for the skillful way in which they have--in the highest tradition of statesmanship--moved the Senate of the United States forward, and the House of Representatives forward, to a point where we can overwhelmingly endorse this legislation today.

MR. CHURCH. I thank the Senator very much for his generous comments.

I simply want to stress my personal indebtedness to the distinguished Senator from New York for his cooperation, and also to the other members of the Committee on Foreign Relations, who throughout this legislation have worked to perfect a bill that would command overwhelming support here in the Senate.

I speak to those Senators of the committee who are present, Senator Helms from North Carolina, Senator Percy from Illinois, Senator Hayakawa from California, Senator Muskie from Main, Senator Glenn from Ohio, and all the other members of the Senate Committee on Foreign Relations. My thanks and appreciation are extended to them.

MR. JAVITS. Mr. President, will the Senator yield?

MR. CHURCH. I yield.

MR. JAVITS. I join with my colleague, the chairman, and associate myself with his remarks.

I want to especially thank Senator Percy. I am a lawyer, as everybody knows by now, and I always value being put to my proof, and his assiduous concentration on the terms of this bill, I think, had a great deal to do with my own ability to summon what creativity was required in order to do what he now applauds us for. Without him I do not think it would have been done, and I thank him very much.

MR. DOLE. Mr. President, the House has passed the compromise conference report ton the Taiwan Relations Act by a vote of 339 to 50. The overwhelming support for this legislation, which I hope will be reflected as well in this Chamber, reveals the general satisfaction with the amendments the Congress made to this legislation, which resulted in a complete rewrite of the original administration proposal.

We in the Senate were concerned about our security guarantees to Taiwan and we strengthened that language in the bill--now we have made our position perfectly clear to the People's Republic of China: Not only do we expect the differences between Peking and Taipei to be settled by peaceful means, but we will consider actions taken to ruin the economy of Taiwan as a threat also. This means such practices as excluding them from vital communications and economic organizations around the world or by preventing international trade through discriminating bilateral agreements.

I am still not convinced the Carter administration bargained with sufficient diligence on the issue of official relations with Taiwan. President Nixon and Ford could have normalized relations with Peking any time in the last 7 years on these terms. I do believe that the Senator from Kansas and his many colleagues have made the very best of a poor situation, by [amending this legislation to include cer]tain rights and privileges for Taiwan, and the final result is that our future relations will be conducted almost as they once were, official relations in all but name.

This past weekend Peking heavily criticized these actions by the Congress. I welcome this criticism. It means we have gotten out point across. The PRC now knows exactly where we stand on the Taiwan question. Let Peking not forget that the United States has a strong strategic interest in the Asian Pacific area, and still has close ties of friendship and harmony with our allies, the people of Taiwan.

Source: *Congressional Record* (Excerpts). House, March 5, 13, 1979. Senate, March 7, 29, 1979. Hearings on Taiwan Relations Act.

TRA17

AN AIR TRANSPORT AGREEMENT
BETWEEN THE AMERICAN INSTITUTE IN TAIWAN AND
THE COORDINATION COUNCIL FOR NORTH AMERICAN AFFAIRS
(TO SUCCEED ALL PREVIOUS AIR TRANSPORT AGREEMENTS)

The American Institute in Taiwan (AIT) and the Coordination Council for North American Affairs (CCNAA), in order to promote extensive, close and friendly commercial, cultural, and other relations; desiring to facilitate the expansion of air transport opportunities on the basis of competition among airlines; desiring to make it possible for airlines to offer the traveling and shipping public a variety of service options at the lowest prices that are not predatory or discriminatory and do not represent abuse of a dominant position; wishing to encourage individual airlines to develop and implement innovative and competitive prices; desiring to ensure the highest degree of safety and security in air transport and reaffirming their grave concern about acts or threats against the security of aircraft, which jeopardize the safety of persons or property, adversely affect the operation of air transportation, and undermine public confidence in the safety of civil aviation; desiring to maintain and expand air services by concluding an agreement to succeed all previous Air Transport Agreements;

Have agreed as follows:...

Article 2

DESIGNATION AND AUTHORIZATION

(1)   Each party may designate as many airlines as it wishes to conduct air transportation in accordance with this Agreement and may withdraw or alter such designation. Such designation shall be transmitted to the other party in writing and shall identify what type or types of air transportation the airline is authorized to conduct. Types of air transportation are specified in Annex I and Annex II...

Article 5

SAFETY

(1)   Subject to Article 32 (b) of the Convention, each party shall recognize as valid, for the purpose of operating the air transportation provided for in this Agreement, certificates of airworthiness, certificates of competency, and licenses issued or validated by the other party and still in force, provided that the requirements for such certificates or licenses at least equal the minimum standards which may be established pursuant to the Convention....

Article 6

AVIATION SECURITY

The Parties, recognizing their responsibilities to develop international civil aviation in a safe and orderly manner, reaffirm their grave concern about acts or threats against the security of aircraft, which jeopardize the safety of persons or property, adversely affect the operation of air transportation, and undermine public confidence in the safety of civil aviation. To this end, each Party:

(1)   shall ensure the observances of the provisions of the Convention on Offenses and Certain Other Acts Committed on Board Aircraft, signed at Tokyo on September 14, 1963, the Convention for the Suppression of Unlawful Seizure of Aircraft, signed at The Hague on December 16, 1970, and the Convention for the Suppression of Unlawful Acts Against the Safety of Civil Aviation, signed at Montreal on September 23, 1971;

(2)   shall ensure that maximum aid is provided with a view to preventing unlawful seizure of aircraft, sabotage to aircraft, airports, and air navigation facilities, and threats to aviation security; give sympathetic consideration to any request for special security measures for aircraft or passengers to meet a particular threat; and, when incidents or threats of hijacking or sabotage against aircraft, airports or air navigation facilities occur, assist in the facilitation of communications intended to terminate such incidents rapidly and safely....

Article 10

FAIR COMPETITION

(1)   The designated airlines of each party shall have a fair and equal opportunity to compete in the air transportation covered by this Agreement.

(2)   Each party shall ensure that appropriate action is taken to eliminate all forms of discrimination or unfair competition practices adversely affecting the competitive position of the designated airlines of the other party.

(3)   Unilateral limitations on the volume of traffic, frequency or regularity of service, or aircraft type or types shall not be imposed, except as may be required for customs, technical, operational or environmental reasons under uniform conditions consistent with Article 15 of the Convention.

(4)   Designated airlines of either party shall not be subjected to a first refusal requirement, uplift ratio, no-objection fee, or any other requirement with respect to the capacity, frequency or traffic which would be inconsistent with the purposes of this Agreement.

(5)   Designated airlines shall not be required to file schedules, programs for charter flights, or operational plans for approval, except as may be required on a non-discriminatory basis to enforce uniform conditions as foreseen by Paragraph (3) of this Article or as may be specifically authorized in an Annex to this Agreement. If filings are required for information purposes, the administrative burdens of filing requirements and procedures on air transportation intermediaries and on designated airlines shall be minimized....

Article 13

SETTLEMENT OF DISPUTES

(1)   Any dispute arising under this Agreement which is not resolved by a first round of formal consultations, except those which may arise under paragraph 3 of Article ll (Pricing), may be referred to arbitration in accordance with the procedures set forth below, unless the parties agree on other procedures.

(2)   Arbitration shall be by a tribunal of three arbitrators. Within 30 days after the receipt of a request for arbitration, each party shall name one arbitrator. Within 60 days after these two arbitrators have been named, they shall by agreement appoint a third arbitrator, who shall act as President of the arbitral tribunal.

Article 14

TERMINATION

Either party may, at any time, give notice in writing to the other of its decision to terminate this Agreement. This Agreement shall terminate at midnight (at the place of receipt of notice to the other party) immediately before the first anniversary of the date of receipt of the notice by the other party, unless the notice is withdrawn by agreement before the end of this period.

Article 15

ENTRY INTO FORCE

This Agreement will come into force on the date of signature. In witness whereof, the undersigned, being duly authorized, have signed the present Agreement. Done in duplicate at Washington in the English language this 5th day of March 1980.

Konsin C. Shah, Representative   David Dean
Coordination Council for North   Chairman of the Board
American Affairs   and Managing Director
                                   American Institute in Taiwan

Source: American Institute in Taiwan, Arlington, Virginia (Excerpts).

TRA18   STATEMENT BY JAMES LILLEY
                  Johns Hopkins School for Advanced International Studies
                          Washington, DC, March 7, 1980.

              SECURITY CONSIDERATIONS IN TAIWAN'S FUTURE

In my view, there are 5 major threats to the future stability and security of Taiwan--

    A world of U.S. economic recession
    A Taiwanese/Mainlander polarization on Taiwan
    A serious intrusion from Peking
    The death or loss of key leadership on Taiwan
    An Asian regional war or Sino-Soviet military confrontation

    These five threats or phenomena occurring individually or in tandem could, in my
view, cause a significant loss of stability in Taiwan. For instance, the impact of an external
event such as a world wide recession could exacerbate Taiwan/Mainlander relations by causing
a severe economic depression in Taiwan, leading to a bitter competition for jobs and a resulting
loss of confidence in a Mainlander-controlled central government. The unfortunate death of
a key central leader such as President Chiang Ching-kuo would undoubtedly cause even greater
loss of confidence, and could result in actions and reactions in the leadership. The social fabric
of Taiwan could be affected resulting in a destruction of the careful balance that exists now.
I do not mean to suggest Taiwan is unstable in relative terms, it is not. Taiwan was able to
sustain, as predicted by the U.S. Government, the shock or normalization as well as the way the
United States handled it with Taiwan.

    Strong private sectors in the United States and Taiwan not only sustained the
relationship but even advanced economic ties between the United States and Taiwan during this
first post-normalization year. The U.S. private sector demonstrated clearly and concretely its
confidence in Taiwan in the fact of uncertainties growing from often unfriendly U.S.
Government attitudes and actions which made its job of governing that much more difficult.

    Most recently, the riots in Kaohsiung on 10 December 1979 dramatized the complex
and potentially explosive relations between Taiwanese and the Mainlanders. The problem
centers on the issue of minority control of the central government which faces increasing
pressures by the Taiwanese for a larger say in the future of Taiwan. It is obviously not as
simple as that. The Taiwanese are factionalized and the rioters of Kaohsiung were isolated
from the Taiwanese mainstream by the extremity of their actions. On the other hand, the riot
had broader implications. It was linked to the issue of freedom of the press (the publication
Formosa was involved in the riots and has been closed), human rights (the riot took place on

Human Rights Day and resulted in a mass arrest of opposition leaders and there was the link to the United States through the American wife of one of the riot leaders. She was deported to the United States earlier. It also followed in the Chung Li riots of 1977 which was the first riot in Taiwan in 20 years.

Taiwanese who represent an overwhelming proportion of the population are still largely kept out of key roles in the military and security forces in Taiwan. Mainlanders in fact represent less than 15 percent of a population of 17 million. Taiwanese are in the central government but not in proportion to their actual numbers. They control business and finance but are not in control of key government ministries which influence the economy. Mainlander control of key security forces (NSB, MJIB, the Taiwan Garrison Command) remains strong as does the Mainlander control of the upper echelons of the armed forces but there are constraints on this control. As the Kaoshiung riots indicated, the regular troops cannot be pushed too far. The rank and file are Taiwanese and there are probably limits to the actions they will take against fellow Taiwanese.

The essential dilemma is this: If a peaceful solution is advanced with Peking leading to closer ties and a semblance of the reunification Peking seeks, then this, under current circumstances, must be negotiated by Mainlanders on Taiwan who are in actual control there. The Taiwanese who prefer a status closer to independence would be deeply suspicious of Mainlanders on Taiwan who seek closer ties with Peking. If it were moving too fast, the Taiwanese could erupt and violently challenge the right of the Mainlanders to decide their fate. Hence, Chiang Ching-kuo who is the inheritor of his father's one-China policy takes a very tough position on negotiating with Peking. He is tougher than many Taiwanese. At the same time he maintains the claim of only one China, in part because he realizes increasing pressure for Taiwan independence could result from any dilution of his unrealistic one-China policy. Taiwan independence would be a serious provocation to the People's Republic of China and could force an unwanted military showdown. It could also lose partners such as the United States which has warned Taiwan against moves towards independence.

It is probable that if Taiwanese gained control of the central government there would be in all likelihood a movement away from Peking and towards a legal independent status. This would be particularly dangerous if it were precipitous stemming say from the sudden death of a key leader on Taiwan. The important issue is how fast and what form will increased Taiwan participation in government take. If Taiwan extremists were to increase their strength rapidly and manipulate a precipitous takeover, serious destabilization could result especially if Taiwan independence were stressed. On the other hand, if more moderate Taiwanese moved in through attrition and through an evolutionary process then there would be considerably less of a threat especially if the one-China policy were temporarily maintained, at least verbally.

Fortunately, good sense and hard materialism prevail in Taiwan supported by a strong economy. Foreign investment and foreign exchange earnings are high, unemployment in a very crowded country is low, worker motivation is generally good. A problem would arise if worldwide recession or even a serious U.S. recession changed the foreign trade and investment balance. A measure of the importance of the U.S. factor is that 40 percent of Taiwan's exports go to the United States. Taiwan is heavily dependent on trade and investment to sustain its economy. If its exports were cut and new markets not found which could well be the case in a widespread recession, then Taiwan would suffer and the effects would spill over from the economic sector into the social sector. Serious dislocations could result brought about by unemployment, economic insecurity and a loss of confidence in the ability of the Taiwan Government to take care of its people, in short the mandate of heaven.

Taiwan dependence on Mid-East oil is a major influence on its economic development. Seventy-eight percent of its energy came from oil in 1977 as opposed to 26 percent in 1967 and the oil import bill in 1978 was close to 2 billion U.S. Although Taiwan has an enlightened program of switching to nuclear power, this is a long way off and will not replace a continuing need for major imports of Mid-East oil. Sharp rises in oil prices coupled with a loss of exports could result especially if Taiwan's oil dependence reaches 80 percent in the 1980's as predicted by the Far Eastern Economic Review.

THE PEKING FACTOR

The Taiwan Government has insisted that Peking represents the greatest threat to its survival. Taiwan cites Peking's aim to reunify Taiwan with the mainland of China, its refusal to renounce force, and the aggressive aims of a Communist state as evidence of this continuing threat. Taiwan says Peking only changes tactics (from belligerent to peaceful) but its objective to absorb Taiwan remains unshaken. In Deng Xiao-ping's major tasks for the 1980's "Bring about the return of Taiwan to the motherland and accomplish the unification of the motherland" is named as Task No. 2 just behind opposing hegemonism (U.S.S.R.) and safeguarding world peace. Taiwan claims this is a clear message of intent.

The image of the United States Taiwan attempts to portray is of a United States tricked by Peking into meeting its three conditions without exacting any from Peking. The United States has, in Taiwan's view, sold out an ally (itself) which had never wronged it and the United States has compromised its principled stand of support in free enterprise systems by recognizing a communist one. The United States in addition, according to Taiwan, has "abandoned" a country which had a superior human rights record to the one it recognized.

Underneath this rhetoric which is still useful with certain groups in the United States there is in Taiwan a clearer recognition of the realities of its situation. First, the United States is essential as a partner if Taiwan is to maintain an important degree of autonomy. Taiwan's more sophisticated arms are almost exclusively U.S. supplied. More important, the Taiwan Relations Act, signed by the President, carries language to the effect that the use of anything other than peaceful means to determine the future of Taiwan is to be considered a threat to the peace and security of the western Pacific and of grave concern to the United States. The United States maintains relations with security elements on Taiwan to support its position in supplying and, if necessary, defending Taiwan. The U.S. statements here are not empty posturing. Taiwan's forces of close to 474,000 men include over a million reservists as well as over 300 combat aircraft which are considered superior to any aircraft possessed by the PRC. Military analysts here have concluded that armed attack on Taiwan is not a viable Peking option for the foreseeable future (5 years to be more specific).

What is unhealthy and destabilizing is the heavy concentration of the forces of Taiwan and the PRC facing each other, pumped up with hostile propaganda on both sides, drawing scarce resources and funds away from productive sectors of their respective economies. Taiwan has made no move to decrease the over-extended armed forces on Quemoy and Matsu which are estimated at one-fourth of Taiwan's ground forces. Peking keeps its troops on the coast opposite Taiwan at high levels. There appears, however, to be less likelihood that Chinese attack will take place on these offshore islands despite their obvious vulnerability. They do represent a geographical symbol of linkage between Taiwan and of the one-China policy espoused by both sides. If these islands were taken over by China, Taiwan would appear more isolated and separated from the Mainland. Thus, on the one hand, there are too many troops crowded on these islands in an overblown gesture of defiance. On the other hand, their pressure represents a practical move to make the cost of take-over high enough so Peking would prefer not to risk the bloodshed as well as disapproval from new western partners and Japan.

Some encouraging signs of cooperations between Peking and Taiwan are beginning to appear trade and commerce have picked up in the Taiwan Strait and in Hong Kong between the Mainland and Taiwan there is a civilized code of behavior worked out among pragmatic Chinese to get fishing done by both sides and to supply scarce goods to the other side. Similarly, Pratas Reef, Nationalist-held island southeast of Taiwan, lies close by the offshore block being surveyed by Phillips Petroleum for the PRC. No serious problems have arisen as U.S. boats conduct their seismic survey for the PRC around the Nationalist-held island.

Taiwan could be seriously affected by a regional war say in Korea which would bring the Soviet Union into confrontation with the United States albeit through surrogates. It's true that Taiwan benefitted from the first Korean War of 1950 when the United States ordered the Seventh Fleet to protect Taiwan; however, this time the communists are considerably stronger militarily and probably would not undertake an adventure in Korea without a clearcut chance of success. The loss of its ally South Korea would be a serious blow to Taiwan as would the resulting security threat to a much more vulnerable Japan.

A Sino-Soviet military confrontation could help Taiwan by weakening and diverting the PRC which Taiwan still chooses to identify as the principal threat. On the other hand, it could result in a much closer relationship between the United States and the PRC and a diminution of Taiwan's importance to the United States. In sum, Taiwan benefits essentially from a peaceful environment in Asia. Disruptions to the economy of the East Asian region caused by war cannot but hurt Taiwan in the long run.

With this as a backdrop, let us now consider the future of Taiwan and conditions which could lead to a more secure Taiwan recognizing that there are areas of confrontation as well as accommodation between the two sides. But first I must emphasize that the major initiatives for changes should come from the Chinese themselves on both sides of the Strait. As for common interests and in areas of accommodation, I would note that both sides have:

A need for peace and stability in the West Pacific and no desire to use arms to achieve aims.
A friendship with, and security linkages to, the United States and Japan.
Common recognition of the Soviet Union as a major threat.

Linguistic historic and cultural ties between Taiwan and Fukien Province are particularly strong and there is, also, and expansion of contacts overseas between Chinese and those from Taiwan between journalists, students, delegates at international meetings.

Potential for cooperation in economic areas which could benefit both sides and Peking and Taiwan economies are in many ways complementary. In addition Taiwan's commercial opening to East European Soviet Bloc countries is a break in a long-standing policy of no dealings with communist countries. Indirect trade with the PRC is at the same time increasing thus portending a healthy liberalization of trade contracts. Neither Peking nor Taiwan has acted to boycott or severely penalize companies trading with the other which is a good sign.

In confrontation, Peking and Taiwan
Have a long historical record of animosity and distrust--the legitimacy of Taiwan's Mainlander-controlled government rests on a claim to all of China.

[Have c]ompeting claims for sovereignty over potentially rich offshore oil areas.

[Have d]ivergent rates of growth (Taiwan's living standard surpasses China's. Its per capita GNP is estimated at 3 times that in China.) Different solutions to economic problems --China's are primarily Marxist/pragmatic; Taiwan's are free enterprise/pragmatist.

Each side represents a threat both real and potential to the other. Peking challenges the right of the Taiwan government to control its own affairs. Taiwan represents an alternative route to economic progress beyond any current plans in Peking. Taiwan's proximity to outward-looking and often troubled province of Fukien poses a dilemma - how to exploit the ingenuity and contacts of the Fukienese without inviting an uncontrollable degree of external contamination. Hong Kong's economic contamination of Kwang-tung Province may be greater but Hong Kong is a military and political eunuch representing no real threat.

Taiwan perceives advantages in dramatizing its confrontation with Peking to the United States. Taiwan appeals to a constituency of strong right-wing groups in the United States who distrust Peking, while it attempts to build broader support for continuing independence from Mainland hegemony. Arms sales to Taiwan not only increase its leverage in dealing with Peking but also drive a wedge between Peking and Washington. On Peking's side, despite a clear victory in normalization negotiations, there are concerns that forces in Taiwan favoring increasing independence will grow and at this stage there is not a great deal Peking can do about without endangering its important links with the United States and Japan. Should Peking's leadership in future become more divided and the struggle more acute centering on issues not necessarily related to Taiwan, then a lack of resolution of the Taiwan question in Peking's favor could be used against those who negotiated the arrangement. Taiwan might not be the real issue but Taiwan itself is emotional enough to Peking so that it could be used as a club to beat an old antagonist who might be stumbling anyway. One need only recall the stridency of the Gang of Four's position on Taiwan in the summer of 1976 in contrast to the more balanced approach of the other leaders to appreciate the possibility of use of this issue in the future.

Peking is currently engaged in united front tactics to reunify Taiwan with the Mainland the more forceful word "liberate" Taiwan has been temporarily dropped. Taiwan's stubborn attitude resisting Peking's overtures has placed it on the defensive but the measures themselves do not appear particularly effective yet. These measures involve encouraging family contacts, inviting Chinese back to China, suggesting opening up direct mail links and encouraging some aspects of direct commerce as well as a less strident brand of propaganda aimed at Taiwan. Peking apparently recognizes that exploiting troubled Taiwanese/Mainlander relations on Taiwan is not currently in its interests. Over the long term, however, Peking is seeking to build a strong constituency among the Taiwanese for its own reunification policy. This requires slow careful organizational work against a formidable security force on Taiwan itself. But Peking wants to be able to exert influence through the building of a support organization so that should Taiwan become more vulnerable in the future, then Peking would be in a better position to gain its objectives.

The future of Taiwan's security lies in stressing those points of common interest mentioned earlier. A basis for cooperation lies in the exploitation of the great potential in oil resources under the East China Sea. The Chinese have shown common sense in suggesting shelving the sovereignty issue with Japan in the Diao Yu Tai or Senkakus and getting on with joint oil exploitation. Taiwan has shown similar common sense in handling the Pratas Reef problem.

Japan and Taiwan both have a need for fossil fuel energy supplies closer at hand than the Persian Gulf. The East China Sea may have these. U.S. investment and oil technology, the best in the world, would, of course, be required to develop these resources in cooperation with the other interested countries, China, Japan and Taiwan.

The jurisdictional problems cannot be minimized but are not insoluble. Negotiations are already underway between China and Japan on the Diao Yu Tai or the Senkakus and surrounding waters. Because the problems concerning offshore areas and are not continental, they are apart from the sacred land concept and hence more negotiable.

Security arrangements should be undertaken by the participating countries. First, to protect the huge investment in rigs, barges and facilities necessary to exploit the oil resources--and, second, to protect the sea supply lines to the consumers. This would induce cooperative guarantees from China, Japan and the United States to preserve the peace and stability of the entire area including the Diao Yu Tai or Senkakus, the Pescadores, Taiwan and surrounding waters. The clear message to the common threat, the U.S.S.R., perceived as such by all participants would be to stay out and not interfere in the cooperative efforts of the countries concerned to exploit the oil resources there. This would have to be backed up by strong naval forces--United States, Japanese and those of China and Taiwan.

There would be no direct threat to the Russians as the area in question would be south of Japan and well distanced from Soviet territorial waters. Similarly it should not offend ASEAN as the area would be north of Taiwan. The South China Sea area where the United States is carrying on seismic surveys for the Chinese would not be included, at least initially.

Taiwan not only has the strategically located port of Keelung which could best support East China Sea oil operations but it has refining and petrochemical facilities which could use Peking's crude oil and gas. Taiwan's advanced shipbuilding facilities and steel capacity would be important to any growing oil producing capability in the area. Far fetched as it may seem now, the pure economics of the advantage of cooperation could, over the long term, overcome suspicions and hostility which prevail now.

Source: *Taiwan: One Year After United States-China Normalization*, Committee on Foreign Relations, U.S. Senate and Congressional Research Service, Library of Congress, U.S. Government Printing Office, Washington, DC, 1980. pp. 140-144.

TRA19

IMPLEMENTATION OF THE TAIWAN RELATIONS ACT:
THE FIRST YEAR

AIT PROBLEMS

During the first few months of its operation AIT experienced a number of problems. Most of these have now been overcome. The uniqueness of the mechanisms, and a lack of procedures within the State Department to deal with a privately incorporated non-profit institute, caused most of these initial difficulties. The few problem areas that remain unresolved result, for the most part, from overly rigid Administration policy directives.

The AIT offices in Taipei and Kao-hsiung, for example, are expected to perform almost all the same functions of an embassy. Washington, however, restricts AIT's Taiwan offices to 55 Americans--about half the number the United States formerly employed at the Embassy.

In addition, AIT, before issuing a new immigrant visa must receive an authorization from the U.S. Consulate in Hong Kong. Hong Kong does almost all the work on processing immigrant visas. This system works, but it is costly and cumbersome. Administration spokesmen justify this procedure by arguing that AIT personnel are not Government employees and the law requires visas to be issued by a U.S. Consular officer.

Another problem area is the State Department's refusal to allow AIT use of the computer facilities at the Regional Finance Center operated by the American Embassy in Bangkok. This causes serious problems for AIT's budgeting and accounting personnel. A new manual system that has been introduced is too complicated and has caused repeated delays and higher administrative costs.

The TRA intended that the private institutes--AIT and CCNAA--would have responsibility for conducting the unofficial relations between the United States and Taiwan. Consequently, AIT officials on Taiwan are instructed not to visit government offices. Taiwan officials resent this restriction and complain that there are occasions when meeting outside their offices is inconvenient and unnecessary. They argue that direct contact should be permitted in emergency situations. They would want similar privileges for CCNAA personnel in Washington. In practice, Taiwan attempts to downplay CCNAA-Taipei's role in an effort to force AIT personnel to meet with government officials as much as possible. Thus, much of AIT's business dealings with Taiwan must be conducted informally.

OTHER PROBLEMS

The State Department's position on the number of CCNAA branch offices permitted in the United States is inconsistent with section 10(b) of the TRA. That section specifically called on the President to allow Taiwan to maintain "the same number of offices and complement of personnel as were previously operated in the United States"...Prior to derecognition, Taiwan maintained fourteen consulates in the United States. Nevertheless, the number of CCNAA offices is now down to nine. Taiwan hopes eventually to open new CCNAA branches in such places as Boston, Kansas City, and Guam, where there had previously been ROC consulates. The Administration's argument that Taipei wants the additional branch offices primarily to offset Peking's gains in establishing contact with the Chinese-American communities in those cities is less than credible.

The United States has also been slow to provide adequate security for CCNAA personnel stationed in the United States. Certain officials have been threatened with death, and on at least two occasions, CCNAA offices have been damaged or broken into. Although Deputy Secretary of State Warren Christopher and his party received deplorable treatment from crowds of angry Chinese during a visit to Taiwan shortly after derecognition, such incidents have not recurred and all AIT installations and the homes of its employees are protected.

The Administration seems to equate protection of CCNAA and its employees with the issues of diplomatic privileges and immunities. It has, therefore, procrastinated on finding a workable solution to the problem. For the staff, the practical imperatives of protecting guests in our country--whether they be in an official or unofficial capacity--far outweigh any negative signals that such a gesture might send to the PRC.

Taiwan officials also believe that the United States is purposefully undermining Taiwan's international position by encouraging other nations to recognize the PRC. In the words of one official, "please don't twist arms to shift recognition from Taiwan to the PRC." This is in response to the growing feeling of isolation Taipei feels as its official representation overseas dwindles. The process began with Peking assuming the China seat at the United Nations in 1971, but accelerated again after the United States and the PRC established normal diplomatic relations. Taiwan perceives that each country that follows the U.S. lead must have been influenced by the United States.

Similarly, officials blame the Administration for Taiwan's failure to participate in the Winter Olympics. They credit the International Olympic Committee with handling the dispute evenhandedly until the United States intervened. A letter sent by the State Department th the USOC at the eleventh hour outlined the Administration position that the U.S. recognizes the PRC and only accepts as official the PRC flag and national anthem. The Justice Department was also asked by State to intercede with the Appellate Court on grounds that the Taiwan question was a political, not a legal issue.

ARMS SALES

Two problem areas--arms sales to Taiwan and the status of treaties and agreements--have most separated the Administration from the Congress. In both cases the Executive Branch has not adequately consulted with the Congress before making important decisions. This is apparently due to the sensitivity the Administration attaches to all aspects of United States-China policy.

The dispute over arms sales began immediately after the President's announcement in December 1978 that the United States intended to normalize its relations with Peking. Although the PRC refused to renounce the use of force to settle its dispute with Taiwan, the United States agreed to let its Mutual Defense Treaty lapse December 31, 1979. Administration spokesmen announced that there would be no new arms sales to Taiwan in 1979, but that arms sales would resume in 1980 on a "limited and selected" basis.

The draft legislation submitted to Congress, however, made no mention of arms sales, except for a vague reference to "other relations." The Congress believed that this badly understated the importance of our commitments to Taiwan and instead inserted the following more specific language:

> ...The United States will make available to Taiwan such defense articles and defense services in such quantities as may be necessary to enable Taiwan to maintain a sufficient self-defense capability.

> The President and Congress shall determine the nature and quantity of such defense articles based solely upon their judgement of the needs of Taiwan...

The intent of this formulation was to replace the Administration's "limited and selected" arms sales formula with a more expansive U.S. commitment to include those arms legitimately needed for Taiwan's self-defense. Legislative history also indicates that it was the drafters' intention that such sales should proceed without regard to PRC sensibilities.

Despite this legislative mandate, pleas from Taiwan, and continuous prodding from individual members of Congress, the Administration continues to agonize over the arms sales question. Although its January announcement that arms sales would resume was received favorably in both Taipei and Washington, the failure to approve or even address Taiwan's top priorities--an advanced fighter (the FX), the Harpoon (naval) missile and the Standard (air defense missile--raised questions about the willingness of the United States to improve and modernize Taiwan's defensive military capabilities. The emphasis in the initial approvals was on providing additional quantities of systems already in Taiwan's inventory and postponing decisions on major qualitative improvements. This was combined with promises that the Administration anticipated more approvals later in the year. However, it is questionable whether such an incremental approach will resolve the controversy surrounding the sophisticated items on the list. The Administration's fear of such sales damaging its China policy persists. No one, therefore, is inclined to develop a long range sales strategy for Taiwan.

For Taipei, this poses the practical problem of planning its military modernization program without benefit of essential information. Taiwan, for example, programmed an advanced fighter to replace its F-104s, F-5As and F-5Bs beginning in 1981-1982. The United States originally approved this proposal in 1974 believing that a follow-on aircraft was necessary and feasible. Now, even if the Administration approves the FX this year, Taipei would be two to three years behind schedule because deliveries could not begin until 1983 or 1984.

The uncertainty surrounding the advanced fighter request also complicates Taiwan's decisions on filling other requirements. Taipei acknowledges that the cost of its complete list of eighteen items, which represents a long-range modernization program, far exceeds its ability to pay for them in any one year. With only limited resources, however, officials are reluctant to make commitments for lower priority items until they receive definite assurances that they will be able to purchase their high-cost priorities, such as the FX and the Harpoon missile.

The Administration's failure to take into account fully Taiwan's training needs and support requirements also threatens, over time, to reduce Taipei's military capabilities. State Department guidelines permit technical training in the United States for military personnel below the rank of major. These courses emphasize the nuts and bolts of operating and maintaining equipment purchased from the United States, but do not provide information on either tactics or command and control. The United States offers such information only in its professional courses. Taiwan, however, is excluded from participating by State Department directive in these courses. Taipei will not feel the full effect of this denial for several years, because many of its officers have recently graduated from a wide range of courses, and it will take time for their knowledge to become outmoded. When it does, however, the impact, although difficult to measure, will be substantial.

The refusal of the State Department to allow the U.S. military to ship explosive materials to Taiwan is another instance of the rigid application of arbitrary implementing directives. The Administration prohibits any direct U.S. military contact with Taiwan. U.S. law, however, requires certain categories of explosives to be shipped only by approved U.S. military contractors. In this case other means of delivery are not available, and as a result purchases have stacked up in U.S. warehouses.

TREATIES AND AGREEMENTS

The issue of treaties and agreements reflects another basic difference in assumptions and attitudes between Congress and the Amdinistration. The intent of Congress was clearly to provide in the Taiwan RElations Acts a framework both for the continuation in force of existing agreements and for the conclusion of new agreements between AIT and CCNAA, with the same legal status as international agreements. The preservation of such important agreements as the Friendship, Commerce, and Navigation Treaty--the basic bilateral framework for most relations between the United States and other countries--was an element in the effort of Congress to reassure the government and people on Taiwan of the continuity of our non-military relations. In that sense, continuation of the form and status of these existing agreements was as important as their substance. Although this preference for continuity did not mean a rigid prohibition against the amendment or termination of agreements, the expectation was that only the Mutual Defense Treaty and its associated military agreements would have to be terminated in the near future.

The termination of the 1946 air transport agreement therefore caught most members of the Congress by surprise. Some members perceived a general policy in the Administration of converting all the existing agreements over time to agreements between the Institutes. Whether or not there was such a policy--and the Administration subsequently assured the Congress that there was not--the failure of the Administration to anticipate the need for terminating or renegotiating certain agreements, and to consult adequately on this issue, raised Congressional concerns about the good faith of the Administration in preserving existing ties and increased the insecurity of Taiwan officials about U.S. intentions.

This was especially unfortunate in view of the fact that the new Institute-to-Institute aviation agreement was substantially more advantageous to Taiwan than the old agreement. Whether or not it would have made sense in this case, the general option of maintaining existing agreements and simply renewing or amending them with Institute-to-Institute agreements where necessary--rather than terminating the former and replacing them completely with the latter--has apparently been avoided by the Administration. Another illustration of this preference is the new science and technology agreement, which is substantively the same as the one that expired but which replaces rather than extends it.

A second example of this difference in Congressional and Administration expectations about treaties and agreements with Taiwan relates to their treatment in the Treaties in Force (TIF) publication. TIF is the authoritative compilation of all treaties and other international agreements legally binding upon the United States and is a basic reference for lawyers, judges and diplomats at home and abroad. The Administration's original proposal was that not only the Institute-to-Institute agreements but also the existing pre-1979 treaties and agreements with the Republic of China would be excluded from TIF. Following objections from both Senator Javits and Congressman Zablocki to this approach, the Administration announced that it would publish the pre-1979 agreements in TIF, but include a notation that Institute-to-Institute agreements would appear only in the Federal Register. To do otherwise, argued Deputy Secretary Christopher, "would unnecessarily jeopardize important elements of our China policy."

In addition to the considerable confusion and inconvenience which such an approach will cause, the TIF episode typifies the inclination of the Administration to avoid even minor objections from the PRC at the expense of the relationship with Taiwan. This relationship, as codified in the Taiwan Relations Act, is certainly unprecedented and extraordinary both in U.S. law and in international law, but it was clearly the intention of Congress to make it so and to preserve certain legal ambiguities and diplomatic anomalies rather than to resolve them, consistently in favor of the PRC.

UNOFFICIAL RELATIONS AND THE PRC

The problems noted above appear to stem primarily from the Administration defining "unofficial relations" too narrowly, and interpreting the TRA somewhat differently than the

Congress intended. In fact, the Executive Branch appears at times to be implementing that version of the Act which it drafted, not the TRA passed by Congress and signed by the President.

The Administration's notion of what future U.S.-Taiwan relations ought to be presumably developed during and shortly after negotiating the terms and conditions of normalization. The term "unofficial" was coined to distinguish it from the U.S. official relations with the People's Republic. Beyond this vague notion of "unofficiality," however, the new relationship appears, in practice, to have been developed through a series of discrete, ad hoc Administration decisions, each one generally erring on the side of caution, and downplaying the relationship with Taiwan in the interest of avoiding confrontations with Peking.

Conflict between the Administration and Congress on this issue has existed from the beginning. Rather than accepting the Executive Branch's view of future United States-Taiwan relations--and in particular giving first priority to PRC sensitivities--the Congress legislated a relationship which is considerably more substantial than the one contained in the draft legislation first submitted by the Administration. That draft authorized only "...the continuation of commerical, cultural, and other relations between the people of the United States and the people of Taiwan..." Although Congress retained this phrase, it went much further and declared that it was the policy of the United States. "...to preserve and promote extensive, close, and friendly commercial, cultural and other relations between the people of the United States and Taiwan..." It also felt compelled to add specific provisions for arms sales and to provide more detailed security assurances for the island. In the House-Senate Conference to work out differences in the Act, House conferees adamantly refused to accept even the word "unofficial" when describing the unique and unprecedented relations embodied in the TRA.

In making these changes, Congress knew that its actions might be objected to by Peking (which they were), but decided that they were necessary for the effective workings of this new relationship with Taiwan and that there was a certain acceptable minimum basis for continued relations with an old ally. Despite these changes, the PRC agreed to proceed with its new relationship with the United States.

Peking, whatever its initial doubts about the extent of our relations with Taiwan, has received tangible benefits from recognition. It is unlikely, therefore, that Peking will reverse this process as long as the United States holds to its position on derecognition, and maintains the Shanghai Communique formula that "Taiwan is a part of China" and that the United States "does not challenge that position." On the other hand, Peking will come to expect a certain pattern in United States-Taiwan relations which it will regard as normal and, thereafter, would have good cause to object to departures in practice which might suggest an "upgrading" in relations. In short, the United States should make clear now, and stabilize, the pattern of United States-Taiwan dealings which everyone is prepared to live with, taking into account the minimum essential elements mandated by Congress.

From Taiwan's point of view, it has been faced with a series of Administration actions which increase insecurities and raise questions about the depth and reliability of U.S. concern and commitment. Given its present isolation, the officials on Taiwan view such signals as being far more significant that the PRC, which is, after all, more in command of its own future.

Source:　　*Implementation of the Taiwan Relations Act: The First Year*, Committee on Foreign Relations, U.S. Senate. U.S. Government Printing Office, Washington, DC, 1980. pp. 8-13.

TRA20   **1980 REPUBLICAN PLATFORM STATEMENT**
                      REGARDING TAIWAN

Asia and the Pacific

The United States is and must remain a Pacific power. It is our vital interest to maintain U.S. guaranteed stability in the area. Republicans recognize the dangerous shifts in power that have accelerated under the current Democratic Administration. The balance on the Korean peninsula has shifted dangerously toward the North. Soviet naval forces in Asia and the Pacific have steadily increased and are now at least equal to U.S. naval forces there. Unilateral cancellation by the United States of the mutual defense pact with Taiwan and the abrupt announcment of withdrawal of U.S. ground forces from Korea, have led countries throughout the region to question the value of alliance with the United States.

A new Republican Administration will restore a strong American role in Asia and the Pacific. We will make it clear that any military action which threatens the independence of America's allies and friends will bring a response sufficient to make its cost prohibitive to potential adversaries.

Japan will continue to be a pillar of American policy in Asia. Republicans recognize the mutual interests and special relationships that exist between the two countries in their commitment to democracy and in trade, defense, and cultural matters. A new Republican Administration will work closely with the Japanese government to resolve outstanding trade and energy problems on an equitable basis. We strongly support a substantially increased Japanese national defense effort and reaffirm that our long-range objectives of military security and a balancing of the expanded Soviet military presence in the region are of mutual interest.

Republicans recognize the unique danger presented to our ally, South Korea. We will encourage continued efforts to expand political participation and individual liberties within the country, but will recognize the special problems brought on by subversion and potential aggression from the North. We will maintain American ground and air forces in South Korea, and will not reduce our presence further. Our treaty commitments to South Korea will be restated in unequivocal terms and we will restablish the process of close consultations between our governments.

We reaffirm our special and historic relationships with the Philippines, Singapore, Malaysia, Indonesia, Thailand, New Zealand, and Australia. Republicans will recognize the long friendship with these countries and will cultivate and strengthen our dipomatic and trade relationships.

We deplore the brutal acts of Communist Vietnam against the people of Cambodia and Laos. We recognize that the suffering of refugees from these ravaged countries represents a major moral challenge to the world and one of the great human tragedies of modern times. A Republican Administration will work actively to bring relief to these suffering people, especially those who have sought refuge in Thailand. We value the special contribution the people of Thailand have made to the refugees by opening their borders and saving hundreds of thousands of them from death, and we pleadege to provide full economic aid and military material to assist Thailand in repelling Vietnamese aggression.

We believe that no expanded relations with Communist Vietnam should be pursued while it continues its course of brutal expansionism and genocide. We pledge that a Republican Administration will press for full accounting of Americans still listed as missing in action.

Recognizing the growing importance of the People's Republic of China in world affairs, Republicans--who took the historic initiative in opening the lines of communication with that nation--will continue the process of building a working relationship with the PRC. Growing contacts between the United States and the People's Republic of China reflect the interests of both nations, as well as some common percentions of recent changes in the global military balance. We will not ignore the profound differences in our respective philosophies, governmental institutions, policies, and concepts of individual liberty.

We will strive for the creation of conditions that will foster the peaceful elaboration of our relationship with the People's Republic of China. We will exercise due caution and prudence with respect to our own vital interests, especially in the field of expanding trade, including the transfer of sophisticated technology with potential offensive military applications. The relationship between the two countries must be based on mutual respect and reciprocity, with due regard for the need to maintain peace and stability in Asia.

At the same time, we deplore the Carter Administration's treatment of Taiwan, our long-time ally and friend. We pledge that our concern for the safety and security of the 17 million people of Taiwan will be constant. We would regard any attempt to alter Taiwan's status by force as a threat to peace in the region. We declare that the Republican Administration, in strengthening relations with Taiwan, will create conditions leading to the expansion of trade, and will give priority consideration to Taiwan's defense requirements.

Source: Republican National Committee, Washington, DC.

TRA21   CANDIDATE RONALD REAGAN'S STATEMENT ON TAIWAN
                        AUGUST 25, 1980 (EXCERPT)

Ten days ago George Bush and I met with you here in Los Angeles on the occasion of his departure for Japan and China, a trip he undertook at my request. As we stressed at the time, the purpose of the trip was to provide for a candid exchange of views with leaders in both countries on a wide range of international topics of mutual interest. Ambassador Bush returned last evening, and has reported his findings in detail.

We now maintain full and friendly diplomatic relations with China. This relationship began only a few years ago, and it is one which we should develop and strengthen in the years ahead. It is a delicate relationship, and the Reagan-Bush Administration will handle it with care and respect, with due regard for our own vital interest in the world generally, and in the Pacific region specifically.

China and the United States have a common interest in maintaining peace so that our nations can grow and prosper. Our two-way trade has now reached approximately $3.5 billion annually, and China's program of modernization depends in a major way on Western and U.S. technology.

Along with many other nations, we and China share a deep concern about the pace and scale of the Soviet military buildup. Chinese leaders agree with Japanese leaders that the

United States must be a strong and vigorous defender of peace, and they specifically favor us bolstering our defenses and our alliances.

It is quite clear that we do not see eye to eye on Taiwan. Thus, this is an appropriate time for me to state our position on this subject.

I'm sure that the Chinese leaders would place no value on our relations with them if they thought we would break commitments to them if a stronger power were to demand it. Based on my long-standing conviction that America can provide leadership and command respect only if it keeps its commitments to its friends, large and small, a Reagan-Bush Administration would observe these five principles in dealing with the China situation.

Guilding Principles for the Far East

First, U.S.-Chinese relations are important to American as well as Chinese interests. Our partnership should be global and strategic. In seeking improved relations with the People's Republic of China, I would extend the hand of friendship to all Chinese. In continuing our relations, which date from the historic opening created by President Nixon, I would continue the process of expanding trade, scientific, and cultural ties.

Second, I pledge to work for peace, stability and the economic growth of the Western Pacific area in cooperation with Japan, the People's Republic of China, the Republic of Korea and Taiwan.

Third, I will cooperate and consult with all countries of the area in a mutual effort to stand firm against aggression or search for hegemony which threaten the peace and stability of the area.

Fourth, I intend that United States relations with Taiwan will develop in accordance with the law of our land, the Taiwan Relations Act. This legislation is the product of our democratic process, and is designed to remedy the defects of the totally inadequate legislation proposed by Jimmy Carter.

By accepting China's three conditions for "normalization," Jimmy Carter made concessions that Presidents Nixon and Ford had steadfastly refused to make. I was and am critical of his decision because I believe he made concessions that were not necessary and not in our national interest. I felt that a condition of normalization--by itself a sound policy choice--should have been the retention of a liaison office on Taiwan of equivalent status to the one which we had earlier established in Beijing. With a persistent and principled negotiating position, I believe that normalization could ultimately have been achieved on this basis. But that is behind us now. My present concern is to safeguard the interests of the United States and to enforce the law of the land.

It was the timely action of the Congress, reflecting the strong support of the American people for Taiwan, that forced the changes in the inadequate bill which Mr. Carter proposed. Clearly, the Congress was unwilling to buy the Carter plan, which it believed would have jeopardized Taiwan's security.

This Act, designed by the Congress to provide adequate safeguards for Taiwan's security and well being, also provides the official basis for our relations with our long-time friend and ally. It declares our official policy to be one of maintaining peace and promoting extensive, close, and friendly relations between the United States and the 17 million people on Taiwan as well as the 1 billion people on the China mainland. It specifies that our official policy considers any effort to determine the future of Taiwan by other than peaceful means a threat to peace and of "grave concern" to the United States.

And, most important, it spells out our policy of providing defensive weapons to Taiwan and mandates the United States to maintain the means to "resist any resort to force or other forms of coercion" which threaten the security or the social or economic system of Taiwan.

This Act further spells out, in great detail, how the President of the United States, our highest elected official, shall conduct relations with Taiwan, leaving to his discretion the specific methods of achieving policy objectives. The Act further details how our official personnel (including diplomats) are to administer United States relations with Taiwan through the American Institute in Taiwan. It specifies that for that purpose they are to resign for the term of their duty in Taiwan and then be reinstated to their former agencies of the U.S. Government with no loss of status, seniority or pension rights.

The intent of the Congress is crystal clear. Our official relations with Taiwan will be funded by Congress with public monies, the expenditure of which will be audited by the Comptroller General of the United States; and Congressional oversight will be performed by two standing Committees of the Congress.

Your might ask what I would do differnetly. I would not pretend, as Carter does, that the relationship we now have with Taiwan, enacted by our Congress, is not official.

I am satisfied that this Act provides an official and adequate basis for safeguarding our relationship with Taiwan, and I pledge to enforce it. But I will eliminate petty practices of the Carter Administration which are inappropriate and demeaning to our Chinese friends on Taiwan. For example, it is absurd and not required by the Act that our representatives are not permitted to meet with Taiwanese officials in their offices and ours. I will treat all Chinese officials with fairness and dignity.

I would not impose restrictions which are not required by the Taiwan Relations Act and which contravene its spirit and purpose. Here are other examples of how Carter has gone out of his way to humiliate our friends on Taiwan:

o   Taiwanese officials are ignored at senior levels of the U.S. Government.
o   The Taiwan Relations Act specifically requires that the Taiwanese be permitted to keep the same number of offices in this country as they had before. Previously, Taiwan had 14 such offices. Today there are but nine.
o   Taiwanese military officers are no longer permitted to train in the United States or to attend service academies.
o   Recently the Carter Administration attempted to ban all imports from Taiwan labeled "made in the Republic of China," but was forced to rescind the order after opposition began to mount in the Congress.
o   The Carter Administration unilaterally imposed a one-year moratorium on arms supplies even though the Act specifies that Taiwan shall be provided with arms of a defense character.
o   The Carter Administration abrogated the Civil Aviation Agreement with Taiwan, which had been in effect since 1947, in response to demands from the People's Republic of China.

I recognize that the People's Republic of China is not pleased with the Taiwan Relations Act which the United States Congress insisted on as the official basis for our relations with Taiwan. This was made abundantly clear to Mr. Bush, and, I'm told, is clear to the Carter Administration. But is is the law of our land.

Fifth, As President I will not accept the interference of any foreign power in the process of protecting American interests and carrying out the laws of our land. To do otherwise would be a dereliction of my duty as President.

It is my conclusion that the strict observance of these five principles will be in the best interest of the United States, the People's Republic of China and the people on Taiwan.

The specific implementation of these duties will have to await the results of the election in November, but in deciding what to do I will take into account the views of the Peoples's Republic of China as well as Taiwan. It will be my firm intention to preserve the interests of the United States, and as President I will choose the methods by which this shall best be accomplished.

Source: Reagan Campaign Press Release, August 25, 1980.

TRA22   **AMERICAN INSTITUTE IN TAIWAN**
                                    1700 N. Moore St.
                                        17th Floor
                                Arlington, Virginia 22209

                                                                September 4, 1980

Mr. Konsin C. Shah, Representative
Coordination Council for North
 American Affairs
5161 River Road
Washington, D.C. 20-16

Dear Mr. Shah:

I refer to discussions between representatives of the American Institute in Taiwan, hereinafter referred to as "the Institute," and representatives of the Coordination Council for North American Affairs, hereinafter referred to as "the Council," and wish to proposed the following general provisions to further scientific and scholarly cooperation between the people of the United States of America and the people on Taiwan. It is agreed that this Agreement succeeds all previous agreements, programs and arrangements in scientific and technological cooperation, except those concluded between non-governmental bodies of both sides.

1.   The aim of the cooperation will be to increase the contacts and cooperation between our scientists, engineers, scholars and institutions of research and higher learning and to provide them with more frequent opportunities to exchange information, ideas, skills and techniques, and to attack problems of common interest.

2.   The scope of the cooperation will cover all recognized branches of science and technology including social sciences, and will include to the extent the Institute and the Council agree thereon: cooperation between institutions; exchange of scientists, engineers and scholars;

pursuit of joint research projects; consultations; exchange of information; and discussion and planning of cooperative activity between the scientists, engineers and scholars of the two sides.

3.   Responsibility for ensuring proper coordination and implementation of the programs under this Agreement, including in appropriate cases the encouragement of the participation of scientists, engineers, scholars, agencies or institutions of third parties in particular joint programs, will be vested in the Institute and the Council. These two entities will work in close consultation for the planning, reviewing and implementation of the joint programs. This will be effected by periodic meetings as mutually agreed. In carrying out these responsibilities the Institute and the Council may utilize the services of advisers, consultants and contractors as necessary to accomplish the purposes of the Agreement and to continue the Satisfactory and mutually beneficial cooperative science program which both sides have had under previous agreements. Copies of contracts between the Institute and the Council and their respective principal contractors will be made mutually available.

4.   The Institute and the Council will facilitate the entry into and exist from the United States and Taiwan of persons and equipment involved in programs indicated pursuant to the Agreement. Equipment shall be admitted free of customs charges.

5.   Information derived from the programs undertaken under this Agreement shall be made available to the world scientific community through customary channels and in accordance with the normal procedures of the participating entities.

6.   Any patent rights that arise under this Agreement shall be subject to the following provisions: (1) The Institute, and its designated advisers, consultants and contractors, shall have and dispose of all patent rights within the United States; (2) the Council, and its designated advisers, consultants, and contractors, shall have and dispose of all patent rights within Taiwan, and (3) either the Institute or the Council, or their designated advisers, consultants and contractors, may seek patent rights in other countries provided that any entity that obtains patent protection in other countries shall make an offer through either the Institute or the Council to the other party to share equitably in the costs and benefits of such rights in other countries; and (4) patents that are obtained in the United States or Taiwan hereunder shall be subject to royalty-free nonexclusive and assignable licenses to the other party.

7.   Each side shall normally bear the costs incurred in the discharging of its respective responsibilities under the joint programs, including the costs of its particpating scientists, engineers and scholars; in exceptional cases the costs for a particular joint program shall be borne according to special arrangements mutually agreed upon. The obligations of the Institute and the Council under any program shall be subject to the availability of funds.

This letter and your reply confirming the contents thereof on behalf of the Council will constitute an Agreement between the Institute and the Council. The Agreement shall enter into force on the date of your letter in reply and remain in force for five years unless terminated earlier by either party upon six months' wirtten notice to the other party. It may be extended or amended by mutual written agreement of the two parties. The termination of the Agreement shall not affect the validity of any programs already in progress hereunder.

Sincerely,

David Dean
Chairman of the Board
and Managing Director

COORDINATION COUNCIL FOR NORTH AMERICAN AFFAIRS
OFFICE IN U.S.A.
5161 River Road, Washington, D.C. 20016

September 4, 1980

Mr. David Dean
Chairman of the Board
and Managing Director
American Institute in Taiwan
1700 North Moore Street, 17th Floor
Arlington, VA 22209

Dear Mr. Dean:

I have the honor to acknowledge receipt of your letter dated September 4, 1980...

In reply I have the honor to accept, on behalf of our Council, the foregoing understandings and to confirm that the aforesaid letter and this reply shall constitute an Agreement between the Institute and the Council.

Sincerely yours,

Konsin C. Shah
Representative

Source: American Institute in Taiwan, Arlington, Virginia.

TRA23   **AGREEMENT ON PRIVILIGES, EXEMPTIONS AND IMMUNITIES**
BETWEEN
THE AMERICAN INSTITUTE IN TAIWAN
AND
THE COORDINATION COUNCIL FOR NORTH AMERICAN AFFAIRS

Whereas the American Institute in Taiwan (AIT) has been incorporated in the District of Columbia as a private, non-governmental entity whose employees are private citizens, whereas the Coordination Council for North American Affairs (CCNAA) has been established in Taipei as an organization outside the governmental structure whose employees are non-active duty personnel, AIT and CCNAA (hereafter referred to as "the counterpart organizations") have reached the following agreement:

ARTICLE 1

The CCNAA may establish an office in the metropolitan area of the District of Columbia and branch offices in eight cities within the United States and such other additional localities as may be agreed upon between the counterpart organizations. The Institute may establish an office in Taipei and a branch office in Kaohsiung. The Institute may operate a Chinese language school in Taipei, a trade center in Taipei and cultural centers in Taipei and Kaohsiung, each of which offices shall be considered an integral part of the Institute.

ARTICLE 2

(a) Each counterpart organization shall undertake to ensure that the other counterpart organization and its personnel will receive all privileges, exemptions and immunities as set forth herein and to take all possible measures, as appropriate, to secure adequate protection of the other counterpart organization's premises and personnel, so as to facilitate proper execution of that organization's functions.

(b) No person shall be entitled to the benefits of this agreement unless he or she (i) shall have been duly notified to and accepted by the receiving counterpart organization as a designated employee of the sending counterpart organization, or (ii) is a member of the family of one of the foregoing accepted or designated employees.

(c) The receiving counterpart organization shall facilitate issuance of identification cards to persons who are entitled to the benefits of this agreement.

(d) The sending counterpart organization shall notify the receiving counterpart organization of the termination of services or of the departure of any person entitled to the benefits of this agreement.

(e) Should the receiving counterpart organization determine that the continued presence of any person entitled to the benefits of this agreement is not desirable, it shall so inform the sending counterpart organization. After such person shall have had a reasonable length of time to depart, to be determined by the receiving counterpart organization, he or she shall cease to be entitled to such benefits.

(f) No person shall, by reason of the provisions of this agreement, be considered as receiving any privileges or immunities other than such as are specifically set forth herein.

ARTICLE 3

Each counterpart organization shall facilitate the issuance of appropriate visas for staff members of the other organization and their family members.

ARTICLE 4

(a) The sending counterpart organization shall be free to communicate for all purposes related to the performance of its functions and shall enjoy inviolability for all correspondence related to its functions.

(b) The bag carrying the correspondence referred to in the preceding paragraph and other articles related to the performance of the counterpart organization's functions shall neither be opened nor detained.

(c) The packages constituting such a bag must bear visible external marks of their character and may contain only documents or articles intended for the performance of the organizations designated functions.

(d) The designated carriers of such bags, who shall be provided with a document indicating their status and the number of packages constituting such bags, shall be protected in the performance of their functions. The designated carrier shall enjoy personal inviolability and shall not be liable to any form of arrest or detention.

(e) The sending counterpart organization may designate such carriers *ad hoc*. In such cases the provisions of paragraph (d) of this Article shall apply, except that the privileges and immunities of an *ad hoc* carrier shall cease when the bag in his charge shall have been delivered to the consignee.

(f) Bags carrying such correspondence and articles may be entrusted to the captain of a commerical aircraft scheduled to land at an authorized port-of-entry. The captain shall be provided with a document indicating the number of packages constituting the bag, but the captain shall not be considered to be a designated carrier of such bags. The sending counterpart organization may send one of its members to take possession of such a bag directly and freely from the captain of the aircraft.

ARTICLE 5

(a) The wages, fees or salaries of any designated employee of a sending counterpart orgnaization, except nationals and permanent residents of the jurisdiction in which the receiving counterpart organization is located, to the extent such wages, fees or salaries are received in connection with the performance of authorized functions, shall be exempt from taxation imposed by the central or local authorities of the jurisdiction in which the receiving counterpart organization is located.

(b) Wages, salaries and fees paid by the sending counterpart organization to its designated employees, except nationals and permanent residents of the jurisdiction in which the receiving counterpart organization is located, shall not be subject to withholding for purposes of taxation by the central or local authorities of the jurisdiction in whicht the receiving counterpart organization is located. The sending counterpart organization is located. The sending counterpart organization and its officers and employees, other than nationals of the jurisdiction in which the receiving counterpart organization is located, shall be exempt from making contributions for unemployment or similar insurance, social security, or other programs adopted by the central or local authorities of the jurisdiction in which the receiving counterpart organization is located.

(c) The property and assets of the sending counterpart organization, and any successor organization thereto, wherever located and by whomsoever held, shall be immune from forced entry, search, attachment, execution, requisition, expropriation or any other form of seizure or confiscation, unless such immunity be expressly waived. The archives and documents of the sending counterpart organization shall be inviolable at all times and wherever they may be.

(d) Real property used for the performance of the sending counterpart organization's authorized functions and for which the counterpart organization would be liable for payment of taxes shall be exempt from central and local taxation of the jurisdiction in which the receiving counterpart organization is located. The property, income, operations, and other transactions of the sending counterpart organization shall be exempt from taxation by the central and local authorities of the jurisdiction in which the receiving counterpart organization is located. The exemptions provided in this Article, however, shall not apply to any property which is not used for the purposes of the sending counterpart organization or successor organizations.

(e) Designated employees of each sending counterpart organization shall be immune from suit and legal processes relating to acts performed by them within the scope of their authorized functions, unless such immunity be specifically waived by the sending counterpart organization.

(f) The receiving counterpart organization shall undertake to ensure that the designated employees of the sending counterpart organization shall be exempt from payment of central and local sales taxes, except those normally included in the price of goods and services. This exemption shall not, however, extend to charges for specific services rendered.

(g) The designated employees of the primary office of a sending counterpart organization, except persons who are nationals or permanent residents of the jurisdiction in which the receiving counterpart organization is located, shall be exempt from all taxes and dues imposed by central or local authorities of the jurisdiction in which the receiving counterpart organization is located in connection with the ownership or operation of a motor vehicle. The receiving counterpart organization shall undertake to ensure that these employees shall also be exempt from payment of central excise taxes on gasoline, diesel fuel and lubricating oil.

(h) A sending counterpart organization and its designated employees and their families, except nationals or permanent residents of the jurisdiction in which the receiving counterpart organization is located, shall be entitled, insofar as customs duties, customs clearance, and internal revenue taxes imposed by reason of importation of baggage and effects, as well as laws regulating entry into and departure from the jurisdiction in which the receiving counterpart organization is located, alien registration and fingerprinting, and registration of foreign agents are concerned, to the privileges, exemptions and immunities equivalent to those accorded under similar circumstances in the United States to public international organizations, their officers and employees as well as members of their families.

(i) With respect to the treatment of authorized communications and imposition of taxes for authorized communications, a sending counterpart organization shall be entitled to privileges, exemptions and immunities equivalent to those accorded a public international organization in the United States.

ARTICLE 6

(a) Each counterpart organization shall possess the capacity:

(i)   to contact;
(ii)   to acquire and dispose of real and personal
        property; and
(iii)   to institute legal proceedings.

(b) In order that it may effectively perform its functions, each sending counterpart organization shall enjoy in the territory in which the receiving counterpart organization is located, immunity from suit and legal processes equivalent to those enjoyed by public international organizations in the United States.

ARTICLE 7

This agreement may be modified at any time by mutual consent.

ARTICLE 8

This agreement is effective on the date of signature and will remain in effect indefinitely. It may, however, be terminated by either party upon one year's prior written notice to the other party or, otherwise, by mutual agreement.

IN WITNESS WHEREOF the undersigned duly authorized for this purpose, have signed this agreement.

DONE at Washington, DC, on this 2nd day of October 1980.

FOR THE AMERICAN INSTITUTE   FOR THE COORDINATION COUNCIL
IN TAIWAN: FOR NORTH AMERICAN AFFAIRS:

DAVID DEAN   KONSIN C. SHAH

Source: American Institute in Taiwan, Arlington, Virginia.

TRA24   COMMENTATOR OPPOSES U.S. ARMS SALES TO TAIWAN

HK310807 Beijing RENMIN RIBAO in Chinese 31 Dec 81 p. 6.

[Commentator's article: "China Resolutely Opposes Foreign Arms Sales to Taiwan"]

[Text]
It is now 3 years since China and the United States established diplomatic relations. During these 3 years, Sino-American relations have developed very well in the political, economic, scientific and technological and cultural fields, as a result of the common efforts of the governments and peoples of the two countries. This conforms to the common aspirations and interests of the Chinese and American peoples and has been sincerely supported by them.

However, to put it bluntly, there has always existed an obstacle on the road of the development of Sino-American relations, and that obstacle is the question of U.S. arms sales to Taiwan. Reports from Washington make it clear that not only is the U.S. Government prepared to continue selling arms to Taiwan, it is in fact considering an escalation of this action and has even declared time and agina that China has not right to interfere in the matter. In this way the gravity of the probme is increased and, as a reulst, the problem has not reached a point where it absolutely must be solved.

The Chinese Government's stand on the Taiwan issue has always been perfectly clear: There is only one China, Taiwan is part of China, and the Government of the People's Republic of China is the sole legal government of China. An important principle in the establishment of diplomatic relations between China and other countries is clear acknowledgement of China's stand on the Taiwan issue. The Chinese people resolutely oppose any attempt to create two Chineas or one China and one Taiwan. After China and the United States released the

Shanghai communique in 1972, there was a long delay beofre formal diplomatic relations between them were finally established in 1979, and this was caused by the equivocal U.S. attitude on the Taiwan issue. Everyone is aware of this.

China's attitude toward foreign arms sales to Taiwan is also very clear. We have consistently been opposed to other countries selling arms to the Taiwan authorities. Since any country establishing diplomatic relations with China acknowledges that there is only one China, that the PRC is the sole legal government of China, and that Taiwan is part of China, it should obviously not sell arms to the Taiwan authorities, who constitute a local force in China. Anyone who acts in this way is violating China's sovereignty and interfering in China's internal affairs. Naturally, the United States is no exception in this respect. The Sino-American Shanghai communique and the communique on the establishment of diplomatic relations between the two countries clearly stated that the U.S. Government recognizes China's stand on the Taiwan question and agrees to handle relations between the two countries in accordance with the five principles of respect for national sovereignty and territorial integrity, nonencroachment on other countries, noninterference in other countries' internal affairs, equality and mutual benefit, and peaceful coexistence. Hence, after China and the United States established diplomatic relations, the U.S. Government should not have engaged in any more activities in violation of China's sovereignty and of interference in China's internal affairs, such as by selling arms to Taiwan. On the one hand, the United States has recognized that Taiwan is part of China, and, on the other, it has regarded Taiwan as an "independent political entity," and has also supplied arms to support this local regime in opposing the legitimate Chinese central government which the United States has recognized. This behavior obviously violates the principles of the communiqe on the estalishment of Sino-American diplomatic relations, and is also prohibited by the principles of international law. The Chinese Government has reapeatedly expressed its solemn and just stand regarding this erroneous attitude of the U.S. Government ever since diplomatic relations were established between the two countries. The Chinese Government publicly declared on 16 December 1978, the day of the release of the communique on the establishment of Sino-American diplomatic relations: "The U.S. side had mentioned in the negotiations that it will continue to sell a limited amount of defensive arms to Taiwan following the normalization of relations.

Source: FBIS PRC International Affairs, United States, 31 December 1981. p. B1

TRA25   Document 496

Transcript of a White House Press Briefing,
July 6, 1981, 12:38 p.m. (Extract)

UNOFFICIAL RELATIONS WITH TAIWAN

        Q. Do you have any response to the Taiwan story that the President intends to increase ties with Taiwan?

        Mr. Speakes: As you know, our law specifies that the relationship with the Taiwan Government is non-governmental. We have no intent to alter that form of the relationship.

Other than that, I don't have anything to add to it.

Q. What about the angle that you are going to permit them to set up more sort of unofficial consulates?

Mr. Speakes: On that, I don't have any comment. These are not liaison offices or consulates. They are unofficial offices and--

Q. Well, I used that phrase for lack of a better one. I couldn't think of--

Mr. Speakes: The act does provide for this, but right now I have no comment.

Q. What are you commenting on? I mean, you are negatively commenting on the story in the Post today that it's not true that we're upgrading our relationship?

Mr. Speakes: The only thing I'm saying is that we have no intention to alter the form of our relationship which is non-governmental.

Q. But that doesn't answer the question.

Mr. Speakes: What's the question?

Q. The question is: If it's not governmental to up the level of relationship with Taiwan--these unofficial offices--

Mr. Speakes: I had no comment on that. It's been the Administration's policy to treat the people of Taiwan with dignity within the context of these unofficial relations and we have, from time to time, had unofficial contacts with representatives of Taiwan, and we will continue to do so, but entirely within the context of the U.S. law.

Q. You are not changing the relationship in any way, then, even outside of government strengthening the ties?

Mr. Speakes: This was a speculative story based on comments made in Taiwan. There have been no official statements from the U.S. Government about any change. You are centering in on the Boston--on the question--there have been some stories about opening an office in Boston. That I have no comment on.

Q. Why don't you tell me, Larry? Are you going to open one or not?

Mr. Speakes: I don't want to say.
Q. Why?

Mr. Speakes: I just don't.

Q. I don't understand why you are commenting on part of it. Why can't you say?

Mr. Speakes: I just don't want to comment on it.

Q. Is it part of secret diplomacy?

Mr. Speakes: No.

Q. The President during the campaign said that he, under the governmental act, he could upgrade the kind of relationship unofficially with them, and he planned on doing so. Are you saying he is no longer planning on doing that?

Mr. Speakes: I'm saying that we do not plan to change the non-governmental relationship. I'm having no comment on the openings of the offices.

Q. Larry, there is still another question on whether he wants to improve the relations with Taiwan within the context of this non-governmental relationship, which is what Reagan had kind of indicated that he wanted--

Mr. Speakes: As you know, since this January 20th there have been numerous unofficial contacts with the government of Taiwan, with the respresentatives of Taiwan. We are continuing on a much more frequent basis than the previous administration. As I say, they are more frequent and probably more cordial than they were in the previous administration.

Q. Would you say that there is an effort to try to improve that relationship?

Mr. Speakes: I don't want to say that. Lou. That is what I'm not saying. I'm just saying that there has been no--

Q. If they are more cordial, is that not an improvement?

Mr. Speakes: That has been the outcome, yes. And there have been more frequent meetings.

Q. You don't want to characterize that as improvement?

Mr. Speakes: No. I'd rather you characterize it and not me.

Q. If you do intend to open an office in Boston, will the American people be notified?

Mr. Speakes: They will.

Q. When?

Mr. Speakes: Before it opens.

Q. But why is it a secret? I don't understand.

Mr. Speakes: Well, Helen, maybe there's no decision yet.
Q. Why don't you say that?

Mr. Speakes: I didn't want to put it in those terms, but if you would like to, there has been no decision yet.

Source: *American Foreign Policy Documents*, 1981. Department of State Publication, U.S. Government Printing Office, Washington, DC, 1984. Document 496, pp. 958-959.

TRA26   U.S. RELATIONS WITH CHINA

                              BY JOHN H. HOLDRIDGE

Statement before the House Foreign Affairs Committee on July 16, 1981. Ambassador
Holdridge is Assistant Secretary for East Asian and Pacific Affairs.

    I am pleased to have been invited here today to try to answer your questions about
U.S. policy toward the Peopel's Republic of China and Taiwan. To begin, let me review our
strategic interests in a sound, healthy relationship with China.

    o   Our security and that of Japan, South Korea, and our ASEAN (Association
of South East Asian Nations) friends has been demonstrably enhanced by the growth of close
U.S.-China ties. We gain very positive benefits both in the Asian and in the global balance of
forces.

    o   In the Taiwan Strait, tensions are at an all-time low.

    o   China is supportive of our global and regional efforts to strengthen our defense
posture and alliance structure against expansionism by the Soviets and their proxies.

    o   Throughout most of the Third World we no longer compete with the Chinese
as rivals. Instead our policies are often complementary.

    o   In short, the U.S.-China relationship is a major component in our global and
regional security policies.

    o   The number of bilateral agreements with China has grown rapidly in the past
2-1/2 years. Trade--including the provision of most-favored-nation status--textile, civil aviation,
and maritime agreements have been signed. A consular convention has been approved by the
Senate Foreign Relations Committee and submitted to the full Senate for action. Joint
economic, commerce, and science committees have been formed and meet regularly to
coordinate cooperation in their respective fields. China is eligible for Customs Cooperation
Council and Eximbank credits as well as OPIC (Overseas Private Investment Corporation)
insurance in order to help support U.S. exports to China. An active consultative relationship
has taken shape, through which our two countries seek to discuss and, when appropriate,
coordinate our remarkably convergent policies over practically the entire spectrum of global and
regional issues.

    Both sides have welcomed these developments and look forward to further
improvement in the relationship. They form the healthy substance necessary for a viable, long-
term relationship. Without going into unnecessary detail, the results have been dramatic. In
the first quarter of this year, China became our third leading export market in Asia, behind
Japan and the Republic of Korea. It is now our third largest agricultural market in the world.
Our ships and planes have begun regularly scheduled service to the other's shores, and tourism
is expanding, as is educational exchange and cooperation in science and technology. All of this
has been accomplished without detracting from our continued nonofficial relationship with the
people of Taiwan, whom we are treating with the dignity befitting old friends.

Reagan Policy Review

    The starting point for this Administration's policy toward China can be found in
President Reagan's statement of last August 25, that our China relationship is global and

strategic and one that we should develop and strengthen in the years ahead. In this context, we undertook an extensive policy review to assess our China relationship on the premise that China is not our adversary but a friendly, developing country with which, without being allied, we share important strategic interests.

o   We deicded to liberalize further our export controls over dual-use technology sales to China and, perhaps more importantly, to implement the new procedures effectively.

o   We are considering possible legislative changes to amend U.S. laws which treat China as a member of the Soviet bloc. We intend to work closely with the Congress on this.

o   We concluded that we should revise the regulations on international traffic in arms to permit the licensing of commercial sales to China on a case-by-case basis.

Export Controls

Our export control policy toward China is designed to strengthen our economic involvement in China's modernization by raising the level of technology that will be routinely approved for sale to China. Our interest in a successfully modernization China is clear. Only the interests of our adversaries would be served by a weak China that had failed to modernize or a China that, in its frustration, had turned away from moderation and cooperation with the West.

Our export controls for China should reflect its role as a friendly, nonadversary state, clearly differentiating China from the Soviet bloc and minimizing the regulatory burden on U.S. companies. We want to help U.S. companies employ their technology edge fully and gain greater opportunities in the China market. Participating in China's economic development benefits business and strengthens bilateral ties. We want to have China look to us as a trusted supplier. Shackling U.S. business would not only cost us money but cause us to miss a unique opportunity to build a viable relationship with a quarter of the world's population.

Legislation

Some statutes remain on the books which inhibit the expansion of our relations with China. Some of these laws were enacted to protect against the difficulties arising from interaction between market and nonmarket economies and should be viewed in this context. Nevertheless, a number of these statutes prohibit cooperation with China by the U.S. Government or private industry due to Beijing's earlier association with the Soviet bloc. As secretary Haig informed the Chinese during his recent trip to Beijing (June 14-17), the Reagan Administration is currently reviewing such legislation and will seek appropriate congressional action to end past discrimination no longer consistent with our present strategic relationship. We will consult with the Congress closely on this subject.

In particular, we are reviewing the Foreign Assistance Act of 1961, the Agricultural Trade Development Assistance Act (PL 480), the Trade Agreements Extension Act (which prohibits imports of seven categories of furs from China and the Soviet Union), and the Trade Act of 1974.

The restrictions excluding China from development assistance, PL 480, and the export of furs are based primarily on that country's previous relationship with the Soviet Union and are not consistent with the current global situation. Thus, we believe these laws should be amended. Ending these restraints would not entail any specific U.S. obligations but would bring our laws up to date and remove self-imposed restraints that are not shared by our competitors from Europe or Japan. By doing so we would be improving our flexibility. Such steps as sales of PL 480 grains or extensions of development assistance would still be done on a case-by-case basis, if at all. Indeed, we have no current plans to offer such assistance to China and would only consider such a step following review of its economic consequences and appropriate consultations with Congress.

On the other hand, the restrictions on our relationship with China created by the Trade Act of 1974--including those on extension of the generalized system of preferences (GSP), trade agreement requirements, and market disruption--appear to be based primarily on the special concerns arising from the interaction of market and nonmarket economies. We see no reason to change statutes for China which simply recognize that nonmarket economies operate differently than market economies. This does not mean that we have foreclosed extending GSP to China at an appropriate time, but this would only be done in the context of China's having met the conditions that the law requires of nonmarket economy countries.

Munitions Control

The steady development of our relations with China over the last several years, as well as our evolving strategic cooperation, make it inappropriate for us to maintain the tight controls on munitions exports to China that we do on such exports to adversaries. A flat prohibition on sales to China, a friendly country, chiefly benefits its opportunistic and aggressive neighbor. This decision is not a decision to sell any specific weapons systems or military technology; it will merely enable Beijing to make requests to purchase from U.S. commercial sources any items on the U.S. munitions list, including weapons. We are by no means committed to approving such requests but only to considering them on a case-be-case basis just as we do for all other friendly nations.

We do not expect this to lead to a sudden or uncontrolled surge of U.S. weapons sales to China. First of all, our own intentions are to move slowly, with appropriate caution and to insure that any weapons are only defensive in character. The Secretary made clear in Beijing that, as far as defensive exports are concerned, we intend to proceed in a gradual and careful way, bearing fully in mind the concerns of and, as appropriate, consulting the Congress, our firends, and allies. Thus, we are not seeking to press arms on China or to move recklessly.

Secondly, we do not believe the Chinese will come forward with massive requests. There are budgetary and foreign exchange constraints and practical difficulties in integrating the most sophisticated technology into their own systems.

Neither we nor the Chinese seek an alliance or an otherwise dramatically expanded security relationship. While they view our willingness to consider military equipment transfers as one measure of our intent to pursue a long-term strategic association with them, they also recognize that we still treat them in a different fashion from our close allies, particularly in the sharing of sensitive technology. For us, the critically important thing is that we are now willing, for the first time, to deal with China in this area similarly to the way we deal with other friendly nations--in the Middle East, Latin America, Africa, and Asia.

Foreign Military Sales

In your letter inviting me here, you have asked that I address the question of foreign military sales (FMS) for China. In the absence of FMS eligibility, the legislated $100-million ceiling on commercial exports of defense equipment and services would act as a barrier to large Chinese purchases. The time may come when we will need to address this question, but we are not seeking to make China eligible for FMS cash sales at this time. FMS credits or FMS-guaranteed loans to China are even more premature though we will be prepared to address such issues on their merits, should they arise.

Conclusion

We see these initiatives as natural developments in the positive evolution of our relations with China over the last decade. We intend to implement these policies in a measured, controlled manner, reflective of third-country interests. We do not see a closer relationship with China as directed against the interests of any other country. Instead, we perceive an historic opportunity to build constructive, friendly relations with a country which is a future world power occupying a strategic position in the Asia-Pacific region and on the Eurasian landmass. Our long-term objective is to enhance greatly the stability of the region by strengthening U.S.-China ties.

As I have indicated, this in no way means that we will ignore Taiwan. We want to continue to improve the substance of our unofficial relations with the people of Taiwan. On his trip, the Secretary told the Chinese that we would continue to manage these relations--as we have since normalization--on the basis of the joint communique. As we have consistently stated, our own law establishes a basis for the continuation of these unofficial relations. It is clear that we have certain differences over Taiwan, which, of course, include the sale of defensive arms. We listened to Chinese views, and we made our views known. I think both sides came away from these meetings with a greater awareness of the other's sensitivities over Taiwan.

Both the Chinese and we realize the for the foreseeable future the political significance of the steps we have taken will far outweigh the immediate military and economic consequences. These are, however, very important gestures aimed at consolidating a long-term relationship in which we will hope to be able to continue to engage our Chinese friends in a positive foreign policy dialogue--particularly in Asia--and to build a network of reinforcing ties which, while leaving us free to pursue internal and foreign policy goals independently, will nonetheless insure cooperative and friendly U.S.-China relations well into the 21st century.

Source: *U.S. Department of State Bulletin*, Volume 81, July-December, 1981, pp. 38-
               40.

TRA27   PRC NINE-POINT PROPOSAL FOR REUNIFICATION
               SEPTEMBER 30, 1981

Marshal Yeh Chien-ying made a "nine-point proposal" on September 30, 1981 to the Kuomintang (Chinese Nationalist Party) in the Republic of China (ROC) in Taiwan for a settlement of the major issues he claimed were dividing the Chinese people on both sides of the Taiwan Strait. The points are listed below, with a brief of the ROC response to each proposal.

Point 1--In order to bring an end to the unfortunate separation of the Chinese nation as early as possible, we propose that talks be held between the Communist Party of China and the Kuomintang of China on a reciprocal basis so that the two parties will cooperate for the third time to accomplish the great cause of national unification. The two sides may first send people to meet for an exhaustive exchange of views.

Response--The record shows that the problem cannot be solved by talks. In the 1920s and 1930s, and again after World War II when U.S. General George Marshall tried to get the Chinese Communist Party (CCP) and the Kuomintang (KMT) to resolve their differences by talks, all these efforts failed. Peaceful reunification cannot be solved by the KMT and CCP alone. It must be decided by the whole body of the Chinese people.

Point 2--It is the urgent desire of the people on both sides of the Straits to communicate with each other, reunite with their relatives, develop trade and increase mutual understanding. We propose that the two sides make arrangements to facilitate the exchange of mails, trade, air and shipping services, and visits by relatives and tourists as well as academic, cultural and sports exchanges, and reach an agreement thereupon.

Response--The CCP is pretending to offer to the people on Taiwan what they deny to the people under their control. People on the Mainland are not free to travel. The CCP is not serious about free exchange of mail, trade and transportation. To the CCP, trade is an extension of politics.

Point 3--After the country is reunified, Taiwan can enjoy a high degree of autonomy as a special administive region and can retain its armed forces. The central government will not interfere with local affairs on Taiwan.

Response--No mention is made of the Republic of China. Clearly, the Chinese Communists would control the local government on Taiwan. They oppose the Taiwan Relations Act and the sale of U.S. arms to the ROC. The CCP speaks of "a high degree of autonomy" but their record of reducing the "special administrative region" of Tibet to a serfdom shows what could happen to Taiwan.

Point 4--Taiwan's current socio-economic system will remain unchanged; so will its way of life and economic and cultural relations with foreign countries. There will be no encroachment on the proprietary rights and lawful right of inheritance over private property, houses, land and enterprises, or on foreign investments.

Response--The Republic of China already has all these rights, and thus has nothing to gain from this proposal.

Point 5--People in authority and representative personages of various circles in Taiwan may take up posts of leadership in national political bodies and participate in running the state.

Response--The Chinese Communists think only in terms of "tso kuan," getting a high position in government. The people in the ROC think of a government post as a service, careers undertaken to benefit the people and not to enrich bureaucrats and give them power over others.

Point 6--When Taiwan's local finances are in difficulty, the central government may provide subsidies.

Response--The Chinese Communists cannot finance modernization. The foreign exchange reserves of the mainland are some U.S. $2 billion compared with U.S. $9 billion for Taiwan. Per capita income on Taiwan is ten times that of the mainland.

Point 7--For people of all nationalities and public figures of various circles in Taiwan who wish to come and settle on the mainland, it is guaranteed that proper arrangements will be made for them, that there will be no discrimination against them and that they will have freedom of entry and exit.

Response--How can the Communists offer freedoms to the 18 million people on Taiwan that they deny to the billion people on the mainland? The people in the PRC may not travel nor change jobs without government permission. As for settlement on the mainland, who on Taiwan would want to go?

Point 8--Industrialists and businessmen in Taiwan are welcome to invest and engage in various economic undertakings on the mainland, and their legal rights, interests and profits are guaranteed.

Response--This is what the Chinese Communists told foreign investors and overseas Chinese investors, and the capitalists who stayed on the mainland, but they all found that they could not control their own business.

Point 9--The reunification of the motherland is the responsibility of all Chinese. We sincerely welcome people of all nationalities, public figures of all circles and all mass organizations in Taiwan to make proposals and suggestions regarding affairs of state through various channels and in various ways.

Response--The ROC has repeatedly made one suggestion: that the Chinese Communists renounce their false and alien ideology and return to Sun Yat-sen's Three Principles of the People and to the Constitution of the Republic of China. They do not answer. They fear that the spirit of Taiwan, the Constitution and the Three Principles will overcome Communism and assure one free China.

Source: Excerpts from Report, "Is the 'Nine-Point Proposal' a Yesable Solution?," China Mainland Affairs Research Center, Taipei, Taiwan, May 1982.

TRA28   DOCUMENT 499

Transcript of an Interview With the Secretary
of State (Haig), Cancun, Mexico, October 22, 1981 (Extract)

CHINESE CONCERN WITH THE U.S.
RELATIONSHIP WITH TAIWAN

Mrs. Sawyer: Let me ask you about one of the bilateral meetings. We are told--some of the Chinese delegation have been telling some members of the press anyway--that they will downgrade U.S.-Chinese relations, perhaps even ask that the Ambassador be recalled if the United States sells advanced weaponry to Taiwan. Is that the impression that you got from your meeting, that that would be the consequence?

Secretary Haig: I think I've had that impression from the outset of our incumbency here in Washingston. The Chinese have been very clear about expressing concern that if we handle the armament question on Taiwan insensitively, it is going to result in a setback in our relationships. I don't think it's shattering because those relationships are built on more profound, fundamental interests. But it would represent a setback. Now we have told them that we are conscious of that, but we have also told them that they must be conscious of our obligations to meet our commitments to the people of Taiwan and to live by the law of the Taiwan Relations Act which the President intends to do. We have made no decision to sell anything, and we are now looking very carefully at what Taiwan's true defense needs are in the aircraft sector.

Source: *American Foreign Policy Current Documents*, 1981. Department of State Pub-
                 lication, U.S. Government Pringing Office, 1984. Document 499, pp. 964-965.

TRA29   Document 501

Testimony by the Secretary of State (Haig) Before the
House Foreign Affairs Committee, November 12, 1981 (Extracts)

PROPOSED SALE OF AIRCRAFT TO TAIWAN

Mr. Derwinski: Let me switch continents for a moment. Is there any truth to the Washington rumor that, for all I know it might come from a certain well-known Pennsylvania Avenue office staff, that you are in disagreement with them on the proposed sale of aircraft to the Republic of China?

Secretary Haig: I don't think there is any position on that subject. I see some speculation in the press from time to time, but let me assure you there has been no deicsion, no decision in principle on that subject. It is an issue that is extremely sensitive not only here in the United States but in Peking and probably in Taiwan as well. That is an issue on the horizon, so what you see as speculation could be misinformed, and it would have to be.

Mr. Solarz: One final question, if I might, Mr. Secretary. You will recall that a few months ago the Subcommittee on Asian and Pacific Affairs unanimously recommended in a letter to the President that we not proceed with the sale of the FX to Taiwan at this time. The subcommittee letter argued that this sale was militarily unnecessary, and, from a political point of view, could create a serious dislocation in our relationship with the People's Republic of China. I gather you have already testified that the Administration hasn't made a final decision on this issue yet.

Secretary Haig: Hasn't even made a preliminary one.

Mr. Solarz: But would you agree that were we to go ahead, that it could have potentially serious adverse consequence for our relationship with Peking?

Secretary Haig: I think I would agree without a question, and I have been on the record on this in the past, that this is an extremely sensitive question in Peking, and we have got to proceed with utmost respect for that sensitivity.

Document 502

**Remarks by the Secretary of State (Haig), Palm Beach,
Florida, November 14, 1981 (Extract)**

U.S.-CHINA DIFFERENCES CONCERNING TAIWAN

Q. Mr. Secretary, would you care to comment on our relations with Red China?

Secretary Haig: The question was our relationships with Red China. We, as you know, have just completed the visit of the People's Republic Foreign Minister, Huang Hua, to China [the United States], and we had the first meeting of President Reagan with the new Premier of Communist China at Cancun.

In general our relationships are on a sound and maturing basis in economic and security-related dialogues. There is, of course, a very worrisome specter on the horizon and that is the differences between the United States and Peking on the subject of Taiwan and military assistance to Taiwan.

China recently put out what they called their Nine Points for the achievement of one China and the reintegration of Taiwan with the Chinese Mainland. These were rather remarkable points. They call for peaceful integration. They recognize the federalism in Taipei and the ability of them to maintain their own political, economic, and security framework. So these were not meaningless proposals, but in the period ahead it's going to be essential that both Peking and the United States handle this particular question with great sensitivity and care. Beyond that I think the prospects are good.

Source: *American Foreign Policy Current Documents*, 1981. Department of State
               Publication, U.S. Government Printing Office, 1984. Document 501-2, p. 966.

TRA30   **Document 483**

**Statement Read by the Department of State Acting
Spokesman (Romberg), January 11, 1982**

NO SALE OF ADVANCED FIGHTER
AIRCRAFT TO TAIWAN

Since the beginning of this administration, the President has been conscious of the need to carry forward the unofficial poeople-to-people relationship between the United States and Taiwan, and he has expressed on many occasions his personal concern for the continued well-being of the people of Taiwan.

This administration has attached a high value to fulfilling the longstanding policy of the U.S. Government with respect to providing such defense articles as may be necessary to enable Taiwan to maintain a sufficient self-defense capability.

Concerned agencies of the U.S. Government, including the Departments of State and Defense and other national security elements, have been addressing the question of Taiwan's defense needs over a period of many months, and have taken into careful consideration the many factors which bear on the judgments which must be made in implementing this policy.

On the basis of this study, the administration has already taken steps to sell Taiwan items necessary for self-defense. We anticipate further steps of this sort.

A judgment has also been reached by the concerned agencies on the question of replacement aircraft for Taiwan. Their conclusion is that no sale of advanced fither aircraft to Taiwan is required because no military need for such aircraft exists.

Taiwan's defense needs can be met as they arise and for the foreseeable future by replacing aging aircraft now in the Taiwan inventory with comparabel aircraft, and by an extention of the F-5E coproduction line in Taiwan. The details have not yet been worked out. The President has approved these recommendations.

Document 484

**Transcript of an Interview With the Secretary of State
(Haig), February 5, 1982 (Extract)**

"EXTREMELY SENSITIVE DISCUSSIONS"

Q. Despite the decisions on not selling advanced jets to Taiwan, the Chinese still seem to be hammering away on the question of Taiwan and infringements on their sovereignty. How do you see Chinese-American relations developing? Are they deteriorating as the Chinese press seems to make out?

A. I think our first principle is to recognize we highly value good relations with China. That is our policy, and I think also you have to make the point that a great deal has been achieved over the decades since the Shanghai communique in which I myself was intimately involved, and that we are determined to do all we can to preserve these achievements.

We have taken a number of important initiatives to advance the relationship with the People's Republic of China. It goes without saying that since the beginning of this administration, we have also had to face continuing disagreement with Peking over our arms sales to Taiwan. We made clear in a bipartisan spirit the United States position at the time of normalization, and the Chinese Government went ahead, knowing our intentions. Still the United States recognizes this is an area to be approached with prudence and discretion.

We carried forward the policy enunciated at the time of normalization, but any examination of our actions will show that we have taken a very careful account of Chinese concerns.

We have also undertaken extremely sensitive discussions with Peking since Foreign Minister Huang Hua visited Washington last October, including Assistant Secretary Holdridge's visit to China last month.

It would be counterproductive to go into details because things are at a delicate stage; but speaking candidly, some difficult issues are involved. We are now making a major effort to bridge these differences. I will be just as frank when I tell you I am not in a position to predict the outcome.

Q. Are there still plans to have talks with the Chinese on arms sales to them? Are they in abeyance?

A. It is clear that that subject is hostage, in effect, to a resolution of these differences I have talked about.

Source: *American Foreign Policy Current Documents*, 1982. Department of State
              Publication 9415, U.S. Government Printing Office, Washington, DC, 1985.
              pp. 1025-1026.

TRA31   Document 485

Exchange of Letters Between President Reagan and
Chinese Premier Zhao, February 28, 1982

TENTH ANNIVERSARY OF THE SHANGHAI COMMUNIQUE

Esteemed Mr. President: On the occasion of the tenth anniversary of the issuance of the Joint Communique in Shanghai by the People's Republic of China and the United States of America, I wish to extend, on behalf of the Chinese Government and people and in my own name, our cordial regards and good wishes to Your Excellency and the Government and people of the United States.

The Joint Communique issued by China and the United States a decade ago was a historic document, which started the process of normalization of relations between China and the United States and subsequently led to the establishment of diplomatic relations between them. During this period, our two sides have had extensive contacts and exchanges in many fields, thus enhancing the understanding between the governments and deepening the friendship between the peoples. The development of Sino-U.S. relations is not only in the fundamental interests of our two peoples, but also conducive to the maintenance of peace and stability in Asia and the world as a whole.

Both the Chinese and American peoples hope that Sino-U.S. relations will continue to move ahead in the years to come. I believe that these relations will continue to develop so long as both governments adhere to the principles jointly established in the Shanghai Communique and the Communique on the Establishment of Sino-U.S. Diplomatic Relations and overcome the obstacles currently existing in the relations between the two countries. The Chinese Government is willing to make efforts together with the U.S. Government towards this end.

Sincerely,

ZHAO ZIYANG

Dear Mr. Premier: Ten years ago today the United States of America and the People's Republic of China issued the Shanghai Communique. In the ensuing decade, and particularly since the establishment of full diplomatic relations between the two countries on January 1, 1979, our relations with your government and people have greatly expanded, and our contacts have embraced almost all areas of human endeavor.

Our bilateral ties now encompass trade, banking, maritime affairs, civil aviation, agriculture, educational and scientific exchange, technology transfer and many other fields. Well over one hundred thousand Americans and Chinese now flow back and forth between the two countries each year, and our relations continue to develop through both people-to-people and diplomatic channels.

These concrete manifestations of good relations between the people of the United States and China are not only in the interests of the two countries. They enhance the prospects for peace and stability throughout the Asia-Pacific region, and beyond.

As we enter the second decade since the issuance of the Shanghai Communique, our desire is to build an even stronger bilateral and strategic framework for long term friendship between our two nations. It is appropriate for me, at this time, to reaffirm the positions agreed to by both sides in the Shanghai Communique and the Joint Communique on the Establishment of Diplomatic Relations between the United States of America and the People's Republic of China and to declare my government's willingness to work with our counterparts in Beijing to overcome differences and deepen U.S.-China ties.

On behalf of the American people, I extend the hand of friendship and warmest wishes to the Government and people of China on this historic anniversary.

Sincerely,

RONALD REAGAN

Source: *American Foreign Policy Current Documents*, 1982. Department of State Publication, U.S. Government Printing Office, Washington, DC, 1985. pp. 1027.

TRA32   Document 486

**Letter from President Reagan to the Vice Chairman
of the Chinese Communist Party (Deng), April 5, 1982**

U.S. INTEREST IN RESOLVING
U.S.-CHINESE DIFFERENCES

Dear Mr. Vice Chairman: The establishment of diplomatic relations between the United States and China was an historic event which improved the prospects for peace and served the interest of both our peoples. Yet we now find ourselves at a difficult juncture in those relations.

I am writing to you because it is important for the leadership of both our countries to resume the broad advance to which you have contributed so much. This is particularly important today, as we face a growing threat from the Soviet Union and its satellite nations throughout the world. Though our interests and thus our policies are not identical, in Afghanistan and Iran, in Southeast Asia, in my own hemisphere, and in the field of nuclear weaponry, your nation and mine face clear and present dangers, and these should impel us toward finding a firm basis for cooperation.

We have come far together in a very short time. I strongly support the continuation of this progress. We must work together to expand the benefits to both our countries. My administration has taken a number of initiatives to further this process, and we intend to do more.

Clearly, the Taiwan issue has been a most difficult problem between our governments. Nonetheless, vision and statesmanship have enabled us in the past to reduce our differences over this issue while we have built a framework of long-term firendship and cooperation.

The United States firmly adheres to the positions agreed upon in the Joint Communique on the Establishment of Diplomatic Relations between the United States and China. There is only one China. We will not permit the unofficial relations between the American people and the people of Taiwan to weaken our commitment to this principle.

I fully understand and respect the position of your government with regard to the question of arms sales to Taiwan. As you know, our position on this matter was stated in the process of normalization: the United States has an abiding interest in the peaceful resolution of the Taiwan question.

We fully recognize the significance of the nine-point proposal of September 30, 1979. The decisions and the principles conveyed on my instructions to your government on January 11, 1982 reflect our appreciation of the new situation created by these developments.

In this spirit, we wish to continue our efforts to resolve our differences and to create a cooperative and enduring bilateral and strategic relationship. China and America are two great nations destined to grow stronger through cooperation, not weaker through division.

In the spirit of deepening the understanding between our two countries, I would like to call your attention to the fact that Vice President Bush will be traveling to East Asia toward the end of April. The Vice President knows and admires you. He is also fully aware of my thinking about the importance of developing stronger relations between our two countries. If it would be helpful, I would be delighted to have the Vice President pay a visit to Beijing, as part of his Asian trip, so that these matters can be discussed directly and personally with you and other key leaders of the People's Republic of China.

Sincerely,

RONALD REAGAN

Source: *American Foreign Policy Current Documents*, 1982. Department of State Publication, U.S. Government Printing Office, Washington, DC, 1985. Document 486, p. 1028.

TRA33   **Document 487**

**Letter from President Reagan to Chinese
Primier Zhao, April 5, 1982**

"IN THE CONTEXT OF PROGRESS TOWARD A
PEACEFUL SOLUTION, THERE WOULD NATURALLY
BE A DECREASE IN THE NEED FOR ARMS BY TAIWAN"

Dear Mr. Premier: The present state of relations between our two countries deeply concerns me. We believe significant deterioration in those relations would serve the interests of neither the United States of America nor the People's Republic of China.

As the late Premier Zhou Enlai said in welcoming President Nixon to China in 1972, "The Chinese people are a great people, and the Amercian people are a great people." We are strong, soverign nations sharing many common interest. We both face a common threat of expanding Soviet power and hegemonism. History has placed upon us a joint responsibility to deal with this danger.

The differences between us are rooted in the longstanding friendship between the American people and the Chinese people who live on Taiwan. We will welcome and support peaceful resolution of the Taiwan question. In this connection, we appreciate the policies which your government has followed to provide a peaceful settlement.

As I told Vice Premier Huang in Washington, we welcome your nine-point initiative.

As I also told the Vice Premier, we expect that in the context of progress toward a peaceful solution, there would naturally be a decrease in the need for arms by Taiwan. Our positions over the past 2 months have reflected this view. We are prepared, indeed welcome, further exchanges of view in the months to come. I hope you share my conviction that the United States and China should work together to strengthen the prospects for a peaceful international order. While our interests, and thus our policies, will not alwasy be identifcal, they are complementary and thus should form a firm basis for cooperation.

In my letter to Vice Chairman Deng, I have suggested that a visit to Beijing by Vice President Bush at the end of April could be a useful step in deepening the understanding between our two countries. The Vice President will be traveling in Asia at the time, and could visit Beijing if you feel it would be useful.

Sincerely,

RONALD REAGAN

Source: *American Foreign Policy Current Documents*, 1982. Department of State Publication, U.S. Government Printing Office, Washington, DC, 1985. Document 487, p. 1029.

TRA34   Document 489

Letter from President Reagan to the Chairman of the Chinese Communist Party (Hu), May 3, 1982

VICE PRESIDENT BUSH TO DISCUSS ISSUE OF U.S. ARMS SALES TO TAIWAN

Dear Mr. Chairman: The visit of Vice President Bush to China affords a welcome opportunity to convey my regards to you.

As sovereign nations, our two countries share a common responsibility to promote world peace. We face a grave challenge from the Soviet Union which directly threatens our peoples and complicates the resolution of problems throughout the globe. It is vital that our relations advance and our cooperation be strengthened.

Vice President Bush is visiting China as my personal emissary. He is prepared to discuss a wide range of issues of mutual concern. My sincere hope is that we can achieve, through discussions, enhanced mutual understanding, at the highest levels of our governments.

Among the issues the Vice President will address is the question of United States arms sales to Taiwan. This remains an area of residual disagreement, as our governments acknowledged at the time of U.S.-China normalization. I believe, so long as we exercise the statesmanship and vision which have characterized our approach to differences over the past decade, we will be able to make progress toward the removal of this issue as a point of bilateral contention.

In the meantime, as stated in my recent letters to Vice Chairman Deng and Premier Zhao, the United States will continue to adhere firmly to the positions agreed upon in the joint communique on the establishment of diplomatic relations between the United States and the People's Republic of China. Our policy will continue to be based on the principle that there is but one China. We will not permit the unofficial relations between the American people and the Chinese people on Taiwan to weaken our commitment to this principle.

On this basis, and with good faith on both sides, we are confident that a means can be found to resolve current differences and deepen our bilateral and strategic cooperation. It is my hope that you and I will have an opportunity to meet soon. Please accept my best wishes in your efforts to build a secure and modernizing China.

Sincerely,

RONALD REAGAN

Source: *American Foreign Policy Current Documents*, Department of State Publication, U.S. Government Printing Office, Washington, DC, 1985. Document 489, p. 1030.

TRA35   Document 492

Report Issued by the Senate Foreign Relations Committee, May 28, 1982 (Extract)

CHINESE ELIGIBILITY FOR U.S. ASSISTANCE PROGRAMS

Sec. 110 --   Eligibility of the People's Republic of China for Assistance

Section 110 adds a new Section 620(y) to the Foreign Assistance Act. It is an amendment proposed by Senators Hayakawa and Glenn which would allow the President to authorize foreign assistance to the People's Republic of China provided the President certifies to the Congress that such assistance is important to the security of the United States. The provision overrides the prohibition against foreign assistance to China contain in Section 620(f). The Hayakawa/Glenn amendment substituted for an administration proposal which would have struck the People's Republic of China and Tibet from the list of prohibited nations. The Committee, in making this change, recognizes that the People's Republic of China, although it has a communist form of government, is a non-allied nation which plays a helpful strategic role.

The Committee received assurances in a letter, dated May 13, 1982, signed by Assistant Secretary of State Powell A. Moore that no military assistance program is being contemplated for China. The letter further states that if, in the future, the initiation of military assistance is contemplated, the Senate Foreign Relations Committee will be consulted and the administration will proceed through the normal statutory process before funds can be expended. The Committee has been further assured that the Administration does not contemplate using reprogramming authority to provide military aid to China. It is the Committee's understanding, based on these assurances, that further congressional action is required beyond that taken in this legislation for China to become a recipient of U.S. military aid. The text of the Committee letter requesting assurances on military aid and the Administration's response are as follows:

U.S. Senate,
COMMITTEE ON FOREIGN RELATIONS
Washington, DC, May 3, 1982.

Hon. Alexander Haig, Jr.,
Secretary of State,
Washington, D.C.

Dear Mr. Secretary: We are writing in regard to the Administration's request that China be made eligible for foreign assistance. As you know, the Administration has proposed changes in the foreign assistance legislation to achieve this purpose.

Our understanding is that the Administration plans no bilateral assistance programs, Public Law 480 programs, or military assistance programs to China at this time, although the Administration would like to invite China to participate in several exchange and multilateral technical assistance programs proscribed by current law.

In principle, we do not object to the Administration's plans. But there are some concerns about the extensiveness of future programs to China and their effect on other ongoing assistance programs in an increasingly austere aid budget. We also have reservations about extending military assistance to China.

Bilateral assistance programs, as well as military assistance, for China would have to be considered by Congress through the normal authorization and appropriations processes. On the issue of military assistance, we would like assurance that the Administration will not use reprogramming authority to provide military assistance to China without first going through the normal authorization and appropriations processes, thus requiring further Congressional action beyond that taken this year.

Sincerely,

CHARLES H. PERCY,
Chairman
S.I. HAYAKAWA,
Chairman
Subcommittee on East Asian and Pacific Affairs
CLAIBORNE PELL
Ranking Minitory Member
JOHN GLENN
Ranking Miniority Member
Subcommittee on East Asian and Pacific Affairs

DEPARTMENT OF STATE
Washington, DC, May 13, 1982

Hon. Charles H. Percy
Chairman, Senate Foreign Relations
Committee.

Dear Mr. Chairman: I have been asked to respond to the letter which you and Senators Hayakawa, Pell, and Glenn sent to Secretary Haig on May 3 concerning China and amendments to the existing legislation on foreign assistance. I wish to reaffirm the assurances given your Committee on April 26 in testimony by Acting Assistant Secretary for East Asian and Pacific Affairs Thomas P. Shoesmith and to assure members of your Committee that no military assistance program is being contemplated for China.

Let me emphasize that the Administration's proposal to make China eligible for foreign assistance and Public Law 480 should in no way be construed as a request for the authorization or appropriation of funds. The request has no budgetary impact and is not designed to provide military assistance to China.

Rather, our intent was to remove outdated prohibitions which are inconsistent with our foreign policy and with our treatment of China as a friendly, non-allied country with which we share important strategic interests. The Administration has no present intention of proposing a Public Law 480 program, or an economic or military assistance program for China. If the prohibition on assistance is eliminated, however, we do intend to consider Chinese participation in certain on-going technical assistance programs for which funding is already available. We have already provided your Committee a paper describing the types of programs in which China might participate.

If, in the future, we should contemplate initiating assistance programs for China, we would at that time consult with the appropriate Committees of the Congress. Following such consultations, it would of course be necessary to proceed throught the normal statutory process before funds could be expended.

We respect to your question on reprogramming, you can be assured that the Administration does not contemplate using the reprogramming authority to provide military assistance to China. If, at a future data, we propose to initiate military assistance to China, we would provide the details of such assistance in connection with our request for the authroization of foreign assistance funds for that year. The Congressional action we are requesting at this time is designed only to establish treatment for China consistent with our treatment of other friendly, non-allied nations.

I trust this letter responds to the concerns raised by you and your colleagues.

With cordial regards,

Sincerely,

POWELL A. MOORE
Assistant Secretary for Congressional Relations

The Committee commends the Agricultural Committee for its timely consideration of the Administration's proposal regarding Public Law 480 Food for Peace and supports the Agriculture Committee's decision to write report language which would state that the Administration's proposed amendment making China eligible for Public Law 480 is unnecessary. It is the Agriculture Committee's judgement that if the President believes that China neither dominates nor is dominated by a world Communist movement, he is free to designate China as a "friendly country" and, therefore, eligible for Public Law 480 under existing law.

The Committee found that, from a foreign policy point of view, the Agriculture Committees' views noted above are consistent with the Foreign Relations Committee's views. Because initiation of a Public Law 480 program would have important foreign policy implications, not only in regard to U.S.-PRC relations, but also in regard to its potential effects on other foreign nations, the President should also notify the Committee on Foreign Relations at least 90 days in advance of implementation of any Public Law 480 program with China. In a situation where Public Law 480 title II might be used to respond to a specific emergency, the Committee recognizes that it might be impossible to provide notification the full 90 days in advance and would accept the Administration's bet efforts to provide prior notification.

Source: *American Foreign Policy Current Documents*, 1982. Department of State Publication, U.S. Government Printing Office, Washington, DC, 1985. Document 492, pp. 1032-1033.

AGREEMENT BETWEEN THE AMERICAN INSTITUTE IN TAIWAN AND THE COORDINATION COUNCIL FOR NORTH AMERICAN AFFAIRS CONCERNING FISHERIES OFF THE COASTS OF THE UNITED STATES

The American Institute in Taiwan (hereinafter AIT) and the Coordination Council for North American Affairs (hereinafter CCNAA)

Considering their common concern for the rational management, conservation and achievement of optimum yield of fish stocks off the coasts of the United States;

Recognizing that the United States has established a fishery conservation zone within 200 nautical miles of its coasts within which the United States exercises exclusive fishery management authority over all fish and that the United States also exercises such authority over the living resources of the continental shelf appertaining to the United States and to anadormous species of fish of United States origin; and

Desirous of establishing reasonable terms and conditions pertaining to fisheries of mutual concern over which the United States exercises exclusive fishery management authority;

Have agreed as follows:

ARTICLE I

The purpose of this Agreement is to promote effective conservation, rational management and the achievement of optimum yield in the fisheries of mutual interest off the coasts of the United States and to establish a common understanding of the principles and procedures under which fishing may be conducted by the people and vessels of the parties represented by CCNAA for the living resources over which the United States exercises exclusive fishery management authority as provided by United States law...

ARTICLE III

...1. AIT is willing to allow access for foreign fishing vessels to harvest, in accordance with terms and conditions to be established in permits issued under Article VII, that portion of the total allowable catch for a specific fishery that will not be harvested by United States fishing vessels and is determined to be available to foreign fishing vessels in accordance with United States law.

ARTICLE X

...CCNAA shall take all appropriate measures to assist in the enforcement of laws of the United States pertaining to fishing in the fishery conservation zone and to insure that each vessel of the parties represented by CCNAA that engages in fishing for living resources subject to the exclusive fishery management authority of the United States shall allow and assist the boarding and inspection of such vessel by any duly authorized enforcement officer of the United States and shall cooperate in such enforcement action as may be undertaken pursuant to the laws of the United States.

ARTICLE XI

1.   AIT will impose appropriate penalities, in accordance with the laws of the United States, on vessels of the parties represented by CCNAA or their owners or operators, that violate the requirements of this Agreement or of any permit issued hereunder.

2.   Arrested vessels and their crews shall be promptly released, subject to such reasonable bond or other security as may be determined by the court.

3.   The representatives of the United States will recommend to the court in any case arising out of fishing activities under this Agreement that the penalty for violation of fishery regulations not include imprisonment except in the case of enforcement related offenses such as assault on an enforcement officer or refusal to permit boarding and inspection.

4.   In cases of seizure and arrest of a vessel of the parties represented by CCNAA by the authorities of the AIT, notification shall be given promptly informing the CCNAA of the action taken and of any penalities subsequently imposed...

ARTICLE XVI

...1.   This Agreement shall enter into force on a date to be agreed upon by exchange of notes, following the completion of internal procedures of both AIT and CCNAA, and remain in force until July 1, 1987, unless extended by exchange of notes between the Parties. Notwithstanding the foregoing, either Party may terminate this Agreement after giving written notice of such termination to the other Party six months in advance.

2.   This Agreement shall be subject to review by AIT and CCNAA two years after its entry into force at the request of either or upon the conclusion of a multilateral treaty resulting from the Third United Nations Conference on the Law of the Sea.

IN WITNESS WHEREOF, the undersigned, being duly authorized for this purpose, have signed this Agreement.

DONE at Washington, June 7, 1982, in English.

FOR THE AMERICAN INSTITUTE   FOR THE COORDINATION COUNCIL
OF TAIWAN: FOR NORTH AMERICAN AFFAIRS:

DAVID DEAN   TSAI WEI-PING

Source: American Institute in Taiwan, Arlington, Virginia. (Excerpts).

AMERICAN INSTITUTE IN TAIWAN
1700 N. Moore St.
17th Floor
Arlington, Virginia 22209
(703) 525-8474

August 17, 1982

Dr. Tsai Wei-ping, Representative
Coordination Council for
  North American Affairs
5161 River Road
Bethesda, MD 20816

Dear Dr. Tsai:

Given our mutual desire to ensure the continuation of uninterrupted maritime trade and the safety of life at sea, I propose that prior to some mutually agreed date assurances be provided to the American Institute in Taiwan (the "Institute") that all ships under the registry of the party represented by the Coordination Council for North American Affairs (the "Council") which are used in bilateral trade have been inspected and are in compliance with the requirements of the 1974 International Convention for the Safety of Life at Sea (1974 SOLAS), a copy of which is enclosed. Compliance with the 1974 SOLAS Convention requirements will be indicated by the carriage aboard such ships of valid certificates attesting to that fact. Such certificates shall be in the same form as those called for in the 1974 SOLAS Convention. Their carriage shall enable such ships to trade at the ports of the party represented by the Institute in the same manner and under the same conditions as ships of signatories to the 1974 SOLAS Convention.

Reciprocally, assurances should be provided that, inasmuch as the party represented by the Institute is a party to the 1974 SOLAS Convention, the carriage of valid 1974 SOLAS Convention certificates on merchant ships under the registry of that party after May 25, 1980, the date the 1974 SOLAS Convention entered into effect, will enable them to trade at ports of the party represented by the Council in the same manner and under the same conditions as ships under the registry of the party represented by the Institute trade at ports of signatories to the 1974 SOLAS Convention.

If these arrangements meet with your approval, I propose that this letter and your letter in reply serve as a basis to establish the procedures described.

Sincerely,

David Dean
Chairman of the Board
and Managing Director

Enclosure:
  1974 Safety of Life at
  Sea Convention (not included)

COORDINATION COUNCIL FOR NORTH AMERICAN AFFAIRS
OFFICE IN U.S.A.
5161 River Road, Washington, D.C. 20016

September 7, 1982

Mr. David Dean
Chairman of the Board
and Managing Director
American Institute in Taiwan
1700 N. Moore St.
Arlington, VA 22209

Dear Mr. Dean:

This is to acknowledge receipt of your letter of August 17, 1982...

In reply, I wish to express, on behalf of the Coordination Council for North American Affairs, our willingness to provide the American Institute in Taiwan reciprocally with the assurances as specified in your letter, and our concurrence with your suggestion that this correspondence of ours will serve as a basis to establish the procedures described.

Sincerely,

TSAI WEI-PING
Representative

Source: American Institute in Taiwan, Arlington, Virginia.

TRA38

Document 496

Statement by President Reagan,
August 17, 1982

ADMINISTRATION POSITION ON THE JOINT COMMUNIQUE

The U.S.-China Joint Communique issued today embodies a mutually satisfactory means of dealing with the historical question of U.S. arms sale to Taiwan. This document preserves principles on both sides, and will promote the further development of friendly relations between the governments and peoples of the United States and China. It will also contribute to the further reduction of tensions and the lasting peace in the Asia/Pacific region.

Building a strong and lasting relationship with China has been an important foreign policy goal of four consecutive American administrations. Such a relationship is vital to our long-term national security interests and contributes to stability in East Asia. It is in the national interest of the United States that this important strategic relationship be advanced. This communique will make that possible consistent with our obligations to the people of Taiwan.

In working toward this successful outcome we have paid particular attention to the needs and interest of the people of Taiwan. My longstanding personal friendship and deep concern for the well-being is steadfast and unchanged. I am committed to maintaining the full range of contacts between the people of the United States and the people of Taiwan--cultural commercial, and people-to-people contacts--which are compatible with our unofficial relationship. Such contacts will continue to grow and prosper, and will be conducted with the dignity and honor befitting old friends.

Regarding future U.S. arms sales to Taiwan, our policy, set forth clearly in the communique, is fully consistent with the Taiwan Relations Act. Arms sales will continue in accordance with the Act and with the full expectation that the approach of the Chinese Government to the resolution of the Taiwan issue will continue to be peaceful. We attach great significance to the Chinese statement in the communique regarding China's "fundamental" policy; and it is clear from our statements that our future actions will be conducted with this peaceful policy fully in mind. The position of the United States Government has always been clear and consistent in this regard. The Taiwan question is a matter for the Chinese people, on both sides of the Taiwan Strait, to resolve. We will not interfere in this matter or prejudice the free choice of, or put pressure on, the people of Taiwan in this matter. At the same time, we have an abiding interest and concern that any resolution be peaceful. I shall never waver from this fundamental position.

I am proud, as an American, at the great progress that has been made by the people on Taiwan, over the past three decades, and of the American contribution to that process. I have full faith in the continuation of that process. My administration, acting through appropriate channels, will continue strongly to foster that development and to contribute to a strong and healthy investment climate, thereby enhancing the well-being of the people of Taiwan.

Source: American Foreign Policy Documents, 1982. Department of State Publication, U.S. Government Printing Office, Washington, DC, 1985. Document 496, p. 1040.

TRA39

Document 497

Statement by the Spokesman of the Chinese Ministry of Foreign Affairs, Beijing, August 17, 1982

CHINESE STATEMENT ON THE
JOINT COMMUNIQUE

1. Following discussions, the Government of the People's Republic of China and the Government of the United States of America have reached agreement on the question of United States sale of arms to Taiwan. The two sides have released the joint communique simultaneously today.

The United States sale of arms to Taiwan is an issue which affects China's sovereignty. Back in 1978, when the two countries held negotiations on the establishment of diplomatic relations, the Chinese Government stated in explicit terms its opposition to the U.S. arms sales to Taiwan. As this issue could not be settled at that time, the Chinese side suggested that the two sides continue discussions on the issue following the establishment of diplomatic relations. It is evident that failure to settle this issue is bound to impair seriously the reations between the two countries.

With a view to safeguarding China's sovereignty and removing the obstacle to the development of relations between the two countries, Premier Zhao Ziyang held discussions with President Ronald Reagan on this issue during the Cancun meeting in Mexico in October 1981. Subsequently, Vice Premier and Foreign Minister Huang Hua continued the discussions with Secretary of State Alexander M. Haig, Jr., in Washington. As from December 1981, the two sides started concrete discussions through diplomatic channels in Beijing. During this period, U.S. Vice President George Bush, entrusted by President Reagan, paid a visit to China in May 1982, when he held discussion with the Chinese leaders on the same subject. The joint communique released by the two sides today is the outcome of repeated negotiations between China and the United States over the past 10 months. It has laid down the principles and steps by which the question of U.S. arms sales to Taiwan should be settled.

2. The joint communique reaffirms the principles of respect for each other's sovereignty and territorial integrity and noninterference in each other's internal affairs as embodied in the Shanghai Communique and the joint connunique on the establishment of diplomatic relations between China and the United States. Both sides also emphatically state that these principles continue to govern all aspects of their relations. That is to say, the question of U.S. arms sales to Taiwan must be settled on these principles. Needless to say, only by strictly observing these principles in dealing with the existing or new issues between the two countries will it be possible for their relations to develop healthily.

3. In compliance with the above principles governing the relations between the two countries, the U.S. arms sales to Taiwan should have been terminated altogether long ago. But considering that this is an issue left over by history, the Chinese Government, while upholding the principles, has agreed to settle it step by step. The U.S. side has committed that, as the first step, U.S. arms sales to Taiwan will not exceed, either in qualitative or in quantitative terms the level of those supplied in recent years since the establishment of diplomatic relations between the two countries, and that they will be gradually reduced, leading to a final resolution of this issue over a period of time. The final resolution referred to here certainly implies that the U.S. arms sales to Taiwan must be completely terminated over a period of time. And only a thorough settlement of this issue can remove the obstacles in the way of developing relations between the two countries.

4. In the joint communique, the Chinese Government reiterates in clear-cut terms its position that "the question of Taiwan is China's internal affair." The U.S. side also indicates that it has no intention of infringing on Chinese sovereignty and territorial integrity, or interfering in China's internal affairs, or pursuing a policy of "two China" or "one China, one Taiwan." The Chinese side refers in the joint communique to its fundamental policy of striving for peaceful reunification of the motherland for the purpose of further demonstrating the sincere desire of the Chinese Government and people to strive for a peaceful solution to the Taiwan question. On this issue, which is purely China's internal affair, no misinterpretation or foreign interference is permissible.

5. It must be point out that the present joint communique is based on the principle embodied in the joint communique on the establishment of diplomatic relations between China and the United States and the basic norms guiding international relations and has nothing to do with the "Taiwan Relations Act" formulated unilaterally by the United States.

The "Taiwan Relations Act" seriously contravenes the principles embodied in the joint communique on the establishment of diplomatic relations between the two countries, and the Chinese Government has consistently been opposed to it. All interpretations designed to link the present joint communique to the "Taiwan Relations Act" are in violation of the spirit and substance of this communique and are thus unacceptable.

6. The agreement reached between the Governments of China and the United States on the question of U.S. arms sales to Taiwan only marks a beginning of the settlement of this issue. What is important is that the relevant provisions of the joint communique are implemented in earnest, so that the question of U.S. arms sales to Taiwan can be resolved thoroughly at an early date. This is indispensable to the maintenance and development of Sino-U.S. relations.

Source: *American Foreign Policy Current Documents*, 1982. Department of State Publication, U.S. Government Printing Office, Washington, DC, 1985. Document 496, pp. 1040-1042.

TRA40

U.S.-CHINA JOINT COMMUNIQUE

Following is a statement by John H. Holdridge; Assistant Secretary for East Asian and Pacific Affairs, before the House Foreign Affairs Committee on August 18, 1982. Also included are the texts of the U.S.-China joint communique and President Reagan's statement of August 17.

Yesterday the United States and the People's Republic of China simultaneously issued a joint communique. During the past months, the Administration has benefited from consultations with members of this committee on this sensitive subject. I am glad to be able to continue our discussion of these issues in a public forum. I would also like to express our appreciation for the way the committee has cooperated with us in maintaining the confidentiality of our discussions with the Chinese; this has been vital, and we appreciate it.

As we went into these negotiations we had two things in mind--our historic obligations to the people of Taiwan and our important and growing relations with the People's Republic of China. Throughout the entire period of our discussions with Beijing, we were guided by these dual considerations. It is a fundamental national interest of the United States to preserve and advance its stretegic relations with China. At the same time, we have obligations to old friends; and we are not going to turn our back on them.

I am glad that we have been able to arrive at a communique with the Chinese that demonstrated their recognition of our determination on this score. Despite the difficulties it obviously causes them, they were willing to join with us in *modus vivendi* which will enable us to continue our relationship because of the important interests involved for them. Such an outcome is of vital importance to our national interest. Three Administrations before us have worked very hard to establish and expand this relationship, and we would have been derelict if we had not made every effort to find a way around the problem that threatened it.

A Valued Relationship

I think it would be useful to take a few minutes to examine the reasons why we value this relationship so highly. One of the major reasons is strategic. Prior to 1971 we had a hostile relationship with China. It was costly. We fought the Chinese in Korea. We almost came to a major war over Quemoy and Matsu. The Chinese worked hand in hand with the Soviets against us in Vietnam. We had to maintain a naval presence between Taiwan and the mainland. China identified itself with support for guerrilla movements on the soil of many of our allies and friends. Furthermore, a large part of our defense resources were allocated on the premise of a hostile China. Last, and perhaps most important, these 1 billion people were not identified with our interests as we faced the Soviet Union.

Starting in 1971 we have changed this situation. Thanks to a productive relationship between the United States and China, Taiwan has never been more secure and prosperous. We no longer have to plan for China as an enemy. We can now think about China as a country with which we might cooperate in certain significant areas. China's relations with our allies in Asia have improved. These 1 billion people are cautiously moving into the mainstream of the world's cultural and economic life. Their isolation is dissolving. Trade has increased. Eight thousand Chinese students are now studying in the United States. Investment opportunities are opening and our parallel interests in containing, the Soviet Union have been repeatedly reaffirmed.

All of these things represent solid, vital benefits to our security and well-being. We were not going to let these achievements disappear into rancor and hostility if we could possibly avoid it. We went after both of the objectives I mentioned at the outset, and I believe we have succeeded.

Reaffirming Fundamental Principles

Let me now turn to yesterday's communique. The communique reaffirms the fundamental principles which have guided U.S.-China relations since the inception of the normalization process over 10 years ago. This reaffirmation is significant; it illustrates the strength and the durability of these principles.

On this foundation, the United States established relations with China which have been economically beneficial to us and which have greatly enhanced our vital strategic interests. At the same time, we have maintained and strengthened our commercial and cultural relations with the people of Taiwan. We have achieved these important goals without impairing the security of the people of Taiwan, and, indeed, because of these improved relations between China and the United States, Taiwan has never been more secure.

The communique also addresses an issue which was not resolved at the time of normalization of relations--the question of U.S. arms sales to Taiwan. During discussions leading to normalization, China demanded that arms sales be terminated. We refused. I can say here that our negotiations almost foundered over this issue. China ultimately agreed to proceed with normalization despite this disagreement but reserved the right to raise this issue again. When it did so, we agreed to engage in discussion to determine whether an understanding could be reached. The alternative to our agreeing to hold such discussions would clearly have been the beginning of a process of deterioration in our relations--deterioration that could have led us back toward hostility since the issue itself was volatile and basic. We would have been irresponsible had we allowed such a process to start.

We undertook these discussions, therefore, with the hope that a formula could be found which would permit the continued growth of our relations with China, but also with the firm resolve that there were principles regarding the security of Taiwan which could not be compromised. Those principles, embodied in the Taiwan Relations Act, commit the United States to sell to Taiwan arms necessary to maintain a sufficient self-defense capability.

Aware of our consistent and firm opposition to the use of force against Taiwan, the Chinese during these discussions agreed to state in very strong terms their policy of pursuing a peaceful resolution of the Taiwan issue and described this policy as "fundamental." The Chinese insisted, however, that we agree to the ultimate termination of arms sales. We refused because the level of our arms sales must be determined by the needs of Taiwan, and we could not agree to a termination date, as the Chinese demanded, which might impair our ability to meet those needs.

At the same time, we recognized that China's peaceful policy bore directly on the defense needs of Taiwan. So long as that policy continued, the threat to Taiwan would be greatly diminshed. As I have just noted, assurances of such a continuity were provided when the Chinese began to describe their peaceful policy on the resolution of the Taiwan question as, as I have just said, "fundamental," which contains the connotation of unchanging and long term. We were thus able to consider a policy under which we would limit our arms sales t the levels reached in recent years and would anticipate a gradual reduction of the level of arms sales. We were not willing, however, to adopt such a course unconditionally.

While the Chinese were willing to state their peaceful policy in strong terms, they at first resisted any relationship between that policy and our arms sales to Taiwan. The Chinese resisted their relationship because of their view that the sale of arms to Taiwan constitutes an interference in China's internal affairs. We rejected any language to this effect in the communique.

We also stressed that as a matter of fact and law, any adjustments in our arms sales to Taiwan had to be premised on a continuation of China's peaceful policy. We therefore maintained, and the Chinese ultimately agreed, that the statement of our policy in paragraph 6 be prefaced by a phrase that related it to the continuation of China's peaceful approach. This is the genesis and purpose of the phrase "Having in mind the foregoing statements of both sides" which precedes our statements in that paragraph. Thus, our policy is predicated on China's commitment in paragraph 4 to a peaceful approach and our acknowledgment of that approach in paragraph 5.

Let me summarize the essence of our understanding on this point: China has announced a fundamental policy of pursuing peaceful means to resolve the longstanding dispute between Taiwan and the mainland. Having in mind this policy and the consequent reduction in the military threat to Taiwan, we have stated our intention to reduce arms sales to Taiwan gradually and said that in quantity and quality we would not go beyond levels established since normalization. This follows from a literal reading of the communique. While we have no reason to believe that China's policy will change, an inescapable corollary to these mutually interdependent policies is that should that happen, we will reasses ours. Our guiding principle is now and will continue to be that embodied in the Taiwan Relations Act: the maintenance of a self-defense capability sufficient to meet the military needs of Taiwan, but with the understanding that China's maintenance of a peaceful approach to the Taiwan question will permit gradual reductions in arms sales.

Questions have been raised concerning whether the wording of the communique adequately conveys the meaning which we ascribe to it. I believe that it does or I would have recommended against its approval. The present wording evolved from 10 months of intense negotiations in which fundamental principles were at stake on both sides. The language necessarily reflects the difficult compromises which were reached.

We should keep in mind that what we have here is not a treaty or agreement but a statement of future U.S. policy. We intend to implement this policy in accordance with our understanding of it. I hope I have made that point abundantly clear in my remarks today. I can further assure you that, having participated closely in the negotiations, I am confident that the Chinese are fully congnizant of that understanding.

Returning now to the document itself, let me recapitulate and emphasize a few key features.

First, the document must be read as a whole, since the policies it sets forth are interrelated.

Second, as I have previously noted, the communique contains a strong Chinese statement that its fundamental policy is to seek to resolve the Taiwan question by peaceful means (paragraph 4). In this context, I would point out again that the reference to their "fundamental" policy carries the connotation in Chinese of "unchanging and long term."

Third, the U.S. statements concerning future arms sales to Taiwan paragraph 6) are based on China's statements as to its fundamental peaceful policy for seeking a resolution to the Taiwan question and on the "new situation" created by those statements (paragraph 5). This situation is new because, for the first time, China has described its peaceful policy toward Taiwan in the terms I have outlined. Thus, our future actions concerning arms sales to Taiwan are premised on a continuation of China's peaceful policy toward a resolution of its differences with Taiwan. This is indicated by the words at the beginning of paragraph 6 that "Having in mind the foregoing statements of both sides, the United States Government states..." We have no reason to think that the Chinese will change this fundamental policy, but if they should, we would, of course, reexamine our position.

Fourth, we did not agree to set a date certain for ending arms sales to Taiwan and the statements of future U.S. arms sales policy embodied in the communique do not provide either a timeframe for reductions of U.S. arms sales or for their termination. The U.S. statements are fully consistent with the Taiwan Relations Act, and we will continue to make appropriate arms sales to Taiwan based on our assessments of their defense needs, as specified by the act.

Substance of Discussions

So much for what is in the actual communique. Over the past several months, there has been considerable speculation about the substance of our discussions with the Chinese. As you know, we have not felt free to comment on such speculation while our talks were underway. Therefore, it might be useful at this point to clarify our stand on a number of issues which have surfaced in such speculations.

As to our position on the resolution of the Taiwan problem, we have consistently held that it is a matter to be worked out by the Chinese themselves. Our sole and abiding concern is that any resolution be peaceful. It follows that we see no mediation role for the United States nor will we attempt to exert pressure on Taiwan to enter into negotiations with the People's Republic of China (PRC).

I would also call your attention to the fact that there has been no change in our longstanding position on the issue of sovereignty over Taiwan. The communique (paragraph 1) in its opening paragraph simply cites that portion of the joint communique on the establishment of diplomatic relations between the United States and the PRC in which the United States "acknowledged the Chinese position" on this issue (i.e., that there is but one China and Taiwan is a part of China).

It has been reported in the press that the Chinese at one point suggested that the Taiwan Relations Act be revised. We have no plans to seek any such revision.

Finally, in paragraph 9 the two sides agree to "maintain contact and hold appropriate consultations on vilateral and international issues of common interest." This should be read within the context of paragraphs 8 and 9, which deal with the two sides' desire to advance their bilateral and strategic relations. It should not be read to imply that we have agreed to engage in prior consultations with Beijing on arms sales to Taiwan.

We hope and expect that this communique, and the step forward which it represents in the resolution of U.S.-Chinese differences on this issue, will enhance the confidence of the people of Taiwan, whose well-being and prosperity continue to be of the utmost importance to us. From the President on down, we have acted in a way which seeks to enhance the future security and prosperity of the people of Taiwan, and I call your attention to the emphasis on this matter in the President's statement which was released simultaneously with the release of the communique yesterday.

Removal of the arms question as a serious issue in U.S.-China relations will help to insure that both countries can continue to cooperate on mutually shared international objectives, e.g., deterring Soviet aggression in East Asia and removal of Vietnamese troops from Kampuchea. It will ease fears by American friends and allies that the general peace and stability in the Asia/Pacific region could be undermined. By defusing the difficult issue of arms sales, we will open the way for an expansion of U.S.-China relations in a broad range of economic, cultural, scientific, and technological areas as well as in people-to-people contact.

In conclusion, I would like to quote a paragraph from the statement issued by President Reagan yesterday:

> Building a strong and lasting relationship with China has been an important foreign policy goal of four consecutive American Administrations. Such a relationship is vital to our long-term national security interests and contributes to stability in East Asia. It is in the national interest of the United States that this important strategic relationship be advanced. This communique will make that possible, consistent with our obligations to the people of Taiwan.

U.S.-CHINA JOINT COMMUNIQUE, AUGUST 17, 1982

1. In the Joint Communique o the Establishment of Diplomatic Relations on January 1, 1979, issued by the Government of the United States of America and the Government of the

People's Republic of China, the United States of America recognized the Government of the People's Republic of China as the sole legal government of China, and it acknowledged the Chinese position that there is but one China and Taiwan is part of China. Within that context, the two sides agreed that the people of the United States would continue to maintain cultural, commercial, and other unofficial relations with the people of Taiwan. On this basis, relations between the United States and China were normalized.

2. The question of United States arms sales to Taiwan was not settled in the course of negotiations between the two countries on establishing diplomatic relations. The two sides held differing positions, and the Chinese side stated that it would raise the issue again following normalization. Recognizing that this issue would seriously hamper the development of United States-China relations, they have held further discussions on it, during and since the meetings between President Ronald Reagan and Premier Zhao Ziyang and between Secretary of State Alexander M. Haig, Jr., and Vice Premier and Foreign Minister Huang Hua in October, 1981.

3. Respect for each other's sovereignty and territorial integrity and non-interference in each other's internal affairs consistute the fundamental principles guiding United States-China relations. These principles were confirmed in the Shanghai Communique of February 28, 1972 and reaffirmed in the Joint Communique on the Establishment of Diplomatic Relations which came into effect on January 1, 1979. Both sides emphatically state that these principles continue to govern all aspects of their relations.

4. The Chinese Government reiterates that the question of Taiwan is China's internal affair. The Message to Compatriots in Taiwan issued by China on January 1, 1979 promulgated a fundamental policy of striving for peaceful reunification of the Motherland. The NIne-Point Proposal put forward by China on September 30, 1981 represented a further major effort under this fundamental policy to strive for a peaceful solution to the Taiwan question.

5. The United States Government ataches great importance to its relations with China, and reiterates that it has no intention of infringing on Chinese sovereignty and territorial integrity, or interfering in China's internal affairs, or pursuing a policy of "two Chinas" or "one China, one Taiwan." The United States Government understands and appreciates the Chinese policy of striving for a peaceful resolution of the Taiwan question as indicated in China's Message to Compatriots in Taiwan issued on January 1, 1979 and the Nine-Point proposal put forward by China on SEptember 30, 1981. The new situation which has emerged with regard to the Taiwan question also provides favorable conditions for the settlement of United States-China differences over the question of United States arms sale to Taiwan.

6. Having in mind the foregoing statements of both sides, the United States Government states that it does not seek to carry out a long-term policy of arms sales to Taiwan, that its arms sales to Taiwan will not exceed, either in qualitative or in quantitative terms, the level of those supplied in recent years since the establishment of diplomatic relations between the United States and China, and that it intends to reduce gradually its sales of arms to Taiwan, leading over a period of time to a final resolution. In so stating, the United States acknowledges China's consistent position regarding the thorough settlement of this issue.

7. In order to bring about, over a period of time, a final settlement of the question of United States arms sales to Taiwan, which is an issue rooted in history, the two governments will make every effort to adopt measures and create conditions conducive to the thorough settlement of this issue.

8. The development of United States-China relations is not only in the interests of the two peoples but also conducive to peace and stability in the world. The two sides are

determined, on the principle of equality and mutual benefit, to strengthen their ties in the economic, cultural, education, scientific, technological, and other fields and make strong, joint efforts for the continued development of relations between the governments and peoples of the United States and China.

9. In order to bring about the healthy development of United States-China relations, maintain world peace, and oppose aggression and expansion, the two governments reaffirm the principles agreed on by the two sides in the Shanghai Communique and the Joint Communique on the Establishment of Diplomatic Relations. The two sides will maintain contact and hold appropriate consultations on bilateral and international issues of common interest.

Source: *Weekly Compilaton of Presidential Documents*, August 23, 1982, p. 20.

TRA41   Document 498

STATEMENTS BY MEMBERS OF THE SENATE FOREIGN RELATIONS COMMITTEE AND BY THE ASSISTANT SECRETARY OF STATE FOR EAST ASIAN AND PACIFIC AFFAIRS (HOLDRIDGE), AUGUST 17, 1982

"OUR POLICY IS PREDICATED ON CHINA'S COMMITMENT....AND TO A PEACEFULE APPROACH"

The committee met, pursuant to notice, at 2:20 p.m., in room 422, Dirksen Senate Office Building, Hon. Charles H. Percy (chairman of the committee) presiding.

Present: Senators Percy, Helms, Hayakawa, Mathias, Pressler, Pell, Glenn, Tsongas, and Dodd.

THE CHAIRMAN. It is a pleasure to welcome back once again Ambassador Holdridge to the committee.

It is my understanding, Ambassador Holdrigde, that you have come to explain to us and elaborate on the President's announcement this morning concerning our relations with China and Taiwan. We particularly welcome your appearance this afternoon on this subject.

As you know, over the period of almost a year the committee has been in contact with you and other officers of the Department on the administration's policy toward China and Taiwan. These sessions have been most helpful to the members of the committee in understanding the problems you confront in pursuing U.S. interests in our dealings with China and Taiwan.

I commend you, former Secretary Haig, Secretary Shultz, and the President on your forthright and candid approach toward the committee. The approach has greatly assisted the committee in fulfilling its constitutional role in the field of foreign affairs.

Our discussions on U.S. policy toward China and Taiwan over the past year have been a model of the consultative process of which both branches of our Government can be justifiably proud. I thank you for your role in that process.

Our sessions during this process, however, in deference to the administration's wishes, have been in executive session and classified to protect the confidentiality in diplomatic discussions. I believe we have made clear that many of us have had reservations about the administration's reluctance to expose its China-Taiwan policy to public discussion and debate.

As I said to you during our meeting in June, it is only as a result of public discussion that general bipartisan support of our policy emerges. Only through public debate can you be assured the administration has defined a national interest which must underlie any enduring policy in a way that is satisfactory to the country as a whole.

Today we begin this practice, and the policies you have devised must stand the test of that debate and time. The committee intends to hold hearings subsequent to this one on our relations with China and Taiwan in an effort to encourage the development of a consensus, and we seek your assistance in doing so. We anticipate further hearings in the near future.

In considering the President's announcement this afternoon we want to give particular attention to two areas. First, we have undertaken certain solemn obligations to the people on Taiwan as embodied in the Taiwan Relations Act overwhelmingly passed by the Congress in 1979. These obligations must be upheld. A policy statement cannot change a public law.

Second, we as a nation value our relationship with the People's Republic of China. We have a number of strategic interests in common. Our relationship has expanded over the last decade. Although our trade with Taiwan is double that with the PRC, trade with the PRC has increased many times over, and this growth promises to continue.

In my view, our relationship with China is to our benefit and should continue to expand and improve. I realize that this is a difficult problem. These two objectives can sometimes be in conflict. Under these circumstances a certain amount of ambiguity may be helpful as long as it does not undermine our basic, fundamental objectives or prejudice what we might want to do in the future. There may be ambiguity in the communique, but there can be no ambiguity in implementing the Taiwan Relations Act. We must assure that Taiwan's legitimate defense needs are met as the Taiwan Relations Act requires of us.

We look forward, Ambassador Holdridge, to your views on how we can achieve these ends and to your explanation of some of the wording in the communique, which on the face of it appears troublesome.

Senator Pell.

SENATOR PELL. Mr. Chairman, I want to second your excellent opening statement. The points you raise are important. I would add that at first blush the joint China-United States communique seems fair. However, on further examination I find myself very concerned with the interests of the native Taiwanese, some 16 million people out of a total Taiwan population of 18 million, or pretty close to 90 percent of the people. Too often our discussions of China-Taiwan policy assume that the hopes, dreams, and aspirations of the native Taiwanese are shared by the mainland Chinese authorities in power on both sides of the Taiwan strait. In fact, nothing could be further from the truth.

The evidence of this is the martial law that has remained, in effect, in Taiwan for over 30 years. The results of these are apparent when you talk to native Taiwanese without any chaperones or advisers around. And I think we should bear in mind the old idea of self-determination. We fought World War I with that as one of our goals. We have forgotten it in many places since.

I believe that given a free choice, the Taiwanese would opt for a separate identity--a free and independent Taiwan. Unfortunately, I conclude after having read the communique and examining it more carefully and noting the inherent contradiction between "peaceful reunification," mainland China's position, and "peaceful resolution," our hope, that it could make it more difficult, if not eliminate the possibility altogether, for the people on Taiwan to choose a free, independent democratic government. And when I say independent I mean independent of mainland China.

I hope I am wrong but if not, I believe we cannot stand by and condone PRC pressures on Taiwan to bend to its desires. This must be a choice freely made not by the Government on Taiwan governing by martial law, but by the people of Taiwan.

Thank you.

THE CHAIRMAN. Senator Glenn.

SENATOR GLENN. I would like to make a short opening statement.

Along with the chairman and other members of the committee I helped draft the legislation which became known as the TRA, so we, better than most perhaps, know what we intended to accomplish in that act. And I can tell you that in my considered judgment the communique announced today does undermine the spirit and intent of the TRA.

Three years ago the executive branch appeared before this committee arguing that the United Stataes intended to sell arms to Taiwan indefinitely, but that this need not be mentioned in the legistation we were considering at that time, the Taiwan Relations Act. Administration spokesment went further and indicated that the President might, in fact, veto a bill that contained specific arms sales assurances for Taiwan. I am glad to say that Congress failed to blink in that confrontation.

In President Reagan's words 2 years ago, the Congress was clearly unwilling to buy the Carter plan which it believed would have jeopardized Taiwan's security. The TRA that passed the Congress with almost unanimous support contained our pledge that:

"The United States will make available to Taiwan such defense articles and defense services in such quantity as may be necessary to enable Taiwan to maintain a sufficient self-defense capability, and the President and Congress shall determine the nature and quantity of such defense articles and services based solely upon their judgment of the needs of Taiwan."

The legislative history demonstrates beyond a doubt that the intent of this passagae was to insure that arms sales decisions, albeit prudent and cautious, would be made in Washington, not in Peking or Taipei.

Now, because we anticipated the PRC would pressure us to end or limit Taiwan arms sales, we provided in the act a framework for the executive branch to resist such pressures. Without these written assurances and confidence that the President would faithfully carry out the TRA, I seriously doubt that the Congress would have been prepared to go along with normalization and the PRC demand that we terminate the Mutual Defense Treaty with Taiwan.

The communique announced today discards that very carefully crafted framework, the heart of the TRA, in favor of an arms sales formulation negotiated under Chinese threats of a retrogression of United States-PRC relations.

As you might expect, under such circumstances the new restrictions on arms sales leave much to be desired. President Reagan indicates that based upon the Chinese statements, particularly the statement that "Peaceful reunification" is a "fundamental policy of the PRC," he was able to impose further restrictions on arms sales to Taiwan.

These new restrictions include: No. 1, agreeing that the United Stataes "does not seek to carry out a long-term policy of arms sales to Taiwan." No. 2, "Arms sales to Taiwan will not exceed, either in qualitiative or quanitative terms, the level of those supplied in recent years." No. 3, that the United States "intends to reduce gradually its sales of arms to Taiwan." And No. 4, this will lead "over a period of time to a final resolution."

I should also note in passing that President Reagan's concessions came just 2 years after candidate Reagan pledged that he "would not impose restrictions which are not required by the Taiwan Relations Act and which contravene its spirit and purpose."

Not only do these restrictions contravene the spirit and purpose of the TRA, they are exactly the sort of PRC-imposed conditions we sought to avoid when we drafted the act. Moreover, the restrictions set forth in the communique unfortunately do not resolve the fundamental differences between the United States and the PRC on Taiwan arms sales questions. They merely postpone the day of reckoning. I think that is a very importan point. The Chinese continue to oppose arms sales, asserting it infringes on their sovereignty and is an interference in the internal affairs.

Under these conditions, agreeing on limits to gradually reduce and ultimately end arms sales puts us in an impossible position. Soon the Chinese will return with more demands and insist we finally resolve the issue, and we can expect that. We will be in the unfortunate position of having limited our argument to when, not if, a cutoff should occur. Based upon past precedent, I anticipate we will not have to wait long before the PRC makes these new demands known.

Let me close by issuing a communique of my own. I can assure you there will be a retrogression in this committee's relations with the Bureau if the action the executive branch has taken results in any major or significant change in the relative military balance that exists today between Taiwan and the PRC.

We want that balance to be maintained, and if implementation of the communique causes a deterioration in Taiwan's capability and an improvement in the PRC's relative military advantage, as a starter I would like your commitment you will not orchestrate a reduction of Taiwan's military capabilities and will notify us on each occasion you are required to disapprove U.S. industry contacts with Taiwan or deny an arms sales request made by the authorities on Taiwan.

As I indicated a few weeks ago, obviously we must be prudent and cautious in our arms transfer decisions. Gratuitous sales protect no one. But when we appear to bend to Chinese pressures on each and every sale we make to Taiwan, it is inevitable that Taipei begins seriously to doubt whether we will live up to our solemn responsibilities.

A State Department spokesman has urged me not to worry and indicated that "our relations with China are predicated on our expectation that the Taiwan issue will be resolved peacefully by the Chinese people themselves." In fact, they are so confident the issue can be resolved peacefully, they state that it is in this context that we have been and will continue to judge Taiwan's defense needs.

Unfortunately, I am not quite so sanguine. If Taiwan decides it wants to reunify with the mainland, everything will work out fine. But if the present or future leaderships decide reunification is not in the island's interest? What then?

Warren Christopher told the Foreign Relations Committee during the TRA debate that:

> "It is our position that if there is to be a reunification, it is of great importance that it be peaceful and not be destabilizing in the area. But we do not have a position of encouraging the people on Taiwan to do something against their will'.

That was an excellent policy then; it is one I fully endorse today. However, if maintaining Taiwan's free choice means supplying needed and selected defensive arms to the island to maintain the balance we have tried to maintain, even over Peking's objections and in the face of threats to downgrade United States-PRC relations, then so be it.

Mr. Chairman, I would harken back to President Reagan's statements when he was a candidate. On August 25, 1980, he stated: "We should not impose restrictions which are not required by the Taiwan Relations Act and which contravene its spirit and purpose." He went on to comment by a use of examples of the Carter administration where they refused to open consulates on behalf of Taiwan; yet just last month we postponed a Boston consulate opening. He said the Carter administration had a 1-year moratorium on arms sales. Yet, we have not sold arms in this administration either.

He talked about the difficulty the Carter administration had caused by refusing to train Taiwan military officers here. We are not now doing that. He went on the state:

> "I recognize the PRC is not pleased with the Taiwan Relations Act which the U.S.Congress insisted on as the offical basis for our relationship with Taiwan. This was made abundantly clear to Mr. Bush and I am told clear to the Carter administration. But it is the law of our land."

Than at a later point he said:

> "As President, I will not accept the interference of any foreign power in the process of protecting American interests and carrying out the laws of our land. To do otherwise would be a dereliction of my duty as President."

Thank you.

THE CHAIRMAN. Thank you very much.

Secretary Holdridge, the Chair will break the precedent of having opening statements by just the Chair and ranking minoritry member in this case.

We have met with you for over a year. Members have observed silence as a result of coming out of those meetings. And I think in the exchange that we have had, and the confidential nature of that exchange, it is well now to permit all members who want to make statements to make their views known publicly on this important issue.

Senator Pressler, I will call on you next to rotate sides.

SENATOR PRESSLER. Mr. Chairman, I will be brief.

Let me say that this announcement by the administration at this time is very ill conceived, because it does not achieve any foreign policy objectives. The point is that we have had trade with both Chinas. We have had relations with both.

I recently visited both. We were going along quite well. If a change of this magnitude occurs, which as my colleague has pointed out violates our law, it should be for some clear foreignb policy objectives. And I would like to hear in public what the immediacy of this was, what caused us to do this now, what foreign policy objectives are we achieving.

Let me also say that I have felt for some time that we did not have need for change, that things were going well; and granted the People'sRepublic of China was making some alleged threats, but China needs the trade, and China wants the relationship with us. Both countries do. I do not think we should have yielded to those threats, if we did so at this time. I fear that down the road there are those in the State Department who would like to see us engage in the sale of arms to the PRC or be involved in an aid program there or some sort of relationship such as that. I am opposed to that. I am for trade and a two Chinas policy, but we already have that.

Let me also say that although I respect our chairman's analysis that this was a model of consultation, I would have to politely disagree. Most of the consultations we have had have been under the ground rules that they were confidential, and the options presented to us in the time of this decision were very ambiguous. I would not agree that this is a model for consultation with Congress in advance of a decision because we were under very great restrictions not to repeat or analyze in public some of the things said.

Also, it came as a complete surprise to me that this was going to occur at dawn today. In fact, I found out about it from a phone call at 6:30 this morning; but that is, I guess, the way it was done. The point is, if I saw a clear foreign policy objective that we were achieving with this decision, I would probably go along with it because I believe in real politics. I have served in the Army in that area of the world. I think that we are abandoning one of our best friends, in essence, in terms of the way this will be perceived.

If the decision helped to achieve something in trade or achieve something in terms of our national interest objectives, I would probably be for it, but I cannot see why it is being done at this time and in this fashion.

Mr. Chairman, I yield back the balance of my time.

THE CHAIRMAN. Thank you very much.

Senator Hayakawa.

SENATOR HAYAKAWA. Thank you, Mr. Chairman.

The unveiling of the latest joint communique between the United States and the PRC leaves much to be desired. As a semantic purist I am somewhat disturbed by the lack of clarity in the languagae. I am afraid unless one looks very closely at the whole document and what is said and what is not said, it appears as though the United States is turning its back on the people of Taiwan. However, I believe there is enough ambiguity so that no one need take any offense.

The wonderful thing about language is its ability to mean whatever we may want it to mean. As a psychologest I recognize that what we have here is a situation not uncommon in human affairs: a totally ambiguous situation. In one sense Taiwan and China are one country because they both say so. Taiwan says China is one country, and the PRC says China is one country. But in another sense they are not one country.

There are many ambiguities in everyday life with which one lives. Often we condemn them as hypocrisies, but life always puts us into situations in which we have to live this these hypocrisies and endure them, hoping that some day a consistent or rational point of view can prevail, perhaps even with a solution which is not yet thought of.

If you look at the present situation between Taiwan and China where they are making toally inconsistent and incompatible assertions about each other, the PRC is saying that Taiwan is really one of our provinces, and we have complete authority over Taiwan, so that if you, the United States, sell them arms, you interfere in ou internal affairs. But we go ahead and sell Taiwan arms, and the PRC does not start a war over it. They do nothing more than make a big squawk and accept what is essentially an illogical situation.

I think that we will have to live with this ambiguity for some time to come. Insofar as any of us on any side of this problem insist we be perfectly logical about it, we will perpetrate some awful injustice on somebody. The only way to guarantee a minimum of justice for perhaps a few decades to come is to accept this ambiguity, to accept this, shall we say, hypocrisy on all sides.

It seems to me that this joint communique is just another one of the necessary ways of enduring this illogic, and even though it has been called another temporary palliative, it may have positive, permanent consequences insofar as it places the burden on the PRC to resolve their differences with Taiwan only through peaceful means; and that we have asked them to underline, and they have. Nonetheless, the United States must be diligent about assessing the intent of the PRC. We must look to what they do and not just what they say. And we, too, must live by this same standard and watch what we do and what we say.

The American people through President Reagan have given assurances to the people of Taiwan that we will not abandon them, and we must make sure that we keep our word and continue to abide by these assurances.

Thank you, Mr. Chairman.

THE CHAIRMAN. Thank you, Senator Hayakawa.

Senator Tsongas.

SENATOR TSONGAS. Mr. Chairman, I am curious about the Secretary's position. I have just an observation.

Last night before the Red Sox game there was a fellow on television who bore an uncanny physical resemblance to President Reagan, and he called for tax increases that outrages supply side economists and have been enthusiastically endorsed by the ADA. And today we consider a communique involving Taiwan and the PRC and the United States, which, if promulgated by a liberal Democrat, would have had this place surrounded by hostile elements all day long.

I guess you have to conclude in Washington if you wait long enough, anything is possible. And I would be curious as to the Secretary's position.

I would also like to read the analysis of the statement by those who were here today, because I do not understand them either; and I would be curious as to how those in our midst who are not from the United States interpret what has been said today to their own people. I would be rather curious.

Thank you.

THE CHAIRMAN. Thank you, Senator Tsongas.

Senator Mathias.

SENATOR MATHIAS. Mr. Chairman, I wait with breathless anticipation for the testimony of the witnesses today. I will just say that I think Senator Hayakawa has given us an interesting historical perspective on this problem and has, I think, said it in the kind of context in which we must view it.

A two-China policy was, I suppose, a comforting concept to some Americans, but it aroused only contempt in both the People's Republic of China and in Taiwan. And if a two-China policy is not a reality in China, then it is only an illusion, and the sooner we clear our vision of it, the better off we will be.

Thank you, Mr. Chairman.

THE CHAIRMAN. Thank you, Senator Mathias.

That is as good a buildup as any witness has ever had. It is a challenge to you, I am sure. We will be anxious to hear from you.

**STATEMENT OF HON. JOHN H. HOLDRIDGE,
ASSISTANT SECRETARY, BUREAU OF EAST ASIAN
AND PACIFIC AFFAIRS, DEPARTMENT OF STATE,
ACCOMPANIED BY WILLIAM F. ROPE, DIRECTOR OF
THE OFFICE OF CHINESE AFFAIRS; AND
DONALD C. FERGUSON, TAIWAN COORDINATION
ADVISER, BUREAU OF EAST ASIAN AND PACIFIC AFFAIRS.**

Thank you very much, Mr. Chairman. I appreciate the chance to meet the challenge.

I would like to introduce, on my right, Mr. William Rope, the Office Director for China, and on my left, Mr. Don Ferguson, the Office Director for Taiwan. I am straddling in the middle. I guess I am in the middle of the Taiwan Strait here. (Laughter)

Let me say, Mr. Chairman, I much appreciated your words yesterday about consultations and again today, and I want you to know that we will do everything in our power to meet the continued obligation to consult with you on matters such as this which we regard as being of transcendental importance, and we will try to keep the standard up as high as you said it was. Let me continue.

Mr. Chairman, this morning the United States and the People's Republic of China simultaneously issued a joint communique. Now, during yesterday's hearing and on prior occasions, members of the committee have expressed the view that public hearings on the course of our policies toward China should be held at the earliest possible date. I agreed with that view and I am glad to be able to continue our discussion of these issues in a public forum.

I would also like to express our appreciation for the way the committee has cooperated with us in maintaining the confidentiality of our discussions with the Chinese. This has been vital, and without this confidentiality, I don't know whether we would have reached the stat we reached today in terms of issuring a joint communique. We are very appreciative of the confidentiality which was maintained.

Mr. Chairman, I think you have stated the problem we face very accurately. As we went into these negotiations, we had two things in mind, our historic obligations to the people of Taiwan and our important and growing relations with the People's Republic of China. Throughout the entire period of our discussions with Beijing, we were guided by these dual considerations. It is a fundamental national interest of the United States to preserve and advance its strategic relations with China. At the same time we have, as you said, obligations to old friends and we will not turn our backs on them.

I am glad we have been able to arrive at a communique with the Chinese that demonstrated their recognition of our determination on this score despite the difficulties it obviously causes them and that they, too, because of the important interests involved for them, were willing to join with us in a modus vivendi which will enable us to continue our relationship.

Again, as you and I have pointed out, such an outcome is of vital importance to our national interest. Three administrations before us have worked very hard to establish and expand this relationship, and we would have been derelict if we had not made very effort to find a way around the problem threatening it.

Mr. Chairman, I think it would be useful to take a few minutes to examine the reasons we valued this relationship so highly. One of the major reasons is strategic. Prior to 1971, we had a hostile relationship with China. It was costly. We fought the Chinese in Korea. We almost came to a major war over Quemoy and Matsu. The Chinese worked hand-in-hand with the Soviets against us in Vietnam. We have to maintain a naval presence between Taiwan and the mainland.

China identified itself with support for guerrilla movements on the soil of many of our allies and friends. Furthermore, a large part of our defense resources were allocated on the premise of a hostile China. Lastly and perhaps most importantly, these 1 billion people were not identified with our interest as we faced the Soviet Union.

Starting in 1971, we changed the situation. Thanks to a productive relationship between the United States and China, Taiwan has never been more secure and prosperous. We no longer have to plan for China as an enemy. We can now think if China as a country with which we might cooperate in certain significant areas. China's relations with our allies in Asia have improved.

These 1 billion people are cautiously moving into the mainstream of the world's cultural and economic life. Their isolation is dissolving. Trade has increased. Eight thousand Chinese students are now studying in the United States. Investment opportunities are opening and our parallel interests in containing the Soviet Union have been repeatedly reaffirmed.

As an illustration of one of the benefits to both parties of this relationship, I want to introduce into the record as a part of my statement an article by Christopher Wren in this morning's New York Times. It describes the contributions to mutual understandings of the United States-Chinese cooperation in the field of management training in Dalian, China.

All of these things represent solid benefits to our security and well-being, Mr. Chairman. We were not going to let these achievements disappear into rancor and hostility if we could avoid it. We went after both of the objectives you have outlined, and I believe we have succeeded.

Let me turn to this morning;s communique. It reaffirms the fundamental principles which have guided United States-Chinese relations since the inception of the normalization process over 10 years ago. This reaffirmation is significant. It illustrates the strength and durability of these principles. On this foundation the United States established relations with China which have been ecomonically beneficial to us and which have greatly enhanced our vital strategic interests.

At the same time, we have maintained and strengthened our commercial and cultural relations with the people of Taiwan. We have achieved these important goals without impairing the security of the people of Taiwan, and indeed, because of these improved relations between China and the United States, Taiwan has never been more secure.

The communique also addresses an issue which was not resolved at the time of normalization of relations, the question of U.S. arms sales to Taiwan. During the discussions leading to normalization, China demanded that arms sales be terminated. We refused. China agreed to proceed with normalization despite this disagreement but reserved the right to raise this issue again.

I can say here, Mr. Chairman and members of the committee, I believe it is well known that the normalization negotiations almost foundered on this whole question of continued U.S. arms sales to Taiwan, and it was only at the last minute by, I would say, a very statesmanlike decision on the part of the leadership of the People's Republic of China that the decision was made to go ahead, but it really was touch and go.

When China agreed to proceed with normalization despite desagreement on arms sales to Taiwan, it reserved the right to raise the issue again. When it did so last year, we agreed to engage in discussions to determine whether an understanding could be reached. The alternative to our agreeing to hold such discussions would clearly have been the beginning of a process of deterioration in our relations, deterioration that could have led us back toward hositility. Since the issue itself was volatile and basis, we would have been irresponsible had we allowed such a process to start.

To address Senator Pressler's question, our foreign policy objective was to preserve a valuable relationship which otherwise might well have and probably would have undergone a serious and possibly fatal deterioration. We undertook these discussions, therefore, with the hope that a formula could be found which would permit the continued growth of our relations with China, but also with the firm resolve that there were principles regarding the security of Taiwan which could not be compromised.

Those principles embodied in the Taiwan Relations Act commit the United States to sell to Taiwan arms necessary to maintain a sufficient self-defense capability. Aware of our consistent and firm opposition to the use of force against Taiwan, the Chinese during these discussions, and I mean the most recent ones, agreed to state in very strong terms their policy of pursuing a peaceful resolution of the Taiwan issue, and eventually came to describe this policy as "fundamental."

The Chinese insisted, however, that we agree to the ultimate termination of arms sales. We refused because the level of our arms sales must be determined by the needs of Taiwan, and we could not agree to a termination date as the Chinese demanded which might impair our ability to meet those needs. At the same time, we recognized that China's peaceful policy bore directly on the defense needs of Taiwan. So long as the policy continued, the threat to Taiwan would be diminished.

As I have noted, assurances of such continuity were provided when the Chinese began to describe their peaceful policy on the resolution of the Taiwan question as, as I havae said, "fundamental," which contains the connotation of unchanging and long term. Let me say this again: which contains the connotation of unchanging and long term. We were thus able to consider a policy under which we would limit our arms sales to the levels reached in recent years and would anticipate a gradual reduction of the level of arms sales.

We were not willing, however, to adopt such a course unconditionally. While the Chinese were willing to state their peaceful policy in strong terms, they at first resisted any relationship between that policy and our arms sales to Taiwan. The Chinese resisted this relationship because of their view that the sale of arms to Taiwan constitues an interference in China's internal affairs. We rejected any language to this effect in the communique.

We also stressed that as a matter of fact and law, any adjustments in our arms sales to Taiwan had to be premised on a continuation of China's peaceful policy. We therefore maintained, and the Chinese ultimately agreed, that the statement of our policy in paragraph 6 of the joint communique be prefaced by a phrase that related it to the continuation of China's peaceful approach.

This is the genesis and purpose of the phrase "having in mind the foregoing statements of both sides" which precedes our statements in that paragraph. Thus, our policy is predicated on China's commitment in paragrapgh 4 to a peaceful approach and our acknowledgment of that approach in paragraph 5.

Let me say this again. Our policy is predicated on China's commitment in paragraph 4 to a peaceful approach and our acknowledgment of that approach in paragraph 5. Let me summarize the essence of our understanding on this point. China has announced a fundamental policy of pursuing peaceful means to resolve the long-standing dispute between Taiwan and the mainland.

Having in mind this policy and the consequent reduction in the military threat to Taiwan, we have stated our intention to reduce arms sales to Taiwan gradually and said that in quantity and quality we would not go beyond levels established since normalization. This follows from a literal reading of the communique.

While we have no reason to believe that China's policy will change, an inescapable corollary to these mutually interdependent policies is that should that happen, we will reasses ours. Our guiding principle is now and will continue to be that embodied in the Taiwan Relations Act, the maintenance of a self-defense capability sifficient to meet the military needs of Taiwan, but with the understanding that China's maintenance of a peaceful approach to the Taiwan question will permit gradual reductions in arms sales.

During our meeting yesterday, questions were raised concerning whether the wording of the communique adequately conveys the meaning which we ascribe to it. I believe it does or I would not have recommended its approval. The present wording evolved from 10 months of intense negotiation in which fundamental principles were at stake on both sides. The language necessarily reflects the difficult compromises which were reached.

Source: *American Foreign Policy Current Documents*, 1982. Department of State Publication, U.S. Government Printing Office, Washington, DC, 1985. Document 498, pp. 1042-1050.

TRA42

ROC STATEMENT ON AUGUST 17 COMMUNIQUE, AUGUST 17, 1982

With regard to the Joint Communique issued on August 17, 1982 by the government of the United States of America and the Chinese communist regime, the government of the Republic of China hereby reiterates its solemn position that it will consider null and void any agreement, involving the rights and interests of the government and people of the Republic of China, reached between the United States government and the Chinese communist regime.

The government of the Republic of China makes further declarations as follows:

The supply of adequate defensive weapons to the Republic of China is an established arms sales policy of the United States of America, formulated by and executed with the stipulations of the Taiwan Relations Act. Now the United States government has mistaken the fallacious "peaceful intention" of the Chinese communists as sincere and meaningful and consequently acceded to the latter's demand to put ceilings on both the quality and quantity of the arms to be sold to the Republic of China. It is in contravention of the letter and spirit of the Taiwan Relations Act, for which we must express our profound regret.

The Chinese communists would always justify the means they choose to employ in attaining their aims. The alternating employment of peace talk and military action is their traditional, inveterate trick. The Chinese communists are exerting all efforts in waging an international united fron campaign, with a view to further isolating the Republic of China. They are seeking all possible means to interrupt and discontinue U.S. arms sales to the Republic of China, trying to pave the way for their military invasion of this country. It is a serious mistake that the United States government, failing to comprehend the real nature of the trick and fraud of the Chinese communists, unwittingly issued the above-said document jointly with them.

During the process of discussions on the so-called Joint Communique, the U.S. side has kept the government of the Republic of China informed of its developments, and at the same time the government of the Republic of China has presented to the United States its consistent position of firmly opposing the issuance of such a document. On July 14, 1982, the U.S. side, through appropriate channels, made the following points known to the Republic of China that the U.S. side:

1. has not agreed to set a date for ending arms sales to the Republic of China,
2. has not agreed to hold prior consultations with the Chinese communists on arms sales to the Republic of China,
3. will not play any mediation role between Taipei and Peiping,
4. has not agreed to revise the Taiwan Relations Act,
5. has not altered its position regarding sovereignty over Taiwan,
6. will not exert pressure on the Republic of China to enter into negotiations with the Chinese communists.

We earnestly hope that the United States government will not be deceived by but will see through the Chinese Communists' plot in attempting to annex our base of national recovery and to divide the free world. We also hope that the United States, upholding her founding spirit of freedom and justice, will fully and positively implement the Taiwan Relations Act to continue providing us with defensive arms so as to maintain the stability and prosperity of the Republic of China and to safeguard the peace and security of the Asian-Pacific region.

Source: Furnished by the Coordination Council of North American Affairs, Washington, DC.

TRA43

The Chairman. Senator Glenn
Senator Glenn. I would like to make a short opening statement.
Along with the chairman and other members of the committee I helped draft the legislation which became known as the TRA [Taiwan Relations Act]; so we, better than most perhaps, know what we intended to accomplish in that act. And I can tell you that in my considered judgment the communique announced today does undermine the spirit and intent of the TRA.
Three years ago the executive branch appeared before this committee arguing that the United States intended to sell arms to Taiwan indefinitely, but that this need not be mentioned in the legislation we were considering at that time, the Taiwan Relations Act. Administration spokesmen went further and indicated that the President might, in fact, veto a bill that contained specific arms sales assurances for Taiwan. I am glad to say that Congress failed to blink in that confrontation.
In President Reagan's words 2 years ago, the Congress was clearly unwilling to buy the Carter plan which it believed would have jeopardized Taiwan's security. The TRA that passed the Congress with almost unanimous support contained our pledge that:

The United States will make available to Taiwan such defense articles and defense services in such quantity as may be necessary to enable Taiwan to

Maintain a sufficient self-defense capability, and the President and Congress shall determine the nature and quantity of such defense articles and services based solely upon their judgment of the needs of Taiwan.

The legislative history demonstrates beyond a doubt that the intent of this passage was to insure that arms sales decisions, albeit prudent and cautious, would be made in Washington, not in Peking or Taipei.

Now, because we anticipated the PRC would pressure us to end or limit Taiwan arms sales, we provided in the act a framework for the executive branch to resist such pressures. Without these written assurances and confidence that the President would faithfully carry out the TRA, I seriously doubt that the Congress would have been prepared to go along with normalization and the PRC demand that we terminate the Mutual Defense Treaty with Taiwan.

The communique announced today discards that very carefully crafted framework, the heart of the TRA, in favor of an arms sales formulation negotiated under Chinese threats of a retrogression of United States-PRC relations.

As you might expect, under such circumstances the new restrictions on arms sales leave much to be desired. President Reagan indicates that based upon the Chinese statement, particularly the statement that "Peaceful reunification" is a "fundamental policy of the PRC," he was able to impose further restrictions on arms sales to Taiwan.

These new restrictions include: No. 1, agreeing that the United States "does not seek to carry out a long-term policy of arms sales to Taiwan." No. 2, "Arms sales to Taiwan will not exceed, either in qualitative or quantitative terms, the level of those supplied in recent years." No. 3, that the United States "intends to reduce gradually its sales of arms to Taiwan." And No. 4, this will lead "over a period of time to a final resolution."

I should also note in passing that President Reagan's concessions came just 2 years after candidate Reagan pledged that he "would not impose restrictions which are not required by the Taiwan Relations Act and which contravene its spirit and purpose."

Not only do these restrictions contravene the spirit and purpose of the TRA, they are exactly the sort of PRC-imposed conditions we sought to avoid when we drafted the act. Moreover, the restrictions set forth in the communique unfortunately do not resolve the fundamental differences between the United States and the PRC on Taiwan arms sales questions. They merely postpone the day of reckoning. I think that is a very important point. The Chinese continue to oppose arms sales, asserting it infringes on their sovereignty and is an interference in their internal affairs.

Under these conditions, agreeing on limits to gradually reduce and ultimately end arms sales puts us in an impossible position. Soon the Chinese will return with more demands and insist we finally resolve the issue, and we can expect that. We will be in the unfortunate position of having limited our argument to when, not if, a cutoff should occur. Based upon past precedent, I anticipate we will not have to wait long before the PRC makes these new demands known.

Let me close by issuing a communique of my own. I can assure you there will be a retrogression in this committee's relations with the Bureau if the action the executive branch has taken results in any major or significant change in the relative military balance that exists today between Taiwan and the PRC.

We want that balance to be maintained, and if implementation of the communique causes a deterioration in Taiwan's capability and an improvement in the PRC's relative military advantage, as a starter I would like your commitment you will not orchestrate a reduction of Taiwan's military capabilities and will notify us on each occasion you are required to disapprove U.S. industry contacts with Taiwan or deny an arms sales request made by the authorities on Taiwan.

As I indicated a few weeks ago, obviously we must be prudent and cautious in our arms transfer decisions. Gratuitous sales protect no one. But when we appear to bend to Chinese pressures on each and every sale we make to Taiwan, it is inevitable that Taipei begins seriously to doubt whether we will live up to our solemn responsibilities.

A State Department spokesman has urged me not to worry and indicated that "our relations with China are predicated on our expectation that the Taiwan issue will be resolved peacefully by the Chinese people themselves." In fact, they are so confident the issue can be resolved peacefully, they state that it is in this context that we have been and will continue to judge Taiwan's defense needs.

Unfortunately, I am not quite so sanguine. If Taiwan decides it wants to reunify with the mainland, everything will work out fine. But what if the present or future leaderships decide reunification is not in the island's interest? What then?

Warren Christopher told the Foreign Relations Committee during the TRA debate that:

> It is our position that if there is to be a reunification, it is of great Importance that it be peaceful and not be destabilizing in the area. But we do not have a position of encouraging the people on Taiwan to do something against their will.

That was an excellent policy then; it is one I fully endorse today. However, if maintaining Taiwan's free choice means supplying needed and selected defensive arms to the island to maintain the balance we have tried to maintain, even over Peking's objections and in the face of threats to downgrade United States-PRC relations, then so be it.

Source: Hearings before the committee on Foreign Relations, U.S. Senate, 97th Congress, August 17, 1982. U.S. Government Printing Office, Washington, DC, 1982. pp. 2-4

TRA44

Statement by the Chairman of the House Foreign Affairs Committee (Zablocki) and Testimony by the Assistant Secretary of State for East Asian and Pacific Affairs (Holdridge) Before the House Foreign Affairs Committee, August 18, 1982

QUESTIONS RAISED BY THE JOINT COMMUNIQUE

The committee met at 11:20 a.m. in room 2172, Rayburn House Office Building, Hon. Clement J. Zablocki (chairman) presiding.

CHAIRMAN ZABLOCKI. The committee will please come to order.

We meet today to hear from the administration justification of the policy decision, announced yesterday by the President, affecting United States relations with the People's Republic of China and Taiwan.

That policy decision, made public in the form of a communique issued jointly by the authorities in the People's Republic of China and in the United States, essentially pertains to the question of Taiwan. It sets out policies of both countries toward Taiwan.

In light of the obligations under the Taiwan Relations Act , this joint communique is understandable causing controversy. Therefore, we have invited an administration spokesman, the Honorable John H. Holdridge, Assistant Secretary of State for East Asian and Pacific Affairs, to appear today to explain the circumstances that surround this important foreign policy action and to answer questions that the committee members may have.

Frankly, in my opinion the joint communique raises serious questions and concerns.

First, procedurally, the way the communique was negotiated and drafted seems to have violated the spirit if not the letter of the Taiwan Relations Act. That act makes clear United States policy statements on how United States policies would be formulated. It clearly states that the nature and the quantity of the defense materials sold to Taiwan would be determined solely and I emphasize solely by the judgment of the U.S. President and the U.S. Congress.

Indeed, many Members of Congress agreed to adopt the provisions of the Taiwan Relations Act in the spring of 1979 only with the clear understanding that the People's Republic of China would in no way have veto power over United States decisions affecting Taiwan's security needs and defense equipment requirements.

Yet, the joint communique issued yesterday almost entirely devoted to matters of great security important to Taiwan was apparently the product of secret negotiations between the United States and the People's Republic.

Second, the joint communique in substance makes several U.S. policy commitments for example, to deny a long-term policy of arms sales to Taiwan, to set qualitative and quantitative ceilings on arms sales to Taiwan and, ultimately, to reduce arms sales to Taiwan entirely.

In this regard, the Taiwan Relations Act makes it U.S. policy to accomplish the very opposite, to assure that Taiwan remains eligible to receive U.S. arms in such quantity so as to enable Taiwan to maintain sufficient self-defense capability.

The joint communique seems to prejudge future security needs of Taiwan, to rule out enhancement if needed for its defensive capability. It seems to leave Taiwan with no better prospect than obtaining obsolete equipment from the United States in progressively smaller amounts.

It was always my impression that the Carter administration, which negotiated the joint communique of January 1, 1979, also envisioned that arms sales would continue with no discriminatory restraint applied to Taiwan, except for the calendar year 1979 during which the security treaty was being terminated and no new arms sales commitments would occur.

This being the case, the decision made public yesterday in Washington and Peking seems to represent a new foreign policy departure. As reported in the press, the People's Republic of China believes, they have really dictated to us and have won their case.

Secretary Holdridge, we look forward to your testimony regarding these concerns. There remains great anxiety about U.S. policy toward Taiwan that his decision only further excites.

We welcome you today and expect your help in explaining the reasoning behind this policy decision and how you expect U.S. policy will be followed in the future. If you will proceed, Mr. Secretary.

CHAIRMAN ZABLOCKI. Thank you, Mr. Secretary.

Apparently the very basis of this communique is what you described as China's "fundamental" policy. It is your understanding, and hopefully, it will be the case, that they will resolve their differences with Taiwan in a peaceful manner.

You do say repeatedly that "should" there be reason to believe that China's policy will change from what is now the understanding in the communique, we will reassess our policy. How long will it take to reassess and make a determination?

MR. HOLDRIDGE. I would imagine, Mr. Chairman, that such a reassessment could occur quite rapidly.

CHAIRMAN ZABLOCKI. On the basis of the track record in the executive branch, in other areas, we wait 6 weeks sometimes.

MR. HOLDRIDGE. Well, again, Mr. Chairman, I am quite sure that we would respond in a timely manner to any shift in China's policy.

Let me say again here that we have no reason to believe that China's fundamental policy of peaceful resolution of the Taiwan question would in fact change.

CHAIRMAN ZABLOCKI. On the basis of this communique, what is the status of the prospective aircraft sales to Taiwan which were under consideration for several months?

MR. HOLDRIDGE. That notification will go to the Congress before the Congress goes into recess. The paperwork is now underway and I would anticipate that the notification could go forward as early as tomorrow.[51]

CHAIRMAN ZABLOCKI. Now, on the basis of the communique, if it is determined that Taiwan indeed does need certain upgrading of, for example, their communications, or transportation, or indeed some military equipment, would upgrading be possible?

MR. HOLDRIDGE. Well, let me say that we are fully confident, Mr. Chairman, that within the provisions of the joint communique and in accordance with the Taiwan Relations Act, we will be capable of meeting Taiwan's needs.

CHAIRMAN ZABLOCKI. In paragraph 7 of the joint communique, there is the statement that "the two governments" -- meaning the United States and China, the People's Republic of China -- "will make every effort to adopt measures and create conditions conducive to the thorough settlement of this issue"; that is, the arms sales issue concerning Taiwan.

What would "conducive conditions" be?

MR. HOLDRIDGE. I would put it in simple terms, Mr. Chairman. We can say that each side will continue to do what it says it is going to do. That is, the Chinese would continue to maintain and pursue their fundamental policy of peaceful resolution of the Taiwan question, and we would carry out the policies that we have outlined in paragraph 6.

CHAIRMAN ZABLOCKI. And how would you, Mr. Secretary, answer questions expressed on Taiwan? I am sure there was some reaction. For example, how would you respond to the concerns expressed by Premier Sun that peace proposals from Peking, particularly the nine point proposal, are just other forms of Communist struggle and that they presume that Taiwan is a subordinate provincial government, not an equal negotiating partner?

MR. HOLDRIDGE. I would like to draw your attention, Mr. Chairman, to the fact that we have a distinction between what the Chinese state in paragraph 4, and what we state in paragraph 5. They talk about a policy of peaceful reunification of Taiwan with the motherland. We talk about the peaceful resolution of the Taiwan question.

Our wording was accepted in the joint communique by the Chinese side, so that in effect we are not committed to supporting any particular content of what the People's Republic of China should propose. We look at this, their two statements about their fundamental policy of peaceful resolution of the Taiwan question, as we put it, in just those terms. We do not take any position on how the resolution of this dispute should be accomplished.

As I mentioned, we are not trying to put any pressure on Taiwan to do anything or to take any particular position. Our only role in this matter is to maintain that the resolution of the differences should be by peaceful means.

CHAIRMAN ZABLOCKI. On page 10 of your statement you say:

"By defusing the difficult issue of arms sales, we will open the way for an expansion of United States-China relations in a broad range of economic, cultural, scientific, and technological areas as well as in people-to-people contact."

Is there any security cooperation implication in the communique?

MR. HOLDRIDGE. Well, we did not address the question of security, Mr. Chairman, in the course of our discussions.

You may recall that as of last year we announced a revision in the policy which would permit the Chinese to come to us if they wanted to purchase weaponry. We said that we would consider any such request on a case-by-case basis, and this would be done in conjunction with consultations with the Congress and also taking into account the views expressed by friends and allies.

The ball is still in the Chinese court, they have not responded to this proposal and the matter still rests in limbo. And, as I said, we did not address the question of a security relationship in our discussions leading to the joint communique.

CHAIRMAN ZABLOCKI. Thank you, Mr. Secretary.

[51]On August 19, the Department of Defense announced that the administration had formally notified Congress of its approval of the sale of 60 F-5E and F-5F aircraft to be coproduced in Taiwan, at an estimated cost of $240 million. The announcement read in part as follows:
"The Taiwan Relations Act states that the United States will make available to Taiwan defense articles and services in such quantity as may be necessary to enable Taiwan to maintain a sufficient self-defense capability. The proposed sale of 60 additional F-5E/F is consistent with U.S. law and policy.
"Improvement of its air defense is one of Taiwan's highest military priorities. The proposed sale would sustain Taiwan's air defense capability and thus contribute to both Taiwan's security and the maintenance of regional stability. The relative power balance in the Taiwan Strait area has not changed appreciably since normalization of relations betweeen the United States and China. However, attrition of aging F-100, F-104, and F-5A/B aircraft between now and 1986 could degrade Taiwan's air defense capability. Accordingly, Taiwan relies increasingly on the F-5E/F and needs to procure additional aircraft to compensate for these projected losses.
"The sale of this equipment and support will not affect the basic military balance in the region."
(Department of Defense files)

[51]Source: *China-Taiwan: United States Policy: Hearing Before the Committee on Foreign Affairs, House of Representatives, Ninety-seventh Congress, Second Session* (Washington, 1982), pp.1-19.

Source: *American Foreign Policy Current Documents*, 1982. Department of State Publications, U.S. Government Printing Office, Washington, DC. Document 499, pp. 1051-1053.

TRA45   CHINA-TAIWAN: UNITED STATES POLICY

WEDNESDAY, AUGUST 18, 1982

HOUSE OF REPRESENTATIVES,
COMMITTEE ON FOREIGN AFFAIRS,
Washington, D.C.

The committee met at 11:20 a.m. in room 2172, Rayburn House Office Building, Hon. Clement J. Zablocki (chairman) presiding.

Chairman ZABLOCKI. The committee will please come to order.

We meet today to hear from the administration justification of the policy decision, announced yesterday by the President, affecting United States relations with the People's Republic of China and Taiwan.

That policy decision, made public in the form of a communique issued jointly by the authorities in the People's Republic of China and in the United States, essentially pertains to the question of Taiwan. It sets out policies of both countries toward Taiwan.[1]

In light of the obligations under the Taiwan Relations Act, this joint communique is understandably causing controversy. Therefore, we have invited an administration spokesman, the Honorable John H. Holdridge, Assistant Secretary of State for East Asian and Pacific Affairs, to appear today to explain the circumstances that surround this important foreign policy action and to answer questions that the committee members may have.

Frankly, in my opinion the joint communique raises serious questions and concerns.

First, procedurally, the way the communique was negotiated and drafted seems to have violated the spirit if not the letter of the Taiwan Relations Act. That act makes clear United States policy statements on how United States policies would be formulated. It clearly states that the nature and the quantity of the defense materials sold to Taiwan would be determined solely--and I emphasize solely--by the judgment of the U.S. President and the U.S. Congress.

Indeed, many Members of Congress agreed to adopt the provisions of the Taiwan Relations Act in the spring of 1979 only with the clear understanding that the People's Republic of China would in no way have veto power over United States decisions affecting Taiwan's security needs and defense equipment requirements.

Yet, the joint communique issued yesterday--almost entirely devoted to matters of great security important to Taiwan--was apparently the product of secret negotiations between the United States and the People's Republic.

Second, the joint communique in substance makes several U.S. policy commitments--for example, to deny a long-term policy of arms sales to Taiwan, to set qualitative and quantitative ceilings on arms sales to Taiwan and, ultimately, to reduce arms sales to Taiwan entirely.

In this regard, the Taiwan Relations Act makes it U.S. policy to accomplish the very opposite, to assure that Taiwan remains eligible to receive U.S. arms of a defensive character and in such quantity so as to enable Taiwan to maintain sufficient self-defense capability.

The joint communique seems to prejudge future security needs of Taiwan, to rule out enhancement if needed for its defensive capability. It seems to leave Taiwan with no better prospect than obtaining obsolete equipment from the United States in progressively smaller amounts.

It was always my impression that the Carter administration, which negotiated the joint communique of January 1, 1979, also envisioned that arms sales would continue with no discriminatory restraint applied to Taiwan, except for the calendar year 1979 during which the security treaty was being terminated and no new arms sales commitments would occur.

This being the case, the decision made public yesterday in Washington and Peking seems to represent a new foreign policy departure. As reported in the press, the People's Republic of China believes, they have really dictated to us and have won their case.

Secretary Holdridge, we look forward to your testimony regarding these concerns. There remains great anxiety about U.S. policy toward Taiwan that this decision only further excites.

We welcome you today and expect your help in explaining the reasoning behind this policy decision and how you expect U.S. policy will be followed in the future. If you will proceed, Mr. Secretary.

STATEMENT OF HON. JOHN H. HOLDRIDGE, ASSISTANT SECRETARY OF STATE FOR EAST ASIAN AND PACIFIC AFFAIRS

Mr. HOLDRIDGE. Thank you very much, Mr. Chairman. Let me say that I welcome this opportunity to appear before you and to deal with the concerns which you have just expressed to me.

Yesterday, the United States and the People's Republic of China simultaneously issued the joint communique. During the past months, the administration has benefited from consultations with members of this committee on this sensitive subject. I believe you will recall, Mr. Chairman, that I have been in touch with you from time to time, as I have with other members of this committee. So, I would state here that I believe that you have been kept generally apprised of the direction in which we have been going and the issues that have arisen as we have addressed the problems before us.

I am glad to be able to continue our discussion of these issues in a public forum. I would also like to express our appreciation for the way the members of the committee have cooperated with us in maintaining the confidentiality of our discussions with the Chinese; this has been vital and we appreciate it.

As we went into these obligations, we had two things in mind--our historic obligations to the people of Taiwan and our important and growing relations with the People's Republic of China. Throughout the entire period of our discussions with Beijing we were guided by these dual considerations. It is a fundamental national interest of the United States to preserve and advance its strategic relations with China. At the same time, we have obligations to old friends and we are not going to turn our back on them.

I am glad that we have been able to arrive at a communique with the Chinese that demonstrated their recognition of our determination on this score. Despite the difficulties it obviously causes them, they were willing to join with us in a modus vivendi which will enable us to continue our relationship because of the important interests involved for them. Such an outcome is of vital importance to our national interest. Three administrations before us have worked very hard to establish and expand this relationship, and we would have been derelict if we had not made every effort to find a way around the problem that threatened it.

Mr. Chairman, I think it would be useful to take a few minutes to examine the reasons why we value this relationship so highly. One of the major reasons its strategic. Prior to 1971 we had a hostile relationship with China. It was costly. We fought the Chinese in Korea. We almost came to a major war over Quemoy and Matsu. The Chinese worked hand in hand with the Soviets against us in Vietnam. We had to maintain a naval presence between Taiwan and the mainland.

China identified itself with support for guerrilla movements on the soil of many of our allies and friends. Furthermore, a large part of our defense resources was allocated on the premise of a hostile China. Last, and perhaps most important, these 1 billion people were not identified with our interests as we faced the Soviet Union.

Starting in 1971, we have changed this situation. Thanks to a productive relationship between the United States and China, Taiwan has never been more secure and prosperous. We no longer have to plan for China as an enemy.

We can now think about China as a country with which we might cooperate in certain significant areas. China's relations with our allies in Asia have improved. These 1 billion people are cautiously moving into the mainstream of the world's cultural and economic life. Their isolation is dissolving. Trade has increased. Eight thousand Chinese students are now studying in the United States. Investment opportunities are opening and our parallel interests in containing the Soviet Union have been repeatedly reaffirmed.

All these things represent solid, vital benefits to our security and well-being. Mr. Chairman, we were not going to let these achievements disappear into rancor and hostility if we could possibly avoid it. We went after both of the objectives I mentioned at the outset, and I believe we have succeeded.

Let me now turn to yesterday's communique. The communique reaffirms the fundamental principles which have guided United States-China relations since the inception of the normalization process over 10 years ago. This reaffirmation is significant; it illustrates the strength and durability of these principles.

On this foundation, the United States established relations with China which have been economically beneficial to us, and which have greatly enhanced our vital strategic interests. At the same time, we have maintained and strengthened our commercial and cultural relations with the people of Taiwan. We have achieved these important goals without impairing the security of the people of Taiwan, and indeed because of these improved relations between China and the United States, Taiwan has never been more secure.

The communique also addresses an issue which was resolved at the time of normalization of relations--the question of U.S. arms sales to Taiwan. During discussions leading to normalization, China demanded that arms sales be terminated. We refused. I can say here, Mr. Chairman and members of the committee, that our negotiations almost foundered over this issue.

If you will recall the situation which was in existence at the time of normalization--that was in December 1978--looking behind the scenes I can assure you that the negotiations were most tense and the critical element was the continued insistence on the part of the United States on arms sales to Taiwan. It came within a hair's breadth of a failure, that negotiations process.

China ultimately agreed to proceed with normalization despite this disagreement but reserved the right to raise the issue again. When it did so, we agreed to engage in discussion to determine whether an understanding could be reached. The alternative to our agreeing to hold such discussions would clearly have been the beginning of a process of deterioration in our relations--deterioration that could have led us back toward hostility since the issue itself was volatile and basic. We would have been irresponsible had we allowed such a process to start.

We undertook these discussions, therefore, with the hope that a formula could be found which would permit the continued growth of our relations with China, but also with the firm resolve that there were principles regarding the security of Taiwan which could not be compromised. Those principles, embodied in the Taiwan Relations Acts, commit the United States to sell to Taiwan arms necessary to maintain a sufficient self-defense capability.

Aware of our consistent and firm opposition to the use of force against Taiwan, the Chinese, during these discussions, agreed to state in very strong terms their policy of pursuing a peaceful resolution of the Taiwan issue and described this policy as fundamental. The Chinese insisted, however, that we agree to the ultimate termination of arms sales. We refused because the level of our arms sales must be determined by the needs of Taiwan and we could not agree to a termination date, as the Chinese demanded, which might impair our ability to meet those needs.

At the same time, we recognized that China's peaceful policy bore directly on the defense needs of Taiwan. So long as that policy continued, the threat to Taiwan would be greatly diminished.

As I have just noted, assurances of such a continuity were provided when the Chinese began to describe their peaceful policy on the resolution of the Taiwan question as--as I have just said--fundamental, which contains the connotation of unchanging and long term. We were thus able to consider a policy under which we could limit our arms sales to the levels reached in recent years and would anticipate a gradual reduction in the level of arms sales. We were not willing, however, to adopt such a course unconditionally.

Chairman ZABLOCKI. Mr. Secretary, the House is in a rollcall and we will suspend for 15 minutes in order for Members to respond to the rollcall. Excuse us.

[Recess.]

Chairman ZABLOCKI. The committee will please come to order. We will resume the testimony from Secretary Holdridge. Mr. Secretary?

Mr. HOLDRIDGE. Thank you, Mr. Chairman, I will now continue.

I would like to recapitulate. You left just as I was getting down to some of the crucial elements of my statement. So, let me go back just one bit and say that really the beginning of a breakthrough in our series of discussions with the Chinese began when they began to describe their policy of a resolution of the Taiwan question as "fundamental" which contained the connotation of "long term" and "unchanging." And under those circumstances we could begin to contemplate being able to reduce arms sales--as I say again, under those circumstances. We were not willing, however, to adopt such a course unconditionally.

While the Chinese were willing to state their peaceful policy in strong terms, they at first resisted any relationship between that policy and our arms sales to Taiwan. The Chinese resisted this relationship because of their view that the sale of arms to Taiwan constitutes an interference in China's internal affairs. We rejected any language to this effect in the communique.

We also stressed that as a matter of fact and law, any adjustments in our arms sale to Taiwan had to be premised on a continuation of China's peaceful policy. We, therefore, maintained--and the Chinese ultimately agreed--that the statement of our policy in paragraph 6 be prefaced by a phrase that related it to the continuation of China's peaceful approach.

This is the genesis and purpose of the phrase, "Having in mind the foregoing statements of both sides" which precedes our statements in that paragraph. Thus, our policy is predicated on China's commitment in paragraph 4 to a peaceful approach and our acknowledgement of that approach in paragraph 5.

Let me repeat this for emphasis because this is an extremely important aspect of the joint communique. "Our policy is predicated on China's commitment in paragraph 4 to a peaceful approach and our acknowledgement of that approach in paragraph 5."

Let me summarize the essence of our understanding on this point: China has announced a fundamental policy of pursuing peaceful means to resolve the longstanding dispute between Taiwan and the mainland. Having in mind this policy and the consequent reduction in the military threat to Taiwan, we have stated our intention to reduce arms sales to Taiwan gradually, and said that in quantity and quality we would not go beyond levels established since normalization.

This follows from a literal reading of the communique. While we have no reason to believe that China's policy will change, an inescapable corollary to these mutually interdependent policies is that should China change its policy, we will reassess our policy.

Our guiding principle is now and will continue to be that embodied in the Taiwan Relations Act; the maintenance of a self-defense capability sufficient to meet the military needs of Taiwan, but with the understanding that China's maintenance of a peaceful approach to the Taiwan question will permit gradual reductions in arms sales because, clearly, the need will be reduced.

Questions have been raised concerning whether the wording of the communique adequately conveys the meaning which we ascribe to it. I believe that it does or I would have recommended against its approval.

The present wording evolved from 10 months of intense negotiations in which fundamental principles were at stake on both sides. The language necessarily reflects the difficult compromises which were reached.

We should keep in mind that what we have here is not a treaty or an agreement but a statement of future U.S. policy. We intend to implement this policy in accordance with our understanding of it. I hope I have made that point abundantly clear in my remarks today. I can further assure you that, having participated closely in the negotiations, I am confident that the Chinese are fully cognizant of that understanding.

Returning now to the document itself, let me recapitulate and emphasize a few key features, and then I will be happy to take your questions.

First, the document must be read as a whole since the policies it sets forth are interrelated.

Second, as I have previously noted, the communique contains a strong Chinese statement that its fundamental policy is to seek to resolve the Taiwan question by peaceful means. In this context, I would point out again that the reference to their "fundamental" policy carries the connotation in Chinese of "unchanging and long term."

Third, the U.S. statements concerning future arms sales to Taiwan [paragraph 6] are based on China's statements as to its fundamental peaceful policy for seeking a resolution to the Taiwan question and on the "new situation" created by those statements [paragraph 5].

This situation is new because, for the first time, China has described its peaceful policy toward Taiwan in the terms I have outlined. Thus, our future actions concerning arms sales to Taiwan are premised on a continuation of China's peaceful policy toward a resolution of its differences with Taiwan--our future actions concerning arms sales to Taiwan are premised on a continuation of China's peaceful policy toward a resolution of its differences with Taiwan.

This is indicated by the words at the beginning of paragraph 5 that, "Having in mind the foregoing statements by both sides, the United States Government states * * *." We have no reason to think that the Chinese will change this fundamental policy but if they should, we would, of course, reexamine our position.

Fourth, we did not agree to set a date certain for ending arms sales to Taiwan and the statements of future U.S. arms sales policy embodied in the communique do not provide either a timeframe for reductions of U.S. arms sales or for their termination. The U.S. statements are fully consistent with the Taiwan Relations Act and we will continue to make appropriate arms sales to Taiwan based on our assessments of their defense needs, as specified by the act. And, of course, as I have just mentioned, if there is a continued peaceful situation maintained by the Chinese, observance of the fundamental policy of peaceful resolution of the Taiwan question, the need for arms can diminish.

So much for what is in the actual communique. Over the past several months there has been considerable speculation about the substance of our discussions with the Chinese. As you know, we have not felt free to comment on such speculation while our talks were underway. Therefore, it might be useful at this point to clarify our stand on a number of issues which have surfaced in such speculations.

As to our position on the resolution of the Taiwan problem, we have consistently held that it is a matter to be worked out by the Chinese themselves. Our sole and abiding concern is that any resolution be peaceful. It follows that we see no mediation role for the United States, nor will we attempt to exert pressure on Taiwan to enter into negotiations with the People's Republic of China.

I would also call your attention to the fact that there has been no change in our longstanding position on the issue of sovereignty over Taiwan. The communique [paragraph 1] in its opening paragraph simply cites that portion of the joint communique on the establishment of diplomatic relations between the United States and the People's Republic of China in which the United States "acknowledged the Chinese position on this issue" that is, that there is but one China and Taiwan is a part of China.

It has been reported in the press that the Chinese at one point suggested that the Taiwan Relations Act be revised. We have no plans to seek any such revisions.

Finally, in paragraph 9 the two sides agree to "maintain contact and hold appropriate consultations on bilateral and international issues of common interest." This should be read within the context of paragraphs 8 and 9 which deal with the two sides' desire to advance their bilateral and strategic relations. It should not be read that we have agreed to engage in prior consultations with Beijing on arms sales to Taiwan. I hope that addresses your concern, Mr. Chairman, that policy is made in Washington, D.C., by the administration and by the Congress, and not by Beijing.

We hope and expect that this communique, and the step forward which it represents in the resolution of United States-Chinese differences on this issue, will enhance the confidence of the people of Taiwan whose well-being and prosperity continue to be of the utmost importance to us. From the President on down, we have acted in a way which seeks to enhance the future security and prosperity of the people of Taiwan, and I call your attention to the emphasis on this matter in the President's statement which was released simultaneously with the release of the communique yesterday.

Removal of the arms question as a serious issue in United States-China relations will help to insure that both countries can continue to cooperate in mutually shared international objectives, for example, deterring Soviet aggression in East Asia and removal of Vietnamese troops from Kampuchea. It will ease fears by American friends and allies that the general peace and stability in the Asia/Pacific region could be undermined. By defusing the difficult issue of arms sales we will open the way for an expansion of United States-China relations in a broad range of economic, cultural, scientific, and technological areas as well as in people-to-people contact.

In conclusion, I would like to quote a paragraph from the statement issued by President Reagan yesterday:

Building a strong and lasting relationship with China has been an important foreign policy goal of four consecutive American administrations. Such a relationship is vital to our long-term national security interests and contributes to stability in East Asia. It is in the national interest of the United States that this important strategic relationship be advanced. This communique will make that possible, consistent with our obligations to the people of Taiwan.

Thank you very much, Mr. Chairman.

Source: Hearings before the Committee on Foreign Affairs, U.S. House of Representatives, 97th Congress, 2nd Session, U.S. Government Printing Office, Washington, D.C., 1982, pp. 1-8.

TRA46   TAIWAN COMMUNIQUE AND SEPARATION OF POWERS

I. Finding

The Subcommittee on Separation of Powers of the Committee on the Judiciary, having studied the issue of whether the President violated the constitutional principle of separation of powers when he issued the United States-Communist China joint communique of August 17, 1982 (hereinafter, "joint communique" or "communique"), because the policy enunciated in the joint communique appears to be a significant departure from the statutory policy enacted by the Congress, finds that the definitive legal statement of U.S. policy concerning arms sales to Taiwan is set forth in Taiwan Relations Act of 1979, Public Law 96-8, April 10, 1979, 93 Stat. 14,22 U.S.C. 3301 et seq., that the statements of arms sales policy announced in the joint communique constitute an apparent change in arms sales policy from that stated in the act, but that the interpretation given by the administration to the statements of policy in the joint communique is generally consistent with the requirements of the act.

II. Background Information

(A) The Background of the Taiwan Relations Act of 1979

On December 15, 1978, President Carter, without any prior consultation with Congress, announced the establishment of full diplomatic relations between the United States and the People's Republic of China, to become effective January 1, 1979. In order to recognize the Communist regime on the mainland as the "sole legal Government of China," recognition which the United States had previously accorded the Chinese Government on Taiwan, the Republic of China, the United States chose to meet the three demands of the Communist regime and terminate formal diplomatic recognition of our longtime friend and ally, the Republic of China.*¹*
In addition to severing official diplomatic ties with the Republic of China, the President also unilaterally denounced the 1954 Mutual Defense Treaty between the Republic of China and the United States. However, the remaining 55 or so treaties and the many other agreements and programs between the two countries were to remain in force, and the President said, "the people of our country will maintain our current commercial, cultural, trade, and other relations with Taiwan through nongovernmental means." "Taiwan Communique and Separation of Powers: Hearings Before the Subcommittee on Separation of Powers of the Senate Committee on the Judiciary," 97th Congress, 2nd session (hereinafter referred to as "Hearings") 156 (1982) (statement by President Carter to the Nation, Dec. 15, 1978).
Thus, while the United States was ostensibly acknowledging the position that "there is but one China and Taiwan is part of China," Hearings, at 155 (statement by President Carter, Dec. 15, 1978), and withdrawing all official, governmental recognition from the Republic of China, the President was also proposing to maintain unofficial treaty, that is, legal, relations with the same entity, now denominated "the people on Taiwan," even while establishing official governmental relations with the Communist regime on the mainland. On December 30, 1978, President Carter issued a memorandum to all departments and agencies. This memorandum said, in part:
In order to effectuate all of the provisions of this memorandum, whenever any law, regulation, or order of the United States refers to a foreign country, nation, state, government, or similar entity, departments and agencies shall construe those terms and apply those laws, regulations, or orders to include Taiwan. Hearings, at 160.
This multilevel arrangement with the governments in China was unique and needed legitimization by Congress.*²* To accomplish this, the administration preferred legislation, H.R. 1614 and S. 245, "to promote the foreign policy of the United States through the maintenance of commercial, cultural, and other relations with the people on Taiwan on an unofficial basis."

The administration proposal, however, encountered immediate widespread criticism. While the administration bill responded more or less directly to the concern of the business community that the stability of our commercial intercourse with Taiwan would be undermined by the abrogation of treaties and agreements other than the defense pact, the bill was roundly criticized in Congress and elsewhere for failing to provide adequately for the security needs of our longtime allies on Taiwan and thereby for the security and peace of the entire region.[3]

The administration defended its proposal by assuring Congress that the term "other relations" appearing in the proposed legislation was intended to include military and security relations. However, Congress believed that some more explicit statement of our commitment to the security of Taiwan was necessary, especially in light of Vice Premier Deng Xiaoping's repeated refusal to rule out the use of force to reunite Taiwan and the mainland.[4]

Accordingly, an alternative version of the Taiwan implementing legislation (H.R. 2479) was substituted for the administration bill, was approved by Congress, and was signed into law by the President. This law, known as the Taiwan Relations Act of 1979, clearly and directly addresses the vital question of America's moral and strategic commitment to Taiwan's security as well as addressing the problem of insuring so far as possible the stability necessary to foster commercial relations between our country and the Republic of China.

(B) Pertinent Provisions of the Taiwan Relations Act

The act sets forth America's policy on arms sales to Taiwan and the means of implementing the policy. Whereas the administration's proposal subsumed the question of our continuing commitment to Taiwan's security under the term "other relations,"[5] the findings of the Taiwan Relations Act announce immediately and unmistakably our fundamental concern with the security of Taiwan:

SEC. 2. (a) The President having terminated governmental relations between the United States and the governing authorities on Taiwan recognized by the United States as the Republic of China prior to January 1, 1979, the Congress finds that the enactment of this Act is necessary--

(1) to help maintain peace, security, and stability in the Western Pacific;

The act then establishes the policy of the United States in this regard:

SEC. 2. (b) It is the policy of the United States--

(2) to declare that peace and stability in the area are in the political, security, and economic interests of the United States, and are matters of international concern;

(5) to provide Taiwan with arms of a defensive character;

Section Three of the act implements the policy set forth above by mandating the supply of arms and services to Taiwan and requiring the President and Congress to determine jointly the quality and quantity of such arms.

SEC. 3. (a) In furtherance of the policy set forth in section 2 of this Act, the United States will make available to Taiwan such defense articles and defense services in such quantity as may be necessary to enable Taiwan to maintain a sufficient self-defense capability.

(b) The President and Congress shall determine the nature and quantity of such defense articles ad services based solely upon their judgment of the needs of Taiwan, in accordance with procedures established by law. Such determination of Taiwan's defense needs shall include review by United States military authorities in connection with recommendation to the President and Congress.

In sum, the Taiwan Relations Act clearly expresses the intent of Congress regarding (1) the maintenance of Taiwan's defensive capability and security, (2) the joint determination by the President and Congress of matters regarding the commitment of the United States to the security of Taiwan, and (3) the continued stability of our commercial relations with Taiwan detailed elsewhere in the act.

(C)   The United States-Red Chinese Joint Communique of August 17,

On August 17, 1982, the President and Communist China issued a joint communique , the main purpose of which was to address the issue of the continuing United States arms sales to Taiwan.   This issue was dealt with in the framework of the "reaffirmation" of "the fundamental principles which have guided United States-China relations since the inception of the normalization process over 10 years ago."   Hearings, at 178 (statement by John H. Holdridge, Assistant Secretary of State for East Asian and Pacific Affairs before the House Committee on Foreign Affairs, Aug. 18, 1982).   The "fundamental principles" cited in the communique refer to the problem of defining Taiwan's legal relationship to the Government of the mainland--the so-called Taiwan question.

The question of the legal relationship between Taiwan and the Communist government has haunted our negotiations with the Communist regime from the beginning.   In the 1978 negotiations which led to the normalization of relations with the Peking government, the Communist regime agreed that the United States would "maintain cultural, commercial, and other unofficial relations with the people of Taiwan."   Hearings, at 155 (statement by President Carter, Dec. 15, 1978); see also Hearings, at 178 (joint communique, par. 1).   However, the Communists demanded that arms sales to Taiwan cease.   According to Assistant Secretary Holdridge:

> During discussions leading to normalization, China demanded that arms sales be terminated.   We refused.   I can say here that our negotiations almost foundered over this issue.   China ultimately agreed to proceed with normalization despite this disagreement but reserved the right to raise this issue again.   When it did so, we agreed to engage in discussion to determine whether an understanding could be reached.   Hearings at 178.

The discussion anticipated by the two parties in 1978 began in 1981, ten months before the issuance of the joint communique.   Again, according to Assistant Secretary Holdridge, the Communist Chinese demanded that "we agree to ultimate termination of arms sales," and again we refused:

> We refused because the level of our arms sales must be determined by the needs of Taiwan and we could not agree to a termination date as the Chinese demanded, which might impair our ability to meet those needs.   Hearings, at 179.

However, the administration did find it significant that twice since the announcement of normalization of relations in December 1978, the Communist government announced a "fundamental policy" of peacefully resolving the Taiwan question.   With the announced intentions of the Communist regime in mind,[6] the administration stated its own intentions regarding arms sales in paragraph 6 of the joint communique:

> 6.   Having in mind the foregoing statements of both sides, the United States Government states that it does not seek to carry out a long-term policy of arms sales to Taiwan, that its arms sales to Taiwan will not exceed in qualitative or in quantitative terms, the level of those supplied in recent years since the establishment of diplomatic relations between the United States and China, and that it intends to reduce gradually its sales of arms to Taiwan, leading over a period of time to a final resolution.   In so stating, the United States acknowledges China's consistent position regarding the thorough settlement of this issue.   Hearings, at 178.

It is this language of the joint communique, when juxtaposed to the sections of the Taiwan Relations Act setting forth U.S. policy regarding arms sales to Taiwan and the implementation of that policy, that gives rise to the serious separation of powers issues that the subcommittee has studied.

III. Subcommittee Action

The subcommittee held 3 days of hearings. On September 17, 1982, oral testimony was received from:

Hon. Steven D. Symms, U.S. Senator from Idaho;
Hon. Richard Stone, former U.S. Senator from Florida and co-sponsor of the Taiwan Relations Act of 1979;
Dr. Ray Cline, Georgetown Center for Strategic and International Studies;
Ambassador leonard Unger, former Ambassador to the Republic of China;
Prof. A. James Gregor, Institute for International Studies, University of California at Berkeley; and,
Prof. Harold Hinton, George Washington University.

The witnesses testifying at the September 27, 1982, hearing were Davis Robinson. Esq., Legal Advisor, Department of State, and Theodore Olson, Esq., Assistant Attorney General, Office of Legal Counsel, Department of Justice. The Honorable Paul D. Wolfowitz, Assistant Secretary of State for East Asian and Pacific Affairs, testified at the final hearing on March 10, 1983. See Hearings, part 2, for March 10 transcript.

In addition to the testimony of these distinguished witnesses, the subcommittee received written testimony from the following individuals:

Hon. Barry Goldwater, U.S. Senator from Arizona;
Hon. Gerald Solomon, U.S. Representative from New York;
H. O. Reinsch, president, Bechtel Power Corp.;
David M. Kennedy, chairman of the board, and W. N. Morell, Jr., president, USA-ROC Economic Council;
Prof. Morton A. Kaplan, University of Chicago.

IV. Preliminary Statement of the Issue

The issuance of the joint communique by the President of the United States and the Government of Communist China presents the problem of a possible violation of the separation of powers principle which underlies the U.S. Constitution. Congress, the legislative or policymaking branch of the National Government, declared the U.S. policy regarding arms sales to Taiwan in the Taiwan Relations Act, and according to the American constitutional scheme of government the President as the chief executive officer is charged with the duty to carry out the statutory policy of the Nation. However, the U.S. policy statements in the joint communique, and in particular in paragraph 6 of the communique, appear to deviate considerably from the policy set forth in the act.

If the communique does in fact purport to state official U.S. policy, and if that policy does in fact depart from the statutory policy, then the departure presents a prima facie case of failure by the President to execute faithfully the laws of the United States and also a case of his unauthorized making of the U.S. policy instead of executing it. Both of these possibilities are violations of the principle of separation of powers, because each branch of the National Government is charged with the duty to exercise certain powers and not to exercise others. It is the function of the executive branch to administer lawful U.S. policies and not to formulate policy which ignores or purports to supersede U.S. law.

Therefore, the separation of powers issue may be reduced to two questions: first, "What is the legal and political nature of the joint communique?" and second, "Is the policy stated therein a legally significant departure from the policy set forth in the Taiwan Relations Act?" Since the separation of powers issue presupposes that the Congress acted constitutionally when it enacted the Taiwan Relations Act, the study of the problem must begin with an analysis of the constitutional basis of the legislation.

V. The Constitutionality of the Taiwan Relations Act

Neither the administration nor critics from other quarters have questioned the constitutional validity of the act. The statements by President Reagan and by Assistant Secretary Holdridge which accompanied the announcement of the joint communique on August 17, 1982, specifically acknowledged the overriding authority of the act as regards U.S. arms sales policy toward Taiwan. Hearings, at 179. Subsequent statements by Assistant Secretary Powell Moore and by Legal Adviser Davis Robinson of the Department of State as well as the answers by the Department to the written interrogatories propounded by the subcommittee reiterated the position of the administration that the Taiwan Relations Act is the law of the land and that the joint communique is fully consistent with the act. Hearings, at 96, 145-46, 182-83.

Most recently, Assistant Secretary Paul Wolfowitz repeated this position at the March 10, 1983, hearing:

> I seek only to fulfill the President's personal commitment to implement our policies, including the Joint Communique in a manner fully consistent with U.S. law, including the Taiwan Relations Act....Let me say in my own words that it is correct that the administration believes that and insists that our policies will be consistent with the Taiwan Relations Act. "Taiwan Communique and Separations of Powers--Part 2: Hearings Before the Subcommittee on Separations of Powers of the Senate Committee on the Judiciary" (hereinafter, "Hearings, part 2") 7, 12 (1983).

The Taiwan Relations Act may be grounded on either of two constitutional foundations. The first and most obvious basis is the power of Congress "to regulate Commerce with foreign Nations," article I, section 8. clause 3 of the Constitution. The establishment of policy regarding the peacetime sale of arms and services to the people on Taiwan is an exercise of this constitutional power.

It may be objected, however, that the derecognition of the Republic of China together with the affirmation that there is only one China and that the Peking government is the sole legal government of China consigns Taiwan to something other than "nation" status. Far from detracting from the constitutional validity of the Taiwan Relations Act, this latter account of the nature of the legal entity which is Taiwan served the Senate Committee on Foreign Relations as the premise for its constitutional justification of the act:

While it is true that the President has some "constitutional responsibility for the conduct of the foreign relations of the nation," it is not true that he possesses all powers granted by the Constitution to do so; his exclusive authority to recognize and to negotiate with foreign governments has never been construed as having in any way narrowed or diminished the many powers of the Congress over foreign affairs matters, including the power to regulate commerce with foreign nations (art. I, sec. 8, cl. 3), to spend for the general welfare (art. I, sec. 8, cl. 1), and to control Federal expenditures (art. I, sec. 9, cl. 7). It is these powers upon which many of the provisions of the bill are based, and it is the Committee's judgment that the enactment of these provisions is legally required--not simply politically desirable, but legally required--if the President is to be enabled to continue to conduct the myriad programs concerning Taiwan. The reason is that the statutes authorizing such programs invariably authorize the President to carry out those programs only with respect to foreign countries, nations, or states, and the President, on December 19, stated that, as of January 1, 1979, "Taiwan will no longer be a nation in the view of our own country." S. Rept. No. 7, 96th Congress, 1st Session 41 (1979). See also Hearings at 13 (statement of Richard Stone).

On the basis of the foregoing arguments, the subcommittee finds that the Taiwan Relations Act is clearly a legitimate exercise of the legislating power of the Congress under the Constitution.

VI. The Legal and Political Nature of the Joint Communique

The administration insists that the joint communique is not an executive or international agreement giving rise to legal rights and legal obligations. Hearings, at 109-10 (statement of Davis Robinson). The Congress has been told by former Assistant Secretary Holdridge that it is a "modus vivendi," an "understanding," and "a statement of future U.S. policy"; legal Adviser Robinson stated that it is "a statement of policy," "a statement of intention," and "a statement of expectations"; and present Assistant Secretary Wolfowitz testified that it is "a framework for managing our differences with the Chinese over a matter of great sensitivity to us both." In his testimony before the subcommittee, Mr. Robinson, the chief legal counsel to the Department of State, described the communique at some length:

At the outset, it is important to define with precision the legal character of the August 17 communique. It sets forth parallel and interrelated statements of policy by the United States and China. It is not an international agreement and thus imposes no obligations on either party under international law. Its status under domestic law is that of a statement by the President of the United States of a policy which he intends to pursue. Like any other Presidential policy, it must be executed in full compliance with all relevant laws. The President has made clear his firm intention to do so.

It is beyond question that the President possesses full constitutional authority to issue statements of the foreign policy which he intends to pursue. Such statements of the Executive's policy are recognized as being at the heart of the Executive's prerogatives in the conduct of U.S. foreign relations. The communique is an example of such a statement of policy and that is clearly within the authority of the President.

The issuance of the communique did not encroach on any constitutional or statutory power of the Congress. The chairman's August 20 and 24 letters suggest that the Taiwan Relations Act limits or otherwise regulates the President's authority to issue expressions of Executive policy with respect to Taiwan in the absence of some action by the Congress. Upon careful further consideration, I have reconfirmed our earlier conclusion that the act imposes no requirements upon the President that have not been satisfied. Hearings, at 95.

This characterization of the joint communique by the administration poses at least two problems. First, although the Department of State spokesmen emphatically refuse to describe the joint communique as a "legal" agreement, the subcommittee notes that the distinction between "legal" and "nonlegal" or "political" agreements among nations often has little real significance. This is especially true in that area of international relations concerned with strategic and military arrangements, the area into which fit both the joint communique and United States-Taiwan arms sales agreements. It is seldom anticipated by the parties to these agreements--whether the agreements are denominated "understandings," "modi vivendi," or "parallel statements of policy"--that the rights and obligations established thereby will be tested in domestic courts or international tribunals.

Thus, it is not the "legal" in the sense of the "justiciable" character of the communique but its "legal" character as determined by our fundamental law, the U.S. Constitution, that is of primary concern to the subcommittee. This concern by Congress is also warranted because the Federal judiciary, an all likelihood, would refrain from adjudicating the instant constitutional questions posed by the joint communique, holding instead that the issues are "political questions" to be resolved between the executive and legislative branches through the political processes set forth in the Constitution. Of course, even if the courts did exercise jurisdiction, the Congress, as a coequal branch of the national government and trustee of our fundamental law, is empowered and obligated to investigate any colorably constitutional issues resulting from actions by the executive branch and to determine for itself the nature of the problem and the best remedial steps to take.

The present controversy also points to the inseparability of law and policy in the statements given and the actions taken in the management of the Nation's foreign affairs. See Hearings, at 111-14. In order to determine whether the joint communique is a proper and legal exercise of executive branch power, the Congress must be able to determine the actual policy which is reflected in the joint communique or which the communique is intended to justify. Therefore, both because of this inseparability of law and policy and because it is the function of Congress to set both the domestic and the foreign policy of this Nation, the subcommittee must inquire into the policy actually being pursued by the President and into the political nature of the agreements our country enters and the nature of the rights and obligations acquired thereby.

The Department of State concedes that the joint communique does indeed create obligations of a nonjusticiable or political type:

While the communique may not be an international legal agreement enforceable in courts of law, is it not the case that the communique is intended to create certain reasonable expectations by each party? Hearings, at 131-32 (interrogatory No. 26).

Yes, while the joint communique is not an international agreement, it contains parallel statements by the United States and the People's Republic of China of policies which our respective Governments intend to pursue. Such a document may create reasonable expectations by each party. On our part, we expect the Chinese to maintain their policy of seeking a peaceful resolution of their differences with Taiwan. Hearings, at 146 (answer No. 26).

Assistant Secretary Holdridge, in his August 17, 1982, testimony before the Senate Committee on Foreign Relations, expressed concisely the political nature of the joint communique:

We have come to an agreement--not an agreement but an understanding with the People's Republic of China, and I think they expect us to carry it out in good faith as we expect them to carry out in good faith the commitment to carry out a fundamental policy of working toward the peaceful resolution of the Taiwan question, so there is an obligation on both sides. Hearings, at 131 (quoted in interrogatory No. 26).

And, in his March 10, 1983, testimony before the subcommittee, Assistant Secretary Wolfowitz also referred to the "agreement" aspect of the communique when, on at least two occasions, he referred to the "formula agreed to in the joint communique," Hearings, part 2, at 9, 11, and when he stated that the administration "intends to comply with the policies as expressed in the August 17 communique," and that "[w]e fully expect the Chinese to do the same." Hearings, part 2, at 9. The subcommittee submits that there is a very fine line, easily blurred, between an "agreement" between nations and an "understanding" or "modus vivendi." It is not clear that the Department of State has always kept this distinction firmly in sight.

Since the communique was first announced, the Communist Chinese have markedly emphasized its nature as an "agreement" and also emphasized the obligations it imposes upon the United States, even while they deny that the communique records the "commitment" adduced by Assistant Secretary Holdridge. See below, p. 17. Red China has repeatedly characterized the U.S. statements as "commitments," "undertakings," and "principles to be adhered to by the United States. As shall be pointed out in the next section of this report, this is not the only area of deep disagreement between the United States and Red China in the interpretation and very conception of the joint communique.

The description of the joint communique as a "statement of policy" intended to encourage significant reliance by each of the parties involved points to a second problem presented by Legal Adviser Robinson's statement--the question of what the administration means by "statement of policy." Of this second problem, the explanations offered by the Department of State do little to assist the subcommittee.

In the foregoing testimony of Mr. Robinson, he refers to the "legal character" of the communique as:

--"parallel and interrelated statements of policy by the United States and China;"

--"a statement by the President of the United States of a policy which he intends to pursue;"

--"statements of the foreign policy which he intends to pursue;"

--"statements of the Executive's policy;" and

--"expressions of Executive policy." Hearings, at 95.

Such statements are "at the heart of the Executive's prerogatives in the conduct of U.S. foreign relations," but the policy "must be executed in full compliance with all relevant laws." Id. (Mr. Robinson's statement is almost identical to the statement in the letter of Sept. 14, 1982, from Assistant Secretary Powell Moore to Chairman East. Id., at 182.)

If all that is meant by the Executive prerogative asserted here by the Department is the President's discretion to publish or to rearticulate U.S. policy where, as here, that policy has been definitively expressed in legislation, the subcommittee finds the assertion unexceptionable. The standard applicable to presidential publication is simply that of accuracy in the restatement of lawful, U.S. policy, and the function of the subcommittee is to determine whether the statements in the joint communique are accurate restatements of the policy set forth in the act.

However, two things cast doubt on this interpretation: first, the use of the terms "Executive's policy" and "policy which the President intends to pursue" rather than the term "U.S. policy"; and, second, the marked difference in the apparent substance of the policy statements in the joint communique from the substance of the policy declared in the Taiwan Relations Act. These facts intimate that the Department has in mind something different from mere rearticulations of the policy stated in the Taiwan Relations Act. Unfortunately, the replies of the administration to questions by the subcommittee do not clarify what this difference is.

In response to questioning by the subcommittee at the hearing on September 27, 1982, the representatives of the administration had this to say:

Mr. Robinson....I want to emphasize that the joint communique is not a legally binding international agreement creating obligations and rights under international law. It is a statement of policy. It is a statement of intention. It is a statement of expectations. It is based upon understandings. *Certainly a communique of this nature cannot bind any future President of the United States.*

On the other hand, *it is a statement of the policy of this administration....*

      *   *   *   *   *

*

Mr. Olson....As Mr. Robinson stated, *the incumbent President, in making a statement of policy, could not bind his successors, and neither this President nor any successor can change the Taiwan Relations Act.* As you have pointed out, it is an enactment of this body, and only this body can change it. The implementation of the United States-China joint communique, which is a statement of policy, must be in accord with the Taiwan Relations Act. Hearings, at 109-10 (emphasis added).

In contrast to this testimony which maintains that the validity of the policy statement of the joint communique is coextensive with the tenure of the administration of Ronald Reagan, the Department of State elsewhere has sought to identify the statements in the communique as the U.S. arms sales policy. Thus, in answer to interrogatories which asked "the nature of the policy called 'executive's policy' or 'policy of the President'" and whether "such policy [is] distinct from official U.S. policy," the Department responded:

> 20. The "policy of the President" is the policy which the President adopts in the exercise of his constitutional and statutory authority. Such policy is the policy of the United States. As noted [in the responses to previous interrogatories], the policies of the United States expressed in the joint communique are fully consistent with the Taiwan Relations Act, and the President has clearly stated his intention of implementing those policies in a manner consistent with U.S. law.

> 21. As stated in response to Question 20, there is no distinction between the policy of the President (or Executive) and the policy of the United States concerning U.S. arms sales to Taiwan. Hearings, at 145.

The problem posed by the latter account is that the official U.S. policy concerning arms sales to Taiwan is declared in the Taiwan Relations Act and is not coterminous with the tenure of this or any other administration unless and until the act is amended by Congress. This is clearly expressed in Assistant Attorney General Olson's testimony.

In an effort to determine the administration's conception of the nature of the policy statements in the communique, the subcommittee finds that the statements of the Department of State support the following inference. The joint communique is a formulation of the means by which this particular administration intends to implement the policy of the Taiwan Relations Act. According to this explanation, the act "enunciates in general terms the policy of the United States," Hearings, at 145 (answer No. 22), or embodies the principles of U.S. policy, Hearings, at 110 (Mr. Olson quoting earlier testimony of Assistant Secretary Holdridge), while the joint communique, pursuant to section 3 of the act, articulates the formula for implementing the general policy. Hearings, at 145 (answer No. 22); Hearings, part 2, at 9, 11 (statement of Assistant Secretary Wolfowitz).

Ignoring for the moment the fact that the Taiwan Relations Act does not delegate to the President alone the task of formulating the steps needed to implement the policies declared in section 2 of the act,[7] this account of the statements in the joint communique as a pronouncement of the means by which this administration intends to carry out the general principles in section 2 has the virtue of tying together the above and other statements of the Department. Thus, this formulation of the steps which this administration intends to take in order to carry out the policy in the Taiwan Relations Act (1) would not necessarily bind other administrations, (2) would be U.S. policy, though not in the same sense as the policy declared in the act, and (3) would be governed by the act and would have to be consistent with the statements of policy in the act.

What obscures this explanation is the failure of the Department of State to distinguish explicitly the provisions in the joint communique as statements of means from the provisions in the act as statements of objectives. The danger in this failure is that some may forget that it is the Congress, not the executive branch, that has the constitutional function of formulating U.S. foreign policy. Because of this plenary power of making policy, the Congress prescribes the specific policymaking functions of the Executive. Congress may indeed delegate considerable discretion to the President in the area of foreign affairs, but such delegation cannot be found in the Taiwan Relations Act. It becomes misleading, then, to speak of "Executive's policy" as identical with "U.S. policy," especially in this case where the Congress has exercised its constitutional power of declaring U.S. policy in a duly enacted piece of legislation. There is certainly a sense in which the steps intended to implement the policy declared in legislation may also be considered "U.S. policy," but there is also a sense in which they may not: this latter sense has been obscured by the various statements of the Department of State spokesmen.

There is a further problem with all of the explanations of the nature of the joint communique by the Department of State, and that is the problem of the authority of the executive branch to formulate unilaterally any policy whatever regarding arms sales to Taiwan. Apart from the statement by a member of the Committee on Foreign Relations that the process leading to the creation of the joint communique had been a "model" of executive branch-legislative branch cooperation, the express statements of other members of Congress during the hearings of August 17 and 18, 1982, and the inferences reasonably drawn from their questions to the representatives of the Department of State during those hearings indicate rather clearly that many members of the Senate and the House did not believe that the joint determination mandated by section 3(b) of the act did in fact occur.[8]

In sum, the subcommittee finds that the Department of State has not offered consistent, intelligible accounts of either the legal and political nature of the joint communique or the nature of the policy stated therein. In drawing the inferences stated above, the subcommittee concludes that the administration may well have exceeded the bounds of its statutory duty set forth in section 3 of the Taiwan Relations Act insofar as it acted unilaterally in formulating implementary policy. Nevertheless, the primary issue is whether the policy reflected in the communique is in fact consistent with the declarations of the Taiwan Relations Act. This issue is the subject of the following section.

VII. The Policy Stated in the Joint Communique

The controversy provoked in the country by the joint communique focuses almost exclusively on the statements of the United States found in paragraph 6:

1. The United States does not seek to carry out a long-term policy of arms sales to Taiwan;

2. United States arms sales to Taiwan will not exceed, either in qualitative or quantitative terms, the level of those supplied in recent years since the establishment of diplomatic relations between the United States and China; and,

3. The United States intends to reduce gradually its arms sales to Taiwan, leading over a period of time to a final resolution.

It is difficult to square these statements of policy with either the statement in section 2 of the Taiwan Relations Act that it is U.S. policy "to provide Taiwan with arms of a defensive character" or the statements in section 3 of the act outlining the means by which the U.S. policy is to be implemented.

In the first statement the United States appears to declare its intention to terminate arms sales to Taiwan at some time before the "long term;" the Taiwan Relations Act, however, place no temporal limits on our policy of making such sales. The intention to terminate arms sales seems also to be reflected in the third statement: a gradual reduction of arms sales leading to a "final resolution" is a statement most reasonably construed to mean a gradual reduction leading to eventual termination. This, indeed, is the interpretation that the Red Chinese have given to the statement since August 17, 1982. The act, however,
says nothing about gradual reductions of arms sales: the level of arms sales is to be determined solely on the basis of Taiwan's defensive needs (section 3).

In statement two, it is declared that our arms sales to Taiwan will not exceed the highest levels of quality and quantity since the establishment of diplomatic relations between the United States and Red China, but again there is no foundation in the act for qualitative and quantitative caps on arm sales.

The interpretation given these policy statements by the Peking government serves to confirm the inferences drawn by the witnesses and the subcommittee. On August 17, 1982, in a statement accompanying the issuance of the joint communique, the Chinese Ministry of Foreign Affairs cited the policy statements in question and noted, "The final resolution referred to here certainly implies that the U.S. arms sales to Taiwan must be completely terminated over a period of time." Hearings, at 194. Again, on October 10, 1982, a Red Chinese commentary stated:

The joint communique of the Chinese and U.S. Governments stipulated the principle of a phased and eventually complete solution to the issue of U.S. arms sales to Taiwan, that is, the United States must gradually reduce its arms sales to Taiwan and completely halt them after a time. Hearings, at 205.

The Department of State, however, denies that termination of arms sales was agreed to in the communique or was even contemplated by the United States, and the Department explicitly rejects the Red Chinese interpretation. Hearings, at 127 (interrogatory No. 16) and 143 (answer No. 16). The Department states:

As noted above, the term "final resolution" refers to a resolution of the differences between the U.S. and China on the question of U.S. arms sales to Taiwan. The Communique does not provide for termination of such arms sales and does not specify the time or form that a resolution of these differences might take. Hearings, at 142-3 (answer No. 15(c)).

Assistant Secretary Powell Moore, in response to a letter addressed by the chairman of this subcommittee to Secretary Shultz, also made this point:

With regard to your concern that the Communique implies a commitment on the part of the U.S. to a termination of U.S. arms sales to Taiwan, I can assure you that the Communique mandates nothing of the sort. Rather, the Communique sets forth a policy regarding future arms sales to Taiwan which is premised on an assessment of Taiwan's defense needs, the standard established in Section 3 of the TRA. Hearings, at 188.

And President Reagan, in a recently published interview, stated:

If the day ever comes that those two [Taiwan and Red China] find that they can get together and become one China, in a peaceful manner, then there wouldn't be any need for arms sales to Taiwan. And that's all that was meant in the communique. Nothing was meant beyond that. We're not going to say, "well, just as time goes by, we're going to reduce the arms to them." No, we hope for a peaceful resolution of this issue. Hearings, part 2, at 58.

This was reiterated by Assistant Secretary Wolfowitz in his testimony:

While we do not seek to carry out a long-term policy of arms sales to Taiwan, we did not agree to set a date for ending arms sales, nor did we agree to consult in advance with the PRC on arms sales to Taiwan. And I would again like to emphasize very clearly, there is no time limitation in that communique. We do not accept such a time limitation. As the President has made clear in his remarks, we do not necessarily accept the interpretation that a final resolution of the arms issue would necessarily mean a termination. Clearly, movement toward resolution of that issue is going to depend on how the Chinese themselves on both sides of the Strait move toward resolution of their own differences.
Hearings, part 2, at 11-12.

Regarding the gradual reduction of arms sales and the caps on the quality and quantity of arms sold, the administration also maintains that the correct interpretation of the communique represents a policy position that is consistent with the Taiwan Relations Act. On October 6, 1982, President reagan declared that there has been "no reversal on our Taiwan policy," that "our Taiwan friends are going to continue to get everything they need for their own self-defense," and further:

If the People's Republic keeps their word that they, for the first time, said that they would try to resolve their differences peacefully and arrive at a peaceful reunification. Yes, then there would be no longer any need for us to provide defense weapons, and there would be a decline and an end at that time, but only linked to that promise of a peaceful reunification. Hearings, at 181 (remarks by President Reagan to Republican candidates).

Again, in an interview published on February 26, 1983, President Reagan was asked:

QUESTION. But what if there is, say progress of a sort, mild progress of a sort, but the Mainland feels that it has a sovereign right to increase and modernize its military arsenal? what happens at that point to Taiwan? Do we still go along with the idea that their military cannot be upgraded?

ANSWER. No, we're doing all the things that we have always done. The shipments are regularly going on.
Hearings, part 2, at 58.

Later in the same interview, President Reagan was again asked about our ability to upgrade Taiwan's defenses in light of the joint communique:

QUESTION. But the key point is, are we allowed to upgrade Taiwan's defenses, especially if the Mainland upgrades its defenses? The Taiwanese, I was told, are not even allowed to get certain defensive weapons from us because these defensive weapons hadn't gone to them prior to the issuance of the Communique.

ANSWER. We're giving them what we mutually agree upon when their people come here and sit down and go over their defense needs, and, as the Taiwan Relations Act requires, we will continue to address their capabilities and their needs dependent on the situation in the region. Hearings, part 2, at 58.

Secretary of State Shultz reiterated this earlier this year:

I think what is said in the communique simply describes that following the statement made on the Chinese side that the situation is peaceful but the level of arms needed basically is a reflection of the conditions that exist. If there is a peaceful situation, one could expect the level of armaments to decline, but that doesn't change our commitment that any resolution of the issues would be by peaceful means.
Hearings, part 2, at 57.

And Assistant Secretary Wolfowitz testifies quite clearly on this point:

We quite logically recognize the direct relationship between Taiwan's defense needs and China's peaceful policy, and in this context agree to reduce gradually the quantity and quality of our arms supplies to Taiwan.
Hearings, part 2, at 11.
As I see it, the standard for judging the flow of military equipment to Taiwan under the TRA is Taiwan's defense needs. We expect that so long as China maintains its nonthreatening posture toward Taiwan in accordance with the policies we set down in the communique, Taiwan's defense needs will gradually diminish. I, therefore, believe the communique to be consistent with the Taiwan Relations Act as we determined should be the case. As the President has asserted, we do not seek any revision of the Taiwan Relations Act.

Hearings, part 2, at 12.

Finally, regarding the limits on the quality and quantity of arms sold to Taiwan, the administration has recently indicated that here, too, the apparent meaning of the statement in the joint communique is not the actual or intended meaning. At the March 21, 1983, daily press briefing at the Department of State, a Department spokesman responded to questions about projected amounts of arms sales for fiscal years 1983 and 1984:

QUESTION. All right...[the Communist Chinese] said [the projection], in effect, is a reneging on the implied or explicit promise by the United States to have a diminished supply of arms going to Taiwan. Would you comment on that?

ANSWER. Let me just say this on that: First, as I say, the figures are projections, and may not be realized in the course of the fiscal year which are cited. The figures which are cited in that document are $800 million for FY-83 and $780 million for FY-84.

QUESTION. The second figure?

ANSWER. $780 M. Should these levels be realized, they would be fully consistent with the August 17 communique. As the communique says, the reductions will be gradual, and, although there may be occasional fluctuations, the trend will be apparent over time. As the Secretary has said, we intend to keep our commitments.

There are various tables which explain how figures for past years might be adjusted to bring them up to '83 levels in terms of this year's dollars to make comparisons and so on, and that's in [the Congressional Presentation: Security Assistance Programs, FY1984].

QUESTION. You're saying that the figures are consistent with the Taiwan Communique--with the communique of August 17, and the People's Republic says they're inconsistent, and that's the way you're going to leave it at this point?

ANSWER. I can't speak for the Chinese. They have to speak for themselves on this issues.

QUESTION. They have spoken for themselves.

ANSWER. Fine. I am saying to you that, yes, we view these as consistent with the August 17 communique.

QUESTION. It sounds like from that you're saying is you have adjusted the previous sales figures for Taiwan by an inflation factor.

ANSWER. That's right. We haven't adjusted it, but there is provided in the Congressional Presentation Document a table which would give you an inflation index.

QUESTION. Why, then did not the commitments say we will supply less arms adjusted for inflation?

ANSWER. Don, as you know, we haven't tried to get as specific as that. As John Holdridge said before the Senate Foreign Relations Committee in August, we had no figures in mind of any dollar limit. We haven't gotten to that sort of specificity. See also hearings, part 2, at 61.

Thus, it appears that the administration is interpreting the communique to permit the increase in the actual current dollar amounts of arms sales in order to take inflation into account. There has been no statement by the administration, other than the statements of February 26, 1982, by President Reagan, Hearings, part 2, at 58, indicating whether the qualitative limitation is being construed literally.

The Peking regime responded to the August testimony of Assistant Secretary Holdridge, to the october remarks of President Reagan, to the February remarks of President

Reagan and Secretary Shultz, and to the March arms projection of the administration with essentially the same accusation: the United States is not adhering to promises it made in the communique.

On August 20, 1982, Red China characterized the statements of Secretary Holdridge as "distorted interpretations of certain contents in the communique," and called his refusal to indicate a schedule for arms sales reductions and termination an attempt "to evade U.S. responsibilities." Hearings, at 196-97. In response to the President's October statement that there has been no reversal of our policy toward Taiwan and that Taiwan will get everything they need for their defense, Red China said, "U.S. President Ronald Reagan violated the Sino-United States joint communique in a statement yesterday by making China's peaceful reunification a prerequisite for an end to the sales of U.S. arms to Taiwan." Hearings, at 203. President Reagan's remarks in the February 26, 1983, interview were called "statements deviating from the 17 August Sino-American joint communique." Hearings, part 2, at 63. And on March 18, 1983, it was reported that Red China protested the rising arms sales to Taiwan projected for fiscal years 1983 and 1984. Hearings, part 2, at 63.

The rationale used by the administration both to justify to the Communists the refusal to terminate sales to Taiwan in light of paragraph 6 of the joint communique and to justify to Congress the permissibility of making any statements of intention to reduce arms or to limit their quantity or quality is that the Taiwan Relations Act mandates only that the United States provide the arms needed "to enable Taiwan to maintain a sufficient self-defense capability." (Section 3(b).) The emphasis is placed on the "needs" of Taiwan: this is clear from the statements of President Reagan quoted above and from the statements of Assistant Secretary Holdridge that are cited in the interrogatories of the subcommittee to the Department of State. Hearings, at 118-23 (interrogatories Nos. 1-10), 138-40 (answers Nos. 1-10), and from the testimony of Assistant Secretary Wolfowitz on March 10, 1983, Hearings, part 2, at 7-12.

The argument takes as its point of departure section 3 of the act, which requires the United States to supply Taiwan with the defensive weapons necessary for its security. The "needs of Taiwan" referred to in section 3(b) naturally depend upon the existence and the specific nature of a military threat to Taiwan. If Red China no longer constitutes a military threat to Taiwan--that is, if the so-called Taiwan question were removed--then the defense needs of Taiwan would be correspondingly eliminated.

The statements in paragraph 6 of the joint communique, continues the argument, are premised upon the statements by Red China in paragraph 5. Thus, in implementing the policy of the Taiwan Relations Act, the joint communique represents an understanding that in return for Red China's policy of striving for a peaceful resolution of the Taiwan question, the United States will (1) cap our arms sales qualitatively and quantitatively, (2) reduce the sales gradually, and (3) consider, as one possible alternative, the termination of arms sales to Taiwan. Hearings, at 143 (answer No. 17); Hearings, part 2, at 11-12 (statement of Assistant Secretary Wolfowitz).

Like the accounts offered by the Department to explain the nature of the joint communique, this argument raises several serious questions. The linchpin of the argument is the assertion that the U.S. actions are premised upon Red China's peaceful policy toward Taiwan, but the Peking regime has repeatedly and unequivocally denied this conditionality. In a statement issued on August 20, 1982, in response to the testimony given by Assistant Secretary Holdridge to the Senate Committee on Foreign Relations and the House Committee on Foreign Affairs, the Red Chinese said:

Here, it should be pointed out once again that U.S. arms sales to Taiwan and China's efforts for peaceful resolution of the Taiwan issue are two separate questions of an entirely different nature. In what way the Taiwan issue is to be resolved is purely an internal affair of China, brooking no external interference. In the communique, the Chinese Government reiterates its policy of striving to resolve the Taiwan issue peacefully and its stand that the Taiwan issue is China's internal affairs. This can in no way be explained as any commitments China made to the United States, and any misrepresentation of a U.S. stop of arms sales to Taiwan as having to be premised by peaceful resolution of the Taiwan issue will be a continued, premeditated interference in China's internal affairs. Hearings, at 197.

To underscore this interpretation, the Communist Chinese have repeatedly refused to renounce the possibility of using force to unite Taiwan with the mainland. Hearings, at 202 (statement of Huang Hua, Oct. 6, 1982).

According to the Peking view, the U.S. policy statements in paragraph 6 depend upon or have in mind not Red China's commitment to a fundamental policy of peaceful resolution of the Taiwan issue, but the principles governing relations between the two countries, namely, "the principles of respect for each other's sovereignty and territorial integrity and noninterference in each other's internal affairs as embodied in the Shanghai communique and the joint communique on the establishment of diplomatic relations between China and the United States." Hearings, at 194 (statement of the Ministry of Foreign Affairs, Aug. 17, 1982).

Second, the rationale is stated at times in a way that seems to assume that if Red China alone poses no threat to Taiwan or poses continually diminishing threat, then reduction of American arms sales is justified and is consistent with the Taiwan Relations Act. This, however, ignores the fact that the Congress, in drafting the act, deliberately refused to cast the statutory commitment to the security of Taiwan in the exclusive terms of a threat by mainland China.[9]

Even the statements by the President indicating that the reunification of China would eliminate the need for arms sales to Taiwan because, presumably, Taiwan as an independent nation would no longer exist are not free from difficulties. For one thing, the subcommittee is aware of no documented case of a free nation deciding of its own volition ("peacefully") to become part of an imperial Communist power. Certainly, the past record of Red China's conquests of Tibet and the Paracel Islands,[10] the persistent refusal by Peking officials to rule out the use of force to reunify China, and the repeated assertions by the government and people of Taiwan that they will resist Red Chinese hegemony provide a less than persuasive historical basis for the belief that the peaceful reunification of Taiwan and the mainland is possible in fact or in principle.

Second, the assumption that peaceful reunification entails the end to Taiwan's independent need for defensive arms ignores one of the key documents upon which this administration bases its hope for a peaceful resolution of the problem--the September 30, 1981, "nine point statement." Hearings, at 190. Points 3 and 4 of the "reunification proposal" state:

3. After the country is reunified, Taiwan can enjoy a high degree of autonomy as a special administrative region and it can retain its armed forces. The central Government will not interfere with local affairs on Taiwan.

4. Taiwan's current socioeconomic system will remain unchanged, so will its way of life and its economic and cultural relations with foreign countries. There will be no encroachment on proprietary rights and lawful right of inheritance over private property, houses, land and enterprises or on foreign investments. Hearings, at 190.

This proposal thus contemplates an independent military for Taiwan even after "reunification." But the subcommittee, again referring to the historical record of Red China's reliance upon armed force to conquer the lands which were once a part of imperial China and to the irrefutable record of gross deceit and the resort to armed might demonstrated by the Communist regimes throughout the world, concludes that recent statements such as the nine point proposal and the 1979 New Year's Day "message to compatriots on Taiwan" provide exceedingly long odds against which to gamble the welfare and security of a free, friendly people.

Thus, the interpretation given to the communique by the administration is not free from problems. It may also be noted that if the future Red Chinese attitude and military posture amounts in fact to a lessening of the military threat--actual and potential--toward Taiwan, the development of a corresponding decrease in Taiwan's security needs may justify a gradual reduction as well as a qualitative and quantitative limitation on arms sales consistent with the Taiwan Relations Act. If the communique itself promotes this change in the attitude of Peking, it will have served a desirable goal. However, if the United States reduces and limits the arms sold to Taiwan without referring to the actual or potential threat of Red China and the consequent needs of Taiwan, or if a threat to the security of Taiwan is posed by forces other than Communist China, such action on the part of the United States will violate both the letter and the intent of the act and, therefore, the constitutional separation of powers.

In sum, the interpretation given to the crucial statements in paragraph 6 by the U.S. Government affords grounds for considerable relief regarding the intentions of this administration toward the security of Taiwan and regarding the lawfulness of its arms sales policy in light of the Taiwan Relations Act. The articulated and demonstrated intention of the administration to avoid a literal interpretation of the communique and to continue to provide arms in response to the proven needs of Taiwan represents sound foreign policy as well as legal and constitutional actions if limited to circumstances described above.

VIII. CONCLUSIONS

The subcommittee draws the following conclusions on the basis of its investigation into the questions posed by the issuance of the joint communique:

1. The administration has not offered clear and consistent accounts either of the nature of the joint communique or of the legal nature of the policy statements made therein.

2. The apparent meaning of the U.S. policy statements in paragraph 6 of the communique is inconsistent with the policy set forth in the Taiwan Relations Act.

3. The administration, in particular President Reagan, has repeatedly articulated an interpretation of these policy statements which is generally consistent with the Taiwan Relations Act. This interpretation is manifested in recent statements and actions by the administration.

In response to requests by the subcommittee for an Executive order or some similar official statement which memorializes this interpretation of the joint communique, spokesmen for the administration have stated on several occasions that such action is unnecessary in light of the statements which appear in the record of the hearings of this subcommittee.[11] Most recently, Assistant Secretary Wolfowitz reiterated this position in both his testimony before the subcommittee and in a subsequent letter to the chairman.[12] In his letter, the Assistant Secretary said:

In line with the President's firm commitment to carry out our policy expressed in the joint communique in a manner fully consistent with the TRA, I feel that there is no need for the President to issue an Executive order clarifying the intent of the communique. Such an Executive order would in my opinion be redundant, and therefore unnecessary. Hearings, part 2, at 14.

The subcommittee notes the repeated statements by the administration that the Taiwan Relations Act is the law of the land and that the policy stated in the joint communique is consistent with the act. The subcommittee also notes with approval the repeated statements in recent months of interpretations of the communique that are consistent with the act. In light of these statements and of the finding that the joint communique represents a policy implementation formula that binds only this administration, the subcommittee is persuaded that an Executive order, though still desirable, is not necessary in order to clarify for all interested parties the intended and actual meaning of the communique.

The subcommittee questions, however, the wisdom of the effort of the administration to negotiate and issue this communique on U.S. arms sales. The communique can hardly be characterized as an "understanding" or "modus vivendi" when the parties publicly disagree on the meaning of every significant pronouncement in the document--that is, the nature of Red China's reunification policy toward Taiwan, the meaning of the U.S. statements in paragraph 6, and the conditionality of U.S. Arms sales policy upon Communist Chinese policy and actions. Further, the "exceedingly obscure" language of the communique, to quote Professor Gregor, has unnecessarily provoked the American Congress and the American public, the governments of Communist China and of free China, and the governments of our allies and antagonists throughout the world to wonder not only about our arms sales policy toward Taiwan but also about the significance that they may prudently attach to our public pronouncements of foreign policy. The subcommittee concludes that the issuance of the communique was most unfortunate and unwise.

[1]"As a result of the normalization agreement between the United States and China, the United States met Peking's longstanding 'three conditions,' the 'derecognition' of Taipei, the termination of the Mutual Defense Treaty, and the withdrawal of U.S. forces from Taiwan." "Implementation of Taiwan Relations Act--Issues and Concerns: Hearings Before the Subcommittee on Asian and Pacific Affairs of the House Committee on Foreign Affairs." 96th Congress, 1st session iv (1979) (preface by Representative Lester L. Wolff, chairman of the subcommittee); see S. Rept. No. 7, 96th Congress, 1st session 9 (1979).

[2]S. Rept. No. 7, 96th Congress, 1st session 41 (1979).

[3]See S. Rept. No. 7, 96th Congress, 1st session 7-8 (1979); H. Rept. No. 26, 96th Congress, 1st session 4-5 (1979).

[4]See S. Rept. No. 7, 96th Congress, 1st session 10-17 (1979); H. Rept. No. 26, 96th Congress, 1st session 5-6 (1979).

[5]"Taiwan: Hearings on S. 245 Before the Senate Committee on Foreign Relations," 96th Congress, 1st session 23-24 (1979) (testimony of Warren Christopher, the Deputy Secretary of State).

[6]The Peking Government disagrees with the United States on this point. Whereas the U.S. position has been that the statements in paragraph 6 of the communique are premised on Red China's statement of its intent to pursue a policy of peaceful reunification of Taiwan and the mainland, the Red Chinese maintain that the statements in paragraph 6 are premised on the "principles governing the relations between the two countries," and that the policy it chooses to pursue in the effort to reunify the two parts of China "is purely China's internal affair, no misinterpretation or foreign interference is permissible." Hearings at 194-95 (statement by the Communist Chinese Ministry of Foreign Affairs, Aug. 17, 1982).

[7]Section 3(b) of the Taiwan Relations Act states in part: "The President and the Congress shall determine the nature and quantity of such defense articles and services based solely upon their judgment of the needs of Taiwan, in accordance with procedures established by law."

[8]Assistant Secretary Wolfowitz sought to reassure the subcommittee on this point: "You expressed in last fall's hearings your fear that Congress, which had asserted its voice in the Taiwan Relations Act might be deprived of its policymaking function. Clearly, this is not

and will not be the case. I say this confidently not because I understand the legal impediments, but because I understand Congress [sic] desire to assure the well being of the people of Taiwan expressed in the act to be reflected fully in the President's own wishes." Hearings, part 2, at 7.

[9]The debates in committee and on the floor of both Houses of Congress make it quite clear that the principal threat contemplated by the members of Congress was that of the Red Chinese, and the Senate amendments to S. 245 contained explicit references to Red China in this regard. However, in the final version passed by both houses, all reference to specific countries had been eliminated, and the Senate Report indicates that all threats to Taiwan's security were to be covered by the Act. See S. Rept. No. 7, 96th Congress, 1st session 31 (1979); H.R. Rept. No. 26, 96th Congress, 1st session 5-6 (1979).

[10]See Michel Peissel, "The Secret War in Tibet" (Boston, 1972); Hearings, at 40 (statement of A. James Gregor).

[11]Hearings at 109-10 (response of Legal Adviser Davis Robinson) and at 188 (letter from Assistant Secretary Powell Moore).

[12]Hearings, part 2, at 13.

Source: Report on the Taiwan Relations Act and the Joint Communique, Committee
               on the Judiciary, U.S. Senate, U.S. Government Printing Office, Washington,
               D.C., June 1983, pp. 1-20.

TRA47   AGREEMENT ON TRADE IN COTTON, WOOL
         AND MAN-MADE FIBER TEXTILES AND TEXTILE PRODUCTS
                               BETWEEN
               THE AMERICAN INSTITUTE IN TAIWAN
                                AND
         THE COORDINATION COUNCIL FOR NORTH AMERICAN AFFAIRS

1. (a) The term of this Agreement will be the six-year period from January l, 1982, through December 31, 1987. Each "Agreement Year" shall be the twelve-month period from January 1 to December 31, with the first Agreement Year commencing on January l, 1982, and ending on December 31, 1982.
    (b) This Agreement will supersede the agreement relating to Trade in Cotton, Wool and Man-Made Fiber Textiles and Textile Products dated June 8, 1978.

2. (a) Textiles and textile products covered by this Agreement are those summarized in Annex A.
    (b) Tops, yarns, piece goods, made-up articles, garments, and other textile manufactured products, all being products which derive their chief characteristics from their textile components of cotton, wool or man-made fibers, or blends thereof, in which any or all of those

fibers represent either the chief value of the fibers or 50 percent or more by weight (or 17 percent or more by weight of wool) of the products, are subject to this Agreement.

(c) For the purposes of this Agreement, textile products shall be classified as cotton, wool or man-made fiber textiles if wholly or in chief value of any of these fibers...

DONE at Washington, D.C., on this 18th day of November, 1982.

FOR THE AMERICAN INSTITUTE   FOR THE COORDINATION IN TAIWAN
         COUNCIL FOR NORTH   AMERICAN AFFAIRS

David Dean, Chairman of the Dr. Tsai Wei-ping,
Board and Managing Director Representative

Source: American Institute in Taiwan, Arlington, Virginia (Annex A not included).

TRA48   AGREEMENT CONCERNING THE TAIPEI AMERICAN SCHOOL

BETWEEN

THE AMERICAN INSTITUTE IN TAIWAN

AND

THE COORDINATION COUNCIL FOR NORTH AMERICAN AFFAIRS

ARTICLE I

The Taipei American School (TAS) will be deemed a contractor of the American Institute in Taiwan (AIT). The contract between TAS and AIT is attached as Annex 1 to this Agreement for reference. AIT will inform the Coordination Council for North American Affairs (CCNAA) of any change in the nature of the contractual relationship between AIT and TAS prior to the effective date of change.

ARTICLE II

TAS shall have the capacity to incur debts, and to enter into and perform contracts, and to own and dispose of property in connection with its functions not consistent with this Agreement.

ARTICLE III

So long as its contract with AIT remains in effect, TAS shall enjoy the following privileges in connection with its functions thereunder:

1. TAS shall be allowed to import all equipment, materials, motor vehicles and

supplies reasonably required for school use, as certified by the educational authorities concerned in Taipei, free from customs duties, taxes and other charges. Upon approval by the appropriate authorities concerned in Taipei, such equipment, materials and supplies likewise may be reported by TAS free from customs duties, taxes and other charges.

2. On the basis of such certification by the authorities concerned in Taipei, TAS shall be allowed to exchange New Taiwan Dollars for United States Dollars for the purpose of importing educational equipment, materials, books and supplies.

3. TAS shall be exempt from income tax, business tax, and all other taxes imposed under the law of the authorities represented by CCNAA in the most favorable manner and to the extent as a fully qualified Chinese private school foundation. However, the tax exemptions accorded to TAS under the preceding text shall not exceed those enjoyed by TAS as of January 1, 1979.

4. TAS shall be allowed to select its own personnel and to determine its own curriculum, rates of tuition and other policies.

5. TAS shall report directly to and be subject to the supervision of the educational authorities concerned in Taipei...

ARTICLE VIII

This Agreement shall be effective on the date of signature, provided, however, that the privileges enjoyed by TAS and its personnel during the period from JAnuary 1, 1980, to the date of this Agreement are hereby ratified, This Agreement shall remain in effect unless and until terminated by either party on one year's notice.

Done at Taipei, on this third day of February, 1983.

James R. Lilley	Raymond S. H. Hoo
Director	Chairman
American Institute in	Coordination Council
Taiwan	for North American
	Affairs

Source: American Institute in Taiwan, Arlington, Virginia (Excerpts).

TRA49

98th CONGRESS
  1st SESSION   **S. RES. 74**

Expressing the sense of the Senate concerning the future of the people on Taiwan.

IN THE SENATE OF THE UNITED STATES

FEBRUARY 28 (legislative day, FEBRUARY 23) 1983

Mr. PELL (for himself, Mr. GLENN, and Mr. KENNEDY) submitted the following resolution, which was referred to the Committee on Foreign Relations.

RESOLUTION

Expressing the sense of the Senate concerning the future of the people of Taiwan.

Whereas February 28, 1983, marks the eleventh anniversary of the Shanghai Communique signed by the United States and the People's Republic of China;

Whereas the communique and the 1979 United States-People's Republic of China normalization agreement greatly improved relations between Washington and Beijing;

Whereas peace has prevailed in the Taiwan Strait since the normalization of relations between the United States and the People's Republic of China;

Whereas maintaining a sound United States-People's Republic of China relationship serves the interest of both countries and the interests of peace in the Pacific region;

Whereas the United States has also pledged in the Taiwan Relations Act to continue commercial, cultural, and other relations between the people of the United
States and the people of Taiwan; and

Whereas the United States established diplomatic relations with the People's Republic of China in the expectation that the future of Taiwan will be determined by peaceful means:
Now, therefore, be it

> *Resolved*, That it is the sense of the Senate that Taiwan's future should be settled peacefully, free of coercion, and in a manner acceptable to the people on Taiwan and consistent with the laws enacted by Congress and the communiques entered into between the United States and the People's Republic of China.

Source: Senate Resolution 74, Expressing the Sense of the Senate concerning the Future of the People of Taiwan.   98th Congress, 1st Session.   U.S. Government Printing Office, Washington, DC, 1983.

TRA50   **AMERICAN FOREIGN POLICY, 1983**

Document 467

Testimony by the Assistant Secretary of State for East Asian and Pacific Affairs (Wolfowitz) Before

a Subcommittee of the House Foreign Affairs Committee, February 28, 1983 (Extract)[8]
U.S.-China Relations 11 Years After the Shanghai Communique

MR. WOLFOWITZ.

I have submitted a slightly longer statement for the record. In the interest of time, I will try to keep my opening remarks here to 10 minutes.

Mr. Chairman, developing a strong, stable, and enduring United States-China relationship is an important element of President Reagan's foreign policy. For compelling historical reasons, that goal has occupied a central place in the foreign policies of four successive administrations. We should not forget that, in the more than two decades preceding the Shanghai communique,[9] United States-China relations were deeply hostile.

China was a large and menacing power with which we maintained no human communications, cultural contact, or economic relations. We were at war in Korea. We nearly came to war over Quemoy and Matsu. And we supported opposite sides in Vietnam.

Indeed, China actively supported insurgencies on the soil of many of our Asian allies and friends. At great cost, we maintained a significant naval presence between Taiwan and the mainland, and at the same time we faced a growing threat from the Soviet Union.

By 1972, it had become clear to both the American and Chinese leadership that continuation of this hostile atmosphere was in neither country's interests. The result was a reconciliation of historic importance. Developments since then have demonstrated the importance of the productive and cooperative relationship that followed.

Let me mention just three instances that illustrate how far we have come and what has been achieved.

Perhaps nothing more dramatically illustrates the changes of the last 11 years than the fact that China is today a major restraint on Vietnamese aggression in Asia.

As another important indicator of change, our economic relations have grown substantially. Bilateral trade with China has risen from zero to more than $5 billion per year.

Perhaps most important of all for the long-term relationship between the United States and China, cultural relations and personal ties have resumed at many different levels. People-to-people contacts have virtually exploded. Nearly 10,000 Chinese students are studying at American universities, more than 100 Chinese delegations per month are visiting the United States, and over 100,000 Americans are visiting China each year. These exchanges bring to each of our societies an increasingly sophisticated appreciation of the other.

In my prepared statement, I mention many other benefits. These include that we no longer have to plan or spend to confront a Chinese threat; it includes agreement on the Soviet threat and parallel interests in containing the Soviet Union in Afghanistan and elsewhere; it includes a useful dialogue on a wide range of important regional and international problems on which China has developed a more constructive regional and cooperative approach.

Despite problems, East Asia has emerged during this period as one of the more stable and prosperous regions of the world, with China playing an increasingly responsible regional role. Even Taiwan has never been more prosperous and the situation in the Taiwan Straits is peaceful.

These benefits are the fruits of a wide variety of agreements that have established the framework for an extensive relationship. Throughout the normalization process, we have consistently adhered to three fundamental principles and realities:

First, that China is already a significant factor in Asia, and is destined to be an important element in international affairs in the future, a power with which we hope to work constructively and cooperatively for mutual benefit.

Second, that the United States and China share certain common and important international perceptions and concerns, and that the development of United States-China relations serves the interests of both our peoples and the cause of peace and stability in East Asia and the world.

And third, that progress in United States-China relations can be made without sacrificing the interests of our friends and allies in the region or our valued commercial, cultural and other unofficial relations with the people of Taiwan.

Adhering to these fundamentals, in 1979 we negotiated a normalization agreement which established diplomatic relations between the United States and China[10] and under which it was understood that commercial, cultural, and other contacts with the people of Taiwan would from then on be conducted on an unofficial basis.

Reflecting the importance that they placed on good relations and their confidence in the relationship's evolution and progress, both sides chose to move ahead with normalization even though not all of our differences had been resolved.

Among the differences left unresolved by the normalization communique was the question of arms sales to Taiwan. In the August 17 joint communique of last year, we provided a framework for managing our differences with China over this highly sensitive matter. However, the lengthy and intense negotiating process placed a considerable strain on the relationship.

One result was a pause in high-level contacts and exchanges, a part of our relationship with China that is particularly important for clearing up misperceptions and for building the confidence on which progress in the relationship depends.

Thus, the Secretary's objectives in visiting Beijing early last month were to put United States-China relations back on a stable, realistic footing, to resume the process of building confidence and trust, to continue our dialogue on important international issues, and to address openly and honestly the various bilateral issues that commanded attention on both sides.

In my prepared statement which I have submitted for the record I have described some of the results of that trip. Since I am sure we will discuss the trip in the period for questions that follows, let me just say here that Secretary Schultz and Foreign Minister Wu Xueqian succeeded in restoring the international dialogue to its rightful place in the relationship. It was a dialogue of high quality, providing that while China may not yet be among the world's wealthiest nations, it is among the more sophisticated, with a decidedly global approach.

Our delegation could not help but be impressed with the serious, constructive, and realistic approach that the Chinese leadership took in our discussions on a wide variety of key issues, including the continued threat posed by Soviet power and expansionism, restoring peace and independence to Afghanistan and Kampuchea, and even on issues where we disagreed in important respects, such as the question of progress toward peace in the Middle East, the question of Namibian independence and the desirability of the withdrawal of Cuban troops from Angola.

China and the United States will undoubtedly continue to have some differences over Taiwan. However, the relationship with China is important enough to us--and, it seems, also to the Chinese--that we will work hard to manage those differences in a way that preserves our focus on shared bilateral and international concerns.

The Secretary's visit was not intended to and did not attempt to renegotiate or go beyond the August 17 communique or earlier communiques that previous administrations had negotiated with China concerning the Taiwan issue. But the Secretary did reassure the Chinese that, consistent with our intent to rebuild mutual trust and confidence, we will faithfully carry out the policies enunciated in those three   communiques, and we are confident that the Chinese will do the same.

That is the key, I believe, to managing effectively our differences over Taiwan. At the same time, we have consistently made clear to China that we have a deep interest in the well-being of the people of Taiwan, as reflected in the Taiwan Relations Act,[11] and will continue the productive, unofficial relationship that we have with them.

The common interests and constructive attitude which we found in many aspects of the international sphere are even more markedly present on bilateral matters. I have cited earlier expansion of economic, cultural and personal relations that provide important advantages to both nations.

Naturally, such increased contacts will, on occasion, lead to increased frictions. It is inevitable, as relations mature and develop and as trade and exchanges advance and multiply, that the attendant bilateral problems grow more complex. This is especially the case for two countries which maintain fundamentally different systems.

The technology transfer issue is a good example of a problem that is born of progress. Since 1979, and particularly during this administration, we have worked hard to facilitate Chinese access to advanced American technology. Licenses issues have gone up roughly 300 percent in the last 3 years.

Secretary Shultz made clear to the Chinese that we intend to support their modernization efforts, and that we will continue to provide them with a broad range of American technology from agricultural know-how to advanced scientific information. Most of these item, in fact, are not subject to export controls. Some are

We intend to administer those regulations in a manner that supports China's development and maintain only those restrictions that are necessary for national security purposes. Secretary Shultz encouraged the Chinese to consider the vast range of items made available in the past few years, to appreciate how far we have come in this area, and to work with us to streamline both their bureaucratic practices and our own in order to smooth the interaction between our two economies.

Looking back over the events of the last month, as well as the rapid progress of United States-China relations over the past 11 years, it is noteworthy that both sides, despite the peaks and valleys that have characterized episodes in the development of the relationship, continue to place a high value on it. Both sides wish to preserve what has been accomplished and to move forward where possible and where mutually beneficial.

As the Secretary noted to the Chinese, enduring relationships more often emerge from a process of working out arrangements for dealing with seemingly intractable disputes than from dealing only with the easy problems. Given the progress made thus far and the undeniable benefits to both sides, it is clear that there will be no turning back.

Some difficult problems lie ahead in United States-China relations. We intend to deal with them fairly and openly, and not to take the relationship for granted. With good will, with appreciation of the value of the relationship, with adherence to our own basic principles, and with Chinese reciprocity--for good relations are a two-way street--the prospects for further progress are encouraging. the stable and enduring relationship that we seek is important to the healthy economic growth that both countries desire and makes an important contribution to regional stability and to world peace.

Thank you.

Mr. Solarz. Thank you very much, Mr. Secretary.

I do not think you have to be concerned that anything you have said in you testimony will unduly discomfort our friends in Beijing or elsewhere in the region. It was a very carefully constructed statement.

Let me ask you this: Based on the testimony of your predecessor before this subcommittee, Mr. Holdridge,[12] we were given the impression that our commitment in the August 17, 1982, joint communique to gradually diminish the quality and quantity of our arms sales to Taiwan was based on an understanding with the People's Republic of China expressed in the communique that they would refrain from the use of force as a way of resolving the problem of Taiwan, and that they would, in effect, attempt to resolve the Taiwan problem through peaceful means alone.

Based on Secretary Shultz's discussions in Beijing, would you say that this, in fact, is the Chinese interpretation of the August 17 communique, or, do they have a somewhat different interpretation of the possible use of force as a way of resolving the Taiwan problem in the future?

Mr. Wolfowitz. I have looked at Secretary Holdridge's testimony fairly carefully, and I think it was very correctly stated there.

I do not believe we have an understanding with China; what we have in the communique is a statement by China of their policy and, as I think Secretary Holdridge said in his testimony both here and in the Senate, our statements about arms sales are premised on that Chinese statement about their policy.

That is a relationship which the Chinese have made some statements about. They feel that, in the first place, they are under no commitment to us, even with their opening statements and, of course, they continue to disagree even with the statement of arms sales policy that we have asserted.

I think the key to working out our differences is that we proceed through actions, not by discussion one another's words; that is, they continue their fundamental peaceful policy and we continue our policy on arms sales. The theoretical difference will then be worked out in practice.

Mr. Solarz. They said in the joint communique that it was their fundamental policy "to strive for a peaceful solution to the Taiwan question."

Was there any discussion of the meaning of that statement in any of the discussion Secretary Shultz had in Beijing?

Mr. Wolfowitz. The Secretary's general approach to this communique was not to try to clarify or elaborate pieces of it, which would amount in fact to trying to go beyond very carefully arrived at language; but to say that we have both made commitments, we have both made statements of policy in the communique, and that the President has instructed me, Secretary Shultz, to tell you directly, and in his name, that we are going to carry out our obligations under that communique and, of course, we expect you to carry out yours.

Mr. Solarz. Are you saying there was no discussion of the attitude or position of the People's Republic of China with respect to the possible use of force as a way of resolving the problem of Taiwan in the discussion that Secretary Shultz held?

I mean, you are saying, in effect, that all he said about this was that everything was said in the communique where you expressed your position and we expressed ours, so let's move on and talk about other things, but we expect you to live up to your statements and we will live up to ours. There was no further discussion of what the words meant?

Mr. Wolfowitz. That is essentially correct.

Mr. Solarz. Would it be fair to say that based on the actual wording of this communique, while the People's Republic of China said it was its fundamental policy to strive for a peaceful solution of the Taiwan question, it clearly does not completely exclude the use of force, in the sense that the People's Republic of China says its policy is to strive for a peaceful resolution, but it doesn't go on to say that there are no circumstances under which in would use force?

Would that be an incorrect interpretation?

Mr. Wolfowitz. I think that is why they are insisting on the point that they have made no commitments. But they have made a statement of policy, and I think the point is not to look at hypotheticals of what might happen if either on of us departed from the statements of policy made in the communique but, rather, to say that if we both follow these parallel courses of policy there is a way in practice to manage the differences of principle.

Mr. Solarz. I am going to ask you the kind of question which is asked of students who seek admission to Talmudic or Jesuit academies. I am going to read to you two statements and I would like you to tell me how they are consistent with each other.

The first statement comes from paragraph 6 of the United States-China joint communique of August 17, 1982, which I gather was reaffirmed, in effect, through Secretary Shultz's discussions in Beijing. We committed ourselves, you have just testified, to carrying that communique out. In the communique it says in paragraph 6 that the United States "intends to reduce gradually its sales of arms to Taiwan leading over a period of time to a final resolution."

Yet the President, in a recent interview which he gave to *Human Events*, said the following:

"If the day ever comes that those tow find that they can get together and become one

China in a peaceful manner, then there wouldn't be any need for arms sales to Taiwan, nd that is all that meant in the communique. Nothing was meant beyond that. We are not going to say, well, just as time goes by we are going to reduce the arms to them. No, we hope for a peaceful resolution of this issue."[13]

On the one hand, the communique says it is our intention to reduce gradually sales of arms to Taiwan over a period of time; on the other hand, the President says that we are not going to say, "Well, just as time goes by we are going to reduce the arms to them."

Can you perhaps reconcile this seeming contradiction?

Mr. Wolfowitz. Well, I hope if I succeed I won't be forced to become a Jesuit or a Talmudist.

But it is a valid question. I think it is important, perhaps first of all, to recognize that on the one hand you are dealing with a carefully crafted negotiated document; and on the other hand you are dealing with an interview. Very much like a line of questioning here, the interview bears in from a certain direction and is asking a certain question.

I think the basic question that is being asked there as you read it in context is how on Earth could the United States have made this commitment to a gradual reduction? I think the President's answer is really a very direct version of what I just said a few minutes ago about the more carefully crafted language of the communique, which is that it is not merely as time goes by that we talk about reducing arms, but in the context of a Chinese statement of a fundamental policy of peaceful approach to the problem.

[8]*United States-China Relations 11 Years After the Shanghai Communique Hearings Before the Subcommittee on Asian and Pacific Affairs of the Committee on Foreign Affairs. House of Representatives, Ninety-eighth Congress. First Session* (Washington, 1983). pp. 3-6, 17-19. For Wolfowitz's prepared statement, omitted here, see *ibid*, pp. 7-16.

[9]For text of the joint U.S.-People's Republic of China statement issued at Shanghai, February 27, 1972, see *Public Papers of the Presidents of the United States: Richard Nixon, 1972* (Washington, 1974). pp. 376-379.

[10]For the text of the Joint Communique issued on December 15, 1978, which established diplomatic relations between the United States and the People's Republic of China as of January 1, 1979, see *American Foreign Policy: Basic Documents, 1977-1980*, pp. 967-968.

[11]P.L. 96-8, approved April 10, 1979; for text, see *ibid*., pp. 989-994.

[12]John H. Holdridge, then Assistant Secretary of State for East Asian and Pacific Affairs, testified before the House Foreign Affairs Committee on August 18, 1982, on the joint communique signed the previous day. For an extract of his testimony and text of his statement be for the Senate Foreign Relations Committee on August 17, 1982, se *ibid*., 1982. pp. 1042-1053.

[13]*Human Events*, February 26, 1983. pp. 1-19. The President's statement was in response to a question about the sale of arms to Taiwan.

Source: *American Foreign Policy Current Documents*. Department of State Publication

Document 468

Transcript of the Department of State Daily Press Briefing, March 21, 1983 (EXTRACT)

SALE OF ARMS TO TAIWAN

Q.   Some stories coming out over the weekend indicate the United States has now "announced," or made known in some way, what the level of arms to Taiwan is to be for this year. How was that done?

A.   Don, there was a Congressional Presentation Document that was sent up to the Hill some time ago -- I would guess almost 2 weeks ago. It's an open, unclassified document that went up to the Hill. I think it is that document which makes these various estimates or projections public.

Q.   Would you get those and make them available to us, because we've repeatedly asked the question in the past about these levels, and the answer was given that they had not been established?

A.   Well, projections -- Again there are projections -- I will check and see whether the Congressional Presentation Document is available. I'm not sure that we're the ones to do that.

Q.   Is it a State Department document?

A.   I don't know the answer to that. But again, let me say to you that, again, they are projections; they may not be realized. I think that the thing to do perhaps is to look at that, and then come back with some specific questions. There is some guidance which I think could be useful. But I don't think addressing it in the abstract is going to be very productive.

Q.   Could you get the guidance plus the document or whatever it is, so we could find out what is being talked about when they, the Chinese are complainig about something that we've never heard of up to now?

A.   The document, I will see where the document is available. If it's available here, we'll be happy to make it available.

Q.   The Chinese say that the projected level is $1.6 billion annually, something in that order --

A.   No, no, no. They didn't say annually; they said over a 2-year period.

Q.   All right, a 2-year period. And they said that, in effect, is a reneging on the implied or explicit promise by the United States to have a diminished supply of arms going to Taiwan. Would you comment on that?

A.   Let me just say this on that: First, as I say, the figures are projections, and may not be realized in the course of the fiscal years which are cited. The figures which are cited in that document are $800 million for FY-83 and $700 million for FY-84.

Q.   The second figure?

A. $780 million. Should these levels be realized, they would be fully consistent with the August 17 communique. As the communique says, the reductions will be gradual, and although there may be occasional fluctuations, the trend will be apparent over time. As the secretary has said, we intend to keep our commitments.

There are various tables which explain how figures for past years might be adjusted to bring them up to '83 levels in terms of this year's dollars to make comparisons and so on, and that's in that same document.

Q.   You're saying that the figures are consistent with the Taiwan communique -- with the communique of August 17, and the People's Republic says they're inconsistent, and that's the way you're going to leave it at this point?

A.   I can't speak for the Chinese. They have to speak for themselves on this issue.

Q.   They have spoken for themselves.

A.   Fine. I am saying to you that, yes, we view these as consistent with the August 17 communique.

Q.   It sounds like, from what you're saying, you have adjusted the previous sales figures for Taiwan by an inflation factor.

A.   That's right. We haven't adjusted it, but there is provided in the Congressional Presentation Document a table which would give you an inflation index.

Q.   Why, then, did not the commitments say we will supply less arms adjusted for inflation?

A.   Don, as you know, we haven't tried to get as specific as that. As John Holdridge said before the Senate Foreign Relations Committee in August, we had no figures in mind of any dollar limit. We haven't gotten to that sort of specificity.

Q.   You've gotten to it now, right? That is what you're telling us.

A.   Not in terms of a limit. I'm not trying to set limits. I'm just trying to explain to you what is in the document to the extent that I can without your having it in front of you, and why it is not inconsistent with the August 17 communique.

Q.   This August 17 communique is all about limits. You're now citing some figure, but you're saying they're not limits?

A.   For example, let me give you one example, if I have a figure. I'm not sure I do.

The 1979 level, for example, was $598 million which, if adjusted for inflation, would be $830 million in 1983 dollars. But I'm not again -- no, I'm not trying to set a benchmark or a specific limit.

Q.   What's the point of producing figures then?

A.   Just because it is assumed that there would be questions about how this fits with previous years' sales.

Q.   Alan, a minute ago you said you were trying to explain why these levels are consistent with the communique, and maybe I'm being obtuse, but I didn't hear anything you said that explains why they are. I heard you say that they are. Why are they consistent?

A.   As I said before, as the communique says, the reductions will be gradual and, although there may be occasional fluctuations, the trend will be apparent over time. I've just given you a figure for example, 1979, which adjusted into 1983 dollars is $830 million as compared with the projections.

Again, I've got to stress they're projections of $800 million for FY-1983 and $780 [million] for FY-84.

Source: *American Foreign Policy Current Documents*, Department of State Publication, U.S. Government Printing Office, Washington, DC, 1983. Document 468, pp. 1000-1002.

TRA52   **Document 475**

Statement by the Deputy Assistant Secretary of State for East Asian and Pacific Affairs (Brown) Before the Senate Foreign Relations Committee, November 9, 1983[33]

PROPOSED SENATE RESOLUTION ON THE FUTURE OF TAIWAN

Thank you, Mr. Chairman.

May I say that we share the concerns of the Congress expressed in the resolution which you are considering.[34] We have made clear our concern for a peaceful solution to the Taiwan issue in a number of joint documents with the People's Republic of China. For example, the U.S. Government's Policy concerning the future of Taiwan and its people has been stated in the Shanghai Communique and reiterated in the 1979 Joint Communique Establishing Diplomatic Relations.

In the February 1972 Shanghai Communique, the U.S. side stated: "The United States acknowledges that all Chinese on either side of the Taiwan Strait maintain there is but one China and that Taiwan is a part of China. The U.S. Government...reaffirms its interest in a peaceful settlement of the Taiwan question by the Chinese themselves."

The United States reaffirmed this statement in the 1979 communique normalizing relations and stated: "The United States continues to have an interest in the peaceful resolution of the Taiwan issue and expects that the issue will be settled peacefully by the Chinese themselves."

This consistent position has two main points: One, the resolution of the Taiwan issue is a matter for the Chinese themselves to decide; and, two, the United States has an interest in having that resolution be peaceful.

The U.S. Government, therefore, has not expressed any opinion on what form the ultimate resolution might take nor the procedures which the Chinese should follow to arrive at it, other than that those procedures should be peaceful.

It is this position which is reflected in the Taiwan Relations Act.

The Taiwan Relations Act emphasizes that "the U.S. decision to establish diplomatic relations with the People's Republic of China rests upon the expectation that the future of Taiwan will be determined by peaceful means," and that the U.S. Congress considers it to be of grave concern to the United States "any effort to determine the future of Taiwan by other than peaceful means."

I would like to say a word about the resolution you are considering and its possibile effect on U.S. relations with China.

The reference in the congressional resolution calling for a settlement of Taiwan's future "free of coercion and in a manner acceptable to the people on Taiwan" could be considered the addition of new and undefined elements to the U.S. position on Taiwan.

These provisions do not contradict U.S. policy. However, we believe this new and different iteration of U.S. policy may be unnecessary and even unhelpful since it may appear to qualify the expression of the U.S. policy which has been contained in formal statements such as the Shanghai and normalization communiques.

I have been asked to comment on the likely reaction by the People's Republic of China to your resolution.

The People's Republic of China has consistently expressed its intense opposition to the Taiwan Relations Act, contending that it constitutes an dinterference in China's internal affairs and that its substance is counter to the commitments undertaken by the U.S. Government in the communique on the establishment of diplomatic relations with China.

The People's Republic of China further asserts that domestic legislation in the United States ought not to take precedence over governmental agreements concluded between nations. Officials of the People's Republic of China make these points without fail in any conversation with U.S. officials or private citizens which touches upon resolution of the Taiwan issue.

It is reasonable to assume that the People's Republic of China would respond along similar lines to the passage of the resolution you are presently considering. The People's Republic of China regards settlement of the Taiwan issue as solely an internal affair of China. Thus, it can be be expected to contest strongly the right of any other State to legislate on this question.

In recent months, our relations with the People's Republic of China have been developing in a very positive fashion. We have seen visits to Beijing by Secretaries Schultz, Baldridge, and Weinberger as well as Dr. Keyworth, and last month we received the Chinese Foreign Minister, Wu. As you know, a visit by Premier Zhao Ziyang is planned for January, and the President will visit China in April 1984.

A number of significant bilateral agreements are currently being negotiated. A healthy and developing relationship between the United States and the People's Republic of China contributes to the overall stability of the Western Pacific region and, thus, to continued prosperity and development of Taiwan.

The extent to which passage of the resolution would cast a shadow over these positive developments in United States-PRC relations is subject to debate, but this is a factor that should be considered by the resolution's sponsors.

In sum, while we do not consider the amendment to be inconsistent with our policy, its passage has the potential to cause complications in our relations with China.

Thank you.*

*   Senate Resolution 74 passed the Senate Foreign Relations Committee on November 15, 1983, but was never acted on by the full Senate. Ref.: Document 476, *American Foreign Policy Current Documents*, 1983, p. 1012.

[34]Senate Resolution 74, introduced by Senators Claiborne Pell, John Glenn, and Edward M. Kennedy on February 28, 1983, stated that it was the sense of the Senate that "Taiwan's future should be settled peacefully, free of coercion, and in a manner acceptable to the people of Taiwan and consistent with the laws enacted by Congress and the communiques entered into between the United States and the People's Republic of China. (*ibid.*, pp.3-4)

Source: *American Foreign Policy Current Documents*, 1983, Department of State Publication, U.S. Government Printing Office, Washington, D.C. 1983, Document 475, pp. 1010-1011.

TRA53   **Document 478**

Response by President Reagan to a Question Asked During an Interview, December 15, 1983[39]

U.S. Relations With China

I don't think they do. I know that the People's Republic of China is uncomfortable with our position on Taiwan. But we have reiterated time and time again to them that the people of Taiwan are longtime friends and, in fact, once were allies of ours. We have recognized that there is one China and that its capital is Peking. But we believe that the differences between Peking and Taiwan should be settled by peaceful negotiations.

We can't cast aside one friend in order to make another. We have argued to representatives of the People's Republic that they themselves should take some comfort from that because it's assurance to them that we wouldn't throw them aside to make friends with someone else.

I think we've made great progress. I know that sometimes the Government of the People's Republic has to speak out about this issue, but our trade relations and cooperation in the area of high technology, all of these things represent milestones and successive steps in improving our relations.

[39]Source: White House Press Release, December 19, 1983, Office of the Press Secretary to the President; also printed in *Weekly Compilation of Presidential Documents*, December 26, 1983, pp. 1715-1716. President Reagan was interviewed by Marvin Stone and Joseph Fromm, both of *U.S. News & World Report*, in the Oval Office of the White House. The

questioner asked what the President considered would be necessary to develop closer relations with China and whether U.S. ties with Taiwan inhibited this.

Source: *American Foreign Policy Documents*, 1983, Department of State Publication, U.S. Government Printing Office, Washington, D.C., Document 477-8, p. 1013.

TRA54
97 STAT. 1286   PUBLIC LAW 98-181--NOV. 30, 1983

ASIAN DEVELOPMENT BANK

SEC. 1002. The Asian Development Bank Act (22 U.S.C. 285 et seq.) is amended by adding at the end thereof the following:
"SEC. 27.(a)(1) The United States Governor of the Bank is authorized to subscribe on behalf of the United States to one hundred twenty-three thousand three hundred and seventy-five additional shares of the capital stock of the Bank.
"(2) Any subscription to the capital stock of the Bank shall be effective only to such extent or in such amounts as are provided in advance in appropriation Acts.
"(b) In order to pay for the increase in the United States subscription to the Bank provided for in subsection (a), there are authroized to be appropriated, without fiscal year limitation, $1,322,999,476 for payment by the Secretary of the Treasury.
"(c)(1) The Congress hereby finds that--
         "(A) the Republic of China (Taiwan) is a charter member in good standing of the Asian Development Bank;
         "(B) the Republic of China has grown from a borrower to a lender in the Asian Development Bank; and
         "(C) the Republic of China provides, through its economic success, a model for other nations in Asia.
"(2) It is the sense of the Congress that--
         "(A) Taiwan, Republic of China, should remain a full member of the Asian Development Bank, and that its status within that body should remain unaltered no matter how the issue of the People's Republic of China's application for membership is disposed of;
         "(B) the President and the Secretary of State should express support of Taiwan, Republic of China, making it clear that the United States will not countenance attempts to expel Taiwan, Republic of China, from the Asian Development Bank; and
         "(C) the Secretary of the Senate and Clerk of the House shall transmit a copy of this resolution to the President with the request that he transmit such copy to the Board of Governors of the Asian Development Bank.
"SEC. 28. (a)(1) The United States Governor of the Bank is authorized to contribute on behalf of the United States $520,000,000 to the Asian Development Fund, a special fund of the Bank.
"(2) Any commitment to make the contribution authorized in paragraph (1) shall be made subject to obtaining the necessary appropriations.
"(b) In order to pay for the United States contribution to the Asian Development Fund

provided for in this section, there are authorized to be appropriated, without fiscal year limitation, $520,000,000 for payment by the Secretary of the Treasury."

Source: *U.S. Statutes at Large*, 98th Congress, 1st Session, 1983, Volume 97, p. 1285.

TRA55
AMERICAN INSTITUTE IN TAIWAN   March 1, 1984
   1700 N. Moore St.
     17th Floor
Arlington, Virginia 22209
   (703) 525-8474

Dr. Fredrick F. Chien
Representative
Coordination Council for
  North American Affairs
5161 River Road
Bethesda, MD 20816

Dr. Dr. Chien:

     I have the honor to refer to the understandings reached during our recent discussions on Taiwan's rice exports. I wish to obtain your confirmation that the attached memorandum correctly reflects those understandings. I further wish to confirm that these understandings will be implemented solely through measures taken or imposed by authorities on Taiwan.

               Sincerely,

               David Dean
               Chairman of the Board
               and Managing Director

Coordination Council for North American Affairs

   Office of the Representative

               March 1, 1984

Dear Mr. Dean:

     I have the Honor to refer to your letter of March 1, 1984, concerning the recent discussion on our rice exports. I wish to confirm that the memorandum enclosed with your letter correctly reflects those understandings. I further wish to confirm that these understandings will be implemented solely through measures taken or imposed by authorities on Taiwan.

                                                              Sincerely,

Mr. David Dean
Chairman of the Board   Fredrick F. Chien
  and Managing Director   Representative
American Institute in Taiwan
1700 N. Moore St.
Arlington, VA 22209

                                                    March 1, 1984

                        Memorandum of Understanding

         The following represents the agreement reached by the American Institute in Taiwan (AIT) and the Coordination Council for North American Affairs (CCNAA) concerning exports of rice from Taiwan:

(1) exports from Taiwan of Provincial Food Bureau rice stocks will not exceed a total of 1.375 MMT (milled basis) during the period of CY 1984 through 1988, allocated as follows:

1984 - 375,000
1985 - 300,000
1986 - 275,000
1987 - 225,000
1988 - 200,000

(2) each of the annual levels for 1985-1988 set forth in (1) may be increased by an amount no greater than 10% of the annual level for that year, provided that total exports over the five year period do not exceed 1.375 MMT;

(3) the rice referred to in (1) will be offered for export sale for shipment only to countries whose annual per capita income was at or below $795 in 1981 (as reported by the World Bank - see attached list);

(4) consultations between AIT and   CCNAA will be held with respect to all issues relevant to the agreement on an annual basis, or at any other time at the request of either party.

(5) exports of rice in the form of grant aid are not subject to restriction.

_____

As used in this understanding the term "exports" refers to actual shipments without regard to the date on which the shipment contract was signed...

Source: American Institute in Taiwan, Arlington, Virginia.

TRA56
AMERICAN INSTITUTE IN TAIWAN   November 7, 1984
   1700 N. Moore St.
     17th Floor
Arlington, Virginia 22209
   (703) 525-8474

Dr. Fredrick F. Chien
Representative
Coordination Council for
  North American Affairs
5161 River Road
Bethesda, MD 20816

Dr. Dr. Chien:

     I refer to my letter of August 23, 1982 to Dr. Tsai Wei-ping and your letter to me of January 27, 1983 regarding an agreement on probabilistic risk analysis (PRA) between the American Institute in Taiwan, hereinafter referred to as "the Institute," and the Coordination Council for North American Affairs, hereinafter referred to as "the Council." That agreement, hereinafter referred to as the "PRA Agreement," entered into force on January 27, 1983, the date of your letter to me.

     Considering Articles 6 and 12 of the PRA Agreement, the Institute proposes to expand the PRA program by adding a Severe Accident Response Study(SARS). This SARS would cover the Second Nuclear Power Station (KUOSHENG). The objective of the SARS would be the development of a technical independent study of effective means to control or reduce the risk of severe accidents in a reactor typical of U.S. design. Severe accidents are defined as those which involve substantial core damage or core melt. The Institute also proposes to expand the PRA program to include cooperation, similar to that presently in effect for the KUOSHENG PRA, in any PRA undertaken on the MAANSHAN reactors.

     The Council is already well underway with the PRA   study of the Second Nuclear Power Station (KUOSHENG). With growing expertise in this type of analysis and with already demonstrated expertise in nuclear plant construction, test, operation, and analysis, the Council is uniquely qualified to conduct severe accident application studies of the type proposed. Also, benefits to both parties would be apparent as a result of cooperation on any PRA conducted at MAANSHAN. The proposed contributions of the Institute and the Council are as follows...

The Institute shall:

1.   Provide access to all current results of the Accident Management Study being conducted by Battelle-Columbus Laboratories for the USNRC (statement of work attached). This study will cover a BWR with Mark I containment and a PWR with large dry containment, reactors similar to the First Nuclear Power Station and the Third Nuclear Power Station.

2.   Provide the results of the Severe Accident Risk Reduction Program (SARRP) and the Accident Sequence Evaluation Program (ASEP) which will provide data to focus attention in the SARS on the most effective means to control or reduce risk.

3.   Provide support for any PRA conducted on the Third Nuclear Power Station in a manner similar to the support provided on the PRA conducted on the Second Nuclear Power Station.

The Council shall:

1.   Analyze accident response and management procedures for the important accident sequences which best utilize existing plant equipment taking into account plant procedures, controls, interlocks, etc., existing at the time of initiation of the analysis.   These analyses shall consist of selecting the important accident sequences, one at a time, and identifying operator responses which could be taken to arrest or at least delay the course of these sequences. The analyses shall give full consideration to plant equipment, as built, and to existing instrumentation, training and procedures. These analyses shall include, where necessary, additional estimates of plant thermal-hydraulic and other responses during the accident phases of heatup, core uncovery, and core melt.

2.   Repeat the analyses of item 1 above with selected changes in plant equipment.

3.   Provide a report on the results of items 1 and 2 in the form of analyses of cost-effective and otherwise reasonable responses to severe accident sequences, including: (a) procedure changes; (b) use of plant components and systems not customarily called upon to perform safety functions; (c) simple equipment changes related to (a) or (b); and (d) enhanced training, instrumentation, or diagnostic tools. Emphasis should be on symptom-oriented procedures, with due consideration given to possible misleading information or symptoms.

4.   Provide the results of any PRA conducted on the Third Nuclear Power Station in the same manner as agreed for the Second Nuclear Power Station.

       The Institute shall furnish access to information identified in item 1 above immediately and on a continuous basis thereafter. The Institute will furnish an initial report and briefing in Taipei on Item 2 by the end of March 1985. The Council will provide SARS reports on the following schedule.

       Report on KUOSHENG

              Draft   1/86
              Final   7/86

       Report on MAANSHAN

              Draft   6 months after the draft PRA
              Final   12 months after the draft PRA

       This letter and your reply confirming the contents thereof on behalf of the Council will constitute an agreement between the Institute and the Council. The agreement shall enter into force upon the date of your letter in reply.

                                        Sincerely,
                                        David Dean
                                        Chairman of the Board
                                        and Managing Director

Attachment:
Statement of Work

Source: American Institute in Taiwan, Arlington, Virginia.

TRA57
AMERICAN INSTITUTE IN TAIWAN   January 22, 1984
   1700 N. Moore St.
     17th Floor
Arlington, Virginia 22209
   (703) 525-8474

Dr. Fredrick F. Chien
Representative
Coordination Council for
  North American Affairs
5161 River Road
Bethesda, MD 20816

Dr. Dr. Chien:

    Given our mutual desire to ensure the continuation of uninterrupted maritime trade and the prevention of pollution from ships, I propose that assurances be provided to the American Institute in Taiwan (the "Institute") that all ships under the registry of the party represented by the Coordination Council for North American Affairs (the "Council") which are used in bilateral trade are designed, equipped and operated in accordance with the Protocol of 1978 Relating to the International Convention for the Prevention of Pollution from Ships, 1973 and its Annexes I and II (MARPOL 73/78), a copy of which is enclosed. Compliance with MARPOL 73/78 requirements shall be indicated in part by the carriage aboard ships of valid certificates and record books etc... such as those called for in Marpol 73/78. Such documentation shall be in the same form as called for in MARPOL 73/78. Their carriage shall enable such ships to trade at the ports of the party represented by the Institute in the same manner and under the same conditions as ships of contracting governments to MARPOL 73/78, as provided for in Article 5 (4) of that treaty.

    Reciprocally, assurances should be provided that, inasmuch as the party represented by the Institute is a contracting government to MARPOL 73/78, compliance with those provisions by merchant ships flying its flag shall enable them to trade at ports of the party represented by the Council in the same manner and under the same conditions as ships under the registry of the party represented by the Institute trade at ports of contracting governments to MARPOL 73/78.

    If these arrangements meet with your approval, I propose that this letter and your written reply serve as a basis to establish the procedures described.

Sincerely

Enclosure: David Dean
        (1) MARPOL 73/78   Chairman of the Board
                                                          and Managing Director

Coordination Council for North American Affairs
Office in U.S.A
5161 River Road, Bethesda, MD 20816

Mr. David Dean
Chairman of the Board
and Managing Director   January 31, 1985
American Institute in Taiwan
1700 N. Moore St.
Arlington, VA 22209

Dear Mr. Dean:

This is to acknowledge receipt of your letter of January 22, 1985, in which you wrote:

"Given our mutual desire to ensure the continuation of uninterrupted maritime trade and the prevention of pollution from ships, I propose that assurances be provided to the American Institute in Taiwan (the "Institute") that all ships under the registry of the party represented by the Coordination Council for North American Affairs (the "Council") which are used in bilateral trade are designed, equipped and operated in accordance with the Protocol of 1978 Relating to the International Convention for the Prevention of Pollution from Ships, 1973 and its Annexes I and II (MARPOL 73/78), a copy of which is enclosed. Compliance with MARPOL 73/78 requirements shall be indicated in part by the carriage aboard ships of valid certificates and record books etc... such as those called for in Marpol 73/78. Such documentation shall be in the same form as called for in MARPOL 73/78. Their carriage shall enable such ships to trade at the ports of the party represented by the Institute in the same manner and under the same conditions as ships of contracting governments to MARPOL 73/78, as provided for in Article 5 (4) of that treaty.

Reciprocally, assurances should be provided that, inasmuch as the party represented by the Institute is a contracting government to MARPOL 73/78, compliance with those provisions by merchant ships flying its flag shall enable them to trade at ports of the party represented by the Council in the same manner and under the same conditions as ships under the registry of the party represented by the Institute trade at ports of contracting governments to MARPOL 73/78.

If these arrangements meet with your approval, I propose that this letter and your written reply serve as a basis to establish the procedures described."

In reply, I wish to express, on behalf of the Coordination Council for North American Affairs, our willingness to provide the American Institute in Taiwan reciprocally with the assurances as specified in you letter, and our concurrence with your suggestion that this correspondence of ours will serve as a basis to establish the procedures described.

Sincerely,

Fredrick F. Chien
Representative

Source: American Institute in Taiwan, Arlington, Virginia.

TRA58   Coordination Council for North American Affairs
Office in U.S.A
5161 River Road, Bethesda, MD 20816

February 14, 1985

Mr. David Dean
Chairman of the Board
and Managing Director
American Institute in Taiwan
1700 North Moore Street, 17th Floor
Arlington, VA 22209

Dear Mr. Dean:

    Reference is made to your letter of November 7, 1984, addressed to me proposing bilateral cooperation on Expansion of the PRA Agreement Between AIT and CCNAA to Conduct A Severe Accident Response.

    I have the honor to accept, on behalf of our Council, the foregoing understandings and to confirm that the aforesaid letter and this reply shall constitute an agreement between the American Institute in Taiwan and the Coordination Council for North American Affairs.

Sincerely yours,

Fredrick F. Chien
Representative

Attachment:
Statement of Work

Source: American Institute in Taiwan, Arlington, Virginia.

TRA59
I. 3 Jun 85

C H I N A
HONG KONG MEDIA ON CHINA

HU YAOBANG INTERVIEWED BY PAI HSING'S LU KENG

HK010420 Hong Kong PAI HSING in Chinese No 97, 1 Jun 85 pp 3-16

[10 May Beijing interview with PRC General Secretary Hu Yaobang by PAI HSING director Lu Keng]

On March 1985... I learned from Hong Kong sources that Hu Yaobang would visit the South Pacific in mid-May, and that he had agreed to meet me when he returned to Beijing from his visit to the South Pacific.

*   *   *

The talk touched upon the problem related to China's reunification, the current political situation on the Chinese mainland, and other various matters related to freedom of the press, economic reform and so on. It also touched on Hu Yaobang's recent visit to North Korea and other questions related to international affairs except for diplomatic issues. We hereby publish the dialogue between them:

*   *   *

Recently, people abroad have been worried about and concerned over the attitude of the CPC toward the Taiwan issue. Since the agreement reached between China and Britain on the question of Hong Kong, it is quite obvious that the CPC Central Committee has found the pattern, namely, "one country, two systems," for settling the issue. However, the Taiwan authorities are unwilling to accept the concept because under "one country, two systems," Taiwan's position will be limited to a local government. According to Professor Qiu Hongda, an authoritative scholar in the United States, this would forfeit Taiwan's international dignity, because a special administrative region is tantamount to a local government. Moreover, all its laws would be determined by Beijing's NPC.

How Will the CPC Deal With Taiwan?

Hu: It is now a local government. It is also in essence a local government.

Lu: However, in light of a legally constituted authority, it regards itself as a central government. In addition, there are 23 countries which recognize this government.

Hu: Even in this case it cannot represent the mainland and is in essence a local government. Naturally, we also cannot represent this government, so we consider it as a special zone. Is this not reasonable? You were talking about international....

Lu: International dignity.

Hu: With regard to international dignity, we should stress overall international dignity and not petty international dignity. In this respect, our outlook should be based on the whole of China and the descendants of the Yellow Emperor. This is what we mean by overall international dignity. As to Taiwan's international dignity, it is only a tottering, petty international dignity.

Lu: People in academic circles like to find historical precedents when examining issues. Studying world history, they have discovered that the unification of many countries has gone through a gradual process. Take the unification of the German nation, for instance. it developed from a confederation into a federation; again, take the United States, from 1776 to 1789 it spent 13 years developing from a confederation into a federation.

Hu: Neither Germany nor America had become nations at that time! The case of the mainland and Taiwan is different, since they were long ago parts of the same country, but the 36 German states at that time represented a number of separate political entities and had certainly not formed a unified country.

Lu: That is so. Their development into a country was slow. However the Taiwan side holds that Communist Chin's power has not extended to Taiwan. Although, since the founding of the state in 1949, China has announced that the areas under its control include Taiwan, however, its political power has not been truly extended to them over there.

Hu: The whole world now acknowledges that [blank space for two characters] Taiwan, and Hong Kong all belong to one China. It was a unified China after World War II.

Even the Americans say that there is one China. Nixon, Carter, and Reagan all acknowledged this point. Even Mr. Chiang says there can only be one China! It is like having three ranks of seniority in one large family: We are the most senior; Taiwan is second; and Hong Kong is third. This large family is precisely the People's Republic of China. All of us have set up this signboard.

* * *

Lu: There is now a view on the Taiwan side, and also similar views abroad, to the effect that the CPC Central Committee states that it wants a peaceful solution and friendship with Taiwan. But at the same time it is adopting various measures in the international field to isolate and deal blows at Taiwan, for instance, by informing all countries that they should not accept Taiwan visas, and by trying to kick Taiwan out of the Asian Development Bank, and so on. They say that this is ruthlessness and diametrically opposed to the professions of friendly consultations.

Admitting That China Does Not Have the Strength for the Time Being

Hu: There are two opinions in the world. One is that we only think of having Mr. Chiang Ching-kuo from Taiwan as a counterpart in the talks but the Taiwanese people and the other parties or factions may not necessarily agree.

Another is what a subordinate of Mr. Chiang Ching-kuo has said: On the one hand, you want to hold peace talks; on the other hand, you also want to isolate us. We do not think these two opinions are clever.

Lu: The CPC Central Committee has repeatedly indicated its readiness to solve the Taiwan issue by peaceful means. Why does it not simply renounce the use of force?

Hu: That is impossible.

Lu: Why?

Hu: Because if we make such a promise, they (referring to Taiwan) will be all the more free from anxiety. Ha, ha....

Lu: Oh! Do you mean they will be even more unwilling to have anything to do with you?

Hu: Of course. Everybody in the world knows that we do not have the strength for the time being. We indeed do not have the strength....

Lu: You are very frank. That is where you are terrific. You neither conceal the truth nor use diplomatic language, but simply say "we do not have the strength for the time being."

Hu: Yes. This temporary period may last 4, 5, 7, or 8 years. After we succeed in developing the economy, we will naturally have the strength. Military strength is based on economic power.

Lu: Right.

Hu: For example, if we are economically powerful in 7, 8, or 10 years, we shall be in a position to modernize our national defense. If the broad masses of the Taiwan people wish to return and a small number of people do not wish to return, it will be necessary to use some force.

Lu: There is still one point, general secretary. Please do not be offended, but I have been to Taiwan and I am aware that most of the people of Taiwan are not willing to return....

Hu: That is true. But I believe more and more people will be willing, not day by day, but year by year. Probably this corresponds with the facts.

*   *   *

Lu: He also mentioned this issue, saying that China has the strength to enforce a blockade. In your view, China does not have enough strength even now. Will this blockade be enforced some years later?

Hu: That depends. If we have the strength to enforce a blockade and if Taiwan vehemently opposes reunification, we shall have to consider enforcing a blockade.

If a Blockade I Imposed, There Will Certainly Be A Counter Blockade

Lu: Do you know Mr. Tao Pai-chuan?

Hu: I do.

Lu: He is a famous Taiwan political commentator. He has strength of character. I visited him on 1 April this year in San Francisco. He said that if the CPC imposed a blockade on Taiwan, Taiwan would certainly counter-blockade, and this would lead to a war. Will this not run counter to the CPC's wish?

Hu: If we have the capability to enforce a blockade, we will surely have the methods to deal with a counter-blockade. Only when we are sure of complete victory shall we take this step. Here, let me tell you a story. When a million of our bold warriors crossed the Chang Jiang to the south in 1949, Chairman Mao also though over questions carefully, one of them being what if the United States should carry out armed intervention?

Lu: Oh, did you consider the possibility of U.S. intervention at that time?

Hu: Yes, it was decided then that, if the United States should carry out armed intervention, we would fight it out. At that time, the main force, such as the 2d and 3d Field Armies, and a portion of the 4th Field Army were concentrated along the Chang Jiang. At that time our troups numbered 4 million. We deployed 2 million troops in that area, preparing to fight it out there. Therefore, once we decide to enforce a blockade, it will be easy to deal with Taiwan. We will also take foreign countries into consideration.

Lu: Speaking of foreign intervention, of course, the United States will probably intervene. If the United States intervenes, would you still be sure of success?

Hu: We shall do this only when we are sure of success.

Lu: This means that once you decide to enforce a blockade on Taiwan, you have taken U.S. intervention into account and are sure of success, are you not?

Hu: Not necessarily U.S. intervention. It may just be foreign intervention.

*   *   *

Why Did You Ask Reagan for Help in Opposing U.S. Intervention

Hu: We are still opposed to U.S. intervention!

Lu: But why did His Excellency Mr. Deng ask British Prime Minister Mrs. Thatcher to take a letter to U.S. President Reagan, hoping that President Reagan would do his best to promote a peaceful settlement in the Taiwan Strait?

Hu: I am not very clear about this.

Lu: According to Elder Sister Deng, the greatest obstacle to the Taiwan issue seems to be the United States.

Hu: That is so.

Lu: Do you hold the same view?

Hu: That is our unanimous view. In two periods before the Cultural Revolution, that is, in the early and late of 1950's, were it not for U.S. support for and blood transfusions to Taiwan, the Taiwan issue would have been solved. It was another problem during the Cultural Revolution. Were it not for the continuing U.S. support and blood transfusions, the Taiwan issue would probably be solved now.

Lu: Oh?

Hu: Therefore, the United States is quite unfriendly in its behavior toward China's reunification and the Taiwan issue.

Lu: On this point, I think you have underestimated the strength of Taiwan.

Hu: We have not underestimated it.

Lu: Your estimation is based too much on emotion, and not sufficiently on reason. I other words, you think that Taiwan does not have any strength and that it mainly relies on the United States; in fact Taiwan has a great deal of strength.

Hu: We have full estimates of two things, three if you like. First, their armed forces are powerful.

Lu: They have 600,000 trained troops.

Hu: Their military installations....

Lu: To a certain extent, their military installations are unbreakable.

Hu: Unbreakable? I do not fully agree.

Lu: I know you will not agree.

Hu: They are quite powerful. In addition it is not at all easy to cross the sea and fight!

Lu: That is so. The Taiwan Strait is so wide.

Hu: In short, they have a certain strength. We understand that they have built installations on the island. During our visit to South Pacific countries, they told us that our naval forces are not strong enough, whereas they have a natural naval strength and plenty of sharks.

Hu: We do not underestimate their economic strength. I said a moment ago that there might be a third point. The United States gives them support. This is the most important point.

Lu: But U.S. support is not given for nothing; it is realized through trade contracts.

Hu: Ay! The United States gives them powerful political support.

Source: FBIS-China, 3 June 1985 (Excerpts).

TRA60   Proposed Sale of Aircraft Avionics Components to China

by James R. Lilley

Statement before the Senate Foreign Relations Committee on April 29, 1986. Mr. Lilley is Deputy Assistant Secretary for East Asian and Pacific Affairs.[1]

I am pleased to be here today to discuss the proposed sale of aircraft avionics components to the People's Republic of China (P.R.C.) for the use in the modernization of the F-8 high altitude air defense interceptor.

This proposed sale has focused attention on our military cooperation with China. Much has been said about this cooperation. As the Congress considers this issue, it is important to maintain our perspective as to what our cooperation is and what it is not and to base our discussion on how this issue fits into both our broader policy toward China and developments in the region.

The last four Administrators have worked to develop stronger relations with the People's Republic of China. Since the establishment of diplomatic relations in 1979, U.S.-China ties have broadened significantly. The strengthening of our bilateral relationship has resulted in many benefits to the United States, including increased trade, extensive contact between the peoples of our nations, cooperation in educational and cultural spheres, and a wide-ranging exchange of views on regional and global issues during high-level visits. Although we don not always agree on international issues, our dialogue has increased understanding of our disagreement between us. Moreover, friendly relations between the United States and China have contributed to a reduction of tensions i the Asia-Pacific region.

U.S. Military Cooperation

A part of our growing relationship is the increased cooperation in the military sphere, including sales of some defensive arms to China. This limited military cooperation is based on the important parallel interests. Foremost among these is a common security concern--the threat posed to both of our countries and the entire Asia-Pacific region by the Soviet Union. The willingness of the United States to sell specific defensive weapons or technologies to the P.R.C. is based on a thorough analysis of each item's utility for enhancing Chinese defensive capabilities, taking into full consideration the political-military environment and the interests and concerns of our other friends and allies in the region.

The proposed program for an upgrade of 50 F-8 air defense interceptor aircraft, to be completed about 1995 or 1996, will contribute to China's ability to defend its airspace against the threat from the Soviet Union. The program was very carefully reviewed to insure that the upgrade would not provide an offensive capability that could be threatening to allies and friends, including Taiwan, in the region.

Our military cooperation with China is proceeding cautiously and deliberately. We believe that the proposed program to assist with the upgrade of the F-8 defensive interceptor aircraft is an area where cooperation to strengthen China's defensive capabilities will not concomitantly jeopardize the security of other Asian friends and allies. We believe strongly that our trade, political, and military ties with the P.R.C. than by refusing to assist them in their modernization efforts in all appropriate areas of activity. The current trend in U.S.-China relations is a positive trend which is aimed at contributing to the security not only of China and the United States but our other friends and allies as well.

For nearly a decade, China has sought to modernize four key sectors--industry, agriculture, science and technology, and military. A key element in these modernizations is the acquisition of foreign technology. The military element is the fourth priority and has been severely constrained by budget limitations despite having to face 49 Soviet divisions comprising half a million men on the Sino-Soviet border as well as up to 44 Vietnamese divisions in the south. Major efforts are underway to reduce the number of soldiers by 1 million men as well as to reform leadership, organization, training, and military doctrine. The goal is a leaner, better equipped, better trained and organized, and better led armed force so as to meet China's main security threats. The budget constraints, however, have delayed procurement and production of new equipment, and China's defense industries have increasingly been civilianized to produce nonmilitary consumer goods. The hope is to obtain needed defensive equipment from abroad, although such procurement will continue to be limited by the increasing lack of foreign exchange.

Regional Considerations

As we consider our military cooperation with China, we have carefully considered the opinions of our friends and allies in East and Southeast Asia. We have made it clear that our cooperation is limited to defensive equipment. We believe these countries understand our rationale and appreciate our caution. While some of them still are concerned that we will move beyond our well-defined limitations, their reactions have been muted.

There has been concern expressed about the impact of this sale on Taiwan. It is, indeed, true that Taiwan is distressed about U.S. military assistance to the P.R.C. and support for the F-8 in particular. However, we believe that if this single program of assistance to a small number of aircraft is put into the proper perspective it will be difficult to claim that it potentially constitutes a significantly increased threat to Taiwan. Taiwan is a dynamic, vigorous society, It has a rapidly growing economy and a stable political system, and these two factors are key deterrents to efforts by anyone seeking to alter the course of developments there by force. I need cite only a few statistics.

Taiwan's per capita gross national product is currently over $3,000 a year and there is every reason to believe that by the end of the century it will rise to $12,000. In addition, every increase in prosperity is equitably distributed, further encouraging economic development and reducing social tensions. Taiwan's total trade was $50.8 billion in 1985, putting it into the top 15 trading entities in the world. Taiwan is the fifth largest trading partner of the United States with a total trade in 1985 of $22.8 billion. Taiwan's foreign exchange holdings are $28 billion.

By many other yardsticks also, Taiwan is a significant actor on the Asian scene. Taiwan's economy is now graduating into the high technology manufacturers which should permit its export economy to grow. Although understandably concerned by the military situation, Taiwan remains confident in maintaining the growth of its economy and in continuing its political progress with stability. Foreign as well as domestic investors give the practical vote of confidence on which taiwan's prosperity and stability rests. We, therefore, think that there are good grounds for Taiwan to continue to act with confidence.

Even though the situation has occasionally been tense in the Taiwan Strait, it has been basically peaceful for nearly 30 years. This can only be explained by a complex of factors-- political, economic, and psychological, as well as military. we believe that this realistic appraisal is shared by the government in Beijing. It has authoritatively stated that its fundamental and consistent policy is peaceful reunification. That policy was at the center of the negotiations which led to the August 17, 1982, joint communique. In that document, the United States acknowledged this fundamental Chinese policy. As stated in then Assistant Secretary [of East Asian and Pacific Affairs John H.] Holdridge's August 18, 1982, statement before the House Foreign Affairs Committee, our willingness to make "adjustments in our arm sales to Taiwan had to be premised on a continuation of China's peaceful policy." He went on to say that "while we have no reason to believe that China's policy will change, an inescapable corollary to these mutually interdependent policies is that should that happen, we will reassess ours."

Although there have been occasional, troubling remarks suggesting possible future military actions and Beijing declines to renounce formally the use of force to resolve what it considers to be an internal matter, we believe that Beijing this issue rather than facilitate its settlement.

Taipei has responded negatively to Beijing's overtures for formal talks about reunification, beginning with political talks about three areas of interim contracts (trade, visits, and communications) on the grounds that Beijing's proposals are not sincere. However, the substance about which Beijing wishes interim talks has been developing. Trade over the years has been increasing, and 1985 trade nearly doubled over the previous year to a level of $1.1 billion in two-way trade, much of it Taiwan, exports. There are increasing contacts between individuals and private organizations in key areas such as science, technology, and culture. While direct communications are opposed by Taiwan, indirect communications assure that the positions of each side is understood by each other. There may eventually be an interest in greater contacts provided they are to their mutual advantage.

A key aspect of Taiwan's confidence is the U.S. commitment. the Taiwan Relations Act is a fundamental affirmation of the strong support which the United States gives to Taiwan and of the interest which the United States has in having any resolution of the future of Taiwan by the Chinese themselves be peaceful. Lest this support be seen merely as verbal and moral, the Taiwan Relations Act specifies that "the United States will make available to Taiwan such defense articles and services in such quantity as may be necessary to enable Taiwan to maintain a sufficient self-defense capability." this has been a consistent policy since the enactment of that legislation in 1979, and we see no sentiment for changing that policy. In 1982 at the signing of the joint communique, the United States realized that this complicated statement, arrives at after extensive negotiations, gave grounds for concerns on Taiwan, an six reassurances were given Taiwan. In addition to stating that the United States "had no intention whatsoever to revise the Taiwan Relations Act" and "had not agreed to hold prior consultations with the People's Republic of China." We believe that Taipei and Beijing both understand the firmness of the United States in implementing the Taiwan Relations Act. Our arm sales have been significant. Although decreasing gradually as agreed to in August 17, 1982, communique, they have remained adequate given the current situation in the Taiwan Strait. In addition, Taiwan is increasing its reliance on indigenous efforts for reasons of national pride as well as sound economic grounds. We have, for many years, supported this Taiwan policy, and we will continue to do so.

This Administration seeks the continuation of our growing ties with China while maintaining our firm commitment under the ties with China while maintaining our firm commitment under the Taiwan Relations Act to the security of the people of Taiwan. We remain optimistic about the future and believe our willingness to cooperate with China in its modernization efforts--including cautious and prudent cooperation in the field of military modernization--will provide stability and peace in the East Asia region in the years ahead.

[1]The complete transcript of the hearings will be published by the committee and will be available from the Superintendent of Documents, U.S. Government Printing Office, Washington, D.C. 20402.

Source: *U.S. Department of State Bulletin*, Volume 86, July-December 1986.

TRA61
AMERICAN INSTITUTE IN TAIWAN
1700 N. Moore St.
17th Floor
Arlington, VA 22209

GUIDELINES FOR A
COOPERATION PROGRAM IN LABOR AFFAIRS
BETWEEN
THE AMERICAN INSTITUTE IN TAIWAN
AND
THE COORDINATION COUNCIL FOR NORTH AMERICAN AFFAIRS

1.   Background

Cooperation between scientists, engineers, scholars, and institutions from the United States and Taiwan is furthered pursuant to an Agreement dated September 4, 1980, between the American Institute in Taiwan (hereinafter referred to as "the AIT") and the Coordination Council for North American Affairs (hereinafter referred to as "the CCNAA"). The "Taiwan Relations Act" (Public Law 96-8, April 10, 1979) authorizes the continuation of commercial, cultural and other relations between the people of the United States and the people on Taiwan...

2.   Program Goals

To increase contacts and cooperation between personnel of our two sides who are engaged in labor affairs; to provide such personnel opportunities to exchange information, ideas, skills and techniques; to enhance opportunities to collaborate in solving problems of common interest; and to utilize special facilities or research opportunities available. Cooperation may be, inter alia, in the areas of vocation training, employment service, employment standards, occupations safety and health, mine safety and health, and labor statistics. The types of cooperative activities may include the exchange of information, including publications, visits, seminars and workshops, and research...

...Other areas of cooperation may be added as may be mutually agreed to by the AIT and the CCNAA, with the concurrence of the DOL [Department of Labor in Washington] and the MOI [Ministry of Interior in Taipei].

AMERICAN INSTITUTE IN TAIWAN	COORDINATION COUNCIL FOR NORTH AMERICAN AFFAIRS
JOSEPH B. KYLE	CHI CHEN

Source: American Institute in Taiwan, Arlington, Virginia, (Excerpts).

TRA62
AMERICAN INSTITUTE IN TAIWAN
Taipei Office
7, Lane 134, Hsin Yi Road, Sec 3, Taipei Taiwan
Telephone: 709-2000 Cable AITAIWAN TAIPEI

May 8, 1986
AIT B-291

Mr. Robert Shiching Hsiao
Chief, Business Division
Coordination Council for
  North American Affairs
133 Po Ai Road

Dear Mr. Hsiao:

As evidenced by a recent unanimous resolution of the Security Council of the United Nations, there is a growing consensus that terrorism attacks all systems of law and order. The International Civil Aviation Organization, as part of the effort to combat terrorism against civil aviation, has approved amendments to Annex 17 of the Chicago Convention which, among other things, include a recommendation that appropriately strong language on aviation security be included in all bilateral civil aviation agreements.

The subject of aviation security is treated in Article 6 of the "Air Transport Agreement between the American Institute in Taiwan and the Coordination Council for North American Affairs," which was signed in Washington, DC on March 5, 1980. However, the language contained in Article 6 of the aforementioned agreement is not as adequate as that recently developed by the International Civil Aviation Organization. Accordingly, I propose that the present Article 6 of the Agreement be replaced by a new Article 6, the text of which is enclosed. The new Article 6 is closely based on ICAO suggestions.

This letter and your reply accepting the contents thereof will constitute an agreement between the American Institute in Taiwan and the Coordination Council for North American Affairs to replace the present Article 6 of the Agreement with a new Article 6. The new Article 6 will enter into force upon the date of your letter in reply and will remain in force for the life of the Agreement.

Sincerely,

Philip T. Lincoln, Jr.
Chief
Economic/Commercial Section

COORDINATION COUNCIL FOR NORTH AMERICAN AFFAIRS
133 Po Ai Road, Taipei, Taiwan
Republic of China

Ref No: (75) CCNAA 0986

July 28, 1986

Communications Programs Office
American Institute in Taiwan
Taipei Office
7, Lane 134, Hsin Yi Road, Sec. 3, Taipei

Attention: Ms. Deborah R. Schwartz
Acting Chief
Economic/Commercial Section

Dear Ms. Schwartz:

This refers to Mr. Lincoln's letter (AIT B-291) of May 8, 1986 and its enclosure proposing a revision of Article 6 of the "Air Transport Agreement between the Coordination Council for North American Affairs and the American Institute in Taiwan, "which was signed in Washington, DC on March 5, 1980.

In reply, we are pleased to inform you that we accept the proposed contents of the new Article 6 and that your letter and this letter will constitute an agreement between the American Institute in Taiwan and the Coordination Council for North American Affairs to replace the present Article 6 of the Agreement with this new Article 6 and that the new Article 6 will enter into force on today's date and will remain in force for the life of the Agreement.

Sincerely yours,

Robert Shiching Hsiao
Chief
Business Division

RH/sc

Source: American Institute in Taiwan, Arlington, Virginia.

TRA63
AMERICAN INSTITUTE IN TAIWAN
1700 N. Moore St.
17th Floor
Arlington, Virginia 22209
(703) 525-8474

July 19, 1986

Dr. Fredrick F. Chien
Representative
Coordination Council for
  North American Affairs
5161 River Road
Bethesda, Maryland 20816

Dear Dr. Chien:

I refer to discussions between representatives of the American Institute in Taiwan (hereinafter referred to as "AIT") and the Coordination Council for North American Affairs (hereinafter referred to as "CCNAA"), which took place in Hawaii during the period May 28-30, 1986, in Washington, DC during the period June 24-29, 1986, and in Geneva, Switzerland during the period July 10-12, 1986. The discussions concerned exports of cotton, wool, man-made fiber, silk blend and other vegetable fiber textiles and textile products exported from taiwan to the United States of America. As a result of these discussions, I propose, on behalf of AIT, the following Agreement relating to trade in cotton, wool, man-made fiber, silk blend and other vegetable fiber textiles and textile products between AIT and CCNAA.

1.   This Agreement modifies and extends the Agreement between AIT and CCNAA dated November 18, 1982...

TERM

2.   (a) The term of this Agreement shall be from January 1, 1986 through December 31, 1988, except as provided in paragraph 15.

(b) An "agreement year" shall be a calendar year commencing on January 1 and ending December 31.

FOR THE COORDINATION COUNCIL INSTITUTE FOR NORTH AMERICAN AFFAIRS	FOR THE AMERICAN IN TAIWAN
DR. FREDRICK F. CHIEN Representative	MR. DAVID DEAN Chairman of the Board and Managing Director

COORDINATION COUNCIL FOR NORTH AMERICAN AFFAIRS
Office in U.S.A.
5161 River Road, Bethesda, MD 20816

October 22, 1986

Mr. David Dean
Chairman of the Board and Managing Director
American Institute in Taiwan
1700 N. Moore Street
Arlington, VA 22209

Dear Mr. Dean:

I wish to refer to your letter of July 19, 1986, which was an agreement between AIT and CCNAA relating to trade in cotton, wool, man-made fiber, silk blend and other vegetable fiber textiles and textile products.

The above-mentioned amendments and changes are acceptable to us. Accordingly, this Agreement modifies and extends the Agreement between AIT and CCNAA dated November 18, 1982 and shall be the bilateral instrument which governs textile trade between Taiwan and the United States of America.

Sincerely,

Fredrick F. Chien
Representative

Source: American Institute in Taiwan, Arlington, Virginia. (Excerpts.)

TRA64

AGREEMENT BETWEEN THE AMERICAN INSTITUTE IN TAIWAN
AND THE COORDINATION COUNCIL FOR NORTH AMERICAN AFFAIRS
CONCERNING BEER, WINE AND CIGARETTES

The American Institute in Taiwan (AIT) and the Coordination Council for North American Affairs (CCNAA) agree that the following guidelines regarding the importation, distribution and sale within Taiwan of beer, wine and cigarettes shall be effective January 1, 1987:

I.   Definitions

For purposes of this Agreement:

A.   The "importer" of U.S. wine, beer and cigarettes shall mean the Taiwan Tobacco and Wine Monopoly Bureau (TTWBM).

B.   "Merchandise" shall mean still and sparkling grape based wines (CCCN 2205 and 2206), coolers and other fermented beverages including non-grape based wines (CCCN 22207), cigarettes (CCCN 2402 and beer (CCCN 2203) produced in and exported from the United States and counted for customs statistical purposes as an export from the United States to Taiwan.

C.   "Commercial importer" shall mean exclusive and non-exclusive representatives, distributors, subdistributors, agents, wholesalers and licensed retailers, who have a commercial relationship with U.S. suppliers of merchandise.

D.   "U.S. suppliers" shall mean producers, export trading companies, brokers and other entities which export merchandise.

E.   "Retailer" shall mean an establishment, facility or outlet operated under a valid TTWMB license to sell TTWMB products.

II.   Importation Procedures

A.   Commercial importers shall be allowed to import into Taiwan, through TTWMB, the merchandise. A commercial importer may purchase from a number of U.S. suppliers of merchandise. A commercial importer shall be responsible for the performance of and shall direct all functions and activities relating to the importation proces,s including securing an import permit from the Board of Foreign Trade in the same of TTWMB and letters of credit or other payment documents...

. . .

IV.   Pricing

A.   All prices for each brand or style of the merchandise shall be established solely on the basis of freely competitive market forces in Taiwan. Commercial importers may not be required to provide notification more than ten days in advance to TTWMB of the anticipated retail prices at which beer, wine, wine coolers and cigarettes shall be sold or of any changes thereto.

VII.   Labeling and Packaging

A.   Cigarettes: A health warning shall appear on each pack of cigarettes. The warning shall be in the Chinese language on the side of the package and shall be identical to the text of the TTWMB health warning. The typesize, typeface and format shall be essentially equivalent to the current TTWMB health warning. Date of packaging shall be on the inside foil of each pack of cigarettes in industry accepted nomenclature. The nomenclature key shall be given to CCNAA.

B.   Beer. The date on which the product is inserted in its container shall be visible on the bottom of each retail container in industry accepted nomenclature. The nomenclature key shall be given to CCNAA. U.S. firms may ship beer products to Taiwan in their containers as produced in the United States without change.

C.   Wine. Retail containers shall be labeled to provide an accurate description of the product.

VIII.   Penalties

In the event of suspected noncompliance with these guidelines by commercial importers, TTWMB shall notify in writing the suspected violator of the alleged violation, the time period within which such violation must be corrected or discontinued, and the penalty to be imposed by TTWMB should the violation not be corrected or discontinued with that time period. A determination by TTWMB of any penalty shall be guided by the applicable laws and regulations. CCNAA and AIT shall consult before the imposition of any penalty which has the effect of preventing the importation or distribution of U.S. beer, wine and cigarettes.

IX.   Consultations

A.   AIT and CCNAA agree to consult promptly at the written request of either party on any matter relating to the sale of U.S. merchandise in Taiwan.

B.   CCNAA reserves the right to change the status of TTWMB as well as laws and regulations governing TTWMB whenever it deems appropriate. In the event that the status of TTWMB as described in this Agreement is modified, AIT and CCNAA shall consult prior to such modifications to ensure that the market access provided for under this Agreement is not impaired and that any new laws and regulations in Taiwan shall be applies in a nondiscriminatory manner.

Done, in duplicate, at Washington, D.C. this 12th day of December, 1986.

FOR THE AMERICAN INSTITUTE   FOR THE COORDINATION COUNCIL
IN TAIWAN   FOR NORTH AMERICAN AFFAIRS

DAVID DEAN   DR. FREDRICK F. CHIEN
Chairman of the Board   Representative
and Managing Director

Source: American Institute in Taiwan, Arlington, Virginia, (Exerpts).

AGREEMENT BETWEEN THE COORDINATION COUNCIL FOR NORTH AMERICAN AFFAIRS AND THE AMERICAN INSTITUTE IN TAIWAN IN CERTAIN MACHINE TOOLS

Recognizing the spirit of cooperation in which the Coordination Council for North American Affairs (CCNAA) and the American Institute in Taiwan (AIT) have consulted on matters of interest to either party, and recognizing the need for a framework for trade in certain machine tool products between the territories represented by CCNAA and AIT, CCNAA and AIT has agreed as follows:

1.   BASIS OF THE AGREEMENT

The objective of this Arrangement is to provide a framework for trade in certain categories of machine tools between the territories represented by the parties in order to maintain sufficient capacity in the territory represented by the AIT for production of certain machine tools required for the security of the territory represented by AIT. To this effect, CCNAA shall ensure that the competent authorities in the territory represented by CCNAA shall for the period January 1, 1987 through December 31, 1991 restrain exports destined for consumption in the territory represented by AIT of products described in paragraph 2.A. of this Arrangement (the "arrangement products").

2.   DEFINITIONS

The following definitions apply to this Arrangement:

A.   "Arrangement product" means the products (assembled or unassembled) listed in Appendix A to this Arrangement, including kits. That Appendix contains a description of each product as well as the current tariff classification number of each product in the territory represented by AIT under the "Tariff Schedules of the United States Annotated" ("TSUSA") and in the territory represented by the CCNAA under the "Classification of Import and Export Commodities" used in that territory. If any change in these classification numbers occurs during the period that this Arrangement is in effect, Appendix A shall be modified to reflect such change. the TSUSA item number controls the definition of each arrangement product.

. . .

3.   EXPORT LIMITS

A.   Between January 1, 1987 and December 31, 1991, CCNAA shall ensure that in each calendar year export licenses shall be issued to exporters in the territory represented by CCNAA for each of the following categories of arrangement products destined for consumption in the territory represented by AIT in quantities that shall not exceed in the aggregate the following percentages of the projected apparent consumption in the territory represented by AIT for each product category ("export limit") for the relevant period:

DESCRIPTION		PERCENTAGES
(1)	Numerically controlled lathes	3.23
(2)	Non-numerically controlled lathes	24.70
(3)	Milling machines	19.29

(4)   Machining centers   4.66

. . .

13.   ENTRY INTO FORCE AND THREE YEAR REVIEW

This Arrangement shall enter into force upon the date of signature. At the end of the third year of this Arrangement, AIT and CCNAA shall thoroughly review the effectiveness of this Arrangement in meeting its objectives, and, if both parties agree, shall consult each other as to whether the duration and other terms of the Arrangement should be modified.

. . .

Done, in duplicate, at Washington, D.C. on this 15th Day of December, 1986.

FOR AIT   FOR CCNAA

DAVID DEAN   DR. FREDRICK F. CHIEN
Chairman of the Board   Representative
and Managing Director   Coordination Council for
American Institute   North American Affairs

Source: American Institute in Taiwan, Arlington, Virginia (Excerpts).

TRA66   March 10, 1987

AMERICAN INSTITUTE IN TAIWAN
1700 N. Moore St.
17th Floor
Arlington, VA 22209
(703)525-8474

Dr. George K.C. Liu
Director
Science Division
Coordination Council for
North American Affairs
4201 Wisconsin Avenue, NW
Washington, DC 20016-2137

Dear Dr. Liu:

On September 4, 1980, Mr. David Dean, the then Chairman of the Board and Managing Director of the American Institute in Taiwan (AIT), and Mr. Konsin C. Shah, the then Representative of the Coordination Council for North American Affairs (CCNAA), signed an agreement to futher scientific and scholarly cooperation between organizations in the territory represented by AIT and organizations in the territory represented by CCNAA.

This Agreement, which is known as the Cooperative Science Agreement, expired on September 4, 1985. I herewith propose that the Cooperative Science Agreement be renewed and extended without limit...

This letter and your signed acceptance of the contents thereof on behalf of the Coordinations Council for North American Affairs shall constitute a renewal and extension without limit of the Cooperative Science Agreement between the American Institute in Taiwan and the Coordination Council for North American Affairs effective retroactively from September 5, 1985...

Sincerely,

Accepted by:

Joseph B. Kyle
Corporate Secretary

George K.C. Liu
Director, Science Division
Coordination Council for
North American Affairs

Source: American Institute in Taiwan, Arlington, Virginia.

TRA 67   **Guidelines
for a
Cooperative Program in Atmospheric Research
between
The American Institute in Taiwan
and
The Coordination Council for North American Affairs**

1. Background

Cooperation between scientists from the United States and the territory represented by the Coordination Council for North American Affairs (CCNAA) is furthered pursuant to an agreement dated September 4, 1980 between the American Institute in Taiwan (AIT) and the CCNAA. The "Taiwan Relations Act" (Public Law 96-8, April 10, 1979) authorizes the continuation of commercial, cultural and other relations between the people of the United States and the people in the territory represented by CCNAA...

2. Program Goals

To increase cooperation between atmospheric scientists in the United States and Taiwan Area Mesoscale Experiment (TAMEX), during the months of May and June 1987. The objective of TAMEX is to improve understanding and prediction of heavy rainfall that can lead to flash flooding in Taiwan... The TAMEX program envisages cooperative research, scientific visits and the exchange of scientific information.

. . .

6.   In addition to the TAMEX program, other cooperative projects in atmospheric research may in the future be mutually agreed to by AIT and CCNAA...

Signature   Signature

George K. C. Liu [s]   Joseph B. Kyle [s]
Director, Science Division   Corporate Secretary
Coordination Council for   American Institute in Taiwan
  North American Affairs

Date: May 4, 1987   Date: May 4, 1987

Source: American Institute in Taiwan, Arlington, Virginia, (Excerpts).

TRA68   THE LIFTING OF
                        THE CHIEH-YEN (EMERGENCY) DECREE
                             IN THE TAIWAN AREA:
                             OFFICIAL STATEMENT OF
                             THE GOVERNMENT OF
                           THE REPUBLIC OF CHINA
                                 JULY 14, 1987

     In 1949, the nation was in a state of total armed rebellion by the Chinese Communists, and thus in a crisis of survival. To ensure the security of the "bastion of reconstruction," the Government had no other choice but to decree a state of Chieh-yen (hereafter, "emergency") in the Taiwan area. Over the past thirty-some years, the Government has on the one hand implemented emergency measures to a very limited degree, but on the other, has actively promoted constitutional democracy, and made outstanding achievements in the areas of political democracy, economic prosperity, cultural development, and social stability. In this process, the actual effect of the emergency measures on the citizenry has been minimal. Some citizens of the Republic of China even now do not know that the Taiwan area has been in a state of emergency all these years.

     During this emergency period, the Government held firm to its resolution to actively implement constitutional democracy at a steady pace. Accompanying growing prosperity and universal education, ROC citizens have in recent years shown great interest in public affairs and an increased desire to participate in government. These factors have served to lay a firm foundation for full implementation of constitutional democracy. In order to accelerate the promotion spirit of the Constitution, to make government more democratic and society more open, and to improve the people's well-being, the Government is declaring the lifting of the Emergency Decree in the Taiwan area starting from midnight tonight. This decision is truly a milestone in the history of the development of constitutional democracy in the Republic of China.

According to the provisions of Martial Law, the Emergency Decree is a measure that permits the implementation of military control and military justice. Therefore, the lifting of the Emergency Decree has substantive significance in at least three areas.

First, it heralds the reduction of areas under military control, and expansion of the functions and powers of civilian administrative and judicial authorities. For example, civilians will no longer be tried in military courts; and even servicemen on active duty will not be tried in military courts, if the offense is a minor misdemeanor. Also, supervision of entry into and exit from the country will now be assigned to civilian police authorities, and regulation of publications will be transferred to the Government Information Office of the Executive Yuan.

Second, civil rights will be greatly expanded. For example, the right of the people to engage in political activities will from now on be protected and facilitated by law. To this end, after the passing of the "Law on the Organization of Civic Groups" and the "Law on Assembly" by the Legislative Yuan in the near future, people may, in accordance with the law, organize political parties and other associations, and assemble and march publicly.

Third, administrative authorities must adhere to the law. After the lifting of the Emergency Decree, many activities will no longer be restricted, and the administrative scope of the various government authorities will no longer be vague and open to interpretation, as was the case during the emergency period; regular civilian law will govern. This will allow the general public and the legislature to better exercise their supervisory functions.

However, the Chinese Communist threat to the Republic of China has not diminished, and Communist infiltration and subversion will continue to be a danger to our security. For this reason, our country is still in a period of mobilization for the suppression of the Communist rebellion, and is in no case in a state of carefree peace and prosperity. Just as Premier Yu Kuo-hwa pointed out: "The lifting of the Emergency Decree means only that our government and people have the ability to manage any eventual crisis they may face in a democratic manner; it does not mean that threats to the nation's security no longer exist." Accordingly, there are a number of preventive measures that must be taken. To safeguard the nation's security and protect social stability after the lifting of the Emergency Decree, the "National Security Law during the Period of National Mobilization for Suppression of the Communist Rebellion" was drafted. It was written in the spirit of minimizing legislative restrictions, and incorporates standards adopted by other countries in the areas of entry and exit, searches and inspections for public security, coastal and mountain defenses, and matters not yet within the jurisdictional domain of other laws currently in effect, which pertain to national security. It is hoped that this law will help pave the way for constitutional democracy on the one hand, and on the other, protect national security, social stability, and the people's welfare.

We must point out that the greatest difference between the National Security Law and the Emergency Decree is, as mentioned in the preceding, that military control will be greatly reduced. Especially significant is that non-military personnel will no longer be subject to military trial, and even servicemen on active duty will be tried in civilian courts, if their offense is a minor misdemeanor. At the same time, civil rights will be greatly expanded. Administrative and judicial matters that could be handled by the highest commanding officer during the emergency period will now be released from military control. Thus there is a great difference between the mandates of the National Security Law and the Emergency Decree. Some critics have said that the National Security Law is only a "repackaging" of the Emergency Decree, and that the lifting of the Emergency Decree will impose even more restrictions than the decree itself did. This is a completely false assertion.

The Constitution endows the President with the prerogatives of commutation of criminal sentences and rehabilitation of rights. Since the main purpose of lifting the Emergency Decree is to ensure that civilians will no longer be tried in military courts, the Government has decided to offer commutation of sentences and rehabilitation of rights to civilians who were tried in military courts during the emergency period and who are currently serving prison sentences. This is to promote social harmony, and encourage such individuals to improve themselves; and allow them to once more have the opportunity to make contributions to society. It is our hope that all citizens of the Republic of China will appreciate the significance of this event, and work together to open this new phase in our nation's development.

After more than thirty years of efforts, our national development now has a firm foundation, and our people are diligent and responsible. Thus, we are full of confidence in our future.

President Chiang recently pointed out: "The lifting of the Emergency Decree at this juncture is a clear demonstration of the Government's sincerity and integrity; it is the beginning of a new stage in the journey upon which the country has embarked, and a declaration of our confidence in the future of our country." The President also stated that the lifting of the Emergency Decree "will usher our country into a new era" in which "our society will be more democratic, freer, more prosperous, and more progressive."

Today, as we welcome the arrival of this new era, it is our fervent hope that all our compatriots at home and abroad will unite and work together toward further strengthening the "bastion of national reconstruction," and toward the reunification of China.

Source: Statement by Dr. Yu-ming Shaw, Director-General of the Government Information Office, Executive Yuan, Republic of China, July 14, 1987.

TRA69   REMARKS OF THE HONORABLE VINCENT SIEW
DIRECTOR GENERAL
BOARD OF FOREIGN TRADE
MINISTRY OF ECONOMIC AFFAIRS

JULY 21, 1987

Ladies and gentlemen, I am pleased to be here today as part of our thirteenth Special Procurement Mission since 1978. These Missions are but one of many ways in which the

Republic of China on Taiwan is seeking to improve its trade relationship with its most important economic and political partner, the United States.

We understand, perhaps more than most people, the importance of mutually beneficial international trade. After all, Taiwan is a small island occupying an area of land only one-third that of the state of Ohio. Only one quarter of our land is arable and we have very few natural resources. Thus, we rely very heavily on international trade in order to survive economically.

The United States is our largest trading partner. Trade between the United States and the Republic of China amounted to $24.4 billion and represented almost 40 percent of all of ROC's foreign trade in 1986.

Despite its size, the Republic of China offers U.S. exporters a significant, lucrative export market, and in fact, about 22 percent of all of the imports to Taiwan are from the United States. In comparisons, however, only about four percent of U.S. imports come from Taiwan. On a per capita basis, we buy about four times as much from the United States as Americans buy from us.

My country is among the biggest buyers in the world of American agricultural commodities and products. All, or virtually all, of our imports of soybeans and corn come from the United States, as do most of our imports of tobacco and apples. In fact, despite our relatively small population of only 19 million people, we buy more American apples than any other nation in the world. We are also the third largest buyer of U.S. corn, barley, and soybeans.

. . .

This Special Procurement Mission is our largest mission to date. In travelling to 22 states and Washington, D.C., we intend to finalize contracts for approximately $2.4 billion of purchases, including $400 million of agricultural products and $2 billion of industrial products. These purchases will increase the total Buy American program purchases to approximately $10.4 billion since 1978.

We are not here, however, merely to finalize contracts for purchases to which we have already agreed. We also come with a shopping list for future purchases of an additional $2.5 billion of industrial products that are produced in the United States. Formosa Plastics Corporation is interested in purchasing around $700 million in petrochemical and other types of equipment. Taiwan Power Company is interested in purchasing $400 million of power equipment. China Steel Corporation, Retire Service Engineering Agency, Evergreen Corporation and others are interested in purchasing over $500 million worth of machinery. Taipei City Police are interested in purchasing approximately $15 million of computer equipment. Various hospitals are interested in purchasing over $30 million in medical equipment. We hope that, during this mission, we will be able to begin the process of purchasing all of these and other products from American suppliers. To this end, we are holding a series of seminars in four major U.S. cities, Columbus, Ohio, Chicago, Illinois, Dallas, Texas, San Francisco, California.

. . .

We believe that through efforts like this Procurement Mission, we can demonstrate our openness to your products, our commitment to increase our imports of U.S. products. We believe that by working together we can develop the type of commercial ties which benefit both our nations. To succeed we need your help. We need your help in convincing your countrymen that we are sincere in our efforts. We treasure very much the close trade relationship we have had with the United States in the past and we look forward to improving the relationship even further in the future.

Source: Coordination Council for North American Affairs, Washington, D.C. (Excerpts).

TRA70   Agreement for a
                              Cooperative Program in the
                             Sale and Exchange of Technical,
                               Scientific, and Engineering
                             Information between The
                               American Institute in Taiwan
                                           and
                   The Coordination Council for North American Affairs

I.   Background

Cooperation between scientists, engineers, scholars, and institutions from the territory represented by the American Institute in Taiwan (hereinafter referred to as "the AIT") and the territory represented by the Coordination Council for North American Affairs (hereinafter referred to as "the CCNAA") is furthered pursuant to an Agreement dated September 4, 1980, between the AIT and the CCNAA...

II.   Program Goals

A. To search for and collect scientific, technical, and engineering information in the territory repre-sented by the AIT and the territory represented by the CCNAA, and to make such information available to business, industry and the general public either directly or through business services. The AIT is authorized to offer, in association with its contractor, the NTIS [National Technical Information Service], products and services for sale on a self-sustaining basis, and is authorized to issue schedules of fees to achieve this end.

B. It is in the interest of the CCNAA in association with its contractor, the STIC [Science and Technology Information Center], to open new and public access to technical information products and services, to develop facilities in the territory represented by the CCNAA for acquiring information, and to further scientific, technical, and industrial development in the territory represented by the CCNAA.

C. The CCNAA has, in association with its contractor, the STIC, the facilities, personnel and expertise to assist the AIT, in association with its contractor, the NTIS, in searching for and identifying scientific, technical, and engineering information that is not generally available in the United States.

D. This Agreement is entered into with the understanding that the CCNAA, in association with its contractor, the STIC, will provide scientific, technical, and engineering information originating from the territory represented by the CCNAA suitable for announcement and sale through the AIT, in association with its contractor, the NTIS...

. . .

XV.   Duration

This agreement will become effective upon signature of both parties and will remain in effect for 3 years unless terminated earlier in accordance with Article XVI or renewed in accordance with Article XVII.

XX.   Program Expansion

A. In the interest of both parties, a mutual exchange of services that will enhance the fulfillment of this Program may be negotiated and performed, subject to funding limitations.

B. These services may include makeup, printing, and distribution of local language promotional materials, equipment, or consulting services.

C. Such services will be defined in separate task orders which will require the approval of the Agreement's signatory authorities.

. . .

American Institute in Taiwan   Coordination Council for
                                                                    North American Affairs

Joseph B. Kyle   George K. C. Liu
Corporate Secretary   Director, Science Division

Date: Nov. 17, 1987   Date: November 17, 1987

Source: American Institute in Taiwan, Arlington, Virginia (Excerpts).

33. Source: *The Future of Taiwan: Hearing Before the Committee on Foreign Relations, United States Senate, Ninety-eigth Congress, First Session, on S. Res. 74* (Washington, 1984), pp.6-7.

About the Authors

William M. Carpenter is a senior consultant to SRI International on international security affairs. He was for many years Assistant Director of the Strategic Studies Center of SRI International. A retired Navy captain, he served in command and staff assignments at sea and in Japan in three wars, and also in planning and policy offices in Washington before extending his career into the research field of international security studies with a specialty in East Asian affairs. He has made many visits to East Asian countries and is the author or co-author of many studies and articles on international affairs.

Stephen P. Gibert is Professor of Government and Director of the National Security Studies Program at Georgetown University. In 1980 he served on the Defense Advisory Group for President Reagan. He was Director of a Village Research Project in Thailand, Advisor to the Burmese Government in Rangoon, and Editor of *International Security Review*. He is the author of *Northeast Asia in U.S. Foreign Policy* and *Security in Northeast Asia*, as well as other works on international security affairs and American-Asian relations. His Ph.D. is from Johns Hopkins University.

Harold Hinton is Professor of Political Science and International Affairs at The George Washington University. His experience in Northeast Asia includes military service during and after World War II and extensive professional travel since 1961. He is the author of many books and articles on the international politics of Northeast Asia, including the forthcoming *China and the Superpowers*. He has taught in the National Security Studies Program since 1979. His Ph.D. in Modern Chinese History is from Harvard University.

Martin Lasater was formerly the Director of the Asian Studies Center at the Heritage Foundation and currently teaches at the U.S. Naval War College. He is a former staff member of the House Appropriations Committee, taught for two years in Taiwan, and heads his own consulting firm. Mr. Lasater is a specialist in Sino-American relations, particularly the security and strategic dimensions. His publications include *The Taiwan Issue in Sino-American Strategic Relations, The Security of Taiwan* and numerous articles. His Ph.D. is from The George Washington University.

Jan S. Prybyla is Professor of Economics at the Pennsylvania State University. He is a recognized expert on comparative economic systems, socialist economies, and the economies of the People's Republic of China and the Republic of China on Taiwan. Dr. Prybyla is the author of several books including *The Chinese Economy: Problems and Policies* and *Issues in Socialist Economic Modernization*. He has written many articles on East Asia and has travelled extensively throughout the region. His Ph.D. is from the National University of Ireland.

INDEX

Acheson, Dean, 10
Aero Industry Development Center, (AIDC), 43
Afghanistan, 13
Allgeier, Peter, 65
American Institute in Taiwan, (AIT), 14
AOC International, 60
Argentina, 66
AT&T, 67
August 17 Communique, See Shanghai Two
Bashi Channel, 33,44
Bolshevik, 6
Brazil, 66
Brown, Harold, 30
Bush, George, 15,38,39
Cambodia, 13
Canton (Guangzhou), 7
Capetronic, 60
Cathay Group, 20
Carter, Jimmy, 1,2,13,18,28,29,30,36,37,46
Chennault, Gen. Claire L., 7
Chiang Ching-kuo, 20,21,22
Chiang Kai-shek, 6,7,9,11
China. See Peoples Republic of China
China Problem, 1
Chinese Revolution (1911-1949), 1,5-9
Chou En-lai, 12
Chungking (Chongquing), 8
Clark, William, 39
Communist International (Comintern), 6
Communist Party of China (CPC), 27
Confucianism, 21
Congress (U.S.), 1,2,13,14,16,18,30,36,39,46,59,63
            See Also: Formosa Resolution, House Foreign Affairs Committee, House
            Subcommittee on Asian and Pacific Affairs, Taiwan Relations Act, War Powers Act,
            Senate Foreign Relations Committee
Coordination Council For North American Affairs (CCNAA), 14,15
Dang wai, 19.20
Democratic Centralism, 6
Democratic Progressive Party (DPP), 20
Deng Xiaoping, See Teng Hsiao-ping
Digital Equipment, 60
Double Ten, 5
Dulles, John Foster, 11
East Sea Fleet, (PRC), 32
Eisenhower, Dwight D., 10
European Economic Community (EEC);
            Exports to Taiwan, 68
Five Conditions, 35
Flying Tigers, 7
Ford, Gerald, 28

Formosa Resolution, 11
Four Tigers, 18
France, 66
Fukien, 9
General Electric (GE), 60
Generalized System of Preferences (GSP) 56, 63,
        See Also Most Favored Nation Clause.
General Agreement on Tariffs and Trade, (GATT), 65,66
General Dynamics, 36
Government of the Republic of China, (GRC), 8,9,14,22,27
        Reform program, 9
        see also, Republic of China
Great Leap Forward, 11
GTE, 67
Haig, Alexander, 15,38,39
Hainan, 8
Hau Pei-tsun, 21
Holdridge, John, 16,38,40,41
Hong Kong, 18,21,35,61,62
House Foreign Affairs Committee, 37
House of Representatives, (U.S.) 2, See Also Congress (U.S.)
House Subcommittee on Asian and Pacific Affairs
        (U.S. Congress), 37
Hsinchu Science-Based Industrial Park, 62
Hu Yaobang, 35,38,43
Huan Guo-cang, 35
Human Rights, 18
IBM, 60
India, 66
Indochina, 10
Iron Triangle, 2
ITT, 67
Japan, 7,8,33,59,62
        Colonial rule of Taiwan, 9
        Exports to Taiwan, 68
Japanese, Occupation of China 6
Jiangxi, See Kiangsi
Joint Communique on the Establishment of Diplomatic Relations (U . S . - P R C),
                                                                29,38,40,41,42,43,44,46
Jones, Gen. David, 30
Kennedy, John, F., 11
Kennedy, Sen. Theodore, 18
Kiangsi (Jiangxi), 6
Kissinger, Henry, 1,12,28
K-Mart, 60
Korean War (1950-53), 1,28,54
Kuomiantang (KMT), 3,6,7,8,9,20,27
Leach, Rep., 18
Lee Huan, Gen., 21
Lee teng-hui, 20,21,22
Lenin, Vladmir, 6
Levin, Sen. Carl, 18
Liu, Henry, 18

Long March, 7
Lu Keng, 35
Manchu Dynasty, 5
Manchuria, 7
Mao Tse-tung (Mao Zedong), 6,8
McArthur, Gen. Douglas, 10,27
Most Favored Nation Clause, 56,66
Matsu, 31
Mattel, 60
Mutual Defense Treaty (US-ROC) 1,12,18,27,29,54
Mutual Security Treaty, 13
Nanking, 6
National Peoples Party, See Kuomintang
National Security Council (U.S.), 16
National Security Law, 21
Neo-Marxist Dependency Theory, 51
Netherlands, 32,37
New Industrialized Countries (NICS), 52,61
New Taiwan Dollar, 61
Nixon, Richard M., 1,12,28
Northern Expedition, 6
Northrop Corp., 36
Organization for Economic Cooperation and Development (OECD), 66
Pai Hsing, 35
Pearl Harbor, 7
Pell, Sen. Claiborne, 18
People's Liberation Army (PLA), 31,35
Peoples Republic of China (PRC), 1,2,14,27,28,29,30,31
         Attack on Vietnam, 35
    Normalization of relations with U.S., 13,29
         See Also: East Sea Fleet, Joint Communique, Shanghai Communique, Shanghai Two,
         Sino-American Relations, Sino-American Talks, Sino-Japan War, Sino-Soviet Alliance
Phillippines, 22,45,61
Quemoy, 10,11,31
Quemoy Crises (1954,1958,1962), 27
Radio and Television Broadcasting Law, 66
Reagan, Ronald, 15,17,37,38,39,40,43,46
Red Army, 6
Red Guard, 35
Republic of China, (ROC; Taiwan);
         Air-defense system, 33,34
         Agriculture, 11
         Anti-sub warfare, 32
         Armed Forces, 42,44
         Board of Foreign Trade,66
         Economic Record 51
         Economic Relations with U.S., 51-69
         Exports, 52,55,57
         GNP, 52
         Imports from U.S., 64
         Heavy industry, 11
         Military power, 32,33
         Military relations with U.S.,27-50

Mutual Defense Treaty with U.S., 1,12,18,27,29,54
Mutual Security Treaty, 13
Sino-Soviet Alliance, 10
Sino-Soviet relations, 18
See Also Sino-American relations, Shanghai Communique, Shanghai Two,
Republic of Korea, 10,18,22
Robinson, Davis, 41
Roosevelt, Franklin Delano, 7
San Min Chu, 6
Schwin, 60
Sears Roebuck, 60
Senate Foreign Relations Committee (U.S.), 1,30,31,32
Seventh Fleet (U.S.), 27
Shanghai Communique (Feb. 1972), 1,12,28,29
Shanghai Two (August 17, 1982), 17,36
Shultz, George, 17,18
Siemens of West Germany, 67
Singapore, 18,51
Sino-American Relations, 15,16,28,29,36,37,46
Sino-American Talks (1955,1958), 11
See Also Shanghai Communique, Shanghai Two
Sino-Japan War, (1894-1895), 27
Sino-Soviet Alliance, 10
Sino-Soviet relations, 44
Smith, Adam, 52
Snyder, Admiral Edwin k., 32
Solarz, Rep. Stephen, 18
South Korea, See Republic of Korea
Exports, 7,10,61
Soviet Union, see USSR
Stilwell, Joseph, W., 7
Sun Yet-sen, 5,6,9,20
Sweden, 65
Taiwan, see Republic of China
Taiwan Control Yuan, 19
Taiwan Legislative Yuan, 19,20
Taiwan National Assembly, 19,
Taiwan Relations Act (TRA), 1,2,15,17,18,29-31,36,38,39,40,41,46,58
Taiwan Stock Exchange, 65
Taiwan Straight, 10,11,18,33,34,36,41,42,44
Teng Hsiao-ping (Deng Xiaoping), 13,35,38,39,45
Thailand, 61
Three Conditions, 1
Three Obstacles, 1
Texas Instrument (TI), 60
Three People's Principles (San Min Chi I), 5
Tibet, 8
TRA, See Taiwan Relations Act
Truman, Harry S., 27
TRW, 60
United Nations (UN), 28
United Nations Security Council, 27,28
United States, 8,12,14,22,29,33

Arms Sales to ROC, 1,16,28,30,37,41,42,45
China Policy, 15
Copyright laws, 19
Derecognition of ROC, 44,58
Economic Relations in East Asia, 52
Joint Communique with PRC, 29,38,40,41,42,43,44
Military relations with Taiwan, 9,10,11
Mutual Defense Treaty with ROC, 1,12,18,27,29,54
Mutual Security Treaty, 13
Normalization of relations with PRC, 12,13,18,19
Trade with ROC, 66
See Also, Congress (U.S.), Formosa Resolution, Taiwan Relations Act, Sino-American
Relations, Sino-American Talks
USSR, 1,8,61
Ussuri River, 35
Vietnam, 32
Vietnam War, 28
Voluntary Export Restraint, 63
See Also U.S. economic relations with ROC.
Wang Chien-shien, 66,67
Wang Laboratories, 60
War Powers Act, 14
West Germany, 65
Wilson Sporting Goods, 60
World War II (WWII), 27,33
Xinhua, 38
Yenan, 8
Yu Kuo-hua, 21
Yuan Shih-kai, 5
Zhao, Ziyang, 16,17,38,39
Zhu Qizhen, 43